WITH THE YANKS IN KOREA

VOLUME 1

BRIAN CULL
AND DENNIS NEWTON

GRUB STREET · LONDON

Published by
Grub Street
The Basement
10 Chivalry Road
London SW11 1HT

British Library Cataloguing in Publication Data
Cull, Brian
  With the Yanks in Korea
  Vol. 1: the first definitive account of British and Commonwealth
  participation in the air war, June 1950 – December 1951
  1. Great Britain, Royal Air Force – History 2. Korean War,
  1950-1953 – Aerial operations, British 3. Korean War, 1950-1953 –
  Aerial operations 4. Commonwealth countries – Armed forces
  I. Title II. Newton, Dennis W.
  951.9′04248

ISBN 1-902304-49-7

Typeset by Pearl Graphics, Hemel Hempstead

Printed and bound in Great Britain by
Biddles Ltd, Guildford and King's Lynn

PUBLICATIONS

Brian Cull is the author of the following Grub Street titles:
Air War for Yugoslavia, Greece & Crete 1940-41 with Christopher Shores & Nicola Malizia
Malta: The Hurricane Years 1940-41 with Christopher Shores & Nicola Malizia
Malta: The Spitfire Year 1942 with Christopher Shores & Nicola Malizia
Bloody Shambles Volume One with Christopher Shores & Yasuho Izawa
Bloody Shambles Volume Two with Christopher Shores & Yasuho Izawa
Spitfires over Israel with Shlomo Aloni & David Nicolle
Twelve Days in May with Bruce Lander & Heinrich Weiss
Wings over Suez with David Nicolle & Shlomo Aloni
249 at War
The Desert Hawks with Leo Nomis
Hurricanes over Tobruk with Don Minterne
Spitfires over Sicily with Nicola Malizia & Frederick Galea

Dennis Newton is the author of the following titles:
A Few of "The Few"
Australian Air Aces
First Impact - Australians in the Air War 1939-40
The Devil at 6 O'Clock

CONTENTS

ACKNOWLEDGEMENTS

Six or seven years ago, aviation writers Brian Cull and Dennis Newton at opposite ends of the planet were unknowingly working on the very same subject – a book about British and Commonwealth aircrew who served with UN forces in the Korean War; both independently contacted John Davies of Grub Street Publishing with their proposals, following which he wisely suggested a collaboration: Volume One of *With the Yanks in Korea* is the result of their efforts; Volume Two will appear in due course.

Brian Cull. First and foremost, as ever, my thanks go to my wife Val for her continuing understanding and encouragement, seeing me through another difficult period; she also spent many, many hours typing and editing, trying to make sense of our scribbled notes and sometimes incoherent offerings.

Whilst Dennis concentrated mainly on the activities of RAAF and SAAF units and personalities, I endeavoured to seek information regarding the RAF and RCAF pilots who flew with the RAAF and USAF in the Korean War. I thank the following for their contributions, without which this account would be much the poorer: Sqn Ldr C.I. 'Joe' Blyth DFC AFC RAF, who kindy provided the Foreword in addition to recollections and photographs; Air Vice-Marshal J.E. Johnson CB CBE DSO DFC RAF; Lady Barbara Wykeham, widow of Air Vice-Marshal Sir Peter Wykeham KCB OBE DSO DFC AFC RAF (formerly Wykeham-Barnes); Mrs Phyllis Bodien, widow of Wg Cdr H.E. 'Joe' Bodien DSO DFC RAF; Air Commodore P.H.L. Scott AFC RAF; Sqn Ldr J.A.O. Lévesque DFC(US) RCAF; Lord Norton, Anthony and Charles Adderley in connection with the late Grp Capt The Honorable Michael Adderley OBE AFC; Air Vice-Marshal Sir Alan Boxer KCVO CB DSO DFC; Mrs Jean Daniel, widow of Sqn Ldr S.W. Daniel DSO DFC DFC(US); the late Sqn Ldr Allan J. Simpson DFC RCAF; Lt Cdr Peter Lamb DSC AFC RN; Ken Sims DSM RN, TAG Association.

My thanks go out to Czech researcher/writer Tomas Polak, co-author of *Stalin's Falcons*, without whose excellent translations of Russian documents and articles details of the Soviet MiG units would be very sketchy; New Zealand author Paul Sortehaug for supplying a copy of the logbook relating to the late Air Vice-Marshal M. Scannell DFC AFC RAF, and other contributions; Carol Adamczyk, Publishing/Rights Assistant at Motorbooks International of Osceola USA for permission to quote extensively from *MiG-15* by Yefim Gordon and Vladimir Rigmant; Frank Olynyk of Ohio USA for providing additional details of USAF claims and losses; Andy Thomas for information regarding the BCOF Japan; Canadian author Carl Mills of *Canadian Pilots in Korea* Project; Canadian author and publisher Larry Milberry; Alexander Mateev (via David Nicolle) for translations; Hans-Dieter Seidl, author of *Stalin's Eagles*, for information and translations; American author and Korean War expert Bob Dorr for encouragement; Yannis Trypitsis of Athens for information and photographs relating to the Greek Dakota Flight; old friends Russell Guest, Norman Franks, Chris Shores, co-author of *Stalin's Falcons*, Mike Schoeman, and Bruce Lander, for various invaluable contributions and assistance; staff of Bury St Edmunds Public Library; staff of Public Record Office, London; staff of the Fleet Air Arm Museum, Yeovilton; and of course my good friend, gentleman and scholar Jack Lee and his charming wife Hilda; Chris Thomas for his excellent artwork on the dust jacket, and John Davies of Grub Street for his editing and publishing expertise.

Brian Cull,
Suffolk,
England

Dennis Newton. My part in this book could similarly not have been compiled without the generous assistance of many former Korean War veterans. Among those who have kindly provided recollections, anecdotes, access to logbooks, photographs, etc, which have enhanced this history, are included: The late Air Vice-Marshal J.I. 'Bay' Adams CBE DFC AFC RAAF; Colonel R.M. Begbie RA; Grp Capt M. Cottee AFC RAAF; Wg Cdr R.C. Cresswell DFC DFC(US) RAAF; Air Vice-Marshal J.H. Flemming RAAF; Lt(P) P.H. Hancox GCM RAN; Grp Capt G.R. Harvey DFC DFC(US) RAAF; Air Commodore D.W. Hitchins AFC RAAF; Capt I. MacDonald RAN; Lt Colonel D.G. MacLeod RCA; Flt Lt K. Meggs DFM RAAF; Cpl K.P. Melican RAAF; Grp Capt L. Reading DFC RAAF; Flt Lt C. Sly DFM RAAF; Flt Lt S.W. Williamson DFC RAAF.

My thanks also to various organisations including Australian Archives; Research Library, Australian War Memorial; Aviation Historical Society of Australia; South African Defence Force Archive, South African Korean War Veterans Association; British Army Flying Museum; Civil Aviation Historical Society of Australia; RAAF Fighter World Williamtown; RCAF Association; Australian Naval Aviation Museum; Public Relations Office (Air), RNZAF; The Chosin Few; USAF Historical Research Centre, Maxwell AFB; and the History Section, Office of the Greek Air Force.

I am particularly indebted to my good friend the late Bob Wills of the Aviation Historical Society of Australia for photographs, research and contacts (sadly, Bob was tragically killed in an aircraft accident early this year); Keith Meggs DFM, President of the Aviation Historical Society of Australia, who so willingly shared photographs of his time in Korea; researcher Colonel Dirk Stoffberg of Pretoria who made so many visits to the South African Defence Force Archives on my behalf; fellow researcher Mike Taylor and his wife Helen for their enthusiastic help and support; Phil Doyle for allowing access to his huge library of aviation books and magazines; Lt Cdr R.E. Geale MBE RAN, Randall Green, Research Curator Monica Walsh and Debbie Poulter, of Point Cook RAAF Museum; Wg Cdr John Quaife and Flg Off 'Homer' Simpson of 77RAAF Squadron for their enthusiastic support; Brigadier John E. Lello SAAF of the South African Korean War Veterans Association; Mr Ian Smith of the AWM Research Library; Librarian Mr H.W. Foot, British Army Flying Museum; Leon Murtagh; David Scott; Doug Norrie; Alex Vassallo; Nikolas Bouras; Lex McAulay; Jim Thorn; David Wilson; Stewart Wilson; John Foreman; Wg Cdr J.A. Treadwell RAAF; and the late Bryan Philpott. Last, but by no means least, my thanks to my good wife Helen for her infinite patience and co-operation.

Dennis Newton,
NSW,
Australia

FOREWORD

Squadron Leader C.I. 'Joe' Blyth
DFC & Bar, AFC & Bar, US Air Medal, RAF

I was posted to Korea in March 1951 to assist members of 77 Squadron RAAF to convert from the piston-engined P-51D Mustang to the twin-jet Gloster Meteor F8 fighter, with which it was about to be re-equipped. Three other members of the RAF Mission accompanied me. Although we were not officially authorised to fly operational sorties with 77 Squadron RAAF, I and my RAF companions managed to wangle the odd flight or two, initially flying the Mustang and later the Meteor. In fact, both Flt Lt Max Scannell, the RAF Mission leader, and myself completed over 100 operational sorties in Korea! These involved bomber escort, air-to-ground – and air combat with the deadly Russian-flown MiG-15 jet fighters. Although the MiG-15 was superior in performance to the Meteor, we held our own in combat and managed to shoot down two or three for similar losses to ourselves. I thoroughly enjoyed my time in Korea and was sorry to leave my new found Aussie friends.

This book, the first of two volumes highlighting the British and Commonwealth participation in the Korean airwar, pays tribute to the young airmen on both sides who found themselves thrust into the first major post-World War II conflict – the opening rounds of the power struggle between East and West which witnessed the tragic loss of so many thousands of mainly innocent lives so soon after the war to end all wars.

Brian Cull and Dennis Newton provide an accurate and fascinating account of that almost forgotten war, a war that erupted 50 years ago this year, and one we can now read about within the pages of this fine study.

Joe Blyth
Squadron Leader RAF (Retired)

INTRODUCTION and PREAMBLE

Korea, annexed by Japan following the Russo-Japanese War of 1904-5, had been promised its freedom by the WWII Allies at the Cairo Conference in December 1943. This decision had been reaffirmed in the Potsdam Proclamation of 26 July 1945. The surrender of Japan following the dropping of the atomic bombs in August 1945 resulted in a rapid re-occupation by the Allies of the territories occupied by the Japanese. A hurried Allied agreement established the 38th degree of latitude as an arbitrary dividing line across Korea. North of this line the USSR accepted the surrender of Japanese forces, while those south of the line surrendered to American troops. Following the surrender, the Russians took the 38th Parallel to be a political boundary and along it they effectively lowered what Winston Churchill called the 'Iron Curtain':

> "Just as the Russians, at this period, were securing control of North Korea for a Communist régime, the only credentials that the Americans sought to establish for the prospective masters of South Korea were their hostility to Communists and willingness to do business with the Americans." [1]

In South Korea the Americans installed Maj-General Henry 'Hap' Arnold as Military Governor who, in October 1945, created a Korean Advisory Council which was supposed to be a representation of the South Korean political spectrum, although it excluded members of the anti-American, pro-Communist Korean Democratic Party, mainly nationalists who had been members of the anti-Japanese resistance organisation, who understandably believed they should inherit the future leadership of Korea.

With South-East Asia and the various island territories being thus secured, plans were also developed for an Allied occupation of the Japanese Home Islands themselves. The need for occupation was largely to ensure that the disarmament and demilitarisation clauses of the surrender were rigidly adhered to. The occupation force was, naturally, largely American but nations of the British Commonwealth which had fought such effective campaigns in Burma and the South Pacific were also invited to send contingents to the Occupation Force. During September 1945 various Commonwealth governments quickly assessed their level of commitment to the proposed Occupation Force. The Australians decided to contribute land, sea and air contingents, for example. Others were less generous, or less able. The Force would be under the overall command of the Supreme Allied Commander, General Douglas MacArthur of the US Army, and the air element would come under the control of the US Far East Air Force. Over the succeeding months arrangements for the despatch and support of the British Commonwealth Occupation Force (BCOF) continued.

The rôles of the Allied occupation forces were the safeguarding of Allied bases and installations, and the demilitarisation and disposal of Japanese war installations, armaments and military infrastructure. In addition, the Allies conducted regular patrols to ensure that there were no covert Japanese military movements or preparations. The British Commonwealth Force was given responsibility for the Hiroshima and Yamaguchi Prefectures of western Honshu. The Air Component was to comprise two Day Fighter Wings and supporting air and ground elements with the HQ and major base being at Iwakuni on the Inland Sea, some 450

---

[1] See *The Korean War* by Max Hastings.

miles west of Tokyo. The RAF would contribute two Spitfire squadrons and the RIAF one, whilst the RNZAF would send a Corsair squadron and the RAAF three squadrons equipped with Mustangs. The Force would be supported by transport and liaison aircraft based in theatre and from home bases, and would be under the command of Air Vice-Marshal C.A. Bouchier CB CBE RAF.

By early 1946 preparations for the move of the various air units allocated to BCOF were nearing completion, the first to move being the three Mustang squadrons of the RAAF's 81 Fighter Wing from Labuan in Borneo. The main party left by sea on 11 February, followed by the first aircraft from 76RAAF on 28 February, each section escorted by a Beaufighter or Mosquito. They were ferried via the Philippines and Okinawa and arrived in Japan on 9 March. 82RAAF was next, beginning to move on 2 March and arriving between the 13th and 18th, but not without mishap. One of its last sections, comprising a Mosquito and three Mustangs, ran into bad weather some 60 miles short of its destination. All four aircraft crashed with the loss of all five aircrew. The arrival of 77RAAF by 22 March completed the Wing, which soon became established at Bofu.

Meanwhile, in early March, the ground elements of the three Spitfire squadrons – 11 and 17 Squadrons of the RAF, plus 4RIAF – left Singapore by sea for Japan. At the same time 14RNZAF with 24 Corsairs left Auckland on the deck of the light carrier HMS *Glory* for the journey north. They arrived at Iwakuni AFB in late March after which the aircraft were lifted onto lighters and ferried ashore, where they were stripped and cleaned after the long voyage. The BCOF's Air Component's final operational elements, the Spitfire XIVs, departed Singapore on the carrier HMS *Vengeance* on 17 April, arriving in Japan at the end of the month. These aircraft were also lifted ashore and inspected before being flown to the designated Spitfire base at Miho on the north-west coast of Honshu. The RAF's 17 Squadron moved in on 2 May, 4RIAF on the 6th, and 11 Squadron RAF arrived the next day. The Force was completed by numerous support units and personnel and by Dakota IVs of the RAF's 1315 Flight, which also absorbed the Auster Vs of 1 and 2 Casualty Evacuation Flights. The Flight was apparently later upgraded to the status of Communications Squadron. By mid-1946 the BCOF consisted of land, sea and air elements numbering in excess of 35,000 personnel. Over 6,000 of these comprised the Air Component.

Both Iwakuni and Miho were former Japanese bases and showed the ravages of Allied air attacks and of stripping by the local populace after the war – a kind of scorched earth policy. Nonetheless, with a lot of effort by various engineering and construction units like the RAAF's No5 Airfield Construction Unit they were gradually made more habitable. This was helped too by welfare services provided by unsung organisations like the WVS and NAAFI. Flying began as soon as the units had aircraft available. The Kiwis got off to a bad start when, on 20 April 1946 during one of 14RNZAF's first flights, Corsair NZ5635 crashed and burned on take-off at Iwakuni killing the pilot. The Australians soon began patrols and the Spitfire squadrons became operational later in May. 17 Squadron suffered the Air Component's first RAF fatality when, on 27 June 1946, Spitfire RM967 crashed near Iodoe resulting in the death of the pilot.

Fighter aircraft from the various Commonwealth squadrons were quickly into a routine of flying surveillance patrols over the Yamaguchi, Hiroshima, Tottori and Shimane Prefectures, and the island of Shikoku, which were in part to 'show the flag' to the Japanese populace. They also acted as a deterrent to any possible resurgence of Japanese militarism. Patrols continued through the summer with each of the units becoming more settled in their Japanese surroundings. The support Flights were also busy and personnel from all units assisted with projects within local communities. During December some of 1315 Flight's Dakotas helped in flying humanitarian relief supplies to the Kobe area following an earthquake there. The communications provided by the support units was invaluable. For example, during the winter when Miho was cut off by snow one of the Austers flew a doctor in from Iwakuni to operate on a seriously ill airman, whose life was thus saved.

Transport aircraft from the home country, or in the case of the RAF from FEAF bases in Singapore, ran flights into Japan providing a vital logistic and morale-boosting link to home. Dakotas were the usual aircraft used, the RNZAF schedule was for example provided by

41RNZAF, and took a week on the long haul up the Pacific. These transport sorties were not without risk as illustrated on 6 April 1947 when Dakota NZ3547 was taking tour-expired Corsair pilots home. Between Manila and Morotai the port propeller 'ran away', but despite appalling tropical weather conditions then prevailing, the pilot skilfully brought the crippled aircraft into a safe landing. He subsequently received a well-earned AFC for a superb piece of flying. By this time, in addition to surveillance patrols, all the squadrons flew full training programmes, including air-to-ground firing and bombing. Unfortunately, during one firing detail on the Yonage range on 30 May 1947, an 11 Squadron Spitfire hit the ground, killing the pilot. Shortly afterwards the Indian squadron suffered a severe loss when in bad weather on 11 June 1947 two Spitfires (SM925 and TX979) flew into high ground at Okatama while in cloud. Both pilots were killed. With the impending independence of India from Britain, 4RIAF was recalled and, on 19 July 1947, it handed its Spitfires over to the RAF and left for home where it re-equipped with newly acquired Tempests. During this period, in addition to more normal duties, some of the RAAF Mustangs were used for anti-malarial mosquito spraying.

By the end of 1947 it was apparent that there was little threat of a resurgent Japanese militarism and thus the Occupation Force was serving little real purpose. Plans were therefore drawn up for the rundown and withdrawal of the BCOF. For the Air Component the reduction was rapid and on 23 February 1948 both 11 and 17 Squadrons disbanded. During that month 14RNZAF moved its Corsairs to Bofu AFB to be replaced at rebuilt Iwakuni AFB by the three RAAF Mustang squadrons. The rundown then began in earnest with most of the RAF contingent leaving Japan by 31 March 1948, leaving just the support aircraft of 1315 Flight and the Communications Squadron. The RAAF and RNZAF detachments continued for a few more months, though 14RNZAF ceased operations in August and returned to New Zealand. The Squadron's 19 surviving Corsairs were assembled in a large pile at Bofu and burnt on 10 October 1948. Later that month both 76RAAF and 82RAAF disbanded, leaving just 77RAAF as the sole remaining operational element. On 1 November 1948, the BCOF announced the disbandment and withdrawal of all units, except 77RAAF, and the end of the Air Component, which effectively ceased to exist on the 15th of that month.

While all remained relatively peaceful in the Japanese Islands as the population struggled to come to terms with the new postwar world, a few miles to the west the titanic struggle between the American-backed Chinese Nationalists led by Chiang Kai-shek and Soviet-supported Chinese Communists led by Mao Tse-tung was drawing to its fateful conclusion. The civil war, which had erupted in July 1946, saw the Nationalists pushed further and further eastwards until their only refuge was the tiny offshore island of Formosa. By October 1949 the ground war was virtually over, and by the end of the year the Chinese People's Liberation Army had reached the border of French Indo-China. Many Nationalist aircraft had fallen into Communist hands including quantities of ex-USAF P-47 and F-51 fighters, B-25 and B-26 medium-bombers and ex-RCAF Mosquito fighter-bombers. In July 1949, the Russians sent a military mission to Peking, and, by February 1950, Russian technicians and advisors were instrumental in setting up a jet-pilot training programme. About 200 WWII-vintage La-9, La-11, and Yak-9P fighters were supplied, together with a few MiG-9 jet fighters[2]; in addition, bomber regiments were formed with Pe-2 and Tu-2 light-bombers, and Il-2 and Il-10 ground-attack aircraft.

Meanwhile, after two years of unsuccessful attempts to reach agreement on a plan for the unification of Korea, the United States referred the problem to the United Nations, which then undertook to establish an independent Korean government following nationwide elections. The USSR refused to co-operate in this so, on 15 August 1948, the Republic of Korea was formed in the southern zone by American-supported Dr Syngman Rhee[3], with Seoul as its capital. Declaring this action to be illegal, the USSR created a similar puppet government – the Democratic People's Republic of Korea – with its capital at P'yongyang and with Russian-

---

[2] The MiG-9 was a twin-jet, straight wing aircraft based on a German design, which first flew in 1946.
[3] 73-year-old Korean-born Dr Rhee had been imprisoned as a young man for political activities and, on release, went to America where he graduated from both Harvard (MA) and Princeton (PhD). He returned briefly to Korea in 1910 before settling in America.

trained Marshal Kim Il-sung[4] in charge, who soon organised a North Korean People's Army. Allegedly, Soviet troops evacuated the north in December 1948, while US troops completed evacuation of the south in June 1949, although a small American military advisory group remained to organise the Republic of Korea Army. More than a year of continuous bickering, cross border raids, sabotage, terrorism, and guerrilla action harassing the south was reported, without breaking down the South Korean government. Alarmed by a serious incident in May 1949, South Korean forces penetrated up to two and a half miles into North Korean territory, and the British Foreign Secretary requested an assessment of the situation from the War office. A response was duly received:

> "In the past it has always been our view that irrespective of strengths the North Korean forces would have little difficulty in dealing effectively with the forces of South Korea should full-scale hostilities break out. This somewhat naturally (since they raised, equipped and trained South Korea forces) was not the American view. Recently, however, they have been coming round to our way of thinking regarding the capabilities of the respective forces.
>
> On the question of aggression by the North, there can be no doubt whatever that their ultimate objective is to overrun the South; and I think in the long term there is no doubt that they will do so, in which case, as you so aptly remark, the Americans will have to make a rather handsome contribution of equipment to the military strength of Asiatic Communism. As to their method of achieving their objective, short of World War III beginning, I think they will adopt the well-tried tactics of preparing the country from within rather than resort to open aggression, although 'frontier incidents' will doubtless continue.
>
> Regarding American policy, if in fact one exists, towards South Korea, I can only say we know little, and of their future intentions even less. Whilst being in no doubt about future North Korean (or Soviet) plans regarding South Korea, we think an invasion unlikely in the immediate view; however, if it did take place, I think it improbable that the Americans would become involved. The possession of South Korea is not essential for Allied strategic plans, and though it would obviously be desirable to deny it to the enemy, it would not be of sufficient importance to make it the cause of World War III. Meanwhile, we must accept an uneasy *status quo* and hope for the best."

The officer commanding the American Military Assistance Group in Korea, Brig-General W.L. Roberts, was similarly asked for his opinions of the current situation by the Director of Plans at the Pentagon; his response was more forthright and frank, and differed in its conclusions and suggestiveness:

> "If South Korea is called upon to defend itself against aggression from the North, its ground army is capable of doing an excellent job. If American advisers are present it will do an even better job, for we have found the Americans are leaned on more heavily the rougher it gets. In other words, the advisers will almost command except in name.
>
> All G-2 sources tell that the North Koreans have up to 100 Russian planes and a training program for pilots. You know and I know what 100 planes can do to troops, to towns and to transport on roads. So, if South Korea were attacked today by the inferior *[sic]* ground forces of North Korea plus their Air Corps, I feel that South Korea would take a bloody nose. Again then, knowing these people somewhat I feel they would follow the apparent winner and South Korea would be gobbled up to be added to the rest of Red Asia.
>
> This is a fat nation now with all its ECA [Economic and Cultural Aid] goods, with warehouses bulging with plenty of rice from a good crop, even if their finances are shaky with great inflationary tendencies. It is getting into the position of an excellent prize of war; strategically it points right into the heart of Japan and in the hands of the enemy it weakens the Japanese bastion of Western defense."

---

[4] Marshal Kim Il-sung had been a minor guerrilla leader fighting the Japanese in Manchuria in the 1930s before joining the Red Army and reportedly seeing much action during WWII. He returned to Korea in 1945 as a Kapitan. By early 1948 he was leader of the 100,000-strong North Korean People's Army.

General Sir Anthony Farrar-Hockley, himself a veteran of the Korean War, offers an insight to the thinking leading up to the invasion:

"Evidence suggests that Il-sung had proposed invasion to Stalin early in 1949 and discussed the matter with Mao Tse-tung, Chairman of the Chinese Communist Party in October 1949; that Stalin consulted Mao during his visit to Moscow on 16 December 1949, and approved the operation in February 1950. The Communist guerrilla war in the southern half of Korea was losing momentum and was being defeated by local security forces. But NKPA lacked the means to sustain an offensive and from February 1950 Stalin began to provide war material, moved from Russia into North Korea by the railway system of North-East China. The end of June 1950 was chosen for the opening of the invasion so as to permit the transplantation of rice shoots in the summer rains. It was expected the operation would be complete by the first rice harvest in August." [5]

This assessment is supported by the memoirs of Nikita Khrushchev – future Soviet Premier who succeeded Stalin on the latter's death – in which he admitted that North Korea's military leaders lusted after the fertile land further south:

"The North Koreans wanted to prod South Korea with the point of a bayonet. Kim Il-sung said that the first poke would touch off an internal explosion in South Korea and that the power of the people would prevail . . . He told Stalin he was absolutely certain of success. I remember Stalin had his doubts. He was worried the Americans would jump in, but we were inclined to think that if the war was fought swiftly – and Kim Il-sung was sure that it could be won swiftly – then intervention by the USA could be avoided." [6]

Meanwhile, trouble continued to flare up further north. Although the Chinese Nationalists had been pushed back to Formosa and the island remained under constant threat of invasion by Communist forces, the United States now took a stance and publicly announced its continued support for Chiang Kai-shek and his diminished military forces. This support encouraged the Chinese Nationalist Air Force to carry out strikes against mainland targets, the Chinese crews unknowingly meeting Russian-flown La-11s and MiG-15s on several occasions. For example, on 28 April 1950, Maj Yuri Keleinikov of the 29th Guards Fighter Air Regiment (GuFAR) shot down a CNAF P-38 which came down on the island of Zhoushan – the first-ever air victory for the MiG jet fighter. Just over two weeks later, on the night of 11 May 1950, a CNAF B-24 was shot down by a MiG-15 flown by Kapt I. Shinkarenko, also of the 29th GuFAR[7]. There had also been a number of serious incidents involving Soviet and US aircraft in the area, including two shortly after the end of WWII when, during the first, Yak-9s attacked and damaged a B-29 which was forced to carry out an emergency landing, followed by a second similiar action two months later. On this occasion the American aircraft was attacked by Soviet P-39s.

Since the end of WWII the USAF and RAF had been conducting spy flights along the vast borders of the Soviet Union, using bases in West Germany, Alaska, the Middle East, and Japan, to test the defences for electronic detecting technology including radar, and to search for airfields and missile sites. The Americans took the lead with converted USAF B-29s and USN P-2Vs fitted out with the latest electronic equipment, while the RAF was busy operating mainly from bases in Iraq, Egypt, Crete and Cyprus over the Soviet Union's southern borders, and from Hong Kong over islands held by Communist China, using initially long-range Mosquito PR34s.

---

[5] See *The British Part in the Korean War, Volume One: A Distant Obligation* by General Sir Anthony Farrar-Hockley DSO.

[6] See *Khrushchev Remembers*. In June 1999 it was announced that Nikita Khrushchev's son Sergei, then aged 63, had been granted US citizenship, having resided in the United States since 1991. It is difficult to imagine what his father would have made of the complete turn-around in US/Russian relationships.

[7] In April 1951, two CNAF B-26s were shot down by La-11s from the 351st FAR flown by Lts P. Dushin and V. Sidorov, and later that month Maj Nikolai Gushev of the same unit reported shooting down two CNAF F-51s. The air shooting war would continue above the Formosan Strait for many years to come.

The Hong Kong-based RAF crews returned on occasion having been fired upon by Communist anti-aircraft gunners but, as far as is known, no aircraft was lost or even damaged. USAF RF-80As of the 8th Tactical Recon Squadron operating out of Misawa AFB in Japan had also been carrying out spy flights over the Soviet Pacific islands and had even penetrated the mainland as far as the city of Vladivostok. Then, following the outbreak of the Korean War, the USAF transferred its 324th Recon Squadron equipped with RB-29s to Yokata AFB in Japan, from where it monitored, in addition to the North Korean defences, Russian activity along the Gulf of Anadyr and the Kamchatka Peninsula.

* * *

As recorded, the BCOF had been but a small contribution to the mighty United States Far East Command under General MacArthur, and the Air Component a minor part of the powerful USAF Far East Air Force commanded by General George E. Stratemeyer which comprised the US 5th Air Force (Maj-General Earle E. Partridge) based in the Japanese Home Islands, the US 13th Air Force based at Luzon in the Philippines, and the US 20th Air Force divided between Okinawa and Guam. By the beginning of 1950, the mainstay of the US 5th Air Force's capability were the three Wings equipped with F-80C interceptor/fighter-bombers – the USAF's first operational jet – which had recently converted from the F-51D Mustang, while, in support were two all-weather fighter units equipped with F-82G Twin Mustangs, and two squadrons with B-26 medium bombers:

8th Fighter-Bomber Wing comprising 35th, 36th and 80th FB Squadrons equipped with F-80Cs, plus 68th FAW Squadron with F-82Gs, at Itazuke AFB, Honshu.

35th Fighter Interceptor Wing comprising 39th, 40th and 41st FI Squadrons equipped with F-80Cs, plus 339th FAW Squadron with F-82Gs, and 8th Tactical Reconnaissance Squadron with RF-80As, at Yokata AFB, Honshu.

49th Fighter-Bomber Wing comprising 7th, 8th and 9th FB Squadrons equipped with F-80Cs at Misawa AFB, Honshu.

3rd Bombardment Group comprising 8th and 13th Bombardment Squadrons equipped with B-26s at Johnson AFB, Honshu.

374th Troop Carrier Wing comprising 6th and 22nd Troop Carrier Squadrons equipped with C-54s at Tachikawa AFB, Honshu.

At Okinawa, available to provide prompt support for the Japanese-based units, were the three squadrons of F-80Cs of the US 20th Air Force's 51st Fighter Interceptor Wing, plus an all-weather squadron with F-82Gs; while Guam was the home to the mighty 19th Bombardment Wing with three squadrons of B-29 heavy bombers, plus a long-range reconnaissance unit (the 31st SRS) equipped with RB-29s. Yet a further wing of F-80C fighter-bombers was based in the Philippines as part of the US 13th Air Force. At the beginning of June 1950, the US FEAF possessed a grand total of 1,172 aircraft of all types including some in storage and a few in salvage. Less than half this total was possessed by operational units, which included 365 F-80Cs, 32 F-82Gs, 25 RF-80As, 26 B-26s, 22 B-29s, and six RB-29s.

* * *

The sole remaining squadron of the BCOF's almost extinct Air Component, 77RAAF with its 26 F-51D Mustangs at Iwakuni AFB (see Appendix VI for details), was itself on the verge of being withdrawn to Australia in June 1950 when the Korean War broke out, by which time it had on strength 26 fully trained but mainly inexperienced pilots, of whom only a handful had flown operationally during WWII. These included the CO, Wg Cdr L.T. Spence DFC, and B Flight commander, Flt Lt J.I. Adams who was known to his friends as 'Bay', a veteran of the fighting in Northern Europe. Sqn Ldr Graham Strout was deputy commander. All the pilots were members of the RAAF.

A Flight	**B Flight**
Flt Lt S. Bradford	Flt Lt J.I. Adams
Flt Lt T.W. Murphy	Flt Lt G.R. Harvey
Flg Off K. McLeod	Flt Lt C.R. Noble
Flg Off T.E. McCrohan	Flg Off W.C. Horsman
P2 R.F. Fairweather	P1 B.F.S. Nicholls
P2 L. Reading	P2 G. Thornton AFM
P2 W.M. Garroway	P2 J.H. Flemming
P2 D.C. Ellis	P2 W.B. Rivers[8]
P3 M.J. Cottee	P3 R.E. Trebilco
P3 G.I. Stephens	P3 W.P. Harrop
P3 A.R. Turner	P4 K.E. Royal
P3 A.T. Stoney	

A reinforcement pilot in the guise of Flt Lt Leo Brown arrived from Headquarters where he had been acting as aide-de-camp to Lt-General Sir Horace Robertson, the Australian GOC BCOF, while Flt Lt Craig Kirkpatrick, the Squadron Intelligence Officer, was also an operational pilot. The Squadron also had on strength a WWII-vintage Wirraway trainer (A20-750), an Auster V for light communications work – probably an aircraft of the RAF's defunct 1315 Flight – and the services of an RAAF Dakota commanded by Flt Lt D.W. Hitchins (see Appendix III for biographical details relating to a number of the afore-mentioned RAAF pilots).

The NCO pilots were distinguished by the newly introduced Pilot 1 to Pilot 4 grading which replaced Sergeant, Flight Sergeant, and Warrant Officer 1st and 2nd Class ranks, and wore a laurel wreath badge on both sleeves in place of normal NCO stripes. After graduation as a pilot, one star inside the laurel wreath denoted the rank of Pilot 4 (P4). Although this rank entitled the wearer admission to the Sergeants' Mess, it was deemed equal to a Corporal for general ranking purposes and less than a Corporal for disciplinary purposes. After six months service as a pilot, a Pilot 4 was automatically promoted to Pilot 3 (P3), equal in status to a Sergeant but lower for disciplinary purposes. Pilot 2 (P2) equated with Flight Sergeant and Pilot 1 (P1) with Warrant Officer. The RAF, originator of this short-lived, ill-fated system, had dispensed with it by 1950 as unworkable. The RAAF however persevered for some while longer. Laurel leaves or stripes, the Squadron's NCO pilots found themselves in an anomalous situation in that USAF fighter aircrew were all commissioned officers. An indication of the comforts the officers and NCOs were accorded while stationed in Japan were recorded by RAAF Press Officer (and later Official RAAF Historian) Flt Lt George Odgers:

> "After the day's work the men relaxed in the comfortable mess ante-room where the yell 'boy-san' brought a Japanese waiter running to take orders for drinks from the bar. The Japanese girls [who worked on the base as typists, room girls, waitresses and kitchen maids] were clean, hard-working, and most polite and ladylike. Each single officer and non-commissioned officer had a room girl assigned to him to make his bed, wash and iron clothes, shine shoes, sew and mend. He was certainly well looked after and all he had to do in return was to give an occasional 'presento' of chocolate, cocoa or soap. No sooner did the airman discard a dirty shirt or pair of trousers than the girl would pounce on them and begin immediately to wash them. They would even pull the shoe laces out of shoes and wash them!
>
> New arrivals suffered some embarrassment when the girls, with a more balanced sense of modesty than the average Westerner, didn't bother to leave the room when they were dressing or undressing. The first reaction was to hurry them outside the door and close it behind them, but in time one got used to this kind of thing. The old occupation hands

---

[8] P2 Wally Rivers, flying Mustang A68-722, had survived a recent air collision with a Royal Navy Firefly flown by Lt(P) A. Baillie of 827 Squadron from HMS *Triumph* off Kure, Japan; both aircraft plunged into the sea with the loss of the Firefly's observer, Cmd Ob Gibbons, the two pilots having baled out safely.

seemed to have a monopoly of the cute-looking 'girl-sans' and the newly-arrived servicemen would usually be assigned the culls who, although extremely efficient, were sometimes as ugly as sin." [9]

On 2 March 1950, a committee of the UN Commission on Korea, a body set up to foster the peaceful unification of North and South, recommended the appointment of trained military observers to help in its work of checking and reporting incidents that might lead to military conflict along the 38th Parallel. After an interchange of cables between the Australian Mission to the United Nations and the Departments of External Affairs and Defence in Canberra, the Australian government provided two observers, Maj F.S. Peach from the Australian Army, and Sqn Ldr R.J. Rankin RAAF. Other member nations had also been invited to provide representatives but by late May 1950 the only observers with the Commission in Korea were the two Australians. For fourteen days, 9-23 June, Peach and Rankin visited ROK troops along the 38th Parallel, inspecting dispositions, weapons, command posts, and interviewing commanders and intelligence officers to gain as complete a picture as possible of activities on both sides of the line. When they returned to Seoul, they reported:

> "The principal impression left with the observers after the field tour along the 38th Parallel is that the South Korean Army is organised entirely for defence, and is in no condition to carry out an attack on a large scale against the forces of the North. No reports have been received of any unusual activity on the part of the North Korean troops that would indicate any imminent change in the general situation on the Parallel."

On the very next day came the invasion.

77RAAF had just completed its last scheduled flying programme on 23 June, and when the final flight of Mustangs touched down on the concrete runway at Iwakuni AFB the pilots thought it was for the last time. Next day there was a huge farewell party. Little did they know what fate had in store for them. At 0400 next morning, the North Koreans launched their attack while some of the last festivities at Iwakuni were still going on. Ops at Itazuke AFB rang with the news, which was greeted with total disbelief by the Australians. But these fragmented reports, as they came in, suggested something bigger than just a border skirmish, and the RAAF Squadron was immediately placed on standby together with units of the US 5th Air Force.

---

[9] See *Across the Parallel* by George Odgers.

PART ONE

LAND-BASED AIR OPERATIONS

Korea 1950-1951

The invasion of South Korea by forces of the North exploded out of the darkness without warning on Sunday 25 June 1950, at 0400 Korean local time. Spearheaded by 150 Russian-built T-34 tanks, seven divisions of North Korean infantry under Marshal Choe Yong Gun attacked in the breaking light across the 38th Parallel. Taken completely by surprise, lightly-armed South Korean forces wavered and broke. As the tanks rumbled towards their initial objectives, the towns of Kaesong and Chunch'on, more North Korean infantry and marines landed from a fleet of small craft on the east coast near Kangnung. At 0800 Kaesong fell, but it was not until just after midday that P'yongyang radio announced a formal declaration of war. The North Koreans proclaimed to the world that their invasion was in response to an attack from South Korea. A report drafted by the two United Nations observers just prior to the attack showed, however, that nothing could have been further from the truth.

Garbled radio messages of what was happening in South Korea in those early hours were picked up in Japan, resulting in a standby F-82 of the 68th FAWS being scrambled at 0400 from Itazuke AFB to investigate. The crew, 1/Lt George D. Deans and his radar operator 2/Lt Marvin R. Olsen, were given a vector to Seoul and instructions to fly up to the 38th Parallel and report on any activity seen on the main roads and railroads. About ten miles south of the line they reported sighting a large military convoy on the road, all on the move southwards, as Olsen recalled:

> "When we arrived in the area, it was overcast with tops of about 8,000 feet. Deans flew us out over the water for letdown, using our airborne search radar – mounted on the central wing between the two fuselages in an enormous housing. We broke out at about 2,000 feet, just west of In'chon, and we proceeded to Kimpo airfield before heading north towards the 38th. About ten miles south of the line we saw a huge convoy of vehicles, over 58 tanks, trucks, and assorted vehicles on the road, when we stopped counting, all on the move. George took us back to 8,000 feet so we could report back what we had observed . . ." [1]

This flight would be retrospectively recorded as the first operational mission flown by the USAF in the Korean War.

---

[1] See *Mig Alley* by Larry Davis.

CHAPTER I

INVASION: DAYS OF CRISIS

June – July 1950

"Our first burst hit the rear of the fuselage and knocked some pieces off. The Yak pilot
racked it over in a steep turn to the right and we gave him another burst along the right wing.
This set the gas tank on fire and took the right flap and aileron off . . ."[2]

1/Lt Carl Fraser, radar operator aboard an F-82 of the USAF's
68th FAW Squadron flown by 1/Lt William G. Hudson who was credited with the first
kill of the Korean War, on 27 June 1950

While Korean fought Korean on the ground, the cloudy conditions which prevailed over Seoul
until about noon had prevented the North Korean Air Force (NKAF) from entering the arena,
but at 1315, as the skies cleared, two NKAF Yak-9s buzzed Youi-do and Kimpo airfields near
the capital although they then returned northwards without attacking. However, later in the
afternoon, four more Yaks strafed the area around Seoul Railway Station. Then, at 1700, two
Yaks strafed Kimpo, hitting the control tower, a fuel dump, and an American Military Air
Service (MATS) C-54 transport which had been grounded with a damaged wing. Four other
Yaks simultaneously strafed Youi-do airfield and damaged an AT-6 (the armed version of the T-
6 Texan trainer) of the Republic of Korea Air Force (ROKAF). Two hours later, at about 1900,
six more Yaks again carried out a strafing attack against Kimpo where the damaged MATS
transport aircraft was now destroyed. Eager to retaliate, though poorly equipped, the ROKAF
sent AT-6s to the battle zone during the evening, where they dropped a number of 15kg bombs
on the enemy's advancing columns. Neither of the Korean Air Forces could boast a modern
armoury, as their comparative strengths on the eve of the invasion would indicate:

Republic of Korea Air Force (ROKAF)
Commanded by Maj-General Kim Chung Yul, the ROKAF possessed 10 AT-6s, 8 L-4s and
4 L-5s supplied by the United States and located at Kimpo and Youi-do airfields, with
detachments at Suwon, Taegu, Kwangju, Kinsan, and Cheju-do. The ROKAF also
possessed at least one Japanese Army Type 95 biplane trainer, a legacy from WWII, and
later modified a crash-repaired AT-6 by fitting floats from a former Japanese Navy A6M2
Rufe floatplane and wingtip tanks from a USAF F-80. A total of 102 pilots were currently
on strength, of whom 30 were fully trained.

North Korean Air Force (NKAF)
The NKAF was commanded by Maj-General Wang Yong, a Soviet-trained former bomber
pilot, and possessed a total of approximately 70 Yak-7, Yak-9, La-7 and La-11 Soviet-built
WWII-vintage fighters, plus 65 Il-2 and Il-10 ground-attack aircraft, all supplied by the
Russians. In addition there were 22 Yak-18 trainers and eight Po-2 biplane trainers. The
majority of the combat aircraft were based on two airfields near P'yongyang, the North
Korean capital, and at the airfield at Yonpo on the east coast. There was also an airfield at
Wonsan, and advanced landing strips were under construction near the 38th Parallel at
Sinmak, P'yongyang, Kumsong, and Kansong.

---

[2] See *Mig Alley*.

Back in Seoul, at a few minutes before midnight, the US Ambassador to Korea informed General MacArthur that he intended to evacuate women and children from the capital, since the situation was clearly worsening. The Supreme Commander was advised that the evacuees were to be loaded on to several merchant freighters currently in harbour at Inch'on and would be sent to the Japanese port of Fukuoka as soon as possible in the morning, at which MacArthur agreed to provide fighter cover for the operation. At 0045 on the morning of 26 June, FEAF HQ in Japan was ordered into action and Colonel John M. White, commander of the 8th FBW at Yokata AFB, was tasked with the protection duty. He envisaged some difficulties in carrying out this duty, since fighter cover work was normally a job for long-endurance conventional aircraft rather than fuel-hungry jets. His 68th FAWS had only a dozen operational F-82s available, and the 5th Air Force's initial reaction was to request the use of 77RAAF's Mustangs at Iwakuni AFB to solve the problem, but MacArthur refrained from using them because the Australian government had not yet taken a stand on the Korean situation. Instead, the 339th FAWS was ordered to move its F-82s from Yokata AFB to Itazuke and eight more F-82s of the 4th FAWS were also ordered to Itazuke. To clear the ramps to receive these additional fighters, the C-54s of MATS currently stationed at Itazuke were moved to nearby Ashiya AFB.

Evacuation operations therefore began in Seoul during the early morning hours of 26 June under an air umbrella of F-82s. The fighters were initially instructed to remain offshore at all times and only shoot in defence of the freighters. However, in an ever-changing scenario, instructions were later amended to allow them to patrol inland to cover truck convoys moving from Seoul to Inch'on, although in general the fighter patrols remained over Inch'on harbour. The American pilots did not have to wait long before NKAF fighters appeared on the scene when, at 1330, two of four patrolling F-82s were jumped by a single Yak-9 or La-7 – the Americans were unsure of its identity. Uncertain whether to return fire, the F-82s took evasive action and the NKAF fighter climbed vertically into the overcast and was not seen again. By the evening the ROK Army was virtually routed and North Korean tanks were at the outskirts of Seoul, the unprotected South Korean capital.

Next day, General MacArthur directed the FEAF to protect fully the evacuation of American civilians from Kimpo and Inch'on. In the light of the aggressive action by the NKAF fighters, USAF fighters covering the evacuation ports were released from their previous restrictions. They were now cleared to return hostile fire and to pursue the attackers, while the FEAF was authorised to initiate combat operations against any potential threat to the safe continuance of the evacuations. Thus, American fighter pilots soon found themselves embroiled in a series of actions. The first clash occurred during the morning as C-54s from Japan were engaged in evacuating American civilians from Kimpo when five aircraft, initially identified as Yak-9s but which were apparently a mixture of La-7s and La-11s, appeared and were promptly intercepted by four F-82s of the 68th FAWS. Three of the North Korean fighters were shot down, the first kill of the war[1] being credited to the crew of 1/Lt William G. Hudson (pilot) and 1/Lt Carl Fraser (radar observer), who saw the pilot bale out, as remembered by Fraser:

> "Our first burst hit the rear of the fuselage and knocked some pieces off. The Yak pilot racked it over in a steep turn to the right and we gave him another burst along the right wing. This set the gas tank on fire and took the right flap and aileron off. By this time we were so close we almost collided with him. I could clearly see the pilot turn around and say something to the observer. Then he pulled his canopy back and climbed out on the wing. Once again he leaned in and said something to the observer. But he was either scared or wounded as he never attempted to jump. The Yak pilot pulled the rip-cord and the chute dragged him off the wing just before the ship rolled over and went in." [3]

The downed pilot was seen on the ground surrounded by ROK soldiers but the Americans learned later that he had been killed when he opened fire at the South Koreans. Meanwhile, a second fighter identified as a La-7 was shot down by 1/Lt Charles B. Moran, whose own

---

[3] See *Mig Alley*. Initially believed to have been a Yak-9, Hudson's victim was eventually credited as a La-11 but was apparently a Yak-7U.

aircraft had sustained damage to its tail unit, and a third was claimed by the CO of the 339th FAWS, Maj James W. Little (a WWII seven-victory fighter ace), whose patrol was flying at a higher altitude. Two more were claimed probably destroyed by his pilots. Shortly afterwards, four patrolling F-80s of the 35th FBS sighted eight Il-10 ground-attack aircraft approaching and, in the first ever combat by USAF jet fighters, four of the NKAF aircraft were shot down, two being claimed by 1/Lt Robert E. Mayne and one apiece by Capt Raymond E. Schillereff and 1/Lt Robert H. Dewald. The encounter clearly demonstrated to the Americans that jet fighters were far superior to older conventional aircraft types.

The only aircraft available with the range to strike effectively at targets in Korea from the FEAF's Japanese bases were B-26 of the 3rd BG, usually stationed at Johnson AFB in central Honshu. However, at the time of the invasion its two combat squadrons were away in southern Japan; the 8th BS was at Ashiya on the island of Kyushu participating in air defence exercises with the US 20th Air Force on Okinawa, while the 13th BS had just moved into Matsushima AFB in southern Honshu for Group manoeuvres. With its personnel and resources thus spread over three separate Japanese bases, the 3rd BG was thrown into turmoil when orders to initiate combat operations came. As luck would have it, the positioning of the 8th BS at Ashiya AFB, the nearest FEAF facility in Japan to the fighting in Korea, was fortuitous, and the 13th BS was ordered to join it there.

The 8th BS, despite having only four aircraft available for operations, was detailed for night interdiction duties and, on the night of 27/28 June, these were despatched to attack North Korean armoured units north of Seoul. Bad weather and darkness prevented the crews from locating their targets and all returned with bombs intact. A second strike was also abandoned for the same reasons but next morning (28 June), the 3rd BG put a dozen aircraft into the air including nine of the 13th BS to attack the rail marshalling yards at Munsan near the 38th Parallel. This marked both the B-26's début over Korea and the first strike of the Korean War by US aircraft. Shortly after take-off the aircraft flown by 1/Lt Remer L. Harding was obliged to turn back with problems. In poor weather, the B-26 crashed while attempting to land at Ashiya, its crew becoming the first USAF fatalities of the war. Meanwhile, the remaining B-26s, despite having failed to rendezvous with the intended F-82 escort from Okinawa, continued to the target and once there split into groups. Following what the crews believed had been a successful mission, the B-26s strafed and rocketed enemy troops in the area. Several aircraft sustained superficial damage and one, piloted by 1/Lt Raymond J. Cyborski, went further west than planned. Cyborski apparently lost control while letting down through clouds over the sea and the aircraft crashed, only the navigator (1/Lt Lister) surviving the bale out to be picked up by a Japanese fishing boat. Another aircraft, flown by 1/Lt Monte Ballew, was damaged by small-arms fire during the attack and successfully carried out an emergency landing on one engine at Suwon, where the aircraft was abandoned. A third 13th BS aircraft, that flown by 1/Lt Darrell B. Sayre, was also lost.

During the afternoon, at 1330, four Yaks appeared unannounced over Suwon airfield and strafed the flak-damaged B-26 and an unserviceable 68th FAWS F-82. Five hours later, shortly before dusk, a further six Yaks swept over Suwon just as a C-54 transport of the 22nd Troop Carrier Squadron was on its finals. Despite damage to his aircraft, the pilot managed to turn away and head for Ashiya where he landed safely, but a second C-54 on the ground was strafed and went up in flames. By the evening of the 28th Seoul had fallen to the North Koreans, together with nearby Kimpo airfield, as ROK forces continued retreating towards Suwon. Among those captured at Seoul and interned were the British Minister and his Vice-Consul[4].

---

[4] The Vice-Consul was George Blake, who was also a member of the British Secret Intelligence Staff; he remained in Communist hands until the end of the war by which time his political sympathies had crossed the divide. He was recruited by the KGB and on release spied for the Soviets until his exposure in 1961 when he was tried for espionage, found guilty and sentenced to 42 years imprisonment. However, five years later he escaped from prison and defected to Russia. When one considers that Kim Philby was the First Secretary at the British Embassy in Washington, and that Guy Burgess was Second Secretary, while Donald Maclean was the Head of the American Department in London – all later self-confessed Communist agents – it is little wonder that the Americans believed their Intelligence Service was being compromised.

Other diplomats included the French Consul-General and members of his staff, while many missionaries and nuns were rounded up and similarly interned. All were taken to P'yongyang.

Air cover continued to be handled mainly by F-80s and F-82s but, particularly because of the limited availability of the latter, it was vital to find another alternative. The Australian government was still waiting to see the reaction of the UN, so Mustangs belonging to 77RAAF remained unavailable. A solution was soon forthcoming when it was revealed that approximately 30 retired USAF F-51Ds had been stored in Japan during the change-over to jets, and that another ten were being used by the fledgling ROKAF. It transpired that ten South Korean pilots, the majority with experience from WWII, had been selected to fly their aircraft to Itazuke AFB for further training. Now, with the arrival of the 8th FBW at Itazuke, it was decided to organise the ROKAF F-51s into a composite unit of US and ROK pilots under the command of Maj Dean E. Hess, a WWII veteran. The Koreans began intensive training immediately, eager to fly in combat and, within two weeks, the composite unit would be formed into the 51st (Provisional) Squadron and transferred to Taegu airfield, a forward base on the Korean peninsula some 60 miles north of Pusan.

B-29s of the 19th BG were in action on the morning of 29 June when nine of the heavy bombers raided Kimpo airfield from 3,000 feet. Three Yak-9s attempted to interfere but one was claimed shot down by the air gunners and a second was damaged. In the afternoon B-26s carried out an attack on P'yongyang airfield and on bridges spanning the Han while escorting F-82s bombed and strafed troops, aircraft of the 68th FAWS using napalm for the first time in Korea. A lone Yak-3 attempted to intercept the B-26s but was claimed shot down by S/Sgt Nyle S. Mickley, a gunner aboard one of the light bombers. Elsewhere F-80s joined in ground strafing sorties while others patrolled the Han, making five separate interceptions of Communist aircraft attempting to strike at Suwon airfield two of which (an La-7 and an Il-10) were claimed shot down by 1/Lts William T. Norris and Roy W. Marsh of the 8th FBS. In the meantime the ROKAF F-51s were put to immediate operational use, American pilots flying them as part of the escort provided for General MacArthur's personal C-54 during his visit to Pusan on the afternoon of 29 June, additional escort being provided by F-80s. Also on board the VIP aircraft was a press contingent with included Australian war correspondent Roy Macartney:

> "Thursday 29 June was one of those incredibly crowded days that come to a man perhaps once in a lifetime. Taking off at Haneda at dawn, we flew in MacArthur's private plane *Bataan*. Aboard were all MacArthur's top generals including Stratemeyer, Commander of the Far East Air Force, which made us all feel better about probable air cover as we speculated over a possible encounter with Yaks. MacArthur paced up and down the plane, puffing at his corn-cob pipe. Taking a vacant chair, he turned to the press and gave us his lucid assessment of the Far Eastern situation. He had apparently already decided there was little chance that South Korean ground forces would be able to repel the Communist invaders and thought the task would require American troops. We landed on the Suwon strip, flanked by the remains of two or three planes shot up on the ground the previous day by Yaks. MacArthur immediately lunged into conference with President Rhee, Ambassador Muccio, Brig-General John Church (commander of his advance headquarters), and South Korean officers. The news he heard was not good." [5]

While MacArthur was thus in conference at Suwon's schoolhouse, four aircraft tentatively identified as Yak-9s, but believed to have been three Il-10s escorted by a lone La-7, approached Suwon as if to attack the airfield. Patrolling F-51Ds of ROKAF aircraft flown by American pilots intercepted, and all four intruders were shot down, two of the ground-attack aircraft falling to 1/Lt Orrin R. Fox and the other to 1/Lt Richard J. Burns, while the La-7 was shot down by 1/Lt Harry T. Sandlin. As a result of the air action one North Korean pilot was seen to bale out and land in the midst of some South Koreans. He did not survive. However, a second NKAF pilot, a Major, was taken prisoner and later allegedly told his captors that their Soviet advisors had ordered them to bomb South Korea as they were aware that the South Korean air

---

[5] See *With the Australians in Korea* by Norman Bartlett (Editor).

force possessed only a few small aircraft. The prisoner apparently also revealed that the NKAF possessed only 80 pilots of whom ten were assessed as 'good' and 40 others as 'fair', which led FEAF Intelligence officers to concur that Soviet instructor pilots were possibly participating in these initial attacks on South Korea[6]. The Supreme Commander was amongst those who witnessed the action. War correspondent Macartney summed up the busy few hours:

> "In a few crowded hours we drove to the front line on the Han, were buzzed by one of our own F-80 jet fighters, saw American planes knock down two Yaks [sic] over Suwon, watched as President Rhee and Ambassador Muccio plunged into the muddy paddy fields as an ill-fated Yak attacked the strip from which we were preparing to take-off in an L-5 . . . and then slipped off the ground in *Bataan*, once more ourselves . . ." [7]

Following his brief inspection of the ROK defences on the Han, MacArthur authorised immediate strikes against NKAF airfields north of the 38th Parallel, the 3rd BG launching 18 B-26s to attack Heijo airfield near P'yongyang at dusk. The elated crews returned with claims for at least 25 North Korean aircraft destroyed on the ground, and the destruction of a lone Yak which attempted to intercept. One B-26 of the 13th BS was lost with the death of the pilot, 1/Lt William T. O'Connell. It was of vital importance for photo-reconnaissance flights to visit the NKAF airfields, this task falling to four RF-80As of the 8th TRS which were now operating from Itazuke AFB. As one USAF officer wrote:

> "On 26 June 1950, the 5th Air Force found itself looking northward through a pair of opaque glasses. Tactical and strategic information needed by the UN forces was totally lacking due to the veritable blackout of North Korea imposed following the close of WWII. Recon, the only solution to the problem, consisted at this time of one photo-jet squadron and one gun-camera lab, not a very impressive array of equipment to say the least. More was needed, in fact, much more if we were to ferret out the information vital to waging a successful campaign of any proportion. Immediately a call was rushed to HQFEAF for recon. The report was negative. There was none to be had in the Far East Command. The request was then relayed to HQUSAF. All that was available, though not combat ready, was the 162nd TR Squadron (night photo) and the 363rd Recon Technical Squadron." [8]

The latter two units were despatched forthwith but would not arrive in Japan until August. Until then, the RF-80s of the 8th TRS would have to bear the brunt of the necessary sorties. At least their speed would prevent interception by the NKAF's piston-engined fighters. The first such flight was undertaken by 1/Lt Bryce Poe II, a successful sortie and was celebrated as the first ever operational USAF jet reconnaissance sortie[9]. But first priority was for USAF strikes against Communist forces massing on the north bank of the Han, 15 B-29s of the 19th BG being diverted from a planned airfield strike to carry out attacks on the troops and their transport, using 250-lb fragmentation bombs, while B-26s rocketed and strafed convoys in the Seoul area.

The last day of the month brought further success for the F-80s when two Yak-9s were shot down by 1/Lts Charles A. Wurster and John B. Thomas of the 36th FBS, this unit also losing an aircraft when it collided with high tension cables while ground strafing. The American pilot was able to reach friendly territory before baling out. Following this loss it was decided to employ FEAF F-80s exclusively for air combat duties. Because of the superior range of the F-51D over the shorter duration jets, the piston-engined aircraft were well suited for operations across the Inland Sea; they were capable of remaining longer over the combat zone for air fighting, for ground-attack, and for escorting B-26s from southern Japan. As a result of this

---

[6] It is interesting to note that Russian ace Kapt Grigorii Ges of the 176th GuFAR included amongst his victories an F-82; as far as can be determined, no F-82s were ever engaged in combat with MiG-15s.
[7] See *With the Australians in Korea*.
[8] See the history of the 67th TRW.
[9] 1/Lt Poe was amongst those pilots of the 8th TRS who had participated in spy flights over Soviet Pacific islands and the mainland city of Vladisvostok prior to the outbreak of the Korean conflict.

assessment, it was decided that three of the F-80 wings were to be re-equipped with F-51Ds on their way from the United States; the first of the re-equipped units, the 40th FIS, would arrive at Po'hang on the east coast of Korea by the middle of the month.

* * *

During an emergency meeting of the UN Security Council in New York, on the afternoon of the invasion, it was agreed that the crisis demanded international police action, but in response to the UN's show of support for the plight of the South Koreans, the Russian Deputy Foreign Minister, Mr Andrei Gromyko, made a scathing radio attack on the United States for giving air and sea support to South Korea. He argued that the Security Council resolution was illegal because of the absence of two permanent Council members, China and the USSR, although China was represented legally by the Nationalists, since the UN refused to recognise the Peking Communist Government. Meanwhile in Canberra, Mr R.G. Menzies, the Prime Minister of Australia, announced that two Royal Australian Navy ships in Japanese waters, the destroyer HMAS *Bataan* and the frigate *Shoalhaven*, had been placed at the disposal of the United Nations in support of the Republic of Korea. At the same time, units of the US Navy and the British Far Eastern Fleet began moving towards the coasts of Korea. In Britain, Prime Minister Attlee and Chiefs-of-Staff were in the dark as to American intentions and accordingly signalled the Chairman of the British Joint Services Mission in Washington, Marshal of the Royal Air Force Lord Tedder:

"Prime Minister is anxious to obtain some idea of the American Plan of Campaign in Korea as indeed we are, since British and Commonwealth forces are now taking part.
2. We assume that the American intention is to clear the territory up to the 38th Parallel. The following questions are therefore relevant:
(a) What American forces are immediately available and what reinforcements are envisaged?
(b) Is it the intention to use land forces if this becomes necessary?
3. As the Americans have committed themselves to restore *status quo* the US Chiefs-of-Staff are doubtless making some appreciation of what this is likely to entail including the timing. We would be very grateful for their views on this in due course.
4. We realise that the US Government cannot commit themselves at the present time but we are most anxious to know unofficially the way the Chiefs-of-Staff are thinking. A preliminary indication of their views early next week would be of the greatest value."

Lord Tedder was able to respond within hours:

"Following points arose in personal talk with Bradley [General Omar Bradley, Chairman of US Joint Chiefs-of-Staff] on his return from the White House.
2. Immediate action in Korea is to put combat group by air and sea to secure port on SE coast. Bradley's view is that of the four [US] divisions in Japan MacArthur could with safety employ two in Korea if necessary. If more were to be needed in Korea their places in Japan would have to be filled from the US. President has authorised employment of US naval and air forces north of the 38th Parallel against the North Korean forces.
3. At this morning's meeting at the White House which was a non-party one representing all parties and both Houses [of Congress] hope was expressed that all nations would make some definite contribution to the UN forces in Korea even though the main burden inevitably American and such contributions in most cases merely token ones. Bradley said that UK and Commonwealth contributions widely and genuinely appreciated, both as regards their promptitude and scale. He realised our already heavy commitments in Far East but said that if, repeat if, a land force contribution, however small, could be added it would have excellent political effect in sealing even more firmly our complete unity on this issue.
4. Bradley said his view, and I understand the US Chiefs-of-Staff view, is that the Soviet has no desire for a war at this stage. On the other hand this affair is a warning to us to overhaul our plans and preparations against the major threat, and we touched on problems of higher direction, command, state of present planning purely in exploratory fashion.

5. Am sure I need not emphasise that above was all given in confidence on purely personal basis . . ."

This assurance of American intent seemed to satisfy Prime Minister Attlee and the British Chiefs-of-Staff, at least for the time being.

The American Army's four divisions in Japan were all under strength and currently under training, though on 1 July, 400 infantrymen and a battery of artillery from the 24th Division were airlifted to Pusan in an immediate show of support for the ROK forces. General Robertson, Commander of the BCOF in Japan, now signalled 77RAAF to prepare for combat. General MacArthur had asked the Australian Government for the Squadron and Robertson was anticipating Canberra's response, which came next day, together with approval for UN forces to use Iwakuni AFB. With the Australian Government's commitment to make the base available, the 3rd BG began to transfer its B-26s from Johnson AFB.

*   *   *

July 1950

Meanwhile, at 0500 on 2 July, one week after the North Koreans had launched their offensive, a section of 77RAAF's Mustangs took off from Iwakuni for their first operation of the war. There were three separate missions. The first involved a flight of four Mustangs flown by Sqn Ldr Graham Strout (A68-803), Flt Lt Stuart Bradford (A68-799), Flt Lt Tom Murphy (A68-708), and P3 Milt Cottee (A68-707) tasked to escort USAF C-47s bringing back wounded personnel from Korea. Flt Lt Bradford was forced to abort when his radio became unserviceable, the remaining three Mustangs following when the American aircraft failed to rendezvous. The second mission consisted of eight Mustangs led by Wg Cdr Spence (A68-809) ordered to escort 17 B-26s of the 3rd BG while they bombed railway bridges over the Han south of Seoul. Shortly after take-off one Mustang (A68-757 flown by P2 Jim Flemming) had to abort and return to Iwakuni but the remaining fighters rendezvoused with the medium bombers over Tongnee near Pusan. The American air gunners regarded the seven RAAF fighters with obvious suspicion at first, particularly as they were expecting high cover, not a close escort. With the Mustangs weaving from side to side just above, the formation set course for the target. Some flak was encountered near Seoul but none of the aircraft was hit, and the bombing was successful. On the way back to Japan, two F-80s, apparently suspicious of the RAAF roundels, made a firing pass at one of the Mustangs but Flg Off Bill Horsman (A68-772) saw the threat in time and avoided being hit by turning inside the less manoeuvrable jet fighters.

The third task of the day called for six Mustangs to escort nine B-29s of the 19th BG on a bombing mission to Yonpo. The heavy bombers had come from the huge US base at Okinawa to rendezvous with the RAAF fighters over Kangnung on the east coast of Korea, 12 miles south of the 38th Parallel. Splitting into pairs, the Mustangs took up positions on either side and above the bombers. It was an easy mission and no opposition was encountered. The Australians had a good view of the mighty B-29s as they droned lazily over their target and unloaded. Flashes from exploding bombs could be seen among the buildings. Anti-aircraft fire was inaccurate, black puffs of bursting shells falling below and behind the bombers. The whole attack lasted only a few minutes. By the end of the day 77RAAF had flown a total of 16 sorties, with two aborted, without loss. This successful though unspectacular start gave no indication of a tragedy which was about to occur.

An unusual report reached FEAF HQ during the day. American pilots had sighted what they believed was a Tu-4 bomber, the Russian copy of the B-29, flying in a northerly direction over Suwon escorted by two La-7s. If correct, this was alarming news. Tu-4s were not known to be in the NKAF inventory, and a Russian or Chinese presence could have far-reaching consequences. According to the observers, none of the aircraft carried any identification markings. But the alarm soon passed when it was realised that this sighting was quite likely part of the B-29 mission to Yonpo escorted by 77RAAF Mustangs, while enquiries confirmed that the USAF also had RB-29s operating from Japan without any identification markings. Nonetheless, USAF fighter pilots were told to be vigilant and, in one instance, 1/Lt Harry White of the 339th FAWS flying an F-82 was ordered to intercept one of these RB-29s which had suffered radio failure, and escort it to Misawa AFB. Since it was virtually identical to the

Tu-4, its actual identity could not be confirmed until it was on the ground. White had been ordered to shoot it down if it made any aggressive moves. Fortunately for the American crew, it did not.

On the ground, the advanced guard of the 24th Division moved forward to take up positions blocking the North Koreans at Osan, as far north on the main road from Seoul as possible. Their follow-up force, the first sea-borne contingent of American troops, was shipped to Pusan. After two days of delay because of bad weather, Maj Hess led the American instructors attached to the ROK, and six of the Korean pilots, to Taegu airfield (known to the USAF as K-2[10]). By now the North Koreans had already crossed the Han and were pressing the ROK Army southward. The South Korean pilots flew their first missions on 3 July in spite of their lack of proper combat training, and set fire to a fuel dump, destroyed some trucks and killed an estimated 30 enemy troops near Seoul. The next day, however, the senior Korean pilot, Colonel Lee Keun Sok, who had flown for the Japanese during WWII and allegedly had some 20 air victories against American aircraft, was lost when his aircraft crashed while attacking a tank in the Anyang area, south of Seoul. Although their job was actually the training of the ROK pilots and maintenance crews, the American instructors soon became involved in ground support missions themselves, and thereby were the first American pilots to fly from the old, Japanese-built bases in South Korea.

The RAAF was back in action at 1400 on 3 July, when eight Mustangs, each armed with six 60-lb rockets, took off from Iwakuni to attack enemy troop movements along the main highway between Suwon and P'yongtaek. Wg Cdr Spence (A68-809) led one section while Flt Lt Bay Adams (A68-772) led the other. Before leaving, the CO had voiced doubts about the assigned target area because it seemed too far to the south. He checked with the 5th Air Force Tactical Control Centre at Itazuke and received assurance that the North Koreans had advanced that far. Sweeping over the assigned area, where a river estuary and a railway junction were clearly pinpointed, the Australians found a train just begging to be attacked. After double checking the location, Adams declared that he was going after the train with his section. Lining up the locomotive, he was down to 1,500 feet and about to open fire when he noticed a symbol marked on the train. It was a red and blue orb divided by a curved line through its centre. South Korean markings! Scanning the map on his knee, Adams checked the pinpoints again. He was obviously in the right place. It seemed probable that the North Koreans could have captured the train and were using it for their own purposes. By radio he called to an American Forward Air Control (FAC) aircraft which was further south, and received an assurance that the area was under enemy control. Thus convinced, Adams brought his section round again but, as he prepared to attack, the locomotive was suddenly blown off the rails and over onto its side before he could open fire. Looking up, Adams saw that the CO's section was attacking from the opposite direction. Having been robbed of the train, Adams ordered his section to concentrate on a nearby convoy of trucks and, for the next 20 minutes, the Mustangs spent their time rocketing and strafing every vehicle they could find. When they finally departed they left behind total carnage.

Later, four more Mustangs led by Flt Lt Tom Murphy escorted B-26s of the 3rd BG to bomb a target south of Seoul, where they encountered medium but inaccurate flak. On returning to Iwakuni, Mustang A68-753 crash-landed although P2 Les Reading escaped injury. That evening, as the Australians were celebrating the success of their earlier mission, news came through that there had been an appalling mistake. The trucks they had attacked had been carrying ROK reinforcements and the advance battalion of the US 24th Division, the first American troops to be rushed to Korea. They had suffered severe casualties, including 29 fatalities, and the train had been loaded with ammunition. Australian war correspondent Roy Macartney was with the Americans at the time and on the receiving end of the attack:

---

[10] Since American airmen had been experiencing trouble with the similarity and pronounciation of Korean place names, FEAF Headquarters assigned a K-for-Korea site number to each airfield in Korea. For example, Pusan was K-1, Taegu, K-2; Po'hang, K-3; Sach'on, K-4; Pusan East, K-9; Chinhae, K-10; Suwon, K-13; Kimpo, K-14; Youi-do, K-16; P'yongyang, K-23; and so forth.

"In P'yongtaek, I tasted to the full the bitter irony of not only being strafed by Australian planes, but by the very men with whom I had been drinking a few days before – Lou Spence, Bay Adams and others. The 5th Air Force headquarters had included P'yongtaek among the squadron's opportunity targets, so the Australian pilots hit it hard. In a terrifying half-hour, while being rocketed and machine-gunned from daringly low altitudes, I lost my glasses so was at least spared the shock of positively identifying my drinking partners. The Americans took it very well. The infanteer seems to have a philosophical resignation about this sort of thing . . . Their main loss *[sic]* was the detonation of a South Korean ammunition train lying in the P'yongtaek siding." [11]

The story of the catastrophe soon reached the US wire services, United Press and Associated Press, and was given a wide distribution in the United States. Investigations into the incident revealed that lengthy delays had occurred between the initial report of a North Korean convoy on the move being received by General MacArthur's Headquarters in Tokyo, and it being passed onto 5th Air Force Operations. It transpired that several hours had passed before the report was acted upon. The officers concerned noted the delay, and estimated where they thought the trucks might have reached by the time the Mustangs could arrive. They were not even aware that American and South Korean troops were in the area. An inquiry cleared the Australians of blame and subsequently 77RAAF received apologies from 5th Air Force commanders but, exonerated or not, the shock of killing men of their own side was something that could not be forgotten.

Soon after this tragic episode, MacArthur instructed the establishment of a realistic bomb line which was to be updated throughout each day. He also ordered that both South Korean and American vehicles were to have clearly visible white stars painted on their tops and sides to avoid confusion. A Tactical Air Co-ordination Flight equipped with two L-5G liaison aircraft modified to carry VHF radios was established and, later in the month, a system of FAC was inaugurated in which Army air observers were carried in AT-6G spotter aircraft of the 6148th Tactical Control Squadron, so they could report on enemy activity and direct incoming fighter-bombers onto their targets. For 77RAAF, as the intensity of the operations began to pick up, there was not much time to dwell upon the tragic circumstances. The remainder of the month would see the Australians heavily occupied in trying to slow down the advancing NKPA.

General MacArthur's underlying strategy at this time was that the enemy must, at all costs, be prevented from capturing Pusan in the south, the greatest port in Korea. Its shipping capacity was ten times that of Inch'on on the west coast. Through Pusan's harbour and airfield thousands of men and massive quantities of equipment could be brought in. Pusan and Japan were the two great staging areas and bases of operations from which, when enough strength had been built up, an irresistible, double-pronged counter-attack could be launched. The North Koreans understood the value of Pusan very well, and their primary goal was the swiftest possible capture of the city. This could stop the flow of troops and material into the port and cut off American forces already in Korea from their supply corridor through which ran the main Seoul to Pusan road and railway line – passing through key towns of Suwon, Osan, Ch'onan, Taejon, and Taegu. In addition, supplementary drives along the secondary road and rail lines to the east and west would enable them to encircle their enemy and swoop down on Pusan from all sides. MacArthur's stop-gap force brought in quickly from Japan was far too small and inexperienced to stop the NKPA's onslaught – its job was to delay the enemy's main advance along the Seoul-Pusan road. The more they could slow down the North Koreans, the more time would be available to move troops and supplies into Pusan. The immediate tactic was to force the Communists to sacrifice as much time, as many men, and as much ammunition and fuel as possible. Allied aircraft would attack the lines of communication from the north to prevent reinforcements and supplies from reaching the front; since the USAF had complete control of the air, the North Koreans would not be able to retaliate. The enemy would thus inevitably be weakened by attrition while the Americans grew stronger. The farther south the front moved, the longer, more tenuous and vulnerable the enemy's supply lines would become – and the

---

[11] See *With the Australians in Korea*.

shorter and more secure would be those of the Americans.

Shortly after daybreak on 5 July, the NKPA struck at the US 21st Regiment near Osan. Fighting continued throughout the morning. The enemy threw in a division supported by 30 tanks, odds of eight to one against the inexperienced American troops. The ROK troops fled but the Americans, completely surrounded, held out for seven hours but by 1430 it was all over. The weary GIs had kept fighting until all their ammunition was exhausted. All they could do then was to withdraw as best they could. Misty rain fell, adding to the misery of defeat. By committing the remainder of his troops, the US commander was able to slow down the North Korean advance, trading terrain for time while further American forces were rushed from Japan.

Late in the morning of 6 July, NKPA tanks were reported on the road just north of P'yongtaek and six B-26s were ordered to bomb the bridge across the river passing through the centre of the town. Escort was provided by two sections of Mustangs led by Wg Cdr Spence. No enemy aircraft was sighted nor was any flak experienced and, since there was 10/10th cloud over the target, the results of the attack were not observed, although a convoy on the road north of P'yongtaek was also bombed, rocketed and strafed with some success. However, there were enemy aircraft about. Four aircraft identified as Yak-9s but allegedly bearing ROKAF markings strafed Osan and knocked out a telephone relay station. 5th Air Force Operations telephoned 77RAAF in the afternoon, asking for a flight of Mustangs for an urgent task. Sqn Ldr Strout hurriedly called three standby pilots together. It was late in the afternoon, the quartet taking off at 1737. Strout's aircraft (A68-809) immediately gave trouble in the air and he had to return to Iwakuni. The other three pressed on, Flg Off Ken McLeod (A68-799) taking the lead. Nearing the target area they heard the FAC calling and, after diving through a gap in the clouds, the Mustangs found the US Army L-19 over P'yongtaek. The FAC wanted them to attack a bridge. The Mustangs went in with rockets but the bridge was a sturdily built, reinforced concrete structure and although two rockets hit, they did not make an impression. Two rockets hit the road approaches, while a 20mm flak position was strafed and silenced. Just as the Australian pilots were about to depart they received an emergency call from the FAC, who believed he was about to be attacked by a North Korean Yak fighter. The aircraft was soon spotted by P3 Milt Cottee (A68-813), who pursued and caught up with it. He had it centrally in his sights and was about to press the firing button when he saw the South Korean markings:

"... we saw an aircraft which we weren't very sure what it was, so we set up quarter attacks on this bloody thing. We had the whole thing lined up and recognised it at this stage as a Harvard [an ROKAF AT-6]. There was a Korean in the front and a Korean in the back. It looked as though he was standing up and his hair was streaming back – you could almost hear him scream 'Get away'."

Cottee then noticed P2 Les Reading (A68-726) closing in to attack and tried to warn him. Just at this point the radio transmission button fell out and he could not transmit, but remembering that there was a pencil on his instrument panel, he quickly jammed it into the transmission button socket and activated the radio just in time to prevent Reading from shooting down the spotter aircraft. A further tragedy thus having been averted, the Mustangs escorted the L-19 back to its base at Taejon. By this time fuel was very low and it was much too late to return to Iwakuni, so the Australians spent the night at Taejon. Flg Off McLeod asked for a signal to be sent to Iwakuni, advising of their whereabouts, but there were so many messages going out that their Squadron did not receive it until 0630 next morning.

For 77RAAF, as the intensity of operations began to pick up, so the effectiveness of the enemy's anti-aircraft fire increased. Operations were further complicated by the wet season. Korea could receive up to 16 inches of rain in July and, mixed with the mountainous Korean terrain, this type of weather could prove extremely hazardous. By the morning of 7 July the North Koreans were pushing on from Kangnung, 12 miles south of the 38th Parallel, and, further south, had taken Samchok. The Squadron was ordered to provide an armed reconnaissance to strike at targets of opportunity along road and railway routes on the east coast, where the NKPA was making rapid progress on the road skirting the mountains. Four Mustangs took off, led by Sqn Ldr Strout, and they crossed the coast south of Samchok, penetrated several miles inland and found the railway. Strout gave the order to attack. The Mustangs peeled off in turn and rocketed a railway station. Flt Lt Tom Murphy (A68-765) had difficulty releasing his drop tanks and had to struggle with the jettison toggle before he followed and, when he dived a few seconds later, he saw a blinding flash near the railway line and assumed that his leader had scored a direct hit. But, in fact, it was Sqn Ldr Strout's aircraft (A68-757) that had careered down onto the target and never straightened out, possibly hit by ground fire. Next day, the CO, accompanied by Flt Lts Adams and Noble, overflew Samchok and scrutinised the disintegrated wreck of the Mustang to satisfy himself that the Squadron's deputy commander had perished in the crash. His remains were recovered later and buried at Pusan following a service attended by Squadron personnel.

Two days after the loss of Sqn Ldr Strout, a specially chartered DC-4 airliner landed at Iwakuni carrying the first of what would be many RAAF reinforcements. On board were a dozen fighter pilots, reputedly the best trained men available in Australia, plus 28 ground staff, armourers and fitters. The armourers, after a quick look around at their strange new surroundings, dumped their gear, put on overalls and began immediately to work on the Squadron's Mustangs as they came back from missions over Korea. Their arrival relieved some of the great stress on the handful of men who had been working up to 20 hours a day to keep the Mustangs flying. The new pilots were: Flt Lt C.J. Murray, Flt Lt I.R. Olorenshaw DFC, Flt Lt F.W. Barnes, Flt Lt F.R. Coburn, P2 W.S. Michelson, P2 E.A. Douglas, P2 S.W. Williamson, P3 A. Hankinson, P3 L.R. Klaffer, P3 R.C.A. Hunt, P3 R.O.L. Brackenreg, and P3 R.W. Wittman (see Appendix III).

Owing to the officer-only status of USAF fighter pilots, when Australian NCO pilots landed at American-occupied bases, they were invariably treated as officers and invited to eat and rest in the USAF Officers' Mess tent since there were no other aircrew facilities available. To avoid continual explanations, the RAAF NCO pilots took to wearing Pilot Officer or Flying Officer badges of rank on their flying suits. However, on their return to Iwakuni it was not unusual for them to be rostered for duty as Corporal of the Guard. This was found to be intolerable and a deputation paraded before Wg Cdr Spence to air their discontent. The CO magnanimously saw their point and guard duties were subsequently abolished for aircrew.

The 3rd BG's B-26s were busy again on 9 July, three aircraft visiting the P'yongtaek area in search of the convoy attacked three days earlier. This was successfully located and attacked from low-level, at least six tanks being left burning and numerous trucks and horse-drawn vehicles being destroyed but at a cost. One B-26 was shot down by ground fire. This latest success contributed to a total of 197 trucks claimed destroyed by the FEAF on the roads between P'yongtaek and Seoul in the last three days. During the second week of July the Communists restored the runway of Kimpo airfield and moved in seven camouflaged Yak-9s. They were intended for short-range, hit-and-run attacks against UN ground troops. Apparently aware of the length of time that the 5th Air Force jets were able to remain in the battle area, four of the Yaks bombed and strafed elements of the US 18th Regiment near Ch'ongju on 10 July, and inflicted casualties. Elsewhere, B-26s, F-82s and F-80s strafed, rocketed and bombed a convoy of 150 vehicles seen near P'yongtaek, the aircrews claiming its almost complete destruction during the course of 280 sorties. The convoy had initially been located and attacked by two ROKAF F-51Ds from K-2. Of this highly successful operation, the 5th Air Force's Director of Combat Operations commented later:

> "This attack was considered by many to have been one of the decisive air-ground battles of the entire conflict."

Next day three Yaks surprised and attacked a flight of F-80s that were strafing ground targets near Ch'ongju although the jets were able to make good their escape unscathed by using their superior speed. NKAF pilots were extremely active again on the following day (12 July). In the morning, a B-29 of the 19th BG bombing railway targets near Seoul was trapped by three Yaks and shot down in flames, the crew having baled out first, coming down in the estuary of the Seoul river. A USN flying boat was sent to the area but failed to make any sightings. It was thought at first that survivors may have been picked up by a junk or sampan, but four days later a searching Royal Navy frigate, HMS *Alacrity*, located and rescued seven of the ten-man crew. In the meantime, in the mid-afternoon of the 12th, two Yaks jumped a flight of ground-strafing F-80s near Chochiwon although again the American fighters were able to escape. However, later in the afternoon two Yaks shot down a US Army L-14 liaison aircraft, also over Chochiwon; several other liaison-type aircraft fell to the guns of the Yaks during the early stages of the war. These incidents underlined the necessity of eliminating, once and for all, North Korea's small air arm as an effective fighting force.

Only a week after leaving Australia, Flt Lt Ross Coburn (A68-801) found himself No2 in a flight of Mustangs led by Flt Lt Tom Murphy (A68-803) in an attack at Chochiwon. The 24th Division FAC sent them to attack camouflaged tanks but, to make certain they were not over friendly territory, P2 Tom Stoney (who had been a navigator during WWII) in A68-739 was asked to double-check the position before going in. Once happy with the situation, the Mustangs struck, P2 Bob Fairweather (A68-799) scoring a direct hit on one of the tanks with a rocket, and there were several near misses. One tank disintegrated, scattering debris and wheels over the road. A fuel dump was hit by incendiary bullets which had ricocheted from a tank, and burned fiercely. The four pilots were credited with the destruction of six tanks, the remains of which could be seen for days afterwards. This action was cited when Flt Lt Murphy was later awarded a US DFC. A second strike led by P2 Geoff Thornton destroyed two more tanks.

By 14 July the North Koreans were still advancing freely down the main highway and had begun crossing the Kum River, a natural barrier protecting Taejon. Flying weather that day was bad, and most flights from Japan were forced to abort before reaching the peninsula. In the afternoon, however, it cleared, and Flt Lt Gordon Harvey (A68-739) led a flight of four Mustangs on a strike. At briefing, the pilots had been told to contact the FAC at Taejon, but Harvey could not raise him. However, another was in the air, and he told Harvey to attack a bridge across the Kum near Kingju. Although rockets were seen to strike home, little damage was inflicted. The Mustangs then began to patrol the road north of Kingju, but the FAC had meanwhile found another target and he recalled them to the river, where NKPA troops could be seen trying to get across in boats. They were caught in the open as the Mustangs strafed, coming down to within a few feet of the ground. The pilots could see soldiers trying to get under cover. One group, waiting to cross the river, lay quite still and appeared to the pilots as though they might be dead, until a Mustang headed towards them and they foolishly jumped up and scattered. Two small boats loaded with troops seen half way across the river were duly strafed, the water stained red with their blood. Sprawling bodies were seen draped over the side of the sinking boats. It was estimated that in excess of 40 North Koreans were killed during the attacks.

Although no NKAF aircraft had been encountered by the Australians during their sorties over South Korea, Yaks nonetheless continued to harass USAF aircraft operating in the area, two of which engaged a flight of B-26s over Seoul on 15 July. One of the bombers was so badly damaged that its crew had to make an emergency landing at Taejon. By now American intelligence had established that the Yaks were operating from Kimpo, and, in the afternoon, the airfield was attacked by a flight of F-80s. Two or three of the widely dispersed Yaks were claimed destroyed. Later that day Kimpo was also bombed by three B-29s which cratered its runway. On 77RAAF's last mission for the day, Flt Lt Jack Murray (A68-801) led a flight of Mustangs escorting a flight of B-26s to Seoul. A railway bridge south of the city was bombed. No enemy air opposition was encountered although a twin-engined aircraft was seen on Kimpo airfield.

Two days later Capt Frank B. Clark, an F-80 pilot of 35th FBS, reported shooting down a Yak-9, three more falling to the guns of 36th FBS pilots 1/Lt Wurster (his second victory), 1/Lt Robert D. McKee and 2/Lt Elwood A. Kees on 19 July during a raid on the airfield at P'yongyang by F-80s of the 8th FBG, although 1/Lt Howard O'Dell of the 36th FBS was shot down by another Yak. Seven other F-80s made pass after pass over the airfield and claimed the destruction of 14 NKAF fighters and one twin-engined bomber, which were camouflaged and hidden under the branches of trees alongside the western edge of the field. In a follow-up raid next day, 14 B-29s bombed the runways and dispersal areas of the airfields of P'yongyang and Onjong-ni, two more Yaks falling to the guns of the escorting F-80s, Capt Robert L. Lee of the

36th FBS claiming one and 2/Lt David H. Goodnough of the 35th FBS getting the second. Although it seemed to cause little concern at the time, American pilots reported seeing a swept-wing jet fighter over Ch'ongju on 16 July.

77 RAAF meanwhile continued with strikes from its base at Iwakuni, Flt Lt Fred Barnes (A68-739) leading a dive-bombing attack on a bridge spanning the Kum on 16 July. Two direct hits with 500-lb bombs were registered by Flg Off Ken McLeod (A68-801), and another by his wingman, P2 Jim Flemming (A68-725). Bombs were considered much better that rockets for this type of task, and three spans were destroyed. The bridge had been damaged in earlier raids, and the North Koreans had been trying to repair it. At 1220, Wg Cdr Spence (A68-809) led a section off on a further bombing and strafing mission, each aircraft carrying two 500-lb bombs. GCI directed them to patrol an area of Nasong-ni. Although the Australians could not see the result of their bombing, they were advised that an excellent job had been done. Spence brought his flight to land at Taegu to refuel. While they were down a report came in that NKAF aircraft were strafing Allied troops in the Ansong area. The Mustangs scrambled to intercept, eager for the rare opportunity of engaging in air-to-air combat, but the intruders could not be found. After searching without result, Spence set course for Iwakuni. The CO's section missed another rare chance to have a crack at the Yaks two days later. After flying two missions in which seven trucks and a petrol tanker were destroyed, plus a building set on fire, poor weather prevented their return to Iwakuni. They landed at Taegu to stay overnight. Just 25 minutes later, a message was received that four Yaks were strafing Taejong, and the Australians were asked to intercept. Unfortunately, they were unable to do so because their aircraft had not been rearmed. Two Mustangs were damaged by ground fire on 18 July, Flt Lt Noble's A68-803 returning with holes in its wings, while P3 Richard Turner landed A68-799 with a 20mm shell hole in the fairing of the fin; a third aircraft (A68-737) was damaged when P3 Bob Hunt carried out a belly-landing at Miho.

Taejon fell on 22 July after bitter fighting. This had been the temporary seat of the South Korean Government and its loss was a psychological setback. The Government moved to Taegu while NKPA columns pressed on relentlessly through Simch'on, beyond Taejon. A pair of Mustangs flown by Flt Lt Noble and P3 Milt Cottee were despatched to attack Simch'on on the following day, their napalm bombs setting the town ablaze. Elsewhere, Flt Lt Adams led a section of four Mustangs to attack tanks at Hamchang. Despite low cloud base, P3 Lyall Klaffer scored a direct hit with a rocket, destroying one tank. Flt Off Tom McCrohan and P3 Bill Harrop shared another, blasting it onto its side off the road.

Due almost entirely to the determination of Maj Hess, an attempt to absorb the American pilots then flying with the ROKAF unit into the new 6002nd FBW being formed, failed. Had the Americans transferred to the new unit it would have effectively entailed the disbandment of the ROKAF as a fighting force. The six remaining F-51s were flown to Chinhae (K-10) via Sach'on (K-4) on 22 July, from where they were to continue operations. Although they had already achieved good results with what they had, on their own they could not slow the waves of advancing North Koreans. In fact, in some instances, they caused confusion. Often they drew fire from friendly forces, including USAF aircraft, simply because of their unfamiliar ROKAF insignia. Maj Hess recalled one such incident:

"One morning I was flying out of Chinhae over the 24th Division sector searching for targets when four American aircraft bore in. Eager new pilots, they obviously had never seen the markings on a Korean plane. They only saw the Oriental symbol on the side of mine – and decided it must be the enemy. Two of the pilots got on my wings while the other two stayed behind. One kept firing at my wingtip. They were trying to box me in, force me down, and take the airplane. I made several radio calls to try to identify myself as friendly, but though I could hear them talking back and forth, I couldn't get through. I called to the Ground Controller to advise them who I was. He replied that these were four airplanes working outside their regular sector and that he didn't have communication with them.

We circled for 20 or 30 minutes. When two of the airplanes were tight on my wing, I would adjust the throttle slightly and manoeuvre so that I would overlap one of them; that way they would have hit a team mate had they opened fire. In desperation I took my helmet off, but I was so tanned from flying in the sun that they couldn't distinguish me from the darker Koreans. Then finally, exasperated, I looked down at the pilot I was hugging just as he glanced apprehensively over his shoulder at me, sitting on his back. I thumbed my nose at him, hoping this strictly American gesture might identify me. Shortly after they all decided to go back to Taegu, either because they were becoming uncertain about my identity or because they were getting low on fuel. I then broke away and sought my original target. I often wonder what they thought about the 'North Korean' pilot who thumbed his nose at them." [12]

On another occasion, while flying with 1/Lt George Haines, Maj Hess encountered a Yak-9 strafing American troops:

"We saw a Yak-9 about 1,500 feet above the ground strafing some American forward units along the road. I had expended all my ammunition but I knew George had plenty. I presumed, evidently erroneously, that George knew the procedure for such an attack: going in, I would draw the enemy on my tail and make a turn to the left, letting him stay on me; then Haines was to make a turn to the right, intercept the aircraft, and as he had the ammunition, shoot him. I made the bounce and let the Yak start after me. I kept looking over my left shoulder, wondering when George was going to hit him. When he didn't, I looked over my other shoulder – to see George close on my wing. It was one of those cases where a new pilot, constantly drilled to stick to the lead airplane, got a little buck fever. All I could do was make a quick turn at the Yak to try to bluff him. It worked; he headed for home before he was aware that no one was firing at him.

Back at base Haines was contrite. Once again I had to assure him that he'd have better luck next time. Unfortunately, he never did; he was shot down the next time out. His aircraft hit the edge of a clearing that was under enemy fire. Our ground forces – this time Korean troops – made a thrust to recover him. The were close enough to see that his plane was riddled. They couldn't see anyone in the cockpit, so they assumed that he was slumped down, dead. His body was never recovered." [13]

On the morning of 24 July, NKPA tanks again broke through the American front line at Yong-dong and started advancing down the main highway. Ground control diverted all available fighters and fighter-bombers to the threatened area, FACs directing the bomb and rocket-laden aircraft as they arrived. A flight of RAAF Mustangs reached the breakthrough area about midday, and saw three tanks moving down the highway with their guns firing at positions in the hills. The Mustangs led by Flg Off Bill Horsman, which included one flown by the Squadron IO, Flt Lt Kirkpatrick, taking time off from his normal duties, attacked with rockets. Although the tanks were soon surrounded by rocket craters, they did not appear to be hit. Two, however, stopped dead and a third began retreating back up the road. American artillery and mortars then opened up on the tanks. Horsman called up another flight of Mustangs which were operating further north. Led by Flt Lt Bradford, the four fighter-bombers arrived within a few minutes and destroyed the fleeing tank. Meanwhile, Horsman's aircraft (A68-772) was hit by small-arms fire which cut a fuel line, and he was obliged to land at Taegu for repairs. Two other Mustangs suffered minor damage. Then, six more Mustangs led by P2 Wally Rivers were ordered to the same area, and for some time patrolled the road, shooting up trucks, artillery pieces, tanks and buildings which appeared to house troops. P2 Tom Stoney (A68-763) participated in this action, which was cited when he was later awarded an American DFC.

Two days later RAAF Mustangs attacked enemy installations and equipment in the Pongseang-dong area, an action which saw P2 Jim Flemming (A68-729) awarded a US DFC, the citation of which noted that he had flown through intense and accurate ground fire to destroy four vehicles loaded with stores, and that he damaged two others in addition strafing and rocketing electric power installations and other buildings. Poor weather restricted operations for two days but the Mustangs were in action again on the last day of the month, the Australian pilots flying five missions against an estimated 800-900 North Korean troops established in the hills between Hadong and Chinju. It was later learned that many of the early interdiction missions flown by the USAF, ROKAF and RAAF were of little use in stemming the flow southwards of enemy troops, since few attempts were made to identify movement of the main roads as being that of NKPA forces. The advancing enemy troops simply avoided the main routes if at all possible, particularly in daylight. Tragically, many innocent civilian refugees became casualties of the waves of strafing, bombing and rocketing UN aircraft. USAF Mustang losses were high during the month, the 12th FBS alone losing ten aircraft including that flown by 2/Lt Billie Crabtree, who was killed. Another who was killed, on 6 July, was Capt Ernest Fiebelkorn of the 4th FAWS, whose F-82 crashed in bad weather 45 miles north of Seoul; Fiebelkorn was a WWII fighter ace with nine victories to his credit.

One logistics problem which had developed was promptly dealt with by help from the US Navy. In co-ordinating the ground-attack effort, Tactical Air Control (TAC) crews found themselves seriously overworked. The TAC Flight had two L-5G liaison aircraft modified to carry VHF radios. These two slow and vulnerable aircraft had some narrow escapes while co-ordinating air strikes in support of the 24th Division, and it was realised that faster aircraft would be more suited to the task. The Airborne Control Detachment operating from Taejon was therefore rapidly re-equipped with AT-6 Texans (known as the Harvard in the RAF and Commonwealth air forces) which had a much higher speed, and gave their crews a far better chance of surviving in a hostile environment of enemy fighters and intense ground fire. By late July, however, the number of AT-6s in position was still relatively small. The US Navy quickly covered the shortfall by detailing a flight of AD-2 Skyraiders from the aircraft carrier USS *Valley Forge* to act as control aircraft, working in conjunction with the AT-6s. The Skyraiders, from VA-55, had the capacity to stay over the front line for up to four hours, and this arrangement worked very well until Task Force 77 withdrew for replenishment at sea (see Chapter X). For the most part, the co-operation achieved in this first combined air offensive proved an unqualified success.

Meanwhile the AT-6s, as they became available, were fitted with an F-51 belly tank carrying 40 gallons of fuel to enable greater endurance, two VHF radios for communicating with the FAC and incoming fighter-bombers, and a dozen 15-lb smoke rockets for target marking. When fully-equipped, the pilot and observer had to carry seat packs, parachutes, Mae Wests, flare guns, torches and binoculars. All this extra weight, close on 1,000-lbs, obviously affected the aircraft's performance, and top speed was reduced to about 150mph while climbing speed was cut to 85mph. Comment was made that service ceiling was so low that an AT-6 was vulnerable to just about everything except thrown pitchforks! On one occasion, when jumped by a NKAF Yak, the AT-6 pilot fired his target-marking rockets in desperation, which apparently scared the enemy fighter away.

Due to its commitments in Europe, the Middle East and the Far East – where it was currently involved in Operation 'Firedog'[14] – the RAF was not in a position to provide fighter or bomber squadrons for operations over Korea; nor did the Americans request aircraft from the Allies, since it appeared to have a large, well-equipped air force available for the task in hand. However, there was a shortage of flying boats to patrol the vast tracts of sea and, as a consequence, the AOC Hong Kong, Air Commodore A.D. Davies, accompanied by Sqn Ldr J.W. Helme AFC, the CO of 88 Squadron, arrived at Iwakuni aboard one of the unit's Sunderland flying boats to discuss the facilities available to operate a detachment from there, as part of the British government's contribution to the UN cause. Facilities at Iwakuni, a former Japanese Naval Air training school, were found to be suitable although the hangars and slipways were not large enough for Sunderlands.

---

[14] Operation 'Firedog' was the codename given to the anti-Communist campaign British forces were currently conducting in Malaya where, during the first year of the emergency, some 350 air strikes were carried out by a variety of RAF Spitfires, Tempests, Vampires, Beaufighters, Brigands, Lincolns, Harvards and Sunderlands, supported by Royal Navy Seafires and Fireflies; in addition to air strikes, RAF Dakotas and helicopters, assisted by AOP Austers, were involved in supply-dropping missions, casualty evacuations, and air observation.

Nonetheless, within a day or so three Sunderlands (PP114/B, RN282/C and PP155/F) duly arrived at Iwakuni. Known as the The RAF Sunderland Flight, the detachment was under the command of Flt Lt D.M. Hunter, with Flg Off R.S. Brand and P2 Bartrum as captains of the other two aircraft, and was attached initially to the USN's Fleet Air Wing One. Its main task, in co-operation with the USN squadrons, was one of maintaining a blockage of North Korean ports in conjunction with UN naval forces. The 88 Squadron detachment was to be the start of a monthly rotation by the three squadrons of the RAF's newly formed Far East Flying Boat Wing based at Singapore, the other two being 205 and 209 Squadrons commanded by Sqn Ldr J.E. Proctor DFC, a WWII fighter ace, and Sqn Ldr P. deL. Le Cheminant DFC, respectively (see Appendix III). The Sunderlands were to prove a useful contribution. The commander of the Flying Boat Wing was Wg Cdr Dudley Burnside DSO DFC, a former wartime bomber pilot:

> "By great good fortune I happened to be between postings in Malaya at the time and although I had never been on a flying boat training course, it seemed that I was the only Wing Commander locally available . . . I was indeed a very lucky man, although aware that there would be many an eyebrow raised within the close-knit flying boat community at the impertinent intrusion of this Bomber Command character with not a vestige of verdigris on his cap badge. But this was a war situation and there was no time to send me back to the UK on a Sunderland training course. I was to learn on the job as I went along . . . In due course my cap badge and buttons began to show a glimmer of green . . . ."

On 18 July, Flg Off Bob Brand flew the Sunderland Flight's first operation from Iwakuni, in PP155/F, and patrolled off the Korean coast until darkness. Three weeks later, on the night of 3 August, Brand undertook the Flight's first nocturnal operational sortie, also in PP155/F, searching for North Korean vessels which had been reported transporting supplies and reinforcements for the advancing NKPA, although no sightings were achieved. The Flight initially had only a dozen groundcrew to maintain the three aircraft, and these same men were required to fly as gunners and relief radar operators until reinforcements arrived with the 209 Squadron detachment in mid-August. Owing to the shortage of trained air gunners it was feared that the bulky, cumbersome flying boats would be vulnerable to interception by day fighters from North Korean airfields. Indeed, one of Fleet Air Wing One's aircraft had recently been attacked by a NKAF Yak in the Formosan Straits although it had escaped damage. To have restricted the Sunderlands to within the range of USN and FAA carrier patrols would have rendered them almost valueless, and it was therefore decided to operate them on coastal patrols only at night until the situation improved. Early in August the Sunderland Flight was placed under the control of the newly established USN Fleet Air Wing Six, alongside patrol Squadrons VP-6 equipped with P2V-3 Neptunes, VP-28 (P4Y-2 Privateers), and VP-42 (PBM-5 Mariners).

Additional reinforcements were beginning to arrive in Japan for the Americans, the aircraft carrier USS *Boxer* delivering a total of 145 F-51Ds from California, these having been rounded up from US Air Guard units. With them came 70 experienced pilots. No time was wasted in unloading and making the fighters ready for combat. In a massive and well-guarded operation, the 5th Air Force would have the conversion of six squadrons of F-80s to F-51s completed within three weeks. Many of the pilots involved in the change-over were not too happy, as noted by the 8th FBG's diarist:

> "A lot of pilots had seen vivid demonstrations of why the F-51 was not a ground-support fighter in the last war, and weren't exactly intrigued by the thought of playing guinea pig to prove the same thing over again."

Others were quite happy to change back to the F-51, however, as the Group had lost 17 F-80s in July alone, though not all to enemy action, but nonetheless eight pilots had been killed or were posted missing. The month had started badly when Maj Amos Sluder, the 80th FBS's CO, was shot down by ground fire on the 3rd. Two more pilots were lost on the 7th, 1/Lt Eugene Hansen of the 36th FBS being killed while 1/Lt Donald Sirman of the 35th FBS was captured but died as a POW. Two days later 1/Lt Leon Pollard of the same unit crashed into the sea on the way back to Japan, and 1/Lt James Hughes was wounded in action. Another pilot was lost due to bad weather next day when 1/Lt Schwarz of the 8th FBS also crashed into the sea on returning from a sortie. The CO of the 36th FBS, Maj Richard McNess, was killed in an accident on the 18th, as was 1/Lt Ralph Ellis of the same unit three days later; and on the last day of the month 1/Lt John Netterbald of the 80th FBS was killed when his aircraft crashed on the island of Tsushima.

At about the same time as reinforcements were arriving for the FEAF, Canada made available six C-54 transports of 426 Squadron RCAF for duty with MATS, the aircraft having transferred from Dorval airport near Ottawa to McChord AFB near Tacoma, Washington. Commanded by Wg Cdr C.H. Mussels DSO DFC RCAF, the Squadron's job was to assist with the airlifting of personnel and equipment to and from the Korean theatre of war.

* * *

Meanwhile, on the political front, Britain, Australia and New Zealand announced that each would be sending ground troops to Korea. In an attempt to justify British involvement, Prime Minister Attlee broadcast to a war-weary and impoverished Britain:

> "The attack by the armed forces of North Korea on South Korea has been denounced as an act of aggression by the United Nations . . . If the aggressor gets away with it, aggressors all over the world will be encouraged. The same results which led to the Second World War will follow, and another world war may result. This is why what is happening in Korea is of such importance to you. The fire that has been started in distant Korea may burn down your own house."

Despite the Prime Minister's support for UN military involvement in the Korean crisis, the British Chiefs-of-Staff remained doubtful:

> "Whether the Americans succeed in keeping a foothold in South Korea or have to go back again after a withdrawal, the subsequent campaign, if conducted on ordinary lines, cannot fail to be long, arduous and expensive in human life and material."

And an appropriate cable was sent to 'our man' in Washington, Lord Tedder, Head of the British Joint Services Mission:

> "We may well be faced with the situation that the Koreans as a whole will urge us not to return. In any event, the people who would mainly suffer from any kind of normal 'campaign of liberation' would be the South Koreans, whose villages, roads and railways would be destroyed and their country turned into the usual squalid battlefield . . . We assume there will be no question of using the atomic bomb in Korea. This weapon must in our view be kept in reserve for use in the proper place in the event of a major war with Russia. Anyway there are no suitable objectives for it in North Korea. This is a United Nations police action, and we do not want to kill thousands of civilians and create a radio-active shambles, but with the minimum loss of life and expense on either side, to restore the *status quo* and the integrity of South Korea."

Nonetheless, the British Government committed itself to an additional defence expenditure of £3,400m over three years (increased to £4,700m six months later), while announcing that National Service was to be extended from 18 months to two years. By offering a brigade to the UN Command, Britain was forced to recall wartime reservists, many of whom were only just settling back into peacetime life with their families. The RAF immediately embarked on a policy to greatly increase its annual intake of pilot trainees, from 300 to 3,000, at the same time calling for 500 former navigators to volunteer for further service, while members of the Royal Auxiliary Air Force were called up for three months' continuous training, and 1,000 aircrew reservists were recalled for refresher training. A plan was instituted to double the rate of combat aircraft production, thereby re-equipping more front line squadrons with Meteor and Vampire jet fighters, while ensuring greater availability of the new twin-jet Canberra light-bomber soon to enter service with the RAF.

CHAPTER II

THE AMERICANS ESTABLISH AIR SUPERIORITY

August – September 1950

"Although Korean conditions are peculiar, bullets still hurt, flying is just as difficult – and the men still have the same amount of courage."

Wg Cdr P.G. Wykeham-Barnes DSO DFC RAF,
attached to the 3rd Bombardment Group USAF

On the first day of August four RAAF Mustangs led by P2 Geoff Thornton (A68-709) carried out what had by then become a typical close-support mission covering UN forces in the Chingju area. After making contact with the controller, the Mustangs were directed to attack three anti-aircraft gun positions, which were silenced following their strafing run. The controller then directed the attention of Thornton to a building which housed a number of heavy machine-guns. This was attacked with rockets and then strafed, after which they were called to attack another enemy gun position 200 yards further west, which they again rocketed and strafed although without obvious results. Finally, before departing, the Mustangs strafed a number of NKPA vehicles, claiming five trucks and one tank destroyed, and a further three trucks probably destroyed.

NKPA vehicles were the prime target in all ground-attack operations, but the situation was so fluid that great care had to be taken when striking at targets which were close to the front lines. The local situation rapidly changed without the controlling authorities being immediately aware. Flt Lt Tom Murphy (A68-708) had cause to remember the the the 3rd of July incident' when his section was directed by an FAC to carry out reconnaissance along a road north-west of Hyopch'on. The section sighted ground targets and were advised that they were enemy vehicles. The Mustangs dived to attack and one fired a burst at a truck but, even as he did so, another member of the section noticed a white star on the vehicle and immediately shouted a warning to the others to hold their fire. The FAC was again contacted and he, in turn, contacted the controller. It was only then that confirmation was received that American troops had moved into the area. A near disaster had narrowly been avoided. As it was, the ground battle was going badly for both the Americans – who reported that its force had suffered some 10,000 casualties by the end of the first week of August – and the South Koreans whose Army estimated about 70,000 casualties amongst its ranks, while it was believed the NKPA had lost 60,000 men by this stage of the war.

Elsewhere, the 35th FBS of the 8th FBG had started to receive F-51s to replace the F-80s, but on 1 August the CO, Maj Vincent Cardarello, was killed when his F-80 crashed during a strafing mission. Next day 1/Lt Orrin Fox of the 80th FBS was lost, while 1/Lt Warner Siber of the same unit failed to return on the 4th. A further fatality occurred a few days later when 1/Lt William Morris of the 9th FBS was shot down and killed. There was a shortage of aerial opposition at this time and, instead, marauding American pilots hunted NKAF aircraft on the ground, pilots of the 67th FBS (one of the first F-80 units to convert back to the F-51D) alone claiming the destruction of two Yaks on 3 August by Capts Edward Hoagland and Howard

Price. The 67th FBS suffered its first F-51 casualty next day, however, when Capt Robert Howell was shot down by ground fire. Other F-51 units accounted for an estimated 18 enemy aircraft destroyed or damaged on the ground at Kimpo on 5 August, while a strike against the airfield at P'yongyang next day resulted in claims for a further nine aircraft destroyed and four damaged. Kimpo was again attacked and three more NKAF aircraft were hit but not destroyed. On the same day Maj Louis J. Sebille, CO of the 67th FBS, led what was supposed to be a routine close-support mission near Hamch'ung. A target was sighted but on his first firing pass, one of Sebille's bombs hung up. He made a second pass in an attempt to release it, taking several hits from intense ground fire and, as he pulled out, the bomb was seen to be still lodged in its shackles. This left Sebille with two options; he could head for the nearest airstrip or make yet another pass. He chose the latter. His wingman saw his aircraft absorbing numerous hits and it failed to pull out, crashing into a cluster of enemy vehicles. As a result of his gallant but foolhardy action Maj Sebille was posthumously awarded the Congressional Medal of Honor, the first of only four USAF airmen to receive America's highest award for gallantry during the Korean War.

Following the conversion to Mustangs by the 67th FBS, the 39th FIS stationed at Ashiya AFB also received the type. On the morning of 7 August they flew out of Ashiya with a full combat load to their new base at Po'hang (K-3) so they could fly close-support missions. The Squadron had its first fatality almost immediately when, on 10 August, 1/Lt James I. Mathis failed to return from an early morning mission. At almost the same time another Mustang was lost when 1/Lt Harold Hillery, the only negro pilot in the 39th FIS, had to bale out off the east coast of Korea after engine failure. Fortunately, he was picked up by a US submarine that was on station carrying out an air-sea rescue patrol. Meanwhile, a search conducted by Mathis' wingman failed to find any sight of the downed aircraft. On the plus-side, Maj Arnold Mullins, the new CO of the 67th FBS, claimed three Yaks on the ground during an airfield strafe. On the morning of 11 August, pilots of the 35th and 36th FBS operating from Itazuke flew their first F-51 missions in Korea, losing Capt Charles Brown who was shot down by return fire from a T-34 tank he was attacking. He managed to bale out and was picked up by friendly troops but suffered a broken ankle when he hit the ground. On completion of the mission, the Mustangs returned to Tsuiki for attachment to the 6131st FBW. One aircraft was lost en route although the pilot baled out safely and was rescued from the sea by a Japanese fishing boat. The 80th FBS (which lost 2/Lt Glenn Payne on the 10th to add to its earlier losses) was now the only F-80 unit remaining in the 8th FBG, and for logistical and tactical considerations it was separated from the Group and attached to the 49th FBW at Misawa, which in turn became attached to the 8th FBG for support operations.

Since early July, USAF weather reconnaissance crews flying night sorties over Korea had reported sighting convoys of trucks moving southward, but these choice targets were not attacked since the Americans lacked a night intruder force, although one flight of the 68th FAWS's F-82Gs had been given the task but achieved few tangible results. In desperation, the USMC Squadron VMF(N)-513[1] began to operate from Itazuke AFB with its all-weather Corsairs but with similar lack of success. F-80Cs and F-51Ds were also found wanting, and it was left to the B-26s of the 3rd Bombardment Group to undertake night intruder sorties, these meeting early success in this rôle despite the lack of suitable radar, but due to the shortage of sufficient numbers of aircraft, the Wing's two squadrons alternated between night and day operations, and by mid-August an average of 35 sorties per night were being flown. To help and advise the Americans, a number of distinguished and combat-experienced RAF officers had begun to arrive at FEAF Headquarters in Tokyo, including Wg Cdr J.E. Johnson DSO DFC (see Appendix III), one of the RAF's foremost fighter pilots who was on an exchange posting, as he later recalled:

---

[1] VMF(N)-513 was commanded by Maj Joseph H. Reinburg USMC, a WWII fighter ace with seven victories, who, just prior to the outbreak of the Korean War, had been on an exchange posting with the RAF in the UK, where he was attached to 29 Squadron flying Mosquito night fighters.

"After a year at the Royal Canadian Air Force's Staff College at Toronto I was sent, as an exchange officer, to Tactical Air Command in Virginia. I did plenty of flying from Langley Field AFB, and when the fighter group there got the F86A, I lost no opportunity in checking out in this splendid aeroplane. The Sabre handled as beautifully as the Spitfire; at height, its 5,000-lb of thrust pushed it along at a top speed approaching that of sound, it was supersonic in a very steep dive, and had a good radius of action. And it was just as well I was in good flying practice, for shortly after the Communist troops of North Korea crossed the border, I found myself reporting to the headquarters of the United States Far East Air Forces in Tokyo for another spell of active service."

Another RAF arrival at FEAF HQ was Wg Cdr P.G. Wykeham-Barnes DSO DFC (see Appendix III), a notable night intruder pilot of whom Johnson later wrote:

"To keep the Communists pinned down the Americans flew B-26 intruder missions at night, and since the RAF had much experience of these highly specialised operations, one of our greatest experts, Wg Cdr Peter Wykeham-Barnes, flew to Korea to help. [He] knew that this sort of flying between the mountains called for high skill and he thought that the best crews were usually ex-flying instructors who had plenty of hours and who kept their heads in tricky circumstances."

Of her husband's sudden departure for Korea, Wg Cdr Wykeham-Barnes' wife Barbara (later Lady Wykeham) remembered:

"[Air Marshal] Basil Embry [AOC Fighter Command] selected Peter for this mission, for his excellence in intruder and night operations. He left the day after our daughter Sadie was born (our first) and just had time to say goodbye. He had just paid three months' rent in advance for a cottage in the New Forest (he was Chief Test Pilot at Boscombe Down). We never occupied it."

Wykeham-Barnes arrived at Tokyo aboard a BOAC Argonaut, having departed from London Airport on 8 August, and was immediately taken to FEAF Headquarters where he met General Stratemeyer, Commander of the FEAF, who advised him that he was to organise and train a night intruder force. But first he was to be given a brief tour of the war zone, and was flown by B-17 to Taegu (K-2), from where he was flown by C-47 to Pusan (K-1), as he later recalled:

"General Partridge [Commander US 5th Air Force] met me and set out the situation. 'We are back on our heels around this port' he said, 'We are just holding them out of artillery range of the docks, and we have to keep them weak until our great counter-offensive. If you'll come with me tomorrow, I'll show you the front line.' The General's way of showing me the line was to fly an unarmed Dakota [C-47] very slowly round the perimeter at 1,000 feet. I class this as the most frightening sortie of my whole life, for I could easily see the enemy soldiers, to say nothing of the AA guns. I asked the General why we were not instantly blasted out of the sky. 'They durst not, Commander' he said, jerking his head upwards. 'My fighter boys are above us, and one squirt from them gooks and down they come.' I thought this answer relied too heavily on the good sense of the opposition."

The Wing Commander flew back to Japan the next day aboard a B-26 and landed at Iwakuni AFB where he found himself attached to the 3rd Bombardment Group under the command of Colonel Leland Walker:

"I was allotted a small cell and a strikingly unattractive Japanese lady to make my camp bed. Colonel Walker then fixed for half his aircrew to assemble for a lecture in night ground-attack, the other half to catch the same lecture next day. I therefore delivered two one-hour lectures, hastily improvised, on the techniques used by [the RAF's] No 2 Group Mosquito Force to immobilise the German Army in France, before and after D-Day [6 June 1944]. I explained that the effects of night ground-attack are one-tenth material and nine-tenths paralysis by instilling an exaggerated fear of the aeroplane overhead in the dark. Soldiers usually over-estimate the perception of the night marauder, and fear to move when he is in their area. As the lecture went on I thought I could detect a faint whiff of scepticism. I had met this attitude before in the USA. Americans do not like to be told. They like to be shown. But once they are convinced, they catch on very fast indeed."

Of the task facing Wykeham-Barnes, Wg Cdr Johnson commented:

"[Peter] stressed that the proper navigation of an intruder aeroplane was the most difficult type of navigation. The navigator had few aids, his radar was of little help at low heights, and his aeroplane was often thrown about the sky when the pilot saw and attacked targets of opportunity. Unless their navigation was always perfect, sooner of later they would find themselves draped round a mountain."

During the next two days Wykeham-Barnes familiarised himself with the B-26B, flying BC-297 with Capt Crosby in the co-pilot's seat, and was given the all clear at the end of 75 minutes' flight. Next day he carried out two further familiarisation flights during which he fired the guns, and one night flying sortie:

"[The B-26B] had been hastily fitted with twelve .5-inch forward firing guns, plus two in an after-turret, and she carried eight 250-lb fragmentation bombs. Guns, bombs, and ammunition made a formidable load, and she could just about drag herself off the Iwakuni strip, though once she was up she flew like a Douglas. But she was much too heavy and clumsy for the job. Korea is a 5,000 feet [high] plateau, threaded with the valleys which hold the rivers and communications, and to get at the roads and railways it would be necessary to creep down into these valleys. Not too bad with a moon and no cloud, but with cloud cover and no moon, and with rather casual dead-reckoning navigation, highly disagreeable. When you reached the head of a valley you had to climb 5,000 feet to get out. It was a bit too close for comfort."

At this time the 3rd BG was suffering from an acute shortage of experienced navigators. Flt Lt W.I. Pretty RAAF was a highly skilled navigator and a crew member of the RAAF Dakota attached to 77RAAF at Iwakuni. In addition to his regular flying duties, he volunteered to fly combat missions with the 3rd BG as a navigator of a B-26, and had undertaken his first mission on 1 August. Two weeks later, on the night of the 14th, his aircraft was forced to crash-land on a beach in southern Japan due to enemy action and bad weather; he survived, unhurt.[2]

Meanwhile, for the Mustang units there was no let up. The operations flown by 77RAAF's Flt Lt Bay Adams were typical of the period. On 5 August he led Flt Lts Ross Coburn and Dave Hitchins (the RAAF Dakota pilot who was officially 'resting' between missions) to the area of Pokson-dong where they destroyed a tank before rocketing and strafing the town, starting numerous fires. They landed at Po'hang to rearm but there Hitchins' machine became unserviceable when its canopy refused to close properly. Four days later Adams led four Mustangs on a close-support mission near Ch'unggyo-ri and Chogye, where a town containing many troops and field equipment was attacked and set on fire, and three trucks and an artillery piece were damaged. The aircraft of Adams' wingman, P2 Stan Williamson, was hit by flak, as a result of which he could not lower the flaps and was obliged to head for Po'hang. During the approach his engine seized and he had to force-land on the runway, causing severe damage to his aircraft (A68-775) although Williamson was able to walk away without injury. Five days later (on 14 August), Adams was briefed to provide close-support under the directions of a ground controller near Yongsan-ni where he and his section, which again included Flt Lt Hitchins, attacked an enemy-held hill. The controller reported good results and at least one tank was destroyed.As NKPA troops relentlessly closed in on Taegu, forcing the ROK government to move to its provisional headquarters to Pusan, 5th Air Force fighter-bombers launched a

---

[2] When Flt Lt Walter Pretty RAAF was awarded a US Air Medal in October 1951 he had completed seven missions as a B-26 navigator, most of which had been flown in the face of intense ground fire and adverse weather conditions. Another RAAF veteran, Sqn Ldr Norman Williams CGM DFM (see Appendix III), managed to wangle himself a number of trips as an air gunner on B-29s before joining 77RAAF as a ground officer.

ferocious counter-attack. They were joined in this task by the mighty B-29 bomber force assembled in the Japanese Home Islands and, on the morning of 16 August, the first of 98 heavily-loaded bombers began taking off in waves, all destined for the Waegwan sector where up to 40,000 North Korean troops were believed to be located. Almost 1,000 tons of bombs were dropped on the area, but when RF-80A reconnaissance jets returned with pictures of the aftermath they revealed no evidence of troops or vehicles of any kind. One historian has written:

> "No evidence was ever produced that this mission – the biggest use of air power in direct support of ground troops since the Normandy invasion of 1944 – had killed a single North Korean soldier, and there was certainly no let-up in the heavy Communist pressure against the Allied defences." [3]

NKAF opposition was conspicuous by its absence during the FEAF Bomber Command raids, although a lone fighter identified as a La-7 did attempt to intercept one B-29 of the 307th BG but was driven off by the tail gunner.

On 22 August Wg Cdr Spence (A68-809) set out from Iwakuni at 0800 with three others to attack targets around the perimeter of Pusan, and they did not return until 1840 that evening after flying three close-support missions from Taegu. At least one of their missions was so successful that the FAC cheered them as they went in, then applauded their marksmanship as he saw their bombs and rockets explode exactly where he indicated. The four Australians were weary when they landed back at Iwakuni, where the CO was told that three American generals were waiting to see him and that all the Squadron pilots were gathering in the mess. Dressed as he was, Spence drove to the mess in a jeep where General Stratemeyer greeted him. In an informal, yet moving presentation, the FEAF Commander pinned the US Legion of Merit medal on Spence's sweat-stained shirt. The citation read:

> "Wing Commander Louis T. Spence RAAF has demonstrated outstanding leadership in the preparation of his unit for combat. Under the supervision of this officer, the 77th Squadron RAAF entered combat with all aircraft operational, resulting in immediate and effective air strikes against the aggressors. During the period 16 July to 21 August 1950, a total of 553 combat sorties were flown by this unit with heavy losses inflicted upon the enemy in personnel and equipment. Wing Commander Spence has been a constant source of inspiration to the officers and men in his command. His deep devotion to duty and personal courage reflect great credit upon himself and the RAAF."

Unshowered and unshaved, Spence looked gaunt and tired. The strain of his responsibilities as the commander of a large operational base and as an active squadron commander was beginning to show. Australian war correspondent Frank Clune arrived three days later at Taegu, where he met Sqn Ldr Ron Rankin who was still working there as an Official Observer for the UN:

> "After a tasty lunch, Ron suggests we return to the airstrip. All aboard the jeep to Taegu strip, where we meet our boys of the RAAF in a snack bar filling up between forays over the enemy lines. Geoff Stephens of Launceston tells me that he has made 20 sorties in Mustangs. Pilots usually stay two hours in the air stooging round for a target. Planes carry four rockets, also two huge napalm tanks, which each hold 110 gallons of fluid. These are dropped from a height of about 200 feet on enemy troops, in support of our own troops, where they are in close combat. Napalm is also death on tanks. A napalm tank-drop has an effective area of a thousand square yards. Napalm is a reddish-coloured jelly substance which sticks like treacle to the body, slowly burning the victim. Geoff says he has no qualms about shooting bullets or rockets, which usually kill, but napalm is agonizing. The pilots usually work one day on and one day off, so that all get an even number of flying sorties. Each pilot is supposed to complete 50 missions, or strikes, before he is eligible to return to Australia. So far, the top pilot has been on 43 strikes, and 77 Squadron has made over 1,200

---

[3] See *Korean Air War* by Robert Jackson.

sorties since they arrived early in July. No Australian airmen live in Korea. They leave their
base at Iwakuni in Japan about dawn, and fly to Taegu, where they refuel and load up with
bombs and napalm, ready for action. When they've made enough strikes for one day, home
they fly the 150-odd miles across the China Sea to their base. Seems a long way to go to
work, but it is necessary in case the enemy break through and wipe out their staging point
at Taegu. After yarning with Flt Lt Jack Murray, Don Ellis and Geoff Stephens, I watch
them take-off at 20-second intervals in their Mustangs, on their mission of death. Jack, first
off, circles the strip awaiting his cobbers. Then the flight heads north. Two minutes later
they're only a speck in the sky." [4]

Flt Lt Murray (A68-796) and his section were vectored to rendezvous with the FAC and, as
directed, attacked the villages between Hajang-dong and a river to the west with bombs and
rockets, setting fire to five. Afterwards they strafed three trucks, a tank and a bridge, resulting
in at least one truck being totally destroyed.

On the morning of 23 August, Flt Lt Adams (A68-715) was briefed to lead an armed
reconnaissance by eight Mustangs over the Wonsan and Hamhung areas. They proceeded first
to Wonsan but owing to deteriorating weather conditions they could not go further. They
changed instead to patrol over the roads on the east coast from Wonsan to Chumunjin where
they strafed a convoy of trucks and left several on fire. Next they found a small railway yard
at Uman-ni and severely damaged a goods shed and three box-cars. During the afternoon
Adams was up again, leading three Mustangs on a close-support mission to Tosong-dong.
Following the directions of the controller, the town was attacked and several fires were started,
while two vehicles were strafed. On returning to Taegu, P4 Tom Stoney's aircraft (A68-801)
became unserviceable with an oil leak. This was quickly repaired but in the meantime the other
two had departed on another strike. Instead of waiting for their return, Stoney accepted an
invitation to join three American Mustangs on an armed recce of the railway line from Taegu
through Taejon to Seoul and Kapsong. A large warehouse in a rail yard was bombed and
destroyed, and two trains were rocketed and strafed.

Two days later Flt Lts Adams (A68-715) and Coburn (A68-799) provided close-support
under the direction of a controller and attacked a large building in the town of Kunwi.
Afterwards, they patrolled the road from Kunwi to Andong but no enemy movement was
detected. During another close-support mission two mornings later (on 27 August), Adams
(A68-791) and two others attacked and destroyed an observation post, complete with radio
tower, near Waegwan. Enemy troops and equipment were located in a nearby orchard and were
thoroughly strafed. At least four large vehicles were destroyed and an adjacent bridge set afire.
Shortly afterwards the Mustangs strafed another camouflaged vehicle and left it blazing. A
nearby large haystack, which was hit during the attack, burned with a very thick black cloud of
smoke and was believed to have concealed a fuel storage dump. Next day, during an afternoon
rocket strike on the North Korean airfield at Taejon, no enemy aircraft were seen on the ground,
so Adams and his section delivered their rockets into a radio tower on the adjacent hill.

In the early afternoon of 29 August, Flt Lt Adams (A68-729) led an armed reconnaissance
near Seoul and over the area to the north. The Australians rocketed large factory buildings at
Chinnampo, three trucks were destroyed and, following railway lines, they attacked several
railway trucks and strafed personnel working on a railway bridge. Just over an hour after
landing, Adams was off again on a close-support mission in the Hyopch'ong area. Flg Off Bill
Horsman (A68-715) led another armed recce tasked with checking all the airfields in the Seoul,
Kimpo, Heitaku and Koryo areas, but when they reached Pusan they were ordered to attack
troops crossing a bridge at Hyonpung. These could not be found so they rocketed a dozen huts
nearby which all caught fire and several exploded – obviously full of stores and ammunition.
Prior to flying to Taegu to rearm and refuel, they strafed another village. At Taegu, Flg Off
Horsman joined a second section of RAAF Mustangs about to depart on a strike. Shortly
thereafter, the three remaining Mustangs led by Flt Lt Tom Murphy (A68-782) set off to carry
out the original airfield recce assignment. Since the airfields appeared devoid of aircraft,

---

[4] See *Korean Diary* by Frank Clune.

buildings at Koryo were rocketed and strafed, half a dozen vehicles nearby being left destroyed or damaged. Continuing southwards to Inwonjin harbour they found and strafed a 100-foot metal craft, which burst into flames. Having been repeatedly subjected to small-arms fire, Murphy was not surprised to discover two bullet holes in his aircraft, while P3 Geoff Stephens found another lodged in the propeller of A68-791.

By the end of August, 77RAAF had chalked up a total of 812 sorties for the month, during which it had destroyed 35 tanks, and had probably destroyed or damaged a further 31, in addition to 182 trucks, 30 other vehicles, four trains and 14 box-cars; at least a dozen ammunition and fuel dumps had also been destroyed. Wg Cdr Spence in his report to RAAF HQ Melbourne wrote:

> "The morale of the Squadron could not be better. Aircrew are keen to operate offensively and competition for sorties is most apparent. Ground personnel work long and irregular hours, cheerfully and efficiently. Many members have almost completed their first and second tours, and amongst them are some who are apprehensive of being posted back to Australia."

Commenting on the month's work, P3 Ray Trebilco recorded later:

> "After the landing at Inch'on and the breakout from the perimeter by the 8th Army, the navigational requirements for successful missions and for any diversions during such missions became even more demanding. However, August was the really critical month in my logbook. I flew 25 missions for 58 operational hours. The perimeter held, reinforcements were able to reach Korea, and United Nations forces were able to cross to the offensive. During this critical phase, all missions were different, hazardous, unusual or successful and I wouldn't want to highlight any particular one." [5]

The USAF Mustang fighter-bomber squadrons had been equally busy during the month. For example, the 51st (Prov) Squadron, which had reverted to its original 12th FBS status, had suffered the loss of six aircraft and four pilots killed in action, plus a further three wounded, since the middle of July. Its sister 67th FBS had lost Capt McVail in addition to its CO, Maj Sebille, and Capt Howell. Other F-51 squadrons also suffered grievous losses, the 8th FBW's 35th FBS alone losing 1/Lt John N. Munkres on the 15th, 1/Lt Pat Gilliam a few days later, and 1/Lt Arlin Mullet shortly thereafter, while 1/Lt Charles Wurster of the 36th FBS, who had shot down two Yaks in June and July while flying F-80s, was seriously injured in a take-off accident. Grievous losses indeed, but just four serious incidents during the course of 1,127 operational sorties flown by the 8th FBW in August was good arithmetic as far as 5th Air Force commanders were concerned. The newly arrived 35th FIG had not done so well either, its 40th FIS losing nine aircraft and six pilots during the month; four[6] of these were killed and two were believed to be prisoners.

The effect of continuous air strikes against North Korean ground forces was beginning to show; body counts in areas of these strikes revealed mass slaughter on a grand scale. South Korean troops found the bodies of some 600 enemy soldiers who had been killed in air strikes near Kigye on 26 August, and a further 700 bodies were located north-west of Po'hang as a result of a fighter-bomber strike four days later. Although the FEAF had issued orders that no UN aircraft was to cross the Yalu into Manchuria's airspace, thereby lessening the possibility of any direct intervention in the war by Chinese military forces, two USAF F-51s nonetheless strafed Antung airfield on the wrong side of the Yalu before the month was out (27 August). The offending pilots claimed a navigational error as the cause of their misdemeanour. Peking made issue of the blunder, claiming that three people had been killed and 21 wounded when the F-51s strafed the rail terminal and adjoining facilities at Talitzu, as well as the airfield at Antung. The Americans admitted that their aircraft may have been responsible, and offered compensation, but remained silent when the Chinese accused them of another violation two

---

[5] See *Korea Remembered* compiled by Maurie Pears and Fred Kirkland.
[6] The four known to have been killed were 1/Lts W.R. Brisco Jr, Meade M. Brown, Marlin T. Nolan, and Thelbert B. Wormack.

days later, reporting that US aircraft had opened fire on Chinese fishing boats in the Yalu, killing four and wounding a further seven. Writers for the Communist Chinese official newspaper *Jen Min Jin Pao* (People's Daily) had a field day; one wrote:

> "The US aggressors are simply hordes of inhuman beasts. Their atrocities virtually eclipse those of the Japanese and the Nazis . . ."

Another wrote:

> "Now American planes have made their appearance over our territory. This is not accidental, but a part of the American imperialistic policy . . . China will rise up in unity . . . and, together with the rest of the world, will smash the aggressive plots . . ."

American generals were not shy with the fervour of their jingoistic responses; Maj-General Orvil A. Anderson USAF, commander of the US Air War College, was relieved of his post following his public outburst:

> "We're at war . . . I don't advocate preventive war. I advocate the shedding of illusions. Give me the order to do it and I can break up Russia's five atom bomb nests in a week . . ."

A view that was undoubtedly nurtured by General MacArthur, the Supreme Commander, in the light of later events which saw him, also, relieved of his command. President Truman endeavoured to calm the situation when he declared:

> "We do not want the fighting in Korea to spread into a general war; it will not spread unless Communist imperialism draws other armies and governments into the fight of the aggressors against the United Nations. We hope in particular that the people of China will not be misled or forced into fighting against the United Nations and against the American people who have always been and still are their friends."

Meanwhile, back in Korea and following the successes reported as a result of airfield attacks and air combat, FEAF HQ estimated that by the end of August the NKAF possessed fewer than 20 combat aircraft, and that it would be pushed to launch more that 16 sorties in any one day. Of the period, General Stratemeyer stated later:

> "As it happened, the air battle was short and sweet. Air supremacy over Korea was quickly established. I need not dwell on the fact that had the enemy possessed a modern air force the whole picture in Korea – from the viewpoint of land, sea, and air forces – would have been vastly different."

Wg Cdr Wykeham-Barnes had meantime flown his first operational sortie over Korea on the night of 25 August, accompanied aboard B-26 BC-331 by Captain Oliver Lewis and gunner Sgt May:

> "Our first trip, to P'yongyang, five hours of low level, produced the usual meagre quota of flying targets. Korea was dark as the pit. Because of the total blackout it was just possible to see movement, and only the army moved. We used up our bombs and bullets, and made it back to Iwakuni. Captain Lewis looked a little more cheerful. I gave another talk to the aircrew, stressing the difference between the heavy B-26 and the agile Mosquito, on which my tactics were based. I emphasised the importance of not being too heroic, for a B-26 and crew was a poor exchange for a Korean truck."

The following night the same crew in a different aircraft, BC-297, located a NKPA convoy on which they unloaded their eight 500-lb bombs while strafing. Another sortie was flown by Wykeham-Barnes on the night of 27 August, again with Captain Lewis but on this occasion with S/Sgt Lammin manning the turret of BC-267:

> "We got our sights on a good-sized convoy near Taejon, dived to firing range, and let go with the front guns. Immediately there was a blaze of flame and sparks all around the inside of the cockpit, as the rigged-up wiring of the front guns blew its insulation. I heaved her into

the dark sky, the cockpit filled with smoke. Captain Lewis squirted everything with a portable fire extinguisher. I cut the main circuit breaker, and we were still flying. We limped home damp with sweat and extinguisher fluid."

Capt Lewis, who had been flying F-80s in the States when he received orders to proceed to Korea, was soon carrying out operations as first pilot, and he recalled the confusion and frustration of the early nocturnal operations:

"You can't believe the confusion. They were trying to find some targets in Korea big enough for us to hit. They simply had not crystallised how to fight this type of war, when we had aircraft designed for large-scale formation operations. Trains were the best targets. Hitting one made you feel like a king. But the Koreans got pretty good at blowing off steam from the engines to make themselves hard to see."

Having flown again on the night of 29 August, this time with a new crew – 1/Lt Woodhall and PFC McHale – Wykeham-Barnes intruded the Taejon-Kunsan-Swangju area but without success. The same crew set out two nights later in BC-688. They patrolled the area between Namwon and Yong-dong, where a convoy was discovered:

"PFC McHale on the rear guns engaged a convoy above us on a mountain road. This was the trip on which, after four hours of crawling around the valleys, the navigator confessed he had no idea where we were. This was not disastrous, for if we steered south-east we would pick up the powerful Iwakuni homer. But our pilot-operated M/F was tuned by a handle at the pilot's elbow, and after a couple of turns it released itself and fell onto the cockpit floor. At that moment we seemed very far from Japan. With no radio we began a nightmare search for base, feeling down through cloud for the Korean coast, marking the water's edge by the twinkling lights of the countless fishing boats, out over the dark sea, groping for the coast of Honshu, weaving along the beach until with only 15 minutes of fuel left, we sighted the lights of Iwakuni."

While the RAF Sunderlands continued mainly nocturnal patrols, which included anti-submarine surveillance, P2-V Neptunes of the USN VP-6, each aircraft armed with 16 rockets and 20mm cannon, attacked coastal targets of opportunity, including camouflaged power boats and coastal railway traffic, but on 16 August one aircraft was hit by return fire from a small patrol vessel and ditched with an engine on fire. The uninjured crew was rescued by HMS *Kenya*. As a result of this loss, Wing Six aircraft were ordered not to participate in attack missions unless specifically ordered to do so. Meanwhile, more reinforcements were on their way. HMS *Unicorn*, the Royal Navy's aircraft repair and ferry carrier, together with the cruiser HMS *Ceylon*, arrived at Pusan on 27 August to disembark the first British troops to arrive in Korea – 1/Argyll and Sutherland Highlanders and 1/Middlesex Regiment from Hong Kong, where they had been on garrison duty. The two battalions formed the new 27th British Brigade under the command of Brigadier B.A. Coad CBE DSO. An American negro band played on the quay-side as the troops disembarked and a Korean girls' choir welcomed them with a shaky version of 'God Save the King'. Brigadier Coad was advised that the situation was under control at Pusan and that there was little danger of a Communist breakthrough. However, just four nights later, on 31 August/1 September, North Korean forces forded the Naktong River on submerged pontoon bridges to start their final big assault against the Pusan perimeter.

September 1950
By daylight on 1 September the massive Communist offensive against the Pusan perimeter was in full swing. Apparently heedless of their appalling casualties, the North Koreans attacked in human waves using tactics which were born of desperate realisation that this was their last real chance to drive the UN forces out of Korea. If this offensive failed, depleted by the battles of the preceding weeks and weakened by ceaseless air attack, the NKPA would not be able to withstand a strong UN counter- offensive. The ferocity of the assaults took the Americans by surprise and the Communists raced on to capture Haman. Two North Korean divisions supported by armour crossed the Naktong and occupied Yongsan. By 6 September they had

advanced to within eight miles of Taegu, cutting the lateral Taegu road in two places.

From the very beginning UN fighter-bombers flew almost non-stop in direct support of the Allied ground forces and the Mustangs proved particularly effective. More than once they enabled pockets of encircled US infantry to break out by dropping clusters of napalm on North Korean concentration. Others, hopelessly surrounded where they were, survived thanks to the efforts of the 21st US Troop Carrier Squadron which air-dropped rations and ammunition to them. The situation on the ground was desperate and it was vital for the air forces to cut off the enemy's supplies and pin down his troops. During the afternoon on 1 September, the 5th Air Force's firepower was increased by the arrival of aircraft from Task Force 77 (see Chapter X), which had raced down the Korean coast at top speed from where they had been attacking targets in the north.

Along with units of the USAF and USMC, 77RAAF bombed and strafed troop concentrations and supply routes around the Pusan perimeter. The routine remained as before but with increased intensity. Every morning possible, the Australian pilots were given their general briefing at Iwakuni and despatched in elements of four across the Sea of Japan to Taegu, where they would be assigned targets by an FAC who would also direct the strike. Afterwards, the Mustangs would land at Taegu to refuel and rearm, and then they would be off again on another strike. The pace did not slacken. Sometimes each pilot would fly three or more sorties before returning exhausted to Iwakuni in the evening. Some ground-attack missions were actually being flown in the circuit area around Taegu itself. The Australians took their place, with the Americans, in long queues of aircraft awaiting turn-around and take-off. Sounds of the ground battle could be heard close by, so the urgency of the situation was very clear to the pilots at Taegu. They would contact the FAC during their climb after take-off, receive their target and roll in for a dive-bombing pass as soon as they had gained the necessary altitude. There was never any shortage of targets. Sometimes enemy troops fired on aircraft taking off and landing in the circuit. On the conditions at Taegu, P3 Milt Cottee wrote:

> "We spent much time waiting in that queue at Taegu with the ever-present sound of not-so-distant gunfire to the north. Intelligence briefs received at Iwakuni indicated a firm resolve to hang on to Taegu and to the small perimeter into which we had been pushed. I was most impressed with the continuing supply of ammunition and fuel available. Without complete air superiority of the area we would have been very vulnerable. One day at Taegu my attention was drawn to unusual sounds coming from the strip. I turned in time to see a C-119 transport completing its landing roll with both of its tail booms broken so that the whole tail section was dragging on the PSP. Someone who had observed the landing said it was a normal landing with the booms breaking just after touchdown. I watched with interest over the next couple of weeks as a team made repairs and then, one day, it was gone." [7]

To aid in a quick turn-around, a small party of RAAF ground staff with tents and equipment had joined the Americans at Taegu in the task of rearming and refuelling, working within earshot of the guns at the front. The supply of bombs and rockets, which were being used at such a phenomenal rate, was critical and in order to keep up, General Robertson handed over his VIP Dakota (A68-121) for use to help replenish supplies. Also called in to assist was a visiting RAF Dakota of 110 Squadron flown by Flt Lt Cox DFC, which thereby became the first RAF aircraft to land in South Korea during the war[8]. At times there were so few rockets left at Taegu that the armourers would pull the rockets straight out of the Dakota and on to the wings of the waiting Mustangs. To Flt Lt Dave Hitchins, the Dakota pilot, flying large cargoes of high explosives, sometimes well within range of enemy artillery, was no more than routine:

---

[7] See *Aviation Heritage* Vol.31 No.1.

[8] 110 Squadron RAF was currently based at Singapore with its Dakota C4s, but Flt Lt Cox and his crew were detached to Hong Kong in early September 1950, from where they would make two special flights to Tokyo and six to Iwakuni. It was while at Iwakuni that he was requested to fly to South Korea to lend a hand.

"When the Korean War began, I was the only RAAF transport pilot there [in Japan]. When that side of RAAF affairs became a bit organised, two other aircraft came from Australia (flown by Flt Lt Noel Eliot and Flt Lt Ron Daniel). Later, five more aircraft and crews came to us from 38 Squadron RAAF in Malaya. Initially, there was no appointment to command of the transport crews and, as I had previously been a flight commander, I assumed control – but had no command authority. Belatedly the unit was given an official designation (30 Transport Unit) and Sqn Ldr John Gerber arrived as CO."

Wg Cdr Wykeham-Barnes flew to Pusan via Taegu in a B-26A (BC-366) to see General Partridge again. The General implied that he was happy with the way the intruder programme was progressing, and hinted that he intended to apply to the Air Ministry for his permanent attachment to the FEAF. On leaving the General's headquarters, Wykeham-Barnes was requested to fly the B-26 on an offensive reconnaissance of the area before returning to Iwakuni. By now the 3rd BG crews were going out regularly by night as well as by day, and a 24-hour interdiction plan was established to cover all the routes from P'yongyang southwards. The aircrews were not over-keen, as Wykeham-Barnes noted:

"The fact was that the B-26 was not the right aeroplane, and as the other crews began to go out at night and get results, my admiration for them grew and grew. They showed the same gritty determination as my other hero, the M/Sgt chief cook of the aircrews tented mess. The chiefie never left his easy chair in the centre of his kitchen. Day and night he sat there, seldom dozing, only taking off his clothes for a shower: and the food was excellent, better than in my own mess back in England."

A force of 25 B-29s of the 307th BG was despatched on 2 September to attack North Korean supplies that were building up in Kumch'on, Kochang and Chinju. Next day it was the turn of the 22nd and 92nd Bombardment Wings to provide a force of two dozen B-29s, which began taking off from Yokota AFB at dawn to bomb targets between Pusan and Taegu along the Naktong, where an estimated 50,000 North Koreans were massing on Pusan. One B-29 of the 326th BS was piloted by Capt Cal Alldredge with Wg Cdr Alan Boxer DSO DFC (see Appendix III), a New Zealand-born RAF exchange officer as co-pilot. Also on board the Superfortress, named Miss Spokane, was Australian war correspondent Frank Clune, who wrote:

"Down the runway with a mighty roar the bombers dash at one-minute intervals as a warning light flashes from the control. This is a most tense moment, for many a heavily-loaded plane fails at the take-off, and then it's curtains for all. I have a tip-top view of the tail-end of *Miss America*, our predecessor in the line. Slowly, we inch towards the runway. Foot by foot we straighten out until we're dead in the centre of the runway. At 6.20am we rumble. I thought we'd never take off. But gently we are airborne. We're in the rough at 7.45am as the typhoon coming in from our left creates some turbulence. My narrow chair rolls around. Alan Boxer grabs the controls and wrestles fiercely as we fly through the storm at 10,000 feet. Suddenly we strike a rough patch and drop like a speedy elevator. 8.30am and daylight ahead. We've been typhooned and triumphed.

Now we fly in boxes of four, at 9,000 feet. We are in the rear of the box. The silver bodies of our planes glisten in the sun. We are to fly on visual target, which is at Pyopch'on, 60 miles from where we are, and about 30 miles south of Taegu. This makes me happy, because we have no fighter cover. I have no ambition to be stooging around all over North Korea, where Yaks and Stormoviks [Il-10s] abound. 10am the target approaches, the bombardier begins counting. 'Bombs away!' As the bombardier speaks the fatal words the trio of Superforts ahead spew ten tons of bombs from each of their innards, 40 bombs of 500-lb from each plane. Fascinated, I watch the bombs twisting in the air, dropping on the unseen target below. Then our 40 bombs drop. The bombardier had discharged his cargo about a mile before we were over the target, which was a long bridge spanning the Naktong, over which supplies were being carried by train and truck to the enemy. Below on our right a huge battle is in progress, by the look of the explosions going on." [9]

---

[9] See *Korean Diary*.

All the B-29s returned safely from this mission, one of nine sorties flown by Wg Cdr Boxer during his tour with the 92nd Bombardment Wing, with which he served as Project Officer, receiving the US Bronze Star in recognition for a task well done; he was also awarded the US Air Medal on completion of his tour.

A total of 129 aircraft of the 5th Air Force had flown 249 close-support, 89 interdiction and 35 medium-bomber sorties by the end of the day. The results achieved exceeded all expectations and Communist pressure on the Allied defences had been lifted appreciably although the results were not achieved without loss. The 36th FBS reported the death of 1/Lt James Anderlie, shot down by ground fire, while 77RAAF also suffered a loss. Flg Off Ken McLeod and his Mustang flight were briefed to escort B-29s bombing P'yongyang, which they did without opposition but then McLeod's aircraft (A68-801) began to give problems and he landed at Taegu. The others, meanwhile, looked for the FAC to find them a target on which to use their rockets, but before long fuel began to run low. P3 Bill Harrop called on the R/T saying that he had only 30 gallons left so they all decided to return to Taegu. When some eight miles out, Harrop called again saying he was going to crash because his aircraft was on fire. The FAC, who was following the Australians, saw the Mustang (A68-753) crash-land on the banks of the Naktong. Apparently unhurt, Harrop was observed to clear the aircraft and then lie down in a paddy field where he was seen to cover his white flying overalls with mud before running to a hut in a nearby orchard. While P2 Bill Michelson returned to base to organise a rescue helicopter, P3 Lyall Klaffer remained circling overhead to give Harrop air cover, but his time was limited. Finally, he had no choice but to leave. However, other Mustangs had been called and, when they arrived, the pilots saw Harrop come out of the hut and wave. The helicopter was delayed in answering the call and, although its crew searched for an hour, the downed Australian could no longer be seen and the helicopter returned without him[10].

On 4 September, Allied fighter-bombers destroyed or disabled most of the tanks supporting the two NKPA divisions attacking in the Yongsan sector. As he crossed Tsushima Straits while returning to Iwakuni after a rocket strike at Kigye, Flt Lt Ross Coburn's Mustang (A68-705) developed a glycol leak. The coolant temperature gauge rose and glycol fumes entered the cockpit, clouding up the canopy. With him were Flt Lts Gordon Harvey and Jack Murray, who could see glycol streaming from the radiator shutter. Coburn told Harvey what was happening and that he had decided to head for Bofu AFB, across the mountains. When over the mountains the Mustang began to vibrate violently and to involuntarily lose height. Murray saw the Mustang spiralling down out of control and yelled into his microphone for Coburn to get out. Of the unfolding drama, Flt Lt Odgers later wrote:

> "Coburn had to get out or die. He jettisoned the cockpit canopy, undid the safety harness and disconnected his headphones and throat mike. Then he stood up in the seat, levering himself up in the cockpit, with his right hand on the armour plate at the rear of the cockpit and his left on the windshield. He then dived towards the starboard roundel, pulling his legs up and crossing his arms over his chest. When he felt he was clear of the aircraft he straightened his legs out again and pulled the parachute ripcord, feeling a sharp jerk as the 'chute opened." [11]

Coburn steered the parachute into a clearing on a mountain side and swarms of Japanese seemed to appear all around him almost before he had time to stand up. He waved to show he was uninjured. His rescuers drove him towards Bofu in the back of a three-wheeled truck, but this was intercepted by a jeep from Iwakuni which picked him up and took him back to base, there to enjoy a couple of beers to celebrate his lucky escape. Another F-51 pilot who had a lucky escape on this day was Capt Robert Wayne of the 36th FBS, when he was rescued by an

---

[10] Many months later, when the area had been retaken, P3 Bill Harrop's body was found – he had been shot. Armed with only a .38 pistol to defend himself, he had presumably died either fighting in a lone battle or had been executed after being captured. The Americans awarded him their Air Medal posthumously.

[11] See *Across the Parallel*.

H-5 helicopter flown by 1/Lt Paul van Boven of the 3rd Air Rescue Squadron, operating from Taegu; this was the first-ever combat rescue mission using a helicopter.

Two more B-26 intruder sorties were flown by Wg Cdr Wykeham-Barnes in early September, one on the third night of the month with 1/Lt Baird and S/Sgt Bell in BC-688, when a convoy was attacked on the P'yontaek-Ch'onan road, and two nights later in BC-692 with 1/Lt Dockery and S/Sgt Lammin to the same area. On this latter occasion motor transport was bombed and strafed through gaps in the heavy overcast. This was to prove to be his last flight with the 3rd BG:

> "I had just begun once more to get a feel for the old business when the astral forces which had plucked me out of England exerted themselves once more. General Partridge called on the radio, and told me to get to Tokyo and write him a report. I said good-bye to Colonel Walker and the boys. Five days later I was back in Boscombe Down."

Of his brief time in Korea, Wykeham-Barnes reflected:

> "Korea is not an easy country in which to find one's way about at the best of times. It is rather featureless – all the hills look alike and the rivers flow in every possible direction. It had no system. It is perhaps somewhat ludicrous now to think that the ancient name of this country was. 'The land of the morning calm', when the only certain landmark in Korea is the battle line which can be pinpointed by the burning, the explosions, and the tracer and radio navigation. During my period there, there was a spell of about 24 hours in which communications broke down completely, and we were left to fight the war on our own. Though rather enjoyable in fact, this is certainly wrong in principle. As regards the Australian squadron, the General Commanding the 5th Air Force himself said that it was 'the best squadron I had; the one that set the pace.' They have the highest possible morale, and their standard of maintenance is tremendous."

To replace Wykeham-Barnes (who received the US Air Medal in recognition of his assistance) as RAF advisor to the 3rd BG, the Air Ministry instructed another RAF night fighter ace, Sqn Ldr H.E. Bodien DSO DFC (see Appendix III), a 34-year-old Londoner known to his friends as Joe, to make arrangements to fly to Japan from Hong Kong, where he was currently stationed.

Units of the 27th British Brigade were cast into the fighting on the Naktong on 6 September. For the next fortnight, while they held 18,000 yards of hill front, they had sporadic contact with the enemy and suffered their first casualties while they kept up energetic offensive patrols. Brigadier Coad said afterwards:

> "I had a gap on my left bank between myself and the next American division which started off at 4,000 yards and quite soon increased to 9,000 yards. Into that gap the best part of a North Korean division infiltrated. Life was very interesting, to say the least of it."

While the 27th Brigade held this line, US Marines were speedily sent to Yongsan and they succeeded in driving the North Koreans out of the area in the second battle of the Naktong Bulge. By 7 September the NKPA was being held back all along the line.

At Iwakuni on 9 September, Flt Lt Adams was rostered to lead three other 77RAAF pilots in an attack on an enemy position south-east of the walled city at Mount Kusan. Altogether, 16 UN aircraft were tasked to give an hour of continuous support over the target area prior to the US Army's 1st Cavalry Regiment assault on the position at 1030. Due to bad weather, however, the Australian Mustangs did not take off from Iwakuni until 0933 and, on arriving over the target, they found the area virtually obliterated by cloud and rain. Adams led his section through a small break over the top of the grey shrouded hill and, following the contours of the terrain, dropped napalm. Of the eight containers which were released, only one ignited. In spite of the dangerous cloud cover which cloaked the top of the hill, the Australians rocketed and strafed the unexploded napalm in an effort to cause ignition, but in vain. The area was too wet and the topography of the place made it too dangerous for diving attacks to strafe effectively.

During a close-support mission to the Pusan area that day, Wg Cdr Spence led his Mustangs to Angang-ni where they were instructed to make a napalm and rocket attack on the town. At that stage, the engine of the aircraft (A68-804) flown by Flt Lt Coburn began to run roughly and he had to divert to land at Pusan. The remaining three proceeded to Angang-ni where, again, weather conditions were unfavourable with low clouds around the target making visibility poor and flying dangerous. Napalm had to be delivered in a shallow dive, levelling out for release over the target. While the CO, in A68-809, was coming in from 700 feet, something went wrong. His aircraft was seen to go into an unusually steep dive. P3 Andrew Hankinson saw the aircraft commence to pull out so close to the ground that it pulled heavy vapour trails from its wing-tips, but it was much too late. The Mustang struck the ground in the centre of the town and exploded on impact. There was no possibility of survival. The remaining two pilots continued to attack the town and caused fires, but neither they nor their controller were able to find targets for their rockets, so they returned to Pusan. Flt Lt Coburn was there, where his aircraft required an engine change. Following the death of Wg Cdr Spence, Flt Lt Bay Adams took over leadership of the Squadron in the air while Air Commodore A.M. Charlesworth RAAF, Chief-of-Staff of the BCOF, came from Tokyo to look after administration at the base until a new commanding officer could arrive from Australia.

The assault from the air was unrelenting and, two days later, in a massive combined effort, the 5th Air Force, the US Marines and FEAF Bomber Command flew 683 sorties against the enemy. In the US 2nd Division's sector alone, UN fighter-bombers killed an estimated 1,500 soldiers and destroyed their equipment. By 12 September the worst was over. The threat to the Pusan perimeter was no more and, following the successful USN amphibious landings at Inch'on on the west coast (see Chapter X), North Korea's bid to drive out the United Nations forces and overcome South Korea had failed. General Walton H. Walker, commanding the US Marines, in his praise of the support of the 5th Air Force, said:

> ". . . no commander ever had better air support than has been furnished the 8th Army by the
> 5th Air Force . . . I will gladly lay my cards right on the table and state that if it had not been
> for the air support that we received from the 5th Air Force we would not have been able to
> stay in Korea."

The cost to the 8th FBG was heavy, three experienced Mustang pilots being killed on operations; Capt Harold Webster of the 36th FBS was lost on the 14th, Capt Walter Russell of the 35th FBS two days later, and Capt Edward Onze of the 36th FBS on the 19th. The F-80-equipped 49th FBW had also suffered a number of losses, losing three aircraft in the first five days of the month although only 1/Lt James Petty of the 7th FBS was killed, but on the 14th and 15th three more pilots were lost, 1/Lt Irving May and 1/Lt Paul Kearns of the 8th FBS, and 1/Lt Richard Bartly of the 7th FBS. All, it seems, the victims of ground fire.

Although poor weather hampered air support, the 8th US Army broke out of the Pusan perimeter on the morning of 16 September, with the US 1st Cavalry leading. Preceded by a two-hour artillery barrage (the weather was too wet for heavy bombers) the American forces began to advance up the road towards Taejon and Seoul. The 27th British Brigade was scheduled to cross the Naktong to protect the left flank. This would entail foot-slogging infantry work, supported by US tanks, artillery and aircraft, to clear the enemy from the hills. The 82 B-29s assigned in the early morning to blast a hole in the Communist defences to enable the American troops to break out from Pusan, found the target area completely covered with low-lying cloud. The bomber commander had to divert his force to secondary targets in P'yongyang and Wonsan and, for the remainder of the day, low rain clouds, as a consequence of typhoon 'Kezia', continued to shroud Korea. Before noon, however, F-80s and F-51s found holes in the clouds and attacked NKPA positions from Po'hang to Masan, but from mid-afternoon the weather worsened and nearly all air units were forced to cease operations. Heavy rain showers and overcast skies again hampered heavy bomber operations over South Korea on the 17th, and B-29 activities were restricted to leaflet drops. Nevertheless, 5th Air Force fighter-bombers, guided by FACs, broke through the clouds and made some effective attacks. As the weather continued to clear, the tempo of the air attacks increased. Next day, B-29s accurately carpet-bombed two target areas either side of where the old road and rail bridges crossed the Naktong at Waegwan. Over a 24-hour period, 5th Air Force pilots flew a total of 647 sorties. Not all were successful. On the night of the 21st, a B-29 crew of the 98th BG made a navigational error and bombed Antung's marshalling yard, causing another chilling response by way of a muted warning from the Chinese in its official newspaper *Jen Min Jin Pao*:

> "There is only one explanation: the American imperialists are deciding to extend their armed aggression against China . . . We Chinese people are against the American imperialists because they are against us. They have openly become the arch enemy of the People's Republic of China by supporting the people's enemy, the Chiang Kai-shek clique, by sending a huge fleet to prevent the liberation of the Chinese territory of Taiwan, by repeated air intrusions and strafing and bombing of the Chinese people, by refusing new China a seat in the UN, through intrigues with their satellite nations, by rearing up again a fascist power in Japan, and by rearming Japan for the purpose of expanding aggressive war. Is it not just for us to support our friend and neighbour against our enemy? The American warmongers are mistaken in thinking that their accusations and threats will intimidate the people of China."

Although not a call for immediate action against the UN forces, it served as a serious warning as to which way the Chinese Communists would respond to any further violations of its border. Two days later Chou En-lai, the Chinese Communist Foreign Secretary, cabled UN HQ with his personal warning:

> "This case is even more serious than the strafings by the United States airplanes which occurred formerly . . . [and] exposes more clearly than ever the determination of the United States of America to extend aggressive war against Korea, to carry out armed aggression on Taiwan, and to extend further her aggression against China . . .. The flames of war being extended by the United States in the east are burning more fiercely. If the representatives of the majority of states attending the United Nations General Assembly should still be pliant to the manipulation of the United States and continue to play deaf and dumb to these aggressive crimes of the United States, they shall not escape a share in the responsibility for lighting up the war-flames in the East."

Meanwhile, over the battle front on 19 September, 77RAAF maintained a maximum effort. From their cockpits, Flg Offs Ken McLeod and Tom McCrohan watched the Americans cross the Naktong at two points. As troops from the US 24th Division forged across the river four miles south of Waegwan and headed for Kumch'on, they flushed from cover a group of some 1,500 North Korean soldiers. The bewildered enemy became confused under aerial attack and milled around in the open, where they fell prey to artillery, F-80s, B-26s and the ever-present Mustangs. McLeod and McCrohan, as they dived, could see then NKPA soldiers trying to shelter behind their yellow back-packs. Devoid of transport, they could only take whatever supplies they were able to carry with them. From high above, American aircraft scattered three million leaflets over the battlefield telling them to surrender. As the leaflets came fluttering down, McCrohan suddenly flew through a shower of them and for a heart-stopping instant feared that he was colliding with a flock of birds.

From one sortie Flt Lt Tom Murphy returned with damage to his aircraft's radiator and one wingtip, caused by ground fire as he discharged his rockets at a tank. Later, a ground controller directed Flt Lt Fred Barnes and his section to cover a secondary amphibious landing some 20 miles north of Po'hang. The Mustangs used up their ordnance on the woods edging the beach. ROK troops landing ashore went ahead apparently unopposed. Meanwhile, the Squadron's new CO had arrived, Sqn Ldr R.C. Creswell, another WWII veteran who had previously twice commanded 77RAAF (see Appendix III). He was soon in action and flew his first sortie over Korea as No2 to Flt Lt Bay Adams on 20 September. Within a week he had flown 11 sorties.

On 22 September, 77RAAF flew its 174th strike for the month, an armed recce to Sinmak. Eight Mustangs led by Flg Off Ken McLeod (A68-729) took off from Taegu with an additional aircraft, an American F-51, tagging along for the mission. McLeod contacted the FAC at a village two miles west of Naksong-dong on the Naktong. An estimated 500 enemy troops were reported in the area and napalm was dropped on the village, on an orchard and on troops along the road. This was followed by a thorough strafing before the Mustangs left the area. The formation arrived over Sinmak 55 minutes later, where two camouflaged objects were spotted, one of which was identified as a light aircraft. This, and the other, were strafed and both left in flames. Various large buildings in the area were rocketed and strafed, along with a railway tunnel a mile south-east of the town. One rocket was observed to disappear into the mouth of the tunnel before it detonated. The railway system continued to attract attention and a locomotive was rocketed, strafed and left damaged. This was followed by attacks on two long rows of train carriages at the station, and four box-cars were left on fire. Finally, before returning to Taegu, the Mustang pilots had a close look at Suwon airfield but did not attack because it was found to already be in friendly hands.

The day was also successful for the 27th British Brigade. Early in the morning the Middlesex Battalion attacked some high ground held by the enemy to the right of the track from the Naktong to Songiu, on the road to Seoul. It was the first assault carried out by the British forces and after heavy fighting they were secure in their positions by the evening. With the Middlesex thus safe on high ground to the right of the track, the Argylls had the job of clearing a well-held covered position known as Hill 282, on the left. Two companies advanced before daylight on 23 September and reached the crest of Hill 388, a high point further along the ridge, as the North Koreans counter-attacked. The Argylls held on grimly but about mid-morning their own heavy artillery support abruptly stopped. Five supporting American tanks down on the flat ground could not help because the flat trajectory of their guns would not allow them to engage the enemy artillery and mortar positions. Additionally, the terrain was too rough to allow the Argyll's mortar platoon to move to a more advantageous position. Ammunition ran low. At this stage Maj Kenneth Muir, the Argylls' second-in-command, led a relief party from Battalion HQ to the crest of the hill and took command there. Despite increased mortar fire, particularly from Hill 388, Muir succeeded in tightening his perimeter, evacuating the wounded and inspiring his men to hold on for air support. As his request, by radio, went through to the nearest US Tactical Air Control Post, the Argylls laid out the appropriate recognition panels on Hill 282.

Just after midday a flight of USAF F-51s arrived over the scene. After they circled Hill 282 three times, they came back in to attack. Napalm bombs were dropped, not upon the enemy, but on the already battered Argylls. The American pilots, who had obviously mistaken Hill 282 for Hill 388, followed up by strafing. The tragic attack reduced the fighting strength of the two Scottish companies on the hill to five officers and 35 ORs. All this time the enemy artillery and mortars on Hill 388 remained free from return fire. Maj Muir had to withdraw to a position about 50 feet below the crest, but, once he had evacuated the wounded, he led his small force back up to the crest of Hill 282 and proceeded to repel every enemy attempt to take the position. Muir himself was killed in the action. He was posthumously awarded the Victoria Cross. Menaced from the front and rear as well as from the air, and with its supplies cut off, the NKPA threatening the Argylls broke and disintegrated. The troops either surrendered or changed into the white dress of peasants and melted into the hills.

From the air the Mustang pilots of 77RAAF saw hundreds of such peasants in white clothing walking eastwards in the south coast area, but were aware that enemy troops were mingling with the refugees and there was nothing they could do about it for fear of hitting civilians. However, seven aircraft led by Flg Off Ken McLeod found a lone enemy tank speeding along the road from Waegwan to Kumch'on and stopped it with rockets. When the crewmen climbed out they were cut down by machine-gun fire. It was not unusual for a single RAAF Mustang to join with an American formation in making a strike on enemy positions, P3 Dick Turner accompanying two USAF F-51s to attack positions near Kumch'on. They were joined in time by other RAAF fighter-bombers before all returned safely to Iwakuni.

On 23 September, Flt Lt Adams (A68-813) led four Mustangs on a very successful close-support mission. They found a large number of enemy troops, two field pieces and eight tanks trapped on the road two miles north of Jusong. The target had already been attacked by American aircraft and two of the tanks were burning, one at each end of the concentration so that the remaining tanks could not escape. The four Australian pilots, which included Sqn Ldr

Cresswell in A68-803, strafed the troops and then napalmed, rocketed and strafed the six surviving tanks. One was hit directly with napalm, completely set on fire and destroyed. A second was also set on fire and a third damaged by rockets. As the Australian pilots assembled for a briefing at Taegu next day (24 September), it was obvious that something a little different was happening. The usual close-support missions were to continue but four Mustangs were directed to carry out an armed recce of the airfield at P'yongyang where the NKAF apparently had two aircraft serviceable for operations, while another four Mustangs were to visit the airfield at Onjong-ni where more enemy aircraft had been sighted. Flt Lt Noble was to lead the attack against P'yongyang, and Flt Lt Barnes the other mission. Each aircraft carried napalm in addition to rockets. As Noble's quartet swept over the airfield at P'yongyang the only aircraft the pilots could see were wrecks and dummies. Only one appeared to be intact, tentatively identified as a Yak-3 or Yak-9. The leader's subsequent report revealed:

"It [the Yak] was camouflaged with small boughs and the cowls were off as though it was under maintenance. This aircraft was burnt and destroyed by napalm. The other aircraft on the field were recced but were all dummies or [previously] destroyed and did not warrant further attacks. The heavy storage area indicated in the photograph was attacked again with napalm, with two direct hits . . ."

After 30 minutes over the airfield Noble concluded that the second enemy aircraft – assuming there had been an intact one in the first place – was not present, and they set off on the return journey, heading in the direction of Seoul. Along the way they sighted four trucks, which they strafed. Three burst into flames but the fourth refused to burn, although it was seen to emit smoke. Further south along the road another truck was strafed. Meanwhile, Flt Lt Barnes' flight proceeded to Onjong-ni, diverting around the area of Seoul because it was a zone restricted for USN air operations, and while no aircraft were to be seen on the airfield napalm was dropped on the designated area just in case. For 40 minutes the Mustangs rocketed and strafed blast pens and openings to underground revetments, one of which had wires leading up to what appeared to be a radio room. Hits were registered but there was no way to determine the effectiveness of the attack. Anti-aircraft fire from small-arms came from buildings on the northern side of the airfield. It was moderate but accurate and Barnes' aircraft (A68-715) was hit in the engine and mainplane leading edge, but without any obvious effect. As Barnes led the way back to Taegu, he was contacted by the FAC who asked the Australians to carry out a reconnaissance along the roads between Yong-dong and the Naktong. This they did, and two trucks and a camouflaged vehicle were sighted and strafed. P3 Dick Wittman flew so low during the attack that the starboard wing of his aircraft (A68-765) struck a tree, and although three feet of wingtip was torn away, he managed to fly back to Taegu where he landed without mishap.

That afternoon Flt Lt Noble and his flight were briefed to return to P'yongyang, as the Photographic Interpretation Centre reported that more aircraft had been discovered in a wooded area near the airfield. Noble later recalled:

"The section, armed again with eight napalm bombs, 16 rockets and full ammunition, proceeded to the airfield area and dropped their napalm in the small wooded area just alongside the airfield. The area was carefully scanned before dropping the napalm and this section is of the opinion that there were no aircraft in the wood. However, as briefed to do, they dropped their napalm in this area. Fires were started in the trees. The storage dump on the road on the north-eastern side of the field, which had previously been napalmed, was again attacked with rockets. This dump was in a type of underground tunnel. Rockets entered the mouth of the tunnel and a fire, thought to be an oil fire, was started. An Il-10 on the extreme west tip of the strip, which appeared to be in fairly good condition, and was camouflaged, was attacked by strafing and left afire. The aircraft which had been previously attacked and left burning by this section in the morning was again recced and found to be well burnt out . . ."

On 26 September, the 8th US Army linked up with X Corps at Suwon, cutting the remnants of the NKPA in two. The enemy retreat had ended in complete rout. As the North Koreans scattered into the rugged countryside, more that 125,000 prisoners were taken, together with most of their abandoned equipment. The US 1st Cavalry and 7th Infantry Divisions met as Seoul was being liberated. The 5th US Marines hoisted the Stars and Stripes over the shattered Capital building on the 27th but, shortly afterwards, for diplomatic reasons they were ordered to replace it with the blue flag of the United Nations. Two days later General MacArthur presided over a solemn ceremony in the Capital building to mark the liberation of the city and the return of the government to South Korean President Rhee.

Two enemy aircraft were damaged by 18th FBG pilots making strafing attacks during September, but the F-51 loss rate remained in the enemy's favour. The 67th FBS lost four Mustangs while the 12th FBS lost another two, five of the pilots being reported missing. Most of these losses occurred while the Group was flying missions from K-9 over North Korea where anti-aircraft fire was heavier. There is little doubt that the movement of the 18th FBG into Pusan at this critical time is what saved the perimeter itself from collapsing while the UN attempted to bolster its ground forces. After a relatively quiet period of some six weeks, with the NKAF virtually out of business, North Korean Yaks put in an unexpected appearance on 28 September. One shot down an F-51 of the 39th FIS from which 1/Lt Donald Pitchford was seen to bale out behind UN lines but, after landing, his exact position could not be pinpointed. His body was later recovered. This was the 39th FIS's only fatality of the month, but the 40th FIS lost two more pilots, 1/Lt William Levi on the 7th, and 1/Lt Donald E. Lee on the 27th. Next day 1/Lt Ralph G. Hall of the 35th FBS probably destroyed a Yak on the ground. Two more Yaks were claimed destroyed on the ground by an F-80 pilot – Capt Ernest D. Fahlberg of the 8th FBS – on the last day of the month. The 18th FBG had suffered equally, losing at least six Mustangs to ground fire, and four pilots killed or missing. The effect of the early American air offensive had undoubtedly made a considerable impact on the outcome of the war, and was emphasised later when Senior Colonel Lee Hak Ku, Chief-of-Staff of the NKPA's 13th Division, admitted that his soldiers had began to associate the American jets in particular, with "a certain mystery and thus primitive fear," and added:

> ". . . not only did they [the jets] come in quickly and destroy the target with a great element of surprise, but also that the soldiers feared them because of the great speed and the way the aircraft appeared before the sound of its flight reached them, to make them aware of its presence."

There was still plenty to shoot at on the ground – Lt Colonel Harold Price flying an F-80 of the 8th FBG destroying three Yaks on the 12th to add to the one he had claimed earlier in July – and, in fact, the 8th FBG and 49th FBW could not contain North Korean supply and troop movements. In addition to the shortage of aircraft, the 8th FBG found itself with a major dilemma when pilots started returning from missions reporting that they could not fire their rockets. A problem with the aircraft was suspected but a thorough inspection revealed that the cause was sabotage. It was discovered that the rocket connections had been tampered with by a person or persons unknown, resulting in a malfunction when the pilot squeezed the trigger to fire. The FEAF therefore decided to call in the 51st FIW from its base on Okinawa and, on 22 September, the 16th and 25th FIS flew their F-80s to Itazuke ready for combat where, on the 25th, an F-80 collided with an F-82 of the 68th FAWS; the crew of the Twin-Mustang were killed but the pilot of the F-80 was able to carry out an emergency landing. The 51st FIW's third squadron stayed behind in Japan for defence, but most of its pilots would be able to rotate in and fly missions with the 16th and 25th. Next day, both these squadrons were on operations, the 16th alone notching up 168 sorties in the last days of September. Commencing on 28 September, the 49th FBW began its move to Taegu and thus became the first jet fighter unit to operate in a combat zone under full field conditions, although major maintenance would still be done at Itazuke.

September had seen a marked reduction in combat operations performed by the ROKAF. The FEAF gave a low priority to the fledgling unit due to its limited resources and commitments to other Mustang units. Because of the meagre delivery of ordnance only 21 effective combat sorties could be flown by Maj Hess's pilots. Emphasis was therefore directed into training and checking out as many Korean pilots on Mustangs as possible. To assist this, a detachment from the 3499th Training Aids Wing was assigned to the unit on temporary duty. They arrived just in time to witness an ROKAF pilot make a serious error when he dived inverted straight into the bay. The detachment's job would be to teach the new pilots how to prevent this sort of tragic mistake from happening.

During the month, for three aircraft lost with one pilot killed – albeit the CO, Wg Cdr Spence – and another posted missing (P3 Bill Harrop), 77RAAF had flown 695 sorties, including a total of 52 in one day. Most were in close support of ground forces under the direction of ground and airborne controllers but many others were armed reconnaissance both south of, and beyond, the 38th Parallel. With the fighting apparently racing to a conclusion, the Australian pilots had found they were having to fly longer and longer missions from their base in Japan to find fewer and fewer targets. Damage inflicted on the enemy by the Squadron since its first operation on 3 July was assessed as:

Destroyed: three aircraft on the ground; 49 tanks or self-propelled guns; 225 trucks; 41 miscellaneous vehicles; four locomotives; 19 rail trucks; five bridges; 25 ammunition and fuel dumps; 24 important buildings; and two boats.

Probably destroyed: 10 tanks or self-propelled guns; 18 trucks; eight miscellaneous vehicles; 18 rail trucks; two bridges; and seven important buildings.

Damaged: 17 tanks or self-propelled guns; 21 trucks; five miscellaneous vehicles; four locomotives; nine rail trucks; 25 bridges; 32 important buildings; and one boat.

Probably damaged: 18 tanks or self-propelled guns; five trucks; ten rail trucks; three bridges; and three important buildings.

In recognition of the part played by 77RAAF in the successes achieved by the US 5th Air Force, the grateful Americans presented several decorations to Squadron members towards the end of September. Flt Lts Bay Adams and Stuart Bradford had by then each flown 50 sorties and received US Air Medals. Other recipients were Flt Lt Carlyle Noble and Ops Officer Flt Lt Charles Taplin.

CHAPTER III

ENTER THE MIG, ENTER THE SABRE

October – December 1950

"What are the chances for Chinese or Soviet intervention?"

US President Truman to General MacArthur

"Very little. The Chinese . . . have no Air Force. The Russians . . . are no match for our Air Force . . ."

General MacArthur, in reply

Early in August there had been informal discussions at the United Nations as to whether UN forces should enter North Korea, and on unifying Korea under an anti-Communist government. The chief US delegate to the UN, Warren A. Austin, had spoken before the Security Council and had made the first public statement of that goal. He implied that the United States would be satisfied with nothing less than the unification of Korea under an anti-Communist government. His speech effectively ended the possibility of the fighting finishing with a return of the *status quo*.

The main stumbling block for such a move was a Soviet-backed China on Korea's northern border. As early as 11 August the American Ambassador in London had notified his government that the British military attaché in China had reported observations suggesting that the Chinese could be preparing for war. The fear at the UN was what China would do if UN troops crossed the 38th Parallel, while the Communist government in Peking feared that such a development would expose them to the danger of American invasion of Chinese-administered Manchuria, which they maintained could be co-ordinated with a US-sponsored Chinese Nationalist invasion of southern China mainland. To Chairman Mao and his generals the signs were there that the Americans really were going to launch a 'preventative war' against Communism. The shift in the military balance at that time suggested that the Americans would soon be in a position to do it. Logic dictated that, just as the Americans considered it would be a strategic disaster should Formosa – the last bastion of the Chinese Nationalists – fall into the hands of a hostile Communist China, so it would be a strategic disaster for the Communists should North Korea fall into the hands of a hostile United States. Therefore, Mao decided, if they, the Chinese Communists, intervened in the Korean War it would be no different from the intervention of the Americans in South Korea. But there was more to Mao's thinking than patriotic defence of China's border with Korea:

". . . the concerns behind the decision to enter the Korean War went far beyond the defence of the safety of the Chinese-Korean border. Mao and his associates aimed to win a glorious victory by driving the Americans off the Korean peninsula." [1]

---

[1] See *China's Road to the Korean War* by Chen Jian.

Undoubtedly the Chinese considered the possibility of the Americans using the atom bomb if they intervened in North Korea, the matter being raised by Acting PLA Chief-of-Staff General Nieh Jung-chen with Indian Ambassador K.M. Panikkar during a meeting in September 1950, although Nieh was dismissive:

> "[The People's Republic of China] will not sit back with folded hands and let the Americans
> come to the border . . . atomic attacks might kill a few million people [but] after all, China
> lives on the farms. What can atom bombs do there?"

General Nieh was echoing the words of his leader. Four years earlier Mao Tse-tung had remarked to an American journalist:

> "The atom bomb is a paper tiger with which the US reactionaries try to terrify the people.
> It looks terrible, but in fact is not. Of course the atom bomb is a weapon of mass destruction,
> but the outcome of war is decided by the people, not by one or two new weapons."

Notwithstanding, the threat of the possible use of such weapons was obviously taken seriously since the construction of air-raid shelters was speedily carried out in Mukden, while air-raid drills were conducted in key cities throughout north-east China. The British Consul in Mukden however refused to allow a shelter to be constructed within the grounds of his residence, with the result that he and his staff were expelled. It is not clear if Mao and his generals were aware of the Russian development of their own atomic bomb, first tested on 29 August 1949; if they did know, they would have been comforted by the knowledge that the Americans would be afraid of a nuclear counterblow if they used their bombs against China; if they were not privy to the facts, they nonetheless accepted the calculated risk.

The Russians were similarly determined not to lose North Korea to American influence and control, but did not wish to face the risks that blatant military intervention would surely provoke. So they did all they could to nourish Peking's fears and convince the Chinese that it was in their own interest to intervene if US/UN forces attempted to unify Korea. Unknown to the West, the Soviets had been supplying the Chinese with military hardware and training its pilots to fly its latest jet fighter aircraft, the MiG-15[2]. A Russian training air regiment equipped with MiGs under the command of Marshal of Aviation Krasovskii had been sent from Kubinka to China in February 1950 to establish a training course for Chinese and North Korean pilots, in response to an earlier Chinese request by General Liu Ya-Lou, commander of China's embryonic air force, for military assistance:

> ". . . the CCP Central Committee cabled Liu, instructing him to explore with Stalin whether
> the Soviet Union would be willing to supply the Chinese with 100-200 Yak fighters and 40-
> 80 heavy bombers, to help the Chinese train 1,200 pilots and 500 technicians in Soviet air
> school, and to send air advisers to China . . ." [3]

The Soviet response was positive and when General Liu met Marshal Alexander Vasilevskii, the Soviet Minister of Armed Forces, in Moscow, he was advised by him that Stalin had already ordered the Soviet Air Force to do its best to assist the Chinese. Subsequently, on 15 October 1949, the first batch of Yak-12 trainers arrived in China followed, nine days later, by the first group of 23 Soviet air advisors and, by early December, six aviation schools had been established, four to train fighter pilots and two to train bomber crews. The Soviets also agreed to sell China 434 aircraft (including MiG-9 jet fighters), 185 of which were delivered by the end of 1949. On 14 February 1950, Mao Tse-tung travelled to Moscow where he and Stalin signed the Sino-Soviet Alliance Treaty, at the same time placing an order for a further 586 aircraft including 280 fighters and 198 bombers; this was almost immediately followed by an additional order for another 628 aircraft.

The newly formed Chinese 4th Air Corps was stationed near Shanghai under the command of General Nieh F'eng-chih, formerly of the Chinese 3rd Field Army where he commanded

---

[2] See Appendix V for details of the MiG-15.

[3] See *China's Road to the Korean War.*

27th Corps; his deputy was another former 3rd Field Army leader, Colonel Yü Li-chin, who had been the political commissar to the Chinese 8th Army. They, together with the Russian instructors, were responsible for training Chinese pilots for service in Korea. The Soviet training regiment was followed by the MiG-15-equipped 29th Guards Fighter Air Regiment (GuFAR) of the 50th Fighter Air Division[4] which began arriving in China in August, as part of the specially-formed 64th Fighter Air Corps raised to direct military operations in Korea. The main function of the Corps was air defence of bridges and dams on the Yalu. Reluctant to run the risk of expanding the conflict outside Korea, the Soviets took great measures to conceal participation of its pilots in the air war. Should a Russian pilot be shot down and captured on offensive operations against the UN, the exposure would have obvious and potentially dire consequences.

According to American military assessment, by the end of September south of the 38th Parallel the enemy's back was broken. The next question was whether or not to pursue the remaining North Korean forces all the way into the north of the country and wipe them out. On 1 October, General MacArthur called upon the NKPA to accept unconditional surrender. On the eastern flank however, regardless of MacArthur's ultimatum, the 3rd ROK Division did not wait for a reply. It crossed the 38th Parallel and drove rapidly towards Wosan. Other ROK units began pushing northwards, too. Next day MacArthur isssued orders for the UN ground invasion of North Korea, and a force of B-29s was immediately despatched from Japan to raid a suspected NKPA training centre at Nanam. Returning crews claimed the destruction of 75 per cent of the complex, although a further attack by 13th BS B-26s on the 3rd resulted in the loss of three aircraft and their crews[5]. Four days later (on 7 October) a UN Assembly resolution authorised UN forces to cross the 38th Parallel, apparently unaware of the actual events taking place on the ground. The order was duly passed to all UN ground forces to advance northwards. On the western flank the US I Corps began its attack. To cover it, FEAF air support operations were to be similar to those flown to shield the Inch'on landing in September. Next day (8 October) occurred another serious violation incident when two F-80s of the 49th FBG erroneously strafed the Russian military airfield at Sukhaya Rechka near Vladivostok and damaged nine P-39s of the 821st Fighter Air Regiment. Fortunately, there were no casualties and the Soviets did not respond, except to demote the commander of the 821st FAR for not taking immediate action against the strafing aircraft. The offending USAF pilots were brought to book, as was the commander of the 49th FBG. The official USAF historian wrote:

> "Acting on orders from above, General Partridge relieved the commander of the 49th Group but brought him to Seoul as director of combat operations of the 5th Air Force. A court-martial subsequently refused to convict the two young lieutenants. The men of the 49th Group thought that these actions were somewhat severe, but they wondered what must have been the punishment of the Russian air commander who allowed his airfield to be strafed without mustering any opposition." [6]

On this same date an attack on a target near the Manchurian border was carried out by B-26s with an escort of F-51s, one of which was flown by Cmdt Jan Pretorius, newly arrived senior SAAF Air Liaison Officer, who was on a familiarisation trip to Korea. The South African government had earlier announced its intention of placing a fighter-bomber squadron at the disposal of the UN Command for service in Korea, and its personnel were currently on their way from South Africa. FEAF units were to continue with their current missions but they were also to be prepared, at four days' notice, to mount a paratroop assault, whenever and wherever it might be needed. The FEAF also began moving units into Korean bases:

49th Fighter-Bomber Group with F-80Cs to Taegu (K-2)

---

[4] A Fighter Air Regiment comprised three eskadrilyas (squadrons); a Fighter Air Division comprised two or three Air Regiments, therefore six or nine eskadrilyas.

[5] The three missing aircraft were piloted by Capt Gordon O. Smith, and 1/Lts Francis J. LaBarge and Lucius P. Walton, all of whom were reported killed as were their gunners.

[6] See *The United States Air Force in Korea* by Dr Robert Futrell.

8th Fighter-Bomber Group with F-80Cs to Suwon (K-13)
51st Fighter Interceptor Wing with F-80Cs to Kimpo (K-14)
35th Fighter Interceptor Group with F-51s to Po'hang (K-3), including 77RAAF

The move to Po'hang meant that the Australian Mustangs could strike at targets in North Korea without needing to cover substantial distances. Flt Lt Gordon Harvey recalled:

"Flying out of Iwakuni initially, it had been an unusual kind of war for us up to then because we had the luxury of our home quarters. You were in the air a long time. You usually flew a mission one day and had the next day off. The flight from Iwakuni was probably an hour or an hour-and-a- quarter. In Korea you'd have to cut lunch and be doing these 30-minute missions and you'd finish up back at Iwakuni for dinner. If anyone was damaged you'd always go back to the American bases in the south rather than fly back. While the war was mostly confined to the south-east corner [of Korea] missions were very short but when things opened up and went further north, it became more and more difficult for us because we had to fly further and further to find a target. It was no longer practical for us to operate out of Iwakuni. It was far better for us to go to Korea and join an American outfit, which we did. We became the third squadron of the 35th [Fighter Interceptor Group]. When we moved into Korea they [the operational flights] were much shorter."

Three RAAF Dakotas, flown by Flt Lts David Hitchins, Noel Eliot and Ron Daniel, transported 77RAAF's equipment and ground staff to Po'hang. These Dakotas were also part of the transport force which was required to convey equipment and reinforcements to the 27th British Commonwealth Brigade[7], and to evacuate wounded on their return trips. The move to Po'hang was completed by 12 October and the RAAF Mustangs joined in the 35th FIG's operations from there, commencing the following day. 77RAAF had just received four new pilots – Flt Lt W.V. Gray, P3 C.R.A. Howe, P4 K.H. Foster and P4 Cecil Sly – as replacements, and later in the month Flt Lts Bay Adams and Ken McLeod were among those who departed for Australia, their tours finished.

According to General MacArthur's orders, the US X Corps was to carry out an amphibious landing at Wonsan and attack westwards in time to meet up with the 8th US Army, so enveloping, then closing in on the enemy. The FEAF would support the landings but initially the US 1st Marine Air Wing aboard the USMC carriers would provide close-support for X Corps (see Chapter X). Except for air transport and courier missions, FEAF aircraft were not to enter the area unless at the request of the Corps tactical air commander. By 7 October, when X Corps began to board ship for Wonsan, ROK troops were only ten miles south of the city. They pushed on without delay and by the 10th were fighting in the city streets. Next day they captured Wonsan airfield, where the runways and facilities were found to be in good condition, which enabled FEAF Combat Cargo Command to fly in 130 tons of supplies for the ROK. By 14 October, ROK forces had occupied positions 20 miles north and 12 miles west of the city, while USMC Corsairs from VMF-212 and VMA-312, and twin-engined Tigercats from VMF(N)-542 began to fly covering missions from Wonsan airfield.

The approaches to Wonsan had been heavily mined and the USN Mariners of VP-42 were called in to help locate them. On 10 October, a Mariner crew spotted a field of about 50 mines moored close to the port, although they were unable to destroy any. However, next day, two were detonated by another Mariner. Other minefields near Yo-do island and to the east of Wonsan were discovered by VP-42 and by the end of the month a further six mines had been

---

[7] The 27th British Brigade had been renamed the 27th British Commonwealth Brigade with the arrival of the 3rd Battalion of the Royal Australian Regiment at the end of September. Later, the 16th Field Regiment of the Royal New Zealand Artillery would join the Brigade, while from Canada came a full brigade, and from India the 60th Indian Field Ambulance. At about the same time a 4,000-strong Turkish Brigade arrived, while Thailand sent an infantry regiment, and the Philippines a 5,000-strong military force. Infantry battalions were sent by France, Holland, Belgium (which included a company of Luxembourgers) Greece, and Colombia, while smaller contingents would arrive from Norway and Ethiopia.

destroyed by the squadron, mainly by gunfire. Despite the efforts of the Mariner crews, two USN minesweepers were lost to mines in the area.

As UN ground forces moved up to the Yalu, the Chinese indicated that they intended to make some form of move. Indeed, on 10 October, Chinese Communist Foreign Secretary Chou En-lai warned:

> "Now that the American forces are attempting to cross the 38th Parallel on a large scale, the Chinese people cannot stand idly by with regard to such a serious situation created by the invasion of Korea . . . and to the dangerous trend towards extending the war. The American war of invasion of Korea has been a serious menace to the security of China from the very start."

General Stratemeyer had predicted that this would first manifest itself in the air. He was right. At 0400 on the morning of 14 October, two hostile aircraft, identified as Yak-9s, made a surprise raid on Kimpo (K-14) and dropped a number of small bombs. The attack did no real damage and four F-51s of the 35th FIG were scrambled to search for the origin of the enemy air attack. As they reconnoitred Sinuiju airfield they encountered heavy anti-aircraft fire from the Manchurian side of the Yalu, and one F-51 was shot down. Despite the severity of the loss, it was felt that this was more of an isolated incident rather than a major escalation. To many it appeared that the war would soon be won.

President Truman arrived at Wake Island on 15 October, there to discuss the military situation in Korea with General MacArthur. During cordial, if guarded, discussions, MacArthur informed the President that organised North Korean resistance should soon be over, and that he saw no chance of Chinese intervention. Most UN troops, he suggested, could be withdrawn by Christmas. As well as assuring victory, plans were well in hand for the anticipated forthcoming postwar situation in Korea. The President departed having been reassured that all augered well for a swift conclusion to the fighting.

The Supreme Commander's confidence was undoubtedly shaken, albeit temporarily, when a returning RB-29 crew brought evidence of about 75 fighters parked in neat rows on Antung airfield, just across the Yalu in Manchuria. Many of the fighters pictured were presumably Russian MiG-15s, numbers of which were beginning to arrive at Antung at this time. Further reconnaissance next day however revealed that they had moved on to pastures new – or had 'disappeared' under camouflage netting. But the warning signs were there. Meanwhile, MacArthur issued orders for a planned airborne operation – which entailed paratroops of the US 187th Airborne Regiment, currently standing by at Kimpo, to drop near the town of Sukch'on and Sunch'on, about 30 miles north of P'yongyang – to go ahead. The Americans estimated that up to 30,000 North Korean troops might thereby be trapped between the paratroopers and the advancing UN ground forces. It was hoped that a number of prominent North Korean government officials might also be captured in the operation, and that a train carrying American prisoners from P'yongyang might be intercepted.

Covered by an air umbrella, UN troops advanced rapidly from the south towards P'yongyang. The 1st US Cavalry drove into the North Korean capital on 19 October. In an effort to block the enemy's withdrawal, the 1st ROK Division attacked the city from the south-east, east, and north-east, and captured the two airfields at P'yongyang and Mirim. At the former, an abandoned NKAF Ki-54 Japanese WWII-vintage bomber was found almost intact. On the same day, 5th Air Force fighter-bombers destroyed 34 trucks, five ox-carts, two artillery pieces, a tank, and other enemy equipment in the area to the east of P'yongyang. A particularly successful mission was carried out by 77RAAF when four Mustangs led by Sqn Ldr Cresswell took off to attack targets close to P'yongyang and, after contacting a ground controller, the flight divided. The CO's section was directed to attack an enemy position holding up the UN advance, while the second pair led by Flt Lt Ian Olorenshaw was sent to attack a train seven miles north of the capital. Over the target the two aircraft separated to make individual attacks on opposite ends of the train. Both Olorenshaw and his No2, P3 Eric Douglas, scored hits and both sections of the train caught fire. The box-cars, after burning for some while, exploded violently, and what remained of the train was then strafed. As a result the locomotive's boiler exploded, sending a cloud of steam some 400 feet into the air. This action was cited when Olorenshaw was later awarded a US DFC. While 77RAAF escaped casualties at this time, a number of the American units had suffered severely in recent operations including the 8th FBG which, by the middle of October, had lost 26 pilots killed or missing, including all three squadron commanders, since the beginning of the war. On the 16th, its 35th FBS alone lost three Mustangs but only one pilot, 1/Lt Wayne Rabun, whose aircraft collided with an L-19 spotter; both pilots were killed. The 18th FBG lost at least seven aircraft to enemy ground fire, its 12th FBS alone losing four pilots killed or missing, while the 67th FBS lost three aircraft and one pilot, two others baling out safely[8]. The 35th FIG, to which 77RAAF was attached, lost no fewer than 18 aircraft during the month to all causes, three pilots losing their lives: Capt Beriger Anderson of the 39th FIS, and Capt Glenn Schlitz and 1/Lt Woodrow Burton of the 40th FIS. One American author noted:

> ". . . there were so many bale outs and forced landings taking place that the squadron historians did not bother to report them." [9]

The F-80 units had lost at least eight aircraft by the 20th, including those flown by Capt Thomas E. Myers of the 16th FIS, captured and killed on the 2nd, while 2/Lt William Carter of the 25th FIS was killed next day. Two pilots of the 8th FBS were lost over P'yongyang on the 7th and 8th, while two others had lucky escapes during emergency landings, but 1/Lt Theon C. Eason and Capt Calvin Roraus of the 25th FIS were killed on consecutive days.

Commencing early on the morning of 20 October, paratroops, supplies and equipment were loaded aboard a total of 76 C-119 and 40 C-47 transports at Kimpo airfield. The aircraft were crowded in the extreme. A typical load for a C-119 consisted of 46 fully-armed men and up to 20 bundles of equipment and supplies. The first aircraft was aloft by noon. After assembling over the Han estuary the aerial armada turned northwards along the west coast, escorted by 5th Air Force fighters. Prior to their arrival, 75 F-51s, 62 F-80s and five B-26s bombed, rocketed and strafed the dropping zones. Pilots claimed the destruction of more than 50 enemy vehicles, five fuel and ammunition dumps, 23 ox-carts, four tanks, and a field artillery piece. At 1400 the first paratroops began jumping from the leading aircraft. A total of 1,470 men were dropped at Sukch'on. Twenty minutes later paratroops began landing in the drop zone near Sunch'on. Within an hour 2,860 men and in excess of 300 tons of equipment were off-loaded into the dropping zones. No anti-aircraft fire was experienced at either location, only a few sniper shots. Casualties were extremely light: one man was killed and 46 injured.

Meeting little resistance on the ground, the paratroopers quickly occupied high ground overlooking both drop zones. They discovered that the softening-up attacks followed by the sudden and unexpected airdrop had so alarmed the Communist troops that they had abandoned their strong defensive positions, leaving loaded guns with ammunition alongside. Late in the afternoon elements of the 6th ROK Division by-passed P'yongyang to link up with the paratroopers. Over the next three days additional men, supplies and equipment were airdropped. But, despite the surprise of the airborne landing and the speed of the overland advance:

> "The overall results of the airborne operation were, in fact, mortifyingly small: the 187th US Airborne Regiment had not cut off any sizeable part of the North Korean forces – the main body of the enemy had already withdrawn north of Sukch'on and Sunch'on, and were either north of the Ch'ongch'on River or in the act of crossing it; no important North Korean government officials were captured, for they had fled from P'yongyang eight days earlier; most of the American prisoners had been successfully removed into the remote vastness of North Korea – a search of the area revealed 73 dead American soldiers, who had either been shot or died of dysentery, starvation or exposure. Although the 187th Airborne Regiment

---

[8] The 12th FBS casualties were 1/Lts Donald D. Bolt, Ramon R. Davis, Alexander B. Padilla, and Claude Taylor, while the 67th FBS lost Capt Daniel Leake; Capt Edward Hodges baled out and was rescued by a helicopter, and 1/Lt Owen Brewer was picked up by US troops after baling out.

[9] See *Mustangs over Korea* by David R. McLaren.

had, for the loss of less than 100 battle casualties, killed over 1,000 Koreans and captured 4,000 more, the North Korean Army was still in the war and soon made this abundantly clear." [10]

805 men of the North Korean 239th Regiment were among those killed in the vicinity of the Ch'ongch'on, and a further 681 were taken prisoner.

The 27th British Commonwealth Brigade was denied the distinction of being the first UN unit into P'yongyang, even though it led the way to the outskirts of the city, because it was routed instead through the village of Sangapo. Brigadier Coad had hoped to rest his men and vehicles, but there was no time, as the Brigade was ordered north to link up with the American paratroopers who had engaged a North Korean rearguard force around Yongju. Light opposition was encountered from a group of some 75 enemy troops in the foothills south of the Yongpu but, squeezed from two sides as they were, they did not impede the initial contact between the Commonwealth battalions and the Americans on the evening of 21 October. Next morning, with the Australians in the lead, the Brigade moved north of the town and, for the first time in several days, met significant enemy resistance. Remaining concealed in an apple orchard, a force of North Koreans estimated at 1,000-strong allowed part of the Australian battalion to pass through and then began firing on them from both front and rear. The Australians promptly counter-attacked. In the face of the assault the Koreans suffered heavy losses as they fled their positions. Tanks operating in support of the Australians added to the carnage. For a total of seven wounded, the Australians killed at least 150 of the enemy and took 239 prisoners.

At this time most UN ground troops were more interested in air transport than in air close-support. Following the rapid advance northwards, the FEAF Combat Cargo Command started delivering supplies as close as possible to the fighting troops, and with the capture of the airstrip at Sinmak the Americans were able to fly in some 235 tons of supplies, although the two airfields at P'yongyang soon became the main supply points for the ground forces. General MacArthur's plan was to march X Corps up the east coast and the 8th US Army up the west coast, whereupon the two forces would make a sweeping envelopment of the enemy. Upon reaching the Yalu, X Corps would turn west and drive all enemy forces south of the Manchurian border into the arms of the 8th US Army. Because the rugged, desolate central mountain mass impeded mutual support, these forces acted independently, their disposition co-ordinated and directed by MacArthur himself from his Tokyo HQ. To advance north of P'yongyang the American troops needed 1,000 tons of supplies each day. Meanwhile, the 5th Air Force had been planning to move two wings of F-51s to P'yongyang and these would require 450 tons of supplies daily. To meet both requirements was beyond the capacity of the US Cargo Combat Command; therefore, following talks with the 8th US Army, the FEAF decided to temporarily offer the entire airlift to the Army. To assist the airlift, the 5th Air Force moved small base service units to P'yongyang, Mirim and Yonpo airfields. At the same time, to reduce its own requirements to approximately 60 tons a day, the 5th Air Force's 51st FBW had to establish at Kimpo.

Continuing efforts were made to integrate all the UN air capabilities under one command control. MacArthur decided that the FEAF would exercise co-ordination control over land-based USMC air units and over carrier-based aircraft operating over Korea, effective as soon as X Corps had advanced beyond the Wonsan objective area. On 21 October, ROK I Corps, now under the control of X Corps, forged beyond that area and the new co-ordination control arrangements took effect. Until mid-October the UN Air Forces had restricted their attacks to targets lying within 50 miles of Korea's northern borders. However, as the ROK troops continued their spectacular progress north of the line, this restriction had to be changed to a 'chop line' 20 miles from Manchuria. This did not last long, either. Just a week later MacArthur ordered the abolishment of all restraining lines for the employment of ground troops. General Stratemeyer, FEAF Commander, while cautioning that the Manchurian border should not be violated, instructed:

---

[10] See *Korea: The Commonwealth at War* by Tim Carew.

"Effective immediately, close-support missions when under direct control of tactical air control parties or airborne controllers, may go as close to the border as may be necessary for proper performance of mission."

After waiting six days while USN minesweepers and VP-42's Mariners cleared the channel, X Corps at last made its landing at Wonsan on 26 October (see Chapter X). Three days later, in a landing designed to lighten port requirements, the 7th US Division went ashore at Iwon, about 90 nautical miles to the north-east. In the days that followed, the ROK I Corps continued northwards along the coastal routes towards Ch'ongjin, the 1st US Marine Division marched towards Hamhung and the Ch'ongjin Reservoir (also known as Chosin Reservoir), and the 7th US Division pushed inland towards the Pujon (Fusen) Reservoir area.

The progress of UN ground forces towards the Yalu left FEAF's Bomber Command without full employment, which led the US Joint Chiefs-of-Staff to order the cancellation of strategic air strikes. Since late September and early October a part of the American medium-bomber effort had been directed at suspected enemy training areas. According to intelligence reports, after their débâcle south of the 38th Parallel, the NKPA had been attempting to mobilise six divisions of trainees for a last-ditch defence. To combat this eventuality, the B-29s had raided suspected training centres at P'yongyang, Hamhung, Nanam, and Hungnam, but FEAF then cancelled further raids because of the possibility that UN captives were being held in these complexes. FEAF Bomber Command had also been given the task of destroying the enemy's bridges. Early in October FEAF had supplied a list of 33 bridge targets, all north of P'yongyang and Wonsan. They had been selected to isolate the two areas but, because the ROK advance had been so rapid up the east coast, ten of these targets had to be deleted within a week. On the western flank, in co-operation with the 8th US Army's advance, the bombers had been forbidden to operate south of Sinanju after 18 October, and the FEAF again had to revise its list of bridges which needed to be destroyed. Targets were running out. According to one report, targets were so scarce that on one mission a B-29 had chased an enemy motorcyclist down a road, dropping bombs until one eventually brought him down! Since early in the month the ROKAF had been flying operations from K-16 airstrip at Yogdungpo south of Seoul, and lost two Mustangs to ground fire which cost the lives of 1/Lt Sang Soo Lee and the Squadron Ops Officer, Capt Dean A. Crowell.

The North Korean People's Army had not only been defeated, it had almost been completely annihilated and was no longer an effective fighting force. At its peak it had numbered around 325,000 men. Of these, 145,000 had been captured and 150,000 were estimated to have been killed by the end of October. Expectation of ultimate success was high. It was known, of course, that there were large concentrations of Chinese forces in southern Manchuria but, as long as UN forces remained south of the Yalu, it was considered unlikely that they would deploy in force across the border. Then the first reports of the presence of Chinese troops in Korea came from local inhabitants and filtered through agents to the US Intelligence Service. Later it was reported that some Chinese dead had been identified and there were a few captives. This did not necessarily mean full-scale intervention however; it was argued that they may have merely been observers or technical experts sent to help the North Koreans. On the basis of the small numbers of Chinese prisoners taken by mid-October, it was estimated that there were only some 9,000 Chinese troops in Korea. Nevertheless, the fact that they were there at all was ominous.

What the UN Command had astonishingly failed to discover, despite continuous aerial reconnaissance, was that during the last two weeks of October the Chinese had succeeded in moving some 18 divisions – approximately 180,000 men under the overall command of General P'eng Teh-huai – across the Yalu and deploying them up to 60 miles inside North Korea. They advanced with great skill, moving rapidly on foot, only at night and halting a couple of hours before dawn to camouflage men, animals and equipment. The Chinese 13th Army Group of General Lin Piao's 4th Field Army assembled in concentration areas north of the Ch'ongch'on, stretching from near Kusong on the west flank to Huich'on on the east, where they waited for the advancing 8th US Army. Over a distance of 75 miles lay the hidden 38th, 40th, 42nd, 50th, and 66th Chinese Armies, each of three divisions. During the first half of November they would be reinforced by the 9th Army Group of General Chen Yi's 3rd Field

Army, comprising the 20th, 26th, and 27th Armies, each of four divisions. This force deployed near the Chosin and Fusen Reservoirs. Altogether, nearly 300,000 Chinese, supported by North Korean remnants and guerrillas some 80,000-strong, awaited 150,000 UN troops.

In the last week of October the US I Corps crossed the Ch'ongch'on at Sinanju and pushed towards Sinuiju, while the ROK II Corps advanced northwards on the eastern front. The 7th Regiment of the ROK's 6th Division reached the Yalu at Chosan but the impetus was slowing. Enemy resistance was not collapsing, it was showing signs of increasing. In the air on 24 October Chinese anti-aircraft guns fired on two USMC Corsairs flying three to five miles south of the border. Four days later Communist troops launched strong attacks against the ROK II Corps. As it sought to clear and secure Ch'ongju, the 27th British Commonwealth Brigade found itself faced by a well dug-in enemy in good tactical positions, supported by armour and artillery. Late in the evening of 29 October the Australian battalion repelled a fierce *banzai*-type charge which was broken up by artillery and mortar fire. Ch'ongju was taken for a cost of nine dead and 30 wounded, while more than 150 enemy dead were counted around the battalion's position. After this, the Brigade went into divisional reserve for the US 24th Division, its place being taken by the US 21st Infantry Regiment.

On 30 October, a flight of four Mustangs from 77RAAF carrying out a close-support mission landed at Wonsan to refuel, and then flew to Taegu where they remained overnight. That evening the pilots were entertained in the mess by Wg Cdr Johnnie Johnson, who was currently flying F-80s with the 49th FBG at Taegu, plus the occasional reconnaissance sortie on RB-26s. Also flying B-26s at this time, though operating from Iwakuni AFB with the 3rd BG rather than from Taegu, was Sqn Ldr Joe Bodien RAF, who had commenced ops with the 8th BS at the end of September, having replaced Wg Cdr Wykeham-Barnes as the Group's RAF advisor. 77RAAF still had numerous ground personnel at Iwakuni providing back-up facilities for the Squadron's operations. To relieve 77RAAF of this responsibility, 91 Wing RAAF was officially formed on 20 October and became operational on 1 November. On formation it comprised the HQ of 91 (Composite) Wing, HQ of 77RAAF, HQ of 30 (Communications) Squadron RAAF, HQ of 391 (Base) Squadron RAAF, and HQ of 491 (Maintenance) Squadron RAAF.

November 1950

During the last week in October there were numerous sightings of NKAF aircraft, most of them on airstrips in the area of Sinuiju in the far north-west corner of Korea. There were also reports of jet aircraft activity along the Manchurian side of the Yalu, but the aircraft were always too far distant for any positive identification. American pilots would however be given a closer look at the jets on the first day of November when, early in the morning, a flight of four F-51s of the 67th FBS received a distress call from the pilot of a B-26 of the 730th BS, who reported that he was being attacked by a Yak fighter. Two of the F-51s flown by Capts Robert D. Thresher and Alma R. Flake were despatched to help and arrived on the scene just in time to witness the Yak pull up into what looked like a high-speed stall, and then crash, apparently shot down by the B-26's gunner. While they circled over the wreckage of the Yak another distress call came in, this time from an AT-6 which had been jumped by three more Yaks near Yangsi, about 15 miles south of Sinuiju. The two F-51s headed for the location, where Thresher and Flake identified the attackers as Yak-3s and each shot one down, one crashing in flames.

The action continued during the afternoon following a report from an RF-80 pilot who sighted 15 Yaks parked in revetments on Sinuiju airfield. The 5th Air Force immediately despatched three flights of F-80s to the area, these destroying one Yak and damaging six others. The revetments, however, opened towards the Yalu and the F-80s had to run the gauntlet of AA fire from the Manchurian side of the border, and one of the jets was shot down, Capt Frank van Sickle of the 16th FBS being killed. A second F-80 strike returned later to destroy the remaining Yaks but, by then, all that could be flown had been moved elsewhere. Meanwhile, while two of four more F-51s from the 67th FBS were engaged in a napalm strike, an estimated six swept-wing jets suddenly appeared. Having overcome their initial shock, the American pilots soon realised that their F-51s were able to turn inside the faster jets and, seizing a fleeting chance, 1/Lt William G. Foster (the flight leader) fired a burst at one and saw it starting to trail smoke.

The MiG immediately headed off in a north-westerly direction. Luck stayed with the Americans, allowing 1/Lt George Olsen to gain strikes on the wing of another MiG during a head-on attack, and while 1/Lt Charles Morehouse covered the FAC's AT-6, the fourth member of the flight, 1/Lt Henry L. Reynolds, joined the fight. He was promptly attacked by a MiG coming from 11 o'clock. They exchanged fire and Reynolds, too, reported strikes without being hit himself. As Foster reformed the flight, Olsen was attacked by another MiG but escaped in a dive.

The F-51s had acquitted themselves well in this first historical meeting with MiG-15s. Without loss, they had not only managed to damage three of the jets but had also shot down two Yaks during their patrol. For FEAF Intelligence, the F-51s also were able to provide the first gun-camera film of the MiG-15 in action. The five, not six, MiGs – wearing spurious North Korean Air Force markings – were in fact flown by Russian pilots from the newly arrived 72nd GuFAR of the 151st Fighter Air Divison led by WWII ace Maj Nikolai Stroikov, who confirmed the destruction of one F-51 in the location of Sinuiju (referred to as Singisyu in Soviet records) by St/Lt Vasilii Chizh[11] in this action, which was reported to have crashed about ten miles north-east of Antung. Another section of four MiGs from the same unit, led by Maj A.Z. Bordun, engaged ten F-80s in the Antung area and two were claimed shot down, including one by Lt Khominich which crashed 15 miles south-east of Antung; Capt Frank A. Doyle of the 7th FBS, who failed to return, was presumably his victim. Other MiG pilots, from the 151st FAD's other unit, the 28th GuFAR, also sighted the F-51s but no contact was made.

The two Fighter Air Regiments of the 151st FAD under the command of Polkovnik (Colonel) Ivan Belov – six squadrons of MiGs totalling about 50 aircraft – were currently assembling at the Antung airfield complex, just across the Yalu, as were two more Air Regiments of the 28th FAD commanded by Podpolkovnik (Lt Colonel) Alexi Alelyukhin, a WWII ace with 57 victories (17 shared) to his credit; other MiG regiments were on their way including the first such-equipped Chinese unit and, in parallel with what was happening on the ground, a new and deadly element was being added to the air war. USAF reconnaissance aircraft brought back evidence of major modernisation work being carried out at Antung; whereas the airfield had previously comprised two gravel runways, aerial photographs now revealed the rapid construction of a 6,000 feet-long concrete runway and a hard-surfaced perimeter taxiway, and the installation of early-warning radar with a range of about 150 miles which extended into north-western Korea. For UN aircraft the sky over Korea had suddenly become much more dangerous. By the end of the month most of the squadrons of two Russian Fighter Air Divisions had arrived at Antung, and another Fighter Air Division – the 50th commanded by Polkovnik Viktor Pashkevich – had arrived at Ansham in northern China:

RUSSIAN MIG-15 FIGHTER REGIMENTS, Manchuria
November 1950

Antung

28th Fighter Air Division	Podpolkovnik A.V. Alelyukhin
67th Fighter Air Regiment	Podpolkovnik Zhemchugov
139th Guards Fighter Air Regiment	Podpolkovnik Tolkachev
151st Fighter Air Division	Polkovnik I.V. Belov [12]
28th Guards Fighter Air Regiment	Maj V.I. Kolyadin
72nd Guards Fighter Air Regiment	Podpolkovnik V.F. Mukhin

Ansham

50th Fighter Air Division	Polkovnik V. Pashkevich
29th Guards Fighter Air Regiment	Podpolkovnik D.V. Virich

---

[11] St/Lt Chizh was believed to have been credited with 13 victories while serving with the 69th GuFAR during the latter part of WWII.

[12] Polkovnik Ivan Belov was promoted to Maj-General and took command of the 64th Fighter Air Corps on 25 November 1950, his place as commander of the 151st FAD being taken by Podpolkovnik A.Ya. Sapozhnikov.

177th Fighter Air Regiment   Podpolkovnik V. Terentyev
Chinese 10th Fighter Air Regiment   Lt Colonel Wang Hai

US 5th AIR FORCE FIGHTER SQUADRONS, Korea
November 1950

Kimpo (K-14)
8th Fighter-Bomber Group (F-51D)   Colonel John M. Price
  35th Fighter-Bomber Squadron
  36th Fighter-Bomber Squadron

51st Fighter Interceptor Wing (F-80C)   Colonel John W. Weltman
  16th Fighter Interceptor Squadron
  25th Fighter Interceptor Squadron
  80th Fighter-Bomber Squadron

Taegu (K-2)
49th Fighter-Bomber Group (F-80C)   Colonel Jack S. Jenkins
  7th Fighter-Bomber Squadron
  8th Fighter-Bomber Squadron
  9th Fighter-Bomber Squadron

Po'hang (K-3)
35th Fighter Interceptor Group (F-51)   Colonel Virgil L. Zoller
  39th Fighter Interceptor Squadron
  40th Fighter Interceptor Squadron
  77 Squadron RAAF (F-51)

Pusan (K-9)
18th Fighter-Bomber Group (F-51)   Colonel Curtis R. Low
  12th Fighter-Bomber Squadron
  67th Fighter-Bomber Squadron

*   *   *

On the morning of 2 November, Yaks were already in the air as four F-51s of the 67th FBS arrived over the battle area. One Yak attempted a bounce on 1/Lt James L. Glessner's aircraft but was pursued by Capt Alma Flake who followed it down and pumped bullets into it until finally a wing broke off and it crashed; this was Flake's second victory on consecutive days. In the meantime, Glessner gave chase to another Yak that had come in behind 1/Lt Harold Ausman's aircraft. He caught him near the ground and scored many strikes. Debris flew off as the Yak turned for the border, and before Glessner could line up on it again, it rolled over and the pilot baled out.

Meanwhile, following a mauling of the US 1st Cavalry Division by Communist troops – on which the *New York Times* reported, somewhat alarmingly: "Chinese Communist hordes, attacking on horse and foot to the sound of bugle calls, cut up Americans and South Koreans at Unsan today in an Indian-style massacre . . ." – UN Command ordered the outnumbered 8th US Army to withdraw to the barrier afforded by the Ch'ongch'on in an effort to erect new defences and to prepare for an enemy counter-offensive. For the next three days the Communists attempted pursuit but found themselves subjected to heavy assaults from the air. In one notable action, flights of B-26s kept Chinese troop concentrations near Ch'ongjin under attack for more than 30 minutes, inflicting an estimated 500 casualties.

On 5 November, 77RAAF flew sorties in support of Australian troops for the first time in the war. The Mustangs had not flown any operational sorties on the 4th because of heavy cloud and the rain which turned the newly formed roads around their base into glutinous mud, but next day, with an improvement in the weather although there remained a strong crosswind, the RAAF aircraft were in the air. Over the combat zone, waiting to be called down, they were ordered into action by the Tactical Air Control Party working with the 27th British Commonwealth Brigade yelling into the radio: "Come over here, the Aussies are going to put in an attack." The Mustangs immediately responded, all sections heading for the vicinity of Pakch'on, where they were told to remain until required. To the pilots watching from above there seemed to be hundreds of friendly vehicles moving up and down the road, including many ambulances, while tanks were firing into the hills where the assault was in progress. The Australian battalion was attempting to dislodge Chinese troops from hilltops overlooking the Pakch'on-Sinanju road in the Taeryong River valley. Flt Lt Olorenshaw's section was called in first, quickly using up all their rockets and ammunition. Enemy soldiers were seen to scatter in all directions, following which the FAC sent Flg Off Bill Horsman's section to rocket and strafe trenches on the same hill. The men on the ground – who found jets to be too fast to be accurate – watched fascinated as the Mustangs softened up the opposition; Flt Lt Odgers later described the action:

> "They [Olorenshaw's section] used up all their machine-gun and rocket ammunition and saw the enemy troops scattering all over the place. It was a good feeling to know you were supporting your own boys. Horsman and Stoney stooged around for a while, and then the controller sent them rocketing and machine-gunning the trenches on the same hill. They saw dozens of enemy troops dart out of their positions and run down the valley. Tanks were landing shells on them as the Mustangs attacked. The whole place was alive with aircraft. Sqn Ldr Cresswell led his four-ship flight against tanks and transport. His flight fired eleven rockets at a tank, which toppled over the edge of the road ... They then knocked out two trucks and attacked a village, which replied with anti-aircraft fire but didn't score a hit." [13]

The Australian troop commander described 77RAAF's support as ". . . the closest I have ever seen and we passed our congratulations to the pilots over our air contact wireless." Initially confused, as others were, as to whether this was a full-scale invasion by Chinese troops, General MacArthur decided to act without consulting Washington, and ordered General Stratemeyer to mount a strike by all available Bomber Command B-29s – some 90 aircraft – against the bridges at Sinuiju, over which US reconnaissance pilots reported heavy military traffic crossing southwards; but before the aircraft had taken off, MacArthur received an urgent directive from the Joint Chiefs-of-Staff ordering him "to postpone all bombing of targets within five miles of the Manchurian border until further notice." MacArthur was furious, and responded accordingly:

> "This movement not only jeopardizes but threatens the ultimate destruction of the forces under my command . . . The only way to stop this reinforcement of the enemy is the destruction of these bridges and the subjection of all installations in the north area supporting the enemy advance to the maximum of our air destruction. Every hour that this is postponed will be paid for dearly in American and other United Nations blood . . . I am suspending this strike and carrying out your instructions ... [But] I cannot over-emphasize the disastrous effect, both physical and psychological, that will result from the restrictions you are imposing. I trust that the matter will be immediately brought to the attention of the President as I believe your instructions may well result in a calamity of major proportion for which I cannot accept the responsibility without his personal and direct understanding of the situation." [14]

Having advised the President, the Joint Chiefs-of-Staff lifted the five-mile restriction and authorised him to bomb the bridges – but only up to the middle of the river! They would not permit any violation of Manchurian airspace, which meant that US fighters could not pursue the MiGs across the Yalu, or attack their airfields. The Commander of the FEAF Bomber Command, Maj-General Everett O'Donnell, wrote:

---

[13] See *Across the Parallel*.

[14] See *Reminiscences*.

"We are not allowed to violate Manchurian territory, and by violation of the territory I mean we are not allowed to fly over an inch of it . . . they [the Communists] had their fighters come up alongside and join our formation about two miles to the lee and fly along at the same speed on the other side of the river while we were making our approach. And just before we got to bomb-away position, they would veer off to the north and climb up to about 30,000 feet and then make a frontal quarter-attack on the bombers just about the time of bomb-away in a turn. So they would be coming in from Manchuria in a turn, swoop down, fire their cannons at the formation, and continue to turn back to sanctuary." [15]

Enemy aircraft were encountered in the air again on 6 November, when a section of three F-51s of the 67th FBS on a reconnaissance mission west of Sinuiju sighted six Yaks heading towards them from the north. The American fighters caught the Yaks in the middle of a turn, and the section leader, Capt Howard Price, dived and fired at one which shed pieces as the pilot baled out. Price's wingman, 1/Lt Henry Reynolds, closed in on another of the Yaks but his guns jammed at the crucial moment. Frustrated, he fired his rockets at it but they missed and went underneath the NKAF fighter. Apparently startled, the Korean pilot dived his aircraft away – right into the sights of Price, who shot it down in flames. Price was officially credited with one and one-half kills while Reynolds, who apparently did not make a claim, was given credit for one-half. The 8th FBG also had encounters with enemy aircraft, when a flight of 35th FBS F-51s led by 1/Lt Robert Dewald clashed inconclusively with a single MiG which attacked head-on. A few moments later, a flight of 36th FBS aircraft led by Capt James Glasser was similarly attacked head-on by another MiG. The Russian jet fired at the F-51 formation's No3 man (Maj Schillereff) without effect. Glasser swung his flight around as the antagonist also reversed his course. Two of the American pilots fired at least two bursts of fire, but failed to score a hit. The MiGs were from the 72nd GuFAR, which recorded two kills against the F-51s including one by St/Lt Kuznetsov which allegedly fell about 20 miles south-east of Sinuiju. During the day the MiG pilots flew a total of 31 operational sorties, 23 of these by the 151st FAD.

Next day (7 November) there were no fewer than five separate engagements between F-51s and MiGs. In one of the actions, a flight of four F-51s of the 12th FBS led by Maj Kendall Carlson on a patrol along the Yalu spotted four MiGs taking off from Antung airfield. The MiGs did not bother forming up or attempting to build up airspeed, they just crossed over and attacked head-on. Both formations fired without result on the first pass, but when the MiGs came back Carlson and his wingman were waiting. Carlson saw his fire strike one of the jets along the wingroot – probably the aircraft flown by St/Lt Chizh of the 72nd FAR, whose aircraft was damaged – but he was then forced to break away to evade a second MiG that had swung in on his tail. This MiG hurtled by (without firing according to the American pilot), followed by two others, and sped back across the Yalu. The second MiG was flown by Lt Sanin, Chizh's wingman, who claimed the F-51 shot down. The Americans reported seeing wreckage of an aircraft burning on the ground, and believed that this was the MiG Carlson had hit, but since nobody witnessed the actual impact, the claim was not officially credited. Nor, would it seem, was one lost, since St/Lt Chizh safely returned to base. In another action, Colonel William O'Donnell's flight from the 36th FBS also met four MiGs head-on and a series of dogfights ensued. The Colonel saw his fire hitting one MiG along its fuselage and wingroot, and the jet was last seen heading out to sea trailing smoke; he was credited with its probable destruction. This was possibly the aircraft flown by St/Lt Dubrovin of the 72nd GuFAR who reported being attacked by an F-51. Colonel O'Donnell's wingman, 1/Lt Robert Rohlfs, claimed another as damaged, while Capt Howard Turner reported firing a two-second burst into the fuselage of the last MiG to attack, following which it zoomed to 20,000 feet. That afternoon another flight of 35th FBS F-51s led by its CO, Maj Rayburn Lancaster, also spotted MiGs taking off from Antung. In a brief clash no hits were scored by either side. When the MiGs broke for home an irate Lancaster led his flight after them but the jets were too fast and crossed the Yalu well out of firing range. In all of these encounters, the American pilots considered the MiG pilots revealed a lack of combat experience. Nonetheless, two F-51s were claimed by the

---

[15] See *Reminiscences*.

Russian pilots, one being credited to the 72nd GuFAR and the other to the 28th GuFAR's Maj Viktor Kolyadin, a Hero of the Soviet Union who had 21 victories from WWII.

In the annals of USAF military aviation history, 8 November 1950 was a date of some significance as the Americans recorded that it marked the first ever jet-versus-jet combat[16] (this, as shown, probably occurred on 1 November when a MiG of the 72nd GuFAR shot down a 7th FBS F-80). The day's main event began when 70 B-29s carried out the first mission of a new two-week bombing campaign with a concentrated attack on the town of Sinuiju. The aim was to block the approaches to the critical twin bridges across the Yalu. The operation had earlier been postponed because of bad weather, but on this morning, ahead of the massed B-29 formation, flak-suppressing F-51 and F-80 fighter-bombers now hammered anti-aircraft positions on the south bank of the Yalu around the target with rockets, napalm and machine-guns. High above the B-29s, the top cover flights of 51st FIW F-80s circled watchfully, their pilots examining the sky north of the Yalu. During the increased enemy air activity over the past week seven Yaks had been shot down. There was little to fear from the piston-engine fighters, but the MiGs were a different proposition. Powerless to intervene, the F-80 pilots could only watch as the MiGs took off from Antung. The Americans reported seeing six – although there were actually eight, from the 72nd GuFAR, the sections led by Kapt Afonin and St/Lt Kharitonov – climb to 30,000 feet on the Manchurian side of the river before spearing down in pairs towards the F-80s.

The Americans turned to meet the MiGs. After making one wildly inaccurate firing pass, the MiGs scattered. Five climbed swiftly towards sanctuary on the far side of the Yalu, easily drawing away from the slower F-80s, but the sixth went into a shallow dive and 1/Lt Russell J. Brown of the 16th FIS saw a chance and went after it. Brown's aircraft was heavier than the lightweight MiG and it gradually narrowed the distance as they both plunged down. When Brown opened fire the Russian pilot apparently realised his mistake and started to climb, but it was too late. Pieces flew off and the MiG went down vertically, trailing a long streamer of smoke. Brown believed it crashed and exploded on the banks of the Yalu, and was duly credited with its destruction, but the MiG escaped with damage only and was able to return to Antung. This was apparently Kapt Afonin's *zveno* (flight) which reported twice being attacked by F-80s without sustaining any losses.

Flights of 8th FBG F-51s were again involved in clashes with MiGs during the day. In one encounter, Capt Joseph W. Rogers spotted four MiGs in the sun and climbed his section to meet them. Both he and his No4, Maj William Betha, reported scoring hits on their selected targets before the jets escaped across the Yalu. Their victim may have been the aircraft flown by St/Lt Savin, who landed with minor combat damage, while his leader Kapt Afonin claimed an F-51 shot down. Another section of F-51s, these from the 35th FBS, found itself under attack by four F-80s which had obviously mistaken them for Yaks. Having evaded this assault, the F-51s were then jumped by four MiGs, apparently led by Kapt Pakhomov of the 139th GuFAR, one of which 1/Lt Harris Boyce claimed probably destroyed when it was seen crossing the Yalu trailing smoke. Another pilot was credited with a damaged, although none of the MiGs was hit. On the other side, one F-51 was credited jointly to St/Lts Akimov and Alexeenko of the 28th GuFAR, with a second being claimed by the 72nd GuFAR's St/Lt Shchegolev. Shortly after these actions, with the MiGs now cleared from the sky, the B-29s arrived over Sinuiju and dropped in excess of 580 tons of bombs on the town and the North Korean end of the bridges. Although the approaches to the bridges were heavily damaged, the structures themselves stood firm.

US aircraft attacking bridge targets along the Yalu began to run into increasingly determined opposition from the MiGs. On 9 November, Soviet radar controllers at Antung reported the approach of an estimated 40 B-29s. Six MiGs of the 72nd GuFAR led by Maj Bordun took off

---

[16] Although the RAF had operated Meteor twin-jet fighters during the last year of WWII, they never came into contact with any of the jet fighters and bombers operated by the Luftwaffe. However, the Meteor was used to combat V1 pulse-jet but unmanned flying bombs launched in great numbers against the United Kingdom in 1944, albeit with limited success.

to engage, but met only a flak-damaged RB-29 of the 91st SRS[17] over Sinuiju. In a running battle the reconnaissance aircraft was further damaged following attacks by Maj Bordun and his wingman Lt Dymchenko before it escaped, while the tail gunner, Cpl Harry J. Lavene, claimed one of the attackers shot down. Meanwhile, the severely damaged RB-29 limped back to Johnson AFB where it eventually crashed on landing, killing five crewmen. Pilots from the 72nd GuFAR also reported shooting down two F-80s during the day, these being credited to Maj Stroikov and St/Lt Kaznacheev.

Next day (10 November), Maj Bordun and his *zveno* were again in action when they were directed against two B-29s. As the six MiGs manoeuvred to carry out an attack, four F-80s appeared and these were engaged, Bordun claiming one shot down. Meanwhile, a *zveno* of 28th GuFAR MiGs led by Kapt Korobov sighted two groups of four F-51s, one group of six F-51s and four F-80s. Two of the first group were claimed shot down, including one by Korobov, while the group of six was engaged by St/Lt Pronin's *zveno*, but without result. As they broke away, two F-80s attempted to intercept but were easily evaded. An hour later seven B-29s were reported approaching the Yalu bridges, with an escort provided by USMC Corsairs, eight MiGs of the 139th GuFAR being scrambled to engage. When about ten miles from Sinuiju, Maj Kharkovskii led his *zveno* into the attack and saw his fire striking one of the 307th BG bombers. The damaged aircraft left the formation and Kharkovskii attacked again, shooting it down in flames and seeing it crash about 15 miles north-east of Antung. A second bomber was claimed by Kharkovskii's wingman, St/Lt Akimov, but was obviously the same aircraft as that attacked by his leader since only one B-29 was lost. The other bombers were pursued by St/Lt Zhdanovich's *zveno* without success. Sometime later, during the afternoon, eight MiGs of the 28th GuFAR led by Maj Kolyadin skirmished with ten F-80s near Antung, neither side gaining an advantage.

Maj Kolyadin of the 28th GuFAR led his MiGs into the air during the afternoon of 11 November when aircraft were reported approaching from the south, meeting an estimated 18 F-80s (apparently aircraft of the 25th FIS) near Anju. St/Lt Akimov claimed an F-80 shot down which had manoeuvred onto the tail of Maj Kolyadin's aircraft, but a second MiG flown by St/Lt Nasonov was hit by another F-80, possibly that flown by either Lt Colonel Clure Smith or 1/Lt Garland Hanson, both of whom reported strikes on MiGs they had attacked. The Russian pilot managed to reach Antung where he carried out a crash-landing, but was killed in the process.

Shortly after 0830 on the morning of 12 November, Maj Bordun led eight MiGs of the 72nd GuFAR off from Antung as a force of B-29s approached. Six bombers and escorting F-80s were encountered over the bridge leading to Antung, but as the Russian pilots attempted to engage the bombers they were attacked by eight F-80s, the aircraft flown by Maj Trofimov and his wingman only just managing to evade in time. The two MiG pilots then turned the tables on their assailants but were unable to inflict any damage. Meanwhile, a further eight MiGs of the 28th GuFAR had scrambled from Antung although six had to return immediately when all six pilots were unable to retract their undercarriages, leaving just Kapt Korobov and his wingman to intercept eight B-29s and their escort, which they did but with result. Two more sections from the same unit followed Korobov's *zveno* into the air, these led by Maj Borovkov. Over Antung they spotted six F-80s at a higher altitude and climbed to attack these, but combat was avoided. The bombers were then sighted but before an interception could be made, four F-80s carried out a bounce from astern. None of the MiGs was hit and only St/Lt Pisanenko was able to open fire in defence, albeit without result. The only USAF casualty from this raid, a flak-damaged B-29 of the 98th BG, carried out an emergency landing at a base in South Korea.

---

[17] The 91st SRS had recently replaced the 31st SRS; equipped with an improved version of the RB-29 which could carry up to nine cameras and had improved radar and electronic equipment, would enable the 91st SRS to fulfil its ELINT (Electronic Intelligence) rôle more efficiently. Among other recent arrivals at Johnson AFB were nine specially-adapted B-29s each capable of carrying an atomic bomb; a tenth aircraft had crashed en route killing the unit commander. The B-29s came complete with their bombs but not the nuclear components.

The B-29s were back on 14 November, 21 aircraft from the 19th and 307th BGs attacking the Sinuiju bridges. Initially seven MiGs of the 72nd GuFAR scrambled but were unable to find any targets. An hour later two more groups of MiGs, this time eight aircraft from the 139th GuFAR led by Maj Kharkovskii and the six more from the 67th FAR led by Kapt Sokolov, were scrambled to intercept another raid. An estimated 40 bombers and 20 F-80s were sighted by Kharkovskii's *zveno*, which immediately engaged two sections of B-29s, one of which Kharkovskii claimed shot down in flames, probably aided by his wingman St/Lt Akimov. Another was attacked jointly by St/Lt Kapranov and Lt Kakurin without success. After the initial attack, Kharkovskii and Akimov climbed to 23,000 feet before diving and firing on the next section of bombers, each tackling a different aircraft, the leader reporting smoke and debris from his target. F-80s then intervened but, after shaking these off, Kharkovskii was able to engage a third bomber from which flames were seen to erupt from its port side. He claimed all three bombers shot down. Meanwhile, the 67th FAR MiGs had become involved with the escort, Kapt Sokolov claiming the F-80 which had attempted to engage Kharkovskii. Another pair of 67th FAR MiGs, flown by St/Lts Podgornyi and Kuprik, attacked one of the bombers which was also reported to have crashed in flames. The two Russian pilots then became separated, and Podgornyi carried out a lone attack on another bomber but was hit by return fire (S/Sgt Richard W. Fisher of the 371st BS claimed a MiG shot down), which caused his oxygen bottle to explode and destroy the canopy of his aircraft. Nonetheless, he was able to land safely. Despite the Russian claims, all the B-29s survived although two were badly damaged with wounded aboard. The bomber crews could not understand why they were not allowed to bomb the enemy without restrictions being imposed, and it was possibly following this raid that General MacArthur wrote:

> "One of those bomber pilots, wounded unto death, the stump of an arm dangling by his side, gasped at me through the bubbles of blood he spat out, 'General, which side are Washington and the United Nations on?' It seared my very soul." [18]

The appearance of these Manchuria-based MiGs posed a grave threat to UN air superiority in Korea. To counter this menace the most modern American combat-ready fighter available was urgently needed. The only comparable fighter in service in the West was the North American F-86A Sabre, which was similar in general layout and performance to the MiG. Based in Delaware and equipped with F-86s, the USAF's 4th FIW was ordered to prepare for movement to Korea. It was one of only four existing F-86 wings. The pilots of the 4th FIW were regarded as probably being the best fighter pilots in the USAF; many were combat veterans of WWII and all had extensive jet training, while most had 18 months flying the F-86. Among the distinguished members of the Wing's 334th FIS was an RCAF exchange officer, Flt Lt J.A.O. Lévesque, a 30-year-old native of Montreal who had claimed four German fighters during WWII before being shot down and taken prisoner (see Appendix III). He had been serving with 410 RCAF Squadron flying Vampires before being posted to the United States, and recalled:

> "They [the RCAF] wanted to send me to England to fly Meteors with the RAF, but I didn't want to fly that bloody old plane – with apologies to my Aussie friends who later did. I wanted to go to the States where they had new planes. I was transferred to Langley AFB at the end of May 1950."

Once there, he was soon introduced to the F-86A Sabre:

> "It was like being on a bucking bronco – I didn't ride it, I just hung on. It had lots of power and could turn on a dime. When you pulled back you got a whole lot of air – the stabilizer didn't fight the elevator. This made the aircraft tremendous.
>
> I flew from Langley on alert after 25 June 1950 when the Korean War started. Then we [the 334th FIS] were re-located to Delaware in order to scramble closer to New York where most aircraft incoming from overseas were identified – the Americans never forgot Pearl

---

[18] See *Reminiscences*.

Harbor. After authorisation from the RCAF in Ottawa, I travelled to Delaware by rail and flew next day by USAF military transport to Travis AFB, where I was given several shots for flu, etc. The following day I boarded a C-97 aircraft for Hawaii, then Wake Island, and finally Tokyo. [There] I reported to my Wing Commanding Officer, Colonel John C. Meyer, on a daily basis."

Before leaving for Korea the best aircraft from the other three F-86 wings were swapped with some of the 4th FIW's older machines. Two of the selected squadrons, the 334th and 335th, then flew to the West Coast where aircraft and crews were loaded on the US Army transport USS *Cape Esperance*. Meanwhile, the third squadron, the 336th, went to San Francisco and embarked aboard a Korea-bound tanker, which would arrive at Kisarazu, Japan, some two weeks ahead of the main party. At the same time, the 27th Fighter-Escort Wing commanded by Colonel Ashley B. Packard with its new F-84E Thunderjets was also committed to Korea. The F-84s were faster and more agile than the older F-80s and, therefore, it was believed that they would have a better chance against the MiGs. Like the F-86, the F-84 was armed with six .5-inch machine-guns but had a greater range and could carry two 1,000-lb bombs, two 11.75-inch rockets, or 32 .5-inch rockets. The Group embarked in the light escort carrier USS *Bataan* but neither the F-84s nor the F-86s would reach Korea until early December. Until then the F-80s had the job of maintaining air cover.

As Po'hang was now far behind the bomb-line, General Partridge decided to send the 35th FIG and 77RAAF northwards, to a former Imperial Japanese Navy airfield near the 40th Parallel, near the coastal village of Yonpo, not far from Hamhung; the airfield was codenamed K-27. The Australians had recently lost two of their pilots in tragic circumstances at Po'hang. Members of the unit were accommodated in two tents with primitive electrical power. On the night of 13/14 November, in the tent occupied by Flt Lts Craig Kirkpatrick and Jim Gray, an electrical fault in the wiring near the light bulb caused a fire. It was fanned by gusty winds. The canvas of the tent, which was impregnated with camouflage paint, burned very quickly. Both men apparently had difficulty in disentangling themselves from their sleeping bags before running from the inferno with their clothes ablaze. The alarm had been raised and would-be rescuers wrapped them in coats and smothered their burning clothes, but both men had suffered second- and third-degree burns and secondary shock. After treatment by the American medical unit at Po'hang, they were evacuated via Itazuke AFB en route to the main military hospital at Fukuoka. Kirkpatrick died later in the day, while Gray lingered on until the 20th.

At the new base, K-27, were repairable brick and stone buildings which would provide shelter for the Americans and Australians alike. The men welcomed the chance to exchange their flimsy tents and the other discomforts of Po'hang for the more settled, though colder, circumstances at Hamhung, which they would be sharing with the crews of the USMC Air Wing with its Corsairs, RAAF Dakotas, American C-47s, and the big C-119s which had moved the Group northwards. 77RAAF flew its first operation from Yonpo three days later. An idea of just how cold it was at K-27 was revealed by Flt Lt Fred Barnes:

"Hamhung was a snow-bound field previously used by the North Korean Air Force. For most of us this was the first experience of operating from a snow-covered strip and take-off techniques had to be adapted for the blinding snow flurries of the previous aircraft. The metal skin of the Mustangs was so cold that to touch it with bare hands meant leaving skin stuck to the metal. Yet the ground staff endured these conditions uncomplainingly and our aircraft were always ready and serviceable. It was so cold that by the time we, the pilots, started taxying, the extremities of our feet and hands were entirely without feeling. It was only during the subsequent climb out, as heat flowed into the cockpit, that we went through the agonising burning that restored full feeling to the fingers and toes." [19]

RAAF Dakota pilot Flt Lt David Hitchins recalled the cold and sometimes difficult flying conditions:

---

[19] See *Odd Jobs* by Steve Eather.

"Heavy icing was perhaps the biggest hazard. Crossing the Korea Strait in heavy cloud, it was nothing unusual to hear ice cracking off the wings and thumping against the fuselage. In the early days the runways we used were pretty sloppy with mud, but what used to trick us was that what had been soft mud one day, turned into frozen ridges and hollows the next, so we never knew where we were. Many Korean aerodromes are ringed with mountains. Taking off from a strange one in the dark was no joke."

As the Australians were moving, another five Mustangs and a detachment of ground personnel in two C-47s landed at K-9 airfield near Pusan. The markings carried by these new arrivals were new to the area. They had not been seen in Korea before. This was the arrival of the advance element of the South African Air Force. Back in August the South African government had announced its intention of placing a fighter squadron at the disposal of the United Nations Command for service in Korea. That task fell to 2SAAF Squadron commanded by Cmdt Servaas van Breda Theron DSO DFC, a World War II fighter ace, with Maj Johann Blaauw DFC as his deputy. The flights were commanded by Capt J.F.O. Davis DFC, Capt G.B. Lipawsky DFC, Capt H.O.M. Odendaal DFC, and Capt W.J.J. Badenhorst AFC, all WWII veterans (see Appendix III). Since it had been agreed that no aircraft or technical equipment would be sent from South Africa, all had be purchased locally from UN sources to enable the Squadron to be available immediately on its arrival in Japan. For liaison and communication links with UN Command, SAAF Liaison HQ was accordingly established in Tokyo.

Pilots and ground personnel had departed Pretoria on 25 September and embarked on MV *Tjisidane* at Durban next day. On reaching Yokohama on 4 November, the Squadron went to Johnson AFB where six weeks of conversion training on the F-51 commenced. Meanwhile, an advance flight with support personnel had proceeded almost immediately to Pusan. Here it temporarily joined the 12th FBS which, together with the 67th FBS, formed the 18th FBG. This was an association which would continue for the duration of the war. On arrival at Pusan the South Africans found that all units were in the process of moving to airfields near the front line, and they found that they, too, were to head northwards to the recently captured airfield at P'yongyang East (K-24). In the interim, it was possible for them to learn from the Americans the type of flying operations peculiar to Korea. The emphasis was on the methods of attack, escape, evasion, and rescue.

On 19 November, while ground staff prepared the aircraft of the 18th FBG for action, representatives from all three squadrons attended early morning briefing. It was learnt that the day's operations were to consist of general reconnaissance, fighter escort to bombers, and close-support missions to ground forces. All aircraft flying from K-9 were to land at K-24. Only four of 2SAAF's five Mustangs were serviceable. Cmdt Theron and Capt Lipawsky took off at 0700 on the unit's first combat operation in Korea, a close-support mission which called for bombing and strafing of Communist supply lines in X Corps' sector where the front line crossed the Ch'ongch'on River. With the assistance of a FAC, good results were achieved. The second mission followed later and was flown by Capts Davis and Badenhorst. Next day, Capts Lipawsky and Odendaal successfully attacked a train in a tunnel near Huich'on.

After three hectic days of activity, the 18th FBG completed its move to K-24 on 22 November. This placed the F-51 squadrons much closer to the battle front. Flying from P'yongyang would allow more time to effectively identify targets and negate the need for external fuel tanks. Such advantages, however, were partly offset by the primitive operating facilities. The airfield had one bumpy and short runway and no hangars. In addition, the Korean winter was already causing temperatures to drop below those to which the men were accustomed. There was very little transport available and most equipment had to be manhandled. The mess consisted of an old former NKAF hangar built of wood with gaping holes through which the freezing wind whistled fiercely. Its dirt floor was damp and cold. The temperature reached –3°C. The South Africans were extremely grateful for the warm American clothing with which they had been issued. At this stage more SAAF fighter pilots flew in from Japan and were immediately thrust into battle to check the southward advance of the Chinese. The younger pilots, without experience of WWII, had to learn the hard way.

Another problem was the reality of Communist guerrillas operating behind the UN lines in and about P'yongyang. These sometimes inflicted casualties with the result that local labourers and inhabitants were denied access to the airfields. Some 5,000 such guerrillas were reported to be approaching P'yongyang from the north. Cmdt Theron was informed of the situation by the base commander, as were the American squadron commanders. All personnel were then alerted but there was little they could do because none of the other ranks had been issued with rifles, in spite of frequent requests for them. The danger passed, much to everybody's relief, when paratroopers from P'yongyang chased the guerrillas back into the hills after a brief skirmish.

On the evening of 23 November the air-raid alert was sounded at P'yongyang East, but no enemy aircraft were heard and no bombs were dropped on the airfield. The 'all-clear' was sounded within an hour. Three USAF F-51s had been scrambled but there was no contact, the intruders apparently having disappeared westwards. This routine was repeated over four consecutive evenings. Two enemy aircraft would approach the airfield but then veer away. The 8th FBG at the main P'yongyang base (K-23) was less fortunate and seemed to attract the enemy. The aircraft that made these nightly attacks on K-23 were probably Po-2 biplanes, as it was this type which was used in a similar manner later in the war.

General MacArthur arrived at the 8th Army HQ at Sinanju on the morning of 24 November where, with General Walker, he watched the commencement of the UN offensive that was expected to finish the war. The 8th Army currently comprised I Corps with the US 24th Division, the 27th British Commonwealth Brigade, and the ROK 1st Division; IX Corps with the US 2nd and 25th Divisions and the Turkish Brigade; and the ROK II Corps with the ROK 6th, 7th and 8th Divisions. In reserve was the US 1st Cavalry Division. MacArthur confidently announced that the war would be won in two weeks and the 8th Army would spend Christmas in Japan. As the 8th Army moved off, the US 1st Marine Division prepared to act as the northern arm of a giant pincer movement in which the 8th Army was to be the southern arm. Before flying back to Tokyo, MacArthur decided that he would like to fly along the length of the Yalu to see for himself the bridges and installations, and particularly Sinuiju and Antung. Gesturing his staff to join him, he requested the pilot of his unarmed C-54, Lt Colonel Anthony F. Story, to proceed; he later wrote:

> "When we reached the mouth of the Yalu, I told Story to turn east and follow the river at an altitude of 5,000 feet. At this height we could observe in detail the entire area of international no-man's-land all the way to the Siberian border. All that spread before our eyes was an endless expanse of utterly barren countryside, jagged hills, yawning crevices, and the black waters of the Yalu . . . If a large force or massive supply train had passed over the border, the imprints had already been well-covered by the intermittent snowstorms of the Yalu Valley . . ." [20]

This arrogant and fool-hardy show of defiance which jeapodised not only his own life but those of his staff and pilot – a typical act of MacArthurism – miraculously encountered neither flak nor enemy aircraft. The MiG pilots had missed a rare opportunity.

At 0830 on 24 November, half an hour after the 8th US Army offensive began, 2SAAF's Capt Gordon Lipawsky and Lt D.D. Deans began the first close-support mission of the day. Directed by a FAC, they carried out attacks on a small enemy-held hill, destroying two mortar positions and killing about 50 troops. In the afternoon Capt John Davis and Lt Elmer Wilson claimed the destruction of two vehicles, a self-propelled gun and a supply dump. These were the only two close-support missions flown by the South Africans during the day, although Capt Badenhorst and Lt E.N. Jones flew escort to a USN minesweeper off the west coast near Cho-do island. Next day Capts Lipawsky and Odendaal were joined by Lt F.B. Ritcher in an attack on a village where a concentration of enemy troops was reported; it was later confirmed that some 300 bodies were located following their attack.

---

[20] See *Reminiscences*.

Throughout the daylight hours of 25[21] and 26 November, 77RAAF joined other units of the 35th FIG in flying support missions for the 8th US Army and ROK II Corps. In a typical action, during the morning of the 25th, Flt Lt Fred Barnes led his section of four Mustangs in a rocket and machine-gun attack on enemy troops reported firing on friendly forces from the ridges of a valley at Uhyon-dong. Meanwhile, Sqn Ldr Cresswell with another four Mustangs provided support for the 1st ROK Division at Taech'on. Then another section led by Flt Lt Jack Murray caught an estimated 200 enemy troops marching up a road; these were strafed and rocketed as they tried to disperse into a creek. American losses meantime continued to mount, 1/Lt Harry Sandlin of the 80th FBS being killed in action while flying an F-80 on the 25th, probably the victim of ground fire; he had scored one of the first kills of the war way back in June. Another F-80 pilot was killed next day when 2/Lt Richard L. Scott of the 7th FBS was similarly shot down. The 35th FIG lost two pilots during the month including the CO of the 39th FIS, Lt Colonel Gerald Brown, who was captured. Also captured after being shot down but almost immediately set free again was 1/Lt Allen C. Durgin. He broke his leg when baling out and was quickly captured, given first-aid and then surprisingly released, being picked up by an advanced UN patrol, but 1/Lt George Lulakis, also of the 39th FIS, did not survive a crash near Po'hang following engine problems. The 18th FBG had fared better during recent operations, losing only five aircraft and two pilots (1/Lt Bernard L. Pearson of the 67th FBS, and 1/Lt Frederick G. Hudson III of the 12th FBS) for the month; another pilot had been rescued by helicopter. Two Forward Air Controllers had also been shot down and killed during the month, both spotter aircraft flown by Mustang pilots: Capt Malcolm B. Edens of the 18th FBG going down on the 16th, and Capt Aaron R. Abercrombie of the 39th FIS ten days later. Capt Edens was taken prisoner but died in a prison camp.

The 8th US Army's 'Home-by-Christmas' offensive in the west went well for the first two days, but then turned sour. Chinese bugles heralded the enemy's own offensive. By noon General Walker was reporting to MacArthur that he estimated there were 200,000 Chinese against him, that ROK II Corps had been swept away, and that IX Corps was falling back to cover its exposed flank. On the 27th the 1st Marine Division launched its attack to the west, which gained barely two miles before it was stopped dead when it ran into eight Chinese divisions. Overnight it snowed. The Chinese moved simultaneously against Hagaru-ri and Koto-ri, far to the rear on the main supply route from Hamhung. These attacks continued with increasing intensity and it was clear that the enemy was attempting to encircle and destroy the entire Marine Division. The unexpected Chinese push forced MacArthur to order a switch from the offensive to the defensive, and the commander of the amphibious force was instructed to make preparations to evacuate UN forces in North Korea, while the commander of the US 5th Marines took matters into his own hands and ordered a stand at Yudam-ni, where the Hagaru airstrip had to be held. At Hagaru, two US Army battalions from the 7th Division came in from the east side of the reservoir, adding about 300 combat soldiers to the Marine force. Another group, which had been formed at Koto-ri comprising a collection of Royal Marines, US Marines, and US soldiers, was ambushed as it attempted to join forces with the US 5th Marines and was cut to pieces.

Six close-support sorties were flown by the Mustangs of 2SAAF during the morning and afternoon. Forty miles away at K-27, 77RAAF, together with the other two squadrons of the 35th FIG, was committed exclusively to a maximum effort in support of the embattled Marines who were desperately struggling to survive in the Chosin Reservoir area. Their aircraft, armed with rockets, sped down the runway amid a flurry of snow. Five miles west of Hagaru, at the southern tip of Changjin Reservoir, Flt Lt Ross Coburn led his flight in at low level, raking snow-covered enemy trenches with rockets and machine-gun fire until their ammunition ran out. Later in the morning Sqn Ldr Cresswell's flight dropped napalm and strafed a roadblock

---

[21] On 25 November, during a UN air strike against a CPV headquarters, Mao Tse-tung's eldest son, Mao Anying, who had been appointed General P'eng's confidential secretary, was killed. One source suggested that Mao Anying had been commander of a Chinese MiG air regiment and was among the first Chinese pilots killed in action; this would appear to be nothing but romanticised fiction.

in the reservoir area, while Flt Lt Barnes and P2 Tom Stoney joined two USMC Corsairs operating from K-9 attacking an enemy tank and buildings sheltering troops. During the day 1/Lt William P. Dougherty of the 35th FBS flying from Kimpo reported that he had destroyed a Yak on the ground. A force of B-29s raided Sinuiju on the last day of the month, MiGs from the 29th GuFAR taking off to intercept but failing to make contact.

December 1950

The outcome was different next day (1 December) when three B-29s raided Antung at noon, eight MiGs of the 29th GuFAR's 1st Eskadrilya taking off to intercept. The MiG leader St/Lt P.I. Orlov reported shooting down one of the bombers which crashed 25 miles east of the airfield, while St/Lt G.M. Grebenkin claimed a second although his own aircraft was hit in the canopy by return fire. The Russians claimed that both bombers crashed and that the crews were captured by Korean forces. Meanwhile, 77RAAF flew a maximum effort of 24 sorties to combat the increasingly serious situation in the Chosin Reservoir area, and in support of US troops confronting another Chinese breakthrough near Taech'on, the Australian pilots reporting the best targets they had seen for some time. Eight miles south of the border town of Sakchu, Sqn Ldr Cresswell and his flight found a convoy of vehicles which included tanks and trucks. They were in a mountain pass about two miles long, and had obviously already been attacked. Twenty of the trucks could be seen burning and some exploded as the Mustangs flew overhead. The Australians used up their ammunition, destroying four more trucks and damaging five others. Because there were still many undamaged vehicles, Cresswell called the FAC telling him to send more fighter-bombers to the area.

Supplies and ammunition were air-dropped to the defenders at Hagaru, but not all such operations were successful; one American soldier wrote:

> "Retrieving them [the supply and ammunition containers] was difficult because the Chinese wanted them as much as we did, and some were dropped far out of reach. Of what we got, we found that a lot of the belts and clips [of ammunition] were damaged . . . Our planes were trying to help by dropping napalm between our troops and theirs. As a result some of our men got burned pretty bad and were put aboard the trucks with us wounded. I will never forget the smell of human flesh after that. A lot of them died before too long." [22]

Reports that the enemy was moving under cover of darkness led FEAF to order flare-dropping RB-26s of the 162nd Recon Squadron to operate in conjunction with night intruder B-26s, but the move met with little success. Low-lying fog and haze at night in the mountainous terrain made night attack extremely difficult.

As the UN ground forces retreated back towards South Korea, all available aircraft moved to Yonpo airfield (K-27) inside the Hamhung-Hungnam defence perimeter. Tension mounted as the enemy advanced ever closer to the airfield. Personnel were ordered to carry firearms and to prepare to defend the base. Bad weather hampered aerial operations, although groundcrews worked relentlessly in sub-arctic conditions to keep the aircraft serviceable. Then word was received ordering the 35th FIG, including 77RAAF, to abandon Yonpo. The Australian Mustangs carried out their last mission from the airfield on 3 December, led by Sqn Ldr Cresswell, and completed it by heading south to Pusan. Vital groundcrews and their equipment were hurriedly evacuated by airlift, and the remainder were moved out by sea and land transport. 77RAAF's diarist recorded:

> "An unending stream of aircraft take off and land at Yonpo. They include Mustangs, Wildcats, Corsairs, C-47s, C-46s, C-54s, C-119s and liaison aircraft. Smoke is rolling down from the mountains from the direction of the battle areas around the Chosin Reservoir. Sqn Ldr Cresswell led the last 'four-ship' flight to take off from Yonpo."

One of the RAAF Dakotas taking part in the evacuation had just flown in from Singapore. It was the first of four more such aircraft being introduced to the Korean theatre to support

---

[22] See *The Korean War* by Max Hastings.

77RAAF and British ground units.

On 2 and 3 December, the 27th British Commonwealth Brigade, moving from Chasan to P'yongyang, covered the withdrawal of American troops. In the confused fighting it was mainly the Argylls who bore the brunt of it. By the evening of the 3rd the Brigade had reached the Taedong where, it was anticipated, it might be given the task of holding a bridgehead to cover retreating American and South Korean troops, but this rôle was given to the newly arrived 29th British Infantry Brigade under Brigadier Tom Brodie CBE, which had disembarked at Pusan. It had moved to Kaesong, coming under the command of the US 187th Airborne Regimental Combat Team. After successful opening actions against pockets of enemy guerrillas, by the evening of the 3rd, the 29th Brigade (less the Royal Northumberland Fusiliers, who stayed in the Kaesong area) was deployed to form the bridgehead a few miles north of P'yongyang. Meanwhile, the 27th Brigade continued with its withdrawal, passing through the ranks of the 29th Brigade during the morning of 4 December. At the same time, X Corps was being withdrawn to Hungham as rapidly as possible. General MacArthur decided there was no point in attempting to unite it with the 8th Army to form a defence line. Such a scheme was considered impractical because the line would need to be 150 miles long and held by all seven American divisions, the combat effectiveness of the ROK Army now having to be assessed as negligible. Without massive reinforcement, MacArthur saw no alternative but to carry out successive withdrawals to eventual beachhead bastions from where they could be evacuated. When President Truman learned of the retreat, he sent a message of assurance to MacArthur:

> "We consider that the preservation of your forces is now the primary consideration. Consolidation of forces into beachheads is concurred in."

By now not having complete confidence in MacArthur, Truman ordered his Army Chief-of-Staff, General Joseph L. Collins, to fly to Tokyo. During a press conference at the end of November, the President had said that the United States would use every weapon it had, if necessary, to meet the military situation in Korea. This obvious rattling of the nuclear sabre sent shivers through Europe and brought Britain's Prime Minister Attlee to Washington on 4 December. He urged that an all-out war against China must be avoided and that a ceasefire be sought. Already the debates over the use of nuclear weapons and the limits of the Korean police action war were causing major concern. But when news reached MacArthur of Britain's suggestion that a buffer zone should be established south of the Yalu, jointly policed by UN and Chinese forces, he retorted:

> "The widely reported British desire to appease the Chinese Communists by giving them a strip of North Korea finds its historic precedent in the action taken at Munich in 1938 . . . To give up any portion of North Korea to the aggression of the Chinese Communists would be the greatest defeat of the free world in recent times. Indeed, to yield to so immoral a proposition would bankrupt our leadership and influence in Asia, and render untenable our position both politically and morally." [23]

One fighting withdrawal was being carried out by the US Marines who were heading towards the port of Hungham from where they could be evacuated. On reaching the village of Koto-ri, about seven miles down the valley from Hagaru, they were suddenly cut off front and rear. US Air Cargo Command was called in for airdrops to provide food, ammunition and supplies, and to evacuate the wounded. On the icy ground a rocky airstrip, barely wide enough to accommodate a C-47, was prepared for the emergency flights back and forth from K-27. Taking part in these flights were the C-47s of the newly arrived Greek Flight commanded by Maj John Gorenko RHAF. The nine aircraft[24] of this unit – officially the 13th Transport Flight of the Royal Hellenic Air Force – had staged through Cyprus, Saudia Arabia, Pakistan, India, Thailand, Indochina, the Philippines and Okinawa before arriving at Itazuke AFB on 1 December. Attached to the US 21st Transport Squadron, a detachment was immediately sent to K-27.

---

[23] See Reminiscenses.
[24] The aircraft included 92612, 92616, 92618, 92620/P, 92622/E, 92630/F, 92632/G, and 92637/H.

The Greeks had been given little time to rest or settle in. Due to the seriousness of the situation, they were thrust into operations immediately. Under extremely adverse weather, through snow-storms and under enemy fire, the aircraft flew over hostile territory and landed on the very narrow lane covered with ice to airlift as many wounded as possible to K-27. From there they were carried to the hospital in the rear. The American and Greek aircraft succeeded in rescuing all the wounded, giving the Marines the chance to evacuate the area without being hampered by their casualties. Greek aircraft ferried back at least 1,000 wounded men and flew 30 sorties carrying in cargo. When the capture of Hungham was imminent, the aircraft finally abandoned the airfield and moved south to Pusan. Missions continued from there. These were carried out by an operational echelon consisting of three or four aircraft, while the Flight Headquarters was stationed at Itazuke AFB. For its outstanding work, the Greek Flight received a US Presidential Citation for exceptional bravery "in the difficult operations of evacuating the wounded from the areas surrounded by the enemy." Participating crews were also awarded the US Air Medal.

At Japan's Iwakuni Bay, the Sunderland Flight was ordered to prepare to take part in the evacuation, as recalled by Wg Cdr Burnside:

"On one occasion orders were received to stand by to rescue American Marines and troops from the British Commonwealth in the area of a reservoir in the mountainous backbone of Korea. As much gear as possible was to be removed from the hulls of the Sunderlands to lighten them and provide space inside to accommodate the maximum number of troops. The plan was to risk enemy ground fire and alight on the reservoir, and rescue as many men as we could in rubber boats. In the event the operation had to be cancelled because the water became frozen over and, as a tragic result, hundreds of UN troops were either killed or taken prisoner."

The Sunderlands were far from idle during this period, however, and on 7 December Flt Lt Hunter's aircraft alighted twice in open sea to rescue 23 survivors from the mined Philippine freighter *Joseph S*. All were flown to Kai Tak (Hong Kong), where the flying boat landed in darkness. The flying boats ranged far and wide, as Wg Cdr Burnside recalled:

"At first much of the operational flying from Iwakuni Bay was done by day, but the emergence of MiG-15s flown from their safe airfields in so-called neutral territory on the other side of the Yalu compelled more and more of the sorties to be carried out under cover of darkness. The Sunderlands were no match for this modern enemy fighter. Another enemy was the weather. Many operations had to be flown in temperatures as low as −20°C and the less than favourable weather conditions associated with this part of the Far East, particularly in the winter. This, together with the mountainous terrain around the approaches to Iwakuni Bay, added to the hazards confronting tired Sunderland crews on their long patrols of often ten hours or more. Diversion bases suitable for emergency landings were few and far between and sometimes we had to make for Saigon or Okinawa if cloud prevented us getting into Hong Kong or Iwakuni. On one such occasion I recall having to refuel in Okinawa Bay from petrol lines passed to us over the stern of an aircraft carrier. Juggling with the outboard engines in an endeavour to keep station beneath the great stern towering above us was an interesting but distinctly tricky manoeuvre."

Meanwhile, as the 8th US Army was preparing to abandon the North Korean capital, an RAAF Dakota almost fell into the hands of the Chinese at P'yongyang. It was the second last aircraft to leave the airfield on 4 December. The pilot, Flt Lt Ron Daniel, remembered:

"I landed at P'yongyang with a load of winter clothing for the Australian troops. We had unloaded most of the stuff when an American came running up to see what it was all about. 'Do you see that river?' he asked us. 'The Chinese are just over that water and heading this way as fast as they can make it. The Aussies are setting up to fight a rear-guard action 30 miles south of here. We are all getting the hell out of here and you had better do the same.' We did. But not before we had reloaded our cargo of winter clothes. We did not care to see Australian equipment keeping Chinese soldiers warm even if only as a bonfire burning in P'yongyang."

The same crew was aboard the same Dakota at Suwon two days later, on 6 December, when an 18th FBG F-51, the lead aircraft in a section which was taking off towards it on the runway, failed to clear and struck the cabin. The cockpit was smashed but the crew had ducked below the level of the instrument panel – thus avoiding a similar fate – as recalled by Flt Sgt Leon Murtagh, the co-pilot:

> "Believe me, the sight of a F-51 right on top of us, undercarriage almost retracted, and carrying two drop tanks of napalm and eight rockets, was awesome as it filled the windscreen just before we ducked beneath the glare shield! The Chinese advance was held up sufficiently to allow A65-74 to be stripped of all useful components and then exploded before Suwon was also overcome in the first week of January 1951."

The withdrawal continued. General Walker had drawn four fall-back lines on his map. The first line had been drawn north of P'yongyang but it was overrun before it could be manned. The next line ran along the Imjin north of Seoul. P'yongyang itself was abandoned on 5 December with 8,000-10,000 tons of supplies left behind, broken up or burning.

Due to the vulnerability of the lumbering reconnaissance RB-29s to the MiGs, a detachment of the USAF's new four-jet RB-45C high-altitude photo-reconnaissance aircraft from the 84th BS(L) Squadron was hurried out to Korea and was attached to the 91st Strategic Reconnaissance Squadron at Yokata AFB, Japan. It carried an array of cameras and the latest radar and, with a top speed of 550mph and two .5-inch machine-guns in the tail, it was hoped that it would be more capable of surviving in a hostile sky. These hopes were soon dashed when, on 4 December, one of the detachment's three aircraft, piloted by Capt Charles E. McDonough, was intercepted by four MiGs from the 29th GuFAR led by Kapt Vvedenskii and shot down, the aircraft crashing about 15 miles east of Sensen. The victory was credited to St/Lt A.F. Andrianov. In addition to the normal three-man crew, on board was a senior USAF intelligence officer, Colonel John R. Lovell, who survived the crash and was taken prisoner together with the badly burned pilot; the latter however died a few days later. Following interrogation by a North Korean general, Colonel Lovell was apparently handed over to local towns people, who allegedly beat him to death.

Later in the day, at about 1320, 1/Lt R.R. Hudspeth in an RF-80 of the 8th TRS, being escorted by an 8th FBS F-80 flown by 1/Lt Markette, narrowly escaped similar fates when engaged by another flight of 29th GuFAR MiGs in the same area. While one MiG carried out tail attacks on both aircraft, others boxed-in the two American jets by flying 50 yards off their wingtips as they sped southwards for safety. Although both suffered damage in this unusual form of attack, they were able to escape and reach their base, where Markette carried out an emergency landing; he claimed possible damage to one of the MiGs. Both were undoubtedly attacked by Kapt Stepan Naumenko who was credited with their destruction, although erroneously identifying them as F-84s. St/Lt Konstantin Rumyantsev was lost during this engagement. It was believed that he flew into the ground while pursuing one of the American aircraft, although he may have been the victim of Markette's shooting. The 29th GuFAR's MiGs were successful again next day (5 December) when four led by Maj Yuri Keleinikov encountered eight F-80s near Kaisen-Kisen, the Major claiming one and St/Lt N.N. Petrov of 2nd Eskadrilya a second.

2SAAF safely completed its move to K-13 airfield near Suwon just a few hours before enemy troops reached P'yongyang. K-13 had been judged unfit for jet fighter operations because it possessed a badly damaged concrete runway, but it was from here that the South African pilots continued to stage their dawn-to-dusk close-support missions. The unit lost its first aircraft during the course of a railway interdiction mission on 5 December. Four pilots were ordered to destroy ten UN railway trucks that had fallen into the hands of the Communists on the main line north of Sunan. The mission was led by Capt Gordon Lipawsky, with Lt Frank Ritcher at No2, Capt John Davis at No3, and an American pilot flying in No4 position. En route for the target the American's F-51 developed engine trouble so he returned to base, escorted by Ritcher. Davis moved up onto Lipawsky's wing. When they reached the target area Lipawsky provided top cover while Davis descended to tree-top level to search for the railway trucks.

They were not to be found at the reported position, as he later recalled:

> "Captain Lipawsky, who was covering me, reported a large number of stores on a railway
> siding approximately four miles north of P'yongyang. I made three strafing runs on the
> stores on the southern end of the siding but I could not get them to burn. I then made three
> rocket attacks and the stores started to burn with high flames and white smoke. There was
> another large dump of stores in the centre of the siding. I made two rocket attacks but
> missed the stores. I commenced the third attack from 3,000 feet and pressed it home as this
> was my last rocket. The rocket struck the stores and caused a terrific explosion which
> severely damaged my aircraft [311] and knocked me unconscious for a few seconds.
> Fortunately the aircraft was trimmed tail-heavy due to the speed gained during the dive and
> this enabled it to gain sufficient height to clear some hills which lay ahead. The elevator and
> aileron controls were inoperative and I had to use the elevator trim to climb away . . ." [25]

The ammunition dump had exploded with such concussion that Lipawsky, circling above,
temporarily lost control of his aircraft. When Davis came to his senses he found that his
windscreen and canopy had been blown off, and both mainplanes were full of holes, some as
big as soup plates. Both his ailerons had also been blown off and the engine was streaming
glycol and smoke. To the left of the control column there was a gaping six-inch hole in the floor
of the cockpit. He reported to Lipawsky that his aircraft had been badly damaged and then
transmitted a 'Mayday' call on the emergency channel that was picked up by the area
controller; Davis continued:

> "Once I was clear of the smoke pall hanging over P'yongyang I realised that I was flying
> south-east into enemy lines, so I turned onto a westerly heading in an endeavour to reach
> friendly lines. Immediately after the explosion the engine had started to vibrate but was still
> giving sufficient power to maintain 200mph at 2,500 feet. The coolant temperature gauge
> showed over 150°C – however, the oil temperature remained constant at 80°C for about five
> minutes and then rose rapidly to 150°C. When the temperature reached this figure the
> engine seized. When this occurred I was about three miles from friendly territory . . ." [26]

As it was too low for Davis to bale out, his only chance was to try and force-land on a straight
stretch of road. Unfortunately, his aircraft's speed fell too rapidly for this and he had to crash-
land onto a freshly ploughed paddy field, the wings flattening two small trees on the way.
Although the Mustang was a complete write off, its radio still worked and Lipawsky was able
to inform Davis that a rescue helicopter was not available. On hearing this, Davis suggested
that the road would be suitable for a light aircraft to land. He climbed out of the cockpit and sat
on the crumpled wing to wait. A few minutes later he saw several armed men approaching.
From his vantage point above, Lipawsky assumed they were North Koreans and scattered them
with a couple of strafing runs. Then two F-80s arrived on the scene, offering support, but it was
not long before they and Lipawsky had to leave with fuel running low. When they had gone,
the armed men advanced to within a few yards of Davis and then stopped. For ten minutes they
sat motionless in a semi-circle with their rifles across their knees. Davis was convinced he was
about to be shot but, at last, an old man arose, saluted and held up a South Korean flag. They
were members of the Democratic Youth Party and UN police, operating behind the Communist
lines. They offered to guide Davis to safety, but at that moment an AT-6 flew over and the pilot
dropped a note instructing Davis to burn his aircraft and walk in a southerly direction towards
friendly territory; he set fire to the aircraft as instructed:

> "It was nearly ten minutes before the [fuel] tank blew up and the aircraft started to burn
> properly. I started to walk south but the Koreans would not let me and forced me to walk
> up the road to the north, as they said there were Communist troops in the hills about half a
> mile to the south. The Koreans took me to their village a mile up the road, where [they said]
> I was to be clothed and fed. The T-6 dropped me another note telling me I was going the

25/26 See *Flying Cheetahs in Korea* by Dermot Moore and Peter Bagshaw.

wrong way and that I was not to go north. I managed to get two of the Koreans to accompany me as I thought their rifles might be useful in an emergency, and their knowledge of the country and people would be invaluable in staying away from enemy occupied areas. On my return down the road to where the aircraft was burning, I noticed an L-5 circling the area. The T-6 flew alongside the L-5 and lowered its undercarriage. I realised the L-5 was going to land on the road. The pilot, Capt James Lawrence, with Capt Lewis Millett as observer, made a very skilful landing on the road which was just wide enough for the wheels of the L-5. The observer volunteered to stay on the ground until Capt Lawrence had dropped me.

I discovered later that Capt Millett knew that the area was being approached by enemy troops and, as he did not have a weapon to protect himself, I consider his action very courageous. Before Capt Lawrence returned, Capt Millett was under fire from the hills and, what is more, Capt Lawrence knew this before he landed. Capts Lawrence and Millett, both of the US 26th Division, were on a routine observation flight and were under no obligation to pick me up. The actions of both these officers are deserving of the highest praise." [27]

It was the feeling of all of the South Africans that Lewis Millett should have received the US Congressional Medal of Honor for his courageous action. Instead, he and Capt Lawrence were each awarded the US DFC, as was Capt Lipawsky; in addition, both Americans were given a bottle of whisky by the grateful SAAF unit in recognition of their bravery.

By now the USAF's 4th FIW with its F-86As had arrived in Japan. Unfortunately, when the 336th FIS off-loaded its aircraft, it was found to everyone's dismay, that they had not been waterproofed properly. Salt water corrosion had taken its toll, so much so that only seven aircraft could be made combat ready straight away. The 27th Fighter-Escort Group's F-84Es were in a similar state but it did manage to get one squadron operational, and flew its first combat mission on 6 December from Taegu (K-2), escorting B-29s raiding the towns of Sunch'on, Songch'on, and Sukch'on where significant concentrations of enemy troops had been reported. A Flight of six MiGs from the 29th GuFAR led by Kapt Naumenko intercepted the bombers and claimed three shot down, all of which were reported to have crashed a few miles south of Anju, one being credited to Naumenko; a second was claimed by his wingman Lt K.V. Minn, and the third was awarded to the leader of the third section, Kapt I.F. Bogatyrev. One of the MiGs was hit by return fire with the loss of its pilot, Lt Nikolai Serikov, who was killed. The Russian pilots also reported sighting escorting F-80s and claimed one of these, which apparently crashed north of Sinuiju; it was credited to Kapt V.K. Krymskii. Three more F-80s were claimed by the MiGs next day, one during a morning skirmish by Kapt Vvedenskii, the other two during the afternoon when St/Lts Pavel Pavlenko and M.V. Fedoseev of the 3rd Eskadrilya of the 29th GuFAR each reported shooting down one, but Pavlenko failed to return. It was believed his aircraft crashed due to technical problems. All three F-80s were reported to have crashed south-east of Sinuiju and allegedly all three American pilots were killed.

Next day (7 December) a flight of four F-84s carried out the 27th Fighter-Escort Group's first armed reconnaissance, led by the Group Commander, Lt Colonel Don Blakeslee DFC[28]. Selecting targets of opportunity, the flight fired a total of 32 .5-inch rockets while attacking enemy positions, knocking out several locomotives, a railway marshalling yard, sinking a loaded barge near Chinnampo, and setting fire to three enemy-held villages. The 29th GuFAR's run of success continued over the next few days, its pilots claiming three F-80s on the 9th. The records show that Kapt A.I. Perekrest was the leader of a formation of eight MiGs from the 3rd Eskadrilya which scrambled at 0812 when fighter-bombers were reported approaching. Four F-80s were sighted at 5,000 feet attacking Sensen railway station and, as they climbed after bombing, Perekrest attacked the leader of the second pair, which he shot down. As the MiGs were returning to their base they encountered another four F-80s, one of which was attacked by Perekrest without result. An hour later Kapt Vvedenskii's *zveno* encountered four F-51s in

---

[27] See *Flying Cheetahs in Korea*.
[28] Lt Colonel Blakeslee had served with the RCAF during WWII before transferring to the USAAF. By the end of WWII he had raised his score to 14 (see Appendix III).

the vicinity of Sinuiju but the Americans evaded combat and escaped. In the same area the four MiGs of Kapt Naumenko's *zveno* from the 1st Eskadrilya were attacked by four F-80s while cruising at 20,000 feet. The Russians managed to climb away unscathed while St/Lt I.F. Grechko claimed one of their assailants shot down. Later, shortly after 1410, Kapt Perekrest's *zveno* was again in the thick of the action when four F-80s were sighted below attacking Sensen railway station. However, these were not engaged although another four of the fighter-bombers were. Perekrest and his No2 Lt V.R. Bondarenko each fired long bursts at the rear aircraft which began to smoke and then crashed near Syarenkan station, credit being given to Bondarenko. At least one F-80 was lost during the day with Capt Richard Moore of the 8th FBS being reported missing in action.

The action continued unabated next day, 10 December, the first clash occurring shortly after 0800 when Kapt Naumenko's *zveno* encountered a group of F-80s. The MiGs' first attack was unsuccessful but during a second attempt Naumenko and his wingman shot down one F-80, which burst into flames, and damaged a second. There was a further engagement in the afternoon, with Kapts Vvedenskii and Yurkevich leading eight MiGs against more F-80s. St/Lt Petrov was about to attack one of the fighter-bombers when he noticed a second on his tail. As he broke to port his engine took a hit, although he was able to return to base and land safely. Petrov's wingman, St/Lt Yuri Glinski reported shooting down the leading F-80 which apparently crashed about three miles north of Sensen. There were a number of other skirmishes but neither side was able to gain an advantage[29]. One of the MiGs damaged during this period may have been the victim of Capt Charles E. McDonald MM[30], who was credited with damaging and possibly destroying one of the Russian jets, one of the first such claims by an F-80 pilot.

P1 Geoff Thornton led four Mustangs from 77RAAF on an armed recce on the 11th, covering an area bounded by Seoul, Kojin-ni and Wonsan. The flight split into two sections, with P2 Stan Williamson and P3 Geoff Stephens flying down the east coast road where they set fire to two buildings and damaged another in the dock area at Changjon. Shortly afterwards they came across a group of 15-20 soldiers waving South Korean flags. Being uncertain of their identity, they did not attack but reported their location to the controller before returning to base. Meanwhile, Thornton and his wingman, Flt Lt Des Murphy, had started out towards P'yonggang but were forced to turn back because of heavy cloud. While diving low over a road, Thornton's Mustang (A68-772) struck some wires strung across it, tearing off two rocket pods, cutting the airscrew, and damaging the radiator scoop, port aileron and flaps. The aircraft still responded, so the pair carried on with the mission, both dropping their napalm on buildings in the town of Kumsong, setting two buildings on fire. Their next target was a goods shed in the railway siding at Changdori. Thornton did not discover the full extent of the damage to his aircraft until he had landed at Pusan.

During another MiG/F-80 clash on 12 December, 1/Lt Evan W. Rosencrans of the 16th FIS reported shooting down one of the jets near Sinuiju while flying top cover to other F-80s attacking the airfield; it would seem however that he was awarded only a probable. MiG pilots of the 29th GuFAR reported shooting down a further three F-80s, all of which crashed south-east of Sinuiju, killing their respective pilots. Six MiGs led by Kapt Perekrest attacked the F-80s as they were strafing the airfield, Perekrest shooting down one which crashed about ten miles to the south, while his wingman Lt Bondarenko claimed a second. The leader of another pair of MiGs, St/Lt Fedoseev, claimed a third fighter-bomber from which the pilot was seen to bale out, but it seems that only one F-80 was lost when 2/Lt William Kimbro of the 25th FIS failed to return. On the 14th and 15th, two more F-80s were reportedly shot down by the MiGs, the first by St/Lt Grechko near Sinuiju, the second by Lt Ryzhov, also near Sinuiju, both American pilots reportedly losing their lives when their aircraft crashed near the airfield. These losses cannot be substantiated, however, although two F-80s of the 8th FBS which were also

---

[29] Maj I.F. Pavlov, twice Hero of the Soviet Union, was reported to have been killed in action on this date, 10 December 1950, but was possibly killed in an accident rather than combat.

[30] Capt McDonald had flown Spitfires with the RCAF during WWII (see Appendix III).

attacked by MiGs on the 15th escaped unscathed. These latest victories by the 29th GuFAR gave the Russian pilots an impressive tally of 22 victories since the beginning of the month – 10 F-80s, six F-84s (or 16 F-80s only), five B-29s and an RB-45.

It was not only the Americans who were receiving fighter reinforcements. At Antung air base on 10 December the 1st Eskadrilya of the 177th FAR landed with its MiGs, Kapt P.M. Mikhailov commanding. The 2nd Eskadrilya would arrive a few days later, commanded by Kapt M.Ya. Fomin, but the 3rd Eskadrilya would not fly down from Ansham air base in northern China until the new year. The Regiment was commanded by Podpolkovnik (Lt Colonel) V. Terentyev, and several of its pilots had WWII experience including Kapt I.A. Grechishko of the 1st Eskadrilya, and Kapt S.A. Barsegyan of the 2nd Eskadrilya. The 177th FAR joined the already successful 29th GuFAR as part of the 50th Fighter Air Division; a third unit, the Chinese 10th FAR, would join the 50th Fighter Air Division at Antung at the end of the year. The 177th FAR's 1st Eskadrilya flew its first operational mission from Antung on the day of its arrival but did not make contact with the raiders.

Meanwhile, Johnson AFB near Tokyo became the 4th FIW's new home but Colonel Meyer was anxious to start operations as soon as possible and decided to move an advance detachment to Korea immediately. Named Detachment A, with pilots drawn from the Wing HQ and all three squadrons, the seven serviceable F-86s were sent to Kimpo (K-14) on 13 December, from where an orientation flight was carried out two days later. Flt Lt Lévesque undertook his first operational flight with the 334th FIS on the 16th:

> "I flew as No2 to Colonel Meyer, just two aircraft, over the Yalu, with no MiGs coming to meet us."

The 4th FIW mounted its first offensive sweep of the war on 17 December when four F-86s of the 336th FIS took off from Kimpo at 1405 and headed towards the Yalu. As they approached, they reduced their speed to 400mph in the hope the Communist radar operators would assume this was just another patrol by the slower F-80s. A few minutes after entering the combat area at 27,000 feet, Lt Colonel Bruce H. Hinton spotted a flight of four MiGs – aircraft from the 29th GuFAR led by Maj Yuri Keleinikov – climbing rapidly to intercept. The ruse apparently worked and the Russian pilots seemed not to realise that they were about to meet a new and deadly adversary. Had they done so, they would almost certainly have climbed for altitude on their own side of the Yalu. They found out their mistake as the Sabres came arrowing down towards them. They broke away, diving for the safety of the river but were too late. Hinton manoeuvred the MiG flown by Maj Yakov Yefromenko (the 50th Fighter Air Division's Inspector of Pilots) squarely into his sights and fired three four-second bursts. The MiG began to burn and dropped into a spin. The American pilots stated that it was racked by explosions as it fell. Nevertheless, Yefromenko was able to head for Antung escorted by St/Lt Petrov although he eventually was forced to eject from his smoking jet. Twenty minutes later, over the runway at Kimpo, Lt Colonel Hinton indulged in a traditional victory roll to celebrate the first Sabre kill.

That same day P1 Geoff Thornton led a flight of four RAAF Mustangs to destroy a double-track railway bridge at Sonch'on, only 30 miles from the Manchurian border. It was part of a campaign to cut enemy communications with Manchuria. Thornton took his flight out over the Yellow Sea, crossed the coast into North Korea, and then attacked out of the sun. The pilots could see great craters caused by bombs dropped during previous attempts to blow the bridge on the main line out of Manchuria. Despite anti-aircraft fire, they dropped eight bombs, scoring several direct hits which destroyed two spans and tore up the tracks.

Two Mustangs of 2SAAF led by Capt Wessel Badenhorst were also engaged in a mission in the Sinanju area, where a concentration of concealed enemy vehicles was located in a deep and narrow valley. Several attacks were carried through a screen of machine-gun fire, one vehicle attacked by Badenhorst exploding with such violence that it damaged his aircraft. Undaunted, he continued the attacks with such effect that he personally destroyed at least eight vehicles, gaining for himself the award of a US DFC. Three days later Capt John Davis was similarly awarded a US DFC following his attack on two enemy supply trains at Kimpo by his flight of four Mustangs during a severe snowstorm. Both trains were destroyed by rocket attack and as a result of this highly successful mission, vital equipment destined for the use of the enemy was destroyed. 2SAAF was now ordered to fall back again, this time to Chinhae (K-10) on the south coast, only 30 miles from K-9 from where it had originally started. Although Chinhae's short grass runway was surrounded by such hazards as hangars, a sea wall, and nearby mountains, the new base proved to be a "veritable heaven" after the cold and mud at P'yongyang and Suwon. At the same time, all SAAF personnel still remaining in Japan were flown over to K-10 with the result that the squadron was happily reassembled as a military entity. K-10 would become their home base for the next two years.

At K-9 on 19 December, after a series of incidents, the entire 35th FIG including 77RAAF, was grounded pending an investigation. Mustang engines had been cutting during take-off or were running roughly when airborne. One American pilot, Capt Ralph M. Olsen of the 39th FIS, was killed after ploughing off the end of the runway and crashing into the sea. Another, Capt Robert Shipley, also of the 39th FIS, crash-landed in a paddy field; then Flt Lt Ross Coburn's engine died while taking off before becoming airborne. He only managed to prevent meeting the same fate as the American pilot by braking hard and pulling up short. Sabotage was suspected. Fuel was taken from one of the crashed aircraft for analysis. It was found to contain a significant quantity of foreign material. Dirty petrol rather than sabotage was the probable cause of the accidents, but the latter possibility could not be totally discounted.

The 35th FIG recommenced operations on 22 December after the sabotage scare, but for the 8th FBG it was the end of the line for its Mustangs. The Group was withdrawn to re-equip with the F-80 having lost a pilot (1/Lt Robert R. Williams of the 36th FBS) on its last day of operations. On this date also, 77RAAF lost a pilot when P2 Don Ellis failed to return from a patrol east of P'yongyang. His leader, Flt Lt Gordon Harvey, heard him twice call over the R/T that he was going to crash. Harvey immediately pulled his aircraft round in a tight turn but was too late to see the impact although he could see the Mustang burning on the ground. He was unable to determine the cause although the Mustang (A68-726) had presumably been hit by ground fire.

Meanwhile, following their initial clash with MiGs, pilots of the 4th FIW worked out suitable tactics for the Sabres to combat the Russian jets. Initially flying at about Mach 0.62 in order to save fuel, the Sabre pilots found this put them at a disadvantage because they had to accelerate before clashing with the higher flying MiGs and therefore switched to cruising at Mach 0.85 or more. After a number of inconclusive combats – the 2nd Eskadrilya of the 177th FAR reported its first engagement on the 18th, while next day during the morning sortie Lt Colonel Glenn T. Eagleston, CO of 334th FIS, damaged the MiG flown by Lt Bondarenko of the 29th GuFAR – there occurred another clash on the morning of 21 December. In the ensuing action Kapt Ivan Yurkevich, also of the 29th GuFAR, reported shooting down an F-86 near Bihen – the first such victory claim for the MiGs, although none of the American fighters was apparently lost. Yurkevich's aircraft was then attacked and damaged by Lt Colonel Eagleston, who claimed the MiG as probably destroyed about 20 miles south-east of Sinuiju. After landing, the groundcrew counted 19 holes in Yurkevich's MiG.

It was to be a different story next morning (22 December), when eight MiGs of the 1st Eskadrilya of the 177th FAR led by Kapt Mikhailov bounced a flight of four Sabres. The MiG leader fired three short bursts at one, but without result, shortly before Kapt N.Ye Vorobyov (flying aircraft No04) shot down Capt Lawrence V. Bach, who baled out and was taken prisoner[31]. Kapt Mikhailov's wingman, St/Lt S.M. Akulenko, attacked another Sabre at which he fired four bursts, causing it to emit smoke before it escaped. Revenge was gained a little later when a MiG was claimed at low level some 20 miles south of the Yalu by a USN exchange pilot Lt Cdr Paul E. Pugh, who was flying with the 4th FIW. Later in the day, at 1540, the tables were really turned (according to the Americans) when another flight of eight Sabres clashed with an estimated 15 MiGs near Sinuiju and claimed no fewer than five shot down for no losses. Kills were claimed by Colonel Meyer and Lt Colonel Eagleston (both high-scoring WWII aces,

---

[31] In his book *Spy Flights of the Cold War*, Paul Lashmar writes: "The interrogation [dossier] of the first F-86 pilot to be captured in December 1950 was sent to Stalin . . ."

Meyer with 24 victories and Eagleston with 18½), Capts John M. Odiorne and James O. Roberts, with the fifth falling to 1/Lt Arthur L. O'Connor. Their opponents were actually eight MiGs of the 177th FAR's 2nd Eskadrilya led by Kapt Fomin (flying aircraft No20) who reported shooting down one of the F-86s; two others were claimed by Kapt V.K. Tishchenko and St/Lt P. Ryabov, although no Sabres were lost in this action. However, two MiGs were shot down including that (aircraft No41) flown by WWII veteran Kapt Sasnyk Barsegyan, who was killed. The pilot of the second MiG, St/Lt Alexandr Zub, managed to eject but left it too late and broke both legs on landing. A third MiG, flown by Lt Deinege, was also hit although the pilot managed to return safely. Elsewhere during this day of intensive action, Kapts F.F. Agureev and B. Meleshkin of the 177th FAR's 3rd Eskadrilya each claimed F-80s shot down.

Christmas Eve witnessed further engagements between MiGs and F-86s, pilots of the 1st Eskadrilya of the 177th FAR reporting an action with ten Sabres during which two were claimed by St/Lts D.K. Belikov and V.P. Kobtzev, while several of the MiGs returned with battle damage. Pilots of the 29th GuFAR were also in action, Kapt Stepan Naumenko claiming two F-86s for his fourth and fifth kills of the Korean War, thereby becoming its first ace in only seven combats and 21 operational sorties. According to Russian records, four MiGs led by Naumenko had engaged four F-86s near Sensen at about 0900, while two more MiGs led by St/Lt Orlov flew top cover. Naumenko reported shooting down the first Sabre from about 900 yards, the leader of the second pair. About 50 minutes later another four F-86s were encountered near Sinhoto and these attacked Orlov and his wingman but Naumenko claimed one of these also. Russian sources indicate that one F-86 crashed about 15 miles north-east of Sensen, and another near Tsio-to, and that both American pilots were killed.

There was no let up on Christmas Day either. Capt Homer Hansen of the 36th FBS was killed in action, while Capt Hendrik Odendaal of 2 SAAF won a US DFC for an action on this day when he led a flight of four Mustangs in bad weather conditions to attack an enemy-occupied village at Kwanch'on, which was left burning despite having to fly through a hail of intensive anti-aircraft fire. On another mission, Lt Ed Jones led four more SAAF Mustangs on a close-support mission against Chinese troops dug in along a ridge near P'yongyang. The attack was so successful that, besides being congratulated by the FAC, Jones had the satisfaction of hearing him give the ground commander clearance for an attack. The Squadron also ferreted out Communist troops sheltering in the villages, occasionally seeing them flee with their clothes on fire from napalmed houses. Flying from Chinhae, with the entire Squadron now operational, the sortie rate of 2SAAF quickly rose to average 16 per day, sometimes more. On 27 and 29 December, 20 and 23 sorties were flown respectively. Flights of four aircraft made armed reconnaissances along the main supply routes, seeking targets of opportunity. During an attack led by Cmdt Theron on 28 December against three enemy-occupied houses, Lt Elmer Wilson claimed around 40 soldiers killed by a single rocket attack. Because of staging through K-13, these missions were usually in the vicinity of two-and-a-half hours duration.

There occurred another serious incident involving Russian and American aircraft over Soviet territory on 26 December, when two MiGs from the 523rd FAR intercepted a USAF reconnaissance RB-29, apparently on an ELINT mission, in the vicinity of Cape Seiskora, this being shot down into the sea by Kapt Stepan Bakhaev[32] and St/Lt N. Kotov. There were no survivors.

The MiGs claimed further successes during the early afternoon of 27 December when 18 jets of the 177th FAR's 1st and 2nd Eskadrilyas were scrambled to engage USAF fighter-bombers and their escort. The task of Kapt Agureev's *zveno* was to attack the fighter-bombers while those led by Kapts Mikhailov and Fomin were to engage the covering high-flying Sabres. Mikhailov's eight MiGs climbed to 17,000 feet where they initially encountered four F-86s, then another two, the latter pair being attacked by Kapt Grechishko (flying aircraft No13) of the 1st Eskadrilya who fired two bursts at one, reporting that it escaped south trailing flames and smoke. Meanwhile, Kapt Fomin's *zveno* engaged several F-80s. Two were claimed by Fomin (aircraft No2) and his wingman Kapt Tishchenko. A third was engaged by Kapt

---

[32] Kapt Stepan Bakhaev was later credited with 11 victories during the Korean War.

Kormilkin and his wingman Kapt M.G. Andryushin, who both fired at it before Kormilkin shot it down into the sea; at least one F-80 was lost in which 2/Lt Harrison C. Jacobs was reported to have been killed when his aircraft crashed near Kuwaksan. Elsewhere, a number of Yaks chased a B-26 but it was able to escape. Next day it was the turn of the 29th GuFAR's 3rd Eskadrilya to engage US fighter-bombers, two F-84s being claimed shot down south of Sensen in which both American pilots were reported to have been killed. The Chinese 10th FAR with its MiGs under the command of Lt Colonel Wang Hai[33] had by now arrived at Antung to join the two Russian air regiments on the 50th Fighter Air Division, and flew its first operation on 29 December in conjunction with the 29th GuFAR. Twelve MiGs took off to intercept F-80s near Sinanju, St/Lt Orlov and his wingman St/Lt Volodkin sighting two of the fighter-bombers through gaps in the clouds, each claiming one shot down, but the Chinese flight led by Capt Li Han failed to engage. At least one F-80 was lost, the 8th FBS reporting 1/Lt James G. Clayberg missing, while 1/Lt Bernard Wilkins of the 80th FBS was killed while attempting to carry out an emergency landing at Itazuke, possibly as the result of combat damage.

As UN forces were routed from North Korea in December, NKAF Po-2s followed them south, nipping at their heels with nightly raids, taking advantage of the predominant bad weather to harass the airfields at Suwon and Kimpo. Even so, there was little co-operation between MiG operations and those of the NKAF. The MiGs intercepted UN aircraft or ignored them at will. NKAF daylight operations consisted usually of either Yak-9s or Il-10s, in flights of four or less, but they too appeared to be operating independently of each other. These NKAF day missions were practically inactive by the end of the year, although on 27 December unidentified NKAF aircraft chased after a B-26, while a B-29 crew spotted what were believed to be several Yak-9s over Cheju-do Island, but they did not attack. The latter, however, were probably ROKAF F-51s on a training flight.

On 30 December the MiGs were reported to be up in force. An estimated 36 (*sic*) of the Russian jets crossed the Yalu during the early morning and engaged sixteen F-86s, but they quickly broke off the action and headed for home, their pilots exercising extreme caution but not before a probable was claimed by future ace Capt James Jabara of the 334th FIS. In fact, four MiGs of the 29th GuFAR's 1st Eskadrilya led by Kapt Naumenko had scrambled on the approach of American aircraft, followed by a further 14 led by Maj Keleinikov. Naumenko's *zveno* engaged a pair of F-86s but another pair manoeuvred onto his tail, inflicting some damage to his aircraft, and he was saved only by the quick reaction of his wingman, St/Lt S.M. Lyubimov, who fired at both Sabres. One of the American jets was reported to have caught fire before it crashed about 25 miles north of Sensen. Naumenko was able to land safely at Antung where at least a dozen holes in his aircraft were discovered. The Americans claimed one MiG shot down by their USN exchange pilot Lt Cdr Paul Pugh (his second victory), and a damaged by 1/Lt Richard S. Becker, also a future ace – achieved for no losses.

Although the 4th FIW had claimed the destruction of eight MiGs, plus two more probably destroyed and seven damaged, for the loss of one of its own during the course of 234 sorties during the month, these early encounters left the Sabre pilots convinced that the two fighter types were more or less evenly matched. The advantages enjoyed by one over the other in various aspects almost cancelled out. A telling factor was the comparative skill of the pilots and in this the Americans considered they were overwhelmingly superior. Nonetheless, the MiG pilots had claimed 64 victories by the end of the year including twelve F-86s, and were more than a match for the straight-wing F-84s and F-80s. The 64th Fighter Air Corps admitted the loss of at least nine MiGs and eight pilots during the course of these actions.

While jet fought jet over the Yalu, the Mustangs had continued their less glamorous routine of armed reconnaissances during the month. Early on the 31st, a flight of 2SAAF Mustangs was carrying out a strike on P'ongyang-ni when two unidentified aircraft were spotted approaching, but these turned out to be a pair of 77RAAF Mustangs flown by Flt Lt Ralph Dawson and P3 Sly on an armed recce. As the South Africans completed their attack, the Australians added to

---

[33] Lt Colonel Wang Hai allegedly emerged as the top-scoring Chinese pilot of the Korean War with nine victories.

the carnage by rocketing and strafing several buildings. Sqn Ldr Cresswell later led a strike against villages and targets of opportunity on the road south-east of Kaesong. There was little enemy reaction. Everything seemed unusually quiet.

During the month the 35th FIG reported the loss of one HQ pilot in action (Maj Kenneth S. Hodges), and two 40th FIS pilots shot down by ground fire, Maj Neil Johnson and 1/Lt Olin W. Johnson. In addition, an aircraft of the 39th FIS suffered engine failure shortly after take-off. The pilot baled out and the aircraft crashed into a nearby POW compound, 42 prisoners being killed in the subsequent explosion. The 18th FBG again fared relatively lightly, losing only four aircraft and one pilot (1/Lt Harold J. Ausman of the 67th FBS) although one injured pilot was rescued from enemy territory by helicopter. The USMC unit operating from K-9 also suffered a series of accidents during the month, the most serious occurring when a damaged Corsair attempted an emergency landing while still carrying two 1,000-lb bombs. As it touched down, the bombs tore free and hurtled down the runway; one exploded and inflicted damage to another Corsair and three C-46s. Fortunately, there were no casualties as a result. As the year rapidly drew to its close, a new Mustang unit arrived at Taegu, the 45th Tactical Recon Squadron equipped with RF-51Ds.

Wg Cdr Johnnie Johnson had by now finished his tour with the FEAF, and was able to reflect:

"During the winter of 1950 [between October and December] I was based at Taegu and flew B-26 reconnaissance missions and F-80 fighter-bomber missions, including napalm attacks – not more than a dozen in all. We preferred to fly jets, since having fewer working parts than, say, the F-51 Mustang, they could withstand more flak damage and, not having a propeller, they gave pilots a better view forwards and downwards; also, the cockpit of an F-80 was far quieter than that of an F-51, which made the jets less fatiguing to fly.

There being no air opposition *[sic]*, I flew the reconnaissance version of the sturdy, twin-engined B-26 and took some day and night photographs of enemy concentrations. It seemed odd to fly over those inhospitable hills, over land stripped of all softness, as far north as the Yalu River, and not to see another aeroplane once we had left the vicinity of the ground fighting. I took full advantage of the strange state of affairs and, apart from getting the feel of things, the B-26's long endurance helped me watch the lively fighter-bombers at work.

On my reconnaissance and fighter-bomber missions I never saw a MiG, but in the evenings, when the days work was over and we had showered, changed and supped well, the veterans got together and talked about the MiGs. What bothered us most was not their high performance, but the people who flew them. Who were these chaps? They flew and fought too well to be North Koreans. So they had to be Chinese or Russians. And even if they were Russians they had come a long, long way in the last five years. For in their use of the sun, their finger-four pattern and their line-astern defensive manoeuvres they were strangely reminiscent of the Luftwaffe.

In Korea, unlike previous wars, colonels in their twenties were no longer the vogue. Complicated weapons systems such as the Sabre were best flown by experienced flyers, and experienced flyers were best led by veterans of the Second World War, many of whom added to their tally of German and Japanese victories. Grey-haired, well decorated and often the fathers of many children – one resolute colonel had eight – they were impressive not for their youth but for their age. They were dedicated men; their motto – 'Not the boldest, but the oldest.'" [34]

On a critical level, he added:

"There was a lack of co-operation between the Air Force and the Army at all levels. US Air Force morale was very high, and they thought they were doing a vital job. But there were not many Army officers present at briefings. In the first months, forward air control seemed very limited. Though we called ourselves the UN, there were so few of us [RAF, RAAF and SAAF] I felt very much an observer of an American show." [35]

[34/35] See *Full Circle* by Air Vice-Marshal J.E. Johnson CBE DSO DFC. He received the US Air Medal and Legion of Merit for his services to the USAF in Korea.

Sqn Ldr Joe Bodien was also now coming to the end of his attachment to the 3rd BG, for which he would receive the customary US Air Medal; the citation stated: ". . . In sustained operations against Communist forces, flights were made regardless of the time of day, weather conditions or enemy opposition encountered . . ." Having started off flying with the 8th BS, he finished his tour with the 13th BS, with one short break to recover from frost bite in his left foot from wearing suede shoes rather than regulation heated boots when flying. The FEAF now requested another experienced officer from the RAF to succeed Sqn Ldr Bodien as advisor to the 3rd BG, Sqn Ldr J.F. Sach DFC AFC (see Appendix III) being posted in from FEAF HQ where he had been attached to the Directorate of Operations; his work at FEAF HQ was recognised by the award of the Bronze Star, the citation noting that he had "laboured untiringly and unceasingly to ensure mutual exchange of information pertaining to aerial tactics and techniques . . ." He was now to take on the mantle of RAF advisor to the rapidly-learning American B-26 intruder crews.

US Intelligence estimated that its aircraft had been responsible for killing and wounding around 40,000 of the enemy during the preceding six months, but hinted that something big was now brewing. The Chinese, out of necessity, had developed great skills in camouflage, but the UN pilots could see signs indicating a major build-up of enemy forces near the 38th Parallel. Early on New Year's Eve there was an uneasy calm. Low-hanging clouds and snow showers hampered air strikes all day. At the Imjin, as night advanced, the Chinese Fourth Field Army began an unbroken barrage of mortar fire. At daybreak next morning the Communists launched a nine-division-strong main thrust southwards across the Imjin against Seoul.

CHAPTER IV

THE AUSTRALIANS GET THE METEOR

January – February 1951

"The Meteor is regarded as the most modern type of jet fighter now available and will give
a striking power, speed and manoeuvrability of a kind to add enormously to our air strength."
Australian Premier Robert Menzies

On New Year's Eve 1950-51, showers of snow and low-level cloud banks along the front lines frustrated UN air strikes. Under the cover of these, the Communists launched their main thrust southwards across the Imjin. Heralded by bugles and shrill whistles, Chinese troops swarmed forward in open V formation; the arms of the V were meant to quickly isolate, surround and swamp their objectives. As the battle developed it became clear that the enemy's offensive was aimed at seizing Seoul and the railway centre at Wonju.

The man confronted with this perilous situation was the 8th US Army's new commanding officer, Lt General Matthew B. Ridgway, formerly the US Army's Deputy Chief-of-Staff for Operations in Washington. On his arrival in Tokyo on Christmas Day, General Ridgway had been advised of the death, two days earlier, of General Walton Walker, whose jeep had collided with a ROK weapons carrier north of Seoul while on the way to visit the Commonwealth 27th Brigade. Thrown in at the deep end, Ridgway was given the daunting task of stopping the Chinese and, after a whirlwind inspection, he found that his Army numbered some 365,000 men consisting of mainly US and ROK troops, plentifully supplied and well-equipped but, in terms of morale after the December setbacks, there was an air of gloom and uncertainty as to what would happen next. Encouragingly, there were reliable small contingents from Belgium, France, Greece and the Philippines; and more national contingents of ground troops were on their way. The UN force was deployed in a line running from a point north of Inch'on on the west coast of Yangyang on the east, with I Corps (the US 24th and 3rd Divisions, the ROK 1st Division, the Turkish Brigade and the British 29th Brigade) holding the UN left, west of the Seoul corridor; IX Corps (US 1st Cavalry and 25th Divisions, the ROK 6th Division, the Commonwealth 27th Brigade, the Greek and Philippine Battalions) in the centre; and the ROK I and III Corps on the right. The 1st Marine Division was in immediate reserve and X Corps was re-fitting further south around Pusan. General Ridgway knew that because of their vast manpower resources and comparative lack of industry compared with the West, the Chinese would naturally place their heaviest reliance on the use of infantry. Although he barely had time to assess the situation first hand, he concluded that holding ground was far less important than bleeding the enemy dry. To do this he devised his obscene-sounding 'Meatgrinder' method of fighting, directing that every possible source of mechanised firepower – aircraft, artillery and tanks – was to be devoted entirely to the job of killing Chinese soldiers.

Among the ranks of the British 29th Brigade were two qualified Air OP pilots, Capt R.M. Begbie who was a troop commander in 11 Light AA Battery, and Capt G. Sipthorne who was in the Brigade's C Squadron 7 Royal Tank Regiment, both on non-flying duties. Bob Begbie recalled:

"During this time I saw much of 45 Field Regiment and in particular their OP parties. The terrain was very mountainous and with considerable tree cover – an OP officer's nightmare, as no matter how high he toiled up hills to a point of vantage, the enemy was always behind the next crest. The enemy could also manoeuvre and form up with relative impunity in the many valleys out of sight. But if it was a ground OP officer's nightmare, it was an Air OP officer's paradise – especially in the early stages when the Chinese did not use AA or even small-arms fire, and reacted to air activity by passive measures. If ever there was a combat area where Air OP was so obviously necessary or where the principle of Air OP could be proved or vindicated, it was Korea; and why 29th Brigade – or 27th Brigade, who were first in the country – were not immediately provided with Air OP support, I will never know. Anyway, Colonel Maris Young [OC 45 Field Regt] and I discussed the problem many times, and he proposed that he should contact the Americans – we operated under 1st US Corps – and ask if I, as a trained artillery air observer, could be allowed to carry out some AOP shoots with 45 Field Regt. To my delight the Americans agreed and with reluctant permission from my Battery Commander, I was off like a shot to the US 3rd Light Aviation Section nominated to take me on. Another officer in the Brigade, Capt Geoff Sipthorne, who had some experience flying L-5s in India, was also sent to fly with the 3rd LAS, but after a short attachment he was recalled to rejoin his tank squadron.

Things went fairly well to begin with although most of my work was in support of the Americans. The problem I found was the American way of providing Air OP which, at that time, required a pilot (he could be from any arm) to fly the aircraft while an artillery observer (not a pilot) carried out the shoot. In Korea this worked reasonably well as we operated in conditions of air superiority and the pilot, with negative danger from AA or fighters, could fly straight and level allowing the observer a clear view of the target. But I didn't like being a passenger (we used L-5s) and I never felt really in control of the situation. The main snag however was pilot exhaustion. The American pilots flew all the daylight hours in support of their own troops (or so it seemed), and began to object to the extra chore of flying me around to provide Air OP cover for the British, when they should have been resting. However, one day the Flight Commander asked if I was a current aviator, whatever that meant. I said of course I was, and he replied: 'Well, godammit Begbie, I don't see why we should have to haul your ass round the sky when you could do it yourself!' So, scarcely believing my luck, I was promptly sent off to Japan for 'Flight Physical' at the USAF base in Tokyo. But, while waiting in Korea for my orders to be 'cut', as the Americans say, I was subjected to the swiftest conversion to a strange aircraft type I have ever experienced – and on a small operational strip, too. It consisted of a tired check pilot whipping me off in an L-5, talking to me through two or three circuits and bumps, saying all the time: 'OK! OK! No sweat, Bob, OK! OK! No sweat! No sweat!' After which he got out and disappeared – I didn't see him again until that evening and I can't remember whether or not he ever told me anything more about the aircraft. The same casual approach was the norm to all the later US aircraft to which I converted!

So I lived and operated as an 'American' pilot until the end of my tour in Korea. I dressed like an American – they had better kit, and anyway it stifled questions when I flew the US brass or performed their missions, and my accent must have been convincing. As a concession, when flying British or Commonwealth missions I usually wore my Gunner brevet."

Monday 1 January 1951 – New Year's Day – dawned bitterly cold though bright and clear. Chinese hopes that the poor weather would continue to cover their movements were thereby dashed when it became obvious as daylight approached that conditions had changed completely. This would be the first of five consecutive days of clear flying weather. Fighter-bombers of the 5th Air Force came out in force, its pilots briefed to ruthlessly pound Chinese troops trekking southwards towards Seoul along the highways from Kaesong and Yonch'on – but first they had to be found. Wary of air attack and becoming expert at camouflage, seldom did they show themselves by day, preferring to make full use of the cover of darkness, but they could not hide everything. There remained abundant evidence of their presence in the form of tell-tale foot marks and wheel tracks in the snow. Guided by these, the FACs directed the fighter-bombers in the onerous task of burning villages reported to be housing troops and supplies, as well as destroying trucks and pack animals along the roads and harassing communications by smashing bridges. Bombing villages was not liked and not an intended part of the UN war plan but where they were obviously sheltering enemy troops and war supplies, there was no other option.

At 0630 orders came for the Commonwealth 27th Brigade to move six miles north to help cover the main escape routes from the north. The Australians went further forward to Chokch'ong, six miles north of Uijongbu, and encountered the most trouble. By nightfall on New Year's Day they were cut off. While pulling back down the road towards their own lines their vehicles encountered several road blocks. Lt Colonel Ferguson, who had been attending a conference with Brigadier Coad and was cut off three miles south of his isolated companies, conducted the breakthrough operation over a field radio. Passing a road block, the Australians ran into fire from either side of the road. Machine-gun fire burst a tyre of the Support Company commander's jeep and it toppled into a roadside ditch, wounding one man. The battalion coming behind dismounted from their transports and cleared the flanks, killing seven of the enemy and capturing a light machine-gun. Four Australians were wounded. Next day the Brigade reassembled in Seoul.

During the first two days of January the fighter-bomber flights reported to the Tactical Air Control Centre at ten-minute intervals, and 60% of their missions were successful strikes against close-support targets. Virtually every flight sighted and attacked concentrations of Chinese troops, or buildings that were reported to be giving them shelter. 564 sorties were flown by the end of the first day and this was followed up with 531 more next day, 2 January, a date which witnessed the loss of the 27th Fighter-Escort Group's first pilot in action when Capt Charles E. McWhirk of the 522nd FES failed to return from a sortie. This day also marked 77RAAF's first six months of continuous active involvement in the war. The operations flown that day were typical, with Sqn Ldr Cresswell leading P2 Bill Michelson, and P3s Ron Mitchell and Kevin Foster off on a close-support mission. Just after take-off, the CO's Mustang became unserviceable and he had to abort after calling P3 Hunt in the reserve aircraft to take his place. On arrival at the front line Michelson contacted the FAC, who was acting for the ROK 6th Division, and was directed to attack a village east of Yonduch'on-ni in which enemy troops were reported, which they did. Later, Flt Lt Des Murphy and P3 Roy Brackenreg on an armed recce napalmed a large brick building, around which the tracks of many vehicles could be seen in the snow, and followed this up with a rocket attack on another building in a village near Chorwon, which showed similar signs of military inhabitation. On another sortie P1 Geoff Thornton and P3 Cec Sly, after destroying a camouflaged vehicle south of Hwach'on-ni, damaged a bridge with rockets and strafed personnel seen wearing dark clothing as they ran away. Elsewhere, P3s Ray Trebilco and Ron Howe, on an armed recce from Kaesong to Tongch'on-ni, strafed and set alight camouflaged objects in a village, and then added to the carnage in a village near Taejin-ni that had already been attacked, while Flg Off Les Reading and P3 Keith Meggs followed vehicle tracks leading to a village near Chorwon, which they proceeded to destroy with napalm. They then continued their reconnaissance by following the railway line towards P'yonggang until they found troops hiding under carts on the outskirts of the town. These were strafed. Of these relentless attacks, P3 Milt Cottee commented:

> "Camouflage was not used initially so trucks and tanks were easy to find. Later, enemy losses became so high that movement stopped during daylight hours with trucks and tanks hidden off roads under trees. Tanks would be driven through the sides of houses for cover. Most of these however were easy to find as no attempts were made to cover the tell-tale tracks. Tank tracks ending in a house meant only one thing, and the task of destroying the tank made easy by burning the house. The incendiary rounds in our ammunition simplified the task. Later, camouflage improved and even extended to camouflaging nothing to look like something. But the amateurish approach to this often astounded us. I saw tanks and trucks looking like haystacks on roads. [Once] I saw a gunboat near Wonsan harbour at anchor covered by branches of trees." [1]

---

[1] See *Aviation Heritage* Vol.31 No.1.

On the night of 2/3 January, B-26 night intruders of the 3rd BG were again active despite the difficulties of finding targets. In an effort to alleviate the problem Colonel Reginald J. Clizbe, the 3rd BG's Executive Officer, borrowed a number of high-intensity flares from the US Navy and loaded them aboard a C-47, thereafter launching them over the target area north of Seoul during the course of the next five hours. Each flare would detonate at about 5,500 feet and float down, providing four or five minutes of near daylight illumination. The patrolling B-26 crews were then able to see almost everything that was moving behind the enemy's lines and consequently destroyed or damaged an estimated 30 vehicles that night. Not only did this inhibit the enemy's movements to about a quarter of a normal night's travel, but UN troops noticed that the Chinese were disinclined to attack while the front lines were thus illuminated. The use of the C-47 in this rôle was repeated and became affectionally and quaintly known to US troops as 'The Old Lamplighter of the Korean Hills', and to the B-26 crews as the 'Lightning Bug'.

As well as trying to camouflage their movements by day, the Chinese intensified their reaction to air attack with increased use of light anti-aircraft guns and small-arms fire. While leading an armed reconnaissance well behind Communist lines from Suwon, Lt Deans of 2SAAF found his attention drawn to a large building near Kujo on the east coast. The words 'YMCA Korean Police – Please help' were seen painted on the roof. He made a low pass to investigate further but could see nothing else out of the ordinary. Nor did he notice any ground fire, but it was learned sometime afterwards that the building had actually been set up as a flak trap.

By the third day of the New Year the Chinese 4th Field Army had suffered dreadful losses from 5th Air Force fighter-bomber attacks and 8th US Army ground fire, but it still had sufficient numbers to rout US ground forces defending Seoul. In co-ordination with ROK retirements in central Korea, the American I and IX Corps fell back to the bridgehead defences around Seoul. Almost at once the enemy began crossing the ice-covered Han to the east and west. Instead of inviting destruction, General Ridgway ordered the 8th Army southwards, back to the next defensive line. UN vehicle columns and refugees began to jam the roads as the Americans retreated. The Commonwealth 27th Brigade acted as part of the rearguard for the withdrawal.

The Mustangs of 77RAAF were also in action during the day, Flt Lt Ian Olorenshaw (A68-801) leading a section of four on an armed recce just north of Seoul, where they observed F-80s making high-speed dives at a burning village. A thick haze of smoke covered the whole area. The FAC was unable to offer the Australians a clear target, who were then directed to one some 16 miles north of the capital. It proved to be a bivouac area concealed in a dried-up watercourse covered by sheets of white canvas. Olorenshaw gave the order to attack and the Mustangs made a series of rocket and strafing runs. Many of the Chinese troops clearly panicked, rushing out as the Mustangs struck, and as he made a run, Olorenshaw could see many others hiding under the canvas. During one low-level strafing run P3 Kevin Foster's Mustang (A68-799) hit a tree, causing minor damage to the port mainplane. On completion of the attack, the quartet was ordered to strafe a village further north before returning to Pusan. Another section comprising Flt Lt Fred Barnes and P3 Dick Bessell operated between Kaesong and Pongyang-ni, where they strafed and set alight a camouflaged object and napalmed a gun-towing tracked vehicle about two miles south-west of Ch'uch'on-ni. After strafing other targets without any obvious results, at the village of Wang Po-dong they destroyed a building which, afterwards, emitted thick clouds of yellow smoke. As they approached Pusan on the way home, Bessell's aircraft (A68-791) developed engine trouble and, as he tried to make a force-landing, it crashed to the side of the runway. Fortunately, the pilot suffered only minor injuries but the Mustang was extensively damaged and had to be written off.

Meanwhile, the efforts of the FEAF Bomber Command were directed to attacks against supplies and enemy personnel in the North Korean capital, P'yongyang. Sixty-three B-29s showered incendiary bombs over the city on 3 January. This was followed up by another raid by 60 of the heavy bombers two days later. Even though P'yongyang radio reported bitterly that the entire city burned like a furnace for two whole days, reconnaissance showed that snow on the rooftops helped to curb the spread of the conflagration and only an estimated 35% of the city's built-up area was destroyed. The 5th Air Force flew 556 sorties on 3 January, and a further 498 next day, the day on which Seoul fell to the Communists for a second time. With the 8th Army beginning to break contact with the enemy, the pattern of air attacks was changing. Unlike the first two days when most were strikes against close-support targets, the majority now were armed reconnaissance strikes north of the bomb line.

As UN forces retreated to take up pre-arranged defensive positions from P'yongtack, through Wonju to the east coast, the Commonwealth 27th Brigade withdrew 100 miles to Yoda-ni. In the sector held by the British 29th Brigade, three of the four rifle companies of 1/Royal Northumberland Fusiliers were almost cut off. They resisted stubbornly and though they were not in immediate danger of being swamped, they were trapped and needed to be extracted fairly quickly. The only access to them was by a narrow, ice-covered track which passed through a difficult defile. Together with a company of Fusiliers, 7/Royal Tank Regiment mounted a successful counter-attack with their Churchill 'Flaming Crocodile' tanks. The Churchills were well-armoured and manoeuvrable, and well suited for the difficult Korean terrain despite their age. Two companies were relieved quickly and the third was able to break out before nightfall. Chinese casualties were estimated at around 150.

To the south, 8th Army troops had established defensive positions long enough to allow the removal of the huge stocks of supplies stored at Suwon. During this operation, on 4 January, a C-47 (No617) of the 13th Greek Transport Flight was severely damaged due to the soft and muddy ground of the airstrip while trying to land. The aircraft was later destroyed to prevent it falling into enemy hands. 77RAAF continued small-scale operations and next day (5 January), flights of Mustangs succeeded in making devastating attacks with napalm, rockets and machine-gun fire on villages just south of Seoul. As they swept in low, narrowly avoiding high-tension cables which dotted the area, the flight led by Flt Lt Des Murphy saw Chinese soldiers in quilted uniforms running from burning buildings. Mustangs of 2SAAF were also involved in flying sorties from the advanced airfield at Suwon, and at the end of the day withdrew to the 18th FBG's main base at Chinhae. Then Suwon's buildings were put to the torch. After having flown a further 447 sorties by the close of the day, the 5th Air Force estimated that it had killed nearly 8,000 enemy soldiers and had destroyed or damaged some 6,400 enemy-occupied buildings since the beginning of the offensive on New Year's Eve, though each day the 8th Army estimated the number of air-inflicted casualties to be approximately double those figures claimed by the aircrews. On taking off from K-9 during a morning mission, Capt William Hook of the 40th FIS was killed when he attempted to bale out at low altitude after his engine had seized. Before joining the 40th FIS, Hook had flown with the ROKAF.

Next morning (6 January), P3s Ray Trebilco and Geoff Stephens took off on an armed recce even though the weather was not promising. As the two aircraft approached Munsan, Trebilco happened to glance over his shoulder and noticed a flash on the ground. Receiving no response from his companion over the radio, he turned back and saw the tail of Stephens' Mustang (A68-765) protruding from the burning wreckage close to three houses near Munsan. He circled the spot five times but could see no sign of life, so returned to base. The cause of the crash remained a mystery as there had been no known enemy activity in that area. Stephens, who was flying his 75th operational sortie, had the night before volunteered for a second tour in Korea. His commission came through shortly thereafter, together with the announcement of the award of both the US DFC and Air Medal; the citation for the former read:

> "He performed an act of exceptional achievement while flying over enemy territory in Korea on 20 November 1950. Through adverse weather and extremely rugged terrain he made repeated devastating passes and personally destroyed three anti-aircraft positions and two supply trucks."

That afternoon a storm front moving southwards from Siberia began to work in favour of the Communist advance. Heavy snowstorms and low visibility gave them valuable cover and inhibited further 5th Air Force operations.

Despite the successes being achieved by the 5th Air Force's fighter-bombers, General Stratemeyer had been forced to withdraw the 4th Fighter Wing detachment from Kimpo to the safety of Johnson AFB in Japan, because of the materialising reality that Kimpo would soon be overrun. Of this period the 334th FIS's Canadian pilot, Flt Lt Omer Lévesque, who had by now completed 14 operational sorties including escort missions for B-29s bombing just below the Yalu, recalled:

> ". . . a few MiGs were seen and attacked but I was not lucky; most aircraft flew from Antung and flew in and out south of the Yalu and quickly returned across and we were told explicitly not to follow them. I flew several sorties until 2 January. By then the Chinese Army had surrounded our airfield and the weather became snowy and icy during the night. All F-80s and Sabres were grounded, and all were attached with demolition charges. Fortunately the Allies, including British troops, Turks and other UN ground forces, saved us. However, the next day at noon the sun came out and melted the ice off our aircraft. We all made it back to Johnson AFB in Japan the same day."

On his return to Japan, Lévesque was interviewed by William Stevenson of the *Toronto Daily Star*:

> "The Russian MiGs used to climb up from Antung, just inside the Manchurian border. I could see them kicking up dust as they took off and then watch them climb on their side of the border until they got enough height to attack. They're fast all right but as soon as ever you'd get near enough to shoot they would hightail it over the border again. My biggest concern was to keep out of Chinese hands [understandable, since he had been a POW of the Germans for three-and-a-half years during WWII]. A crash anywhere south of P'yongyang meant you could get picked up by one of the rescue planes. North of there it was better to drop into the mudflats along the coast. If those Chinese ever discovered you were a Sabre pilot they'd have you up before Joe Stalin before you could rattle off your ditching drill.
>
> Upper temperatures get down to 55 below near the Manchurian border, it's so darn cold that if you bale out the sensible thing is to make a free drop for several thousand feet before pulling the rip cord or you'll freeze to death. But at Kimpo it was good and warm – compared to Canada. I soon found that the Canadian winter flying suit was a good deal less cumbersome than the equipment Uncle Sam gave me, but I'm still waiting for my stuff to reach me."

Following the departure of the Sabres from Kimpo, aviation engineers torched the remaining stocks of fuel and napalm, and also set fire to the airfield's buildings to deny their use to the enemy. Unfortunately, the withdrawal to Johnson AFB put the F-86s out of the effective range of the air fighting over Korea, and not unnaturally raised fears that with the F-86s away the MiGs would be able to play havoc with the slower UN jets and piston-engined fighter-bombers. Although the MiGs flew 46 sorties during the first three days of the month, little contact was made with UN aircraft since the action was too far south for them to become involved although the 177th FAR claimed a success on 3 January. Kapt Andryushin of the 2nd Eskadrilya, who was also the Regiment's Navigation Officer, reported shooting down an F-80; three days later Kapt Akulenko of the 1st Eskadrilya claimed an F-84. In addition, a few North Korean airmen did take to the air during this period, carrying out small-scale night attacks in light aircraft over the central front against ROK troops at Yongwol and Kyongpo. Although FEAF intelligence officers predicted that a major and sustained Communist air effort might erupt at any time, General Liu Ya-Lou, Commander-in-Chief of the Chinese Communist Air Force, had his own problems to overcome, not the least of which was the fact that his pilots needed much more experience with their new jet aircraft before they could hope to mount a serious air offensive in Korea. Furthermore, the relatively short-range MiG-15 was designed as a defensive fighter and was considered unsuitable for attacking tactical targets more than 100 miles from its home base. Added to this, Peking was unwilling to allow General Liu to use his air bases in Manchuria for mounting attacks against UN personnel and installations across the border in Korea because of possible American air retaliation against China herself.

Faced with such limitations, General Liu drafted a blueprint for conducting an air war, first to counteract UN air supremacy, and then to support a Chinese offensive on the ground. There were several stages which had to be achieved before such an air offensive could be attempted against the UN with any hope of success. By allowing the Russian MiG regiments to use his bases at Antung, the first step had to be to achieve an area of air supremacy over north-west Korea. This phase would also allow the Chinese MiG pilots of the 10th FAR the opportunity to gain combat experience. Next, having established a working local air supremacy, new airfields could be constructed within the defended area and existing ones repaired. At the same time a programme to build and repair as many other airfields immediately north of the 38th Parallel as possible would be implemented in secret. For protection, automatic weapons and anti-aircraft batteries would be moved in as the work progressed. When the airfields reached the stage of being operational MiG fighters and ground-attack aircraft could be flown in ready to start a full-scale offensive. That was the theory, the intention. But time was needed to implement these measures and in January 1951, to the chagrin of the Chinese ground commanders, particularly General Lin Piao, General Liu was not ready. Liu's plan was targeted to support offensives scheduled for the forthcoming spring so, not only did the Russian/Chinese Air Force fail to support the current thrust, the MiG squadrons were in the main stood down during the first week of the month.

Seizing an opportunity of a break in the weather on 8 January, 5th Air Force F-80s, F-84s and F-51s gave the US X Corps about 50 close-support sorties before the weather closed in again. By 10 January most 5th Air Force units were obliged to stand down from operations, although MiGs were active over North Korea when an estimated 15 of the jets attacked a lone RB-29 over Sinanju. However, when the gunners opened fire the MiGs apparently quickly departed but the fact of their appearance was an ominous indication of what could lay ahead. A second RB-29 of the 31st Recon Squadron did not escape the attentions of the 177th FAR's 1st Eskadrilya, however, the reconnaissance machine being shot down with the loss of six of the crew; five others baled out and were captured by Chinese troops. Ten MiGs led by Maj Mikhailov had been scrambled at 1135 on the approach of the American aircraft. Climbing to 12,000 feet, Maj Vorobyov was the first to sight it in the distance, some 1,500 feet below. The MiGs jettisoned their auxiliary fuel tanks and made a left turn in pursuit. Mikhailov ordered Maj Greschishko's *zveno* to provide cover as he and his wingman Kapt Akulenko went into the attack from astern, opening fire from 1,000 yards, each firing three or four bursts. They were followed by two other pairs led respectively by Majs Vorobyov and Zakhartsev. The reconnaissance aircraft tried to hide in cloud but was repeatedly attacked. With its port wing engulfed in flames, it was last seen entering clouds, but was later reported to have crashed nine miles north-west of Anju. Although most of the Russian pilots fired at the intruder, the victory was credited to Maj Mikhailov.

Next day (11 January), 77RAAF lost an aircraft but fortunately not its pilot. P3 Roy Brackenreg was testing Mustang A68-754 near K-9 when his engine cut out completely at 900 feet. Still some distance from the airfield, he had little choice but to try and crash-land on the waters of Pusan harbour. His chances were far from good. Mustangs were very hazardous to ditch because their large air scoop made them prone to sinking almost immediately – and the water in January was icy and he would not be able to survive in it for long:

> "I jettisoned my canopy when the engine cut and decided to land on the sea in deep water. I knew it was risky, and that the Mustang would sink immediately, but I had no alternative. Although I thought I might not make it, I wasn't going to give up hope by any means. I stared glumly out in front, and felt brassed off to be going like this – it was not even an operational flight. As I got down towards the water I concentrated on flying, and the aircraft splurged on from about three feet. It was going about 80 knots at the time, but the water pulled it up and the nose went down immediately. Water poured in all over me, but this didn't worry me at all. In fact, I had an intense feeling of relief at that moment because I knew I was not hurt. I let the safety harness go, and kicked up out of the cockpit from seven feet under the water and came to the surface."

Brackenreg's luck was doubly in. South African-born Cpl Johannes van Breda from Cape Province and now serving in the US Army was the temporary skipper of a tugboat which was, by chance, only half a mile away from the ditching. He had seen the aircraft ditch and, guided by other RAAF and USAF Mustangs circling and diving overhead, reached the floating Australian pilot in less than three minutes. Brackenreg was suffering from cold and a cut over one eye but was otherwise safe and sound. When the tugboat docked they found Sqn Ldr Cresswell waiting with a jeep to take his pilot back to K-9 and a couple of shots of brandy.

Meanwhile, Flt Lt Coburn's Mustang flight carried out an armed recce checking out the airfields at Hamhung, Yonpo, Sondok and Wonsan but saw nothing, not even any footprints. After attacking a variety of other targets of opportunity and reaching Ch'angjon, the flight set course for home. Just then two unidentified aircraft were sighted east of Wonsan and Coburn ordered a turnabout and detached two Mustangs to investigate. Whoever they were, they did not stay long when they saw the Mustangs approach and drew away using superior speed. Coburn reported later:

> "They were single-engined conventional types, faster than a Mustang and one emitted a streak of black smoke as it accelerated."

Far to the south an F-86 detachment of the 4th FIW returned to Korea to begin flying air-to-ground missions from Taegu. This was the first attempt to use the Sabre as a fighter-bomber, a task for which it had not been designed, and it was limited by its short range and lack of load-carrying ability. Nonetheless, over 150 missions were flown in a short period of time. Another 'first' was achieved during the day when, at General Ridgway's request, ten B-29s of the 98th BG flew a saturation raid against Wonju. The bombs carried were the new proximity-fused 500-lb general-purpose type, designed to burst in the air showering thousands of steel fragments over the target area.

By 15 January General Ridgway was ready to stand and fight. His forces were deployed along a curving line that stretched across the Korean peninsula, with the 8th Army in the west, X Corps in the middle, and ROK troops in the mountainous terrain along the east coast. He ordered a reconnaissance in force, codenamed Operation 'Wolfhound', in which an American regiment re-established contact with the Chinese near Osan. The bulk of the enemy forces, however, were actually farther east, grouped against X Corps, which lost the town of Wonju in bloody fighting next day. Aside from this, a gap had developed between the opposing forces along most of the line as the Chinese withdrew to better tactical positions. An AT-6 of the 6147th TAC Squadron was lost during the day while searching for suitable targets for a flight of USN Corsairs, both Capt Wayne Sawyer and his observer 1/Lt Clinton Summersill surviving the crash-landing. Despite injuries and the cold, they covered 40 miles in under 48 hours to reach safety, eventually being rescued by an ROK patrol; Summersill in particular had suffered severe frostbite and, in order to save his life, both feet were amputated at the ankles.

The day also saw 77RAAF fly one of its most successful strikes for some time – quite by accident. A flight of Mustangs led by Flt Lt Fred Barnes lost its course while on a reconnaissance patrol. It was difficult enough for pilots trying to follow the snow covered roads as they weaved their way north-south along the valley floors, let alone find a target. After unintentionally losing track of the supply route, they found a large supply dump hidden in a draw off a secondary road. Stores were scattered in small piles over an area of 200 yards. For the next 30 minutes the Australians rocketed, napalmed and strafed the area, causing explosions and setting most of the supplies on fire. On another mission Flt Lts Harvey and Dawson flew an armed recce of the area between Wonsan and a point six miles south-west of Taech'on, where a train was reported to be hidden in a tunnel. Arriving at Wonsan, they saw that the snow had been cleared from in and around the railway station. Further on, hundreds of enemy troops were deployed walking either singly or in pairs along the road and railway line. They refrained from attacking these because the distances between the soldiers would have meant wasting too much ammunition. Passing Hamhung, they could see that the railway line was in use from there to towns in the north. Before reaching their designated target, three more railway tunnels were spotted from which either smoke or steam was escaping. When they finally reached the target tunnel, Harvey and Dawson fired three rockets at the entrance, which caused extensive damage to the tracks. Deciding this was enough, they returned to one of the other tunnels and rocketed and strafed the entrance. The tracks were damaged, while heavy clouds of steam billowed from the tunnel mouth. The next tunnel was attacked the same way and with similar results. It had been a satisfying mission and the two pilots returned to base convinced that they had caused extensive damage.

Although the Russian and Chinese-flown MiGs were reluctant to leave the north-western Korea zone and grasp the opportunity to seriously challenge the UN over the battlefield, a few North Korean pilots nevertheless continued taking to the air. Near P'yongyang on the 15th, a single Yak fighter made a firing pass on a flight of B-26s of the 452nd BG. P'yongyang radio gave tribute to the exploits of its Hero Ong and Hero Kim – two celebrated North Korean airmen who apparently daily flew their Yak fighters "to chase American aircraft away" from the capital. Meanwhile, during the hours of darkness North Korean pilots in Po-2 biplanes persistently raided UN ground troops. They created a nuisance but did not inflict much damage. 18th FBG was tasked to raid these airfields and airstrips, losing Capt Joe H. Powers of the 67th FBS in the process; Powers had been credited with shooting down at least 14 enemy aircraft in WWII.

On the evening of 18 January, Sqn Ldr Cresswell addressed his pilots in their quarters, informing them that they were to carry out an important mission next day. Intelligence reports indicated that the Chinese Army had taken over a large complex of nine school buildings in P'yongyang for its headquarters. Joint Operations Control assigned the task of destroying it to the 35th FBG at K-9. On two occasions flights of F-51s from the 39th and 40th FIS had taken off on the mission but each time they had had to abort because of heavy cloud, snowstorms or fog. Now it was 77RAAF's turn to try to reach this target. On this mission, for the first time in the war, the Squadron would be operating at full strength, rather than in flights or sections.

Weather reports for the attack were poor and during the morning of the 19th the sky remained grey, cold and overcast. Morning passed with painful slowness at readiness but at last the word came to go. One by one the engines were started – all except that of Flt Lt Gordon Harvey's aircraft. There was no question of him aborting the mission since he was deputy leader and had to lead the second group. Following standard procedure he ran to the standby aircraft and ordered its pilot out, and taxied out with the others. This was Harvey's 84th combat mission, and his last on Mustangs before he was due to fly to Japan for jet fighter training. At exactly 1300 Sqn Ldr Cresswell's flight hurtled down on the target and released its bombs. They found the anti-aircraft gunners alert and waiting because high-flying B-29s were thundering over the city at the very same time. The Americans were out of sight above the clouds, blind-bombing by radar[2]. Delays in the take-off from Pusan had put the Australians behind schedule. At least if any MiGs had ventured out in the poor weather they would probably be intent on the bombers rather than the Mustangs. Cresswell saw four bombs from his flight burst in the middle of the target area and altogether results were assessed as four direct hits, four near misses and four misses. P3 Ron Howe's aircraft (A68-799) was hit by ground fire but was able to return to base with nothing worse than a damaged elevator. Shortly thereafter, at 1310, Harvey's napalm-carrying Mustangs came skimming low over the roof tops. Harvey could see flashes from exploding bombs among buildings not far off where the B-29s were unloading but there was no time to worry about that. His flight fired their rockets off in salvos and dropped their napalm, scoring several hits with both. During the rocket dive Reading saw flames coming from the engine of Harvey's aircraft (A68-772). He moved in close to his leader, gave him a cut-throat signal and warned him that he was on fire. Then, shortly afterwards, Harvey called over the radio that he was going to belly-land, as he later recalled:

"There was an explosion in the engine. It may have been hit by small-arms fire but there was no concussion, no thud or knock of a bullet striking home, only the explosion. The cockpit was full of oil and smoke and there was no power. I had to find a place to land quickly because it was impossible to gain enough altitude to bale out. There was just one

---

[2] On this date, if not during this raid, a lone B-29 dropped a radio-guided 12,000-lb tarzon bomb from 15,000 feet and demolished two spans of the important railway bridge at Kanggye. The newly developed bomb had first been used the previous month, but due to technical problems only one of the ten dropped had scored a direct hit on its designated target.

chance – if the ice was thick enough on the frozen (Taedong) river below to withstand the
weight of the plane . . ."

Flg Offs Allen Frost and Les Reading, Harvey's two wingmen, followed him down and saw his
Mustang touch down with its wheels up and slide along on the ice and snow towards an island
jutting out of the frozen river. Still intact, it finally slid to a halt. As they swept up and away
they saw Harvey climb out of the cockpit apparently unhurt. On the white landscape below it
was difficult to pick out features but they circled back, using the island as a landmark, and
spotted a running figure they assumed to be their flight commander dashing towards a haystack.
The situation looked bleak. Harvey had come down only four miles north-west of P'yongyang.
A helicopter represented his only chance of rescue, but when Frost radioed a request for one to
be sent the answer came that there were none available. Having ordered the Mustangs to return
home to avoid fuel shortages, Sqn Ldr Cresswell and his section remained to provide air cover
for a rescue attempt or to await relief. Repeated attempts to secure the services of a rescue
helicopter proved fruitless and eventually the Mustangs had to give up and leave. Relief aircraft
covered the area until nightfall but there were no further sightings of Harvey. Nonetheless,
Harvey was alive and free – but his freedom was soon to end. Having emerged from his aircraft
shaken and bruised but otherwise unhurt, he quickly surveyed the scene and realised that the
wide surface of the frozen river was much too open:

> "There was no immediate cover. In the distance on what I assumed to be high river banks I
> could make out a few houses but little else. The only possible place to hide was what
> seemed to be a very large brick building on a hill, possibly the island, a long way off. I set
> out for it across the ice. My progress seemed hopelessly slow – too slow. I was only halfway
> across when they picked me up. A group of North Koreans came running towards me. They
> appeared to be civilians but at least one man was carrying a rifle. There was no escape.
> There was simply nowhere to go and there were too many of them to attempt to fight them
> off. I was quickly hustled to a farmhouse and placed under guard. Outside, from time to
> time, I could hear low-flying aircraft, probably searching for me. An hour ago I'd been up
> there with them. Eventually the sound of planes died away. Shortly after this, soldiers – an
> officer and some men – came and took me away."

Thus, Flt Lt Gordon Harvey had the dubious honour to be the first Australian flier to be
captured during the Korean War[3]. Harvey's was not the only 35th FBG Mustang lost that day,
Capt William S. Matusz of the 40th FIS being shot down and killed by ground fire.

On 20 January it was the turn of the 18th FBG to fly a special mission. Intelligence reported
that a Chinese general, dressed in civilian clothes and supported by 5,000-7,000 Communist
guerrillas, was engaged in turning the local population in the mountains south of the town of
Kwanju in south-west Korea against the UN. The ROK's 11th Division and their advisers had
isolated the guerrillas in an area containing 27 small villages, and the 18th FBG at Chinhae was
requested to provide three flights of four aircraft, one from each of its squadrons which
included 2SAAF, to attack the villages. Five were subsequently totally destroyed and five
others partially destroyed, resulting in over 500 guerrillas being killed. ROK troops then moved
in and accounted for close on 200 more. A week later the 18th FBG received letters from the
Chief of Police and the Governor of Cholla Namdo Province praising the Wing for its support.
With an improvement in the weather, flights of US fighter-bombers were also active, as were
the MiGs, six of 177th FAR's 1st Eskadrilya led by Maj Fomin (flying aircraft No20) meeting
four F-84s strafing ground targets near Kaisen. The Americans spotted the MiGs approaching

---

[3] Flt Lt Harvey was not placed in a POW camp immediately and, for the first five months of his captivity,
he was kept with other prisoners to work in labour gangs around P'yongyang, shifting supplies at night.
He saw for himself the devastation in the centre of the city caused by the B-29 bombings, and likened it
to the scenes of destruction in Berlin in WWII. He and two American officers escaped from their camp
on 28 April 1951 but were caught after six days. On recapture they were treated very badly and one of the
Americans died; Harvey survived being incarcerated in a hole in the ground for 45 days. Thirty-two
months would pass before he would be freed.

and attempted to counter-attack Fomin's *zveno* but were themselves engaged by Maj Andryushin's *zveno*. One of the fighter-bombers started to trail smoke and fell away following an attack by Andryushin, and a second turned on its back apparently out of control while under fire from Podpolkovnik Sychev. Meanwhile Fomin lost sight of his intended victim but then saw another approaching Maj Kormilkin's aircraft; this he attacked, firing four bursts and it was last seen heading towards the mountains. Two victories were awarded, one each for Maj Fomin and Maj Andryushin.

Meanwhile, the Communists had begun repairing the airfields at Sinuiju and P'yongyang, in accordance with the Second Phase of General Liu Ya-Lou's plan. From the point of view of defence, Sinuiju was best placed of the two airfields because it could be covered by the MiG air umbrella from Antung and was protected by heavy anti-aircraft emplacements on both sides of the Yalu. P'yongyang was out of range of the MiGs, but the anti-aircraft defences were steadily increased until there were over 100 guns around the airfield. This heavy defensive screen protecting P'yongyang was a major concern for FEAF Bomber Command.

Apparently realising at last that the F-86s were no longer present, flights of MiGs began appearing further south. In an aggressive mood early on the morning of 21 January, six MiGs of the 29th GuFAR led by Maj Yurkevich bounced four F-84s south of Sinanju, Kapt Perekrest and his *zveno* being ordered to engage. The Americans saw them coming and broke away in time and, although there were several engagements, no claims could be made. However, later that day, the Russian monitoring station reported that one F-84 had crashed as a result of this action and St/Lt Bondarenko was awarded a victory. Just over an hour later, at 0910, Kapt Orlov's *zveno* spotted what they believed were two F-84s near Sensen, and one was claimed by Kapt Grechko; the other was pursued by Maj I.F. Bogatyrev, who noticed several strikes as it twisted and turned to escape. The American jets were in fact F-80s, three from the 8th FBS escorting an RF-80 of the 8th TRS. The reconnaissance pilot was shot down as was 1/Lt Joe L. Dalman, one of the escorting pilots. Six F-84s then appeared and attacked Bogatyrev and his wingman but these were engaged by Orlov's *zveno* and broke away. Two more F-84s then attacked Orlov and his wingman. Despite the skirmishing, neither side was able to make any claims, although the leader of the Chinese flight, Capt Li Han, claimed the first victory in Korea for a Chinese MiG pilot.

An hour later, at 1020, there occurred another clash when six MiGs of the 177th FAR's 1st Eskadrilya led by Maj Mikhailov encountered another four F-84s near Bihen, two of which were promptly claimed shot down, one by Mikhailov and the other by his wingman Kapt Akulenko. Mikhailov then shot down a third after firing five short bursts. Four more F-84s appeared and these were engaged also, two being claimed by Kapt I.V. Popov and Maj Grechishko (flying aircraft No13). Despite these claims only one F-84 was lost in this action. The F-84s of the 523rd FES had been dive-bombing a bridge across the Ch'ongch'on when the MiGs attacked. The American pilots reported that in the battle that followed the MiG pilots chose to dogfight instead of using their usual fast hit-and-run tactics. By doing so they did not keep their advantage, for at the lower altitude the straight-winged F-84s could more than match them in turning ability and Lt Colonel William E. Bertram, the Group's new CO, became the first F-84 pilot to be credited with destroying a MiG when he sent one down which reportedly crashed into the river. Three more 49th FBG F-80s were lost when their pilots, short on fuel, encountered ground fog which completely obscured K-2, and were forced to carry out belly landings alongside the Naktong; all three survived, shaken but unhurt.

The MiGs again encountered US fighter-bombers next day, an F-80 and an F-84 being claimed shot down by pilots of the 177th FAR, which reported that four MiGs led by Maj M.A. Zabavin – two others had returned early – encountered a dozen F-80s and F-84s near Kaisen. Kapt Dovgalya fired at one from 500 yards and saw smoke issuing from it before it disappeared from sight, while Maj Agureev's victim was reported to have fallen away out of control. Maj Meleshkin's combat was more decisive and his target fell in flames.

There occurred another major clash between the Russian jets and F-84s on 23 January. In co-operation with a planned B-29 attack on P'yongyang, eight flights totalling 33 F-84s of the 27th FEG from Taegu set out northwards to strike at Sinuiju airfield. The plan was for two flights to strafe the airfield while the other six flights remained overhead acting as top cover. The eight strafing F-84s were able to make one firing pass before swirling dust clouds were observed at Antung across the Yalu, signalling that MiGs were taking off to intercept. The strafers hastily rejoined their top cover and over the next 30 minutes there developed a furious air battle. The MiGs again demonstrated their advantages in speed and acceleration, but while the F-84s remained below 20,000 feet they were able to fight on equal terms. Able to out-manoeuvre the MiGs at these heights, 1/Lt Jacob Kratt claimed two shot down in less than two minutes and, before the fight was over, two more were claimed by Capts Allen MaGuire and William W. Slaughter. Three more were claimed probably destroyed, and four damaged, all without loss. One of the latter was credited to Capt Vasseure F. Wynn (flying FS-378) who had served with the RCAF during WWII (see Appendix III). Wynn was aged 33, one of the older pilots in the Group. When asked about the younger members, he observed:

> "They've got it, that old enthusiasm. They've got a lot to learn, but they're learning fast. They're quick and they're sharp, and they keep us old-timers on the line. It's good to have them around, even when they call you 'Pops' or 'Pudgy' [to his RAF friends at Malta during WWII he was known as Georgia]."

All three eskadrilyas of the 177th FAR participated in this engagement, the 13 MiG pilots led by Maj Mikhailov reporting both F-80s and F-84s, one of the former being claimed by Kapt Belikov of the 1st Eskadrilya, and one of the latter by Maj Agureev of the 3rd Eskadrilya, who returned with three bullet strikes in his aircraft. Kapt Popov landed with great difficulty at Antung, where 39 bullet and shrapnel holes were discovered; the jet was scrapped. Meanwhile, the 29th GuFAR had scrambled 20 MiGs and were joined by eight more from the Chinese 7th FAR on the approach of the raiders, six aircraft of the 2nd Eskadrilya led by Maj Krymskii making the initial contact at 20,000 feet, meeting eight F-84s. Two were claimed shot down by St/Lt A.K. Kurnosov and Kapt G.P. Chumakov. The 1st Eskadrilya also reported meeting eight F-84s, flying at about 1,500 feet, and claimed three shot down, Maj Bogatyrev, Kapt Orlov and Kapt A.D. Ryazanov being the successful pilots, while Kapt Grechko damaged a fourth. Not to be outdone, Maj Yurkevich's 3rd Eskadrilya engaged six more F-84s at 9,000 feet but were unable to make any claims until Kapt Perekrest dived on two of the American aircraft as they attempted to escape, claiming one shot down from about 300 yards. The Chinese pilots also claimed two F-84s (one possibly by Lt Colonel Wang Hai) but two of the Chinese MiGs were shot down, one pilot being killed, while St/Lt Grebenkin of the 29th GuFAR also failed to return. Later that morning the 49th FBG sent 46 bomb and rocket-laden F-80s to suppress P'yongyang's flak batteries, losing 1/Lt Ralph Jacobs. Immediately afterwards, 21 B-29s on the 19th and 307th BGs arrived from Okinawa and dropped their bombs on P'yongyang's main airfield, the crews believing 90% of them to have hit and cratered the runway, from end to end. There was only light and inaccurate AA fire and no B-29s were damaged. Not far from P'yongyang a flight of patrolling F-51s of the 39th FIS from Pusan was bounced by a pair of Yak-3s. Capt Alexander Currie claimed one destroyed and his wingman, Capt Thomas Manjack, was credited with a probable. It was thought the two NKAF pilots might have been the legendary Hero Ong and Hero Kim.

On 24 January, eight Mustangs – four USAF and four RAAF led by Flt Lt Olorenshaw – were tasked to check the airfield at Kang-dong. There, they encountered "modest and inaccurate" anti-aircraft fire coming from positions near the airfield, but there were no enemy aircraft to be seen on the ground although there were obvious signs of recent activity in the snow. Shortly afterwards, while attacking a nearby village, the engine of Olorenshaw's Mustang (A68-812) suddenly cut out, but picked up again a few seconds later. Despite this hiccup, he made a strafing run using all his ammunition and then returned to Pusan escorted by his wingman. The other two Australians, P3s Dick Turner and Kevin Foster, remained with the American flight, adding to the carnage when they destroyed four barracks-type buildings between Sach'ang-ni and Namch'on-ni.

Next day (25 January), the US 8th Army's I and IX Corps began Operation 'Thunderbolt', a push forward to the Han. At first the 8th Army moved forward against little opposition but after six days the enemy reacted firmly, particularly through the use of their heavy mortar and artillery fire. To cover and direct 5th Air Force's close-support operations for the advance, controllers of the 6147th TAC Squadron staged forward from Taegu West through the old airstrip at Taejon. This way their T-6 control aircraft could patrol in front of the UN ground troops for up to three hours at a time. As they located enemy strongpoints, they would issue warnings over the R/T to the ground commanders below. In order to relay high-frequency transmissions for air strikes from the front lines to the TAC centre, the 6147th Squadron had earlier initiated the procedure of keeping another T-6 aloft midway between the front lines and Taegu. This T-6 had two radio channels for relaying messages, but in practice this relay station would often be swamped with radio traffic. Ready for the drive forward, and beginning on 26 January, the 6147th Squadron put aloft a C-47 airborne relay station with 20 channels of VHF communications and thereby successfully overcame the bottleneck. This C-47 maintained a station 20 miles behind the front lines and passed messages between TAC parties, airborne controllers, fighter-bombers, and the TAC centre. On this date, the 45th TRS, whose pilots had been granted permission to attack targets of opportunity while engaged on reconnaissance sorties, suffered its first battle casualty when Capt Warren Hawks' aircraft was hit by small-arms fire although it was able to return to Taegu and land safely.

Due to the short range of the MiG-15 restricting its operational radius, the 50th FAD arranged for further quantities of jettisonable under-wing fuel tanks to be flown to Antung for the use of the 177th FAR. These arrived aboard Chinese Air Force Il-12 transports, but later they were locally produced. Problems sometimes arose when the pilots attempted to release the tanks, which would not always jettison and therefore caused serious problems when combat was joined. Such was the case on 26 January when Maj Zabavin's 3rd Eskadrilya encountered a dozen US fighter-bombers. Zabavin ordered his pilots to jettison their tanks and prepare for battle, but was unable to release his own, nor could Kapt N.E. Gorokhov release his. Both endeavoured to shake them free by violent manoeuvring, Gorokhov eventually succeeding although he had to return to base, but Zabavin was able to free one only, the other remaining in place and causing the MiG to enter a spin. With great difficulty Zabavin was able to regain control and succeeded in reaching Antung, where his stressed aircraft was found to require a wing replacement. The Eskadrilya's remaining MiGs failed to register any claims nor did it suffer any losses. Elsewhere however, the F-84s of the 523rd FES were again in action when a single Yak fighter bravely, if foolishly, attacked the US jets near P'yongyang, 1/Lt Kratt shooting this down for his third victory in four days. Since it was believed that the gallant Yak pilot might have been the surviving member of the Hero Ong/Hero Kim duo, FEAF monitors tuned in with interest to P'yongyang Radio in the hope that it would announce that both its 'Heroes' were missing. It did not.

Changes were also in the air for 77RAAF. Sqn Ldr Cresswell and Flt Lt Des Murphy had been selected for jet training, as had the missing Flt Lt Gordon Harvey, the former two now flying to Itazuke AFB in Japan where they were attached to the USAF's 8th FBG for conversion to the F-80, following which they would be allowed to fly ten combat missions. Sqn Ldr Cresswell recalled:

> "I had no jet experience so it was decided that three of us, Gordon Harvey, Des Murphy and myself, would fly jets with the Yanks. Des Murphy had already flown Vampires in Australia. We lost Gordon Harvey before we were posted down to Itazuke on the jet course, so only the two of us went."

The purpose of the jet training was to help with the transition of 77RAAF from the propeller-driven Mustang to the Meteor F8 twin-jet fighter, a number of which were on their way to Japan from the UK. Although the Mustang had proved a suitable workhorse for the Australians during the first six months of this undeclared war, the advent of the MiG over Korea had led to demands that 77RAAF should re-equip with a modern jet fighter as a matter of urgency. It was not only piston-engined fighters and bombers that were now under threat, but also the first generation of American straight-wing jet fighters such as the USAF's F-80, the F-84 and the US Navy's F9F. Enquiries were made in Britain and the United States for suitable, currently available, modern jet fighter aircraft. General Sir Horace Robertson GOC BCOF, writing on discussions that he had held with General Stratemeyer, reported that the Commander of the FEAF had stated, ". . . you re-equip 77 Squadron with jet aircraft from British sources as early as you can do it . . ." and held out no hope of the possibility of rearming 77RAAF with second generation American jets as the new F-86 Sabre. Stratemeyer added that it would be the first opportunity the British would have for testing their jets in actual combat. The Americans hoped that this factor might induce the UK to speed up re-equipment of its own fighter squadrons – a number of which still flew Spitfires – in case the fighting should continue or escalate. Unofficially, Sqn Ldr Cresswell was trying to make a private arrangement with the Americans, whereby the Australian squadron would acquire some of the 4th FIW's unwanted, battle-weary F-86s, exchanging their Mustangs one at a time as the Sabres became available once replacements had arrived. The plan was to refurbish these and use them on operations. The scheme fell through when it was learned that the Meteor had been purchased.

The Australian High Commissioner in the United Kingdom, Sir Eric Harrison, had reported in November of the previous year that three types could be acquired from British sources: the de Havilland Venom, the Hawker P.1081, and the Gloster Meteor. For maintenance reasons he gave first priority to the Venom, second priority to the P.1081 and third priority to the Meteor, a design that had been in service with the RAF since 1944. De Havilland could supply 20 aircraft but deliveries would not commence until January 1952, a twelve-month delay that was not acceptable. Hawker's P.1081 was destined never to enter production, but would be a stepping stone in the trail of development towards the formidable Hunter – but all too late for Korea. The third choice Meteor won selection by default[4]. The High Commissioner was advised that 36 Meteor F8s could be supplied to the RAAF, with delivery of the first twelve aircraft within three-four months of signing the contract so that 77RAAF could be re-equipped with the type early in 1951. Since the Meteor F8 equipped most of the RAF's front line fighter squadrons, the British Air Ministry hoped that it would be able to hold its own with the MiG-15, but with its straight-wing, twin-jet configuration it was clearly no match for the Russian swept-wing, single-jet, second generation fighter, as the Australians were to learn to their cost. The Meteor was originally intended to be used in Korea as a ground-attack fighter but the rôle was changed to that of day-fighter because, owing to the lack of shipping space, it would have been difficult to have kept 77RAAF supplied with rockets. Other factors which influenced this decision were (a) the aircraft had not been cleared to carry bombs or napalm tanks, and (b) with the increase in numbers of MiGs on the Manchurian airfields, HQ 5th Air Force was eager to augment the 4th FIW with its F-86s, which was the only Wing being solely employed in the day-fighter rôle.

In the CO's absence, 77RAAF found itself under the temporary command of Flt Lt Olorenshaw who, on 29 January, led a dozen Mustangs as part of a 40 aircraft-strong fighter-bomber strike against targets at P'yongyang. The Australians were positioned on the right flank, the 39th FIS in the centre, and the 40th FIS on the left flank. After take-off, the formation proceeded to the target area but on contacting the FAC the leader was informed that friendly troops had already crossed the bomb-line. The Mustangs were allotted the alternative task of destroying enemy bivouac areas and villages near P'yongyang. The subsequent attack left eight to ten villages burning furiously and was estimated to have killed a large number of enemy troops.

There was an improvement in the weather conditions by the end of the month, which allowed an armed recce by 77RAAF along the Kaesong-P'yongyang-Sunch'on roads on the 30th. Led by Flg Off Dick Wittman, the four Mustangs located a camouflaged tank which

---

[4] The RAAF had evaluated a Meteor F3 shortly after the end of WWII, when it was the only jet fighter in service anywhere in the world which therefore made it exciting and unique, although soon to be overtaken in design and performance by its American and Russian second generation, swept-wing rivals. By 1951 it was already obsolete. The F3 supplied to the RAAF carried both its RAF serial number EE427 and RAAF serial A77-1. It did not survive long in RAAF service, being written-off after a heavy landing at Darwin on 11 May 1947.

exploded after being hit. Haystacks were also strafed, one apparently concealing a fuel dump which erupted into flames. Anti-aircraft fire was experienced as the Mustangs reached the outskirts of Sunch'on and P3 Ken Royal's aircraft (A68-715) was hit twice, one shell punching a hole and shattering his windscreen, although the pilot was not injured and was able to return to Pusan safely. Next day (31 January), Flt Lt Coburn led another patrol to dive-bomb and napalm a road bridge between Singye and Wongyo-ri. The wooden railings and sections of the bridge were set on fire, and nearby houses around which could be seen vehicle tracks were strafed, killing at least five soldiers. Later, a strike led by Flt Lt Olorenshaw found seven camouflaged vehicles near Yangdogwon-ni, which were rocketed and strafed. Although some hits were seen none of the vehicles burst into flames, while small-arms fire struck one of the Mustangs but the damage was minor.

Because their surface supply lines were disrupted by weather and clogged by troops and refugees, the UN ground and air forces in Korea had to rely heavily upon supply by air. During the early part of the month, with the loss of Kimpo, Seoul, and Suwon, only Taegu and Pusan airfields remained to accommodate heavier transport aircraft. The USAF's Cargo Command's capability to lift supplies now exceeded the capability of the available landing grounds to handle them. The old airfield at Taejon was able to support the heavily-laden transport aircraft while the ground was frozen but, when a thaw caused a serious C-54 accident, this field had to be closed to anything heavier than a C-46. First at Wonju, then at Ch'ungju and Andong, US X Corps repaired old airfields and, weighing the hazards against the urgent needs, C-46s and C-47s began flying into these rough landing grounds. Thus, by using improvised and existing strips, Cargo Command in the first 24 days of January managed to airlift just over 5,000 tons of men and materials for the 5th Air Force, and almost 7,500 tons for the 8th US Army. On their return trips from Korea the transports evacuated 10,849 combat casualties to hospitals in Japan.

During the month the RAF Sunderland Detachment based at Iwakuni had been reinforced by the arrival of three more aircraft from 205 Squadron led by Sqn Ldr John Proctor flying PP107; the other two aircraft were RN269 captained by Flt Lt T.A. Bridge, and PP144 (Flt Lt M.F. Aldersmith). The Detachment continued flying anti-submarine and shipping patrols off the east coast, logging 16 operational sorties during the month, not always without incident. While on one such sortie on 15 January, covering the American Fleet Refuelling Group, Flt Lt Herbert Houtheusen and his crew of 88 Squadron's RN282/C were instructed to search for a dinghy in the sea just off the coast near Wonsan. The dinghy was sighted, drifting towards the enemy coast and it contained an occupant. Houtheusen decided that the water was sufficiently calm for the big flying boat to alight and attempt a pick up. The man in the dinghy proved to be an American Corsair pilot, Ensign Edward J. Hossta, whose aircraft had been damaged by anti-aircraft fire during a strike against Wonsan harbour, and had plunged into the sea in flames. Hossta had baled out uninjured but was suffering from exposure. Rescue completed, the Sunderland was able to take off safely and returned to Iwakuni, where the American pilot was admitted to hospital. Flt Lt Houtheusen was awarded the DFC for this rescue. Next day (16 January), Flg Off Bob Brand and his crew of PP155/F sighted a sampan displaying an SOS about 30 miles out from the east coast. It appeared to be carrying about 30 people. The US destroyer *Norris* was contacted, and was on the scene within 30 minutes, safely picking up the occupants who turned out to be Korean civilians. Sqn Ldr Proctor, having flown one long anti-submarine sortie shortly after his arrival, took the opportunity to fly two sorties with the Neptunes of VP-42 and VP-892 at the end of the month. On the return from the second of these, on 28 January, he learned of the tragic accident which had overtaken the crew and passengers aboard Sunderland PP107 which had taken off from Iwakuni to fly to Hong Kong. In poor visibility the flying boat crashed into Mount Morrison on Formosa. Flt Lt D.R. Hobdey, his four-man crew, plus eight passengers all perished in the accident (see Appendix II).

Away from the war, two weeks of lobbying by the US Government had resulted in the United Nations General Assembly branding Communist China as the aggressor in Korea, by a vote of 44 to 7. Most Member States, however, were reluctant to push the issue any further. The General Assembly then voted 42 to 7 to merely study the idea of imposing sanctions on China. None wanted this flashpoint in Asia to escalate further and this probably indicated that they were unhappy with the speedy and forceful way in which the US had pushed the resolution through.

February 1951

The main internal supply system in North Korea was built around the double-track railway line and roadway running from Seoul through Kaesong, Sariwon, P'yongyang and Sinanju, to Sinuiyu and Manchuria. The other main north-south route was the road and railway line running the entire length of the peninsula along the east coast. These two arterial routes were connected by lateral railway lines and roads from P'yongyang to Wonsan, and from Seoul to Wonsan. Roads linking the smaller towns to the main routes and to each other completed the network. To completely sever either was not an easy task as the abundance of sidelines and roads served as alternatives should the main route become unserviceable. Dominated by mountainous terrain, the eastern rail system alone had 1,140 miles of track, 956 bridges and causeways, and 231 tunnels – one bridge for just over every one mile of track and one tunnel every five miles.

Intelligence reports reaching Tokyo indicated that, because FEAF attacks on transportation had seriously hampered the enemy's use of the rail network in north-western and central Korea, the Communists were now making increased use of road and rail routes open to them on the eastern side of the peninsula. North of Hamhung rail travel had made a revival. To sever the east coast rail lines, B-29s of the 307th BG attacked and destroyed nine spans on the railway bridges at Ch'uuronjang, Hongwon, and Tanch'on on 1 February. For the next few days further B-29 raids placed mounting pressure on east coast bridges and marshalling yards – but it was not enough. By 6 February the Communists had become so openly active in north-central and north-western Korea that General MacArthur directed General Stratemeyer to focus combined efforts on the 5th Air Force and the FEAF Bomber Command on these areas until further notice. Orders promptly went out for further B-29 attacks on bridges, points of congestion and tunnel entrances, and for the 5th Air Force to attack rolling stock.

In common with other fighter-bomber squadrons of the 5th Air Force, the 18th FBG which included 2SAAF, concentrated on armed reconnaissance operations. Occasionally there were diversions for close-support or interdiction targets when intelligence managed to find concentrations of troops or supplies. The South Africans paid particular attention to transport routes between Seoul and Sariwon, Wonsan and the Chosin Reservoir, and Wonsan and P'yongyang. Up to 2 February, 2SAAF had been operating in Korea for 54 days and had flown 899 combat sorties for the loss of only one aircraft. The South Africans had been far from inactive during this time, on occasions in January maintaining a sortie rate of around 24 per day. There had been several scares, though, aside from Lt Deans' emergency landing at K-2 early in January, as later in the month Lt Syd de la Harpe's Mustang had been hit in the wing by anti-aircraft fire and, the following day, Lt K. van Heerden had flown into high-tension cables but luckily the aircraft suffered only slight damage to its propeller spinner. But such good fortune simply could not last, and 2SAAF's 900th sortie, on 2 February, saw the end of its exceptional safety record when Lt Elmer Wilson was lost. He had taken off from Chinhae leading four Mustangs on an armed recce of the area around Wonsan. Shortly into the flight his No4 developed engine trouble and had to abort. When the remaining three Mustangs reached the target area, Lt Wilson descended to begin searching for targets, leaving the other two to provide top cover. Just north-east of Wonsan his Mustang (319) was seen to start trailing white smoke, which indicated a glycol leak, probably the result of a hit in the cooling system. The Mustang gained altitude and headed out to sea, Wilson baling out just offshore. His parachute opened and he was seen to make a good descent into the water by the other two members of his section, Lts Mike Frost and Ian Gow, but they saw the parachute sink immediately. They descended to sea level to maintain a watch over their leader, having radioed for help.

Soon they were joined by flights of F-80s and USMC Corsairs and, before long, an SA-16 of the USAF's 3rd Air Rescue Squadron arrived. Despite the cold and choppy sea, the amphibian managed to alight near Wilson, who could be seen in his Mae West, but once down it became increasingly difficult to keep track of the bobbing figure. The Americans could only catch glimpses of him in the high, pitching swells. For 35 minutes they revved the engines and manoeuvred, trying to close the gap enough to throw a line but eventually the Mae West completely disappeared from view. The rescue attempt had to be abandoned and it was presumed that the South African pilot must have perished in the icy water. It was a bad day for the 18th FGB for, apart from the loss of Lt Wilson of 2SAAF, Lt Colonel Milton F. Glessner Jr of HQ was shot down on another sortie and was posted missing, as was Capt Elzeard J. Deschamps of the 67th FBS.

Meanwhile, on the ground, encouraged by his success in the west at the end of the previous month, General Ridgway ordered the US X Corps to move northwards in central Korea. Although opposed by the North Korean II and V Corps, American troops captured Hoensong on 2 February. Next morning, shortly after 0900, MiGs from the 1st Eskadrilya of the 17th FAR were scrambled when reports were received that US fighter-bombers were active, meeting a lone F-80 (although erroneously identified as a two-seater T-33 'reconnaissance' aircraft) some 25 miles north-east of Sinuiju. Kapt Akulenko opened fire and the F-80 was seen to jettison its drop tanks and make a sharp turn to port. Maj Vorobyov and his No2 then attacked and saw strikes as it tried to escape. Vorobyov (flying aircraft 04) fired three more short bursts and the American jet was reported to have crashed 15 miles south-west of Kijio. Later, Maj Zakhartsev's *zveno* encountered two more F-80s, which evaded the initial interception but were followed by Kapt Popov and his wingman, the leader shooting down one south of Kijio. The 35th FBS reported the loss of 1/Lt John Adkins during the day, although apparently not due to combat but rather an accident. He baled out into Fukuoka Bay and was drowned.

This proved to be the last engagement for the 17th FAR, which was withdrawn from operations two days later. The Regiment had claimed between 22 and 27 victories for the loss of three MiGs and one pilot. All three air regiments of the 50th FAD had now completed their tours and were being withdrawn, the 29th GuFAR having been credited with 36 victories for five losses including four pilots, while the Chinese 10th FAR had lost two aircraft and one pilot for three claims. Following these withdrawals, there remained at Antung (temporarily) the 67th FAR and 139th GuFAR of the 28th FAD, although these units were also withdrawn once the replacement 151st Guards FAD comprising the 28th GuFAR commanded by Podpolkovnik Viktor Kolyadin, and the 72nd GuFAR (Podpolkovnik Bordun), plus the attached Chinese 7th FAR, had settled in for its second tour of operations.

The Mustangs of 2SAAF flew four separate armed reconnaissance patrols, each of four aircraft, on 4 February. Each mission lasted between three and four hours duration, and the most successful was led by Cmdt Theron. While patrolling the Singye-Yangdok road his section came across a stationary convoy of 20 well-camouflaged vehicles, which were duly rocketed and strafed. By the time they departed, 13 of the vehicles were on fire. Other sections returned with claims for the destruction of one fuel dump, seven buildings and a further six vehicles, and more were damaged as were two tanks and a bridge.

During the night a number of low-flying C-47s scattered eight tons of roofing nails along four twisting highways south of P'yongyang. Operation 'Tack' was the brainchild of the 3rd BG. The idea was to immobilise enemy supply trucks with punctured tyres so that they would be found in the open early next morning by the UN fighter-bombers and destroyed. While engaged in this activity, Maj Robert V. Spencer encountered three enemy tanks. Hastily pulling his C-47 up out of range, Spencer sent out a call for the B-26 night intruder bombers. When they arrived over the area, he flew along his route again to draw flak and relocate the targets. This done, he flew over yet again to drop a flare so that the intruders could see and destroy the tanks. Next morning UN fighter-bombers were out in force early to reap the anticipated harvest sewn by the C-47s. Their orders were to reconnoitre the highways at first light and destroy all the stranded trucks with flat tyres that they could find. The South Africans flew two missions without finding any crippled vehicles at all. On the whole Operation 'Tack' had been well executed, but it could not be considered as much of a success. Only 28 stationary vehicles were found by the entire 5th Air Force.

On 5 February, three days after capturing Hoengsong, General Ridgway ordered X Corps to implement 'Roundup' and advance towards Hongch'on. That day Maj Arnold Mullins, Operations Officer of the 67th FBS, led a flight of three F-51s against ground targets near Sunan, north-west of P'yongyang, where they claimed the destruction of two locomotives and ten trucks. Just after pulling up from a strafing pass, Mullins unexpectedly spotted a Yak-9 directly overhead. Pulling the nose of the Mustang up, he fired a few bursts and scored direct hits on the enemy's cockpit canopy and fuselage. The Yak took no evasive action and its only manoeuvre was a slow turn before going into a dive to crash and explode. With the MiGs having gained air superiority over north-western Korea, the 5th Air Force instructed its pilots to avoid combat if at all possible in an effort to reduce losses until it was possible to reintroduce the F-86 units. In the airspace between the Ch'ongch'on and Yalu Rivers, the MiGs had achieved local air superiority to such a degree that his pilots could indulge in much needed combat practice, and American pilots now dubbed the area 'MiG Alley'. They were not to know that the main MiG units were being withdrawn to make way for another Fighter Air Division, and that this would not be operational for a few weeks. Meanwhile, RF-80 photo-reconnaissance jets, sometimes alone and sometimes with an F-80 fighter escort, continued to dart to the Yalu to produce photographs of any enemy activity on the ground. The pilots reported that only a quarter of the MiGs they sighted in the air showed aggression, but on at least four occasions during the month the MiG formations attacked. Ever cautious of the danger of interception, the intrepid reconnaissance pilots managed to narrowly escape being shot down each time.

The air-to-ground story was different. UN fighter-bombers were not so fortunate and tragedy struck the South Africans again on 7 February, when Cmdt Theron led a flight of Mustangs on an armed reconnaissance along the Wonsan-Hamhung road. After discharging their rockets against a supply dump, they came across three camouflaged vehicles on the road just north of Yonhung. Their only remaining weapons were their machine-guns. As 2/Lt D.R. Leah in Mustang 307 broke to starboard after his second strafing run, his wing struck the ground. The aircraft cartwheeled and crashed in flames, spreading wreckage over a wide area. There were no obvious signs of ground fire. Doug Leah was 2SAAF's second battle fatality.

In the second week of February the 5th Air Force adopted new initiatives designed to pin down the enemy's elusive supply trucks. Three armed reconnaissance areas covering a band of territory 50 miles north of the bomb-line were established and it made one each of these regions the responsibility of the 18th FBG, the 35th FBG and the 1st US Marine Air Wing. These three wings were ordered to keep relays of F-51s or Corsairs constantly on patrol over their designated areas to locate and attack targets of opportunity. By doing this it was hoped that the pilots would become so familiar with the local geography that they would be able to easily pick out unusual changes to the terrain and so isolate objects that were camouflaged. To help determine the most likely places where enemy vehicles might be dispersed and hidden, the JOC started preparing and issuing every morning master map overlays to each group showing the location of all vehicle sightings reported through the night by intruder and reconnaissance crews. However, there were teething problems, as General Partridge indicated when he addressed the pilots of the 35th FBG including the Australians at K-9, as evidenced in 77RAAF's records:

> "General Partridge had all the pilots at the base called together in the Operations Room where he addressed them. He said there were reports of bombing of friendly troops. All pilots must observe the following rules before they attack targets. Firstly, they must establish exactly where they are. If they are north of the bomb-line it is then permissible to go ahead and bomb. Secondly, if they are south of it, no attack may be carried out unless it is under the control of either an [airborne] controller or a tactical controller on the ground. Thirdly, if the pilot, although he is operating with a controller and has been assigned a target by that controller, yet feels there is the slightest doubt the target is enemy, then he must quit."

Survivors of the Chinese 50th Army continued to resist until 9 February, but then their defences broke and the US I Corps raced northwards to the Han. By dusk on 10 February the port of Inch'on and Kimpo airfield, with its bomb-cratered runways, again belonged to United Nations forces. With this gain, General Partridge impressed upon his staff that he wanted Suwon, Kimpo and Seoul airfields made operational without delay, particularly so the F-86s of the 4th

FIW could be moved back into Korea. However, reports made by the 5th Air Force tactical reconnaissance pilots seemed to suggest that enemy troops were assembling for an offensive. This was indeed the case. General P'eng, commander of the Chinese Volunteers, had been resting and replenishing his forces, but now, because of UN pressure, he felt compelled to counter-attack. Although not fully prepared, he launched his Fourth Phase Offensive in a bid designed in particular to reduce the pressure on Seoul. Beginning after nightfall on 11 February, the Chinese 40th and 66th Armies and the North Korean V Corps attacked along the Hoengsong-Wonju axis.

The new MiG unit, the 151st FAD, reported its first engagement during the afternoon of 10 February, when a dozen fighters – eight from the 28th GuFAR and four Chinese – encountered four F-80s at 20,000 feet south-west of Anju. Kapt Akimov, the formation leader, fired at the leading fighter-bomber and after his fourth burst it exploded, while Kapt Aleexenko shot down the No2 aircraft. As the second pair tried to escape, Kapt Lebedkin claimed one shot down. One of the Chinese MiGs failed to return, but whether the victim of one of the F-80s is unknown. On the morning of 12 February, just as the 5th Air Force's new armed reconnaissance zones were established and the new 'truck hunting' plan was implemented, the Communists, who were desperate to get their supplies through, moved them in daylight. It could not have been a more timely event for the UN fighter-bombers. By the time night fell, 236 enemy vehicles had been destroyed and 83 damaged to set a new day record – an outstanding success, but not sufficient to curb the Chinese offensive. To meet the Communist attack towards Hoengsong on 13 February, General Ridgway reacted quickly by ordering the highest priority for close air support be given to the US X Corps. Fighter-bomber pilots who had been aiding the US I and IX Corps in the west now found themselves operating over X Corps in central Korea. All available aircraft were thrown into the Hoengsong area but the Communists succeeded in capturing the town. During these operations the 35th FBG lost aircraft on successive days, Capt Justice Haythorne of the 40th FIS baling out into the sea but being found dead when a rescue craft reached him, while Capt Clifford Summers of the 39th FIS baled out of his damaged aircraft near Taegu, breaking his leg on landing. An F-80 of the 25th FIS also failed to return on the 12th, with the loss of 1/Lt Edward D. Fleming, reportedly to ground fire although a MiG pilot of the 28th GuFAR, Kapt Viktor Borodin (HoSU), claimed one of eight F-80s encountered near Anju on this date.

The Fourth Phase Offensive then moved against Chipyong-ni, a village lying north-west of Wonju surrounded by mountains and held by elements of the US 2nd Infantry Division. Here the US 23rd Infantry Regiment and the French Battalion commanded by Lt Colonel Raoul Montclar were soon surrounded. This village was situated at the hinge of the sector defence lines manned by the US IX and X Corps; if it fell the whole 8th Army front would be endangered. Recognizing the hazardous situation existing at Chipyong-ni, Generals Ridgway and Partridge gave the 2nd Division the highest priority for air support. Each day, from 14-16 February, ten flights of FAC aircraft maintained constant daylight air patrols over the 2nd Division as long as the weather held. The South Africans flew three missions to help the defenders of Chipyong-ni, all of them against enemy troops in trenches along the mountain ridges. Napalm proved a highly effective and terrifying weapon when employed on such targets.

The MiGs reported further successes against the B-29s on 14 February, ten of the Russian jets having scrambled at 1025 on the approach of the bombers. Led by Maj P.B. Ovsyannikov of the 28th GuFAR, the MiGs were soon joined by two more flown by Podpolkovnik Kolyadin and his wingmen. A dozen F-80s were seen ground strafing south of Huang tsai-tong but these were not attacked, although only Kolyadin and his No2 eventually engaged the bombers, shooting down one and damaging a second before escorting F-80s intervened. One of these was fired at by Ovsyannikov but it escaped, apparently undamaged,

The 14th was destined also to become a black day for 77RAAF. Flying low over the rugged terrain could be hazardous enough at any time but in February the heavy cloud and icy conditions combined to bring about a tragedy when two Australians failed to return from a close-suppport mission, as P2 Stan Williamson recalled:

"It was a pretty bad day. When we finally did go there were only two sections that got off. One went up the east coast which was the more mountainous coast. The west, where we went, was flatter, more of a tidal area. We let down below the cloud. As far as I was concerned, it was the first and only time I've ever fired rockets uphill! You usually fire rockets when you are coming down in a dive, but the cloud base was so far down and these people were somewhere up on the side of the hill. Where they wanted us to put the ordnance in, you just couldn't dive in, so we had to come in level, fire and pull away. That other section went out to the east coast and tried to come in and that's when we lost two fellows. They got fouled up in the mountains . . ."

Bad weather had prevented the other four Mustangs from reaching Wonju and contacting the ground controller for the 2nd Infantry Division. It was decided to abort the mission and jettison the napalm on the east coast before returning to base. As they entered a cloud bank, the Mustangs divided into pairs and began to climb. Minutes later P2 Bill Michelson and his wingman P3 Ray Trebilco heard a voice call over the radio, "I am spinning and am going to bale out". When Michelson and Trebilco broke through the cloud the other two aircraft were nowhere to be seen. They waited but the other two Mustangs did not emerge from the cloud. It was assumed that Flt Lt Keith Matthews (A68-812) and P3 Sinclair Squires (A68-796) had probably collided in mid-air. An exhaustive search was carried out by the Australians next day without result. Neither the men nor the aircraft were ever seen again. Normal missions had to be flown, too, and P2 Williamson was on an armed reconnaissance again, this time with P3 Keith Meggs on his wing. Sweeping low near Seoul they napalmed and destroyed a large school house which had many motor transport and foot tracks around it. South of Yongpyong they damaged a road bridge with their rockets and then used up their ammunition by strafing numerous suspicious bundles on the side of the road. About a mile south of Mansegyo-ri the wreckage of an aircraft was spotted, but on closer scrutiny it appeared to be the relatively old remains of a crashed Royal Navy Sea Fury.

15 February also brought the South Africans another casualty. While flying an armed reconnaissance along the Kaesong-Haeju-Sariwon route, Lt Dereck Doveton and his wingman Lt Doug McKellar found a camouflaged vehicle near Kaesong. They attacked it repeatedly but it was not until after the fourth pass that the target finally caught fire. Doveton instructed McKellar to carry on with the recce while he went in for one final strafing run. It was his undoing. As McKellar climbed away he saw Doveton's low-flying aircraft (304) bounce off a hillside in a cloud of smoke. It somersaulted, crashed into the ground and burst into flames. Doveton had no chance to get out and it would seem that he was probably the victim of ground fire.

Despite the weather, the 2nd Infantry Division at Chipyong-ni had its declining ammunition stocks replenished by a parachute supply drop. Later, a task force of 23 infantry-supported tanks from the US 5th Cavalry set out to relieve Chipyong-ni. Stiff opposition was initially encountered and two tanks were lost, but a breakthrough was made in time to catch a Chinese regiment in the act of forming up for an assault against the 23rd Infantry's perimeter. Dismayed, the Chinese broke and ran – in the wrong direction. They were cut down in a withering crossfire. Elsewhere, X Corps was containing the impetus of the enemy attacks. The success of the Americans at Chipyong-ni was reflected in a rather callous message sent to London by Air Vice-Marshal Bouchier, the RAF AOC Japan:

"The myth of the magical millions of the Chinese in North Korea had been exploded. In the last United Nations offensive, the Americans have learned how easy it is to kill the Chinese, and their morale has greatly increased thereby."

There was now a race between 77RAAF's Flt Lts Fred Barnes and Ross Coburn to reach the 100th mission mark first. Throughout January they had remained neck and neck on the number of sorties flown, and by 15 February the score was at 99 each. Flt lt Olorenshaw had been ahead of both at one time, but while cranking a jeep he had broken a bone in his wrist, and his lower arm had to be encased in plaster. This should have disqualified him from flying but, while Sqn Ldr Cresswell was still absent at Itazuke, he remained the acting CO. After testing his wrist he found he could operate the controls of a Mustang without much difficulty and after only a few days lost from flying, he reintroduced himself to operations and had put himself back into the 100-mission stakes. The weather was poor on 16 February, and effectively curtailed flying. In his capacity as Acting CO, Flt Lt Olorenshaw was instructed to attend a conference of squadron commanders at Taegu that had been called by the 5th Air Force. Here they were told that air interdiction was not working as well as it was hoped. There was positive intelligence that truckloads of supplies were still reaching the Chinese and North Koreans at the front. One method of deception being employed was to drive the vehicles into houses before daylight and then drop a false wall of some kind over them.

The race between Flt Lts Barnes and Coburn finished a dead-heat next day. Both reached the century when they went out on the very same mission, providing close support to the embattled 15th US Infantry Regiment engaged east of Seoul. Flt Lt Coburn led his flight to the vicinity of Sadogam-ni, where they were directed to check out the embankment near Tukto. There were many foxholes but no troops to be seen. Coburn decided that some trees alongside a reservoir to the west were a likely target and these were bombarded with napalm. A large oil fire broke out together with several smaller flare-ups and a fire in a brick building. Smoke billowed up to about 5,000 feet. Other buildings in the vicinity were hit by rockets and strafed. At least three enemy soldiers were killed. An observation post with radio masts on top of it was attacked with inconclusive results. They were obviously in the right place as there was now fairly intense small-arms and automatic weapons fire coming up from the whole area. Barnes' Mustang (A68-780) took a hit in the starboard wing through the roundel and that (A68-725) flown by Flg Off Wittman was hit in the inboard section of the starboard mainplane. Three miles east of Tukto three haystacks and a house were also attacked and destroyed. By the end of the day Flt Lt Olorenshaw, flying on another armed recce, completed his 98th mission. Of the other Australian pilots coming to the end of their tours, P3 Tom Stoney flew his 93rd, and eleven others had flown more than 70 each.

Two days later on 19 February, the Australians classified the weather in the target areas as ceiling and visibility unlimited, allowing the Mustangs to fly 24 sorties. Adding to the 126 missions he had flown in the Pacific War, Flt Lt Olorenshaw notched up his 99th and 100th in Korea. On one of these, with P3 Dick Bessell as his No2, he spotted suspicious looking objects under houses in a village. Closer scrutiny revealed that they were really canvas-covered vehicles; the canvas was the give away, showing up as a dirtier shade of white than the surrounding snow. Using napalm and their machine-guns, they left six large trucks in flames. P3s Ray Trebilco and Kevin Foster destroyed several more trucks found hidden under canvas and bushes at the side of a road. It became obvious that they were loaded with petrol and oil when flames and black smoke billowed out. Elsewhere, the FAC told P2 Stan Williamson, who was leading another flight of Mustangs, that enemy troops were sheltering in a tunnel north of the Han River, near Seoul, so they attacked, letting the napalm tanks skip into the mouth of the tunnel. At least one entered each end of the tunnel and almost certainly would have caused many casualties among the troops inside, provided they were there.

The South Africans employed similar tactics against rail targets using 500-lb high-explosive bombs fitted with 15-second delayed-action fuses. B-26 night intruder crews had reported trains travelling along the supply routes, moving from one tunnel to the next, under the cover of darkness. Reconnaissance pilots on early morning patrols the following day had seen smoke issuing from the very same tunnels. Obviously they were being used as shelters during daylight. Maj Jan Blaauw led a mission to bomb one such tunnel near Ch'ongjin. The eight Mustangs were each loaded with a single 500-lb bomb. Shortly after take-off, one aircraft had to abort. When the remaining seven Mustangs reached the area, Blaauw realised the target area was situated where the surrounding terrain made a glide approach too dangerous. He ordered instead dive-bombing attacks. Although this technique was less accurate, out of the seven bombs dropped, two cut the tracks at the eastern and western ends of the tunnel amd a third entered and exploded inside the tunnel itself, throwing debris out of both ends. F-80s were also in action during the day, 1/Lt Harry Peyser of the 36th FBS crash-landing his AA damaged machine in a river bed. He was seriously injured but luckily a rescue helicopter came to his aid.

A number of accidents occurred at Pusan on 20 February, during which a total of seven

American combat aircraft were either destroyed or damaged. The worst incident happened when a USMC Corsair crashed on take-off with its bombs still on board. As it skidded to a stop its pilot managed to scramble clear, well before the bombs detonated in the resulting fire. Although the explosions were close to 77RAAF's area at the northern end of the strip, there were no casualties and no damage to any of the Australian machines, but one of the 39th FIS's Mustangs was destroyed in the blasts, and two more were seriously damaged while four others received minor damage.

Following the relief of Chipyong-ni, General P'eng's Fourth Phase Offensive had spent most of its energy. The Chinese and North Koreans had been badly hurt by US/UN air and ground action and they had suffered heavy loss of life. Their supplies of food and ammunition were desperately low and there was little they were able to forage in the frozen countryside. On top of this they were threatened by an epidemic of typhus. By 19 February the initiative was unmistakably back with the 8th Army and two days later General Ridgway mounted Operation 'Killer' using his IX and X Corps. The operation was designed to cut off and kill as many of the enemy as possible before they could re-cross the Han. To further weaken Chinese morale Ridgway had leaflets dropped on the retreating troops. They carried a simple message in Chinese: COUNT YOUR MEN.

Flt Lt Des Murphy returned to 77RAAF on 21 February, followed next day by Sqn Ldr Cresswell. Both had been on a jet conversion course with the USAF at Itazuke. They were the only Australians on the big US base and were suitably impressed with the F-80. They found the jets were much less complex to handle than piston-engined aircraft, and following conversion were allowed to fly a few operational missions. Murphy was attached to the 35th FBS, and Cresswell to the 36th FBS. There was a friendly rivalry between the two units to see whose Australian would be the first to fly a mission. Murphy, who had previously flown a Vampire jet in Australia, emerged as the 'winner' but, as his CO remarked, following his own solo on the F-80: "The Yanks very nicely gave me my own personal jet, a T-33 . . ." Such conversion/training flights were not without their share of incidents and, an hour after Murphy had soloed, an American pilot took off in the same machine and a moment later it exploded. His body was recovered from the water but the search for pieces of wreckage continued for days afterwards. Shortly thereafter, Murphy took off with three other F-80 pilots on his first operational jet sortie:

> "We were told to carry out a support operation just near Suwon. American troops were to make an assault on a hill close by. The forward controller told the pilots that as soon as they had given the close support, the ground force would launch an attack and take the hill. So we screamed down on the hill, throwing napalm and rockets at it, and could see the enemy troops running in all directions. It was one of the best operations I had ever been on. We could see exactly what we were doing. The commander of the ground force was talking to us on the radio and said we were putting the stuff right in the vital area."

Afterwards, when war correspondents and the Public Information Office at Itazuke interviewed him, they wrote about the "first Australian to fly American jets in combat" and the occasion rated some exposure in the American press. The two Australians found that the questions of fuel consumption and length of time in the air were always uppermost in the minds of the F-80 pilots. Their standard procedure after take-off was to fly high, let down to operational level, and attack assigned targets with as little delay as possible. During one of his flights Murphy had a more unusual fuel problem. The balance of his F-80 became seriously affected when one of its wingtip drop tanks emptied but the other did not. After a conference with the other pilots in his flight, Murphy decided to try and puncture the tank by firing at it with his .45 pistol. He succeeded. Fuel pressure in the tank forced the remaining fuel out through the hole and the aircraft's balance was restored. In one of his first combat missions Sqn Ldr Cresswell struck trouble. He was flying with three others over the Korean east coast when a number of engine turbine blades shattered. This caused severe vibration, the temperature gauge dropped alarmingly and red warning lights started flashing in the cockpit. He announced the emergency over the radio and headed south to Po'hang safely, and decided to press on to Taegu:

"I was flying up the east coast towards Hungnam. I assume I got hit because I suddenly lost a lot of engine power. There was a lot of bad weather around too. If you're airborne and can fly your aircraft, you lead back with your flight beside you, helping and guiding you, but you actually do the leading. I turned around and flew back. There was certainly damage at the back because there was smoke coming out. I flew through fairly heavy snow – we got used to that there – down around 6,000 feet, may be a bit higher, approaching Taegu. Taegu was a staging post for jets. I asked permission to land. The tower yelled back at me, 'Negative, we've got an emergency landing.' I soon let him know that I was it! I went straight in . . . and got down alright, but the tail fell off . . . burnt out."

Sqn Ldr Cresswell developed a healthy respect for the work that the F-80 pilots had to do:

"On one of my F-80 sorties I was leading an element of two in a flight of four. We were attacking flak – it was a frightening job to attack flak batteries but that was the job of the F-80s. [My No2] got in front of me in the dive for some reason or other. He was hit and blew up. He happened to be the son of the American Secretary of State for the Armed Forces, or something or other. Boy, the enquiry! Here was a foreigner [me] leading an element! My gun camera film actually showed him going in . . ."

The American pilot who was killed was believed to have been Capt Thomas Symington, his aircraft having taken a direct hit while he was attacking an enemy troop position near Seoul on the 13th. A few days later, Flt Lt Murphy's flight was called in to stop a B-26 attacking UN troops. The B-26 pilot obviously did not know exactly where he was and had already made several passes. A voice filled with rage belonging to the American colonel in command of these unfortunate troops boomed over the radio, "I want him shot down immediately!" Murphy recalled:

"I was No2 to the leader, so we flew past and waggled our wings to attract [the B-26 pilot] and let him know that he was doing something wrong. No way in the world did we want to fly in front of him. He had some guns and it may not have been a Yank flying – it could have been a captured B-26. So we went across the top of him and the other pair did the same thing. At this stage the colonel was becoming agitated and wanted to know who was in charge of our flight. The outcome was that we were able, by the four of us flying over his cockpit and waggling our wings, to force the B-26 away. This appeased the colonel, but upset most of us as we had to get a quick target to get rid of the napalm. We had wasted too much time at low altitude."

Before the B-26 left the scene the irate colonel had demanded to know the pilot's name, but what happened to him after he landed, Murphy never found out.

Anticipating that Suwon could be used as a staging post, the USAF moved a refuelling and rearming detachment there on 22 February. At the same time the 334th FIS flew in to Taegu from Japan with its F-86s. One of the pilots was Flt Lt Lévesque, who was amongst those flying CAP sorties in case the Russians carried out a strike against the American bases in Japan; there were many excursions over the sea by Russian aircraft but no encounters:

"I had been sent to north-west Japan [Misawa AFB] and flew CAP over the international waters between Vladivostok and the Sea of Japan until the end of January, completing 26 missions. Then we moved to our main base at Johnson and flew air defence alert missions until 22 February, when we were despatched to Taegu."

The MiGs gained a further success on 23 February, when Maj Ovsyannikov led two *zvenos* to the Anju area where UN fighter-bombers were active. Two F-80s were sighted at 10,000 feet with two more at 18,000 feet, these being pursued by Kapt Pronin and St/Lt Bezmaternykh (who was Kapt Gordeev's No2). Gordeev, unaware that he was alone, was then attacked by an F-80 from astern and his aircraft sustained several hits, forcing him to eject. He landed safely about ten miles south of Anju. The only success was that reported by Maj Ovsyannikov who chased one pair of F-80s and shot down one after firing a long burst. This was probably the aircraft flown by 1/Lt Jack Brock of the 8th FBS, who failed to return. Brock may have been responsible for shooting down Gordeev. The MiGs caught the vulnerable B-29s again two days later, on 25 February, Maj Ovsyannikov again leading a successful mission. The eight MiGs attacked in pairs. The initial interception was unsuccessful but, during the second, two of the bombers were seen to be badly damaged, while two more were hit during a third pass. Four bombers were claimed, one each being credited to Maj Ovsyannikov, Kapt Parfenov, Kapt Pronin, and St/Lt Monakhov, while Pronin's aircraft was damaged by return fire.

Although the Sabres began to fly combat air patrols from Taegu immediately, they had insufficient range to reach any further north than P'yongyang. Despite the intention, they could not stage forward to Suwon because the airfield was too badly damaged to permit its use. Nevertheless, on 26 February, the 5th Air Force informed FEAF that it was again prepared to escort B-29s into north-western Korea. In response, FEAF directed Bomber Command to return to interdiction attacks on targets in that area, beginning on 1 March.

Meanwhile on 23 February, four RAF fighter pilots arrived in Japan on posting to 77RAAF as jet conversion instructors, their task to convert the Mustang pilots to the twin-jet Meteor F8. They were Flt Lt Max Scannell AFC (see Appendix III) from 12 Group HQ, a New Zealander in the RAF, who commanded the detachment, Flt Lt Frank Easley from 63 Squadron at RAF Waterbeach, and Flt Lt Colin Blyth AFC (see Appendix III) and Sgt Reg Lamb from 203 AFS at RAF Driffield. Flt Lt Blyth, known to his friends as Joe, recalled:

> "Reg Lamb of 2 Squadron, 203 AFS Driffield, and myself of 1 Squadron, were posted to 77 Squadron RAAF. Presumably we volunteered. We travelled by Hastings TG531 from RAF Lyneham to Changi, Singapore, with Frank Easley and Max Scannell. The idea was, I believe, also an experiment in rapid transportation of troops; no night stops – refuelling only – to see how fit they were for duty on arrival. In the event, the mixture of nurses (female) and others – apart from Frank, Max, Reg and myself – looked completely bushed. As for we four, we just headed for the bar! The flying time was 36 hours, 20 minutes.
>
> From Changi we left two days later by Dakota for Iwakuni, via a one-day stop in Kai Tak [Hong Kong] ; it was interesting, dodging in and out of cloud around the small mountainous islands to avoid people taking pot-shots at us! Arrival in Japan was 23 January. 77 Squadron RAAF was still busy operating from Pusan (K-9) and things were not in place to commence conversions. We were not supposed to be flying in Korea. However, Dick Cresswell was an operational type and took little persuading to allow us to join the Squadron at K-9. On 27 and 28 February I carried out two familiarisation flights on the Mustang [A68-782] . . ."

The four RAF pilots arrived in Japan one day ahead of the British Light Fleet Carrier HMS *Warrior* which dropped anchor off Iwakuni with a deck cargo of 15 Meteor F8s and two Meteor T7 two-seat trainers. The jets were transferred from the carrier by lighter, and then transported by road to Iwakuni. For protection from the effects of sea salt corrosion they had been covered with black inhibitor, but this had baked hard. To help prepare the aircraft for service, the RAAF found it necessary to employ more local Japanese labour, many of whom had worked in the Japanese aircraft industry before and during WWII. They were keen to work and were respected for their craftsmanship and skill. Although the British authorities had hoped to have ghosted the Meteors to the war zone, the world at large was soon aware of their arrival, as noted by Flt Lt George Odgers:

> "Futile attempts were made to hush up the sending of the British Meteor jets to Korea. A party of Australians who, prior to joining the Squadron, had been sent to England to pick up technical knowledge of the aircraft, were sworn to secrecy. But when the Meteors were on the aircraft carrier *Warrior* at Malta, en route to the Far East, they were photographed by a news photographer. Some time later the aircraft carrier was sighted off Formosa on its voyage home to England, and a report came out of Taipeh that the Chinese Nationalists were threatening to bomb an unidentified carrier reported twenty miles off the west coast of Formosa. British representatives asked the Chinese to delay any contemplated bombing because the carrier 'could be British'. Fortunately, no attack was made." [5]

---

[5] See *Across the Parallel*.

On this same day the first draft of replacement pilots for 2SAAF arrived at Chinhae. Unlike their US and Australian counterparts who, under normal circumstances, flew an operational tour of duty of 100 sorties, the South Africans, after taking stock of the stresses of operational flying coupled with the unpredictable nature of the Korean weather, the vulnerability of the Mustang to ground fire, and the real threat posed by the superiority of the MiG-15, decided on a maximum tour of 75 operational sorties. Among the new arrivals was Cmdt Ray Armstrong, who had been appointed to take over from Cmdt Theron when the latter's tour expired. The new men immediately began an indoctrination and training programme under Capt Badenhorst.

When F-86 FU-271 touched down at Taegu on the morning of 25 February, US groundcrews of the 334th FIS were surprised to see a moustachioed RAF officer climb down from the cockpit, an array of ribbons below his wings denoting the arrival of an obvious fighter ace. This new pilot joining the 334th was Flt Lt S.W. Daniel DSO DFC, a WWII veteran with 16 victories to his credit (see Appendix III). Another RAF exchange officer, Steve Daniel had been serving with the 71st FIS in Pittsburg when the call came through for him to depart for Korea. He arrived at Johnson AFB at the end of January and had been attached to the 335th FIS until familiarised with the locality and operational procedures.

The Australians lost another pilot on 26 February, the eleventh since the beginning of the war. P3 Ken Royal in Mustang A68-704, flying as No2 to Flt Lt Des Murphy, failed to return from an armed reconnaissance mission north of Seoul. Sqn Ldr Cresswell later wrote:

> "The loss of P3 Royal is due to damn bad luck . . .[He was] a lad with a very keen eye for picking up camouflaged targets. He was, at the time of reporting low oil pressure, examining camouflaged objects about ten miles north-west of Seoul. He reported his trouble to his No1, Flt Lt Murphy, then jettisoned his napalm and flew in a southerly direction intending, I think, to cross the bombing line into friendly territory. To do so necessitated a wheels-up landing . . . He did a belly landing, skidded twenty yards, hit a tidal embankment about six feet high and, after hitting, cartwheeled a couple of times which caused the aircraft to turn over on its back into two or three feet of water. We were lucky in having a helicopter within 38 minutes of the crash, [plus] a C-47 and five of our F-51s. Unfortunately the helicopter could not land because of the water, although the pilot said there was no hope of Royal surviving. A ground party reached the aircraft at dusk. The aircraft was under water. We got the body the next day."

The Americans also lost a fighter-bomber pilot on this date, 1/Lt Ray VanBelt of the 36th FBS being shot down by AA during a napalm run at Hengch'on. After the maximum effort needed in the Hoengsong area earlier in the month, the 18th FBG, the 35th FBG, and the 1st Marine Air Wing had settled down to the highly effective armed reconnaissance saturation coverage of their assigned areas. They soon went further and sub-divided their areas into squadron sectors. Flying over the same terrain in pairs day after day, the Mustang and Corsair pilots soon developed the ability to pick out minute changes and detect more and more camouflaged equipment. The 18th FBG, which included 2SAAF, was swiftly building up a reputation as the "ace truck busters of the 5th Air Force". This was due in no small part to the forceful personality and leadership of the Wing's new CO, Colonel Turner C. Rogers, whose doctrine was:

> ". . . Thoroughness is the secret of the successful 'truck hunter' . . . There is only one way to detect camouflaged vehicles, and that is by flying low and slow and thoroughly searching every foot of ground. Every building, haystack, ravine, wooded area, and side road must be checked and then double checked . . ."

Before a day's mission intelligence officers would analyse the preceding night's vehicle sightings and calculate the areas where enemy convoys were likely to take cover before dawn. To do this they estimated a vehicle speed of 15mph. The first pair of Mustangs flying out in the morning would sweep these suspect areas to pick up any vehicles damaged by night intruders, and to oblige the enemy to camouflage before daybreak. The 18th FBG's truck hunters usually spent up to two hours in the target area. By maintaining this constant pressure, the Wing alone accounted for 728 vehicles destroyed and 137 damaged during the month, out of a total of 1,366 (plus 812 damaged) claimed destroyed by the 5th Air Force. Thus pressured from the air, and on the ground by UN forces, the Communists had withdrawn so hastily from the line of contact that they had abandoned much of their equipment. Aside from some desperate delaying actions, all Chinese and North Korean resistance south of the Han had collapsed.

The outstanding work carried out by the South Africans who had, by the end of the month, flown a total of 1,217 operational sorties during the course of 407 missions, was now acknowledged when the Americans awarded DFCs to five 2SAAF pilots; the recipients were Cmdt Servaas Theron, Capt John Davis, Capt Hendrik Odendaal, Capt Gordon Lipawsky and Capt Wessel Badenhorst. In addition, 36 Air Medals, 19 First Oak Leaf Clusters, two Second Oak Leaf Clusters, and three Third Oak Leaf Clusters were presented to the assembled pilots. Earlier in the month there had been a similar ceremony at Pusan when 14 pilots of 77RAAF were awarded US Air Medals, including medals announced for Flt Lt Gordon Harvey (now missing, but a POW) and P3 Geoff Stephens (now misssing, believed killed).

The RAF Sunderland Detachment based at Iwakuni flew a further eight operational sorties during the month, one of which almost ended in disaster for the crew of RN282/C of 88 Squadron. Maintaining the around-the-clock blockade of the North Korean ports in conjunction with the US Navy patrol squadrons required long and arduous flights, often up to 12 hours duration. It necessitated much night flying as well as long daylight patrols, often as far north as Vladivostok. During the long winter months, in the draughty, unheated Sunderlands the temperature often fell to as low as −20°C and the weather made icing a frequent menace. Added to this, the very mountainous terrain around Korea and Southern Japan created another hazard. The safety height for the airfield at Iwakuni was 4,000 feet and frequently the only way in and out of the bay for the flying boats was to either fly over the top at 4,500 feet in dense cloud or to crawl through a narrow gap visually as low as 100 feet or less. During one such patrol on 7 February, RN282/C was forced to turn back with severe engine and airframe icing, its crew having to jettison 1,000 gallons of fuel as the pilot struggled to maintain height and eventually managed to alight safely in the bay. A further four Sunderlands arrived to relieve those currently at Iwakuni, these from 209 Squadron under Sqn Ldr Le Cheminant; the four machines were SZ571/Y captained by Flt Lt B.C. Horsnell, PP198/V (Flt Lt A. Hutchinson), RN303/X (Flg Off K.J. Evans), and SZ560/W (Plt Off L.J. Day).

* * *

During the winter months of 1950/51, 650 captured UN troops, mainly Americans but with a sprinkling of British, were forced to march to a POW camp about 40 miles south-east of P'yongyang. In the harsh conditions, with little food, unsuitable clothing, and no medical treatment – and accompanied by harsh guards – only about 200 survived the march. On arrival, they joined about 500 inmates in what was known as Bean Camp, on account of the diet of soya beans which the prisoners were fed. One survivor of the march was an Australian-born member of the British Army who had been a POW of the Japanese in WWII, who now found himself in the same camp in which he had been incarcerated by his former captors; he even found his initials carved on the wall of a hut. Shortly after the arrival of the latest pathetic intake, a flight of US F-51s strafed the camp and inflicted casualties amongst prisoners and guards. A few weeks later there was another strafing attack by F-51s when it was estimated between 30 and 35 prisoners were killed. Another POW camp was located about eight miles south of P'yoktong, known as Camp V, which housed at this time about 2,000 Americans, mainly from the 1st US Cavalry and 2nd Division, plus a few Commonwealth and Turkish prisoners. By early February 1951, pneumonia, dysentry and malnutrition was rife, and the death rate among the American prisoners, many of whom were teenagers, began to rise alarmingly. One of the handful of American doctors later wrote:

> "They had no discipline. Give them an order and they'd say, 'Go to hell'. Which was just
> what the Chinese wanted. They refused to be ordered about, reasoned with, or forced." [6]

Another reflected on the prevailing attitude of some:

[6] See *The Captives of Korea* by William Lindsay White.

"If a sick man refused to eat, why coax him? When he died there would be more for the strong. However much or little this lack of morale and discipline in the American enlisted men's compound increased the death rate, it shocked those who saw it. Yet the picture was not all black. For every bully who robbed the sick of food there were a dozen who nursed their buddies." [7]

Nevertheless, one British officer reported:

"The spectacle of Americans being taken out of their huts [by other Americans] and left naked to freeze, was something we just did not understand." [8]

By the end of February, when the death rate had reached 28 a day at Camp V, the Chinese allowed small amounts of penicillin and sulphonamides to be used, but without proper food and clothing, and inadequate shelter, the drugs had little effect[9]. Sadly, the war was proving to be one where many atrocities were committed by both sides. There was the shooting by North Korean troops of American POWs, their hands tied behind their backs with barbed wire, during the early days of the war; there was the murder of 100 Americans whose bodies were discovered in a railway tunnel; there was the shooting of 130 Chinese POWs by US Marines as they tried to escape during fighting near Koto-ri in December; there was the random and wanton shooting of suspected Communists by South Korean military police squads, as witnessed by British troops, some of whom complained bitterly to their own MPs or the British press; there was the execution of corrupt South Korean officials by South Korean military police on the orders of President Rhee. These were just a few of the many atrocities by armed men against unarmed men during the first few months of the war. Following one such incident in December, the British Minister in Korea had written to London:

"Besides two instances of mass executions reported in my telegram, a third occurred near Seoul on the evening of 20 December, within half a mile of 29 Brigade Headquarters. It was stopped by British troops on orders from Brigade Headquarters when 20 persons had already been shot, but the execution of 38 more was prevented . . . It transpired that the South Korean military authorities were responsible in this case . . . As the threat to Seoul developed, and owing to the destruction of the death house, the authorities resorted to these hurried mass executions by shooting in order to avoid the transfer of condemned prisoners south, or leaving them behind to be liberated by the Communists . . ." [10]

And not least, there was the inhumane treatment of UN prisoners by North Koreans and Chinese in the various POW camps, which continued throughout the bitter war, a conflict which General S.L.A Marshall, the US Army historian, later called "the century's nastiest little war", possibly not without good cause.

[7/8] See *The Captives of Korea*.

[9] By the end of the Korean War the population of Camp V had risen to around 3,500, but it was estimated that about 1,500 had died in that one camp alone, most in the first three months of 1951. Of the 7,140 Americans to fall into enemy hands, 2,701 died in captivity, as did about 50 of the 1,188 British and Commonwealth POWs. However, none of the 229 Turkish prisoners died in captivity.

[10] See *The Korean War* by Max Hastings.

CHAPTER V

FIRST MIG FOR THE CANADIANS

March – April 1951

"If we had a strong air support, we could have driven the enemy into the sea and the protracted defensive battles raging from 25 January to 22 April . . . should have been avoided."

Assessment by the Chinese Communist Special Aviation Group

The new month opened with the MiGs chalking up another success against UN fighter-bombers. Shortly after 1100, Kapt Borodin led eight MiGs of the 28th GuFAR to patrol in the Sinuiju area where four F-80s were seen strafing ground targets. The leader of the second *zveno*, Podpolkovnik Kolyadin, performed a head-on attack against these without success, although one was claimed shot down by St/Lt Bushmelev, his wingman. Another was engaged by Maj Timofeev and his No2 but this evaded and escaped.

In their quest to block the Communist supply routes from Manchuria, the Americans became over-anxious to strike at the bridges in Korea's north-west, right in MiG Alley, and US Bomber Command was directed to make the first attack on these targets on 1 March, the 98th BG undertaking the mission. But first a formation of F-86s of the 334th FIS operating from Taegu carried out a sweep of the P'yongyang area without incident, Flt Lt Steve Daniel flying FU-080 on this occasion. With F-80s tasked to provide escort, the force of 18 B-29s from Japan encountered unexpected headwinds. They were late for the rendezvous, causing the escorting jet pilots to keep an anxious eye on fuel consumption, which was always a major problem, and it was not long into the flight that they were obliged to return to base. As a result, the bombers had to continue to their bridge target at Kogunyong near Ch'ongju minus their escort. Shortly after dropping their bombs, they were intercepted by six MiGs from the 28th GuFAR led by Maj Ovsyannikov, two of the original eight having had to return with undercarriage problems. The MiG leader spotted four B-29s at 20,000 feet. He ordered Kapt Motov and his No2 to provide cover while he led his *zveno* into the attack. The bombers formed into a tight defensive formation as they headed home but the MiGs were all over them, Ovsyannikov's group having been joined by five more led by Podpolkovnik Kolyadin. In the ensuing running battle, a MiG was claimed shot down by one of the air gunners, Sgt William H. Finnegan of the 343rd BS, but ten of the bombers were damaged, three so badly that rather than risk the flight back to Japan their crews made emergency landings at Taegu. The Russians believed that four bombers had been severely damaged, two of which were reported to have crashed into the sea west of Seksen. Maj Ovsyannikov was credited with shooting down one, shared with his No2 Kapt Pronin, and a second was awarded jointly to Kapts Parfenov and Motov, while others had been engaged by pairs of MiGs led by Kapts Akimov and Gavrovenko. There were no recorded losses for the MiGs.

That same day the Mustang pilots of 2SAAF established a new record by flying 32 combat sorties in a single day. These comprised eight armed reconnaissance missions over the roads north-east of Chorwon, and eight close-escort missions. The most successful armed reconnaissance was flown by Lts Doug McKellar and Des Deans when they discovered seven trucks hidden in an area surrounded by high hills. The topography of the area made the trucks difficult to approach, so the two pilots adopted a different method of attack, one never attempted by 2SAAF before. Instead of coming in at the targets in a shallow dive, as was usual with napalm, they solved the problem by dive-bombing the trucks, and in doing so scored direct hits. Meanwhile, the most successful close-support mission of the day was led by Lt Ed Jones when his sections destroyed two tanks on the southern side of Seoul. Other units of the 18th FBG were not quite as successful, Lt Colonel Robert May, CO of the 67th FBS, being shot down by ground fire although he managed to bale out, and was rescued by a USN helicopter from the heavy cruiser USS *St Paul*.

Although 2SAAF did not take part in night sorties, the South African pilots had a taste of radar bombing procedure when Capt Lipawsky led a four-aircraft flight on an experimental radar-directed bombing mission through heavy overcast. The ground controller directed the flight on four different bombing runs at increasing altitudes before he finally gave the order to release bombs at 22,000 feet. The directions given to Lipawsky were constantly interrupted by other controllers who broke in and, when it was judged that the most suitable position had finally been reached, the South Africans gained little satisfaction in blindly releasing their bombs into cloud. Lipawsky concluded that the whole technique was inefficient but might be vastly improved if a separate radio channel be employed.

Next day (2 March), 2SAAF lost two of its most experienced pilots, both of them WWII veterans. Lt Dennis Ruiter (see Appendix III) was leading four Mustangs north of Wonsan when his aircraft (301) developed engine trouble. West of the target area he reported that his coolant temperature gauge was fluctuating, and decided to return to base escorted by his No2. A few minutes later the Mustang began to trail white glycol smoke and realising that he only had minutes before his engine seized, Ruiter headed out to sea to attempt a force-landing on the beach at Yo-do island. His approach was too high and he overshot, but while turning to port to come round for another run his wing struck the sea. The Mustang crashed into the water and sank out of sight like a stone. Despite circling the spot and thoroughly searching the area, the remaining members of the flight who had followed could find no trace of Ruiter or his aircraft. The second SAAF pilot killed in action that day was Capt Wessel Badenhorst. His mission was to carry out a long-range armed reconnaissance towards a section of the main supply route between Sinanju and Ch'ongju. While crossing over the Ch'ongch'on at an altitude of 500 feet, the flight suddenly came under heavy anti-aircraft fire. Over the radio Badenhorst's shouted warning stopped in mid-sentence, "Look out – there's bags of flak . . ." He had obviously been hit for his aircraft (317) went out of control, climbing and then diving steeply. Urgent calls by the others for him to pull out raised no response and the Mustang crashed and burst into flames.

MiGs were also active during the day, pilots of the 28th GuFAR reporting successes against two F-80s and an F-84. During the first action shortly after 1100, Kapt Akimov's formation encountered four F-80s but were unable to engage successfully. A few minutes later they sighted a dozen more but were forced to return to base owing to lack of fuel, Maj Ovsyannikov's *zveno* providing cover as they landed, before crossing the Yalu to intercept the F-80s. Four of the fighter-bombers were sighted and engaged, Ovsyannikov shooting at one which fell away trailing black smoke, while St/Lt Monakhov hit another. At 1210 Kapt Borodin led off six more MiGs when yet more USAF fighter-bombers were reported to be ground strafing, meeting four F-84s which bounced the third pair led by Maj Korobov. These were spotted in time by the leader of the second pair, Maj Timofeev, who pulled round in a tight turn and shot down the rear Thunderjet, which fell away trailing black smoke.

Next day it was the turn of the 40th FIS to lose a pilot when Capt Edward Williams was shot down by ground fire, while the 45th TRS lost its first pilot to be killed in action when 1/Lt Marshall Summerlin failed to return from a reconnaissance sortie. Lt Piet Swemmer narrowly escaped becoming 2SAAF's third fatality within a few days when, while at the controls of Mustang 305 on 4 March, his engine cut out on take-off. Despite having only limited control, he managed to bring the aircraft down safely in a rice paddy at the end of the runway. He was uninjured although the Mustang was beyond repair. Meanwhile, his companions carried out 16 sorties during the day and destroyed two villages, two warehouses, and a dozen vehicles, and inflicted damage to other villages and vehicles. Not so fortunate was Capt Robert Cannon of the 8th FBS whose F-80 was shot down by ground fire.

After the savage blow struck at the B-29s on the first day of the month, it was obviously necessary for the F-86 to begin carrying out patrols along the Yalu to block the MiGs as soon as possible. To be able to do this they had to move forward to Suwon airfield north of Taegu, since Taegu itself was not ideally suitable for jet fighters even though the 334th FIS persevered, escorting B-29s raiding P'yongyang on 3 March. The runway at Taegu consisted of 7,000 feet of pierced steel planking laid over compacted dirt and clay. While this type of surface had proven adequate for WWII-vintage fighters such as the F-51, landings and take-offs by jet fighters, as well as bombers and transport aircraft, had played havoc with the planking. Jet blast had eroded the natural undersurface, causing dips and holes to form, and pilots complained they were experiencing multiple take-offs before their aircraft finally became airborne. Extreme distortion of the airframe and wings of heavily-laden F-80s and F-84s could be discerned as they struggled into the air. In places the planking had become bent and torn, with sharp edges that projected upwards which were a hazard for tyres and fuel or napalm tanks – with occasional disastrous results. The steel planking had another disturbing feature. It tended to roll forward in front of an aircraft's wheels and, in effect, resulted in an uphill take-off with a consequent loss of acceleration. The only other alternative was Suwon, but this was just a waterlogged, narrow, bomb-pitted concrete runway surrounded by a sea of mud. It lacked a taxiway, so aircraft had to taxi back along the runway while others were coming in to land. The flight surface was so constricted that fighters using this strip had to land one behind the other, risking the turbulence of jet air wash. Despite these drawbacks, the 334th FIS began to stage Yalu patrols through Suwon as from 6 March.

Next day (7 March), rather than attempt a frontal assault across the wide and now thawing Han at Seoul, General Ridgway ordered the US IX and X Corps to attack northwards in central Korea. This attack, called Operation 'Ripper', was designed to create an outflanking bulge east of Seoul from which UN forces could then envelope the capital city. The most critical phase of this operation was expected to be at the beginning as the IX Corps' 25th Infantry Division attempted to establish a bridgehead across the Han near its confluence with the Pukhan, about 15 miles east of Seoul. As it did so, the 5th Air Force mounted some 575 sorties in support. About one-third of these were directed against personnel, supplies and vehicles on the enemy's immediate rear. US fighter-bombers were joined by others from the USMC next day over the bridgehead, while almost two dozen B-29s hit the major supply centre near Ch'unch'on. Bad flying weather the following day reduced the FEAF's effort but the Mustang groups found some worthwhile targets and made effective strikes. Outside Seoul, a single flight of 35th FBG pilots claimed about 100 Communist troops killed and wounded, while near Chorwon the 18th FBG destroyed 22 enemy trucks. The whole of the 27th British Commonwealth Brigade, which had recently been reinforced by the arrival of 2/Princess Patricia's Canadian Light Infantry, launched an attack on high country south of Yangdogwon-ni, a town on the road to Honch'on. The enemy's front line, at this stage, was extended from the mountainous area south of Honch'on, west to the Pukhan which joined the Han just east of Seoul, then along the Han itself westwards through Seoul to the sea. The Argylls, Middlesex and Canadians each advanced without needing to fire a shot, but the 6th ROK Division on the Australian flank failed to cross the road and left them exposed to heavy mortar and rifle fire. Two men were killed and seven wounded. Eight more Australians were wounded before American mortar and New Zealand artillery fire eventually suppressed the enemy mortars and next day the defended ridge was taken without further opposition. The 7th Regiment of the 1st US Marines then established contact on the Commonwealth Brigade's right flank, making the line secure. On the left, the 1st US Cavalry Division and the 24th US Infantry Division completed the UN front which was by now virtually back in control of South Korea.

The 18th FBG lost another aircraft on 8 March when Capt Lucian Schuler of the 67th FBS belly-landed his Mustang at K-13 after being hit near Kaesong. He was fortunate, as next day 1/Lt Gerald Heagney of the same unit was also shot down by ground fire, his aircraft seen to crash into a hillside. It was the turn of 2SAAF to lose another of its experienced pilots on 10 March, when Capt John Davis led a strike against enemy troops entrenched along a ridge near Yandogwon-ni between the Han and Pukham. When they reached the target area the Mustangs encountered intense small-arms fire and, as Davis turned in to attack, his aircraft (321) suddenly fell into a spin. It failed to recover and struck the ground still carrying its full load of napalm and rockets. As the remainder of his flight grimly pressed home their attacks, they could see the wreckage of the Mustang burning fiercely on the ground. His was yet another tragic loss to the South African squadron.

After intense non-stop, day and night work, the airstrip at Suwon was at last declared sufficiently serviceable to be used by the F-86s, following completion of parking space and the setting-up of a tented camp. Accordingly, the 334th FIS moved north from Taegu to Suwon, although, because of the single narrow runway, there remained some risk. Meanwhile, the 336th FIS flew its Sabres across from Japan to take up residence at Taegu. From there the 336th's fighters could stage forward to Suwon each day and then take part in the Yalu patrols. There occurred an inconclusive clash on 11 March when 16 MiGs – ten of the 72nd GuFAR and six of the 28th GuFAR – encountered four F-86s some 3,000 feet above but, as they climbed to engage, the American jets climbed even higher. Only Kapt Dubrovin was able to narrow the range and open fire, albeit with success. Flt Lt Steve Daniel flying FU-160 with the 334th FIS saw his first MiGs, noting that eight plus were engaged without any conclusive results, although Capt Jabara claimed one damaged. With minor exceptions, the tactics employed by the F-86s in their renewed patrols over north-western Korea were the same as those used during December. The flights arrived in MiG Alley at intervals, the leading flight usually going to Sinuiju to stir up a reaction across the Yalu. If swirling dust could be seen on the runway at Antung it indicated that the MiGs were taking off. The F-86 leader would report this fact over the R/T and the other flights would converge on the area.

A dozen MiGs took to the air at about 1015 next day (12 March) – ten from the 72nd GuFAR led by Podpolkovnik Bordun, including one flown by Podpolkovnik Vasilii Mukhin, the commanding officer, and two of the 28th GuFAR led by Podpolkovnik Kolyadin as top cover – when USAF fighters were reported approaching from the south. Having climbed to 39,000 feet, they spotted a dozen F-86s flying in three sections. The first section had begun to descend so Bordun led an attack against the second section, ordering Kapt Guts' *zveno* to engage the third section. Guts went for the leader while St/Lts Chizh and Sokolov took on the No2. Kapt Dymchenko, flying with another *zveno* reported seeing a Sabre fall away, apparently out of control, and this was credited to Kapt Guts. Another was seen to be hit by Podpolkovnik Mukhin. Meanwhile, the 28th GuFAR pair flying top cover – Podpolkovnik Kolyadin and St/Lt Bushmelev – had also engaged the Sabre formation, Kolyadin attacking the leading aircraft of the second section, on which he closed to 400 yards and witnessed his cannon shells striking home, but was forced to break away when two more Sabres intercepted from astern. Returning to base alone, Kolyadin was bounced by four more and, despite his aircraft taking 26 bullet strikes, he landed safely. It would seem that he had been attacked by Lt Colonel Eagleston, who claimed a MiG damaged. Flt Lt Daniel had reported seeing seven MiGs take off from Antung and these trailed his flight as it returned southwards to Suwon.

During the afternoon, while patrolling Sabres converged on a spot where MiGs were reported to be assembling north of the Yalu, another group of ten MiGs of the 28th GuFAR slipped across the river unnoticed and near Namsi bounced a flight of four F-80s of the 36th FBS. The American pilots saw their attackers in time and managed to evade, reporting that two MiGs were seen to collide as they attempted to get on the tail of 2/Lt Charles Blomberg's aircraft. This was an accurate observation and both St/Lt Sokolov and St/Lt Bushmelev were killed as a result of the collision. Although Podpolkovnik Kolyadin claimed damage to one of the fighter-bombers, all four F-80s returned safely, but the 18th FBG lost another Mustang and its pilot during the day, 1/Lt Willis R. Brown of the 12th FBS being shot down and killed by ground fire.

77RAAF, in particular, now entered a brief period of intense operations with its anticipated successes and losses. Flt Lt Olorenshaw led four Mustangs in providing air cover over an American pilot, Capt Allen H. Vanderyerk of the 40th FIS, who had been shot down inside enemy territory at Ch'ongch'on. The RAAF aircraft circled in line astern, firing at nearby ridges and houses to keep enemy troops at bay, while a helicopter performed a rescue. Next day Maj Carl Aubrey, deputy CO of the 40th FIS, was shot down and killed by ground fire. On 13 March, a dawn reconnaissance by Sgts[1] Lyall Klaffer and Dick Bessell discovered what appeared to be a motor vehicle crudely covered with branches and green foliage. As they made a pass they could see their shells ricochet off the target. Assuming it to be heavily armoured, the next pass was made using rockets. At the same time, about one hundred yards away, Klaffer noticed a machine-gun position open fire on Bessell's Mustang as it went in to attack. The camouflage was blown away to reveal a large rock that had apparently been disguised as bait for a trap. Bessell did not realise that his machine had been hit until he saw the hole in its fuselage after landing. Elsewhere, on another mission, Flt Lt Olorenshaw's aircraft was also hit and damaged by ground fire. 2SAAF's deputy CO had a narrow escape, too. Just three days after the South Africans had lost Capt Davis, Maj Jan Blaauw's aircraft was hit in the mainplane by anti-aircraft fire during a strike against some railway trucks. Despite the severe damage he was able to get back to Chinhae and carry out a safe landing.

By 14 March, 77RAAF was flying up to 24 sorties a day in direct support of the slowly advancing ground troops. Seoul was re-occupied by UN forces for the second time when American troops re-entered the South Korean capital without encountering any serious opposition. Next day, while Flt Lt Scannell flew his first operational sortie with 77RAAF – an armed recce to Ich'on in A68-715 – two of the Australian pilots were obliged to crash-land because of anti-aircraft fire following an attack on an enemy village north of Kimpo, when a dozen buildings were destroyed. Sgt Keith Meggs' aircraft (A68-737) was hit over Munsan and rapidly lost oil pressure. As he watched the gauge drop until it went right off the clock, he reported to Flt Lt Murphy who was flying alongside, that he was about to bale out. Murphy advised him that Kimpo was just ahead. He did not know whether the airfield was again in UN hands but considered it the best chance before the engine seized. Flying at very low power he managed to nurse the Mustang to the strip and belly-land safely:

> "As I slid to a halt, I saw a US Marine or Navy Corsair also on its belly a hundred yards away to port. Things were so chaotic about that time that I wasn't sure whether the airfield was in our hands or not. When two Oriental-looking soldiers approached, I climbed on the wing of my plane, loosened the pistol in its holster and tried to figure whether they were Chinese, North Koreans or South Koreans. When they got a little closer they identified themselves as South Koreans, and I knew I was all right. After the two soldiers came up, a US Army jeep came and took me to an aid station somewhere a little south, and it was from here that I was picked up by Lt Ern McQuarrie USAF and flown to Suwon in a Sikorsky S-51 [actually an H-5, which Flt Lt Murphy had called up]. Then by C-47 and C-46 in two stages back to Pusan. I was flying again the next day."

A similar successful outcome was in store for Wt Off Ron Howe who force-landed A68-708 on the bank of the Han after having been hit by ground fire, a rescue helicopter whisking him away to safety within 20 minutes of being brought down. Not so lucky was Capt Clarence V. Slack Jr of the 36th FBS whose F-80 was the latest victim of ground fire. More Sabre sweeps followed, interrupted by an escort to an RB-45 reconnoitring the Kangye area. Flt Lt Daniel reported sighting 30-plus MiGs on Antung airfield on 15 March, and a further seven airborne north of the Yalu, while next day his flight was bounced by at least seven MiGs which caused him to comment, with obvious understatement, that it had been an "anxious moment."

Antung saw the arrival of the 2nd Eskadrilya of the 72nd GuFAR on the 16th while, at 1030, six MiGs of the 28th GuFAR led by Kapt Akimov were scrambled on the approach of UN aircraft from the south. After climbing to 29,000 feet, Akimov received a message that four aircraft were in his vicinity. As the MiGs turned to port Kapt Pisanenko spotted six F-86s 1,500

---

[1] The RAAF had now reverted to its former system of NCO ranks, dispensing with the P1, P2, P3, and P4 for the more familiar and acceptable Sergeant (Sgt), Flight Sergeant (Flt Sgt) and Warrant Officer 1 and 2 (Wt Off 1 and 2).

feet below and went into the attack. The Sabre pilots spotted them in time and broke formation. Akimov pursued the first pair, fired and missed, while Pisanenko was more successful and claimed strikes on the right wing of the leader of the second pair. Meanwhile, a further ten MiGs led by Maj Afonin had arrived, having climbed to 46,000 feet where they sighted eight Sabres but these were already returning southwards. During the afternoon the 151st FAD put 14 MiGs into the air, these encountering ten Sabres at 38,000 feet. The Russian pilots noted that the leading pair was about 20 miles ahead of the pack. Podpolkovnik Bordun led an attack on these two, but they evaded and returned to the south.

The 72nd GuFAR was now getting into its stride, four MiGs being vectored to the Sensen-Antung railway line on the morning of the 17th, where Podpolkovnik Bordun spotted four F-80s strafing targets near Sensen. The MiGs swept into attack, St/Lt Khominich firing at both the leader and his wingman of the second pair before they broke and evaded. Kapt Dubrovin, however, followed one which his colleagues believed blew up under his fire, but he failed to return, his aircraft seen crashing into the mountains. The Americans, from the 36th FBS, reported a slightly different version of events. They stated that the aircraft flown by 1/Lt Howard J. Landry collided with a MiG, which was in turn being pursued by 2/Lt Lloyd Smith who was about to open fire when the collision occurred. The sister 35th FBS also lost a pilot when 1/Lt Donald R. Jenkins failed to return from another sortie. It was the turn of the 25th FIS to lose an aircraft and its pilot next day, 1/Lt Albert H. Bull being shot down by ground fire. None of the three F-80 pilots survived.

The 27th Fighter-Escort Group at Itazuke now received a new pilot, Sqn Ldr The Honourable Michael Adderley AFC and Bar[2], one of the RAF's most experienced instructor pilots and former test pilot at the RAE, who had more recently been attached to Air Headquarters Malaya where he had attended a short course on air-to-ground rocket-firing, flying Vampire jet fighter-bombers. He joined the 523rd Squadron commanded by Maj Albert Fell and commenced familiarising himself with the Group's F-84s, initially flying FS-356, FS-378 and FS-165, before participating in his first operational sortie, an armed reconnaissance, on 19 March in FS-424.

Sgts Lyall Klaffer and Harry Strange of 77RAAF carried out an attack on a village near Wonsan on the 19th, during which Strange (A68-782) reported that his aircraft had been hit by flak and that his engine was losing oil pressure rapidly. Klaffer ordered him to head east for Wonsan harbour where he would be able to bale out near blockading UN ships but, when over the sea, Klaffer was horrified to see the figure of Strange plummet into the water, his parachute unopened. A USN helicopter was quickly on the scene but could find no trace of the Australian pilot, who had only recently joined 77RAAF. It was thought that he might have hit his head as he baled out and been knocked unconscious or perhaps killed outright. An investigation subsequently suggested that his parachute had become detached, causing him to fall to his death. The 45th TRS, which had lost an aircraft two days earlier although the pilot, Capt David Rust, had been rescued by helicopter, lost another on this date, 1/Lt James Nolan being shot down and killed by ground fire.

MiG pilots reported some action during the day, six aircraft of the 28th GuFAR meeting a lone F-80 south-east of Antung in the morning. Despite attention from Podpolkovnik Kolyadin it managed to escape. Later, four F-86s were sighted about 2,500 feet above. The MiGs climbed, allowing Kolyadin to position himself behind the rear Sabre at which he fired, closing to 650 yards, before it dived away. He claimed it probably destroyed. Flt Lt Daniel was involved in this mission (his 22nd operational sortie with the 334th FIS since the beginning of the month) and noted an F-80 escort to Sinuiju, where he strafed a train and observed six MiGs scrambling from Antung although these were not engaged by his flight. Next day (20th March) there was a similar encounter when four MiGs led by Kapt Borodin saw contrails above. Having climbed to 33,000 feet they spotted a section of F-86s approaching and carried out a head-on attack. The Sabres dived away followed by Kapt Sosna, who fired at one but without result.

---

[2] Sqn Ldr Adderley was the younger son of Lord Norton, 6th Baron Norton of Fillongley Hall, whose ancestor had been in the court of King Henry VIII (see Appendix III).

UN fighter-bomber losses continued. Early that morning (20th), two RAAF Mustangs took off in the dark on a road reconnaissance north of Seoul, Sgts Cec Sly and Keith Meggs hoping to catch enemy supply trucks and armour in the open. Having carried out napalm attacks on the villages of Kanam-ni and Powon-ni, destroying several buildings in each, they spotted two camouflaged objects which they attacked. Sly then located a truck which he blew to pieces with rockets, and had just regained his position at 1,500 feet, with Meggs on his wing, when his cockpit suddenly filled with smoke. Meggs could see his companion's aircraft trailing glycol, which quickly thickened, so that Sly was flying blind:

> "My mind was racing as things began to happen quickly. I wound the canopy back to get rid of the smoke. The idea was that when the smoke cleared I would close the canopy again to streamline the aircraft and so have a better chance to reach a safe base or the lines – that was if the cockpit did not fill with smoke again. The altimeter read 3,000 feet . . . but the engine started to backfire and the plane slowed. I knew I wasn't going to make it. My choices were narrowing – ride it down or bale out. I looked around for a landing place. There were boulders everywhere, no clear flat stretches. Riding it down was out of the question. Baling out was almost as risky ... The plane was backfiring badly and losing height . . . and suddenly flames came back out of the exhaust stacks. Keith's voice was yelling in my earphones: 'It's on fire! Get out of it!'"

At 150 knots Sly lowered twenty degrees of flap, trimmed the crippled Mustang (A68-715) to glide and turned it slightly to starboard. He unbuckled the safety harness, then pushed himself up and tried to dive for the roundel, the accepted method of clearing the tailplane while baling out. But something was stopping him. The canopy:

> "I should have jettisoned it. The parachute seat pack was caught behind the edge of the canopy and I couldn't move. The aircraft was going into a vertical dive. I was trapped, pinned by the force of the slipstream which was increasing as the plane picked up speed. I twisted and squirmed trying to break free. With one half of me outside and the other half hooked in, I could neither push myself out nor get back in and try to fly down. All this happened so fast . . . I thought if I could pull my legs up I should tumble out backwards. I managed to bend my legs and suddenly I was free! I did a backward somersault. My headset was wrenched off as I went, but something struck the right side of my head . . ."

He had hit the tailplane but was still conscious – and in the clear, at last. His mind registered a series of impressions:

> "I can remember the Mustang falling away from me . . . pulling the ripcord . . . the rocks below growing rapidly in size . . . a cracking sound as the parachute opened. I was very low (looking down from the other Mustang, Keith Meggs estimated that the 'chute opened at about 400 feet). As I floated down I could hear swishing sounds, like gusts of wind in the fir trees . . . the sound was puzzling – I did not realise until much later that it had been the sound of bullets whipping past. I was being fired upon by enemy infantry, but the shooting did not last long because I was so low."

When he landed, Sly shed his parachute and harness and, drawing his revolver, threw himself down into a nearby ditch. His body ached all over but he did not seem to be seriously hurt, although there was blood on his forehead. He remembered hitting the tail, striking it with the right side of his body. When flying on operations, Sly always carried around his belt a medical pack on one side and on the other two food packs – one standard Australian issue, plus an extra one of American rations. The latter was in a can rather like a large tin of sardines but had been bashed completely out of shape by the tail – and had probably saved him from serious injury. He surveyed his surroundings. He was positioned towards the base of a rocky hill. In front of him was a small stream on the other side of which, further along, appeared to be an orchard. The wreckage of his aircraft was about 50 yards off, and burning fiercely. Ammunition was exploding in the fire, sending bullets flying in all directions. He now discarded his brightly-coloured Mae West as it made him too conspicuous since enemy troops were all around and closing in on the burning Mustang. Before baling out he had heard Meggs calling for assistance and anticipated that a helicopter would soon arrive, and shortly thereafter the first covering aircraft flew over, a flight of four US Mustangs, which circled and then began strafing runs on the surrounding area. A second flight of Mustangs turned up, this time sporting RAAF roundels.

The 3rd Air Rescue Squadron had scrambled an H-5 helicopter immediately on receiving news of the downed Mustang. At the controls was 1/Lt Osbourne McKinzie who was accompanied by medic PFC Chaille. Thirty minutes later, as he approached the pick-up point, McKinzie noticed the orbiting flights of Mustangs and then, on the ground, the wreck of the RAAF Mustang and a parachute nearby. Beyond that, in a ditch, he could see the Australian pilot but, as he made a pass over the area, he observed small-arms fire being directed at his helicopter. The heaviest fire was coming from the orchard across the stream. He quickly gained height so that the fighters could come down and strafe. As the Mustangs hurtled down, firing their guns, launching rockets and dropping napalm, Sgt Sly observed all from the safety of his ditch:

> "I could see the flash of their guns as they attacked and zoomed by. A few seconds afterwards ejected cartridge cases would cascade down onto the surrounding rocks with tinkling, ringing sounds. I could also see rifle flashes from enemy troops firing up at any planes that happened to swoop low, but they did not fire on me."

Coming down for a second time, McKinzie felt his helicopter take hits from accurate ground fire. At 50 feet it was taking too much punishment. Calling over the radio that he was pulling out, he climbed away and turned back for base, the helicopter's engine belching black smoke. He gingerly nursed the ailing machine back to friendly territory, landed, and then decided to continue on to Suwon, where he landed safely. Just how close an escape it had been was revealed during an inspection of the helicopter when 45 holes were found in its fuselage; an intake manifold and oil line had been hit, there were several holes in the engine cowling, and a hole in the rear fuel cell; the ignition harness had been hit and one strand of the rudder cable had been shot away.

Meanwhile, down on the ground, Sly had watched in disbelief and despair as the H-5 had flown away. He had prepared himself for a dash across the open as soon as it landed. Now he felt alone in spite of the orbiting Mustangs, which were working in relays. As fresh, fully-armed flights arrived, those out of ammunition departed. A protective umbrella of 16 aircraft always remained overhead. When one flight roared in to drop napalm on the area across the stream, from whence came the heaviest ground fire, Sly was startled to see two Chinese soldiers clad in quilted khaki uniforms leap up and run away. They were too close for comfort, only about 100-200 yards distant, and he realised he was well within range of a rifle shot. He decided to change position and worked his way further down the river bed until he stopped behind a rock which gave better cover and offered a clearer field of vision. About 20-30 yards away he could see his burnt-out Mustang, the remains of its tail protruding upwards.

The Chinese were still entrenched all around, as he could tell by the gun flashes when they replied to the strafing Mustangs, which included a RAAF flight led by Flt Lt Joe Blyth, who had the fuel tank of his aircraft (A68-813) holed twice, while Sgt Roy Robson's machine (A68-793) was struck on the leading edge of the port wing. Among the covering pilots there remained Sgt Meggs, but having orbited his leader for 70 minutes he was now obliged to return to Suwon to refuel. From Suwon another H-5 had just taken off to go to Sly's aid, this flown by Capt Lynden E. Thomasson with Sgt Okamote as aero medic. Meanwhile, Sly was unaware that, because he had shifted position, the circling fighter-bombers had lost sight of him, and they had requested the services of a spotter aircraft. The AT-6 arrived before Thomasson's helicopter and began to make circuits of the area, searching for signs of the downed pilot. Sly had assumed that he could be easily seen from the air, but he realised his error as he watched the spotter plane searching. It was into its third orbit when it passed close to his position. He broke cover, leaving the shelter of the rock, and waved. One of the Mustang pilots spotted him first and indicated to the AT-6's crew, which dropped down to make certain of the position, but at the same time ran into a fusillade of small-arms fire from the Chinese. The American observer, 1/Lt Brown, was hit in the leg, but the job of the AT-6 was over now and it could depart and leave the rescue to the incoming helicopter crew. It was just on 1000. Sly had been on the ground for two hours when the helicopter came into view. As the Mustangs began concentrated attacks on the surrounding positions, Capt Thomasson started making passes at a likely-looking landing spot, but each time drew fire from the enemy troops. It was obvious that the Chinese were too well entrenched to be completely neutralised. Sly recalled:

> "I could judge from the passes where the helicopter would attempt to touch down. It was now or never, there would not be another chance. Taking advantage of all possible cover, I began to crawl towards the landing spot, timing it with the descending helicopter so that we would arrive together – that way there would be the least exposure and therefore less chance of being hit."

Thomasson, completely disregarding the ground fire, brought the H-5 down to within six yards of where Sly had taken cover. As the wheels were about to touch, the Australian sprang up and, bracing himself against the whirling force of the rotor blades, ran to the helicopter's open door. He threw his revolver in first as the willing hands of Sgt Okamote dragged him on board. On the way back, Sly was able to guide Thomasson around known flak concentrations, and the helicopter touched down at Suwon at 1035. The rescued pilot was taken for an X-ray to determine if he had suffered any serious injuries while baling out. After spending a couple of hours at Suwon, he decided to hitch a ride back to Pusan on a DC-4 which was going that way. He walked across the airstrip and tried to climb on board. It was then that reaction set in and waves of exhaustion and nausea swept over him:

> "I had difficulty walking. I managed to stagger into a first-aid post, where I had a hard time explaining to the orderlies that I'd been shot down and was sick. At first they did not believe me because they did not know of anyone who had been shot down at that time. They could not figure out where I had come from, but in the long run they were convinced. They put me into one of the hospital tents. In the next bed was an American lieutenant by the name of Brown, who had been wounded in the leg by ground fire. I was fascinated to discover that he had been the radio operator of the T-6 which had been called in to find me. He showed me the wound. The bullet had gone straight through."

Sgt Sly was transferred to Suwon hospital for two days and then returned to Pusan on the medical evacuation train. There he spent a week in hospital. Within two weeks he was back on operations. In recognition of Capt Thomasson's courage and skill, the Australians recommended him for the British DFC. It was a popular decision, but for reasons unknown to the men at the front, the medal was never awarded. The Australians, Sgt Sly in particular, were lavish in their praise of the courage and work of the helicopter rescue crews, as indeed were all UN airmen. It was praise well earned. The day after rescuing Sly, Capt Thomasson was involved in another dramatic incident. An American F-51 was extensively damaged during a mission and forced to return to safety behind UN lines. It could not reach an airfield. Thomasson, this time with Sgt Chaille as aero medic, flew to the area where it had come down and landed nearby. Chaille walked over to the force-landed Mustang, looking for the pilot, but when he peered into the cockpit he came face-to-face with a Chinese soldier. Both men were shocked, but Chaille was the first to recover and ran back to the helicopter and informed the pilot, who quickly took off before other enemy soldiers arrived. This was possibly Capt James Kuntz's aircraft. The 67th FBS pilot had baled out near Suwon, to where he had flown his badly damaged Mustang after it had been hit by ground fire.

Another helicopter crew was involved in the rescue of a 2SAAF pilot on 20 March, picking up Lt Steve Armstrong who had baled out of his Mustang (315) following an engine fire. Armstrong came down on a hillside behind the front line south-west of Wonju, where friendly Koreans stayed with him until the helicopter arrived. During another mission on this day, Lt Potgieter suffered a minor wound while patrolling the Imjin in company with Lt Jan Joubert. The South African pair had noticed moderate anti-aircraft fire coming from both sides of the river on the northern side of Munsan. A shell then hit the starboard side of Potgieter's aircraft, piercing the cockpit and passing through the radio control box before knocking his goggles from his face and striking him in the chest. Fortunately for him the force of the shell was all but spent and it caused only a superficial wound, and was not enough to deter him from continuing the mission in which he joined Joubert in strafing and rocketing targets in the Kaesong area before returning to base. The rescue helicopters were kept busy during the day, Capt William Yoakley of the 80th FBS being recovered by a USN machine after he had ejected from his crippled F-80 near Wonsan. Next day the same unit lost another aircraft but on this occasion the pilot, 1/Lt Willie J. Wall Jr, was killed.

By now the Australian pilots had been advised that they would be moving back to Iwakuni very soon to begin training on the Meteor. At the same time they learned that Flt Lts Ian Olorenshaw and Ross Coburn would shortly be leaving the Squadron, tour-expired, and their places as flight commanders would be filled by Flt Lts Des Murphy (A Flight) and Vic Cannon (B Flight). Following the successful rescue of Sgt Sly, during which he helped provide covering support, Flt Lt Blyth, on returning to Pusan, was asked to fly Meteor F8 A77-982 back to Iwakuni. The jet had been flown over to Pusan for local evaluation by Flt Lt Easley.

The Russians reported a further MiG/Sabre engagement on 22 March, when Kapt Akimov led six MiGs of the 28th GuFAR in a climb to 33,000 feet; below, at 26,000 feet, they saw four F-86s. Akimov ordered Kapt Pisanenko and his No2 to climb to 36,000 feet to provide cover while he prepared to lead the other four into a diving attack. At that moment however another eight Sabres approached, one section attacking Akimov's pair. They escaped damage, turning on their assailants, one of which Akimov claimed shot down. Meanwhile, Kapt Garkavenko and his wingman engaged a second pair although no claims were made. In this action 1/Lt Richard Becker of the 334th FIS claimed a MiG probable.

Next day (23 March), with the Sabre screen improving, three formations of B-29s totalling 22 aircraft from the 19th and 307th BGs bombed key rail bridges at Kogunyong, Kwaksan, and Ch'ongju. The most important of these bridges crossed the Yalu at Sinuiju, in full view of the MiG force based at Antung, but the F-86s were able to keep the Russian jets at bay, Lt Colonel Eagleston claiming one damaged. The bombers were thus able to concentrate on the task in hand, and the Sinuiju-Sinanju railway was severed in three places. The MiG pilots – six from both the 28th GuFAR led by Kapt Borodin and the 72nd GuFAR with Maj Afonin at their head – reported meeting 18 Sabres in three groups of six. The latter unit made first contact but the Sabres avoided their attack, Afonin then attacking a second pair and closed to 650 yards on one, which fell away in a spiral dive, while Kapt Volodkin and his No2 attacked another pair. Both fired long bursts with no apparent results. The 28th GuFAR group also engaged four F-86s in a head-on approach but no contact was made. Kapt Borodin then went to the aid of Maj Afonin's *zveno* and personally fired at two Sabres before another – presumably that flown by Lt Col Eagleston – got on his tail and inflicted some damage; six bullet strikes in the port wing and tailfin were revealed on inspection after he had landed back at base. The F-80 units were not quite so lucky during the day, Capt Thomas Van Riper of the 8th FBS being shot down by ground fire, while the 16th FIS's 1/Lt Albert Ware was lost on a test flight.

On the 24th, the B-29s were back and hit two rail bridges immediately south of Manpojin and single bridges at Huich'on, Kunu-ri, and Sukch'on, again immobilising rail traffic on the Manpojin to Sinanju line. Flt Lt Daniel piloted one of the F-86s involved in keeping the way open for the bombers, and although seven MiGs were seen, they remained north of the Yalu. Daniel's flight was again bounced by MiGs during a sweep in the same area next day, but the Sabres were able to evade and there were no casualties, 1/Lt Becker again claiming a probable, although on this occasion his shooting was apparently better than he thought. It would seem that his victim was Kapt Yuri Savinov of the 72nd GuFAR, who was flying as wingman to Maj Afonin when three Sabres were sighted and attacked. Savinov was seen to engage one which went into a spiral dive, but was then attacked by two more, shot down and killed.

The South African Mustangs were also active during the day, Maj Blaauw and Lt Potgieter finding a dozen camouflaged trucks drawn up alongside a road south of Sinmak. The Mustangs were carrying only rockets, but these were used so effectively that ten of the trucks were destroyed and one damaged. More successes against camouflaged vehicles were scored by Capt Odendaal and Lt J.H. Kruger, when they destroyed nine trucks south of Tosan. The South

Africans were congratulated by USAF Generals Stratemeyer and Partridge for their skill in finding and destroying so many vehicles. It was a day of heavy air activity. General Ridgway's strategy of exposing the flanks of the Chinese holding Seoul, and thereby avoiding a costly frontal attack, was so successful that the defenders had withdrawn without fighting. To cut off and destroy as many of the enemy as possible, he ordered a parachute drop near Munsan, 22 miles north-west of Seoul on the Seoul-Kaesong road while, at the same time, he launched a thrust northwards towards the Imjin by the US I Corps. Codenamed Operation 'Tomahawk', the largest airborne operation of the Korean War, the 187th Airborne Regiment was to parachute in to Munsan from a fleet of 120 C-119s and C-46s. They were to be escorted by 16 Mustangs of the 35th FBG, half of them from 77RAAF. The rendezvous was over an island off the east coast, from where they were to escort each wave of transport aircraft to Munsan and attack any opposition from the ground. Four waves would be arriving at ten-minute intervals and the Australians were to take up positions on the right flank, while the USAF F-51s flew on the left. As the first wave came in at about 500 feet there was some light ground fire which two of the American pilots dealt with. One witness was Sgt Bob Hunt of 77RAAF who, with Flg Offs Geoff Thornton and Les Reading, had recently returned from Australia for a second tour of duty:

> "After the first run there was no fire at all from the ground. We saw the red, yellow, blue and white 'chutes open. In the last wave came the heavy stuff – jeeps and guns. One of the parachutes of the jumpers was a streamer, and we could see him battling to get it open. He succeeded finally, when only about 100 feet from the ground."

Although the operation was a technical success, the nine-day interval between the Chinese withdrawal from Seoul and the parachute landings had been enough for most of the enemy to have moved north of the intended blockade position at Munsan. Most of them had already slipped through. Only a few hundred men of the 60,000 it had been designed to trap were cut off. Nevertheless, the paratroop operation now brought the 8th US Army to within 12 miles of the 38th Parallel. The UN air forces flew 800 sorties in support of the operation and this, with another 400 sorties in other areas, made a total of 1,200 sorties for the day. As US I Corps advanced to the Imjin, the focus of 77RAAF's operations returned to armed reconnaissance. The Commonwealth Brigade now joined the 24th US Infantry Division in the mountains of Toebori north of the Pukhan, about 30 miles north-east of Seoul and 15 miles below the 38th Parallel. For the next fortnight the British, Canadian and Australian troops were on foot in rough terrain, among mountains reaching some 4,000 feet, advancing by scrambling over slippery grass along high ridges, here and there mopping up small pockets of Chinese resistance. They were always near the front in a relatively quiet UN advance in force to the 38th Parallel. The helicopters again proved their worth at Munsan. Between 23-30 March the 3rd Air Rescue Squadron was involved in the evacuation of wounded from the fighting. All pick-ups were conducted under heavy mortar and small-arms fire, and a total of 342 casualties were evacuated.

Armed reconnaissance sorties continued unabated, only inclement weather interfering with the pattern of 5th Air Force offensive operations. Although the weather was not really suitable for flying on 29 March, 2SAAF's Lt Des Deans and his wingman nonetheless carried out an armed reconnaissance of the Kaesong area, as witnessed by the glowing citation which accompanied the award of the US DFC to Deans:

> "He led a flight of two F-51 aircraft on a reconnaissance of the Kaesong area which he only reached by dint of extraordinary navigational and aeronautical skill. Flying at dangerously low altitude through constant rain and snowstorms, which had compelled several other flights to return to base, Lt Deans, displaying unwavering tenacity in the face of these odds, reached the reconnaissance area and began his methodical search for targets. His diligence and complete disregard for personal safety led to the location of a large enemy supply dump and motor vehicle which he immediately attacked. So accurately did he direct his armament in successive hazardous attacks that the supplies were completely destroyed and the vehicle severely damaged. Lt Deans only left the scene of devastation after the optimum results had been obtained . . ."

Despite the poor weather, the 19th and 307th BGs again despatched B-29s to strike at the Yalu bridges, but most of the bombers found their assigned targets obscured by clouds and diverted to bomb P'yongyang airfield instead. Three of the 19th Group's B-29s were tasked to attack the Sinuiju bridges using 12,000-lb tarzon bombs but misfortune plagued the mission; one aircraft aborted with mechanical trouble, while a second, carrying the Group commander, Colonel Payne Jennings Jr, ditched at sea and was lost with all on board. Only the third aircraft continued to Sinuiju but its bomb missed the target. Top cover was provided by F-86s of the 334th FIS, one of which was flown by Flt Lt Steve Daniel. He noted that two MiGs were sighted by his flight but no contact was made. The Russians had scrambled 22 MiGs on the approach of the bombers, Kapt Akimov's *zveno* instructed to patrol over the bridges, while Podpolkovnik Trofimov's eight aircraft from the 72nd GuFAR were to engage the escort, and Maj Korobov, the new deputy commander of the 28th GuFAR, was to take his group after the B-29s. Trofimov's *zvenos* duly encountered eight Sabres at 21,000 feet before pursuing a further dozen, without success. Meanwhile, Korobov's group sighted a lone B-29 at 15,000 feet with six F-86s in close escort. Korobov led an attack on the bomber and fired a long burst without any tangible result. Before a second pass could be made eight more bombers with an F-80 escort were sighted. The MiGs went for the rear section of B-29s and fired from long range, this proving sufficient to force them to turn away. There were no further engagements.

The bombers returned next day (30th March), when 38 B-29s of the 19th, 98th and 307th BGs, with F-86s flying top cover and F-80s flying close escort, again raided the bridges over the Yalu at Ch'ongsongjin, Manpojin and Namsan-ni, as recorded by the *Montreal Daily Star*'s correspondent:

> "American B-29s blasted at the doorstep of Communist China today. The most concentrated air bombardment of the war was aimed at four key supply bridges linking Red Manchuria and Korea. At least one Russian-built MiG-15 jet fighter was shot down and two others damaged in two swirling dogfights with American escort jets. A total of 31 *[sic]* MiGs and 35 US jets were involved in air battles, which raged from 20,000 to 30,000 feet over the Korean-Manchurian frontier area."

Two spans of the Ch'ongsongjin road bridge were destroyed, as were two spans of the Manpojin railway bridge. The now-familiar cloud of dust at Antung betrayed the take-off of MiGs but they did not press home their attacks on the B-29s, and only one bomber – an aircraft of the 19th BG – was badly damaged. In return, two MiGs were claimed shot down by the bomber gunners, credit going to S/Sgt Norman S. Greene and T/Sgt Charles W. Summers, both of the 28th BS. According to Russian records, however, a total of 24 MiGs had been scrambled, 16 led by Podpolkovnik Kolyadin of the 28th GuFAR, the remaining eight from the 72nd GuFAR led by Podpolkovnik Trofimov. While Kolyadin's formation attacked an estimated 24 bombers close-escorted by F-80s and F-84s, Maj Ovsyannikov's *zveno* engaged the top-cover F-86s, one of which he claimed destroyed. Meanwhile, Kolyadin led his MiGs into a diving attack from astern, he and his wingman St/Lt Mosyazh attacking a lone bomber of the rear section. Maj Korobov and his No2 also fired on the rear pair of bombers before being forced away by the F-84s. They then attacked the leading section of bombers, which were seen to jettison their bombs, before F-84s again forced them away. Another pair led by Kapt Lebedkin engaged a section of F-86s, forcing them away from their charges but low fuel obliged the MiGs to return to base; en route they spotted a lone B-29 on which they used their remaining ammunition, possibly the same lone aircraft intercepted by Maj Ovsyannikov's *zveno*, which was claimed shot down.

The 72nd GuFAR formation also engaged a lone B-29 escorted by six F-84s south of Sinuiju, and attacked in pairs, all six pilots firing at the bomber, which was claimed probably destroyed. Their task was interrupted by a pair of Sabres which attacked Podpolkovnik Bordun's aircraft, but these were engaged by his wingman and one claimed probably destroyed. Maj Afonin's *zveno* also fired at a lone bomber, Kapt Nolodin pursuing one of the escorting F-80s, but no claims were submitted. Despite claims for one MiG destroyed and one damaged by the Sabre pilots, there were apparently no losses. Capt Jabara of the 334th FIS claimed damage to one of the MiGs before it evaded and escaped, but credit for the downed MiG went to Flt Lt Omer Lévesque, the unit's Canadian pilot who was flying FU-111 on his 43rd operational sortie; he recalled:

> "We escorted the B-29s from P'yongyang to the Yalu. I was flying as wingman for Maj Ed Fletcher, leader of Red Flight. Suddenly the squadron commander called out bandits coming in from the right. We all dropped our auxiliary fuel tanks, and Fletcher spotted two more MiGs at nine o'clock – off our left wing and above us a bit."

The two F-86s turned sharply towards their attackers, who split and veered away. Fletcher and Lévesque pursued them:

> "My MiG pulled up into the sun, probably trying to lose me in the glare. That was an old trick the Germans used to like to do – but this day I had dark glasses on, and I kept the MiG in sight. I guess I was about 1,500 feet away from him. I got in a really nice deflection shot but with those six guns you lost 30 to 40 knots of speed, which was a hell of a lot. I aimed again and fired another burst and, all of a sudden, the flaps came down on the MiG. He kept on turning and I followed him down."

He then fired a one-second burst at closer range and observed the left flap of the MiG to split along the trailing edge. The aircraft snapped violently to the right, paused abruptly in an inverted position and continued in a long glide towards Sinuiju where it was observed to crash and explode. He continued:

> "I started to pull up and saw another MiG diving from above me. I climbed into the sun at full throttle and started doing barrel rolls. The MiG disappeared. I went right through the B-29 formation and they all shot at me! Thank God they missed. I waggled my wings and they stopped firing, but lots of shells had just missed me."

This was the first air combat victory for a Commonwealth pilot in the Korean War, and Flt Lt Lévesque's fifth in two conflicts, having claimed four during WWII. He was awarded the US DFC for this action, to add to his earlier Air Medal. During this mission, or another, the 9th FBS reported the loss of an F-80 and its pilot, Capt Kenneth J. Granberg, apparently to ground fire. It had been a costly month for the F-80 units for, in addition to the ten losses recorded, the 51st FIG reported that 16 more of its aircraft had suffered combat damage with six pilots being critically injured, most through forced-landings on returning to base, while the 7th FBS had two aircraft written off.

Elsewhere that day, Sqn Ldr Cresswell (A68-121[3]) and eight of his pilots, on armed reconnaissance sorties north of P'yongyang, found an abundance of targets in the form of trucks and supply dumps. Flying through heavy small-arms fire, they damaged a dozen trucks and destroyed a tank, two field pieces and an estimated 150 buildings. Flt Lt Scannell participated in this mission flying A68-806, his 17th operational sortie in just over two weeks, as did Flt Lt Blyth, who logged his 27th operational sortie in A68-763.

Next day (31 March), low cloud over the target area brought about a temporary lull in bombing operations against the Yalu bridges. The 98th BG instead sent B-29s to attack the road bridge at Linchiang, but bombing results were poor, probably because of the inexperience of the Group's newly arrived replacement crews. MiG activity was light. Elsewhere, the 12th FBS's 1/Lt James D. Heath was shot down by ground fire, the 18th FBG's fourth fatality of the month. The 45th TRS lost another pilot before the month was out although Capt William Preston survived to be taken prisoner.

During March, 2SAAF flew what would prove to be its greatest number of sorties in a single month of the war, 633 at an average of just over 20 per day. The usage of napalm bombs and rockets also reached its peak. Because of the anticipation of torrential rain in the summer, it was thought that operations would be restricted if heavy air traffic broke up the earth runway at Chinhae, from where 2SAAF had been operating, and the decision had been taken to lay a steel

---

[3] A68-121 was one of the four Australian-built Mustangs to reach Korea.

planking runway. While this work was being done, the South Africans moved temporarily to Pusan East (K-9) where they came under the control of the 35th FBG, and briefly joined 77RAAF. The other squadrons of the 18th FBG were moved to Pusan (K-1). Although not officially cleared to fly operations with 77RAAF, by the end of the month Flt Lt Joe Blyth had been airborne almost every day since his arrival at Pusan on 1 March:

> "During 24 days of March, I flew 28 sorties totalling 91 hours, 15 minutes. CO was 'angry' since I either broke or nearly broke his top monthly record. We mainly carried out close-support and interdiction. I also did escort to photo-recce planes, and was involved in support of downed pilots on two occasions. One 'cutter' mission (long-range targets of opportunity) gave me my first sight of Siberia, south of Vladivostok. We carried, most often, rockets and napalm. It was usually necessary to light the dropped napalm with machine-gun fire, since they did not explode. I recollect rushing in to machine-gun a dropped napalm and saw startled eyes looking up. They were not even running. I didn't touch them, they included children. Bombs were less usual, but when carried we sometimes put one on one wing and a fuel tank on the other. Max [Scannell] had a fright once when the bomb fell off just after take-off from K-9. I picked up some damage from ground fire, but was lucky not to sustain anything too harmful."

The RAF Mission commander, Flt Lt Max Scannell, who had flown his first operational sortie on 15 March, had logged 18 armed reconnaissance and close-support sorties by the end of the month, all without major incident, while Sqn Ldr Adderley, flying F-84s with the 27th Fighter-Escort Group, had by the end of the month logged a dozen operational sorties, apparently all without undue incident[4]. Meanwhile, from its base at Iwakuni, the RAF Sunderland Detachment continued to carry out its varied tasks without major incident during the month, albeit on a reduced scale. Only eight operational sorties were flown. However, one scare had developed early in the month (on 3 March) when 88 Squadron's RN282/C suffered an engine fire although Flt Lt Hunter was able to return to Iwakuni and alight safely.

Shortly before 1030 on the last day of the month, UN forces crossed the 38th Parallel into North Korea for the second time, as an American armoured column pushed warily forward from Uijongbu towards Kumwha. There had been no fanfare or flag waving this time. Everybody knew that the main Chinese armies were still intact. Communist ground opposition was stiffening but the 8th US Army continued to push ahead towards the enemy's vital Chorwon-Kumhwa-P'yongyang communications and supply area, the so-called 'Iron Triangle', at around two miles a day. General Ridgway was aware that the Chinese and North Koreans would not allow the UN forces to breach this area without mounting some kind of major effort. Nevertheless, he persisted because he wanted to straighten the defence lines and maintain the constant pressure. Signs suggested that an all-out Communist offensive could be a reality all too soon.

April 1951

April started with inclement weather, including fog and haze, which hampered UN air support operations by fighter-bombers coming up from the south. Because of the cloudy weather, which would persist for more than a week over the north, FEAF Bomber Command B-29 attacks were diverted away from the international bridges across the Yalu. Next day (2 April), conditions over the southern half of the Korean peninsula improved and operational flying for 2SAAF at Pusan began at 0600. The highlight of the South Africans' day was a mission flown by Capt Odendaal and Lt Jan Kruger who landed back at 1615, claiming the destruction of nine enemy vehicles, plus damage to one more, south of Tosan. Altogether, the Squadron pilots destroyed 19 vehicles, damaged 11 others, and inflicted damage on a dozen villages. During the day there occurred an unusual incident at Itazuke AFB when Capt William Alden, flying an F-80 of the

---

[4] Since his first operational sortie on 19 March, Sqn Ldr Adderley had flown a variety of F-84s by the end of the month including FS-157, FS-334, FS-339, FS-367, FS-378, FS-407, FS-416, FS-424, FS-426, and FS-429, and had logged 30.15 flying hours on the American jet.

8th FBG, hit a dog on take-off and had to abort the mission when he found he could not retract his undercarriage due to the damage inflicted. The fate of the dog was not recorded.

There were now changes for the Russians at Antung, the 324th FAD flying in to replace the 151st GuFAD, which noted that since 8 February its pilots had flown 721 sorties in 99 missions, and had claimed 24 victories in 28 combats. The new Fighter Air Division was commanded by triple Hero of the Soviet Union Polkovnik Ivan Kozhedub, one of Russia's greatest WWII fighter pilots with 62 victories, and comprised the 176th GuFAR commanded by Polkovnik Koshel (also a Hero of the Soviet Union), and the 196th FAR led by Podpolkovnik Yevgenii Pepelyaev. The majority of the pilots had WWII experience, and all had accumulated many hours on the MiG. All were volunteers and had been selected more carefully than those of the earlier FADs. For example, Pepelyaev had some 2,000 flying hours to his credit and had flown the MiG for about a year. The 324th FAD flew its first mission the day after its arrival (2 April) when six MiGs of the 176th GuFAR led by Kapt Sergei Kramarenko were scrambled to investigate approaching aircraft. An RB-45 escorted by ten F-86s was sighted at about 39,000 feet but by the time the MiGs had reached that altitude the intruders were out of range.

Very early on the morning of 3 April, Colonel William McBride, who was now in command of the 18th FBG, called a briefing for his mixed bag of US, Australian, British and South African pilots. The 5th Air Force had decided upon a new strategy designed to disrupt the enemy's road supplies and communications. The fighter-bombers were to blast holes in the road routes behind the front lines by dropping 500-lb bombs every half mile or so along the main highways. This was to be done in such places as narrow defiles, on cliff edges, or near paddy fields where the enemy could not make detours. There was an estimated 2,000 enemy trucks in the forward areas, and these measures, it was hoped, would prevent them returning to their main supply dumps. Additionally, after dark, B-26 intruders would follow up on this tactic by patrolling the roads and attempting to prevent the enemy from carrying out repairs.

The first flight of four SAAF Mustangs took off at 0755 led by Lt Ainsley Cooke. Each aircraft carried two 500-lb bombs. They had the task of bombing the highways around Sinmak where, following their successful strike, the main road was cut in four places. As they made their way home they located and destroyed by strafing two camouflaged vehicles, and damaged at least one other. Eight RAAF Mustangs followed at 0810, one four-aircraft section led by Flg Off Geoff Thornton scoring direct hits on the main road behind the bomb line, making craters about 20 feet across. Pilots however generally found it difficult with bombs to line-up the target because the aircraft tended to twist and roll in a dive. This tendency was accentuated when the bombs were dropped singly. With the bombing part of the mission completed, the aircraft separated into pairs and went off on their normal recce patrols. In the afternoon more bombs were dropped on the roads. Over their assigned drop zone the Australian pilots found that holes had already been blasted there by earlier flights, so they flew further north along the road to unleash their bombs, dive-bombing from 3,000 feet, as Sgt Ron Mitchell reported:

> "One of my bombs hit dead centre and pushed the road apart. Vehicles would not be able to get by that hole because the sides of the road looked very boggy."

Flying behind Flt Lt Frank Easley, Sgt Max Colebrook (A68-123[5]) from Perth recalled:

> "I was the last in a dive-bombing attack on a road, and saw two bombs from the pilot in front of me (Easley) hit fair and square in the middle of the road, blowing huge holes."

Elsewhere, the 39th FIS's Capt Manjack, who had claimed a Yak probably destroyed in January, was himself shot down (by ground fire), and crash-landed behind enemy lines. Despite injuries to his forehead he was able to evacuate his aircraft and was eventually rescued by a helicopter. Four days later a colleague, 1/Lt Siegel Dickman, was similarly rescued after crash-landing north of Singye. Further north on this day of intense air activity, the Sabre patrols up to the Yalu found a MiG force ready and determined to press home its attacks. Fortunately for the Americans, the shooting of the MIG pilots did not match their aggression and, during

---

[5] A68-123 was another of the Australian-built Mustangs.

several lively engagements, the F-86s claimed three shot down for one loss, with victories credited to Lt Colonel Ben H. Emmert Jr (a WWII ace with six victories) who was flying with the 335th FIS, while the 334th's Capt James Jabara gained his first confirmed kill. The third was shared between 1/Lt Roy W. McLain of the 334th and 1/Lt William B. Yancey Jr of the 336th. The 176th GuFAR had certainly come second best to the Sabres on this initial meeting. Eight MiGs led by Kapt Konstantin Sherberstov had scrambled at 0913, meeting a formation of F-84s but failing to gain any successes. They were then attacked by F-86s and St/Lt Pavel Nikitchenko was shot down and killed. Sherberstov's group had been followed into the air by a further eight MiGs led by Kapt Alexandr Vasko (HoSU), a 20-victory WWII ace. These also tangled with the F-86s and, as a result, both St/Lt Reitarovskii and St/Lt Verdysh (Kapt Kramarenko's wingman) were hit and obliged to crash-land at Antung; both were injured. Meanwhile, Kapt Murashev took off at the head of another eight MiGs to join the battle, meeting six F-84s at 13,000 feet. Murashev's *zveno* engaged but were themselves attacked by two F-86s, one of which was claimed shot down by Kapt Yabokov; this was probably Capt Ronald D. Shirlaw, who ejected to become a prisoner. Before the fighting subsided, yet another eight MiGs had taken to the air led by Kapt Boris Bokach of the 196th FAR. They skirmished with four F-86s at about 18,000 feet but without result. MiGs were also encountered by a flight of 36th FBS F-80s and, during a brief skirmish, one was claimed damaged by 1/Lt Willis Jones while one F-80 returned with its fuel tank damaged by a cannon shell.

The Sabres again found the MiGs willing to fight on the morning of 4 April, one of the Russian jets being claimed shot down by Maj Ed Fletcher of the 334th FIS, apparently the aircraft flown by St/Lt Kalmykov of the 176th GuFAR which crash-landed in a paddy field. Eight MiGs led by Kapt Antipov had scrambled and made contact with a dozen Sabres near Tetsuzan, Kapt Ivanov reporting strikes on one which went down trailing smoke, while Kapt Tkatskii pursued two others to 30,000 feet before they escaped out to sea. There occurred another clash in the afternoon when eight MiGs of the 196th FAR led by Kapt Nikolai Shelomonov encountered two Sabres near Antung, one of which flew away towards Anju trailing smoke after being attacked by St/Lt Fedor Shebanov. He was credited with a victory when remains of an F-86 were located on the ground next day. Elsewhere, Kapt Kramarenko's *zveno* intercepted four F-84s without success. Of these early clashes, Kapt Boris Abakumov of the 196th FAR recalled:

> "The day after our relocation [from Anshan to Antung], we had to meet Sabres above the bridge. When in the air, we saw that a narrow bridge to pass motor transport in one direction had been attached to the railway bridge. That day there were multiple cloud layers . . . Enemy aircraft broke out of the clouds and, flying beneath them, combed the battle area at high speed. Then they plunged into the clouds again. Our group was ordered to protect the bridges. We were also commanded neither to enter the clouds nor to engage in combat with the fighters . . . but to wait for a bomber raid. But there were no bombers. In this first fight I saw a pair of Sabres in the clear. I directed my fighter to them but they rushed into the clouds and I saw them no more . . . but from intense communication I understood that somebody was shooting . . . Our first meeting with the enemy had taken place." [6]

While Sabre battled MiG high above, the fighter-bombers went about their business. During one such mission by F-80s of the 25th FIS, Capt Richard Hale's aircraft was hit by ground fire. He managed to belly-land on mudflats near Chinnampo from where he was rescued by a helicopter.

A second Fighter Air Division arrived on the Manchurian border during the day when the 303rd FAD commanded by Polkovnik Georgii Lobov, a WWII ace with over 20 victories to his credit, flew into Mukden with its three regiments of MiGs, the 18th GuFAR commanded by Podpolkovnik Belostotskii, the 17th FAR commanded by Maj Grigorii Pulov, and the 523rd FAR under the command of Podpolkovnik Alexandr Karasyov, Hero of the Soviet Union, another WWII ace with over 20 victories. Together with the 324th FAD, they presented a formidable threat to the air supremacy so far enjoyed by the UN air force.

---

[6] See *MiG-15* by Yefim Gordon and Vladimir Rigmant.

There occurred another clash between Sabres and MiGs on 6 April, eight MiGs led by Kapt Bokach of the 196th FAR meeting 16 Sabres in two equal groups near Tetsuzan. The Sabres were escorting F-80s, which were flying a few thousand feet lower. Bokach's *zveno* attacked the leading group of Sabres while Kapt Abakumov's *zveno* went for the second group. Abakumov fired at the leading aircraft which trailed smoke and was credited as a victory. He then led his *zveno* into a second attack, his No2 St/Lt G. Loktev coming under attack by four more Sabres but managing to evade and return, despite a hole in one wing. Meanwhile, Bokach's *zveno* carried out a head-on attack without result before engaging the fighter-bombers, one of which Kapt Nazarkin claimed shot down in the direction of the sea, having fired nearly all his ammunition at it. Of his combat, Abukumov later recalled:

> "Later, we were told that the Sabre, piloted by USAF Major Crown[7], had bellied in near P'yongyang. He did not have enough fuel to reach base; I had hit his aircraft fuel tanks. He was taken prisoner. The F-86 was disassembled for carriage in two trucks, but American attack aircraft smashed them on the way to our airfield." [8]

At Pusan, Colonel McBride had called a further conference of his pilots to discuss the progress of the road bombing campaign. He said he was satisfied with the results and that he intended to keep on "digging holes" for the next 15 days, adding:

> "After tomorrow, we'll do our ordinary reconnaissances and the last missions of the day will be to bomb the roads so that not even a flea will be able to hop down them. There are a lot of troops abreast the Parallel and the enemy seems to be building up for a counter-attack. This will stop them getting supplies."

The trouble with this type of bombing was that the road surfaces were easy to repair, even if the pilots did manage to bomb right on target. In fact, the enemy had already started repair work. As they flew low, the fighter-bomber pilots could see where the holes had been filled in and the surfaces of the roads rebuilt. In other places, vehicle tracks could be seen skirting around the rims of the bomb craters. This was to prove to be the last mission for the Mustangs of 77RAAF in advance of the move back to Iwakuni to re-equip with the Meteor. This information was received with mixed feelings. The Australians had been integrated with the 35th FBG for six months and many strong friendships between the Australians and Americans had grown during that time. They had met the foe together during the grim days at Po'hang, gone north to Yonpo for the bitterly cold winter fighting, and then flown back to Pusan in the hasty retreat which followed China's entry into the war.

There was sincere regret that the two formations were going to part company. Australian airmen in Korea tended to mix more freely with the Americans than they did with the South Africans. The same was true of the South Africans. Neither Australians nor South Africans mixed as well with each other. To the amusement of the Americans, while the Australians were confiding to them that the South Africans were "rough boys", the South Africans were saying the same thing about the Australians. For the men serving with 2SAAF a political and cultural problem lurked in the background. All were white, mostly of Boer extraction and, in South Africa at this time, the Nationalist government had its strict racial segregation policy in place. Some members of 2SAAF were dismayed to find themselves working and living alongside American negroes who held commissioned rank in the USAF, as were some white American servicemen. No black or coloured could hold a commission in the South African Armed Forces but, at Pusan, South African officers quartered with the Americans and ate in the same mess halls as American negro officers, many of them captains and majors who were senior in rank. A few of the South Africans shook their heads but, in the main, difficulties arising from this were kept in check through the professionalism of all concerned.

On 6 April, the last day of operations for 77RAAF's Mustangs, weather conditions dawned grey and threatening. The early missions took off and among these was a four-aircraft flight led

---

[7] It has not been possible to confirm the identity of 'Major Crown'.

[8] See *MiG-15* by Gordon and Rigmant.

by Flg Off Dick Wittman who, up to then, had flown 98 operational sorties. He was scheduled to fly twice that day so that he could reach his century, and thus become the twelfth Australian pilot to achieve this feat. The flight came across Chinese trucks ranged along the Koksan-Singye road and attacked them with rockets, claiming ten destroyed, which were left burning and billowing heavy black smoke, six probably destroyed and others damaged. After the mission Wittman and the others loaded their parachutes into a jeep and headed back to the parachute store. There, they found American reporter Clete Roberts of *US Television News* waiting for them. Roberts had his camera and equipment set up to record a ten-minute TV interview. According to him, the Australians had not had much publicity in the United States, and he was ready to rectify this, adding that the interview would probably be seen by 20 million people. Thus a show was staged for the camera. Flt Lt Scotty Cadan sat on the bonnet of the jeep with a parachute pack next to him as they drove the jeep into the scene. In the background was a line-up of 77RAAF Mustangs, and revving engines could be heard. The four Australian pilots climbed out of the jeep and were introduced in turn to the American newsman as the close-up shots were taken. Roberts asked about their mission, what the food was like, whether or not they had wives and families. Wittman told of the good luck in "knocking off" the Chinese trucks, how he had just finished his 99th operational sortie, and that he hoped to fly his hundredth that day. The light was poor for ordinary photography, and a cold wind was blowing from the north while rain threatened any moment, but Roberts was unconcerned and completed filming.

According to one of the Australian pilots, the press officer, Flt Lt George Odgers, was always after a good story, so the pilots, with their boyish sense of humour, often conned him by embellishing their successes. Apparently they did so on this occasion and, because of the presence of the TV crew, the story grew even further. Usually they would wait until he was just about ready to send details of the latest 'exploits' out on the wire service before somebody would walk up and quietly say, "you'd better not send that one, George". On a couple of occasions they did not catch him in time and the stories got out and away and, with the passage of time, they became 'fact'. On this occasion the pilots responsible realised they had gone too far with their line-shoot and were on the point of sheepishly admitting the prank when Colonel McBride turned up and congratulated them on what he had seen of their handiwork, since he had just returned from a sortie during which he had flown over the same road and was delighted to see the trucks still on fire, some of them blowing up as he watched. He was even more delighted to find out that the destruction had been caused by "his" Australian pilots. Apparently the facts did not spoil a good story – this time anyway.

Unfortunately for Flg Off Wittman, the perpetrator of the latest prank, the weather closed in and, by midday, all flying had to be cancelled, but not before two more flights had set out on armed recces. One five-aircraft flight led by Wt Off Bob Hunt managed to inflict bomb damage on the Singye road and attack a village near Wongyo, but the next flight encountered heavy cloud and, despite descending to 1,000 feet, the pilots could not see the ground. They jettisoned their bombs in the Naktong and returned to base, having unsuccessfully completed the RAAF's last piston-engined operational fighter mission.

That night the RAAF Squadron invited the Americans, South Africans and locally-based British officers of the Hussars to a farewell party. It started off congenially enough. Like fighter pilots the world over they sang bawdy songs, and the highlight of the evening was when the South African pilots put on a Zulu war dance. They pranced around the bar on their haunches, yelling a blood-curdling chant. The evening was more than memorable – for those who could recall it later – although several unfortunate incidents did take place. In one, a Hussar was pushed through a wall by a stockily-built South African; another man was wounded in the rear by a hunting knife; and another officer was injured when his jeep overturned on the way back to camp from the party. By the morning the quarters were in a sorry state, much to the confusion of the Korean house girls who came along later to clean up. By 8 April, except for a small rear party, the whole of 77RAAF was back in Japan at Iwakuni AFB.

Meanwhile in Korea, on the ground and in the sky, the war continued unabated and without 77RAAF's contribution. During the first week in April, while the B-29s had to wait for promising weather over their assigned target areas, USAF commanders re-thought the problem of their fighter escort. There were still not enough F-86s available and the older F-80s were clearly not good enough for the task – they were fully 100mph slower than the MiGs which were able to break through to the bomber formation before the F-80s could engage. General Stratemeyer was receptive to a suggestion that came from General Curtis E. LeMay, commander of the Strategic Air Command in the United States, to the effect that the F-84-equipped 27th Fighter-Escort Group should be allocated as many escort missions as possible in order to maintain its competence. LeMay's suggestion was passed on to General Partridge with a request for the F-84s to be staged through Korean bases and used for escort duties whenever possible. Accordingly, the 27th FEG was scheduled to escort B-29s of the 98th and 307th BGs as they attacked the railway bridge at Sinuiju and a newly-built road bridge at Uiju, on 7 April.

That morning Itazuke was enveloped in low-lying cloud and visibility was restricted to less than a mile. Nevertheless, the 27th FEG launched 48 F-84s (although not including Sqn Ldr Adderley on this occasion) in 15 minutes and, 500 miles away from base, they rendezvoused with the B-29s within a minute of their ETA. Nearing the Yalu the F-84s flew parallel to the bomber boxes as the F-86s from Suwon flew top cover. Suddenly the MiGs appeared. An estimated 30 of the Russian jets skirmished with the F-84s, attempting to break through the fighter screen to get at the bombers, but only a few succeeded, two of the bombers being claimed shot down by the 17th FAR, one by Kapt Ivan Suchkov and his No2, the other by Kapt Subbotin and his wingman; one B-29 of the 307th BG failed to return, all members of Capt John L. Buckner's crew being reported missing. An F-84 was also claimed by St/Lt Boris Obraztsov of the 176th GuFAR while one of the F-84 pilots claimed a MiG probably destroyed. It would seem that his victim was St/Lt Andryushkov of the 196th FAR, who ejected safely, although it was reported that he fell victim to the F-86s. However, none of the Sabre pilots submitted claims. Two pilots of the 176th FAR reported meeting four F-80s during this or another action on this date, Kapt Suchkov and St/Lt Petr Milaushkin each claiming one damaged. An F-80 of the 8th FBS flown by 2/Lt John E. Thompson failed to return, although its loss was put down to ground fire. Despite the loss of the B-29, General James E. Briggs, commander of the FEAF Bomber Command, later spoke of the fighter protection as being "well-nigh perfect."

Meanwhile, it was fighter-bomber operations as usual for the Mustangs, 2SAAF flying 19 sorties in five missions during the day. A total of four enemy vehicles were claimed, while five villages were napalmed, bombed and rocketed. Lt Steve Armstrong's flight achieved the best results, claiming two of the vehicles on the main highway north-west of Sinmak, as well as attacking a village. That evening, the CO, Cmdt Armstrong, conducted a meeting of all pilots. He reported that, according to information coming in, the UN forces were continuing to advance against stubborn resistance along the front north of the 38th Parallel. Behind the lines numerous enemy vehicles carrying supplies and reinforcements were moving to the front and enemy air activity was increasing. It was decided that defensive tactics would be used against all enemy jets if they were encountered: formations were to stick together and act as a team and the formation leader should reduce altitude, manoeuvre to keep in sight any enemy aircraft positioning themselves to attack, and turn into each attack as it developed. Next day, without any aerial interference, the South Africans claimed the destruction of a further five vehicles and two supply dumps, plus damage inflicted on five more vehicles and no less than 14 villages which were attacked. UN Intelligence estimated that there were now about 70 Chinese divisions south of the Yalu and it was apparent that Communist preparations for their next major offensive were reaching completion.

Kapt Sergei Kramarenko of the 176th GuFAR was in action again on 8 April, his *zveno* intercepting an F-86-escorted reconnaissance RB-45, which St/Lt Ivan Lazutin attacked, although without apparent success. According to Kapt Abakumov of the rival 196th FAR, Lazutin had forgotten to switch over to cannon and "fired" at the American jet with his gun-camera only. Abakumov added:

". . . the target did not wait for the MiG's cannons to place fire on it but headed south quietly." [9]

---

[9] See *MiG-15* by Gordon and Rigmant.

However, the RB-45 was then engaged by Kapt Shelomonov, who fired all his ammunition into it after which it turned over and disappeared into clouds trailing smoke. One report suggests that the damaged aircraft landed near P'yongyang. However, another source credits the 523rd FAR with shooting down an RB-45 which reportedly crashed in flames in the sea. Two more F-80s were lost during one mission, when the aircraft flown by 1/Lt Robert Lempke of the 25th FIS was shot down by ground fire south-west of Song-dong-ni. He baled out safely, but his wingman 1/Lt Edward N. Alpern was then also shot down as he orbited the downed pilot; Alpern was killed and Lempke taken prisoner.

Next day (9 April), MiG pilots of the 176th GuFAR reported meeting two RB-45s (there was only one) escorted by ten F-86s about 30 miles south of Sinuiju. Kapt Murashev decided to attack one of the reconnaissance aircraft but his group was assailed by six Sabres. Kapt Grigorii Ges and his wingman St/Lt Negodaev swung round to engage but the latter suffered engine failure and had to carry out an emergency landing in a paddy field. Another group of MiGs led by Kapt Vasko pursued what they believed to be the second RB-45. As they closed the range, Vasko opened fire and reported seeing several strikes before he engaged one of the escort. The Sabre went down in a spiral dive and subsequently blew up in mid-air, but others attacked St/Lt Lazutin and his wingman St/Lt Fedor Slabkin, shooting down the latter, who was killed. He was the victim of 1/Lt Arthur O'Connor of the 336th FIS, his second victory. During an afternoon sortie on this date, a B-26 was intercepted near Anju by MiGs of the 176th GuFAR and was attacked by Kapt Subbotin, who achieved several hits before it was shot down by Kapt Ges, the twin-engined intruder reportedly crashing near Bata-Jyuan mountain; it is believed the crew survived to be taken prisoner.

The following day (10 April), in another fight over MiG Alley, Russian jets from the 324th FAD were encountered, the air regiments led by their respective commanders, Podpolkovniks Vishnyakov and Pepelyaev. Kapt Soskovets' *zveno* was attacked by four F-86s, one of which St/Lt Viktor Alfeev claimed shot down into the sea, while Capt James Jabara of the 334th FIS claimed a MiG to record his second victory. Meanwhile, Kapt Vasko's *zveno* met four F-80s near Teiju, two of which were claimed shot down by Vasko and his No2 St/Lt Gogolev, while Kapt Kramarenko of the 176th GuFAR reported shooting down an F-84, his first victory – and almost his last:

> "After my first attack, which resulted in shooting down one F-84, I attempted a corrective intended to shoot down a second F-84, but nothing of the sort happened. Making use of manoeuvring advantages of the Thunderjet, the opposing pilot quickly got on my tail, at a distance that could be called critical, or, to be more exact, deadly. Only a quick and very sharp manoeuvre could save me, and I performed it. But I pulled the control stick with such an effort and so violently that my MiG, attaining supercritical angles of attack, entered a spin. It is good that my wingman saw it. When I recovered the aircraft from its spin, my wingman joined up immediately . . ." [10]

The wreck of a MiG was seen in shallow water off Sinmi-do, from which the pilot had apparently ejected. It was presumed to have been Capt Jabara's victim but was probably the MiG shot down the previous day, since none was reported lost on the 10th. The 5th Air Force was naturally anxious to recover the aircraft and the commander of Task Force 95, which was operating in the area, was requested to investigate the possibility of so doing (see Chapter XI).

A further heavy raid had been carried out by B-29s against the railway bridge at Sinuiju on 12 April, after aerial photographs had shown that it was still standing, albeit battered, despite the recent bombing. Forty-eight B-29s from all three bomber groups were made ready for the assault, while F-84s of the 27th FEG provided close escort, and F-86s from Suwon flew top cover, but from the outset things did not go according to plan. Eleven B-29s aborted the mission, reducing the combined bomber force to 39 aircraft, and along the way the three formations became strung out in the target area, compelling the escorting F-84s to split up in an effort to provide adequate cover. This allowed the defending MiGs to concentrate their fire

---

[10] See *MiG-15* by Gordon and Rigmant.

against the weaker formations. Three minutes before they reached the target the 19th BG's eight B-29s were bounced by an estimated 40 to 50 MiGs which had dived through the top cover to get at the bombers, virtually ignoring the slower F-84s, which were not only outnumbered but the tactics employed by the MiGs denied them any advantages. The frustrated and confused pilots fired at anything with swept wings – MiGs and Sabres alike. Meanwhile, two of the B-29s from the 93rd BS dropped away to crash in flames, and five others were damaged. Amongst those lost was the commanding officer, Colonel Douglas H. Hatfield, and Maj Anaclethe DeCesare.

Kapt Ivanov of the 176th GuFAR led the first attack, opening fire on the bomber on the left flank of the first section and observing strikes, while his wingman St/Lt Kochegarov fired on the rear bomber of the same section which began to trail smoke and was reported to have crashed into the sea. At this point Kochegarov was attacked by four F-80s, Ivanov coming to his aid. The pair had been covered in this attack by Kapt Tkatskii and his No2, but they now dived on the second section of bombers, both firing at the same aircraft which was observed to trail smoke from its starboard wing. The third pair of MiGs carried out similar attacks but were engaged by the escorting F-80s and forced away. By now Kapt Shelomonov's group had arrived over Tetsuzan, all four members of his *zveno* selecting different targets but reporting no successes, although Kapt Soskovets' *zveno* did. Three of his pilots fired at the lead B-29 which was reported to have gone down, the victory being credited to St/Lt Fedor Shebanov, while St/Lt Savchenko gained strikes on another. As the MiGs pulled away, an F-80 fired at Shelomonov's aircraft but missed, Kapt Dostoevskii chasing it away. Further attacks were made on the bombers but the only success was noted by Dostoevskii who joined another pair of MiGs firing at a B-29, the bomber seen to fall away trailing smoke.

An estimated 20 MiGs – in fact 14, eight from the 176th GuFAR led by Kapt Sherberstov followed by six more led by Kapt Murashev – then bounced the second American bomber formation, the 307th BG's twelve B-29s. One of the bombers was badly crippled and barely managed to limp back to Suwon, where it had to be written off. Murashev's group attacked first but were unsuccessful. The pair led by St/Lt Shipitsin then attacked another of the bombers, gaining strikes on its starboard wing, while St/Lts Plitkin and Obraztsov scored hits on the port wing of their target. When Kapt Sherberstov's group arrived they observed two groups of bombers south of the bridge. Ignoring the escort, Sherberstov attacked the rear bomber of the first group, which fell away. He then opened fire on another, as did his wingman St/Lt Nikolaev, scoring several strikes. The second pair of MiGs flown by Kapts Subbotin and Milaushkin became embroiled with the escorting F-84s before they were able to break free and engage the bombers, the latter seeing his shots strike the centre fuselage of his target. Four more MiGs from the 176th GuFAR scrambled at the height of the battle, Kapt Vasko leading his *zveno* into the attack against four B-29s and eight F-80s near Antung. He went for the bombers, ordering Kapt Kramarenko to engage the fighters, one of which Kramarenko claimed shot down while his No2 St/Lt Lazutin damaged another. At least one MiG suffered damage, No823 of the 176th GuFAR returning to Antung minus the top of its tail fin and rudder, and with a bullet-riddled port wing and rear fuselage, plus a shattered canopy, although the pilot was unhurt.

Last over the target were the 19 bombers of the 98th BG and they encountered a few wary MiGs but sustained no damage. However, the MiGs were still heavily involved with the earlier bombers, which were now being engaged by another eight aircraft from the 196th FAR led by Kapt Bokach. Having climbed to about 20,000 feet, the Russian pilots sighted two groups of bombers and their escorting fighters. They attacked one section of F-80s and forced them away, before Bokach led his *zveno* against the leading bomber of the second formation, which began to trail smoke following the pass. Two F-86s then attacked Bokach but were chased away by his wingman St/Lt Ivan Larionov. The pair led by Kapt Nazarkin also fired at the leading bomber, Nazarkin setting fire to two engines and also hitting the cockpit before his wingman St/Lt Vermin delivered the *coup de grâce*. As he chased and attacked another of the bombers, Kapt Abakumov passed so close to the aircraft's huge tail that his own aircraft was flipped over by the slipstream. He corrected and re-attacked, firing all his remaining ammunition into the doomed bomber's tail, which fell to pieces. He saw the crew bale out, and the bomber fell away to crash. He then claimed a second shot down. These attacks were covered by Kapt Yakolev and his wingman, the leader getting on the tail of an F-80 which he claimed to have shot down into the sea.

As a result of this series of actions at least ten B-29s, possibly a dozen, were claimed shot down (as against three actual losses and five damaged), the confirmed victories being awarded to Kapts Sherberstov, Ges, Subbotin, Milaushkin (who claimed two but was credited with one only, plus damage to an F-84), Nazarkin, and St/Lts Suchkin, Plitkin, Obraztsov, Kochegarov, and Shebanov, although Kapt Abakumov also claimed two, while Kapt Kramarenko, Kapt Yakolev and St/Lt Fukin each claimed an F-80.

During the early afternoon there occurred another clash when MiGs of the 196th FAR took off to investigate activity near Antung. As Kapt Abakumov's *zveno* was stalking a number of F-84s, a pair of F-86s got on his tail:

"They poured fire on me from their machine-guns. I made a violent half-roll to pull out of the dive. The F-86s dived and pursued me, dropped down when recovering from the dive, and I lagged behind a little. I rushed into the anti-aircraft area. Ack-ack guns cut off the Sabres, and I landed on our airfield. After the landing my technician found eight holes in my MiG-15." [11]

The MiG flown by Kapt Yakolev was also hit and he was wounded in the back, making an emergency landing about 15 miles east of Sinuiju. His wingman St/Lt Zykov claimed damage to one of the attackers, which flew away leaving a trail of smoke.

The escorting American fighter pilots similarly overclaimed during the day's many actions, reporting four MiGs destroyed and six others damaged. Capt James Jabara claimed his third for the month, and the 336th's Lt Colonel Bruce Hinton – the first Sabre pilot to shoot down a MiG, in December 1950 – scored his second kill. The other two were credited to Colonel John Meyer, who claimed a second as damaged, and Capt Howard M. Lane of the 336th FIS. In addition to those claimed by the 4th FIW, the F-84 pilots reported three MiGs as probably destroyed. However, it was the B-29 gunners who were credited with the greatest success, optimistically claiming ten MiGs destroyed, of which seven were awarded[12], although it is doubtful if they actually shot down any. Nevertheless, two were claimed by Sgt Billie G. Beach of the 28th BS, one of the gunners aboard No Sweat, who later recalled:

"I watched as they shot at the tail first, then swung to hit us amidship. They were coming so close I could see the muzzle-blast from their cannon. I started firing as soon as I got one in range . . . and kept firing short bursts until he went out of control about 900 yards out. He went straight down, spinning like crazy . . . four passes later, I spied this other guy coming in low. I picked him up about 1,200 yards out and chopped into him with short steady bursts. That MiG got out about 400 yards, keeled over on its side and went into a headlong dive. I watched it crash and explode on the mountainside . . ." [13]

The damaged B-29, with two engines feathered, eventually bellied in at Suwon. All on board survived unhurt. Although Sqn Ldr Adderley participated in this mission in FS-155, there is no record of him personally being engaged by the MiGs. Many of the bomber crews involved in these relatively ineffective but costly operations were unhappy with the way things were going, including 1/Lt Joe Hilliard, a navigator aboard one of the 307th BG's bombers, who later commented:

"A lot of us thought that if we were taking this thing seriously, we should have been able to bomb across the Yalu. We felt we should have had some better targets, or else some people felt that we shouldn't have been there at all. It was very discouraging when we found that

---

[11] See *MiG-15* by Gordon and Rigmant.
[12] These were credited to Sgt Lyle R. Patterson, Sgt Royal A. Veatch and S/Sgt Robert A. Winslow of the 3rd BS; Sgt Ercel S. Dye and Sgt David R. Stime of the 351st BS; and Sgt Beach of the 28th BS, who claimed two.
[13] See *MiG Alley*.

they were repairing so many of the targets that we were hitting . . ." [14]

Off the coast, because of the two B-29s that went down, Captain P.W. Brock aboard HMS *Kenya* instructed the destroyers HMCS *Nootka*, HMAS *Warramunga* and HMS *Amethyst* to conduct a search for survivors but only one body was recovered from the sea, by the *Amethyst*. The loss of the three bombers was prohibitive and General Stratemeyer directed that B-29 attacks in the Sinuiju area had to be discontinued until they could be better protected. He also had to revise his opinion of the effectiveness of the F-84s. They were much too slow to cope with the MiGs, whose pilots had shown aggressiveness and determination in pressing home their attacks. Forward-based F-86s were better suited to the task, but numbers available were insufficient. In the interim, Stratemeyer assured General LeMay that he would continue to use the F-84s for escort duties when conditions justified their employment. Regarding these latest bomber losses, the official USAF historian commented:

> "Except for the massive Sinuiju railway bridge, which stubbornly refused to fall, the Superfortress attacks along the Yalu had severed most of the key bridges connecting the Communist armies with their logistical base in Manchuria . . . But Bomber Command had been paying heavily for its victories, for in the month prior to 14 April it had lost eight bombers and *their crews* [authors' italics] from combat and operational causes. Counting planes out of commission from combat damage, Bomber Command had only 75 aircraft for operations on 14 April . . ." [15]

In addition to the eight total losses mentioned, at least one further B-29 had been written-off during this four-week period as a result of its crash-landing at Suwon, although the crew had survived.

In the immediate days following the latest B-29 losses, and after further clashes with the MiGs, Sabre pilots agreed that the enemy fighter pilots were continuing to improve. Their tactics were better and they covered each other so well that the Americans were unable to claim any further victories. On 16 April, however, the 334th FIS's RAF exchange pilot Flt Lt Steve Daniel did succeed in damaging a MiG, probably an aircraft of the 196th FAR. While flying FU-080 and leading a flight of four, Daniel encountered six MiGs at 28,000 feet, a height at which the Sabre could out-turn the MiG in level flight and diving turns. He split the enemy formation and pressed home his attack. After placing himself in a firing position and following one MiG through violent evasive manoeuvres, he chased his severely damaged victim to the Manchurian border, firing at every opportunity until he had to turn away. In his logbook he simply noted, "Sweep Antung. 6 MiGs bounced. Self, one MiG damaged", to open the RAF's account in Korea, an action for which the Americans awarded him with the DFC. It would seem that he had attacked a formation of six MiGs led by Kapt Bokach, who reported that he and his wingman were attacked twice by two Sabres, as were the other two pairs, but all returned to base safely. One of the Russian pilots, Kapt Shelomonov of the 196th FAR, reported shooting down an F-80 near Sinbi-to.

As for the UN fighter-bombers, because the MiGs were being kept occupied elsewhere, it meant that they could continue with their work unmolested. Bombing results achieved by 2SAAF on 12 April "were excellent and extensive damage was caused to the highways." The South Africans flew a dozen missions throughout the day, which amounted to 24 effective sorties. The pilots reported that they had probably killed five enemy soldiers and claimed the destruction of three vehicles, plus damage to eight villages, one tank and the entrance to a tunnel. Two days later, Lts Jan Kruger and Syd de la Harpe set a new Squadron record for the number of enemy vehicles destroyed during a single mission when they claimed 18 destroyed out of a convoy of 19 at Songwolli, a side road near Sinmak. More success followed on 16 April, as noted by the Squadron diarist:

---

[14] See *The Korean War* by Max Hastings.
[15] See *The United States Air Force in Korea 1950-1953*.

"Today's bag is the best the Squadron has ever had. The total claims amounted to 32 vehicles, one tank, eight anti-aircraft posts, and four rolling stock destroyed. Seven villages, one vehicle, and eight rolling stock were damaged."

Their day started when Cmdt Armstrong and Lt Kruger took off on an interdiction mission to the area west of Kaesong. At first they could find no targets and were on the point of returning when Kruger spotted 30 trucks hidden in a ravine. Despite the narrowness of the valley, they attacked the trucks, many of which burst into flames and burned intensely. On returning to base Cmdt Armstrong despatched another mission, two Mustangs flown by Lts de la Harpe and Gow, to finish off the job. However, honours for the day went to Capt James Sweeney, whose exploit earned him a US DFC:

"Leading a flight of two F-51 aircraft in the Komch'on area of North Korea, and although the anti-aircraft fire was accurate throughout the period spent in the area, he continued to fly at extremely low altitude investigating suspicious objects. His complete disregard for personal safety and unremitting perseverance was rewarded when he sighted an enemy tank and cleverly concealed anti-tank gun. He unhesitatingly attacked both targets with relentless accuracy and left the area only after the complete destruction of both was assured. In the process the aircraft which T/Capt Sweeney was flying was hit in the left gun bay by an explosive shell which burnt all the rocket and gun electrical wiring. Quite undeterred, however, he continued on his mission and caused severe damage to an enemy village before returning to base . . ."

Having experienced a relatively quiet period concerned mainly with training, Mustangs of the ROKAF were back in action during the day, four aircraft attacking a heavily defended fuel dump north of Inch'on and suffering the loss of Capt Choi Chong Bong. A few days later the ROKAF lost a second pilot when Capt Lee Se Young was killed during a strike against another fuel dump. The F-80s were still causing concern, three pilots being lost in accidents within a few days of each other: 1/Lt Douglas Matheson of the 25th FIS was killed on the 9th, 1/Lt Richard Briggs of the 35th FBS on the 14th, and 1/Lt John King, also of the 35th FBS, next day.

Since February, FEAF photographic interpreters had been pouring over reconnaissance photos showing the enemy was repairing various airfields throughout North Korea. At the beginning of April they reported that the Communists were almost certainly ready to move aircraft into these airfields. Generals Stratemeyer and Partridge were of the belief that the construction programme could only have one logical meaning: the Communists were going to use these airfields to launch an air attack in co-ordination with their imminent new ground offensive. Stratemeyer informed General Briggs to ready his B-29s for raids on the airfields because the job was too big for fighter-bombers alone. Even so, the Communists had such seemingly unlimited resources of impressed labour for repair work that it was unrealistic to expect the B-29s to be able to destroy the airfields. General Briggs had earlier secured permission to wait until the airfields were just about operational before neutralising them and keeping them out of commission with relatively small follow-up air attacks, flown often enough to continually disrupt repair work. But there was a danger, the MiG force. Successful execution of the plan required uninterrupted B-29 attacks, but if the MiGs put up strong resistance as they had done over the Yalu bridges, it might prove very costly. The stage was set, and FEAF photo interpreters declared that the time had come for the airfield attacks. General Stratemeyer ordered Bomber Command to begin airfield strikes next day. Just how serious a threat to the UN forces the Chinese build-up was considered can be judged by the discussions held by US Joint Chiefs and the US State Department and National Security Council on 18 April. General Hoyt S. Vandenberg, Chief of the US Air Staff, commented:

"The problem we have here in Washington is to persuade these governments that we believe that the air build-up is being made with serious intentions. The UK is ready *to sacrifice the brigade it has in Korea if that is necessary to save the British Isles from attack* [authors' italics]. However, we cannot sacrifice nine divisions for that purpose. We have to insist that those governments look at the problem from our point of view . . . As long as they continue to build airfields and to employ Chinese Communist forces, the enemy poses a serious threat. There is talk now about a volunteer air force. That could be the Russian air force. The Russians have 4,000 aircraft in the area. They could use half of that if they thought it could do the job. They could mount an offensive which could seriously upset us. We need earnest efforts to persuade our allies that an air offensive could be serious. We cannot handle this thing on a wait-and-see basis as the UK desires ..."

As with the majority of air actions over North Korea, the success or failure of the FEAF's neutralisation effort depended upon the effectiveness of the F-86 screen. Because the MiG pilots were showing a higher degree of skill with four-aircraft flights and using formations of 16 aircraft, the 4th FIW realised it would need to increase the size of its Yalu patrols, and time them better. With the 334th FIS based at Suwon and the 336th FIS at Taegu, the Wing was not always able to mass its Sabres in MiG Alley. However, the improvement of facilities at Suwon now enabled the 336th FIS to move northward to join its sister unit. This closer contact meant that both squadrons could co-ordinate better and benefit from closer timing between patrols. Between 17 and 23 April, the Sabres maintained an effective barrier in the air at the Yalu so the FEAF's airfield neutralisation programme proceeded without much hindrance. With an average of 12 bombers scheduled daily for the work, the B-29s cratered runways and spread delayed-action bombs at P'yongyang Main, P'yongyang East, Anak, Sariwon Kang-dong, Hamhung, Sinmak, Sunan and Yonpo airfields. Fighter-bombers of the 5th Air Force then made follow-up raids, while B-26 day bombers also added their weight to the attack and B-26 intruders visited the airfields after dark to discourage the enemy's persistent repair efforts. On one occasion a flight of F-86s returning from MiG Alley dropped low and strafed airfield repair workers at P'yongyang. Because the airfield strikes were carried out completely free of enemy air opposition, FEAF airmen commented that it was much like shooting at sitting ducks. Although the Communists patiently continued making repairs to their airfields, FEAF Bomber Command's campaign was judged to be so successful that after 23 April it was able to return to interdiction missions.

Over the Yalu the air war was beginning to heat up again. In order to counter the tactics of the four-aircraft MiG flights, which invariably spilt into pairs when being pursued, one pair climbing and the other diving, F-86 flights were increased from four aircraft to six. This way, four Sabres could follow the climbing MiG pair and two could chase after the diving pair. Pairs of Sabres could then continue to pursue single climbing MiGs as the climbing elements separated again into singles, as they almost invariably did. During a clash between MiGs and Sabres near Tetsuzan on 18 April, the 324th FAD reported shooting down two out of 16 F-86s which were flying top cover for an RB-45, Kapt Shelomonov claiming one, the other being awarded to Kapt Soskovets, while St/Lt Shebanov fired at another, using all his ammunition as he closed to about 200 yards. MiGs were airborne again on 20 April, Flt Lt Steve Daniel of the 334th FIS sighting four during a sweep of the Sonch'on area, but there was no engagement. Benefiting from the closer timing between patrols, and using six-aircraft flights, a dozen Sabres of the 334th FIS, near the end of their patrol on the afternoon of 22 April, encountered a force of 36 MiGs from both FARs which charged across the Yalu, but these ran into the incoming Sabre 336th FIS patrol led by Lt Colonel Eagleston. The Americans promptly claimed four MiGs shot down and another four damaged, the victories being claimed by Eagleston and 1/Lt Yancey of the 336th, and Capt Jabara and 1/Lt Becker of the 334th, Jabara claiming another as damaged. Flt Lt Daniel (FU-317) chased two out of eight he sighted but was unable to close on them. It was Jabara's fourth victory for the month, which made him the leading USAF fighter pilot in Korea. One MiG was shot down, St/Lt Samusin ejecting from his damaged machine at about 6,000 feet, while Kapt Shelomonov landed with six holes in his aircraft. In return two Sabres were claimed, one by Kapt Soskovets and the other by St/Lt Fedor Shebanov, the latter's fifth victory, thereby becoming the second Russian ace of the war, having been credited with four F-86s and one B-29 to date. The Americans reported the loss of two F-84s during the day, the 522nd FES's 1/Lt David P. Barnes being taken prisoner, while 1/Lt Vesley was reported missing, the latter apparently the victim of a MiG pilot.

Two days later the MiGs and Sabres clashed again, on this occasion near Sensen, the MiG flown by Kapt Murashev of the 176th GuFAR being shot down by Lt Colonel William J. Hovde (10½ victories in WWII) of the 4th FIW for no recorded loss. Murashev, who believed he had just shot down a Sabre, ejected safely. A second Sabre was credited to St/Lt Nikolai Sutyagin of the 523rd FAR. One Sabre was reported to have crashed near Teiju and the other on a beach near Teiju. The latter was believed to have been Murashev's victory and according to Chinese troops it carried out an emergency landing. There were several other skirmishes but no decisive results. The MiGs were led by Polkovnik Vishnyakov, who had just been promoted to command the 324th FAD in place of Polkovnik Koshel who had returned to Russia due to ill health. Vishnyakov's aircraft was the target of the Sabre which Murashev claimed to have shot down. Vishnyakov was in the air again next day at the head of a dozen MiGs which clashed with F-86s over Sensen. In a series of swirling dogfights, Kapt Milaushkin's aircraft was hit in the port wing but all the MiGs returned safely. No claims were made.

For several weeks all US intelligence sources, including aerial reconnaissance and interrogations of prisoners, had been pointing to the looming threat of a Chinese offensive. It came on the night of 22/23 April. Employing new troops from Manchuria, the Chinese attacked the 8th US Army along a line south of Kaesong to Chorwon to Kumhwa. They intended to drive the Americans out of Korea, or at the very least, gain ground to use as a bargaining counter should truce talks following General MacArthur's recent dismissal as Supreme Commander. In a dramatic turn of events, General Ridgway, commander of the 8th US Army, acting on a directive from US President Truman, had relieved MacArthur as Commander-in-Chief on 14 April. Frustrated by what he and many other US generals felt was the "no-win" policy pursued by the Truman administration, MacArthur had at times become openly critical of the "accordion fashion" of the fighting in Korea during the spring of 1951. Without clearing the statement with Washington, MacArthur had implied on 24 March that the United Nations might depart from its tolerant efforts to contain the war within Korea. Whether the UN military objective had not been clearly communicated to MacArthur or whether he was so fundamentally lacking in sympathy for the policy that he could not – or did not want to – comprehend it, still remains open to argument. Because of his criticism, it was obvious now to President Truman that there was ample evidence that MacArthur could no longer remain in command, and he issued his dismissal order. Lt-General James A. Van Fleet was ordered to proceed by air from Washington to take command of the 8th US Army and its attached forces. Ironically, the General was privately even more bitter than MacArthur about the stalemate and the Truman administration's "no-win" policy. Following his arrival at Taegu, 8th Army Intelligence greeted their new commander with the news that General P'eng, the Chinese commander, had brought in massive reinforcements from China, and 70 of his divisions were arranged along the battlefield. Radio P'yongyang was making no secrets of P'eng's goals: the complete destruction of UN forces in Korea.

At this time, the 29th British Infantry Brigade occupied a nine-mile front from Choksong to the junction of the Imjin and Hantan. Because the front lay across a natural avenue of approach to Seoul, its position was an important one to hold for as long as possible. On the 29th Brigade's left was the ROK 1st Division and between them the important road junction at Uijongbu, which in turn controlled all the roads in the I Corps area. To the Brigade's right, the UN line turned north. A successful enemy attack could cut off the UN forces to the east. It was an obvious focal point for the Chinese in their attack to break through 8th Army's front. The Imjin was easily fordable at this time of year and proved no obstacle to the Chinese, who began their assault with wave after wave of horn-blowing, cymbal-clanging, shouting troops. During the night, the forward companies were unable to prevent penetration of their positions and confused fighting continued throughout the following day.

Following the UN's renewed advance northwards, the 27th Commonwealth Brigade had been withdrawn into a reserve position near Kapyong for rest and refitting. The Brigade was on three hours notice to move where ever necessary in support of the 1st US Marine, the ROK's 6th Division, or the 24th US Infantry Division. The major Chinese assaults fell on the right flank of the Korean division, which began to collapse, although some elements managed to hold out overnight. Early the next morning, the Brigade commander, Brigadier B.A. Burke, was instructed to move his units to defend the northern approaches of the town, which guarded one of the main east-west communication routes south of the battle line. Burke positioned his units in a naturally strong defensive posture along a line of hills around the confluence of the Kapyong River. His force included 3/Royal Australian Regiment, 2/Princess Patricia's Light Infantry, and the 1/Middlesex. With them went the 5th Regiment of the 1st US Cavalry Division. They dug in as the ROK troops retreated through their lines. The Australians occupied one side of the Kapyong valley and the Canadians the other while the Middlesex held a reserve position. In support were the 25-pounders of the 16th New Zealand Field Regiment.

During the evening of 23 April, the 8th Army began an organised movement to the rear, withdrawing to the east. To the west of the 29th Brigade, which continued to stubbornly block the Chinese push thanks to a gallant stand made by 1/Gloucesters at Solma-ri, other Commonwealth troops of the 27th Brigade supported by the US 1st Cavalry Division held a front of just over a mile wide against a Chinese penetration. The battle shaping up at Kapyong was in fact a succession of actions fought as the Chinese attempted to break through the defending battalions' positions. Beginning that evening, the Australians met the first onrush of the Chinese who had infiltrated with the retreating South Koreans and had to face and repulse successive Chinese assaults throughout the night. The Australian battalion was obliged to give ground next day but the Chinese were unable to penetrate the main positions. Meanwhile, the enemy committed a second division into the battle against the Gloucesters at Solma-ri in order to gain a decisive result. That afternoon, attempts were made to relieve the Gloucesters, who were now completely surrounded and had concentrated for a final stand. Amid the fighting, Lt Philip Curtis led a courageous counter-attack to recover a lost position. He was killed in the action but his gallantry was recognised by the award of the Victoria Cross, posthumously. Meanwhile, Belgian, Filipino, Puerto Rican and American troops, together with the 8th Hussars, tried to break through to the Gloucesters but without success. A formidable artillery barrage and air screen protected them as best they could, and an air drop took in ammunition and essential supplies. After the relief efforts failed, the remainder of the 29th Brigade had to be ordered to withdraw during the night to take up new positions north of Seoul.

Early on the morning of 25 April, the Gloucesters were advised that with artillery support no longer available, they had to try to break out on their own and reach the UN lines if possible. The battalion was under constant fire from the surrounding hills and a full Chinese regiment was battering at its front. Colonel J.P. Carne, the battalion commander, gathered his company commanders together for their last conference. He gave them permission either to surrender or attempt to fight their way out, then announced his intentions to stay with the wounded together with the doctor, the chaplin and the battalion sergeant-major. Most of the survivors headed south towards the UN line but never made it. Only those of D Company, who took a different route, heading north initially before swinging to the west eventually reached safety. These five officers and 34 ORs were the only Gloucesters to report back for duty to Brigade HQ out of the battalion's original strength of 622 men. The 29th Brigade suffered over 25% casualties in the Imjin battle, one entire battalion being virtually wiped out. Large quantities of equipment were lost or destroyed, including several of the new Centurian tanks. On the other hand, the three-day stand frustrated completely the enemy's attempts to break through to Seoul and inflicted disproportionately heavy casualties upon its forces. Unofficial estimates put the enemy dead as something like 15,000. Most of the survivors and the wounded who remained behind before the escape attempt were captured by the Chinese. Colonel Carne, who led the remnants of the battalion into captivity and was responsible for maintaining the morale of the prisoners for the next two years, was later also awarded the VC.

Unable to break through in the battle at Kapyong, the Chinese broke off action around the middle of the third day. Just over half of the 27th Brigade – the two British battalions in the brigade were in the process of being relieved, and one of these played no part in the action at all – had outfought an entire Chinese division. The Australians lost 32 dead, 59 wounded, and three missing who were taken prisoner, and Canadian casualties were ten killed and 23 wounded; but they had all held their ground and some 600 Chinese soldiers had been killed. For the first time in the war, the Australians took large numbers of prisoners, many of them unwounded. The enemy failure at Kapyong demonstrated that the Chinese resources in men and material were not without limit and that the Chinese Fifth Phase Offensive was already beginning to run out of steam. The holding actions fought by the 29th Brigade in the west and the 27th Brigade in the centre earned US Presidential citations for the Gloucesters, 3/Royal Australian Regiment, 2/Princess Patricia's Canadian Light Infantry and A Company, 72nd Tank Battalion of the 2nd US Infantry. Largely thanks to them, the 8th Army's withdrawal was orderly and went according to plan. Just north of Seoul the UN troops dug their heels in and waited for the enemy's offensive to blunt itself against these well-prepared defence positions.

The degree of UN air superiority that had been won over North Korea and the effectiveness of the Sabre screen was best demonstrated by the fact that the Communist ground forces received no support from their air forces during the Chinese Fifth Phase Offensive. During daylight hours, 5th Air Force, US Navy and US Marine close-support aircraft provided support for the embattled troops and these could operate without fear of air attack. When the Communists launched their offensive they exposed their supply lines and road transport to UN air attack, particularly in daylight. As a result of air strikes, the 5th Air Force claimed a total of 2,336 enemy vehicles destroyed and 1,496 damaged during the month, but the cost was high, the USAF alone losing 25 F-51s, 13 F-80s and two F-84s to ground fire. Five of the F-80s went down in a four-day period, 1/Lts Lee G. Schlegal and Cornelius Scott of the 16th FIS both being shot down on the 23rd, 1/Lt James Towle of the 9th FBS next day, when 1/Lt Direck de Rhee Westervelt of the 35th FBS was also killed as he attempted an emergency landing at Seoul City Airport, his aircraft hitting a gun emplacement and inflicting further casualties. On the 26th, 2/Lt Horace Martin of the same unit was shot down by ground fire. Another pilot was lost on the 28th when 2/Lt Kenneth L. West failed to return, while the 49th FBG alone admitted a further six F-80s had to be written off due to battle damage. In addition to the American losses of aircraft to ground fire, MiG pilots of the 303rd and 324th FADs had claimed no fewer than 30 aerial victories during April, comprising 12 B-29s, nine F-86s, four F-80s, three F-84s, an RB-45 and a B-26.

The 39th FIS lost three pilots during this period, both Maj Shelton Monroe and Capt Zack W. Dean losing their lives, and Capt Duncan Palmer being taken prisoner. The 36th FBG again suffered heavy losses, the 12th FBS had three pilots posted as missing on the 30 April alone, Capt Chauncy A. Bennett Jr, who was flying his 100th operational sortie, Capt Graham Smith, and 1/Lt Harry R. Middleton; while the 67th FBS also had three pilots missing, 1/Lt Jack Wright on the 2nd, Maj Herbert R. Andridge on the 10th, and 1/Lt William T. Haskett Jr on the 14th, and another three who were rescued by helicopter from behind enemy lines, 1/Lt Robert Pasqualicchio, Capt James Corn, who was severely injured, and Capt Carl Allen. The RF-51D reconnaissance pilots of the 45th TRS had their worst month to date, losing three pilots killed in eight days – Capt John McCullum on the 10th, 1/Lt Roma C. Foglesong Jr four days later, and Capt Charles J. Brown on the 17th; a further 13 aircraft returned to Taegu with battle damage.

Among the commendations and awards made at this time to individuals and units was a Unit Citation to Colonel Packard's F-84-equipped 27th Fighter-Escort Wing, of which the 27th FE Group commanded by Colonel Bertram comprised the flying echelon, and which included Sqn Ldr Adderley[16] among its numbers:

> "The 27th Fighter-Escort Group distinguished itself by its introduction of combat testing of a new jet fighter in 5th Air Force operations in Korea. During the months of March and April 1951, the 27th attained the highest combat sortie rate among the fighter organizations of the 5th Air Force – claimed 21 aircraft, 18 tanks, 224 vehicles, 22 field pieces, 38 railroad cars, 10 locos, 25 bridges, 7,000 miscellaneous buildings, 3,400 troops estimated killed."

For the South Africans, April nearly passed without loss of any aircraft but, on the last day of

---

[16] During April, in 20 flying days, Sqn Ldr Adderley had flown a further 30 operational sorties, again flying a variety of F-84s including FS-149, FS-155, FS-157, FS-168, FS-333, FS-341, FS-356, FS-364, FS-367, FS-378, FS-394, FS-400, FS-402, FS-407, FS-412, FS-425, FS-428, and FS-429, clocking up an impressive 59.55 operational flying hours for the month.

the month, Lt Piet Celliers in Mustang 313 was shot down behind enemy lines. As the leader of a four-aircraft section, he had been briefed to attack a railway tunnel on the main supply route three miles east of Sinmark. The section released its bombs on the tunnel and then broke into two separate pairs to find targets of opportunity for their rockets. Shortly after leaving the primary target, Celliers' aircraft was seen to be hit by anti-aircraft fire and burst into flames. His wingman, Lt Guy Paterson, saw him bale out successfully near Sinmark. Paterson reported his position to the rescue service and then recalled the other two, Lts Pat Clulow and J.C. Ansell, to help cover their leader. Another flight was diverted after bombing a tunnel in the Sohong area to relieve them, and soon afterwards a rescue helicopter arrived and recovered the downed pilot, who had suffered a wound to his right calf. During the day the South Africans claimed the destruction of one village, five vehicles, three supply dumps, and five box-cars, plus damage to other villages and vehicles. 2SAAF's stay at Pusan East (K-9) had come to an end a few days earlier, and they returned to their former base at Chinhae, where many improvements had been made in addition to those to the runway. Living and recreational facilities had been improved and the infrastructure of the base had been adapted to allow for all-weather operations. In fact, some pilots thought that the new facilities were equal to those of a permanent South African Air Force station back home. With this, the squadrons of the 18th FBG once more began to stage through forward bases for operations.

With the fighter and fighter-bomber pilots taking all the accolades, and the B-29 crews constantly making the headlines, the efforts of the RAF Sunderland Detachment at Iwakuni went almost unnoticed, but hour after hour, day after day, week after week, the flying boat crews carried out their assigned duties, mainly without incident. But not always. On 19 April, while flying from Iwakuni to Kai Tak, PP114/B suffered a No2 engine failure. The pilot, Flt Lt J.R. Douche, shut down and feathered the engine and successfully completed the flight on the remaining three. News also came through during the month announcing that Sqn Ldr John Proctor, CO of 205 Squadron, was awarded a Bar to the DFC he had won way back in 1941 in recognition of his performance during the 1940 fighting in France and the Battle of Britain. Although the Detachment had flown 17 operational sorties during the month, the highest number since the previous December, it was now decided to reduce its commitment in Korea in view of recent developments[17].

Meanwhile in Japan, 77RAAF was getting down to the serious business of converting its pilots to fly the Meteor. After two days free from duty following their arrival at Iwakuni on 8 April, training began again, first on Mustangs and then on the Meteors. The original batch of 15 (plus two T7 two-seat trainers) had been augmented by a further 20 which had arrived aboard HMS *Warrior* from Singapore[18]. Off-loading had begun at once, but not before an incident took place reminiscent of a comic routine. The tail of one Meteor was extended over the side of a lighter and airmen were attaching the lifting sling prior to lifting the aircraft ashore. Some of the Japanese workers had set a barge in motion to pull it in alongside the jetty and, although it was only moving slowly, it appeared certain to crush the Meteor tailplane and rear fuselage. There was no equipment long enough to stop its movement. The mechanics worked at breakneck speed and the aircraft was lifted as quickly as possible, just as the barge grazed the bottom of the Meteor's rudder. In the event, no damage was done. When the new aircraft were checked over it was found that five of the windscreen front panels had cracked in transit. Another point noted was that the black masking tape used at Singapore for sealing off fairings and seams was not as effective as the green masking tape used on the first batch of aircraft. When the black tape was pulled off, it also removed the aircraft's external finish down to the primer coat.

---

[17] 209 Squadron's CO, Wg Cdr Peter Le Cheminant also received a Bar to his DFC shortly thereafter, while 88 Squadron's CO, Sqn Ldr James Helme received the DFC; a DFC was also awarded to Sunderland crew member Master Engineer Loggie Ledingham of 209 Squadron, and a DFM to Sgt Gerard McCourt, while several others received a Mention in Despatches including Flt Lt Hunter of 88 Squadron.
[18] The aircraft of the second batch had been flown out from England via the Middle East and India to Singapore; one (WA935) had gone missing en route on 31 March.

Formal training began on 11 April, with lectures on the new aircraft and its armament, based on notes that had been supplied by the Gloster Aircraft, while the courses were commenced by members of a 13-man RAAF technical team under the command of Sqn Ldr C.J. Leopold that had been to England. Concurrent with the lectures, flying continued with more instrument flight training on Mustangs and the Squadron's Wirraway trainer, A20-750. Influenced by his experience with the Americans, who had stressed that for jet operations over Korea the ability to operate in all weather was a prerequisite, Sqn Ldr Cresswell emphasised practice in instrument flying and Ground Control techniques. After a few weeks of lectures and instrument flying, the Australians had at least two flights in the Meteor T7 two-seat trainer with one of the RAF instructors before proceeding to fly solo in a single-seat Meteor F8. It was a problem to conserve flying hours on the T7 trainers, A77-229 and A77-305. Pilots who had completed their hundred missions in Korea and were on their way home to Australia via Iwakuni were keen to be checked out on the new jets. In addition, pilots who had been ferrying unserviceable Mustangs from Pusan wanted to log some jet experience, thus keeping the servicing mechanics busy from morning till dusk. The four RAF instructors were also kept busy checking-out the eager young Australians, Flt Lt Joe Blyth's logbook revealing flights with newly commissioned Plt Off Lyall Klaffer, Flt Lt Vic Cannon, Flg Off Les Reading, Flt Lt Ralph Dawson, Sgt Tom Stoney, Sgt Max Colebrook, Flt Lt Scotty Cadan, and Sgt Allan Avery DFM[19] – in that order – during the next few weeks. Flt Lt Cannon made the first conversion flight on 17 April. In between his instructor duties, Flt Lt Blyth was able to undertake night flying tests in the Wirraway trainer, with Flt Lt Des Murphy as his pilot. Similarly, during this period, Flt Lt Scannell had been checking out some of the more senior pilots including Sqn Ldr Cresswell, Flg Off Thornton, and the station commander Grp Capt Charlton RAAF. This period was not without its tragedies, Sgt Roy Robson losing his life in Mustang A68-125 (another of the Australian-built Mustangs) while on a night training exercise.

At this time it was announced in Australia that the King had at long last awarded eight British decorations to members of the Squadron. One was a Bar to the late Wg Cdr Louis Spence's DFC, while DFCs were announced for Flt Lt Bay Adams, Flt Lt Stuart Bradford, Flt Lt Carlyle Noble, Flt Lt Ken McLeod, and Flg Off Bill Horsman, all of whom were now back in Australia, while DFMs were awarded to Wt Off Brian Nicholls and recently-commissioned Flg Off Geoff Thornton AFM, the latter having volunteered for a second tour with 77RAAF, as had several others. At about the same time the USAF released the names of two Australians to receive the US DFC, Sqn Ldr Cresswell and Sgt Tom Stoney. Another 31 RAAF pilots were awarded the US Air Medal, General Partridge personally presenting the medals during a parade on the tarmac at Iwakuni. One pilot, Sgt Kevin Foster, was listed to receive an Air Medal but he was in hospital at the station sick quarters. In a gesture that was much appreciated, the General was driven to the hospital after the ceremony, where he met Sgt Foster informally and pinned the medal on his pyjama jacket. During his brief visit to Iwakuni the General took the opportunity to fly one of the Squadron's Meteor trainers (A77-229) and was accompanied by Flt Lt Scannell.

Although the Chinese Fifth Phase Offensive was apparently running out of steam, and the US Bomber Command offensive against the airfields in North Korea had proved effective, the threat of massive Chinese retaliation was not overlooked by the politicians and generals, as witnessed by a telegram sent to British Foreign Minister Herbert Morrison on 31 April by Dean Acheson, the US Secretary of State:

> "Short of a change in the aggressive Communist purpose, I do not see how hostilities can cease. So long as this purpose persists there will be fighting in Korea. So far there has been no indication of a change in purpose. In fact, a new and massive offensive is under way. Under these circumstances, we must fight. And our economic and political measures and attitudes should back up our military ones. We must convince the enemy that a cessation in hostilities is in his interest.

---

[19] Sgt Allan Avery DFM (see Appendix III) was one of the batch of new pilots recently posted to the Squadron to replace those tour-expired.

There are many indications that a major air attack may be launched at any time against the United Nations forces from bases on Chinese territory. If this occurs we must assume that a decision has been made to attempt to drive the United Nations forces from Korea whatever the cost or consequences. Under these circumstances, it may be imperative to attack the bases from which the attack upon our forces comes. Should the air blow be launched against us, the safety of the forces, land, sea, and air, will be gravely imperilled. Time will be a factor of the most vital importance in launching a counter blow against the bases from which the attack comes . . ."

Aware that President Truman had already agreed to strike back at the Chinese should such air attacks be launched from their soil, Foreign Minister Morrison, having consulted the Prime Minister, responded promptly:

". . . the onus will be on China and Russia without whose assistance large scale air attacks would be impossible. On the merits of the case I see no alternative but to meet this new threat by the most effective military means at our disposal, i.e. by bombing the bases from which the air attacks have been launched. If China takes the grave decision to extend the war she must accept the consequences, and I believe that it would be a profound mistake for us to flinch from taking the decision, unpalatable as it is.

I do not doubt that in the long run we would find ourselves participating in action against China if she were to provoke this by air attacks on United Nations forces in Korea, and I believe that the people of this country would understand and endorse that course however much they shared the government's lack of enthusiasm for it."

The world was thus poised on the brink of another major conflict, and with it loomed the real threat of World War III erupting. And this time atomic weapons were available.

CHAPTER VI

THE COMING OF THE METEOR

May – June 1951

"Sqn Ldr Adderley pressed his attacks with vigour and accounted for the destruction of 15 buildings used to store supplies, two large supply dumps, ten troops and other miscellaneous targets . . ."

Extract from the citation accompanying the award of the US DFC to
Sqn Ldr The Hon Michael Adderley AFC RAF, attached to the 523rd FES USAF,
for an action that occurred on 21 May 1951.

Anti-aircraft fire was making life more and more difficult for the UN fighter-bomber pilots. The Communists were determined to better protect their supply routes, supply dumps and airfields from air attack. Besides being expert at camouflage, they also employed a heavy screen of anti-aircraft defence. By May 1951, FEAF intelligence officers had plotted the locations of 252 AA guns and 673 heavy automatic weapons. The AA gun positions were fixed, but the danger along the main supply routes came from truck-towed 37mm Soviet automatic weapons. These were effective against targets up to 4,500 feet and were to take an ever-increasing toll of UN aircraft.

Flying with the 334th FIS during the early afternoon of 1 May, Flt Lt Steve Daniel in FU-109 reported sighting four MiGs during a fighter sweep but was unable to personally engage, although other pilots attacked the four MiGs of Polkovnik Vishnyakov's *zveno* and succeeded in shooting down the aircraft flown by St/Lt Pavel Nikulin. Wounded in the face, he nonetheless managed to eject at about 30,000 feet and was fortunately quickly recovered by Communist troops and taken to hospital for treatment. For the former instructor to the Chinese Communist Air Force it was the end of his Korean tour of operations, in which he had claimed two American aircraft shot down, although he would return to duty with the 176th GuFAR later in the year when it was based at Port Arthur on the Liao-tung Peninsula of Manchuria. A second MiG was hit in this action and Lt Golovachev was also wounded in the head but managed to land safely.

From K-10 (Chinhae) meanwhile, the Mustangs of 2SAAF flew 24 sorties on the first day of the new month, the first mission taking off at 0500. By the end of the day the South African pilots had claimed the destruction of four villages, two vehicles, an AA gun position and a petrol dump, plus two enemy soldiers killed, also inflicting damage on a further nine villages, a road bridge and a tank. On one of these missions, the machines of both Lts Doug McKellar and Gordon Marshall were hit by fire from automatic weapons. Next day saw the South Africans run into further trouble. Maj Jan Blaauw led four Mustangs on an interdiction mission against a railway tunnel between Kaesong and Namch'onjom. The target was attacked without difficulty but on the way home, as the pilots hunted and strafed enemy vehicles, they encountered severe automatic and small-arms fire about three miles south-west of Songan-ni. The No3 aircraft flown by Capt Sweeney was hit in the left aileron and in the starboard side of the cockpit. One bullet penetrated the cockpit and struck Sweeney who suffered a laceration to the right buttock. Bleeding profusely and fighting off unconsciousness, Sweeney managed to fly his damaged Mustang south to the forward airfield at K-16, encouraged all the way by his leader over the radio. He landed safely and then promptly passed out due to loss of blood. After receiving emergency medical attention, he was later transferred back to Chinhae aboard a C-47 and, once there, was declared unfit to fly for six months. Despatched to a hospital in Japan, Sweeney found himself in the same ward as Lt Piet Cilliers.

The big disadvantage of flying from Chinhae for the Mustang pilots of the 18th FBG was its distance from the front line. This situation was rectified as from 2 May when they were instructed to re-arm and refuel at a forward airfield, K-13 at Suwon, which lay 175 miles to the north. The three squadrons of the Wing – the 67th, 12th and 2SAAF – were each instructed to follow a system of rotation. One flight of four aircraft was to be despatched daily from K-10 on a combat mission and afterwards land at Suwon, where the Mustangs were to be re-armed and refuelled and fly a further two missions from that airfield on the same day. The pilots would remain overnight and next day fly one more mission before returning to Chinhae. To service the aircraft, 2SAAF formed and sent a detachment of 22 groundcrew to Suwon but they were soon moved to K-16. The same rotation procedure, but now for K-16 rather than K-10, remained in place for the pilots.

On 3 May, Lt Jan Joubert led off four SAAF Mustangs armed with bombs and rockets on a road-cutting mission, but when they were airborne the controller diverted them to a close-support target south of Koksu-ri on the northern side of the Han, which they reached in rapidly deteriorating weather. Visibility had degenerated even further due to the latest Communist ploy of using smoke generators to thicken the haze over the front and so frustrate attacks from the air. When they reached the designated area, a FAC marked the target with coloured smoke. It was a ridge line along which were well-dug-in enemy positions, but visibility here was no better and the weather was worsening. Threatening grey clouds shrouded the higher surrounding ridges and, as if this was not perilous enough, UN troops were situated nearby, adjacent to the ridge. Joubert was worried that the rockets might fall short and cause casualties to the wrong side. Also, the cloud base was only about 1,000 feet which necessitated a flattish approach that could have led to an error recognising the target during the run in. After the first rocket and machine-gun attacks, the FAC announced that all rockets and shells were concentrated in the target area, and that they should continue with the good work. However, the close proximity of friendly troops still gravely concerned the South Africans, especially when they were spotted so near to one side of the line of fire, jumping up and down and waving eagerly to cheer on the attacks.

When the cloud began to descend even lower, Joubert decided on one more run before calling it a day. The Mustangs had to fly up the slope towards the enemy positions below the ridge line and peel away to starboard after attacking, skimming the tree-covered slope while diving down the road that meandered through the centre of the valley. Lts Micky Rorke and Albie Gotze, flying as a pair, lost contact with each other and the leading pair during the final attack, but after instrument flying through the murk, both safely flew into clearer weather, Rorke being somewhat surprised and elated to see K-11 appear immediately below. The target area had been neutralised and UN troops had little difficulty overcoming what remained of the opposition while taking the ridge. For his leadership, Lt Joubert received an American DFC. After a quiet couple of days or so, 2SAAF's pilots dropped forty 500-lb bombs, released 112 rockets and fired well over 18,000 rounds of ammunition during the course of 20 operational sorties on 6 May. Six vehicles were claimed destroyed as were two supply dumps, while damage was inflicted upon two villages attacked. Lt Kruger's aircraft sustained damage to its tailplane.

Night-intruder B-26s of the 3rd BG were enjoying a rewarding period, having claimed the destruction of 17 locomotives and 227 vehicles during April, and were continuing the good work into May. On the night of 8/9 May, B-26s had attacked road traffic north of Taegwangni. A witness to the destruction caused by the aircraft was a captured American pilot (1/Lt Melvin J. Shadduck), who later escaped and made his way back to friendly territory; on his return he related:

"We came to the place where the B-26 had dumped his load. The place was in an uproar. First we began meeting litter carts with wounded on them, then came hand-carried stretchers, and then handmade, makeshift stretchers, then men carrying others on their backs, and finally carts pulled by mules or Chinese soldiers with ten to 15 dead bodies on each cart . . . I would estimate there were a minimum of 200 wounded and about 12 to 15 carts with the dead ones stacked solid on them. Probably 225 dead. I don't know how many B-26s had attacked, but it sure was a mess . . ." [1]

While the UN fighter-bombers continued to be very active, there was little trade for the F-86 pilots of the 334th FIS at K-13 and on 7 May they traded places with the 335th FIS at Johnson AFB in Japan. However, the 334th's Capt James Jabara, with four MiGs to his credit, was permitted to stay in Korea to fly with the incoming unit in an effort to give him every opportunity to achieve his fifth kill and thereby become the first all-jet air ace. With the return of the 334th to Japan, both Flt Lt Steve Daniel and Flt Lt Omer Lévesque finished their tours, the former having flown 45 operational sorties over Korea, the latter 71 which included 16 air defence sorties from Northern Japan. During one of these he had been instrumental in locating a colleague lost in bad weather and with an ailing engine, guiding him back to Misawa AFB.

Early in the month, 5th Air Force reconnaissance aircraft brought home evidence of increased enemy activity at Sinuiju airfield. Under the umbrella of MiGs stationed at Antung and covered by a bristling collection of anti-aircraft batteries, the Communists apparently felt secure at Sinuiju. Detailed inspection of photographs of the area revealed that new fuel, supply, and ammunition dumps had been built on the fringes of the airfield, and no less than 38 aircraft identified as Yak-9s, Il-10s, and La-5s could be counted dispersed in revetments. It was necessary to neutralise this obvious threat before the airfield and garrison could become operational in support of the flagging Chinese Communist offensive that had so far received no air cover. The probable intention was to employ the Sinuiju aircraft in support of the second wave of their spring ground offensive. At the end of the first week of May, General Partridge concluded that the time was ripe for a massive UN attack and he accordingly ordered Operation 'Buster'.

Therefore, beginning precisely at 1400 on 9 May, 312 fighter-bombers of the 5th Air Force and 1st Marine Air Wing raided Sinuiju airfield while relays of F-86s, F-84s and USMC Panthers flew cover overhead. For this operation, 2SAAF was instructed to fly 16 Mustangs (to be joined by eight more from the 18th FBG) to escort and provide CAP for SA-16s and SB-17s carrying out air-sea rescue work. Maj Blaauw led off four flights of four and waited for business orbiting over the Yellow Sea west of Cho-do Island, to where UN pilots had been briefed to head should they be in difficulties; there they could ditch and hopefully be rescued by one of the amphibians. As waves of 8th and 49th FBG F-80s suppressed flak with proximity-fused bombs and rockets, USMC Corsairs and 18th FBG Mustangs launched bombs, rockets, and napalm against targets in the ten-square miles of the airfield area. This devastating series of air attacks destroyed all of the enemy aircraft on the field, wrecked an estimated 106 buildings, exploded 26 other ammunition and supply dumps, ignited a massive dump of aviation fuel, and inflicted heavy casualties among enemy personnel who streamed out of the buildings to be trapped in the open. As it happened there were no UN casualties during the attack and the South African part in the operation passed without incident. Only one F-84 was damaged and it returned safely to base, as did all UN aircraft. The escort fighters encountered little enemy activity. Around 50 MiGs were seen taking off from Antung but most of these showed no wish to fight. Faced with meeting such a formidable air armada, less than half made fleeting passes across the border into Korean airspace. The pilots of one Sabre flight reported that a similar flight of eight MiGs flew alongside on a parallel course with only the width of the Yalu separating them. Under such circumstances there was little opportunity for air-to-air combat and, consequently, only two MiGs were claimed damaged in the skirmishing, one by an F-86 pilot and the other by an F-84 pilot. The Russian pilots reported a slightly different version of events, six MiGs of the 176th GuFAR meeting four F-84s near Sensen, Kapt Shelomonov engaging one which caught fire and crashed about 15 miles north-west of Teiju, while Kapt Ges claimed a second 15 miles south-west of Teiju. The 523rd FES's Sqn Ldr Adderley participated in this mission, flying FS-425, but it is not known if he tangled with the MiGs.

---

[1] See *The United States Air Force in Korea 1950-1953*.

Although the fighter-bomber units had escaped losses during the attack on Sinuiju airfield, they were not so fortunate next day (10 May) when 2/Lt Frank Bay of the 36th FBS was lost to ground fire. A tragic accident involving another F-80 occurred when two 80th FBS aircraft were taking off from Itazuke. 1/Lt Harry Compton temporarily lost control of his aircraft when one of the wingtip tanks fell off. While attempting to maintain formation, his wingman 2/Lt Joseph Dunaway flew into the side of a house, killing himself and ten Japanese civilians. May was to prove to be another bad month for the F-80 units, the 25th FIS losing two pilots on the 3rd when 2/Lt Charles M. Andrews and Capt Louis Christensen went down to ground fire, the former near Surnan and the latter north-west of Munsami. Further losses were reported on the 12th, the 36th FBS's 1/Lt Lewis Haefele also falling to ground fire, as did 1/Lt Robert Spragins and 2/Lt Robert W. Gillespie of the 16th FIS, the same unit losing two more pilots next day, 1/Lt Adrian Christensen and 2/Lt Frank Frey, while 1/Lt Carl Celeschig of the 36th FBS failed to return on the 14th. That made ten pilots killed or missing in the first two weeks of the month. More were to follow.

By the middle of the month eleven of the original draft of 2SAAF pilots had finished their operational tours and were preparing to return home. One of those due to go was Lt Jan Kruger, but he nearly did not make it. At 0700 on the morning of 11 May, a flight of four Mustangs led by Maj Blaauw took off from K-10 for a road interdiction mission in the Kaesong area north of Seoul. The flight had orders to stage from the forward air base at K-16 so there was a good chance that three more sorties could be flown before returning to K-10. This meant that Lt Kruger might reach his tour limit of 75 operations and soon be on his way back home to South Africa. Two hours later the Mustangs landed at Suwon and, after being refuelled and rearmed, they carried out a second interdiction mission without mishap. At 1530 that afternoon, they took off again for what was Kruger's 74th sortie. It was a road reconnaissance in the Kaesong area. For this mission, Kruger led the flight with Maj Blaauw acting as his wingman.

Kruger attacked a small dam in an attempt to breach it and flood the road below, before continuing to search for targets of opportunity. He and Maj Blaauw flew low while Capt Pat Clulow and Lt Martin Mentz provided top cover. Before long they spotted what appeared to be AA guns and, as the two low-flying Mustangs pulled up and turned for a closer look, Blaauw warned that these had opened fire. Kruger ordered the formation to attack. He selected a gun that was apparently pointing straight at them and blasted it with rockets and shells. Then, coming round for a second attack, he was about to open fire when a shell struck the Mustang's port wing and almost knocked the aircraft (309) over on to its back. Kruger recalled:

> "After recovering, I pulled out of the dive, climbed to about 2,000 feet and turned towards the south. The aircraft seemed to be flying normally, but the port wing was on fire and there was a large jagged hole right through it. The time had come for me to get out quickly. The bale-out proved to be simple enough until the canopy was jettisoned, when flames were drawn into the cockpit. The sequence of my movements as the flames scorched my hands and face are vague, but I remember tumbling through the air, pulling the ripcord and floating earthwards. The parachute opened at no higher than 1,000 feet, and my left shoulder hit the ground while I was trying to stop the 'chute's oscillations. As I was struggling to release the harness, it was obvious that my shoulder was broken and only one arm was useable. While hopping and hobbling towards a shallow donga I found that my ankle was sprained and my left hand and forehead was badly burnt. My feelings at that time are difficult to describe; but I believed that if the Communists captured me I would probably not survive. It was about four in the afternoon and I could hear the guns firing at the three aircraft circling above." [2]

Maj Blaauw told Clulow to gain altitude and contact the rescue service while he and Mentz kept watch over the downed pilot. Every now and again they made a strafing run to discourage the possibility of enemy soldiers creeping towards Kruger's position. Time dragged. By 1715 all three South African pilots were running short of fuel with no sign of the rescue helicopter or an

---

[2] See *Flying Cheetahs in Korea*.

incoming flight to relieve them. Blaauw made a courageous decision and ordered the other two to return to base while he stayed to give cover. He knew full well that if he remained behind he would not have enough fuel to return to base and believed that the Communists would probably shoot him out of hand if he was captured. Nonetheless, he continued to circle and strafe the area from time to time. After another 15 to 20 minutes he was joined, at last, by two USMC Corsairs, but by now his fuel gauge showed empty. The only way he could go was down; Kruger, on the ground, watched the drama unfold:

> "To my utter astonishment and horror, Jan's Mustang approached flying very low and slow, with its canopy open and flaps down. I watched in disbelief as the aircraft [322] crash-landed, wheels up, in a small paddy field nearby. The engine broke away from the fuselage, and seconds later Jan came running towards me through a cloud of dust. There was blood on his face and he seemed to have gone out of his mind shouting 'klippe, klippe!' and darting about like a maniac picking up stones and piling then in a heap. A short while later he explained that a helicopter was on its way and the stones were needed to adjust the centre of gravity of the chopper when it picked us up." [3]

Maj Blaauw, his own face bruised during the crash-landing, helped Kruger to dress his burns and they settled down to wait. There was much gunfire directed at the dozen or so covering American aircraft overhead and then, finally, with daylight rapidly fading, an H-5 helicopter arrived and landed nearby. The pilot and crewman helped the two South Africans climb inside and made a hasty take-off. They were off-loaded at a forward US Army medical unit at last light and Kruger was immediately taken to the operating tent for treatment, while Blaauw telephoned Cmdt Armstrong to report the unusual way in which he had lost his aircraft. He was warmly commended for his action. The Americans were impressed also, awarding Blaauw the Silver Star for his gallantry, the highest award made by the US government to members of foreign armed forces. He was only lightly injured with abrasions and bruises and was off flying for two weeks. The rescue deservedly became one of the legends in the annals of South African military aviation. Lt Kruger was flown back to Chinhae next day and then on to the Australian base hospital at Hiroshima. His 75th and last sortie had been flown in a helicopter.

The South Africans suffered a tragic loss a few days later, on 15 May, when Lt Micky Rorke, one of 2SAAF's most popular pilots, was killed in a take-off accident at K-16 when his aircraft (330) crashed and exploded in flames, as remembered by Lt Gotze:

> "Micky was taking off for an interdiction mission from our advance base. Halfway down the PSP runway was a bump that more often than not seemed to assist a Mustang loaded with bombs or napalm drop tanks, to become airborne . . . when Micky's aircraft reached the bump, it became airborne. Instead of gradually climbing away, the Mustang commenced nosing upwards, possibly because Micky hadn't trimmed the elevator correctly. He must have realised that a stall was imminent, so he jettisoned the two napalm drop tanks, which hit and set fire to a B-26 that had recently crashed on the end of the runway and was being dismantled. Micky's Mustang, now in vertical attitude and totally out of control, collided with the blazing inferno. We stood in total mortification and sheer horror watching the funeral pyre of our friend and comrade-in-arms." [4]

The weather had become much warmer in the first two weeks of May and, at the front, Australian troops had begun wearing summer clothing. On 12 May they had relieved the 1/Middlesex on the right flank of the brigade, when the latter departed for Hong Kong. General Van Fleet visited the Brigade HQ during the day to explain his plan for dealing with the coming enemy offensive. Two days later he ordered the whole 8th US Army to construct three belts of double-apron barbed-wire fencing across the front line. All weapon pits were to have their own wire defences and overhead cover. The Shropshire Regiment joined the Brigade next day and

---

3/4 See *Flying Cheetahs in Korea*.

soon became fully operational, taking over the reserve position vacated by 3 RAR.

On the night of 15/16 May, General P'eng launched the long-awaited Second Phase of his offensive with 21 Chinese and nine North Korean divisions. He attacked all along the line but aimed the weight of the thrust to the east at X Corps – the ROK 5th and 7th Divisions – and the ROK III Corps. As usual, first contact with the Communists was with small units attempting to infiltrate and terrorise. The ROK III Corps was again routed and the enemy succeeded in penetrating the UN line and creating a salient some 30 miles deep. To the right of this, the seasoned ROK I Corps refused to budge but, on the left, the ROK 5th and 7th Divisions were forced to give way under heavy assaults. This in turn exposed the right flank of the US 2nd Division (with attached French and Dutch battalions) which stood firm, despite heavy casualties, and inflicted substantial losses on the Chinese. The 8th US Army again rolled with the punch, trading ground for Chinese lives.

On the opening day of the attack a blanket of rain and fog had provided the enemy with valuable cover. The Communists seemed determined to take their objectives regardless of cost and both fighter- bomber pilots and FAC reported that they made little effort to take cover – at first. Chinese troops continued to march forward even while they were being blasted from the air. Under such circumstances air-support inflicted heavy casualties. On 17 May alone, the US 2nd Division reported that supporting air strikes killed at least 5,000 hostile troops on its front. It was on this occasion that Sqn Ldr Mike Adderley of the 523rd FES flew his 50th operational sortie, in FS-397. Variable weather conditions continued to hamper UN air strikes on the days that followed but in the latter stages, the Communist attacks, which remained vigorous at night, ceased with daylight when UN air power and artillery could intervene. This became the general pattern of the fighting. Once again, the factor of air power coming to the assistance of the ground forces was proving to be decisive. The US X Corps had as much close support as it could profitably employ, despatching aircraft to its divisions as fast as the divisions could handle them, usually three to four strikes an hour. To the west, 2SAAF flew 28 sorties and claimed the destruction of a village, one vehicle and a dozen enemy troops, plus damage to six more villages and the entrances of three tunnels. In the IX Corps sector, the brunt of the attack was born by the 5th US Infantry Regiment, manning outposts in front of the main defensive line. Substantial enemy movement was detected on the 28th Brigade's front during the following day and 3 RAR was shelled during the evening although no casualties were suffered. The 18th US Regimental Combat Team, now on the right flank of 3 RAR, had a more difficult time and, in the early hours of 18 May, Lt Colonel Ferguson became concerned that the Americans might not be able to withstand the pressure. Fortunately, Ferguson's fears were unfounded because the Americans counter-attacked and hurled the Chinese back, repelling the main attack on the 24th Division's front.

General Van Fleet had anticipated where General P'eng's forces would strike and he had established the US 3rd Division and the 187th Airborne Regiment as strategic reserves. They were moved forward quickly to secure the US 2nd Division's open flank while the 1st US Marine Division began making a series of counter-attacks against the eastern edge of the enemy's salient. The Chinese and North Koreans were now over-extended with their supplies and communications under continuous aerial attack and, on top of all this, they were confronted by constant pressure from all sides. The impetus of their offensive was faltering already and they soon began to reassemble and mass their reserves for a renewed attack. As this happened, and when such concentrations could be located, the USAF made great use of its night-bombing aircraft. At around 1800 on 19 May, an area where enemy troops were preparing for an attack was pinpointed. Shortly thereafter, eight B-29s saturated the locality with 80 tons of proximity-fused 500-lb bombs. No enemy charge occurred. That night Chinese soldiers were discovered laying mines in front of the 28th Brigade's Canadian positions. The mines used were particularly effective because they were of timber construction and almost impossible to detect. Normal equipment only indicated metal objects. Over the next three days, three American tanks, two New Zealand trucks and a vehicle of the 60th Indian Field Ambulance were blown up within a mile of the Canadians' positions. By 20 May, the Second Phase offensive had been stopped in its tracks. Other Communist attacks on the western flank north of Seoul, and in the centre down the Pukhon, had also been repulsed. The 28th Brigade advanced that day, dislodging resistance and clearing some 12 miles of rugged hills, ranging between 2,000 and 2,500 feet in height, during the next five days. The Brigade was then transferred from the 24th Division to become again the IX Corps' reserve, situated near Hyon-ni, the starting point of the Brigade's advance late in the previous March.

The enemy continued to be savaged from the air – and the carnage continued. On the night of 20/21 May, fifteen B-29s attacked Chinese infantry reported to be assembling against the US 2nd Division. Infantry patrols went forward next day and found the remains of a group of some 300 fully-armed Chinese soldiers. Next night, X Corps received reports that enemy troops were massing on the roads near Hangye and Ch'unch'on. Eight B-29s hit Hangye and five more bombed the area near Ch'unch'on. When the Communists finally did attack, they could only do so with two battalions and these were easily repulsed. Not even the fanatical Chinese could continue sustaining such losses. There were no major night attacks after 20 May, and it was thought highly significant that the enemy had to fight the offensive without support from the air.

The MiGs were out and about, however, but obviously not in support of the ground offensive. More action erupted in the late afternoon of 20 May, when two flights of F-86s from the 335th FIS on a fighter sweep down the Yalu were jumped by an estimated 50 MiGs. Capt James Jabara (FU-318), detached from the 334th FIS, was in a second formation of F-86s following 15 minutes behind, and was able to hear over the R/T what was happening. Responding to a call for assistance, his group climbed to 35,000 feet and dropped their wing tanks ready for combat, but Jabara found himself in trouble. One of his tanks would not jettison. Standing orders were that a pilot with such a problem should abort his mission, but Jabara was determined not to lose what might be his last chance to become an ace. He told his wingman and joined the fight:

> ". . . three more MiGs attacked us. They overshot me as I turned into them . . . I closed to within 1,500 feet and gave him three good bursts . . . the MiG exploded . . . spotted six more MiGs. I was in a good position so I bounced them. Picking one of them out, I closed the range and got off two good bursts. One more burst caught him right in the middle and he caught fire . . ."

Jabara was then attacked by two more MiGs and radioed for help. Two F-86s came to his aid, 1/Lt Gene Holley attacking one of the MiGs which was pursuing Jabara, and was able to force it away emitting smoke. The Americans emerged from this action claiming three victories, one probable and five damaged, for no losses. Jabara claimed two of the kills for his fifth and sixth victories, establishing himself – or so it was thought – as the first all-jet ace in aviation history, while Capt Milton E. Nelson was credited with the other MiG. The probable victory was credited to 1/Lt Ralph D. Gibson over Sinuiju, while Lt Colonel Eagleston claimed one of the MiGs damaged.

First contact for the MiGs was by ten aircraft of the 18th GuFAR led by Kapt Antonov which took off shortly before 1500 from Antung, to where the Regiment had moved on the 8th. Initially ordered to patrol over the bridge, they were vectored to Sensen where they spotted eight F-86s some 5,000 feet below. These were pursued but there followed only brief skirmishing before the Sabres withdrew out to sea. Meanwhile, two more groups of MiGs from the 196th FAR had scrambled, Podpolkovnik Pepelyaev's two *zvenos* clashing with four F-86s near Tetsuzan, one of which Pepelyaev claimed for his first victory. The second pair of MiGs led by Kapt Bokach, which were covering the attack, saw another three Sabres preparing to engage their leader and went after them. Bokach's wingman St/Lt Zykov straggled and was himself set upon by two Sabres; his aircraft sustained ten strikes and he received wounds to his back but was able to land safely. The *zveno* led by Kapt Nazarkin suffered similarly when it was attacked by another four Sabres, Nazarkin and his No2 Lt Litvinyuk both falling away in spirals following which Nazarkin was shot down, ejecting safely. The victors were themselves pursued by Kapts Abakumov and Kirsonov, the latter the 196th FAR's navigation officer, who claimed one of the Sabres shot down for his first victory. The eight MiGs led by Kapt Shelomonov arrived over Tetsuzan several minutes later, and carried out a head-on attack against four Sabres, followed by a series of twisting manoeuvres as each attempted to gain an advantage. Shelomonov then spotted a lone MiG under attack some 5,000 feet below and dived on the two Sabres. He fired on the leading aircraft, closing to about 900 yards, observing it fall away trailing smoke. The *zveno* led by Kapt Soskovets, which was covering Shelomonov's attack, also engaged four F-86s, the second pair of St/Lts Alfeev and Shebanov emerging successful from the clash and each was credited with shooting down an opponent, Shebanov's victim apparently crashing into the sea; it was the latter's sixth victory and fifth F-86, also making him an all-jet ace. How strange that both Jabara for the Americans and Shebanov for the Russians should become 'the world's first all-jet ace' in the same action. Although the Americans admitted no losses, one of their pilots was reported to be a prisoner of the Chinese.

In the meantime, however, a special unit had arrived at Antung and was attached to the 196th FAR. This was *Grupa NII* VVS, which comprised sixteen MiG test pilots[5] from the Scientific and Research Institute of the Air Force at Chkalovskoye near Moscow, led by Lt-General Alexi Blagoveshchenskii, whose commander flying was Podpolkovnik Dzyubenko. The task of the group's pilots was to gather information about the F-86 and, if possible, to force one of the American fighters to land at Antung. The Soviet authorities were desperate to examine at close range the qualities of the fighter which, if not out-classing the MiG-15, was at least its equal. *Grupa II*'s equipment was the latest enhanced-performance MiG-15bis[6], which was just coming into service with the Soviet Air Force.

On 21 May, Sqn Ldr Mike Adderley led a flight of F-84s of the 523rd FES on a difficult mission in FS-339, an action for which he was awarded the American DFC; the citation noted:

> "Cited for extraordinary achievement – displayed exceptional courage and aggressiveness, and in spite of rain and low clouds which restricted visibility and made attacks extremely hazardous due to the mountainous terrain, Sqn Ldr Adderley pressed his attacks with vigour and accounted for the destruction of 15 buildings used to store supplies, two large supply dumps, ten troops and other miscellaneous targets. His flight was credited with the destruction of over 95% of assigned targets."

Everywhere along the UN lines by 22 May the Communist offensive had totally collapsed in a blood-soaked defeat so costly as to approach disaster. It was estimated that the enemy had suffered a staggering 90,000 casualties. Previously, when their offensives spent themselves, the enemy had been able to withdraw beyond artillery range to reorganise and resupply. This time, however, UN ground forces had recoiled only slightly and the Communist assault forces had hardly cleared their lines of departure. The key to the success of close-support operations continued to be the FAC of the 6147th Tactical Control Group, and during the month two British Army officers – Capt F.A. Cox RA and Capt D.A. Hall RA of 655 AOP Squadron – who had been flying as observers with the 6149th TCS, were awarded British DFCs at the end of their operational tours with the Americans. They were effectively replaced by two Canadian Army officers, Capt H. Hihn of the 2/Royal Canadian Regiment, and Lt D.G. MacLeod of 2/Princess Patricia's Canadian Light Infantry. As with their predecessors, the two Canadians initially spent time in ground school studying maps of the terrain and the language of the air observer, in addition to learning the rudiments of flying an AT-6 against the day their pilot might be killed or otherwise incapacitated in the forward cockpit. In fact, an F-80 pilot of the 8th FBS, 2/Lt Alfred Alverson, was killed during the month while performing FAC duties.

General Van Fleet ordered the 8th US Army to go on the counter-offensive on 23 May. Preparing the way for the attack, 22 Okinawa-based B-29s of the 19th and 307th BGs, together with 11 B-26s of the 3rd BG, bombed enemy positions across the entire front in the greatest single night close-support effort of the war. Following this, US I, IX, and X Corps launched co-

---

[5] In addition to Podpolkovnik Dzyubenko, the pilots included Maj Trofimov, Maj Gulyaev, Maj Mitusov, Maj Perevozchikov, Kapt Malakhin, Kapt Kurashev, St/Lt Alekhnovich, St/Lt Babonin, St/Lt Semenenko, St/Lt Serdyuk, and St/Lt Tikhomirov.
[6] Fitted with the modified RD-45F (Nene II) engine designated VK-1A giving almost 1,000-lb increased thrust.

ordinated assaults designed to cut the enemy's main supply routes, but unfavourable weather conditions during the last week of May hampered both close air support and armed reconnaissance missions. Nonetheless, the enemy was forced into an exodus from South Korea which soon became a headlong flight. By the end of May, UN forces had again advanced to the 38th Parallel, reconquering the ground given up in the Communist spring offensive. In addition to suffering heavy casualties, large numbers of Chinese and North Korean troops began to surrender. Not since the period following Inch'on had so many Communist soldiers given up the fight.

The proximity of K-16 to the front allowed sorties of much shorter duration and this brought about an increase in the sortie rate. A major problem loomed for 2SAAF in that too many experienced pilots looked like completing their 75-sortie operational tours before the end of the month. Their departure would leave few veterans available to train and lead the new batches of expected replacement pilots. To help alleviate the problem, the South African unit was limited to 16 sorties per day until the new pilots, due to arrive within a couple of weeks, had settled in. On 24 May, the Mustang flown by Lt Gotze was hit in the scoop while he was searching for a downed American pilot, but he landed safely after being escorted to K-18. Two days later the weather was so bad that 2SAAF was able to fly only four sorties, fortunately without mishap, but the day turned out far worse for the Greeks who suffered their first serious accident in Korea when Dakota 612 of 13 Flight RHAF, which was now commanded by Maj Panagiotis Demiris, crashed shortly after taking off from Taegu. The transport aircraft, flown by Lt Anastasios Marnyoukas, crashed into a hillside and burst into flames en route to K-5 airfield at Taejon. Killed with Lt Marnyoukas was Lt Nick Mamakis (navigator), and technicians Andreas Artsitas and Spyridon Ekonomopolos, together with 1/Lt Pok Yan of the ROK Army. A Greek army officer later described the incident:

> "There were two aircraft. One pilot had much experience. The other was well trained, but very young and very confident. One pilot followed the other. When the storm came up, the more experienced pilot headed for the ground to get under the clouds. He was slow and careful, and made it safely. The young pilot headed for the clouds to get under them, but he was too fast for his own good. He hit the mountain. We all have to learn, but his is the hard way."

Incessant attacks flown by the FEAF in April had rendered all North Korean airfields unserviceable but, except for the once substantial bases at P'yongyang, Sinuiju, and Yonpo, most NKAF facilities consisted of simple dirt or sod airstrips that were easy to repair. Given a week uninterrupted by bombing, impressed labour could restore any airfield to serviceability and overnight repairs could make some of the dirt airstrips available for light aircraft. Realising that these would probably be used after dark, the 5th Air Force despatched night-intruder B-26s on routine nocturnal surveillance and to harass the labour gangs. On the night of 24/25 May, one patrolling B-26 crew sighted an unidentified aircraft taking off from Yongyu, 25 miles north-west of P'yongyang. As a consequence, a force of B-29s was despatched two nights later to crater the airfields at both Yongyu and P'yongyang.

With Communist troops streaming backwards in great disorder, the fighter-bombers struck telling blows, one flight of four F-80s of the 8th FBG led by 1/Lt Leo A. Higgins alone claiming the destruction of nine trucks and an estimated 200 enemy troops during a mission to Hwach'on on 25 May. Other F-80 units continued to suffer heavy losses including Maj Thomas Harrison, who was lost on his first sortie as CO of the 16th FIS; two more were killed on the 23rd, 1/Lt Donald R. Torstad and Capt Cecil Wright of the 25th FIS, while Capt Charles Chenault of the 80th FBS broke his back when he crash-landed his damaged aircraft near Taegu. In addition, the 8th FBS suffered the loss of 1/Lt Edwin Reeser in an accident on the 25th, and two others were critically injured in accidents. On the same day, in a single strike against enemy troops attempting to withdraw under the protective cover of low-hanging clouds, 16 F-84s of the 524th FES set out late in the afternoon for the Inje area, an estimated 1,000 troops having been spotted by the FAC. Loaded with napalm, the F-84s made their way through heavy rain and cloud-hidden, jagged mountain tops, catching the enemy by surprise, as later recalled by one of the flight leaders, Capt John P. Torland:

> "We came in low on both sides of Inje and could see enemy troops for two miles. We gave them everything we had. It was impossible to estimate how many troops and trucks our flight destroyed. Intelligence lists at least 700 killed or wounded, but I think that was a very conservative number."

In addition to the human casualties, the Squadron was credited with at least 50 vehicles destroyed and numerous pack animals killed. The four flight leaders were each awarded the US DFC, and the remaining pilots received Air Medals or Oak Leaf clusters.

Towards the end of the month, when the 5th Air Force was given the primary responsibility of interdicting the enemy's lines of communications, Maj-General Edward J. Timberlake, the Deputy Commander of the 5th Air Force, ordered the preparation of an air/ground offensive that he named Operation 'Strangle'. Its aim was to paralyse enemy transport in the zone between the railheads at the 38th Parallel and the front lines. The plan divided the key north-south traffic arteries into three sections for intensive attack by units of the 5th Air Force, the 1st Marine Air Wing, and Task Force 77. The intention was to systematically attack bridges and tunnels, and to crater main roads, making wider use of delayed-action bombs. As well as the 'Strangle' attacks, the 5th Air Force and TF77 planned to render key rail and highway bridges unusable with precisely timed fighter-bomber strikes.

Operation 'Strangle' began on the last day of May, and the pattern of attacks went much the same in each of the three sectors. In the west, 18th FBG Mustangs, including 2SAAF, scouted out sections of road and railway where repairs or by-passes would be difficult to make, and pot-hole them with 500-lb bombs, some with contact fuses and some fused for delayed explosions. Filled roadbeds through low, wet ground such as rice paddies, were particularly susceptible to being cut by bombs. B-26s of the 3rd BG sprinkled butterfly bombs at choke points on the enemy's main supply routes. On release, these bomb clusters broke down into a number of smaller packages which fluttered to the ground and lay inert until they were disturbed. North of where the Mustangs were working, F-80 fighter-bombers of the 49th and 51st FBGs meanwhile mounted regular attacks on north-western Korea's rail bridges in the all-out air offensive.

With such intensive activity there was little surprise when the MiGs put in an appearance, a dozen falling upon two B-29s of the 19th BG while they were waiting for their F-86 escort 75 miles south-east of Sinuiju. It was unusual for the MiG pilots to venture so far from the Yalu, and it seemed to the Americans that they may have been a group of trainees, possibly Chinese, because they did not seem to know how to launch a successful attack on the bombers. The MiGs were, in fact, from *Grupa NII* led by Podpolkovnik Dzyubenko, whose section attacked one of the B-29s. Together with his No2, Maj Gulyaev, he opened fire at the right-hand bomber, which was also attacked by St/Lts Babonin and Alekhnovich. As Dzyubenko pulled away from the attack he encountered two F-86s against which he carried out two attacks but without making any claims. Meanwhile, Gulyaev and Babonin again attacked the B-29 but Alekhnovich was fired at by two F-86s and his aircraft was hit, although he was able to return safely to Antung where seven bullet strikes were found in his machine. The other sections were equally unsuccessful in their attacks on the second B-29, the Russian pilots later realising that thay had misjudged the bomber's size and had fired from too great a range. During one attack against this aircraft, St/Lt Semenenko overtook his leader, Maj Perevozchikov, and when he attempted to reform, could not find him. Perevozchikov failed to return and was later reported to have been attacked by two F-86s and shot down. He ejected safely but when his parachute opened he fell out of the harness and was killed. One other MiG returned to base with battle damage. The B-29 gunners claimed one shot down, credit for the kill being given to S/Sgt Michael R. Martocchia of the 28th BS, while two more were claimed by 335th FIS pilots 1/Lt Otis Gordon Jr and 1/Lt Bobbie L. Smith. The American pilots reported that their timely arrival appeared to have caused such confusion among the MiG pilots that they seemed to fire at each other far more than at the American fighters.

While casualties due to enemy action had been relatively light during the month – 59 FEAF aircraft having officially been reported lost to enemy ground fire during April and May, mainly in April – these figures appear to be on the conservative side, since at least 40 aircraft are recorded as having been shot down in April, while the 18th FBG alone lost 25 Mustangs on operations during May, a similar number of F-80s also being lost. The 5th Air Force also revealed that F-80 losses were averaging 18 per month, which meant that if jet fighter-bomber sorties were to be maintained at the current rate, one group would have to convert to F-84s without delay. While the MiG pilots of the 303rd and 324th FADS had experienced a quieter month, with only six claims comprising four F-86s and two F-84s, they had accounted for a considerable number of UN aircraft since their arrival.

The 18th FBG at K-16 had been joined by the 39th FIS early in the month, this unit containing a number of experienced Mustang pilots from the 40th FIS who still had a 100-mission requirement to meet. The Group desperately needed the extra men and machines, a total of 32 aircraft having been lost during the month of which 25 were lost on operations, but apparently only one pilot failed to return, 1/Lt Richard J. Seguin being shot down in flames on 23 May. Meanwhile, the 35th FIG had withdrawn to Johnson AFB in Japan to re-equip, receiving new squadrons: the 40th FIS with F-51s, the 41st FIS with F-80s, and the 339th FIS which was in the process of changing its F-82s for F-94s. During the month an instructor pilot of the 41st FIS was scrambled in his F-80 to shoot down an abandoned but still flying C-119 transport aircraft from which the crew had baled out. This turned out to be the only 'kill' made by the 41st FIS during the war. Although the 45th TRS had eleven of its aircraft damaged by ground fire during the month, none was lost, while Mustangs of the ROKAF had contributed 164 sorties to the war effort in May, also achieved without loss. During the month the CO, Maj Hess, completed his 250th mission.

In addition to the operational losses, the 5th Air Force lost two of its senior aviators during the month in a flying accident involving a T-33 two-seat trainer. Colonel Ashley Packard, commander of the 27th FEW, and Lt Colonel Leland Molland, a WWII fighter ace with $10^{1}/_{2}$ victories, and Acting CO of the 39th FIS but attached to the 8th FBS, were killed when the aircraft crashed 12 miles south-east of Taegu on 16 May while on a weather recce flight. Since the 27th FEG was about to be withdrawn from operations, the 49th FBG was nominated to carry out conversion to the F-84 forthwith, with the 27th FEG providing transitional training. A new group arrived from the United States, the 136th FBW under the command of Colonel Albert C. Prendergast, which was also equipped with F-84s. With the new arrivals settling into Itazuke AFB, they welcomed to their ranks an RAF exchange pilot, Flt Lt P.H.L. Scott (see Appendix III), who had been serving with the 82nd FIS at Hamilton AFB in California. He recalled:

> "In the spring of 1951 I got a letter from a Wing Commander in our Mission in Washington, saying something like this:
>
>> 'We're thinking of sending one or two of our exchange pilots on detachment to Korea, and we're looking for a ground-attack pilot. The trouble is you're a day fighter pilot, and anyway you're married with a young child, so perhaps you're not our man. What do you think?'
>
> It wasn't until much later that I did think – what an extraordinary way of being invited to take part in a war! But at the time my sole thought was to get the necessary ground-attack experience as soon as possible, and I knew just where to go to do that. The USAF had a weapons training base at Nellis near Las Vegas. The colonel of my fighter group made the arrangements and I flew down there. For a week they taught me how to use napalm, drop 500-lb bombs, and fire rockets – three or four sorties every day, and usually an evening one to The Strip in Las Vegas with new friends. After that week it was back to San Francisco, a call to our Mission in Washington and then a week's holiday in Yosemite National Park with my wife and little daughter Carol, before flying off to Tokyo via Honolulu and Wake Island.
>
> My detachment was to the 182nd FBS of 136th National Guard FBW from Little Rock, Arkansas. They were operating from Itazuke on the island of Kyushu, the most southern of all the Japanese Islands, and about 130 miles from the South Korean port of Pusan. So we had to fly 130 miles over the sea before we even got to the Korean peninsula, let alone to

the front line further north. My new friends from Arkansas were great fun, though they didn't know much about the more distant parts of their own country let alone the rest of the world. So I was an oddity with an accent to match. Officers on the base who were not flying lived in the Officers Club in some comfort. But the operational pilots – to keep our minds on the business in hand – lived in little wooden huts quite close to the airfield perimeter track, and I shared one of these with seven pilots from Little Rock for about four months, and we got on fine."

Flt Lt Scott flew his first operational sortie on 29 May – an armed reconnaissance to familiarise himself with the terrain in FS-414 – followed by a napalm and strafing attack next day in FS-461. Both sorties were accomplished without mishap[7].

Meanwhile, 77RAAF's conversion to the twin-jet Meteor was well under way. After graduating to the Meteor F8, the next stage of training for the pilots involved was to familiarise themselves with the aircraft and become proficient in its handling. A flying training programme was put into effect which was based on the RAF Fighter Command Annual Training Syllabus. Because 77RAAF's previous rôle was tactical support, emphasis during the training period was to be placed on high altitude flying, air-to-air attacks using the gyro gunsight, tactical formation flying, fighter versus fighter tactics, approach aids under instrument conditions and high altitude navigation. The majority of the pilots had had little or no practice in high altitude flying so, after their initial conversion, all flying with the exception of armament training was carried out at 30,000 feet or above. A few pilots had never used the gyro gunsight before and, with the exception of those who had recently joined the Squadron, all were out of practice. Exercises using the gunsight were carried out at altitude, the initial practices being started at 25,000 feet and the height was increased as the pilots gained confidence and grew in efficiency.

Some problems were beginning to manifest themselves with the Meteors. For instance, many of the Rolls-Royce Derwent engines were surging at height. It was found that engine RPM had to be reduced by so much that the pilots were not able to maintain formation at altitude, let alone practice for fighting. In the cockpit, the artificial horizon was found to be unsuitable since it took ten minutes to re-erect after toppling. A caging artificial horizon was fitted as a temporary measure and installation of a 360 degree artificial horizon was regarded as urgent.

The lack of navigational aids in Japan and Korea necessitated a very high standard of pilot navigation and called for accurate flight planning. This lack was also aggravated by the extremely high winds encountered at heights above 10,000 feet. Over Japan and Korea during the winter months, an almost permanent jet stream covered the operational area with wind speeds reaching 100-200 knots. Before any operational flight, accurate pre-flight planning had to be carried out. Perhaps most important of all, the minimum amount of fuel needed to return to base had to be determined and included in the pilots' briefing. The possibility of fitting the American radio compass ARN-6 to the Meteor was being discussed. This would help substantially with navigation and give an accurate homing course, thus relieving the pressure on the pilot and undoubtedly reduce the traffic on the emergency radio channel. The difficulties faced were not confined to just those confronting the fighter pilots, as airframe fitter Cpl Dinny O'Brien recalled:

"Our conversion to the Meteor was a thought-provoking exercise. Two field service engineers, one from Rolls-Royce [Mr Jock Gibb], the other from Glosters [Mr Eric Greenwood[8]], provided the instruction. Being in the airframe trade, 'Mr Gloster' taught me what he knew about the jet. While he was very knowledgeable he did teach us a few bad habits which were totally unacceptable by our engineering standards. Some of us had limited experience on Vampires while the remainder were jet illiterate. The pressurisation system was a bit of a worry and cost many rectification hours. Both the canopy seal and the Westland valve, which was located under the seat, caused a lot of system failures. Actually it was a fairly basic aircraft compared with the F-86 and others of that vintage."

---

[7] Flt Lt Peter Scott had survived an F-84 crash in Louisiana shortly before his posting to Korea (see Appendix IV).

[8] Eric Greenwood was Gloster's Chief Test Pilot; he was the first pilot to exceed 600 mph, flying the specially prepared Meteor which later officially raised the World Air Speed Record to 606mph.

Cpl O'Brien had more to add about the Westland valve:

> "Dust and dirt in Meteor cockpits caused a lot of pressurisation problems by blocking the Westland valve filter located under the seat. Rectifying the problem was relatively simple but gaining access to it required some effort. The job involved removing the canopy, disarming and removing the seat, cleaning the valve then replacing the items and doing a pressurisation test. Removal of the canopy and seat was a gut-busting, two-man job. This unserviceability occurred regularly on the last flight of the day. Consequently, the job was more difficult working in the dark using a torch, especially later at Kimpo."

Other factors had the potential to limit the operational use of the Meteor in Korea. This was particularly the case with regard to the incompatability of supplies. American equipment could not be used. American rockets, wireless crystals and oxygen equipment were not compatible and although 20mm ammunition was being used by the US Navy, the shells would need to be re-belted because the American links did not fit the British gun. Fuel was another possible problem. At the time, the USAF was using JP1 aviation fuel but was expected to begin using JP3 aviation fuel in the near future. If, in the course of time, it switched exclusively to JP3 fuel, which appeared to be the intention, JP1 fuel would need to be specially brought in for the Meteors. And there was an urgent need for a refrigeration device to ensure that the cockpit temperature was cool enough for a pilot to wear sufficient clothing to guard against frostbite if he was forced to bale out at height. For evasion and escape, and high altitude bale-outs, it was necessary to wear warm clothing. The most comfortable gear for flying the Meteor at this time was a summer-weight flying suit and underpants but even this was too much when flying below 10,000 feet, besides being totally useless as escape apparel. If forced down during a mission, such scant clothing would do little to enable a pilot to evade capture through some 200 miles of enemy-held territory[9].

On the positive side, the idea of a twin-engined jet fighter had some appeal. One of the main worries of pilots conducting operations over North Korea was the fear of an engine cutting out, particularly when operating from Japan across 200 miles of sea. Two engines obviously gave a better chance. Asymmetric flying training was therefore most important. Few of the Australian pilots had flown a twin-engined aircraft before, let alone a twin with one engine disabled. It was on a practice single-engine exercise that Sgt Dick Bessell took off in Meteor A77-735 on 7 May. This was his seventh flight in an F8 and A77-735 was the same machine he had gone solo in earlier in the month. The cloud base over the airfield was 600 feet and the Meteor was immediately enveloped in cloud after take-off. Bessell was soon lost. He requested a Ground Controlled Approach (GCA), but as he was about to find out, Iwakuni airfield was a notoriously bad site for this method of landing because of the large number of permanent echoes which showed on the display of the GCA scope. USAF pilots had reported difficulty with GCA approaches due to their aircraft not appearing on the display. The operators now experienced great difficulty trying to pick up the Meteor. Bessell's inexperience with the technique caused him to fly around much too fast for the GCA controlling. He would appear as one blip on the screen and then just disappear. A number of patterns were tried without success. After 47 minutes he ran out of fuel. One engine cut out and he had come down through the cloud. He was lucky and broke into the clear at 1,000 feet over a fishing village about eight miles south of Iwakuni. After jettisoning the canopy and applying full flap and dive brakes, he touched down on the water at a speed of 105 knots on a run parallel to the seashore, about a quarter of a mile away. Left rudder caused the aircraft to swing towards the shore. The Meteor remained afloat for ten minutes and Bessell had ample time to inflate his dinghy and paddle ashore.

The aircraft was salvaged by a crew from 491 (Maintenance) Squadron the following afternoon. An aircraft-lifting sling was taken to the scene of the crash on a high-speed launch. A Japanese naval diver attached a wire rope to the aircraft that had by this time settled on

---

[9] Other problems were more easily remedied. During the first three-month period, 14 Meteors had to have their windscreens replaced due to cracking. Orders were issued to routinely cover the windscreens while the aircraft were on the ground to prevent excessive heating of the glass.

the ocean bed. The aircraft was then lifted to the surface by a 40-ton crane on a lighter which come from Kure. The intention had been to attach the lifting sling to the aircraft on the surface of the water with the idea of avoiding extreme damage to the airframe as it was lifted clear. However, the damage on the underside was such that it was decided not to worry and to lift the aircraft straight on the lighter using the wire rope. When the lighter reached Iwakuni, A77-735 was lifted gently ashore. The undercarriage wheels were locked down and the wreckage towed to the maintenance hangar by tractor. After the major components were removed, the airframe was washed down in fresh water from the pumps of the unit fire engine. This was the 77RAAF's first training accident in the conversion to Meteors. Inevitably, it would not be the last.

Shortly thereafter, Flt Lt Steve Daniel[10], having completed his operational tour with the 334th FIS, brought one of the unit's F-86s (FU-318) over to Iwakuni in order to carry out comparative trials against a Meteor F8. The exercise began on the afternoon of 18 May, the Meteor initially in the capable hands of Flt Lt Scannell, flying both A77-949 and A77-734 during the trials, while Flt Lt Blyth was able to get in one flight against the F-86, flying A77-721, as did, it is believed, Flt Lt Easley and Sgt Lamb. In between, Flt Lt Daniel took the opportunity to fly a Meteor trainer to get a feel for the aircraft against which he was competing, while Flt Lt Scannell enjoyed a 45-minute stint in the F-86. Flt Lt Blyth was naturally keen to get his hands on the Sabre, but:

> "I got to within ten yards to enter and fly when the word came from above that no more non-USAF were to fly the Sabre. Oh, well!"

There followed four days of high speed flying and aerobatics, witnessed by those on the ground as both of these very competent pilots carried out the tests within sight of the airfield. It was soon apparent that above 25,000 feet the Sabre was superior and in a long straight and level run, it left the Meteor behind due to its superior Mach number. However, in turning, zooming and in a sustained climb below 25,000 feet, the Meteor had a clear advantage. A serious disadvantage that the British machine did have was the distinct blind spot to the rear caused by the end metal of the cockpit canopy. This point was emphasised in 77RAAF's Monthly Tactical Report:

> "An F-86 aircraft of the United States Air Force was attached to No 77 Squadron for four days to carry out comparison trials against the Meteor, and to make attacks against Meteor formations simulating the tactics adopted by MiG-15 aircraft . . . The most important point that was confirmed during these trials was the extremely poor rearward visibility of the Meteor VIII. To counteract this as much as possible calls for an extremely high standard of formation flying for mutual protection. If aircraft get separated in combat, pilots will have to maintain a constant weave to clear their tails. This weave is not an easy manoeuvre at heights of 40,000 feet."

The Meteors practised basic formations at all altitudes and it was decided to adopt the open battle formation with pairs flying in line-abreast for air operations. The best distance between pairs was worked out to be about 500 yards at 20,000 feet and this was to be increased as height increased, so that at 40,000 feet sections would fly at 1,000 to 1,500 yards distance. American aircraft on fighter sweeps were currently adopting the fluid six formation, an arrangement that increased visual cover but was lacking in manoeuvrability. The Australians decided that this would be too cumbersome for Meteor operations.

It was intended for 77RAAF to return to Korea on 2 June but, before the move could be put into effect, General Robertson, the Australian commander of the BCOF in Japan, who was also administratively responsible for all Commonwealth forces in Korea, intervened. He announced that the Meteors would not be allowed to operate in Korea with each aircraft being fitted with

---

[10] With the F-86/Meteor trials completed, Flt Lt Steve Daniel boarded a Canadian airliner in company with Flt Lt Omer Lévesque and others, bound for Washington via Montreal, where the latter returned to his model wife. Once resettled, Flt Lt Daniel's fiancée Jean flew in from England and the couple were soon married.

an ARN-6 radio compass. Robertson's action was the result of following USAF advice and the decision prompted a high priority search for an ARN-6 to install in a Meteor for proper testing. Some of the components of an ARN-6 were quickly made available. There were a number of minor problems to overcome but these were expertly sorted out by the technicians, although there remained more serious problems to test their skills. For example, faulty readings on jet pipe temperature gauges were experienced. Most of this trouble was traced to the cold junction compensator. When a report of this was forwarded to the manufacturer of this component, it was admitted that a fault existed resulting from the method of manufacture. All the unserviceable compensators were exchanged for a modified type, which proved to be quite satisfactory.

In most aircraft the 20mm cannons were quite trouble-free, but in some a stoppage would occur after only a few rounds had been fired. This situation was improved to some extent by fitting a 14-gauge steel plate at the neck of the ammunition link chute on the inboard and outboard faces, which prevented links from twisting and thereby jamming in the neck of the 'chute. Both starboard guns gave more trouble than the port guns. The guns were made to fire by adjusting the tension on the belt-feed mechanism, and it was noticed that when the guns had fired about 200 rounds, it was then possible to fully tension these springs properly. When reporting these problems it was suggested that if a firing butt had been available, the trouble would not have occurred. The efficiency of the guns gradually improved, and finally reached such a pitch that there was only about one stoppage in every 1,000 rounds fired. Broken cannon sear lugs and faulty ammunition accounted for 60% of these stoppages. Finally, at last, it seemed that 77RAAF's Meteors were ready for action.

June 1951

By the end of May, except for an area around Kaesong in the west, UN ground forces along most of the front were back to the line north of the 38th Parallel that they had occupied in April. Although the Joint Chiefs-of-Staff made it clear to General Ridgway that continued pursuit of the Communists into the far north was out of the question, they somewhat reluctantly accepted his proposal for Operation 'Piledriver' to begin on 1 June, with the primary objective of seizing as much as possible of the area known as the 'Iron Triangle', the enemy's road network above the 38th Parallel. Accordingly, General Van Fleet ordered his US I and IX Corps to advance towards the 'Wyoming Line', some 20 miles ahead. They were given the task of capturing Chorwon and Kumhwa to breach the southern limits of the Triangle.

In the air Operation 'Strangle', the isolation of the enemy sources of supply from the battlefield, continued unabated. Mustangs of the 18th FBG including those of 2SAAF reconnoitred sections of roads and railways where repairs or by-passes would be difficult, and pot-holed them with 500-lb bombs. Some of the bombs were contact-fused and some were delayed-action. The Mustangs were now being fitted with special brackets which enabled proximity-fused bombs to be carried, which meant the fighter-bomber pilots could launch their bombs from higher altitudes, out of reach of enemy ground fire, and still make the bombs explode at heights best judged to kill enemy troops, destroy equipment, or suppress flak. The Mustangs, with their vulnerable engine cooling system, were still suffering the heaviest losses from ground fire. Test flights flown against friendly gun batteries at Seoul airfield revealed that during armed reconnaissance flights the trailing wingmen in the low-level pair were sitting ducks for enemy gunners. In a change of tactics, the 18th FBG decided that the flight leader should fly on the deck searching for targets of opportunity, while the No3 element leader flew at 4,000 feet and looked for flak areas. Meanwhile, the No2 and No4 would follow No3 and keep watch for enemy fighters. In this way three men would cover the one pilot who was flying the reconnaissance below.

On 1 June, Lt Gotze led a flight of four SAAF Mustangs on a low-level armed reconnaissance mission. The Mustangs dropped napalm on a target at Chorwon and then flew northwards to look for targets of opportunity. Near P'yongyang, a South African voice over the radio suddenly announced that his aircraft was burning and he was about to bale out. The pilot could not be immediately identified because he did not use his call sign. Seconds later Gotze realised that his No2, Lt Hector Macdonald in Mustang 332, was missing. The remaining

Mustangs conducted a 30-minute search of the area and Gotze found the remains of an aircraft strewn across a railway line about seven miles south of P'yongyang. His impression was that the machine had attempted a high-speed landing but it was impossible to tell from the wreckage what type of aircraft it had been. There was no sign of the pilot. Macdonald had to be listed as missing in action, assumed killed. However, about six weeks later, a *Voice of India* radio broadcast was picked up in Usakos, South-West Africa, reporting that a certain Lt Macdonald was a prisoner of the Communists. This was confirmed when the missing pilot wrote to his brother four months later. The letter was sent through the offices of the 'Chinese People's Committee for World Peace against American Aggression.'

In air-to-air fighting the MiGs were active again for the second day in a row and again B-29s were the target. The leader of a flight of four bombers of the 343rd BS had decided on a second bomb run over a railway bridge north-west of Sinanju even though their F-86 escort had to leave due to shortage of fuel. A few minutes later they paid the price when 25 MiGs of the 303rd FAD pounced on them from out of the sun. One of the bombers was immediately badly hit and fell, losing one wing on the way down. Two others were damaged but the gunners fought back determinedly and claimed two MiGs shot down, credit for these being awarded to Sgts James C. Davis and Earl A. Kanop. Calls for help over the radio were answered by incoming F-86s of the 336th FIS, and these intervened in time for Capt Richard O. Ransbottom and USN exchange pilot Lt Simpson Evans Jr to claim one apiece. One MiG was indeed lost, St/Lt Yevgenii Stelmakh of the 17th FAR being credited with shooting down one of the B-29s before he was himself shot down. Although he managed to eject, he died from his wounds. Another 17th FAR pilot claimed an F-86 shot down which allegedly fell into the sea south of Sensen. Elsewhere, shortly after midday, MiGs of the 18th GuFAR intercepted F-51s of the 67th FBS, Kapt Lev Shchukin claiming one while another was shared by Kapts Skidan, Solovyev and Kalyuzhnyi, together with St/Lt Akatov. One F-51 was lost and its pilot, Capt Harry C. Moore, was killed when his aircraft crashed in flames into a gulf near Rikaho, having last been seen by his colleagues south of Sinuiju in a dive with four MiGs on his tail. F-84s of the 27th FEG were involved in operations during the day, Sqn Ldr Adderley of the 523rd FES flying FS-400 on this occasion, while 1/Lt Lester K. Sweat of the 522nd FES failed to return. Meanwhile, Flt Lt Peter Scott, in company with other pilots of the 182nd FBS, carried out two sorties, flying FS-166 on the first and FS-411 on the second, on both occasions strafing and bombing enemy troops:

> "We had a long runway at Itazuke, but they strapped so much in the way of ordnance to us – napalm, 500-lb bombs, and rockets that we would never have got airborne but for the help of extra thrust, lasting 30 seconds, from Jet Assisted Take-Off bottles (JATO) attached to each side of the fuselage. We fired our JATO at 100mph, and it was a strange feeling knowing that if it didn't work we'd go off the end of the runway at high speed with a lot of very nasty things hanging from our wings. It was not the sort of departure to appeal to old men – but we weren't old men! Quite a few [182nd FBS] aircraft were damaged but none destroyed [in action], other than the few in the water having run out of fuel on the way back. My CO was killed."

On 2 June two SAAF Mustangs were damaged when pilots in training suffered mishaps while landing at K-10. In the morning 2/Lt Terry Liebenberg's aircraft (303) swung as he touched down and crashed. Liebenberg escaped injury but his aircraft was badly damaged. Shortly after noon, the aircraft flown by 2/Lt R.V. Sherwood bounced badly while touching down and also swung off the runway resulting in another crash. Again the pilot was uninjured, but Mustang 314 was extensively damaged and had to be written off. These incidents were attributed to the unsuitability of K-10 for the transitional training of relatively inexperienced pilots. After this, authority was sought, and received later in the month, from the CO of the 18th FBG for such training flights to take place at the far more suitable K-1 airfield nearby at Pusan. Again the Russians recorded a success against an F-86, Kapt Kramarenko of the 176th GuFAR being credited with shooting one down which reportedly crashed about 15 miles north of Taisen, although this may have been the F-84 flown by Capt Edwin R. Dischinger of HQ Sqn 6160 ABGP, who was reported missing.

At the battlefront, as cloudbursts turned the 8th US Army's lines of communications into quagmires, advancing troops had to depend heavily upon supplies transported in by air. In central and eastern Korea, the US X Corps and ROK I Corps were especially dependent upon air-dropped and air-landed support. Aircrews of the 314th Troop Carrier Group flying at only 800 feet had to thread their C-119s through mazes of mountain peaks to parachute supplies into drop zones that were often inadequately marked. On such missions the supply aircraft were frequently fired upon from the ground but the only losses sustained occurred on 3 June when, in the ROK 5th Division's area, a C-119 formation searching for a vaguely marked drop zone flew through a 'friendly' artillery barrage. Two of the transports were shot down. After this unfortunate accident, orders were issued to supply-dropping crews that they must make positive radio contact with a FAC or a TAC party before entering a drop zone.

On 4 June the SAAF pilots had one of their least successful days on record, claiming only one enemy vehicle destroyed. Low-hanging clouds and pelting rainstorms were continuing to greatly hamper air support and impede the progress of the 8th US Army on the ground. Communist soldiers remained well entrenched, out of sight of marauding UN fighter-bombers. All they could do was to keep up a steady pounding war of attrition against known locations such as caves and bunkers. As ground forces crept forward towards Chorwon and Kumhwa however, the FEAF[11] launched a series of radar-directed attacks against positions in the P'yongyang-Chorwan-Kumhwa triangle. One of these raids was intercepted by MiGs from the 18th GuFAR during the afternoon of 6 June, two F-80s being claimed shot down south of Teisu by Podpolkovnik Smorchkov and Kapt Shchukin. The 45th TRS lost its second aircraft of the month – although reportedly to ground fire – when 1/Lt Willis Thatcher was killed during a low-level sortie, but 1/Lt Francis Johnson of the 16th FIS was attacked by a MiG; he was however able to reach the coast where he carried out a successful ditching. Having evaded capture he eventually returned to friendly territory. At dusk next day (7 June), and continuing at 30-minute intervals throughout the night, a total of 23 bombers – B-26s of the 3rd and 452nd BGs, and B-29s of the 98th BG – began showering proximity-fused, air-bursting 500-lb bombs on enemy troops and supplies.

Two days later (9 June), 2/Lt Terry Liebenberg of 2SAAF was killed when his aircraft (333) crashed while taking off with a full fuel, bomb and ammunition load. Having survived a crash a week earlier, his luck ran out on this occasion. Arrangements were made for the funeral to be conducted at the UN Cemetery at Pusan. With this latest accident, 2SAAF was reduced to 21 aircraft. US fighter-bombers were also having a difficult time, Capt Philip Kuhn of the 12th FBS being shot down by ground fire, although he survived the crash-landing of his F-51 and was rescued by helicopter. Next day, 1/Lt Eric O'Briant of the same unit crashed on take-off from K-16 with a full load. He was more fortunate than 2SAAF's 2/Lt Liebenberg and survived with injuries, but two days later 1/Lt Ronald Cree of the 67th FBS was killed by ground fire when he attempted to carry out an emergency landing in his already damaged F-51. Colonel McBride[12], CO of the 18th FBG, became the next victim of the deadly ground fire when he was hit in the temple while leading a four-aircraft strike, although he managed to return to K-10 and carry out a safe landing, but not so fortunate was Capt Jack Hederstrom of the 39th FIS who failed to return in his F-51 from another sortie. His aircraft was seen to explode against a hillside. On 11 June it was the turn of Capt Kenneth Stewart of the 67th FBS to be rescued from under the noses of enemy troops after his Mustang had been shot down by ground fire. To his rescue came an SA-16 piloted by 1/Lt John J. Najarian, which alighted in the shallow and debris-filled Taedong south of Kyomipo and plucked the grateful pilot to safety.

---

[11] The FEAF was now commanded by Lt-General Otto P. Weyland, who had recently served temporarily as Deputy Chief-of-Staff for Operations, with Maj-General Frank F. Everest in command of the 5th Air Force, having succeeded Lt-General Partridge and Maj-General Timberlake, respectively, both of whom had returned to the United States on completion of their appointments.

[12] On recovery from his injury Colonel McBride did not return to his command but was posted to HQFEAF, where he became Director of Combat Operations.

It was not only UN units which were suffering accidents and consequential losses, for the special Russian MiG unit at Antung, *Grupa NII*, had been disbanded following its disastrous losses which culminated in the death of its commander, Podpolkovnik Dzyubenko, on 5 June when his aircraft crashed and overturned on landing. The unit was disbanded next day after a third pilot had been killed. Some of the pilots transferred to other Antung-based units, while the remainder returned to Russia. The highly ambitious task for which the unit had been formed – to capture an F-86 – had been a miserable failure. The departure of *Grupa NII* from Antung was followed by the arrival of a new unit, the La-11-equipped 351st FAR commanded by Podpolkovnik Ivan Andreevich. Its task was that of night fighter defence. Shortly after arrival at the Antung complex, St/Lt I.V. Gurilov was killed in a night flying accident.

An American tank force drove forward all the way to P'yonggang at the apex of the Triangle and entered the abandoned town on 13 June. General Van Fleet however ordered the American column to withdraw because he feared that it could be ambushed and trapped, although both Chorwon and Kumhwa were occupied. With the hills at the base of the Triangle now in UN possession, the Communists were deprived of an important staging area not only for a new offensive but also for any future attempt to again invade South Korea. Thanks to the improving weather, the 5th Air Force was able to return to its routine of systematic strikes on enemy airfields. A survey of recently-acquired aerial photographs had shown that all known airfields in North Korea had been rendered unserviceable but since then bad weather over the area had temporarily held up the routine of regular attacks. It was feared that this might have been sufficient time for the enemy to repair at least some of these airfields. Unknown to the 5th Air Force, it had actually been long enough for the North Koreans to bring at least Sariwon back up to the capability of operating light aircraft. A small group of intrepid NKAF airmen were assembling there and preparing to take the fight to the Americans. The weapons they intended to employ were small canvas-covered, open-cockpit trainers – Polikarpov Po-2 biplanes, probably among the oldest Soviet aircraft still in service.

Near Seoul in the early morning hours of 14 June, radar operators of the USAF's 606th Aircraft Control and Warning Squadron noticed two blips emerge from the ground clutter on their screens. The unidentified aircraft represented by the blips were flying low, heading in a southerly direction. At around 0315 one of the bogies dropped two bombs on Suwon airfield, just missing a squad of engineers who were making routine repairs to the runway. The second raider cruised unmolested over Inch'on and dropped his two bombs on an 8th Army motor park. The air defences had been taken completely by surprise and both enemy planes escaped northwards. Based on a number of descriptions from various sightings, 5th Air Force intelligence officers were able to identify the low-flying raiders as Po-2 biplanes. The North Korean pilots from Sariwon were starting to hit back, employing the same tactics that the Russians had used successfully in night attacks against the Germans in WWII, and had even used the very same type of aircraft. On the night of 15/16 June, K-16 received another harassing attack by the daring Po-2 pilots, as noted by 2SAAF's diarist:

> "During the night an enemy aircraft bombed and strafed airfield K-16. No casualties or damage were suffered by any of the squadrons in the Wing. This is the first enemy attack experienced by the ground personnel during the present tour of operation in this theatre."

Another strange aircraft, identified as a Blockavidan MBE-2 pusher-type seaplane, made a strafing pass across nearby Kimpo airfield with no results other than some near misses against a jeep-load of policemen. These nuisance raiders were becoming widely known as 'Bed Check Charlies'. RAAF airframe fitter Cpl Pat Melican recalled the reason for this:

> "Because the raider would invariably arrive later than midnight, the air raid alarm would awaken all personnel already asleep who were under orders to go to their places in the allocated slit-trenches where the officer or NCO in charge of the trench would check that all airmen were present. I believe the Americans would go through every tent checking beds to ensure that none of their airmen had slept through the alarm and that it was this precaution that give rise to the raider's name of 'Bed Check Charlie', later abbreviated to 'Bed Check'. Korea is a very mountainous country and the Po-2 would fly to Kimpo along

first RAF pilots to fly on operations
the USAF in Korea, 1950:

left: Wg Cdr Johnnie Johnson DSO DFC.

right: Wg Cdr Peter Wykeham-Barnes
DFC.

Bottom left: Sqn Ldr Joe Bodien DSO
DFC.

Bottom right: Sqn Ldr Jack Sach DFC AFC.

This page: Flt Lt Peter Scott was attached to the 182nd FBS flying F-84s.

Above: Flt Lt Steve Daniel DSO DFC, a successful WWII fighter pilot, flew F-86s with the 334th FIS and was credited with damaging a MiG-15.

Left: Flt Lt Steve Daniel (left) with Flt Lt Omer Lévesque RCAF (third from left) and two American pilots of the 334th FIS.

Air Force F86 A-5-NA
SERIAL NO. 49-1110 A

DEL. NO- GNCOPF-35

CANOPY

HAND GRIP

NO STEP

Above: Flt Lt Omer Lévesque RCAF, attached to the 334th FIS on F-86s, the first Canadian pilot to be credited with shooting down a MiG-15.

Right: A sketch made by Flt Lt Omer Lévesque following his combat with the MiG-15 he claimed shot down.

Above: Three pilots of the RAF Mission engaged in shooting practice; left to right, Flt Lt Joe Blyth AFC, Flt Lt Frank Easley and Sgt Reg Lamb, watched by Flt Lt George Odgers (second from right), the RAAF PRO.

Left: Flt Lt Max Scannell AFC (right), the leader of the RAF Mission sent to Korea to convert pilots of 77RAAF from Mustang to Meteor, chatting with Sqn Ldr Dick Cresswell, CO of 77RAAF.

Above: Wg Cdr Alan Boxer DSO DFC had flown clandestine missions during WWII; from Japan he flew several operations with the 307th BG on B-29s.

Right: Sqn Ldr The Honourable Michael Adderley AFC was attached to the 523rd FES flying F-84s.

77RAAF Mustang pilots...

Top left: Wg Cdr Lou Spence, the CO (KiA 9/9/50).

Top right: Flt Lt Bay Adams (left) and Wg Cdr Lou Spence.

Middle left: P3 Don Ellis (KiA 22/12/50), left, and P3 Geoff Stephens (KiA 6/1/51).

Middle right: P1 (later Flt Lt) Geoff Thornton shows the wire that damaged his Mustang during a low-level attack on 11/12/50.

Left: Flt Lt Gordon Harvey (POW 19/1/51).

More Australian Mustang pilots...

Top: Sqn Ldr Graham Strout (KiA 7/7/50).

Middle left: Sgt Cec Sly.

Bottom left: A dead-heat: Flt Lts Ross Coburn (left) and Fred Barnes congratu[...] each other on reaching 100 missions.

Bottom right: P3 Sinclair Squires (KiFA 14/2/51).

Top: RAAF Mustang A68-708, seen patrolling off the coast, was written-off in a crash-landing on 15/2/51.

Middle: RAAF Mustang A68-791 after P3 Dick Bessell's forced-landing at Pusan 3/1/51.

Left: Symbolic changeover from prop to jet - 77RAAF's last Mustang taxis past a line of Meteors, 4/4/51.

Top: Flg Off Wal Rivers.

Middle right: Flg Off Ken Blight.

Middle left: Flt Sgt Bill Middlemiss.

Bottom: Flt Lt Des Murphy in the cockpit of an F-80 of the 8th FG.

p: 77RAAF personnel at Iwakuni, circa
y 1951:

o row, left to right: Flg Off Ken Blight;
t Keith Meggs; Sgt Allan Avery DFM;
t Off Bob Hunt; Flg Off Dick Wittman;
Off Ray Trebilco DFC; Wt Off Bill
chelson DFC; Sgt Ron Mitchell;
t Keith Foster.

ddle row: Sgt Tom Stoney; Sgt Dick
ssell; Flg Off Les Reading; Flt Lt Leo
*o*wn; Wt Off Alan Philp; Flt Lt Ralph
wson; Sgt Max Colebrook; Sgt Don
*m*it; Sgt Fred Collins; Sgt Reg Lamb

RAF; Flt Lt Frank Easley RAF; Flt Lt
Scotty Cadan; Sgt Cec Sly.

Bottom row: Flt Lt Joe Blyth AFC RAF;
Sqn Ldr Morgan (Admin); Flt Lt Max
Scannell AFC RAF; Mr Eric Greenwood
(Gloster Chief Test Pilot); Sqn Ldr Mike
Kater MC (SMO); Flt Lt Des Murphy; Sqn
Ldr Dick Cresswell; Flt Lt Vic Cannon; Flg
Off Geoff Thornton DFM AFM; Mr Jock
Gibb (Rolls-Royce); Flt Lt Kalucy (Admin);
Flt Lt Ian Lyons (Admin); Wt Off Ron Howe.

Bottom: Flt Lt Max Scannell RAF on
readiness beside Meteor A77-982.

Top left: Sabre v Meteor comparative trials at Iwakuni.

Top right and middle left: Sqn Ldr Dick Cresswell DFC (right) was succeeded as CO of 77RAAF by Wg Cdr Gordon Steege DSO DFC (left).

Middle right: Sqn Ldr David Wilson inspecting damage to Meteor A77-616.

Right: Sgt Bruce Thomson was a victim of the MiGs (POW 1/12/51).

Top left: Flt Lt Scotty Cadan damaged a MiG and an F-86 in combat.

Top right: Sgt Keith Meggs climbing into the cockpit of a Meteor.

Bottom left: Flg Off Bruce Gogerly, the first RAAF pilot to shoot down a MiG (1/12/51).

Bottom right: Sgt Vance Drummond, a New Zealander in the RAAF, was shot down by MiGs on 1/12/51 (POW).

Top: Unusual shot of a Meteor being refuelled.

Above: Flt Lt Joe Blyth's usual mount, A77-189.

Right: Meteor A77-616 after undercarriage collapse on landing, 22/9/51. The GCA tent is in immediate background.

Left: Flg Off Les Reading damaged a MiG on 27/10/51.

ght: Wt Off Ron Guthrie ⟨w⟩s shot down by a MiG on ⟨2⟩/8/51 (POW).

Top left: Meteor A77-316 tailplane damage inflicted by a MiG, 24/10/51.

Top right: Flg Off Phil Hamilton-Foster beside his combat-damaged Meteor A77-316, 24/10/51.

Middle: Sqn Ldr Mike Kater (SMO) and Flt Lt Vic Cannon examine damage to Meteor T7 A77-305, 10/9/51.

Bottom: Damage sustained by Meteor A7 726 in combat, 5/9/51.

lots of 2SAAF... the cost was high:

Top left: Lt Elmer Wilson (KiA 2/2/51).

Top right: Lt Denis Ruiter DFC (KiFA 2/3/51).

Middle left: Capt John Davis DFC (KiA 10/3/51).

Bottom left: 2/Lt T. Liebenberg (KiFA 10/6/51).

Bottom centre: Lt A. G. Frisby (KiA 22/6/51).

Bottom right: Maj L. B. Pearce (KiFA 9/7/51).

Top left: Lt Roelof du Plooy (KiA 23/7/51).

Top centre: Lt Ian de Jongh (KiA 14/8/51).

Top right: Capt Freddy Bekker (KiA 23/7/51).

Middle left: 2/Lt Mike Grunder (KiA 1/9/51).

Bottom left: Lt N. Biden (KiA 5/9/51).

Bottom right: Capt Frank Montanari (KiA 12/9/51).

Top left: 2/Lt Theo Joyce (KiA 29/10/51).

Top centre: 2/Lt Critton Pappas (KiA 4/11/51).

Top right: 2/Lt George Krohn (KiA 24/11/51).

Middle left: Capt Amo Janse van Rensburg (KiA 29/11/51).

Bottom left: Lt Peter Norman-Smith, killed in mid-air collision 3/12/51.

Bottom right: 2/Lt Ken Whitehead, killed in mid-air collision 3/12/51.

Top left: 2/Lt Mike Halley (POW 23/7/51).

Top centre: Lt Denis Earp (POW 27/9/51).

Top right: Lt Chris Lombard (POW 7/10/51).

Middle left: Cmdt Johann Blaauw DFC.

Bottom left: Freddie Potgieter was lucky t have survived when a bullet smashed through his cockpit and knocked his goggles from his face.

Bottom right: Capt Gordon Lipawsky DF

Top: Dramatic image of an armed and ready 2SAAF Mustang being warmed up in the darkness for an early morning mission.

Middle: 2SAAF Mustang 303 undergoing repair at Iwakuni. In the foreground is a WWII Japanese Baka kamikaze rocket aircraft.

Left: 2SAAF Mustang 321 at K-10. Capt John Davis was shot down and killed in this aircraft on 10/3/51.

Top: RHAF Dakota 622/E; note 'Neptune' on nose.

Middle left: 77RAAF's Dakota offloading equipment at Pusan.

Middle right: Flt Lt (Wg Cdr) Dave Hitchins, Dakota pilot, also flew a few ops on Mustangs with 77RAAF.

Bottom left: Sunderland 'B' at rest in Iwakuni Bay.

Bottom right: 77RAAF Meteor overflying Sunderland 'C' at Iwakuni; two USN Mariners can just be discerned at their moorings in the background.

Top: Auster VF639 of 1903 (AOP) Flight
shed on take-off from Fort St. George
6/12/51.

Bottom: Auster WJ358 and the newly
acquired Cessna L-19 (14754) of the RAF's
1913 (Light Liaison) Flight.

ddle: Auster VF498 of 1903 (AOP)
ght.

Top: Canadian Army observer Lt Don 'Bud' MacLeod (left) with his USAF pilot Lt C.F. Doane of the 6149th TCS prior to a mission.

Middle left: Army pilot Capt Bob Begbie, seen with visiting Hollywood actress Lana Turner, quipped: 'Transportation of VIPs was a tough job, but somebody had to do it!'

Middle right: Personnel of the 67th Tac Recon Wing USAF included RAF officers Sqn Ldr Vic de la Perelle (squatting, second right), Flt Lt Eric Roberts DFM (standing extreme left), and Flt Lt John Low (standing fourth right), plus Sqn Ldr Allan Simpson DFC RCAF (standing, second right).

Right: Army pilot Capt Geoff Sipthorne flew observation ops in an L-5 during the battle for Hill 327 in February 1951.

p left: Barrier crash HMS *Triumph* – efly PP585/282 of 827 Squadron.

p right: Lt (P) Stanley Leonard of 807 uadron (HMS *Theseus*) whose Sea Fury s shot down by ground fire on 10/11/50; was rescued by a USAF helicopter.

ttom left: Lt (P) Ian Hamilton, also of 7 Squadron, returned to HMS *Theseus*

by USN helicopter after a very icy dip in the ocean, 18/4/51.

Middle right: Snow-covered Sea Fury of 807 Squadron aboard HMS *Theseus*.

Bottom right: Sea Fury VW558 of 804 Squadron from HMS *Glory* nosed over at Kimpo.

Top: Firefly VT503/204 of 817 Squadron RAN runs into trouble while landing on HMAS *Sydney*.

Middle left: Sea Fury of 805 Squadron RAN landing on HMAS *Sydney*.

Bottom left: The CO's Flight 805 Squadro RAN, HMAS *Sydney*: left to right: Lt Cd (P) W.G. Bowles, Sub Lt (P) F.T. Lane, Su Lt (P) I. MacDonald, Lt (P) F. Sherbourn

Bottom right: A Sea Fury from HMAS *Sydney* dropping 500-lb bombs on its targ

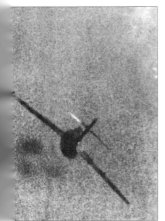

Top: Capt James Jabara of the 334th FIS on return from claiming his fifth MiG to become the USAF's first all-jet ace, 20/5/51.

Middle left: Maj George Davis Jr (left) and Maj Winton Marshall (right) being congratulated by Colonel Ben Preston on gaining their fifth kills on 30/11/51.

Middle right: Capt Vasseure 'Georgia' Wynn served with the RCAF during WWII and flew in defence of Malta in 1942, where he claimed several victories, gaining more after transferring to the USAF. He served in Korea with the 52nd FES on F-84s.

Left: Through the gunsight: a MiG-15 about to become another Sabre victory.

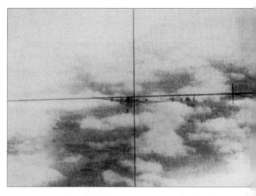

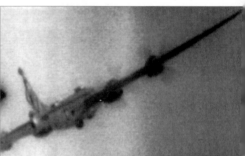

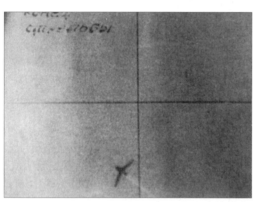

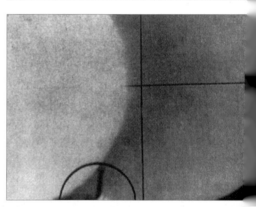

Top left: Kapt Sergei Kramarenko of the 176th GuFAR who was credited with 13 victories.

Through the MiG gunsight (1):

Top right and below: B-29s under attack.

Middle left: Sabre trailing smoke.

Middle right: Doomed F-84.

Bottom: MiG-15 No823 of the 176th GuFAR at Antung showing signs of battle damage following combat on 12/4/51.

 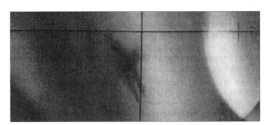

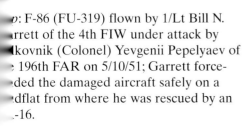

p: F-86 (FU-319) flown by 1/Lt Bill N. arrett of the 4th FIW under attack by kovnik (Colonel) Yevgenii Pepelyaev of 196th FAR on 5/10/51; Garrett force-ded the damaged aircraft safely on a dflat from where he was rescued by an -16.

ddle: The remains of FU-319 were overed by a Soviet salvage team.

Bottom left: Polkovnik Yevgenii Pepelyaev, commander of the 196th FAR, who was eventually credited with about 20 victories during the Korean War.

Bottom right: Polkovnik Pepelyaev's MiG (No325) showing battle damage sustained during the action on 5/10/51.

Top left: St/ Lt (later Major) Pavel Nikulin of the 176th GuFAR was shot down by an F-86 on 1/5/51 but ejected safely although he suffered injuries.

Top right: Two MiG aces, Podpolkovnik Alexandr Smorchkov, left, (15 victories) of the 18th GuFAR and Major Dmitrii Os'kin (11) of the 523rd FAR.

Bottom left: Some of the MiG pilots who engaged Meteors of 77RAAF on 1/12/51. Back row, left to right: Podpolk A. Mituso St/ Lt N. Kravtsov; St/ Lt A. Nikolaev; St/ Lt N. Moroz. Front row: St/ Lt A. Verdysh Kapt G. Ges; Podpolk S. Vishnyakov; St/ D. Fyordorov.

Bottom right: Kapt Grigorii Ges of the 176th GuFAR was credited with eight victories.

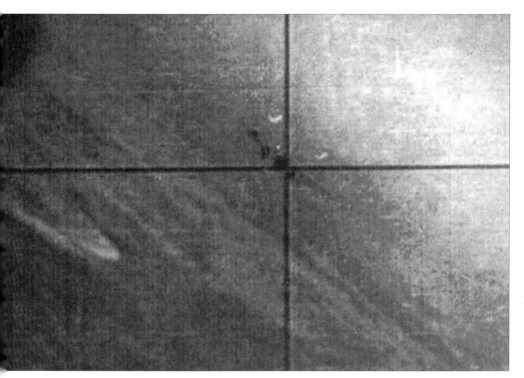

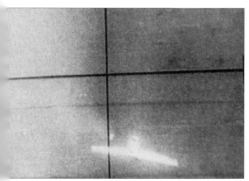

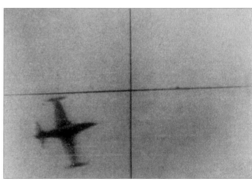

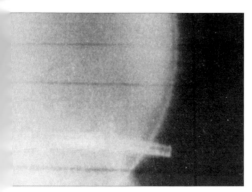

:ough the MiG gunsight (2):

*ɔ: Meteor of 77RAAF under attack by
ɔt Petr Milaushkin of the 176th GuFAR
ɔ claimed two Meteors among his ten
ɔries.*

ldle and bottom left: Polkovnik Yevgenii

Pepelyaev fires at an F-86 on 28/11/51; it
was claimed shot down.

Middle right: F-80 about to enter the
killing zone.

Bottom right: Closing in on an F-84.

Top: Chinese MiG pilots played only a small rôle in air operations until the end of 1951.

Above: Chinese MiGs prepare for an early morning take-off.

Left: Capt Li Han of the Chinese 10th FAR was credited with the first Chinese MiG kill, an F-80 on 21/1/51.

the valleys, below the mountain tops which would conceal his approach from our radar at Kimpo. Eventually, he'd have to climb to bombing level to locate the base and then the radar would detect him and the alarm would be sounded. Often, the first warning would be a rapid firing of four rounds of 40mm shells from the AA battery situated about a hundred yards from our tents, followed by the wailing of a siren that probably shared the good news with the occupants of the nearby village."

On the night of 16/17 June, the pilots of two of the North Korean biplanes achieved a notable success when they arrived over K-13 where they found the area well illuminated. On the perimeter road around the airfield a steady flow of moving vehicles using their headlights outlined the target very nicely for the raiders. Each Po-2 dropped a couple of small bombs, one of which damaged equipment in the 802nd Engineer Aviation Battalion's motor pool, and another, apparently dropped by Lt La Woon Yung, scored a direct hit on the 335th FIS's aircraft parking ramp. One F-86 was completely destroyed and eight others were damaged, four of them seriously. A small convas-covered, open-cockpit biplane trainer had caused almost as much damage to the Sabres as had all of the encounters with MiGs up to that time.

Later that morning F-86s of the 4th FIW patrolling the Yalu encountered a formation of 25 unusually aggressive MiGs from the 303rd FAD. Up to now the Americans had occasionally met extremely able and confident MiG pilots who often flew alone or were seen to be guiding the actions of those with them. These men were thought to be Russian or Chinese instructors whom the Sabre pilots came to call *honchos*, the word *honcho* in Japanese meaning 'boss'; they were, in fact, from the 18th GuFAR and 176th GuFAR. It was now becoming apparent to the American pilots that a new unit of very capable MiG pilots had been assigned to Korea. The skirmish on 17 June however favoured the Sabre pilots, who claimed one MiG shot down by Capt Samuel Pesacreta, and damage to six others without loss to themselves, although the Russian pilots claimed four F-86s in return, two of which were reported to have crashed into the gulf near Sensen as victories of 176th GuFAR pilots Kapts Subbotin (his fourth) and Kramarenko. Another was credited to Kapt Lev Shchukin of the 18th GuFAR (also his fourth victory of which one was shared), but he was himself shot down near Ku-song, ejecting safely, obviously the victim of Capt Pesacreta[13]. The fourth Sabre was claimed by Kapt Dmitrii Os'kin, also of the 18th GuFAR, his first victory.

Next morning (18 June), not discouraged by the results of the previous day's dogfight, an estimated 40 MiGs of the 303rd FAD took off from Antung, including eight from the 176th GuFAR led by Kapt Sherberstov, to engage a force of 32 F-86s in another savage encounter, in which the American pilots claimed five of the Russian jets destroyed for the loss of one of their own flown by Capt William D. Crone, only the second or third F-86 pilot to be lost in air combat to date. Honours for the day really belonged to 1/Lt Ralph Gibson of the 335th FIS who claimed two shot down, the other scorers being 1/Lt James E. Heckman also of the 335th, Maj Richard D. Creighton of the 336th, and Capt Erwin A. Hesse from 4th Group HQ. For the Russians, Kapt Serafim Subbotin was credited with one of the six F-86s the MiG pilots believed they had destroyed, to achieve acedom, but was also shot down, ejecting safely. Of this action he reported that during his first attack he shot down one Sabre, and as he manoeuvred into a dogfight he saw two more attacking a MiG. He fired at one and at the same moment felt hits in his engine, which grated and stopped. Smoke poured into his cockpit, so he jettisoned the canopy and went into a low spiral:

"When I went out of the right-hand spiral I was twice attacked by a Sabre which was following me. It fired all the time. As a result my aircraft was again hit. It continued pursuing and shooting all the time from close range. I extended the air brakes and almost at once I felt and heard grating and saw on the left side of me the fuselage of an F-86 with a broken right wing – the Sabre had crashed into my plane. My MiG began to gyrate from

---

[13] Kapt Lev Shchukin would be shot down twice more before the end of his tour in Korea, ejecting safely each time. He went on to fly a total of 212 operational sorties and amassed a score of 15 victories which made him the joint third highest-scoring Russian pilot of the Korean War.

side to side and I was thrown about in the cockpit. I chose the moment when negative G tore me out of my seat and baled out of the uncontrollable aircraft. My parachute opened successfully and I landed in mountains about 12 kilometres from the town of Teisen."

St/Lt Plitkin claimed another Sabre, while three of the victories were awarded to pilots of the 523rd FAR (Podpolkovnik Karasyov, Kapt Ponomarev, and St/Lt Yakovlev), and these are alleged to have crashed near Teiju, Sintsan and Hakusen, while Subbotin's was reported to have gone down north of Muneri; the sixth victory went to a pilot of the 18th GuFAR, Kapt Tarasov. The series of actions continued for a third consecutive day, Sabres and MiGs becoming embroiled over north-western Korea. In this battle the Americans came off second best for the first time; one F-86 pilot, 1/Lt Robert H. Laier, failed to return to Suwon and was assumed lost (he was taken prisoner but died in captivity), in return for claims of four MiGs damaged. St/Lt Nikolai Sutyagin of the 17th FAR was credited with shooting down one of the two F-86s claimed, his first victory, which crashed near Sensen. A second victory was claimed by St/Lt Shulev of the same unit.

Meanwhile, with the influx of 17 newly arrived replacement pilots, 2SAAF's sortie rate increased to 24 per day, and on 12 June the South Africans had destroyed 16 buildings and damaged six others and a field gun, while on an early morning interdiction mission next day, Lt Freddy Bekker's Mustang was hit in the starboard wingroot by an explosive bullet which severed a hydraulic pipe. He had to land at K-16 without brakes. That day the South Africans claimed the destruction of 43 buildings and three rolling stock plus damage to 16 other buildings. 2SAAF also became involved in the airfield raids, and on 18 June, one flight of Mustangs carrying 500-lb bombs attacked a suspected airstrip at Ongjin and caused five large craters on what was believed to be the runway. In other operations, six buildings, three railway rolling stock and a truck were claimed destroyed, with damage inflicted to five more buildings. In addition, three enemy troops were killed. Contributing again to the campaign against North Korean airfields, next day another flight of bomb-carrying SAAF Mustangs gained four direct hits on the runway of Haeju airfield. In other sorties, 16 buildings were destroyed and 13 damaged. While the South Africans managed to avoid casualties during this period, other squadrons of the 18th FBG were not so fortunate, 1/Lt Bernard Percy of the 12th FBS being shot down by ground fire on 14 June although he was able to bale out and was later rescued by an SA-16. Two days later, the 67th FBS lost 1/Lt Francis Escott and, on the 19th, 1/Lt Lee Harper of the 39th FIS was killed when he baled out at low level from his damaged Mustang. More fortunate was 1/Lt Vernon Burke of the 67th FBS who was rescued by helicopter after he had baled out.

Beginning on 18 June, FEAF Bomber Command put the strength of its medium bomber force behind the 5th Air Force campaign against the North Korean airfields. They worked around the clock. By day, fighter-bombers, light-bombers and B-29s pot-holed the airfields, and at night B-26 intruders made up to five attacks on the airfields that looked as though they might have repair gangs at work. Trouble was brewing elsewhere. For several days reports reaching UN Intelligence suggested that the Chinese and North Koreans were likely to invade the Sinmi-do Islands, just three miles off the western coast of Korea and 70 miles south of the Yalu. The occupants of these islands were considered to be friendly to the UN. With the MiG force now seriously challenging the Sabre screen, an operation such as this so close to the Manchurian border would provide an ideal opportunity for the Chinese Communists to test the ability of their Il-10 ground-attack units to be able to provide local air support.

Early on the morning of 20 June, a flight of 18th FBG Mustang pilots on a sweep of the roads south of Sinuiju looked up to see a mixed gaggle of twelve aircraft identified as Il-10s and Yak-9s on a course for Sinmi-do. The Mustang pilots promptly called for reinforcements and then pulled up to launch an attack. Another flight of F-51s, which took station over Sinmi-do, were soon dogfighting six Yak-9s and a third flight of Mustangs, with F-86s covering, arrived on the scene at more or less the same time as the first MiGs put in an appearance. Mustang pilot Capt James B. Harrison of the 67th FBS, flying in the No3 position, destroyed the leading Yak with a highly accurate full deflection shot. The NKAF pilot baled out and the aircraft crashed into the sea. It was seen burning on the surface of the water before sinking. This brought Harrison's total to eight kills in two wars. Two other pilots from the 12th FBS, Captains Bruce Clark and Landell Hames, each claimed an Il-10 destroyed and 1/Lt James Reintz claimed one damaged, while Lt Colonel R.H. Saltsman, acting Wing Commander of the 18th FBG, claimed a probable. Only Harrison's kill was officially credited by the USAF, and this turned out to be the last official victory awarded to an F-51 pilot during the Korean War. Higher up, the Sabres damaged four MiGs including one by Lt Colonel Ben Emmert of the 335th FIS, but a few MiGs slipped through the top cover and made passes at the Mustangs and shot the wings off the aircraft flown by Capt John J. Coleman of the 39th FIS. The Mustang fell in flames east of Sibito and Coleman had no chance to bale out, having apparently fallen victim to the combined attack of Kapt Grigorii Ges and St/Lt Nikolaev of the 176th GuFAR, although four of the American fighter-bombers were claimed in total by the Russian pilots, the others being claimed by Polkovnik Vishnyakov, Kapt Sherberstov and Lt Golovachev. However, it would seem that Coleman's aircraft was that shot down by Ges and Nikolaev since one of the doomed Mustang's wings damaged the tail of Ges' MiG as the aircraft broke up, while Nikolaev's aircraft was then attacked and damaged by one of the F-86s. Both MiGs were able to return safely to Antung. This ended the air action over Sinmi-do and the CCAF ground-attack force had been turned back. As the MiG pilots returned to base they were attacked by two F-86s and Kapt Skidan was shot down about ten miles east of Sinuiju. He received severe injuries and was rushed to hospital. It is not known if he survived.

The veterans of 2SAAF who had trained the new batch of incoming pilots for combat were now completing their tours, Lt George Sykes flying his 75th sortie on 20 June during a mission when 15 buildings and a road bridge were destroyed, and a further dozen buildings left damaged. Next day, Capt Joubert led four aircraft from K-16 on a road interdiction mission to complete his 100th combat sortie in Korea. This mission brought about two complete road cuts in the Chinnampo area using 500-lb bombs, after which the SAAF pilots proceeded to rocket and strafe buildings that had been allocated as secondary targets. Both Capt Jan Willers and Lt Piet Strydon completed their tours on the same operation. Two replacement Mustangs now arrived from Japan boosting the aircraft strength back to 24 machines.

For more than a week the FEAF crews committed to the airfield neutralisation strikes had been able to carry out their tasks free from enemy air resistance but, on 22 June, the Russians cast their MiGs into the fight. Carrying wing tanks, which they jettisoned prior to combat, the MiGs left their sanctuary across the Yalu, flew above or otherwise evaded the Sabre patrols along the border and penetrated as far south as P'yongyang and Chinnampo. A flight of four Mustangs of the 67th FBS on a rail cutting mission was jumped by six of these MiGs, the fighter-bomber pilots turning in to their assailants to meet them head-on. The Mustang leader, 1/Lt Joseph M. Babsa, scored effective strikes all over the nose of one MiG but then his guns fell silent – he had run out of ammunition. It was a good chance gone and Babsa, who was noted for his aggressive leadership, was left seething with rage. In another clash, F-80s raided Sinuiju airfield and escaped unscathed, while covering Sabres of the 4th FIW tousled with MiGs of the 303rd and 324th FADs overhead. The Russian pilots exploited the advantages of their aircraft to the fullest, especially using the MiG's ability to fly and manoeuvre at high altitudes and out-climb the F-86s. They introduced a new tactic which the American pilots described as a 'Yo-Yo' manoeuvre: first, 20-plus MiGs established an orbiting pattern above the USAF formations; then, preferably from up-sun and usually in pairs, they dived and attacked their targets from high astern, before zooming back up to the orbiting MiGs high in the sky. On this day, for the loss of one F-86 flown by 1/Lt Howard P. Miller Jr, the 4th FIW pilots claimed two MiGs destroyed but only one of the kills received official USAF credit, that of 1/Lt Charles O. Riester Jr of the 336th FIS. For the Russians, St/Lt Nikolai Sutyagin of the 17th FAR claimed two F-86s shot down, and Kapt Serafim Subbotin of the 176th GuFAR reported shooting down a third, while St/Lt Plitkin of the latter unit was shot down, ejecting safely. One American pilot was reported to have been captured by North Korean troops.

2SAAF also lost a pilot on 22 June. At 1055, Cmdt Ray Armstrong led a flight of four Mustangs on a mission to attack enemy supply routes north-west of Namch'onjam, an action for which he was awarded an American DFC, the citation noting that:

". . . as a result of this aggressive air strike, a great number of enemy troops were killed [and] anti-aircraft batteries were discovered and attacked, resulting in the total destruction of two positions [as were] an enemy supply dump and three large barracks-type buildings . . ."

However, when flying at 2,000 feet west of Sibyonni, section leader Lt A.G. Frisby called that he had been hit by ground fire and that he was going to bale out. At 800 feet, Cmdt Armstrong saw the canopy of Frisby's Mustang (337) shoot off and a brown-coloured object fall away from the crippled aircraft before it crashed into the side of a river bed and broke up. No parachute was seen and there was no sign of the pilot. After landing back at K-16, Cmdt Armstrong arranged to lead out another four aircraft for an extra search. Despite close scrutiny of the area they failed to find any evidence of the pilot and had to conclude that Bob Frisby had, in fact, baled out too low and that his parachute had failed to open.

While these major actions were being waged in daylight, at night the little North Korean Po-2s were arriving in the Seoul area with tedious regularity. Except for the destruction achieved at Suwon on 17 June, they accomplished little material damage but were proving to be an irritating thorn in the flesh of the Americans trying to get a good night's sleep. Geared to combat high-performance aircraft, the US air defences were baffled as to how to tackle the problem of the nocturnal marauders. The wood framed, fabric covered biplanes offered poor electronic reflecting surfaces for the radar scopes and even when a raider was located and a night fighter from the 68th FIS or VMF(N)-513 was vectored to intercept, the Po-2's slow speed and extreme manoeuvrability usually allowed it to escape. On several occasions USMC night fighters narrowly avoided collisions with the elusive biplanes because they could not detect them from amidst the ground clutter on airborne radar. But they did not always escape and, on the night of 22/23 June, an 8th Squadron B-26 intruder flown by Capt Richard M. Heyman responded to a call for help from Kimpo's air direction centre and, before overshooting, managed to throttle back sufficiently to shoot down a Po-2 north of Seoul.

There occurred another jet clash next day (23 June), the MiG pilots from the 303rd FAD reporting an engagement with F-86s although these may have included F-80s of the 8th FBS, one of which was seen to be shot down by a MiG; its pilot, 1/Lt Ernest Dunning, was reported missing. Claims for F-86s were submitted by Kapt Grigorii Okhai of the 523rd FAR, his victim reportedly having crashed near Syarenkan, while that claimed by Kapt Ivan Tyulyaev crashed about 20 miles north-east of Teiju. The 4th FIW reported two skirmishes with MiGs during the day, one in the late morning and another in the evening, Colonel Glenn Eagleston claiming MiGs damaged on both occasions. One MiG was shot down during a morning sortie near Sensen, but this was attributed to a recognition error by North Korean AA gunners; the pilot, St/Lt Vladimir Negodaev of the 176th GuFAR, was killed. Meanwhile, SAAF Mustangs were involved in attacks against airfields during the day, including a mission led by Capt Johannes Swanepoel against the revetments at Sariwon airfield. These were protected by 37mm automatic weapons and numerous 20mm and 40mm anti-aircraft guns. Swanepoel led his flight in at 20-50 feet above the ground and covered the target area with napalm. Because of the intense and accurate return fire they did not wait around to survey the damage. For his leadership and aggressive spirit, Swanepoel was awarded a US DFC for this action. Other flights from 2SAAF, each comprising four aircraft, also attacked the airfields at Anak, Sinmak and Ongjin. All aircraft returned safely from these missions.

Next day (24 June), the South Africans were back again attacking the airfields at Sariwon, Anak, Sinmak and Haeju, this time using fused rockets for flak suppression and 500-lb bombs to pot-hole the runways. They flew a total of 22 sorties in seven missions, three of which led to the award of the US DFC to the flight leaders. On one mission, Lt Syd de la Harpe led three Mustangs to attack Sariwon where, despite intense anti-aircraft fire, four direct bomb hits were obtained on the runway and two gun positions were destroyed. This was followed by 2/Lt Bob Staats taking his flight to Sinmak, where the runway was bombed, before launching an attack against rail cars at Kumch'on-ni. A persistent 20mm gun position was silenced by Staats before he led the other three to destroy five box-cars together with the stores they carried. Another mission was led by Lt Gordon Marshall, who took off with his flight at 1945. Together with Capt Larry Eagar, 2/Lt John Howe and 2/Lt Jessie Verster, he was briefed to carry out an interdiction mission north of Kaesong. En route to the target area they heard an FAC calling for support from any flight in the vicinity that could hear him. Marshall diverted his flight in response. The FAC indicated a concentration of enemy troops situated in an almost unapproachable location about 20 miles south-west of Chorwon, where the surrounding terrain was defended by an abundance of automatic weapons and batteries of 20mm and 40mm anti-aircraft guns. Marshall led his flight through the barrier of intense and accurate enemy fire to deliver attack after attack on the target. So heavy was the return fire from the defences that the FAC instructed an incoming USAF fighter-bomber flight to stand-by to fly CAP should any of the Mustangs be hit and forced down behind the lines. Both newcomers Howe and Verster later expressed surprise at having survived. The flight strafed and rocketed enemy troops, killing an unknown number of them, and attacked the gun positions destroying at least one 40mm gun, two automatic gun positions and inflicted damage on another 40mm gun. The courage of these pilots was recognised on 2 July when the Squadron received notification of the immediate award of an American DFC to Lt Marshall and Air Medals to the other three pilots involved[14]. Marshall's citation read:

> "Despite poor visibility and in the face of withering enemy ground fire, Lieutenant Marshall, without hesitation and with complete disregard for personal safety, made successive hazardous attacks with relentless accuracy on the enemy positions. In an exceptional display of aggressiveness and aeronautical skill he engineered the attacks of his flight with such outstanding airmanship that the optimum damage was inflicted against the enemy without the loss of one of his aircraft."

According to Russian records, 24 June was the date of an outstanding success for the MiG pilots of the 303rd FAD, who apparently claimed no fewer than eight F-80s and an F-86 shot down, the latter being credited to a pilot of the 18th GuFAR, and was reported to have crashed about ten miles north of Kokusen. The first action occurred shortly before 0500 when 29 MiGs of the 523rd FAR led by Podpolkovnik Karasyov met four F-80s near Bihen. All four were claimed shot down, one apiece by Kapts Okhai, Popov and Ponomarev, with the fourth credited to St/Lt Razorvin. A few minutes later a further 22 F-80s were encountered, in two groups of six and 16, and these were also engaged; a further four were claimed by Kapts Mazilov and Bakhaev, St/Lts Shatalov and Silkin. The F-80s allegedly crashed over a wide area, one near Serenkan, another near Teiju, a third near Nam-men, and another a few miles north-east of Rakotsin; two blew up in mid-air, and the remaining two fell into the gulf but, as far as can be ascertained, no F-80s were lost on this date. According to available information, F-80s of the 51st FBW were jumped by a formation of MiGs while strafing Sinanju airfield. In the ensuing running battle at low level, where the F-80s retained their advantage, the American pilots escaped unharmed and claimed to have damaged four of the enemy jets. In addition, an aircraft identified variously as an F-94 or a T-33 was intercepted shortly after 0900 by MiGs of the 176th GuFAR and claimed shot down by Kapt Goncharov, the American jet crashing about eight miles north-east of Anju. Apparently the pilot ejected and was taken prisoner, his aircraft probably an RF-80 of the 15th TRS.

It was the turn of the Americans to make a claim on 25 June, Capt Milton Nelson of the 335th FIS being credited with shooting down a MiG for his second victory. The Russian jets were from the 18th GuFAR led by Podpolkovnik Smorchkov whose pilots submitted claims for four F-86s shot down near Teiju. The claimants were Kapts Antonov and Babonin, St/Lts Akatov and Kolpikov. One of the Russian pilots also claimed an F-80 near Tsinnampo. Next day (26 June) the newly arrived pilots of the 136th FBW received their baptism of fire, when six flights of F-84s left Itazuke to escort four B-29s on a strike to bomb the airfield at Yongyu, near Sinuiju. Sixteen of the aircraft were from the Wing's 182nd FBS, and were accompanied by eight more from the 27th FEG. They rendezvoused with the bombers near Cho-do island,

---

[14] 2/Lt Jessie Verster never knew of his award. On 1 July he was killed while ferrying Mustang 328 from K-10 to K-16. His body was recovered from temporary burial near the village of Sosan on the west coast and interred in the UN cemetery at Tandok.

but on the way to the target, one F-84 developed engine trouble and was escorted to the coast where the pilot ejected. He was safely retrieved by an SA-16 amphibian after only a few minutes in the water. As the B-29 formation turned for home after bombing Yongyu, MiGs were spotted coming down in a shallow dive onto them after making a steep approach from six o'clock high. There were 20 MiGs of the 17th FAR and one – apparently that flown by St/Lt Fokin – scored hits on the rearmost bomber, forcing the crew to feather an engine, but the B-29 managed to stay in formation. Meanwhile, 1/Lt Arthur E. Oligher and Capt Harry L. Underwood of the 182nd FBS pounced and shot down one MiG, which blew up upon impact with the ground, its tail section being flung 50 feet clear of the main wreckage by the explosion. This was evidently the aircraft flown by St/Lt Yevgeni Agranovich who was killed about 12 miles south-west of Eidzyu; his colleagues believed that he had just shot down an F-80 before his own demise. In the same fight, 1/Lt Joseph C. Chapman, who had been the first to sight the Russian jets diving to attack, and 1/Lt John M. Hewett Jr, each received credit for damaging a MiG. Flt Lt Peter Scott, who was flying FS-413 on this, his 21st operational sortie, did not make contact with the MiGs, but of this type of mission he later recalled:

> "Some of the time our job was to escort B-29s bombing the North Korean capital of P'yongyang on the Yalu. When we did this – 24 aircraft at a time – we had two extra fuel drop tanks, which we used up first, and just before we reached Pusan, the leader – sometimes it was me – called 'jettison tanks – now', and 48 silver tanks would tumble down slowly into the water, an amazing sight for us from above, and of no little interest, we were told later, to various fishermen below.
>
> The only aircraft that could match the MiG in high level combat was the F-86. Our F-84Es were heavier and under-powered; more suitable for ground-attack. About one mission in four we escorted B-29s bombing P'yongyang, more as a deterrent than anything else. We used to see them [MiGs] in the distance, but we stayed with our bombers."

Top cover F-86s were also engaged by the Russians, one MiG pilot (St/Lt Shatalov) of the 523rd FAR, which had joined the battle, claiming a Sabre shot down which reportedly crashed near Jyunsen, while two more were claimed by the 17th FAR's St/Lts Sutyagin and Shulev. One of these was flown by Colonel Eagleston of the 4th FIW who, however, was able to return safely with his damaged aircraft.

For the South Africans, the close-support missions they flew were different in character on 26 and 27 June, as they provided special cover for a 24th US Division task force which was mounting a thrust from the UN front line east of Kumwha. Throughout the first day, two SAAF Mustang flights each of four aircraft were ordered to remain on a continuous 30-minute alert, ready to go whenever needed. Three missions were flown on the first day and continuous cover was given to the American troops by flights of Mustangs armed with napalm and rockets. Flying over the advancing columns in relays, the South Africans flew 28 sorties in seven missions on the second day, each lasting around two hours, as they dislodged Communist troops from commanding positions on the ridges and silenced hostile artillery batteries. Two days later, 2SAAF pilots were kept busy destroying 19 buildings, a truck, a supply dump and three anti-aircraft positions. Returning from a sortie, Mustang 340 piloted by Capt Hardy Snyman swung on the runway after landing and crashed. Snyman was uninjured but his aircraft was badly damaged.

In two separate instances, on 28 and 30 June, MiGs attacked flights of USAF Mustangs near Sinanju and Songch'on. The American pilots reported hearing radio chatter and even laughter on the enemy's communications channels, indicating that the Russian pilots were confident and enjoying their work. Nevertheless, on each occasion, the Mustangs managed to outmanoeuvre the faster jets and were able to escape safely at treetop level, although the MiG pilots of the 523rd FAR claimed three shot down during the first clash, these being credited to St/Lt Shatalov (two) and Razorvin. One Mustang was lost on this date, but to ground fire when Capt John Crowell's 45th TRS aircraft was hit, necessitating a safe bale out over UN lines. On the last day of the month the 39th FIS lost another Mustang when Capt Charles Sumner's aircraft was hit by ground fire. The pilot was able to reach K-16 where he carried out a successful belly-landing, only for the damaged machine to catch fire; he survived with second degree burns. The FEAF admitted the loss of 22 of its aircraft to ground fire during the month. That night, Capt

Edwin B. Long of VMF(N)-513 was vectored by ground control onto a slow moving bogey flying towards Seoul – another Po-2. Because of his aircraft's superior speed, it took the USMC pilot three passes before he was able to manoeuvre his F7F-3N Tigercat behind the biplane long enough to blast it with his four cannons. The biplane disintegrated and went down in a fiery crash on the side of a mountain.

The last day of the month also saw Sqn Ldr Mike Adderley's 73rd and final operational flight with the 523rd FES when he participated in an interdiction mission flying FS-157. A few days earlier he had his first experience of the use of napalm during a practice sortie, a weapon about which he expressed his disgust. Following the end of his operational tour, he was posted to HQFEAF as Fighter Aircraft Requirements Officer, a position he held until January 1952. As FARO he was required to develop planning factors and make far reaching decisions in the establishment of requirements for fighter aircraft, their equipment modification, and maintenance, for which he would be awarded the US Bronze Star Medal for Meritorious Achievement.

At the Antung airfield complex, the pilots of the 303rd FAD in particular were jubilant after what they believed had been a very successful month, the Division having been credited with 40 air victories – 21 F-86s, ten F-80s, eight F-51s, and one aircraft tentatively identified as an F-94 or T-33 – while the 324th FAR claimed a further six F-86s and one F-80. Seventeen of the victories had been awarded to pilots of the 523rd FAR. USAF losses were far fewer than Russian claims which, up to the end of June 1951, had reached a total of 178 since the first was made on 1 November 1950. Of these, 55 were for F-86s, 44 for F-80s, 32 for F-84s, and 26 for B-29s. According to US intelligence sources, there were now some 445 MiG-15s based in Manchuria. Although only two F-80s had fallen victim to the MiGs during the month, their losses to ground fire were again causing concern at 5th Air Force HQ. In addition to the earlier losses, at least a further four had been shot down by ground fire in the last week of June: 2/Lt Bob A. Lauterback of the 35th FBS failing to return on the 26th, 1/Lts Arthur J. Johnson and John Murray of the 36th FBS being reported missing on the 28th, and 1/Lt Will C. White of the 36th FBS on the 29th, while 1/Lt Warren F. Polk and Capt Edward Miller of the 8th FBS were also lost in action during the month, as was 1/Lt Shuman H. Black of the 25th FIS, while 1/Lt James Kinner of the 8th FBS was lost on a training flight.

25 June 1951 had marked the first anniversary of the North Korean invasion of the south. The FEAF produced sets of statistics to show the extent of the effort its units had achieved in the first twelve months of hostilities: 223,000 sorties had been flown during which 97,000 tons of bombs and nearly eight million gallons of napalm had been dropped, 264,000 rockets fired and 98 million rounds of ammunition expended. It was estimated that 120,000 casualties had been inflicted on the enemy by air attack, while 391 aircraft had been claimed destroyed or damaged in the air and on the ground – including claims for 60 MiGs shot down – 893 locomotives and 14,200 rail cars destroyed, plus 24,000 M/T (827 enemy vehicles were claimed in June, mainly victims of intruder B-26s) and almost 1,700 tanks had been put out of action, not to mention thousands of buildings and hundreds of bridges and tunnels. The cost was high, however, 246 aircraft lost due to enemy action including 188 fighters and fighter-bombers, and 33 bombers, with 187 airmen known to have been killed and 415 missing, plus a further 255 wounded. These figures did not include aircraft and personnel losses suffered by the USN and USMC, nor those of the Royal Navy's Fleet Air Arm (see Chapters X and XI).

Meanwhile, across the sea in Japan, the saga of 77RAAF and its new Meteors continued. The Squadron had suffered two more incidents during its working-up programme – one was relatively minor and the other an enigma. Sgt Keith Meggs and Flg Off Dick Wittman had been up to 40,000 feet just before dawn on 14 June, and were landing together using landing lights. Meggs touched down first in A77-587 but, just before stopping, his radio and landing lights cut out. The following machine, Wittman's A77-373, with its windscreen and side panels misted up obscuring the pilot's vision, slowly taxied into it. Fortunately nobody was hurt but both aircraft were rendered temporarily unserviceable. The top front bulkhead, camera mounting and outboard portion of the main plane on A77-373 was crushed. Repairs to this aircraft were completed by 27 June. It was necessary to change both rear nacelle fixed tail portions and carry out extensive repairs on the inside of the rear fuselage on A77-587, this being out of commission until late August.

The second incident occurred when Sgt Tom Stoney, a veteran of over 100 missions in Korea, took off in the afternoon to perform an acceptance check on Meteor WA944. Once accepted, it was to be allocated RAAF serial A77-231. However, within a few minutes of leaving the ground, Stoney was seen to be descending by parachute with his aircraft making right hand turns around him. It flew around him five times and at one point it was only 20 feet away before it crashed into a hillside four miles west of Iwakuni. Stoney was able to gather his parachute and walk down to a jeep that took him to hospital. There it was discovered that he had sustained a slight injury to his spine and suffered abrasions to his wrist, thigh and tongue. In the subsequent interview Stoney – who came up with a classic quip – "the Meteor is evidently not my métier" – remarked that at the time of the ejection he was leaning slightly forward in the cockpit with his left hand on the throttle and his right hand on the control column. The ejection had been entirely automatic and he had been catapulted up by the ejector seat clear through the canopy which had not been jettisoned. An inspection of the crash site was made and the ejector seat was found about two miles from the main wreckage. When the drogue gun on the seat was inspected it was found that although the firing gun had operated properly, it had not touched the cartridge. It transpired that the barrel of the drogue gun had not been fully screwed home. To circumvent oversights of this nature in the future, it was decided that prior to the installation of the drogue gun, the firing pin would be replaced against a dummy cartridge with a percussion head filled with putty. However, this was not the reason for the ejection on this occasion, and no satisfactory conclusion could be reached. It was never discovered. The incident was recorded in the 91 (Composite) Wing records as ". . . some mechanical fault which caused spontaneous ejection of the ejector seat."

June had lived up to its reputation of being the wettest month of the year in Japan but the real problem facing the groundcrews servicing the Meteors was the manner in which the sun would shine immediately after a very heavy shower of rain. This caused heavy condensation in the rear fuselage. After a weekend of particularly heavy rain, the radio mechanics found that nearly 60 per cent of the aircraft radio receivers were unserviceable. In most instances the trouble was in the relay system situated in the rear fuselage. In some cases there was moisture in the transmitter, but practically all of the trouble was caused by condensation resulting in the shorting of circuits. As a consequence of this, it became standard practice in wet weather for mechanics to remove the radio sets or not to operate them until the rear fuselage had been properly ventilated by the removal of the radio access panel.

Towards the end of the month, despite only a proportion of the Meteors having been fitted with their ARN-6 radio compasses, it became apparent that the Squadron would soon be moving from Iwakuni back to Korea. The two-seat Meteors, carrying radio officers as passengers, were making numerous trips to Kimpo airfield. Then, on 29 June, the day before the departure of the advance party to Korea, a Squadron party was held. It was decided that this should be held in a Japanese hotel and in accordance with Japanese customs. Thus, as the airmen arrived they were required to remove their outdoor shoes and put on the special slippers provided, before being escorted to a large dining room by geisha girls. Sitting cross-legged on the floor at large low-built tables, traditional Japanese food was served by waitresses in colourful kimonos. During the meal, entertainment was provided by geisha girls dancing and singing, accompanied by the samisen. Unfortunately, the free-flowing saki and beer had its effect on the diners and towards the end of the evening the revellers became more and more boisterous. When the party finally ended it was apparent that a Japanese hotel was not suitable for a function of this nature, and due recompense was forthcoming. Next day, 77RAAF finally commenced its move back to Korea when its ground equipment was airlifted to Kimpo by the USAF in 17 C-119s and seven C-54s, while Dakotas of the RAAF's 86 (Transport) Squadron transferred its forward ground personnel. There was more cause for celebration a few days later when a batch of well-earned British decorations was announced for a number of the Australian pilots, most of whom had by now left the Squadron. There was a Bar to his DFC for Flt Lt Ian Olorenshaw, and DFCs for Flt Lts Fred Barnes, Ross Coburn, Jack Murray, and Gordon Harvey (the latter now a POW); DFCs were also awarded to newly commissioned Plt Off Ray Trebilco, and Wt Offs Wally Rivers and Bill Michelson.

The departure of 77RAAF from Japan saw the arrival of another representative air force to the UN's cause. New aircraft markings, those of the Royal Thai Air Force, were to be seen in the FEAF Command theatre of operations for the first time during the month when three Thai

C-47s arrived at Tachikawa AFB in Japan on 23 June. They had departed Don Muang airport near Bangkok five days earlier. In command of the detachment was Sqn Ldr Promoth Puthipanta. The Thai Flight, known as the Royal Thai Air Transport Detachment, was immediately attached to the USAF's 21st Squadron of the 374th Troop Carrier Wing and, because of the language problem, American co-pilots and radio men were assigned to each aircraft. Meanwhile, the Thai aircrews, like the Greeks before them, had to go to school to learn English. In addition to this, and its army and naval units, Thailand's government also despatched three separate medical service elements to assist the UN.

Despite the continued build-up of UN and Communist forces across the 38th Parallel, there was just a hint of peace in the air. Across the world, speaking on a UN radio programme, Soviet Russia's chief delegate to the UN, Mr Iakov Malik, stated that "the Soviet people" believed armistice in Korea on the basis of the 38th Parallel could be possible if both sides really wished to stop the fighting. On the world stage the Korean War was gravely harming the Soviet Union's strategic position in the Cold War between East and West. As a direct result of the conflict, both the United States and Britain had embarked on exceptionally ambitious re-armament programmes for their armed forces, supplying them with an abundance of new and sophisticated weapons. Anglo-American co-operation was at its highest peak since the end of WWII. The United States had gained almost complete control of the United Nations organisation itself, and had managed to place a UN-backed anti-Communist force – army, navy and air force – in the field. West Germany was on its way to sovereign status and re-armament, and Japan was in the throes of being re-armed and allied with the United States. Soviet diplomatic efforts to reverse these trends had failed miserably. On 21 June, just two days prior to Mr Malik's broadcast, a conference in Paris of the Big Four deputy foreign ministers had broken down in outrage when the Soviet delegate had attempted to force through an anti-NATO measure. The NATO alliance had, in fact, been consolidated to the point where a pan-European army led by an American general now looked on the verge of becoming a reality. The continuation of the fighting in Korea was only making things worse. Defusing the situation in Korea was one way in which the Kremlin might slow the impetus of the anti-Communist military build-up and disrupt the success of US diplomacy.

In China, the Peking *Jen Min Jin Pao* newspaper unsurprisingly came out in support of Mr Malik's comments concerning a possible armistice on the basis on the 38th Parallel. It stated that the Chinese people agreed with the Soviet people. Behind the rhetoric, however, it was now apparent even to the most dedicated Communist leaders that the Chinese Army had been terribly mauled and was incapable of defeating the UN in the field. The Communists had lost control of the fortified zones, the Iron Triangle and the important area north of Sowha, areas they had previously used as springboards for their offensives. In China itself, the war was not universally popular and the government had to resort to a policy of repression to stifle criticism. In addition, the Chinese economy did not have the capacity to sustain the burden of continuous all-out fighting and this threatened to have serious financial consequences for the entire Communist bloc, which was being largely carried by Soviet Russia. To add to China's woe, Stalin now expressed his anger over the Chinese Communist Air Force's reluctance to commit its MiG-15s to battle. It was suggested that the CCAF MiG-9 units be used to counter the US/UN bombers and fighter-bombers, allowing their MiG-15s to engage the F-86s, but CCAF leaders were not happy to send the MiG-9s into action over North Korea since they were considered inferior to even the F-84. Orders were issued to the 64th FAD to begin retraining the Chinese 6th, 12th and 14th FARs on the MiG-15.

From Tokyo on the last day of June, as instructed by Washington, General Ridgway made an open broadcast relaying a message addressed to:

> "Commander-in-Chief Communist Forces in Korea
>
> I am informed that you may wish a meeting to discuss an armistice providing for the cessation of hostilities and all acts of armed force in Korea, with adequate guarantees for the maintenance of such armistice . . ."

It sounded simple. The offer was there, placing the burden of initiating dialogue upon the Communists. The question was, would they respond?

CHAPTER VII

THE MIGS GAIN AIR SUPREMACY

July – August 1951

"The first engagements with the Australians showed that their aircraft [Meteors] were not meteors at all. They were inferior to MiGs in all respects . . ." [1]

Lt-General Georgii Lobov, commander of the 303rd FAD

General Ridgway did not have to wait long for a reply to the ceasefire feeler that he had announced on 30 June. In his speech he had suggested that the ceasefire meeting could be held aboard a Danish hospital ship, the *Jutlandia*, in Wonsan harbour. Radio Peking addressed a reply, jointly signed by General Kim Il-sung, as commander of the North Korean People's Army, not as head of the North Korean government, and General P'eng, commander of the Chinese Volunteers. They agreed that it would be desirable to begin talks but proposed that representatives of the opposing sides meet in Kaesong, just below the 38th Parallel. Since, at this time, Kaesong was situated between the lines in no-man's-land, Washington instructed Ridgway to accept the site as suitable for the conference and his agreement followed next day, 3 July. General Ridgway also suggested a meeting of liaison officers to make the necessary arrangements be held on 5 July. The Communists agreed but insisted that the meeting be held on 8 July, a change of date to which the General concurred.

Subsequently, UN liaison officers landed at Kaesong. After exchanging credentials, they conferred on arrangements for the first meeting, which they decided would be held in two days time at the same location – Kwangmun-dong, north of the centre of Kaesong. The first meeting of the main truce delegations was accordingly scheduled for 1000 on the morning of 10 July. The day dawned damp and cloudy with poor visibility that hampered flying, the US helicopters carrying the UN delegation being obliged to fly northwards at a few hundred feet, en route the delegates noticing white-clad Koreans working in the rice paddies waving as they flew overhead. The helicopters landed on a level field near the Kaesong Methodist Missionary compound and the delegation members were met by Colonel Chang Chen San, the North Korean liaison officer. As they climbed into jeeps which were prominently marked by white flags, Communist photographers and newsmen gathered around taking movies and pictures. Armed Chinese troops lined the sides of the landing site. On the ten-minute ride to the so-called United Nations House that had been assigned to the delegation, the road was lined with more armed guards and photographers. The United Nations House itself was also surrounded by prominently stationed guards armed with burp guns. Only after arriving did the delegation learn that the Communists were using a different time: 1000 hours UN time was 0900 hours local time, so the UN delegates were obliged to wait for an hour before the meeting could start.

The UN party comprised Vice-Admiral C. Turner Joy USN, Maj-General Laurence C. Craigie USAF, Maj-General Henry I. Hodes US Army, Rear-Admiral Arleigh A. Burke USN, and Maj-General Paik Sun Yup ROKA. During the delay they discussed their communications

---

[1] See *MiG-15* by Gordon and Rigmant.

facilities, the large number of Communist newsmen and photographers present and the display of armed force. The whole exercise was obviously being carefully staged by the Communists for propaganda purposes, to demonstrate their domination of the situation. The North Korean-Chinese delegates were General Nam Il NKPA, Maj-General Lee Sang Cho NKPA, Maj-General Chang P'yong San NKPA, General Tung Hua CCF and Maj-General Hsieh Fang CCF. During the first meeting, Communist photographers came streaming into the conference room taking more pictures until the UN delegates finally protested. It was then mutually agreed that photographers and newsmen would be excluded from the conference room at least. Nonetheless, at the Military Armistice Conference there were still large numbers of photographers and newsmen all around the conference site and none of them were representatives from non-Communist countries. With this one-sided arrangement the major concern was the propaganda edge. All of the on-the-spot news was obviously open to misrepresentation in the Communist press and UN news agencies had no direct knowledge of what was happening. Admiral Joy read a message on the matter from General Ridgway and the UN delegation finally stated flatly that in future it would bring 20 members of the free press to the conference site. Therefore next morning the UN convoy to the Military Armistice Conference set out with the promised 20 newsmen accompanying but its passage was blocked by the Communists. The newsmen were not permitted to proceed and the UN representatives would not go on without them. This was the final straw and the UN delegation turned about and returned to Munsan. There followed an exchange of notes between General Kim Il-sung and General Ridgway before the matter was finally resolved and the truce talks could proceed. This dispute over newsmen and photographers was just the first of many such side issues and incidents that were to occur as negotiations went on and on, month after frustrating month, and turned into years. Progress was pathetically slow. At the eleventh session of the Military Armistice Conference, which occurred on 27 July, the points under discussion were:

1. Adoption of an agenda.
2. Fixing a military demarcation line between both sides so as to establish a de-militarised zone as a basic condition for a cessation of hostilities in Korea.
3. Concrete arrangement for the realisation of a ceasefire and armistice in Korea, including the composition, authority, and functions of a supervising organisation for carrying out the terms of a ceasefire and armistice.
4. Arrangements relating to prisoners of war.
5. Recommendations to the governments of the countries concerned on both sides.

By the end of the day, an agreement was at least reached on Point 1: the adoption of an agenda for the regulation of the conference itself.

*   *   *

While these peace overtures were going on, UN air operations continued unabated and FEAF medium, light, and fighter-bombers continued day and night strikes against Communist airfields in north-western Korea as directed by General Weyland. Where the enemy's defences warranted, the FEAF co-ordinated its aerial attacks.

On the first day of the new month a Canadian Army officer, Capt Joseph 'Pat' Tremblay of the Royal 22nd Regiment, was airborne in an AT-6G of the 6148th Tactical Control Squadron piloted by Capt Elmer E. Witten. It was Tremblay's initiation into "the mysteries of aerial reconnaissance"; it was also nearly his last flight. Having taken off from P'yongtak, the AT-6 headed for the Imjin, but when north of the river it was hit by a burst of machine-gun fire, as the Canadian graphically recalled:

> "There was a flash, an appalling bang, and bits of glass, metal and fabric were swirling round the cockpit. The plane, hitherto so docile, was all at one behaving like a bucking bronco. As the fragments settled, I saw the peaked cap [of the pilot] slumped back against the headrest, and a hand lying limply along the edge of the cockpit. Later I learned that a .50 machine-gun burst, just missing the spare fuel tank, had angled up into the belly of the aircraft, finishing up a vicious spray of splinters just behind the front cockpit . . . a bullet

had paralysed Witt's spine, and another had pierced his stomach, causing immense loss of blood. I saw a little stream of blood flowing past my right shoe. The thought that Witt might be dead froze me . . ."

Tremblay called anxiously over the intercom to his wounded pilot, and received a feint reply to the effect that he should try to fly the now out-of-control aircraft. Unsure of what to do, Tremblay yanked the control column back and, to his relief, the AT-6 came out of its dive:

"I was not just scared. I was stupefied. The only thing I knew about flying was that, to go up, you pulled the stick back; to go down, you pushed it forward. There was no time for further thought. A wooded hilltop rushed toward us. Blindly I grabbed the rubber-covered broomstick, breathed a prayer – and yanked it backward. We shot up like a whale surfacing in a typhoon. The plane rolled and wallowed, but at least there was now quite a respectable distance between us and the landscape."

In the next few minutes he was able to gain some sort of control over the aircraft, but then realised to his dismay they were heading northwards. By trial and error he succeeded in turning the aircraft on a more southerly course. Although not able to communicate as the intercom had become disconnected, Witten was able to take control as he periodically regained his senses before lapsing back into unconsciousness. Eventually Kimpo airfield came into view and Witten summoned sufficient awareness and strength to make a landing, although the aircraft careered off the runway and came to a rest having shed its undercarriage along the way. But they were safely down, and Tremblay was able to drag Witten out of the cockpit and onto the wing, and from there to a safe distance from the wreck before it caught fire. Capt Witten survived his wounds but remained paralysed from the waist down. He was awarded the US DFC. Capt Tremblay received the Military Cross in recognition of his performance.

The month also started badly for the 45th TRS when it lost its veteran CO, the legendary Colonel Karl Polifka. Hit by ground fire, he attempted to bale out but his parachute snagged on his stricken aircraft and he was killed. Next day, 1/Lt Eugene L. Ruiz of the same unit was also killed as a result of ground fire. On 3 July, while 32 F-84s – including FS-376 flown by Flt Lt Peter Scott – suppressed flak positions in the North Korean capital, six B-29s, escorted by 33 F-86s, rained more than 850 x 100-lb bombs on the runway of P'yongyang's main airfield. Next day the 39th FIS lost a pilot when Capt Raymond Carlson crashed after being hit by ground fire in the area of Huich'on. Twenty-four hours later the same unit lost Capt Walter E. Pittman, who was on his 95th mission, a third pilot from the 39th FIS being shot down two days later, but on this occasion he was rescued. The 8th FBG also lost two pilots during the first week of July, 1/Lt John J. Flournoy of the 35th FBS being shot down by ground fire on the 1st, and 1/Lt Charles H. Blomberg of the 35th FBS six days later. The 13th BS also lost a crew, its first for two months, when the B-26 flown by Capt Donald D. Tegt failed to return.

The MiGs put in an appearance on 7 July, pilots of the 18th GuFAR reporting an engagement with F-86s near Sensen, the Russians returning to Antung with claims for three of their opponents shot down, one each by Kapt Kalyuzhnyi, Kapt Sokhan and St/Lt Akatov. MiGs were also operating from the newly opened Manpo airfield[2], and according to Lt-General Lobov, the commander of the 303rd FAD, a total of 56 MiGs were currently using the two Yalu airfields. Next day (8 July), USAF and SAAF Mustangs flew a 32-aircraft strike against Kangdong airfield, north-east of P'yongyang. The South Africans were briefed to dive-bomb the airfield immediately after the last American fighter-bombers had left the target. To simplify their bombing run, Cmdt Armstrong ordered his two flights of four Mustangs into echelon and led them down the length of the runway. Fifteen of their sixteen bombs exploded on the runway itself. Just after reforming, the South Africans heard an American voice over the radio yell "MiGs!" Sightings of about 20 of the Russian jets were reported in the area. Off to the north Armstrong saw the USAF Mustangs orbiting in a defensive circle and he noticed a MiG trying

---

[2] Manpo airfield had been constructed in record time. Lack of construction equipment did not deter the Chinese and, by use of manpower provided by some 10,000 labourers, a two-mile long concrete runway, as well as taxiways and revetments, appeared within one month from what was once marshland.

to turn with one of the F-51s. At long range, he fired his machine-guns in that general direction in an effort to distract the attacker, and succeeded only too well. A few seconds later the enemy jets shifted their attention to the SAAF Mustangs flying east at 7,000 feet and two MiGs were spotted coming in from the south. Two more stayed higher up as top cover. As the first pair came astern, Armstrong waited for the right moment and ordered a 180-degree turn. The Mustangs turned to face the attack and both MiGs immediately pulled up almost vertically without firing. Provided they could see the MiGs coming in time, the South African pilots found they were able to use the superior manoeuvrability of their slower piston-engined aircraft to stay out of trouble. Another attack was deflected in the same manner. While both sides continued to jockey for an advantage, several bursts of 37mm flak were fired from the ground but none of the Mustangs was hit. Finally, after five minutes of stalemate, the enemy jets turned away, heading north. In fact, it was now the turn of the MiGs to come under attack.

Responding to the call for help, 35 Sabres of the 4th FIW were arriving on the scene. Leading the F-86s was Colonel Francis S. Gabreski, the highest scoring USAF ace in the European Theatre of Operations in WWII with 31 victories to his credit. In the ensuing action he opened his Korean account and added to his record by shooting down a MiG. Two more were claimed by Maj Franklin L. Fisher and 1/Lt Richard Becker of the 334th FIS. Although there were no American losses, MiG pilots of the 176th GuFAR claimed two F-86s shot down, one of which reportedly crashed a few miles south-west of Koburi, while the other was alleged to have crashed into the sea. The claimants were Polkovnik Vishnyakov and St/Lt Verdysh, while St/Lt Pavlovskii and St/Lt Obukhov of the 523rd FAR were shot down, although both ejected safely. Later in the day, Capt Hardy Snyman led a flight of 2SAAF on another successful strike against Ongjin airfield, where six hits were seen on the runway. Another raid followed when two flights of SAAF Mustangs led by Capt John Swanepoel joined to make up a formation of 32 aircraft in a bombing raid against Sariwon airfield. Enemy repair crews were left with a dangerous job that night because the bombs had been fitted with six-hour delay fuses. Next day, 9 July, saw the MiGs active again when a flight from the 176th GuFAR intercepted six B-29s of the 19th BG just as the bombers were turning off their target run over Sinanju airfield. Escorting Sabres counter-attacked and Capt Milton Nelson of the 335th FIS reported shooting down one MiG, his third victory, while B-29 gunner Sgt Gus C. Opfer claimed another destroyed. One of the Russian pilots claimed an F-86 in return.

On 11 July, 2SAAF suffered another casualty when newly arrived Major L.B. Pearce, an experienced WWII pilot (see Appendix III), was killed under circumstances that will never be fully known. Flying Mustang 316, Pearce drifted away from his flight as he was climbing through cloud above Chinhae. He failed to respond when the leader, Lt Marshall, called him on the radio. A search located the remains of his burnt out aircraft which had hit the ground under power some 15 miles north of the airfield. Pearce's body was found nearby in a rice paddy. He had apparently jumped from the Mustang just before it crashed. Elsewhere, 21 F-80s led by Lt Colonel William Betha of the 36th FBS dropped napalm on a target south of Sinuiju and were intercepted just afterwards by 30 MiGs from the 303rd and 324th FADs. While the F-80s were defending themselves, 34 Sabres joined the fray. One MiG was seen to burst into flames and explode in mid-air, while a second fell burning and its pilot baled out: St/Lt Boris Obraztsov of the 176th GuFAR ejected but died from internal wounds, while St/Lt Ivan Larionov of the 196th FAR was killed. They were the apparent victims of the 335th FIS's Capt Milton Nelson, his fourth kill, and 1/Lt Ralph Gibson, his third. Another MiG pilot was seen escaping by parachute when his machine suddenly went into a spin for no obvious reason, while Podpolkovnik Pepelyaev, commander of the 196th FAR, returned to Antung in his aircraft (No325) damaged, it having received three hits. One F-86 was claimed by Maj Mitusov of the 196th FAR, which was reported to have blown up in mid air, and three more were credited to the 176th GuFAR, two of which were alleged to have crashed south-west of Tetsuzan while the third reportedly fell into the sea. One of the these was credited to Kapt Sergei Kramarenko as his fifth victory; another was claimed by Lt Zyuz, and the third awarded to the missing St/Lt Obraztsov. Of the battle, Podpolkovnik Pepelyaev recalled:

"We flew a six-plane combat mission. Six F-86s were ahead of us. Our position was favourable. Knowing that I was protected by my wingman, and that Kapt Nazarkin's flight was high astern, I attacked. I got involved in a turn with a Sabre. But Nazarkin's flight could not provide cover for us. Later he explained he lost sight of us because of the sun. The Americans, having better turning characteristics and knowing that we had no protection, got my wingman at once. We could not even bury Larionov. His aircraft fell into the Yellow Sea. And immediately, a burst of fire hit my MiG-15. The second pair ran in from the right. I realised that help would not be rendered. I threw my aircraft into a spin and went down. An F-86 above me spiralled down, but the pilot had not enough skill to reach me. I rushed into the cloud, turned my aircraft near the water, and proceeded to our airfield . . ." [3]

Although the Sabres were able to keep the MiGs away from the F-80s, the fighter-bomber pilots met a hail of defensive fire from the airfield as they launched their attacks, losing 1/Lt Cecil Rhodes Mohr Jr of the 36th FBS and 1/Lt Irwin E. Taylor of the 80th FBS. The MiGs also attempted to intercept a B-29 raid which was being escorted by F-84s of the 136th FBW, including a formation from the 182nd FBS, one of which was flown by Flt Lt Peter Scott in FS-150. He was amongst those who did, on this occasion, pursue a section of MiGs, albeit without success. One of the MiG pilots from the 196th FAR claimed an F-84 shot down near Simbi-to. This was Flt Lt Scott's 21st operational sortie. Of this period, he recalled:

"Most of our missions involved close-support of front line troops. For these we'd fly up to the front line, letting down to the rendezvous point with a light aircraft [flown by a FAC] equipped with smoke rockets. The pilot would show us where the targets were with these smoke rockets. Napalm – a horrible weapon – we'd drop as low and fast as possible, up to 500mph. Doing this got the adrenalin going because we'd been told that the North Koreans stretched wires across some of the valleys. We fired our rockets and dropped our bombs in steep dives, and when we'd finished we reformed and climbed to about 40,000 feet for the flight back to Japan. We had to get our fuel right because of the 130 miles of water to end up with – diverting into one of the few airfields in Korea was frowned on. Every now and then somebody did run out of fuel in spite of the precautions we took, and ended up in the sea – very unpopular and very expensive."

Before daybreak on 12 July, USMC Corsair pilot Capt D.L. Fenton of VMF(N)-513 intercepted and shot down another Po-2 biplane near Uijongbu. Something else of significance occurred on 12 July. Quite suddenly, the enemy's air offensive in Korea halted. On North Korean airfields labour gangs no longer attempted to fill the bomb craters made by the FEAF's bombers and fighter-bombers. A subsequent report by Communist China's Special Aviation Inspection Group revealed that it had spent two months on the battlefield supervising the repair of 69 airfields which in the end only helped facilitate the operations of 30 aircraft. Such a futile construction effort, the Group asserted, was far beyond the financial power of China to support. The Group also noted that the CCAF Ilyushin ground-attack force had staged just a single raid and that had failed. There was no doubt that the revised air war plan had failed. Probably as a result of this decision, the Po-2 nocturnal nuisance raids also came to a halt following the latest loss. While Communist night operations were proving unsuccessful, the same could not be said for the B-26 intruder crews who continued to take a toll of the enemy's supply convoys. A particular success was scored in the early-morning hours of 14 July by Capt William L. Ford and his crew from the 452nd BG, when they attacked two convoys north of Sinanju. Thirteen trucks were claimed destroyed and 15 damaged as a result of their first bombing and strafing attack, even greater successes being claimed against the second convoy with 25 trucks destroyed and at least 15 damaged. Not bad for a night's work. By the end of the month a total of 711 vehicles destroyed would be added to the B-26s' ever-increasing tally, with more than 1,500 claimed damaged. While waiting for a return to action, 77RAAF's Flt Lt Joe Blyth managed to hitch a ride in a B-26 intruder (BC-953A) of the 90th BS piloted by Capt Gicewicz:

"That night [21 July] saw me co-pilot a B-26C bombing and strafing in the P'yongyang

---

[3] See *MiG-15* by Gordon and Rigmant.

area. Vital actions in the B-26 were wheels-up, hand round cigars (with ash trays fitted as standard!). Very interesting, with the navigator [1/Lt Snyder] calling out heights as we dived into the mountains in the dark, except for lights from the many transports on the move on the ground."

In the meantime, Capt Bob Rogers of 2SAAF led a highly successful Operation 'Strangle' mission on 16 July. He was ordered to lead four Mustangs, each carrying 500-lb bombs and a supply of rockets, on an interdiction mission to the Suan area. His wingman was Lt Frank Montanari and the other members of his flight were Lts Jack Haskins and Brian Martin. The South Africans found the target blanketed by heavy cloud which shrouded the hilltops. What happened next was graphically described in the citation which accompanied the award of the American DFC to Capt Rogers, who had won the DSO and DFC during WWII:

> "The leader searched until he found a gap over the main highway, through which he immediately led the flight on a bombing run. As he pulled out, he discerned an enemy convoy of eleven vehicles and, accordingly, remained below cloud with his wingman. Meanwhile, the element leader had returned through the gap which closed almost immediately, and precluded his rejoining the leader. In constant danger of flying into hilltops which were shrouded and with manoeuvrable space severely restricted, he made a series of relentless attacks with rockets and machine-gun fire, and only desisted after the optimum damage had been inflicted. A final count revealed eight vehicles burning furiously and three more severely damaged. Captain Rogers then climbed up through cloud and joined the element leader who had been unable to locate him in the interim. Through his outstanding disregard of personal safety and his remarkable aeronautical skill, Captain Rogers caused a severe blow to be struck at the enemy."

Despite these successes, 22 July marked the beginning of a spate of losses and tragedies for 2SAAF. The run of bad luck began when the cooling system of Lt Bob Staats' Mustang (312) was damaged by ground fire and he had to abandon his aircraft over Wonsan. The aircraft crashed into the harbour although the pilot had the good fortune to be rescued from his dinghy within just 20 minutes by the crew of an American destroyer. Worse was to follow next day, which became the South Africans' most tragic day of the war to date, when a flight of Mustangs was almost wiped out. The ill-fated flight was led by Capt Freddy Bekker in Mustang 335 and accompanying him were Lt Roelof du Plooy, 2/Lts Tony Green and Mike Halley. They were briefed to carry out an armed weather reconnaissance of the west coast. Each Mustang was loaded with two 500-lb bombs and six rockets. The flight took off at 1505 and proceeded up the Han in battle formation at approximately 1,500 feet. At the mouth of the Han the flight turned east but ran into badly deteriorating weather. In almost no time the cloud base descended to about 700 feet above ground level. After repeated attempts to break through to the north, Bekker decided to abandon the idea and started searching for targets east of Haeju. Finding none, the flight flew farther east along the Han and then proceeded along the Imjin. They were flying in line astern formation with cloud base alternating between 700 and 1,500 feet, but again no targets were in the offing.

The Mustangs then headed for their secondary target at Sibyoni but the weather was worse there and it became impossible to proceed farther north. At 1540, Bekker found a road bridge over the river which he and the others attacked and destroyed. Shortly thereafter, flames were seen emerging from the wing of Bekker's aircraft. Suddenly the canopy of the stricken aircraft flew off and and the pilot could be seen quite clearly in the cockpit as the flames were sucked in, engulfing him. Flying in the No2 position, 2/Lt Green was forced to break away violently to avoid a piece of flaming wing which had broken off in the air as the burning Mustang porpoised twice, lost altitude and plunged into the side of a hill. Tony Green's frantic evasive action took him into the cloud but, nevertheless, he managed to retain control and descended in a steep diving turn to port. As he broke cloud, he passed over the remains of Bekker's burning machine. As he descended he spotted a parachute above at a height of about 200 feet. It was coming down directly over the same position. Over the radio he learned that 2/Lt Halley had been forced to abandon his aircraft (331). Green and du Plooy watched Halley land safely as they circled. He seemed uninjured and waved to them.

By now the weather had grown considerably worse, affecting the radio. The two pilots decided that du Plooy would remain over the area flying a CAP over Halley while Green climbed up to try and establish better radio contact with the rescue organisation. As Green pulled up he came under fire. Tracer bullets hissed past his wing and there were bursts of 20mm fire forward and above his port mainplane. At a higher altitude Green managed to raise the alarm on the emergency channel. He was instructed to proceed to a rendezvous with a helicopter ten miles east of Kaesong. While the helicopter was en route, Green alternated his position between the downed pilot and the rendezvous point. The weather was closing in rapidly and Halley's position was difficult to find in the adverse conditions. He had to stay very low for on every occasion he attempted to climb he attracted ground fire, some of it dangerously close. Over the radio he could hear du Plooy reporting that he was being kept fully occupied making strafing attacks to prevent enemy troops from closing in on Halley.

Two flights of UN aircraft passing overhead heard the South Africans' reports over the radio and offered to help but they were unable to find the location because of the weather. Du Plooy continued his heroic single-handed fight for 45 minutes but at 1630 he announced that his ammunition was exhausted and the enemy was still closing in. Green now spotted the rescue helicopter and was escorting it in when du Plooy reported that it was too late. Mike Halley had finally been captured. The news was relayed to the helicopter pilot and he was instructed to return to base but he refused, stating he would remain standing by just in case. About a minute after hearing du Plooy's voice, Green sighted the smouldering wreck of yet another aircraft, and another parachute. Fearing the worst, he desperately called du Plooy over the radio but there was no reply. Green could not positively identify the wreckage but while circling he ran into intense and accurate anti-aircraft fire and had to take evasion action, dodging in and out of cloud. Meanwhile, the helicopter had entered the flak area and the South African realised it was necessary to escort it out safely before he ran out of fuel. His gauge was already showing just 15 gallons left in his tanks. Green landed safely at base.

A state of shock pervaded the Squadron as the news spread and everybody realised the gravity of what had happened – three pilots and their planes lost in just one mission. It was officially reported months later that Mike Halley was a POW but, although the location of the wreckage of his Mustang (338) was known, du Plooy's body was never found and he was listed as missing. In recognition of his determination and gallantry in risking his own life to defend his wingman, Lt du Plooy was posthumously awarded the US Silver Star.

Next day the South Africans lost another aircraft when Capt Hardy Snyman's Mustang (339) was hit over enemy territory by AA fire but he managed to reach the east coast before the engine seized. He baled out into the sea and this time rescue was at hand and he was promptly picked up by an SA-16. Back at Chinhae it was discovered that his right shoulder had been dislocated when his arm became tangled in his parachute harness. To cap off a disastrous month for 2SAAF, yet another aircraft was lost on 26 July when 2/Lt John Howe had to abandon Mustang 336 after it developed a serious glycol leak. Fortunately he came down in friendly territory and was picked up by a helicopter without difficulty.

While the South Africans were experiencing this run of bad luck, Russian MiG pilots of the 196th FAR reported a field day on 21 July, when ten led by Popolkovnik Pepelyaev engaged a formation of eight US jets which they identified as F-94Fs *(sic)*, claiming no fewer than seven shot down in a major action between Teiju and Anju. Two of the American jets were claimed by Pepelyaev, two more by St/Lt Pupko, and one apiece by Kapts Abakumov, Nazarkin, and Shelomonov. One of the American pilots was apparently captured by North Korean troops, and the body of a second American was recovered. Two of the American jets were reported to have blown up in mid-air. Whatever type of aircraft the MiG pilots engaged, there were no such losses, although it seems probable that they were actually a flight of USMC F-9F Panthers of VMF-311 operating from K-3 Po'hang, which reported an action with MiGs and the subsequent loss of Lt Richard Bell, who was taken prisoner. Of the action, Podpolkovnik Pepelyaev recalled:

"There was a thick fog. The Americans had penetrated Chinese territory a distance of about

120 miles. I had been sitting with my group asking for clearance to take off. We took to the air [after the weather had improved], caught up with the F-94Bs *[sic]*, which were heading south, and attacked them. I shot down one aircraft of this type and afterwards its wreckage was delivered to our airfield." [4]

Kapt Abakumov added:

". . . ten MiGs took-off under Pepelyaev's command. I was in the closing pair. We broke through the clouds together, in tight formation. We proceeded at maximum speed and met the F-94Bs *[sic]*. We manoeuvred to attack them, broke into pairs, and attacked the enemy from different sides. It was Pepelyaev who shot down the first aircraft. He sawed off the F-94's fin with a burst of fire. I sighted the leader and shot at him. My shells had their effect. The F-94 gradually tilted to the left and went toward the ground with its nose down. Only one of the eight F-94s managed to survive in this battle." [5]

By 25 July, 77RAAF with its Meteors was fully established back in Korea once more, ready to operate from Kimpo airfield near Seoul, home of the USAF's Sabre-equipped 4th FIW. The transfer from Japan to Kimpo had taken most of the month. Cpl Dinny O'Brien recalled:

"I was put in charge of an advance party of nine technical personnel to support the first Meteors to go to Korea. Four jets flew to Kimpo and we preceded them in a Dakota. Our task was to maintain and operate them for about a week until the Squadron arrived. American hospitality continued and a USAF liaison officer met us on arrival. When informed that I was in charge he assumed that I was a sergeant. The weather was warm so I wore my shirt sleeves rolled up, so that only the top of my chevrons was visible. This was a deliberate ploy to confuse the Americans as it had been successful to gain entry to the USAF Top Three Club (Sergeants' Mess equivalent) in Tokyo when on R and R [rest and recuperation] leave. The lieutenant provided a jeep and suggested I collect combat rations for my crew. Despite being unfamiliar with this ration I accompanied him to the supply section, where he made the necessary authorisation. To my surprise and joy the rations comprised 200 cigarettes, chocolate bars, gum, tooth brush and paste, razor blades, condoms, cigarette lighter etc for each person. When asked the number of personnel in our crew I promptly replied twenty. To our delight double rations seemed an appropriate reward for being the first RAAF ground crew at Kimpo. Conditions were more tolerable at Kimpo. Our living area was walking distance from the Flight Line, although it was necessary to travel by vehicle to the cookhouse and messing facility. Another bonus was the warm weather. On the negative side, however, were the hot winds, dust and smoke during the stubble and dung burning periods."

Five American C-54 transports flew the initial elements of 77RAAF to Kimpo. The newly arrived ground crews were greeted by driving rain and mud that hampered unloading operations and the establishment of the unit's maintenance facilities. Training commenced, co-ordinating with the GCI station sited near the airstrip. Although the lack of refuelling tankers – there were only two available at the time – restricted initial training somewhat, practice interceptions were begun under GCI control for flights of four aircraft. Despite the limitation, 20 sorties were flown on 27 July, the day that General Robertson sanctioned 77RAAF's return to operational flying, provided the weather at base was within certain limits, mainly a minimum cloud base of 1,000-1,500 feet.

The weather improved for 77RAAF's first Meteor mission from Kimpo airfield on 29 July. The Order of the Day specified a fighter sweep between Songch'on and Ch'ongju in MiG Alley. Anticipation ran high among the Australian pilots over who would take part in this first historic mission. There was excitement mixed with apprehension for those who were selected to fly, and disappointment for those who were not, particularly for the newer men who had been posted in from Australia while the Squadron was in Japan. Among the newcomers were Sqn Ldr David Wilson, former CO of 76RAAF, who had been appointed deputy commander of

---

[4/5] See *MiG-15* by Gordon and Rigmant.

77RAAF, Flt Lt Cedric Thomas DFC, Wt Off Ron Guthrie, Flt Sgt Bill Middlemiss, Sgt Don Armit, and Sgt Allan Avery DFM (see Appendix III). The pilots chosen were:

A77-616 Sqn Ldr R.C. Cresswell	A77-464 Flg Off G. Thornton
A77-854 Sgt F.T. Collins	A77-949 Sgt E.D. Armit
A77-446 Flg Off L. Reading	A77-128 Flt Lt R.L. Dawson
A77-750 Wt Off W.S. Michelson	A77-744 Plt Off R.E. Trebilco
A77-15 Sqn Ldr D.L. Wilson	A77-734 Flt Lt V.B. Cannon
A77-559 Flt Sgt W. Middlemiss	A77-385 Sgt A.J. Avery
A77-959 Flt Lt C.G. Thomas	A77-380 Sgt K.H. Foster
A77-721 Wt Off R.D. Guthrie	A77-911 Wt Off R.C.A. Hunt

Shortly before take-off, Sqn Ldr Cresswell assembled the pilots in the tin shed briefing room, where he described the tactical formation to be flown:

> "The first squadron will fly line-abreast in two sections of four, myself and Thornton, at 35,000 feet, and the second squadron, Wilson and Cannon, will fly the same formation at 30,000 feet. The American F-86 Sabres are to fly at 25,000 feet and 20,000 feet below us. There will be 28 of them. There is to be no unnecessary chattering on the radio. Everybody is to keep a good lookout and report immediately any unidentified aircraft sighted."

Take-off time came quickly and they climbed into their Meteors, aided by the groundcrew. The air soon became saturated with the warm, sickly smell of kerosene vapour as engines roared into life, and at three-second intervals, the Meteors accelerated down the runway and hurtled into the air. On the way to MiG Alley the Australians saw heavy anti-aircraft bursts exploding at 32,000 feet over P'yongyang, but well off target. Flg Off Les Reading recalled:

> "We were patrolling at 35,000 feet. It was a nice clear day. We saw no MiGs airborne, but we did see them on the ground, all shiny with the swept-back wings . . ."

The RAAF's first jet operation thus turned out to be something of an anti-climax. It seemed incongruous to the pilots that the MiGs could be allowed to just sit there on the ground, a juicy target, and remain untouched because they were in Manchuria and yet be permitted to cross the border and attack UN aircraft at will. Although the Australians had not seen the enemy in the air, the Americans they were flying top cover for did make contact as the Meteors left the patrol line. MiG pilots of the 324th FAD reported an encounter with F-86s near Anindo shortly before midday, claiming three shot down by the 17th FAR – two by St/Lt Shulev and the other by Kapt Artemenko – while Kapt Kramarenko of the 176th GuFAR claimed another which allegedly crashed about 15 miles north of Teiju[6]. Later, during the afternoon, Maj Pulov led off another 24 MiGs of the 17th FAR, these meeting F-80s near Etsuhori, of which four were claimed shot down, one apiece by Kapts Artemenko and Ponomarev, and St/Lts Sutyagin and Fokin. These fighter-bombers were apparently from the 16th FIS, 1/Lt William W. McAllister of that unit claiming a MiG destroyed in return – thereby recording the last confirmed kill to be credited to an F-80 pilot during the Korean War. The 154th FBS lost an F-84 and its pilot Capt James R. Overstreet during the day, possibly the victim of one of the MiGs, while the 13th BS suffered its second crew loss of the month when the B-26 flown by 1/Lt John R. Burtis failed to return.

On the morning of 30 July, the 5th Air Force launched a massive fighter-bomber raid against a large ordnance factory complex at P'yongyang. The raid, by a total of 354 USMC and 5th Air Force aircraft was preceded by an attack to suppress flak in the area by almost 100 F-80s. The main operation included 69 Mustangs from the 18th FBG, of which 2SAAF's contribution was a dozen aircraft under the leadership of Capt Bob Rogers. They dropped napalm and strafed an ammunition factory and were credited with achieving 80 per cent coverage of the target.

---

[6] This proved to be the last Russian MiG claim for July, raising the tally to 26 victories for the month; however, on the 31st, two Chinese MiGs attacked a USN PBM Mariner of Fleet Air Wing Six over the Sea of Japan and inflicted much damage, killing two of the crew and wounding two others.

Amongst the day's casualties was 1/Lt Joe M. Babsa Jr of the 67th FBS who was shot down and killed by ground fire. A second Mustang failed to return, 1/Lt Eric F. O'Briant of the 12th FBS being reported missing.[7]

Three SAAF flights returned to P'yongyang on a similar mission in the afternoon but they found the whole area blanketed with cloud, so they had to be diverted to a secondary target. The Australian Meteors flew two close-escort missions of sixteen aircraft each to cover the B-29s and B-26s also involved in these raids. Flt Lt Max Scannell flew on both escort missions, in A77-128 on the first and A77-740 on the second, while Flt Lt Joe Blyth (A77-163) was involved in the B-29 escort mission only. No air opposition was encountered. F-84s from the 136th FBW also participated in the day's events, the 182nd FBS dive-bombing P'yongyang. Flt Lt Peter Scott in FS-365 was involved in this operation, his 40th and final operational flight in Korea. He recalled his final days in Japan:

> "Our squadron pilots got an Air Medal for every eight missions, so I got five but never picked them up because some idiot at the British Joint Services Mission in Washington said we shouldn't accept medals from foreign powers[8]. After I'd finished my allotted time on combat operations, and after a splendid farewell party with my friends from Little Rock in the Officers Club in Fukuoka, I flew off to see how the army and navy were doing. I don't know how I did it, I was only a Flight Lieutenant. I got a flight to Kimpo in a C-47. I spent a very frightening and sleepless night in a fox-hole on the front line with the 11th Hussars near the Imjin River, and then did an artillery spot for the 29th Brigade in an Auster [NJ870] of 1 AOP Flight with Maj Guy[9]. Later I flew out [in an USN TBM piloted by Lt Rich] to the US aircraft carrier *Princeton* off the east coast for a couple of days to see how they did things."

On his return to Itazuke, having bade his final farewell to Korea and Japan, Flt Lt Scott set course for the United States aboard a DC-4, eventually landing back at Travis AFB from whence he had departed at the end of May at the start of his Korean adventure. Once settled in and reunited with his wife and daughter, he rejoined the 82nd FIS at Hamilton AFB to complete his exchange posting with the USAF. One who did not return to the 82nd FIS at Hamilton was Peter Scott's particular friend, Capt Fred Gleason USAF, who had departed for Korea a couple of months before he had:

> "Fred and I had met up again at Itazuke. By then he had done nearly 80 missions in quite a short time, and a few weeks later his CO grounded him for a while, considering that he was suffering from combat fatigue. This didn't suit Fred at all because he had become more and more aggressive towards his Communist foes, and all he wanted to do was to drop or fire as much ordnance at them as possible, as often as possible.
>
> It so happened that the period of Fred's enforced inactivity coincided with his birthday, and he decided to celebrate it in the local town of Fukuoka, at a place called 'The House of Mirrors'. We all knew it well because it was the squadron's favourite place to spend an evening drinking beer and meeting Japanese girls – less formal than the Officers Club, to say the least, though the food wasn't so good. Only those not flying the next day were allowed to take part, and we knew that we could drink quite a bit and stay out late. Towards the end of the evening it became apparent that Fred hadn't been seen for a while, but nobody worried much – he was grown up and there was always more than one reason why someone could go missing at a party in 'The House of Mirrors'. It was not until the evening of the next day that I heard the whole, extraordinary story of Fred's disappearance – from the man

---

[7] While the F-80 units did not suffer any casualties during this strike, and losses were less severe during July as a whole, nonetheless the 49th FBG's deputy commander Maj Marlyn C. Ford Jr was lost to ground fire (on the 14th) as was 1/Lt John S. Starck (on the 18th), and the 8th FBG reported four pilots missing during the month, with the 51st FIG losing two pilots in accidents.

[8] 25 years later, on retiring from the RAF as an Air Commodore, Peter Scott enquired of the USAF to see if he could at last receive his medals, only to be informed that it was too late.

[9] This flight would suggest that at least one Auster was operating in Korea before the arrival of 1903 AOP Flight, possibly a single aircraft detachment from 655 AOP Squadron.

himself, sitting up in Itazuke base hospital, with an armed guard at the foot of his bed!

Fred had had quite a lot to drink, and gradually became more and more fed up with his CO for grounding him, and increasingly angry with North Koreans. In the end he decided to do something about it. He left 'The House of Mirrors', without bothering to put his boots back on (we always took them off on arrival), pinched a Japanese tricycle milk cart parked nearby, and cycled back to the airfield some four miles away – all this at about midnight. He checked in at the guardroom window and, having abandoned his milk cart, he pattered off to the Flight Line. He found his parachute and helmet in the Flight Safety section (open because of night flying) and was eventually helped into an aircraft by an unsuspecting Japanese guard. He was even aware enough to choose one that was marked with red signs as having live ammunition. He strapped in, plugged on his oxygen and radio connections, started up, and taxied out – all of this he could have done in his sleep, let alone after a few beers. The runway and taxiways were lit up to receive an incoming training mission and Fred had no trouble in finding his way to the take-off end of the runway in use. Then the airfield controller said, 'Aircraft taxying out, state nature of mission.' Fred said, 'Secret mission', and took off! The controller immediately grabbed the hot line and made a series of emergency calls to Headquarters and to every airfield in South Korea, warning them to be on the look out for an unexpected visitor.

Fred told me that he flew up the Korean peninsula at high level, past Seoul and the front line, and finally let down near the Yalu as dawn was breaking – further north than any other Allied aircraft had ever flown at low level, and without anything like enough fuel to get back to Itazuke. He loosed off all his ammunition – almost certainly doing no harm apart from waking up a few people, and then headed back for the most northerly fighter base in Korea – Kimpo. There he did a victory roll at low level and landed without saying a word. To cap it all, he even managed to run out of fuel taxiing back to the Flight Line. Put another way, this meant that if he'd left things about 15 seconds later he would have run out of fuel in the air. Anyway, the authorities on the ground were waiting for him. He was surrounded by an assortment of ambulances, fire engines, staff cars and jeeps, and escorted back to base operations, still in his socks. After a good deal of questioning, Fred was flown back to Japan under armed guard and put in the base hospital, where I was allowed to see him that evening and be told his story. Fred was a warm-hearted, friendly man and happily married with two nice children. He was also brave, but the pressure built up and became more than he could handle. He was not court-martialled, but was invalided out on the grounds of combat fatigue and with no dishonour attached to his name. And that was the outcome of what must have been about the most sensational sortie in the whole of the Korean War." [10]

More British and Commonwealth troops were arriving for service in Korea, and to mark the formation of the 1st Commonwealth Division, as the new force was to be known, a ceremony was held at the new Divisional HQ near Tokch'ong. Amongst those present were General Van Fleet, Lt-General Robertson, Maj-General John W. O'Daniel, who had recently taken command of the US I Corps, and Maj-General James Cassels, the new Commonwealth Division commander. The Division was composed of British, Australian, Canadian, Indian and New Zealand units. The British Government provided the bulk of the Division, contributing the commander and most of the headquarters staff, five battalions (one and a half brigades) of infantry, a regiment and a squadron of tanks, a field artillery regiment, an anti-aircraft battery, a heavy mortar battery, an Air OP Flight, a field engineer regiment, most of the Divisional signals regiment, two transport companies, a field ambulance unit and much of the Division's logistic supporting elements. The Australian Government provided one infantry battalion,

---

[10] At Malta during WWII, an American pilot flying Spitfires with the RAF had similarly 'stolen' a Spitfire during a quiet period with the intention of flying to Sicily to carry out an unauthorised, one-man nocturnal operation. However, he responded to a radioed recall and returned to Malta. Threatened with a court-martial, he was instead transferred to one of the RAF's crack Middle East Spitfire squadrons as 'punishment', completing his tour of operations before transferring to the USAAF (see *The Desert Hawks* by Leo Nomis and Brian Cull). There were probably other similar incidents.

while Australian Army officers, particularly of corps other than infantry, were attached widely to the Commonwealth units and headquarters to gain experience in their particular arm or service. The Canadian Government provided three infantry battalions and other elements to make up a full brigade, including armoured, artillery, engineer, transport and medical units. The Indian Government provided a field ambulance unit and the New Zealand Government a field regiment of artillery and a transport platoon. The Commonwealth Division would assume responsibility for approximately nine miles of the front held by the US I Corps. The 1st ROK Division was on the left flank and the 25th US Infantry Division was on the right, at least until replaced by the 1st US Cavalry Division. Within the Division, the 29th Brigade held the left sector of the front, the 28th Brigade held the right sector and the 25th Brigade was in reserve behind the other two. The Division's first major task, commencing at the beginning of August, would be to carry out a series of patrols across the Imjin River in conjunction with elements of the 1st US Cavalry Division.

The air observation unit accompanying the Commonwealth Division was 1903 Independent Air Observation Post (AOP) Flight, which had been stationed at Kai Tak in Hong Kong as part of the British 40th Division. On 14 June it had been notified to prepare for service in Korea to join the 1st Commonwealth Division. The Flight, with its five Auster VIs[11], equipment and personnel, had embarked aboard HMS *Unicorn* on 9 July and sailed from Hong Kong the following day. On board, in addition to six Army pilots under the command of Maj R.N.L. Gower RA, was a full establishment of RAF aircraft mechanics plus Royal Artillery drivers and signallers. Total manpower was around 50 men of all ranks. On arrival at Iwakuni, the Flight came under the administration of 91 Composite Wing RAAF while the Austers were assembled ready for the flight to Korea. To meet up with the flying echelon, the unit's vehicles were taken from Kure to Pusan by sea on a small Japanese ship. As soon as the Austers had been assembled and test flown at Iwakuni, they set out for K-9 airfield at Pusan. At the controls of the five aircraft were Maj Ronald Gower, Capt R.C. Corfield, Capt L.R.B. Addington, Capt T. Fitzgibbon and Capt D.B.W. Jarvis, all Royal Artillery officers (Capt A.G.E. Stewart-Cox RA was the reserve pilot). Initially they flew to Ashiya to refuel, from where they were escorted over the open sea by a Sunderland of 205 Squadron to Pusan, where they landed without mishap. As has been noted, the men of 1903 Independent AOP Flight were not the first British Army pilots to fly in Korea, Capts Begbie and Sipthorne of the 29th Brigade having achieved that honour[12]. The former, who had by now logged many flying hours, recalled:

"When 1903 Air OP Flight arrived in Korea and became established, the requirement for me to carry out Air OP missions for the Commonwealth Division really disappeared and I thought I might have to return to proper soldiering. However, as by this time I had virtually an aircraft of my own (a plush brand-new L-19) and access to a variety of others, it didn't take much to persuade General Cassels that it would be foolish to throw away such a valuable asset to the Division (and incidentally, thereby taking some 1903 Flight aircraft away from their Air OP job). So I continued my American existence until I finished my Korean tour. This coincided with the arrival of 1913 Liaison Flight, who later on having failed to convince General Cassels and our US Corps Command of the virtues of the Auster as a passenger carrier, inherited my L-19. There was some pressure by the British when 1903 Air OP Flight arrived, to have me moved over from the Americans to join 1903 Flight. But, at that time, the Americans, who had by now come to look upon me as part of their establishment and were making normal use of me as a section pilot, raised objections. They

---

[11] The serial numbers of the initial five Auster VIs are unknown but during the course of its stay in Korea, 1903 AOP Flight is known to have used TW626, VF496, VF513, VF525, VF528, VF561, VF568, VF574, VF582, VF663, VF664, VW988, and WJ360.

[12] As recorded earlier, other British Army officers flew as observers with the 6147th Tactical Control Group, two of whom, Capts Fred Cox and Denis Hall of 655 AOP Squadron, had each been awarded the DFC in May. Additionally, Canadian Lt Don MacLeod received the US Air Medal on completion of his tour with the 6149th TCS. Others would follow, all volunteers, from British, Canadian, Australian, New Zealand and ROK units.

were also at that time not willing to let me take one of their aircraft with me, so it would
have been a counter-productive move. In any case, 1903 Flight were not equipped to look
after American aircraft so soon after their arrival."

The UN Command was not very happy with the progress of events on the ground in Korea.
Operation 'Strangle' had been launched at the end of May, coinciding with the UN's counter-
attack towards the 38th Parallel. Initially, it had achieved some successes but it soon became
obvious that airpower alone could not prevent a steady stream of enemy supplies and
reinforcements from reaching the battle line. UN aircraft were not permitted to attack the most
vulnerable parts of the Communist supply system – the sources of raw materials and the places
of manufacture outside of North Korea. Only exposed segments of the distribution system in
North Korea itself could be attacked and these targets narrowed down to the supply routes
themselves (bridges, tunnels, rail tracks, roads); rolling stock (locomotives and box-cars,
trucks, wagons and carts); the personnel who repaired and operated the supply networks; and
the stockpiles of materials and supplies in transit or in dumps. To achieve this end, three
patterns of attack were tried: key bridges were cut by bombing and every effort was made to
keep them cut; a belt was selected across the peninsula and every supply route and target within
it attacked; and widespread damage was inflicted upon the road and rail lines themselves.

On the other hand, there were simply not enough aircraft available to demolish the 956
bridges that had been nominated as targets, nor to block the 231 known tunnels. Darkness
covered the enemy's troop and supply movements. UN aircraft could not find and destroy at
night, nor in poor weather, on anything like the scale they were capable of achieving in
daylight. The Communists were adept at hiding, camouflaging, and dispersing their supplies in
hundreds of caves, tunnels and huts as dawn approached. Attacks upon rolling stock had to
inflict damage at a rate of attrition that exceeded the enemy's capacity for replacement, but this
was not possible to achieve for a prolonged period of time. There was an almost limitless
supply of trucks and trains across the border in Manchuria, so replacement of these material
losses was relatively easy. Because of the unlimited manpower available to the Koreans and
Chinese, attacking the personnel that were operating or repairing the supply routes at night, was
not feasible even if they could be found, identified and targeted.

By mid-July the 8th US Army had achieved its main objectives and pressure on the
Communist ground armies had slackened. No longer hard pressed, the enemy could re-group
his front line troops and afford to resupply them at a more leisurely pace. 'Strangle' operations
bore diminishing results at increased cost as the enemy's anti-aircraft defences improved and
became more prolific. In the forward areas Chinese Army service troops apparently performed
maintenance on the roads serving them while, further to the rear, the North Koreans repaired
damage to the main supply routes. As it continued through July, Operation 'Strangle' produced
poorer and poorer results. In the long run FEAF had to conclude that it was not successful
". . . due to the flexibility of the Communist logistics system." Under the UN's self-imposed
restrictions, except for only very short periods, air power could not isolate the front. [13]

August 1951
Meanwhile, the truce negotiations at Kaesong were not going well. Back on 27 July, attention
had turned to the question of the future demarcation line between North and South Korea. US
negotiators insisted that the new boundary should be the line of contact between the military
forces at the time an armistice agreement was signed. The Communists insisted upon the 38th
Parallel and maintained that they had only agreed to negotiations because the United States and
the UN had said that they would accept a return to the *status quo* that existed before June 1950.
The Americans argued that the topography along the 38th Parallel made that line difficult to
defend. They could therefore only accept a line that was further to the north, where the hill and

---

[13] Despite these misgivings, Operation 'Strangle' would continue in a revised form until the summer of
1952; when it was finally abandoned, the FEAF had lost 343 aircraft destroyed and a further 290
damaged, mostly fighter-bombers, for questionable results.

ridges could be properly fortified. The Communists professed outrage. The Americans countered by saying that it would be worthwhile to give a small amount of territory in return for an end to UN air attacks on North Korea. In reality, what made the issue so emotional for both sides was the perception that the loss of territory would be seen by the world as North Korea's punishment for its aggression. To prod the Communists into compliance, the USAF bombed P'yongyang heavily on July 30 and instigated the continuing naval action in the Han estuary, but the Communists remained impassive and resolute.

Around the conference site itself, the tenuous nature of their situation in this so-called neutral zone continued to rankle members of the UN delegation. Ostensibly for the 'protection' of UN personnel, many well-armed Communist soldiers patrolled the area. The inequality was further emphasised by the fact that UN personnel were completely unarmed. It had become obvious that the lack of real neutrality of Kaesong was having a marked effect upon procedure and the progress of the negotiations. On 4 August, during the lunch recess, a company of heavily-armed Chinese Communist soldiers passed within a few hundred yards of the staff house used by the UN personnel. The delegation felt menaced. It immediately objected to this violation and, as a consequence, General Ridgway subsequently cancelled the talks until such time as the Communists would give an assurance that there would be no more such incidents. Next day General Ridgway, in a message to General Kim Il-sung and General P'eng, formally protested the violation of the neutral zone by the armed Communist troops. Admiral Joy in turn informed General Nam Il, referring to this communication, that UN delegation would remain within UN lines until further notice.

General Nam Il then protested to the UN delegation over the alleged strafing by USAF aircraft of a supply truck belonging to the Communist delegation. He alleged that it had been displaying a white cloth over its hood and carrying a white flag when it was attacked while on its way to Kaesong from P'yongyang. Admiral Joy immediately replied that the Communists had agreed to first communicate such vehicle movements to the UN Commander-in-Chief, and this had not been done. He further pointed out it was known that on numerous occasions the Communists had used vehicles disguised with these markings to move war supplies to the front down the highway from P'yongyang, apparently assuming that they would be protected from air attack. He further declared that the UN Command could not grant blanket clearance to all distinctly marked traffic moving along the main supply route leading to the enemy front.

On August 10 the truce talks resumed. General Nam Il again restated his arguments in favour of the 38th Parallel as the future demarcation line between North and South Korea and then declared that they had nothing more to say. Admiral Joy agreed. The delegates then sat facing each other in unbroken silence for two hours and eleven minutes before the session was finally adjourned. General Ridgway was furious. He recommended to the Joint Chiefs-of-Staff that the talks be suspended unless the Communists accepted the proposed UN line within three days, but was advised to be patient and show restraint. President Truman was of the opinion that the Communists wanted to end the war but that they would only do so after some face-saving delay. He did not want the talks interrupted. During the week after 10 August, the Communists did in fact show signs of relenting, and there seemed to be an increasing willingness to compromise on the issue of the 38th Parallel, which many observers felt was the key question of the negotiations. If that point could be resolved, a truce might well be in the offing.

There began a dramatic turn of events at the truce talks on 19 August, when the Communists suddenly protested that UN forces had seriously violated the neutrality of the Kaesong conference zone. They dramatically claimed that "thirty-plus" UN personnel had entered the Kaesong conference site and killed one of their platoon leaders. In presenting the charge, Maj-General Lee Sang Cho stated:

"... [Platoon commander Yao Ching-hsiang] is the first victim of the efforts for peace, the first to die by faithfully living up to the peaceful agreement. The people of Kaesong are spontaneously holding a memorial service at 1100 this morning. The organisers of this meeting have asked to let you come. I think Comrade Yao was a real partisan for peace, who died for peace, who lived up to the agreement. No one could refuse to show honour to and sorrow for him. I hope you will go to the service with us ..."

UN negotiatiors were taken completely by surprise and denied any knowledge of the alleged attack. Then, after a continued barrage of complaints against the UN Command, the Communists made another shocking charge on the night of 22/23 August. Half an hour before midnight, a radio telephone message was received at the UN Command Base Camp at Musan from the Communists asserting that just ten minutes earlier the armistice conference site at Kaesong had been bombed and strafed by a United Nations aircraft. An immediate investigation was demanded.

By torchlight and in the dead of night, UN liaison officers and interpreters were shown 'evidence' of the attack. On the road leading to the UN delegation house was a crumpled piece of metal resembling an aircraft oil tank. There was no crater under this piece of metal and no scorched earth. Ten feet away there was a small depression about 30 inches in diameter and ten inches deep, possibly made by a partially buried explosive of a force equivalent to a grenade. There was no evidence of burning to be seen, but the Communists declared these two items proved that a napalm bomb had been dropped. North-west of the residence of the Communist delegates, four similar but smaller holes and pieces of duraluminum, some containing flush riveting, were pointed out. They appeared to be pieces of an aircraft fuselage or engine nacelle. Near one of the holes there was a tail fin of a rocket but no physical evidence of a rocket impact. There were no bomb craters, no scorched earth, no rocket furrows and no pieces of metal remotely resembling a bomb casing. Finally, near a sandstone ridge they were shown two more holes about two feet in diameter and one foot deep, that might have been formed by the impact of a small falling object. Near both holes were pieces of aircraft metal showing flush riveting. At the first hole there was the weak smell of gasoline and, adjacent to the hole, about four superficially burned areas three to five inches in diameter. In the vicinity of the second hole there was about 70 square inches of a substance which might have been a poor mixture of napalm that had not been ignited.

In the course of this investigation, several people claimed to have heard the attack and a Chinese Communist soldier gave a supposed eyewitness account – all in front of Communist press reporters who had magically appeared. The man claimed to have seen the aircraft circle around with two bright lights shining ahead, dropping several bombs. The UN liaison officers demanded that the newsmen leave and requested a proper daylight examination of the evidence. A daylight inspection was refused and so far as the Communists were concerned the investigation was completed. By now it was 0430. Demands were made that the UN liaison officers should accept full responsibility for the bombing. They of course refused and repeated their request for a proper daylight inspection which was again denied so the investigation ended in a deadlock.

Next, the matter was referred to the 5th Air Force to check the possibility of a UN aircraft being present in the area. Investigation showed that there had been none, but the 5th Air Force's radar screen had, in fact, picked up an unidentified aircraft proceeding from the west directly towards Kaesong. This aircraft was about two minutes flying time from Kaesong at 2318 on 22 August (the approximate time of the alleged attack was 2320), and then faded from the radar screen. It was reasoned that the fade out was probably due to the aircraft descending behind the hills below radar coverage between Kimpo airfield near Seoul and Kaesong. But who was flying it? The question remains unanswered. It is possible that South Korean guerrillas, or even regular troops, were responsible for the alleged attack on the conference zone on the 19th – if indeed it did occur. President Rhee was against an armistice that would leave Korea divided, and he may well have given secret orders to sabotage the talks. Perhaps, also, it was a South Korean aircraft that made the raid on the night of 22/23 August – if one did in fact take place. But it was also possible that the charges were a Communist ruse to confound the UN Command. The UN liaison team concluded that the night incident had indeed been staged by the Communists themselves – probably making use of one of their own aircraft burning its landing lights to attract attention. It seems likely that only a small number of Communists at Kaesong, including the delegates, liaison officers, and several other selected personnel, knew beforehand of the fraudulent nature of the incident. In any case, the Communists suspended the talks and for 63 days, from 23 August to 24 October, no armistice discussions were held.

* * *

While the negotiators argued at Kaesong, the war in the air over North Korea continued. By the beginning of August, the newly arrived 1903 AOP Flight was considered to be fully operational and was flying from the 1st Commonwealth Division's designated airstrip located some five miles south of the Imjin. After slit trenches had been dug and camouflage for the aircraft and equipment set up and rigged, the Auster pilots began familiarising themselves with their area of responsibility. This was in fact the 1,000 yards of no-man's-land separating the Division from the enemy's front line. As well as this, they took care of another urgent task. In separate aircraft, Capts Fitzgibbon and Stewart-Cox began photographing their machines from all angles in the air. These shots were for distribution to the American front line troops and, in particular, to the AA gunners. This was considered not just highly desirable, but very necessary because most of the Americans had never seen an Auster before. Thereafter, the Flight started the arduous and dangerous business of air observation, locating targets for the artillery and reporting and photographing the incessant ground activity.

August had opened with poor weather particularly for flying, but this did not prevent Capt Larry Eager of 2SAAF from undertaking a close-support mission on 4 August, winning for him an American DFC. He led four Mustangs to the area of Otan-ni where, in the target area, the South Africans found extremely low clouds which shrouded the surrounding hilltops. In poor light, and with limited space to manoeuvre, Capt Eager nonetheless began a series of superbly executed and extremely effective attacks on the enemy troop positions. The citation for his award noted, in part:

> ". . . he made a series of devastating runs which resulted in 100 per cent coverage of the assigned target. Working in close proximity to friendly forces, he so directed his attacks that absolutely no injury was caused them. Showing a sense of devotion to duty and a standard of airmanship away and above that normally expected, he only left the area after the optimum damage had been caused to the enemy potential. His outstanding leadership and complete disregard for personal safety in the face of the marginal weather conditions that prevailed, and against the ground fire encountered, was highlighted in a tribute addressed by the Commanding General 5th Cavalry to the Commanding General 5th Air Force . . ."

At Kimpo that day, 77RAAF was called upon to carry out another fighter sweep along the Yalu. Sixteen Meteors were to be in the target area by 2000. Sqn Ldr Cresswell assembled the pilots together for the general briefing at 1800. He told them that while the Squadron carried out its fighter sweep along the Yalu, F-86s would be flying below them on their own covering fighter sweep. Below the Sabres, F-80s were scheduled to attack road and rail centres used by the enemy to transport ammunition and equipment at night. The rôle of the Meteors and Sabres was to prevent enemy fighters from attacking the fighter-bombers, particularly while they were still heavily loaded with bombs. The F-80s of the 8th FBG were based at Kimpo with the Australians, and 20 of these took off ahead of the Meteors. Fully loaded as they were, the F-80s needed about ten minutes head start to arrive over the target area at the same time. When they did eventually arrive at the rendezvous point, the Meteors manoeuvred into battle formation. Below them, the Australians could see the Sabres on patrol but could not see the fighter-bombers, although they could hear the American pilots talking on the radio as they located their targets.

Across the Yalu the enemy base at Antung could be clearly seen and, around the concrete runway, the dying sun reflected on the wings of highly-polished MiGs. As the Australians watched, they saw six of the jets take off and begin to gain height while still within their Manchurian sanctuary. The word was spread among the Meteor and Sabre pilots, "Swept-wing fighters at nine o'clock, climbing". More MiGs were sighted and the Australians fully expected a battle to develop. Necks were twisted as sixteen pairs of anxious eyes scanned the skies, up and down and from side to side, trying to see as much as possible from the limited rear vision of the Meteor. Not surprisingly, some pilots complained later of stiff neck muscles. Six MiGs paced the RAAF jets, copying their flying tactics, then two turned in as if they were intending to make an attack but, when the Meteors turned to meet them, they veered back to Manchuria.

Although more MiGs then appeared, these also declined to attack. Sqn Ldr Cresswell recalled:

"During our first missions up and down the Yalu, we were paced by the Chinese *[sic]* on the other side trying to work out who and what we were. When we'd turn, they would turn too . . ."

Unknown to the Australian pilots, the pilots at the controls of the MiGs were Russians from the 1st Eskadrilya of the 523rd FAR (the true extent of Russian involvement in Korea was to remain a well kept secret for over 40 years), and they were indeed studying the newcomers. Air-to-air photographs were taken using a special automatic camera installed in the MiG flown by Kapt Dyachenko, and the film was rushed to the intelligence officer of the 64th Fighter Air Corps. The Russians, before long, were able to confirm that British jet fighters had in fact been committed to the Korean War.

On the ground, the new Commonwealth Division's first major task had been to carry out a series of major patrols across the Imjin, in conjunction with elements of the 1st US Cavalry Division on their eastern flank. Both the 28th and 29th Brigades were ordered to send elements of two battalions across the river up to three and a half miles into no-man's-land. The first patrol failed to contact enemy troops, and when heavy rain caused the Imjin to rise by ten, the patrol was marooned on the northern bank. After they had been re-supplied by airdrop – which the hungry troops discovered consisted mainly of canned potatoes – they managed to re-cross the river and reach safety. It was fortunate that they were able do so, because the river was to rise even higher after more heavy rain that began two days after their return. This unsettled August weather was widespread and eventually caused operations from the UN's forward airbase at K-6 to be suspended. On 9 August the Han, also swollen by the summer rains, threatened to flood the runways and dispersal areas at Seoul. Along with others, 2SAAF's re-arming and re-fuelling detachments were withdrawn until the river subsided, and eventually took nine days to do so. When the South Africans were finally able to return to K-16, they were accompanied by all of the Squadron's serviceable aircraft because the southern base at Chinhae was then being threatened by a typhoon.

MiG flights managed to infiltrate through the patrolling Sabres again on 9 August, when they made attacks on the slower F-80s which were fortunate, on this occasion, to escape unscathed despite claims for four shot down by pilots of the 176th GuFAR. However, four MiGs did succeed in intercepting an RF-80, which was badly damaged. Meanwhile, up above, the two Meteor flights led by Sqn Ldr Cresswell and Flt Lt Des Murphy sighted at least a dozen MiGs. These flew west and disappeared behind cloud. Around six minutes later the Meteor pilots saw more swept-wing jets flying south-west from Sakchu. With hearts racing and thumbs resting on firing buttons, the Australians turned in towards the other jets. It was obvious the Meteors had been seen because their opponents jettisoned their wing tanks ready for battle. As the discarded tanks tumbled towards the ground thousands of feet below, the two formations converged and in that instant the Australians recognised the others as F-86s. At the same time, before they opened fire, the American pilots also realised that their bogies were friendly – and a dangerous crisis had been averted. The 8th FBG's F-80s suffered severely next day, losing four aircraft and three pilots. 1/Lt Mark Castelino of the 80th FBS crashed shortly after take-off from Suwon, and was killed; 1/Lt James Kiser of the 36th FBS was shot down by ground fire, while his colleague 1/Lt Henry Nielson ran out of fuel on the return flight and was posted missing; the fourth aircraft crashed on landing.

During an attack by 2SAAF on a road bridge over the Imjin near Chorwon on 12 August, 2/Lt Mike Muller's Mustang (323) was badly damaged by the blast of its own rockets. Although the hydraulic system was put out of action and the rudder cables severed, the South African pilot managed a wheels-up landing at K-2. Muller, who had experienced a similar mishap earlier in the month, was unhurt. Nor was the day free of incident for the Australians. On returning to Kimpo from a fighter sweep, Meteor A77-740 flown by Flg Off Ken Blight was seen to make a normal approach and touch down but, suddenly, the aircraft veered to the left and the port wheel caught in a deep hole, the result of some workings on the side of the runway. The port undercarriage leg sheared off and the Meteor hit some empty oil drums before coming to rest. Blight was unhurt, and lucky – about 200 gallons of fuel still remained in the main fuel tanks. Investigation later revealed that he had made his landing with the windscreen and hood completely misted up. He had not switched on the port demister panel and had depressurised at 10,000 feet on the descent. The Meteor had suffered considerable damage. Besides the sheared-off port undercarriage leg, the undersides of both engine nacelles were badly crushed, and the lower lip of the centre section front spar was ripped over a distance of 12 inches. Also torn were the underside centre section formers and skins, and the leading edges of both mainplanes. The aircraft had to be categorised as only fit for instructional purposes, and was sent back to Australia.

On 14 August mass raids were carried out against P'yongyang, and the Meteors were given the task of close escorting 22 B-29s to a target near the North Korean capital. The method devised for these operations was to use at least a dozen Meteors in three formations of four aircraft in each, staggered some 3,000-5,000 feet above the bombers. These three formations flew on ahead, one overhead and one behind the bomber flight. All three followed a weaving pattern, crossing over the top of the bombers on opposite courses. They were to be the last line of a fighter defence in-depth, with the job of cutting off any MiGs which managed to penetrate the outer fighter screen. Tactically they were hampered by being unable to divert from the bomber formation. Another drawback of this type of escort mission for the fighter pilots was having to concentrate on keeping station, which made it difficult to support each other if the need arose. Nevertheless, it was good for the morale of the bomber crews having a highly visible fighter presence. On this first occasion, 15 Meteors made up the escort. They met the B-29s at the scheduled time and accompanied them to the target without encountering any enemy fighters. Near P'yongyang they were greeted by heavy flak bursts ranging from 23,000-24,000 feet, but these were ineffective.

Mustangs of the 18th FBG, including those of 2SAAF, took part in the attacks on the enemy capital. These missions had to be flown from K-10 instead of K-16, which had been temporarily abandoned because of the flooding. This meant flying nearly twice the normal distance and entailed reducing the amount of ordnance, and effectiveness, by replacing one napalm bomb with a long-range fuel tank. The pilots described these flights as "real bum-busters"! Newly promoted Cmdt Jan Blaauw, who had recently taken command of 2SAAF from Cmdt Armstrong, led the morning raid on P'yongyang with four flights of two aircraft, plus two reserves, in a wing formation totalling 64 aircraft. When they reached the target area, the South Africans dropped their napalm on a cluster of warehouses by the river bank and then strafed two anti-aircraft batteries. During the attack they came under intense ground fire which made several of the pilots somewhat apprehensive when they took off again later on a similar mission. On this occasion, Cmdt Blaauw led the entire fighter-bomber wing of 64 Mustangs, including 17 from 2SAAF. The South Africans were allocated, as a target, a large tank and vehicle repair shop. Using napalm, at least four direct hits were scored on the buildings which were left burning fiercely and were eventually gutted. They then turned their guns on two river boats and a barge which were also claimed destroyed. This time the anti-aircraft guns offered only moderate opposition but as Lt Ian de Jongh (349) was pulling out of his napalm run, he called up to say he had been hit. He announced he was heading for the coast, but did not think he would make it. He called again immediately afterwards to say he was going to bale out.

Lt Willem van den Bos, who was flying in the same flight, saw de Jongh's stricken Mustang streaming glycol as it left the target area. The former had been best man at the wedding of de Jongh's sister to Lt Dereck Doveton (whose death in action was described earlier), so he was very anxious about what was happening. Unfortunately, the napalm tank under the port wing of his aircraft had hung up during the attack and this prevented him for keeping up with de Jongh's machine. When he at last managed to jettison the tank it was too late, his friend had disappeared westward into scattered cloud. Lt de Jongh was never seen or heard of again[14]. Three other SAAF Mustangs received minor damage, while Lt Albie Gotze in Mustang 341

---

[14] Lt Ian de Jongh had been one of South Africa's most talented young athletes. He held the national high-jump record and had the prospect of becoming a future Springbok rugby player.

was obliged to land at K-14 for fuel on the way home. The South Africans flew 35 sorties that day, setting a new record for the 2SAAF in Korea. Six American Mustangs of the 18th FBG[15] also failed to return from these raids, while seven B-26s were also lost over the target area, all victims of the intense and highly accurate anti-aircraft fire.

Launched suddenly and without warning on 18 August, the UN started a new air campaign, this time aimed at North Korea's railway system. Owing to the dwindling success of the Operation 'Strangle' road-interdiction stratagem, alternative plans were laid for an assault on the enemy's rail network by the 5th Air Force and FEAF Bomber Command, in conjunction with USN and USMC air units. In support of the new initiative, Colonel McBride, the 5th Air Force's Director of Combat Operations, explained:

> "We decided to destroy the enemy rail system to where its rail traffic was as near zero as we could make it . . . We are optimistic enough about it to believe that with this programme we can force the enemy to retire from a line generally from P'yongyang through Kowon, which is a line generally 100 miles from and parallel to the Yalu River."

It was reasoned that the UN's air force was not only capable of destroying the enemy rail system, but also of continuing to hinder his highway transport to such an extent that they would not be capable of effectively opposing the 8th US Army. If the railways south of a line between Sinanju and Kilchu were destroyed, the Communists could still supply their forces by increasing the use of their motor transport, but it was thought that escalating the volume of movement of this would also increase the risk of exposure to air attack and prove too costly. Light bombers of the 5th Air Force would hunt trucks as a priority, and natural attrition would take an additional toll. Estimates suggested that Communist transport losses could range up to a prohibitive 7,500 a month. Realising that lateral rail routes on North Korea's H-shaped rail network would be useless if the main north-south routes were destroyed, the heaviest air attacks were the single-track rail lines that connected Huyich'on and Kunu-ri, and Kunu-ri and Sunch'on. Enthusiastic about the prospects of success of the new plan, 5th Air Force officers at a briefing for General Vandenberg used the same code name that they had given to the earlier road-interdiction campaign – Operation 'Strangle'.

Day after day, following 18 August, orders from 5th Air Force HQ specified a 15-30 mile stretch of rail line in north-western Korea for rail-cutting attacks by each of the fighter-bomber groups. Subsequently, along with the rest of the 18th FBG during the last two weeks of August, the bulk of 2SAAF's targets were changed from roads to railway lines. Covered by an F-86 screen, the fighter-bombers usually attacked their designated sections of rail line twice each day, but track-breaking was not a simple task. The Korean railway track was only 56 inches wide and only a direct hit on this narrow-gauge target was effective. Tactics varied according to enemy opposition and the weather. Most air commanders employed group gaggles of 32-64 aircraft and used glide and/or dive-bombing attacks. Glide bombing was regarded as being more accurate but the latter minimised exposure to enemy ground fire. Initially, some fighter-bombers carried 1,000-lb bombs, but as the month wore on the standard ordnance for use against rail tracks soon became two 500-lb bombs. At the same time as the fighter-bomber strikes, B-29s of FEAF Bomber Command attacked key railway bridges at P'yongyang, Sinanju, Sunch'on, and Sonch'on as a second priority to a continued neutralisation of North Korean airfields. As a matter of routine, Bomber Command attacked bridges when photographic reconnaissance showed they were serviceable. On a rail-cutting day, two flights of four aircraft were usually sent out against two bridges. Nature gave Bomber Command a helping hand when flooding of the Ch'ongch'on swept over both the rail and road bridges at Sinanju.

The new UN assault again brought the MiGs into play, and the first day of the offensive, 18 August, saw more Sabre and MiG clashes in MiG Alley. Two of the Russian jets were claimed destroyed without loss, both credited to 1/Lt Richard Becker of the 334th FIS, his third and fourth victories. In return, a pilot of the 176th GuFAR claimed an F-86. Next day, in more air

---

[15] Four pilots were killed: Maj William J. Greene of the 67th FBS, Maj Murrit H. Davis, CO of the 39th FIS, Capt John F. Grossman and Capt John L. Horn, both also of the 39th FIS.

fighting, the contest was a draw after 28 MiGs fought a battle with 30 F-86s. Russian ace Kapt Grigorii Okhai, giving testimony to the toughness of the MiG, recalled later that:

"The enemy was very skilful and dangerous. Pilots on both sides were getting the best out of their aircraft. Neither we, nor they, could shoot down a single aircraft. On completing the battle, our pilot Churkin landed at Antung with 57 rupture holes in his MiG-15 . . ." [16]

Nevertheless, one F-86 was credited to a pilot of the 18th GuFAR. Covered by the Sabre umbrella, the UN fighter-bombers continued with their work, and 2/Lt Tom Sivertsen of 2SAAF carried out a mission that earned him an American DFC. With 2/Lt Jean de Wet as wingman, he led a flight of four Mustangs to the Kumsong area and contacted the FAC. The citation for his DFC recorded what happened next in glowing terms:

". . . this young pilot initiated and directed a succession of devastating attacks against enemy targets with the utmost success. In quick succession, he caused the utter destruction of an extensive enemy supply dump, severe damage to an important road bridge, the annihilation of 55 enemy troops, and the complete destruction of four .50 calibre automatic anti-aircraft guns. Leading the flight like a veteran, and quite oblivious of personal safety, the success attained can only be attributed to his calm direction of every attack, and the aggressive spirit he enthused into every calculated thrust against the enemy. After the aircraft flown by his wingman and the number four had been severely damaged by ground fire, his fiendish determination to obliterate the guns mounted steadily. When his own ammunition was completely expended, he continued to make dry runs over the positions to draw fire on himself and so more clearly pinpoint the target for the remainder of the flight. This intrepid pilot only left the area after he was convinced that the optimum damage had been inflicted against the enemy potential. 2/Lt Sivertsen's exceptional accuracy caused the Controller to express the highest appreciation and admiration for a mission superbly led and executed . . ."

The 18th FBG lost another pilot on this date, 1/Lt Richard Heilands of the 39th FIS being killed in action. At least four F-80s were lost at this time; 1/Lt Bruce Wilson of the 36th FBS hit a high tension cable and was killed, while two days later on the 20th, the 16th FIS had two pilots shot down by ground fire, 2/Lt Edwin F. Tabaczynski and Capt Emmett N. Long, who were both reported missing, while 1/Lt Billy Dixon of the 80th FBS managed to bale out of his crippled jet over Inch'on harbour and was promptly rescued by an H-5 helicopter. The 5th Air Force's night-intruding B-26 crews reported more and more successes against trucks and trains while, during daylight, the fighter-bomber squadrons continued their rail-cutting attacks, and often also caught enemy M/T in the open. Better weather over the target areas and an increased emphasis on dawn and dusk armed-reconnaissance sweeps began to bring in fruitful results, but not every attack met with triumph. The narrow railway lines were not easy targets, and even the multi-track sections were difficult to hit under certain conditions. On 22 August, for example, when two flights of SAAF Mustangs attacked a marshalling yard on the line between Kunu-ri and Such'on they had an uncommon lack of success when a high cross wind made accurate bombing impossible. Two days later, a flight of F-80s of the 16th FIS caught the enemy ferrying a large convoy across the river and this flight, plus two others that were quickly despatched to the scene, accounted for over 40 trucks, 20 railway cars, some supply-laden barges and a large dump of equipment still on the riverbank. In Sabre vs MiG clashes, the Americans claimed two more MiGs shot down, one credited to the 4th FIW's Colonel Ben Preston Jr and the other to Capt Jack A. Robinson of the 334th FIS. Both were first kills. A pilot of the 523rd FAR, probably St/Lt Razorvin, claimed an F-86 shot down in return, which apparently crashed about 15 miles north of Teiju, while a B-29 was also lost to MiG attack.

Meanwhile, two RAAF Meteors and their pilots had been lost in a mid-air collision on 22 August. While returning from a fighter sweep one section was changing from battle formation to line astern when the No2, Flt Sgt Reg Lamb, who was flying A77-354, collided with the No3, Sgt Ron Mitchell in A77-128. Both aircraft were completely wrecked and crashed north of the

---

[16] See *MiG-15* by Gordon and Rigmant.

Han, about one mile apart. Neither man had a chance to bale out and both were killed. They were both experienced operational pilots and serious losses. A Londoner, Flt Sgt Lamb, who had flown at least 30 sorties with the Australians and had been awarded a US Air Medal, had been one of the RAF flying instructors sent out to assist in 77RAAF's conversion from Mustangs, while Sgt Mitchell from Sydney had been flying operations since December 1950 and had also earned a US Air Medal. Cpl Pat Melican recalled:

> "Ron Mitchell and an RAF pilot, Reg Lamb, collided while returning to base at Kimpo and were killed. I was one of the Burial Party flown over to Pusan for their interment in the UN cemetery there. We used an Australian flag and a Union Jack."

Sqn Ldr Dick Cresswell's tour of duty as commanding officer of 77RAAF had ended on 18 August, after a notable 11 months that earned him the DFC in addition to the US DFC and Air Medal. However, it was not quite the end for him in Korea. After handing over to his successor, Wg Cdr Gordon Steege DSO DFC (see Appendix III), Sqn Ldr Cresswell attended ground and air schools for the F-86 and flew a further ten sorties with the 4th FIW as a guest of the US Government before returning to Australia. The new CO, Wg Cdr Steege, had in fact arrived at Iwakuni on a courier flight on 10 May, but had been required to attend an Air Power symposium in England shortly afterwards. His return was delayed several weeks because of an RAF operational commitment in the Middle East, which curtailed transport flights to Japan. He had not previously flown Mustangs or Meteors, but converted to these types before taking over his new command.

The Meteors' first contact with MiGs occurred on 25 August, as a formation of eight aircraft led by Flt Lt Max Scannell provided air cover for RF-80s on a reconnaissance mission south of Sinanju. At 1040, four MiGs were sighted at 25,000 feet. They were aircraft from the 176th GuFAR led by Maj Grigorii Pulov, the commander of the regiment. Maj Pulov and his wingman, St/Lt Nikolai Sutyagin, peeled away and crossed the Yalu to attack. Sgt Kevin Foster spotted them first and called for the Meteor flight to break as tracer passed within 20 feet of his port wingtip. The MiGs then concentrated on Wt Off Bill Michelson's aircraft, tracer passing his port wing before the Russian fighters dived through the formation, heading for the sanctuary of the Yalu. Flt Lt Scannell (A77-982) had seen the two MiGs and he gave chase. He managed to fire off a burst of 20mm cannon at extreme range but could not tell if his target had been hit. He lodged no claim. No Meteors had been hit. It was a vastly different story from the Russian viewpoint, however, with Major Pulov and St/Lt Sutyagin each claiming a Meteor shot down. Two more American Mustang pilots were lost during the day, both Capt David J. French of the 18th FBG and 1/Lt Raymond S. Stewart of the 12th FBS failing to return, the latter later being reported a prisoner. Two others survived when their aircraft were shot down, both baling out safely although one, Capt Lawrence Cookman, suffered burns. In addition, an F-80 piloted by 2/Lt Robert Martin of the 80th FBS was shot down by ground fire, while Capt Gerald Brose of the 30th Weather Squadron, who was attached to the 51st FBG, was also shot down and killed. The 25th FIS lost 2/Lt Robert Lacey to ground fire a few days later.

The British Army pilots of the 1903 AOP Flight had very quickly established themselves and during the first month they carried out 34 shoots with the Divisional artillery. AOP work was showing signs of becoming more lethal when (on 22 August) Capt Derek Jarvis' Auster was subjected to ground fire and one round holed the port flap. It was the first time one of the British spotter aircraft had been hit, but it would not be the last. Four days later a message was received by the Flight that a USAF AT-6 had crashed north of the Imjin, both of the occupants having baled out. Capt Leslie Addington was instructed to set out at once in his Auster to search. At the same time a foot patrol was sent out. Addington found the downed airmen and circled, calling in a rescue helicopter and remained in position ready to call for artillery support should the enemy attack. The helicopter duly arrived and picked up both men without difficulty, then Addington flew on to locate the searching foot patrol. Once found he dropped a message telling them to return to base.

The pressure of Operation 'Strangle' continued unabated and 2SAAF's missions for 26 August were typical. Capt Larry Eager led eight Mustangs as part of a 36-aircraft mission on rail interdiction, followed by an armed reconnaissance of known transport routes on the way home. A large fire was started. Four box-cars were destroyed and 15 damaged in the same area, while one motor vehicle was damaged by strafing and an estimated five enemy troops killed. On another operation, Lt Don Parker led eight more Mustangs in a 36-aircraft mission against a similar rail interdiction target and subsequent armed recce from Ch'onju to Sonch'on. The four aircraft carrying delayed-action bombs obtained four rail cuts and, since no ground fire was experienced, the other four then attacked with conventional bombs, achieving a further rail cut. During the return flight, a bridge was damaged by rocket attack, 150 troops were strafed and a supply dump was also strafed but without any obvious results. All aircraft returned safely.

29 August was to be judgement day for 77RAAF and its Meteors, although the first mission led by Flt Lt Scannell, an escort to B-29s, proved uneventful. A second formation of eight Meteors led by Sqn Ldr Wilson was ordered to carry out a sweep north of Sinanju, these encountering a large formation of MiGs of the 303rd FAD led by Podpolkovnik Belostotskii of the 18th GuFAR. The MiGs were up to intercept a force of incoming B-29s escorted by F-86s, one section comprising Kapt Lev Shchukin and St/Lt A. Asanovskiv attacking four of the Sabres. They fired at one section but then, to avoid being counter-attacked by the other section, zoomed back into cloud cover. When they finally emerged from the clouds they found not Sabres, but Meteors. Sqn Ldr Wilson and his section – Flt Lt Cedric Thomas, Flg Off Ken Blight and Sgt N. Woodroffe – were at 35,000 feet when six MiGs were sighted about 5,000 feet above. Wilson led his Meteors around to the left while maintaining a careful watch for other enemy fighters. Two more MiGs were spotted below and he decided to attack them. Closely followed by his No2, Sgt Woodroffe, Wilson dived but his companion's Meteor suddenly went into a spin from which it did not recover before dropping 5,000 feet. Unaware he was alone, Wilson continued with his attack. His aircraft (A77-616) suddenly shuddered as it took hits. Another MiG was on his tail, flown by Kapt Shchukin. Wilson broke away violently. Fortunately his plight had been seen by the other two Meteor pilots, Thomas and Blight, who chased after his attacker. Shchukin and Asanovskiv zoomed their MiGs upwards and escaped into the upper level of the clouds, leaving the Meteors in their wake. When they emerged again it was into an empty sky. There were no Meteors to be seen. Shchukin was awarded a kill, his fourth victory.

When he was clear of the fight, Sqn Ldr Wilson had time to assess the damage to his aircraft. His port aileron had been shot away and there was a huge hole in the wing. It looked large enough for a man to fit through, such was the power of the MiG's 37mm cannon. He was also losing fuel and this caused him to doubt his ability to reach home, although he was able to achieve this and land relatively safely. He had, however, certainly emerged second best from this first contact with the MiGs. Worse was to come. The second section of Meteors led by Flg Off Geoff Thornton was also attacked by the MiGs. Thornton had spotted the Russian jets diving out of the sun and quickly called out a warning. The Meteors broke as the MiGs made a firing pass, Kapt Nikolai Babonin and his wingman St/Lt A. Svinititskii, also of the 18th GuFAR, selecting the aircraft (A77-721) flown by Wt Off Ron Guthrie:

"My flight was over the mouth of the Yalu when we saw a flight of MiGs running for the border, about 5,000 feet below. We immediately turned to attack. I lagged about 50 yards in making this turn and a flight of MiGs jumped me from above at 6 o'clock. I broke to port but was hit before I could make the move effective. During the break I called to the rest of the flight but found that both my radios had been knocked out. While I was about 40 degrees through the break, two MiGs passed my nose and I turned back to starboard to have a shot at them. I was hit again from behind while firing at one of the pair in front of me. This time my controls failed to respond so, after flick-rolling four times, I abandoned the aircraft by the ejection seat, at about 38,000 feet [when flying at Mach .84]. The seat and oxygen worked perfectly and I floated down uneventfully until I was within about 1,000 feet of the ground, when troops began to fire on me intermittently. As soon as the seat had settled down under its own chute, I separated myself from it and opened my own chute. In all, it was about 28 minutes before I reached the ground. Members of the North Korean Home Guard, assisted by civilians, immediately surrounded me and led me off to the nearby village of Kooson." [17]

The victory was awarded to Babonin, the former test pilot and member of the ill-fated *Grupa NII VVS*, who related that he had opened fire from a distance of 300-400 yards and set one of its engines on fire. Despite being badly damaged, the stricken Meteor managed to continue flying and it appeared to him that the pilot was trying to put up a fight, so he closed to within 100 yards to finish it off. None of the returning Meteor pilots had witnessed Guthrie's fate, but gradually information started to filter in. An F-86 pilot flying at a much lower altitude had seen an aircraft spiralling downwards with smoke pouring from behind. Other American pilots reported seeing a parachute. Since no MiGs had been claimed destroyed that morning, and no American aircraft lost, it was assumed that the burning aircraft was the missing Meteor and that Guthrie may have parachuted out behind enemy lines. It would be many months before confirmation of his capture was announced.

Back at Kimpo, following the return of the Meteors, an inspection of Sqn Ldr Wilson's damaged aircraft revealed that the lever at the rear of the aileron torque tube in the main spar had been practically shot away. A huge hole was torn out of the skin of the aileron and the aileron shrouding was peppered with shrapnel. A shell had also gone through the rear fuselage aft of the IFF aerial, and had ricocheted across the top of the radio compass set, peppered the centre section rear bulkhead and punctured the rear compartment of the main fuel tank about 20 inches from the top of the tank. At least, if nothing else, the Meteor was proving itself capable of taking punishment. This was the first operational loss in 354 sorties flown from Kimpo to date, excluding the two aircraft which had collided when returning from a mission. It was obvious to those involved in the action that the Meteor was no match for the MiG, a view endorsed by 77RAAF's press officer, Flt Lt George Odgers, when he later wrote:

"Few who knew their fighter aircraft believed that the Meteor was a war winner, but after these brief encounters near the Manchurian border the warmly nurtured hope that British military aviation was holding its own was rudely shattered. The Australian pilots had tested out the best fighter that Britain had in production. The lamentable outcome had been one lost and two damaged, while the Australians could not claim even a hit in return. It is true that on both occasions the MiGs had had a tactical advantage. Nevertheless, many of the pilots felt the Meteors were a failure. They had seen with their own eyes the MiG-15s going like 'greased lightning', as they put it. The MiG had turned tighter and pulled up faster." [18]

MiGs were again encountered by 77RAAF on the last day of the month although, on this occasion, there were no fighter engagements, the MiGs going after the B-29s. Flt Lt Des Murphy led one of the flights, Flt Lt Joe Blyth (A77-189) the other, as he recalled:

"We were close escort to B-29s bombing Sunch'on. I think this was a bad one. When the MiGs came we were the rear section – they outpaced us and damaged some of the bombers, further frustrating us by doing rolls over the top of the B-29s after firing . . ."

The MiGs, from the 176th GuFAR, also encountered a formation of F-80s near Anju, four of which they claimed shot down. One was reported to have crashed a few miles south-east of Anju, another near Naidori, and a third was apparently seen to fall into the sea. At least one American pilot was lost, 1/Lt Jack Henderson of the 36th FBS being reported killed in action. The last day of the month also witnessed the loss of another US Mustang pilot when 1/Lt John

---

[17] Wt Off Ron Guthrie remained a POW until after the cease-fire in 1953. After the eventual exchange of prisoners he discovered that his high-altitude bale-out had given him a place in history. It was the first time that a Martin-Baker ejector seat had been used to save a pilot's life in combat. His was the highest known bale-out up to that time, and that his 28-minute descent was also a record.

[18] See *Across the Parallel*.

D. Hoke of the 39th FIS was killed. It had been a bad month for the Mustang units; in addition to the losses previously recorded, the 45th TRS lost an aircraft to ground fire when 1/Lt Donald Dishon was shot down on the 7th, although he was able to force-land in friendly territory. The 8th FBG's tenure at Kimpo was now coming to an end. Two months of operations had clearly shown that fully combat-loaded F-80 fighter-bombers could not use this cramped airfield safely. Although American engineers continued to make good progress reconstructing Kimpo, the airfield's runways were still comparatively short and rough. It was planned that in late August, the 4th FIW and 8th FBG should trade bases. The Sabres did not carry external ordnance and could therefore use the shorter runways, as could the Meteors.

During the middle part of the month, the USAF's 67th Tactical Reconnaissance Wing under the command of Colonel Vincent W. Howard had begun to assemble at Kimpo, where it joined the 8th FBG and 77RAAF. Its tactical squadrons were coming from Taegu and the supporting units from Japan, to bring the Wing together for the first time since its activation. Among the specialists with the 67th TRW was a detachment from the RAF's Photo Intelligence Department commanded by Sqn Ldr Vic de la Perelle, a New Zealander in the RAF. Other personnel included Flt Lt E.A. Roberts DFM and Flt Lt John Low, who would be joined later by Sqn Ldr Allan Simpson DFC RCAF (see Appendix III). None of these officers were required for flying duties. Sqn Ldr de la Perelle was later awarded an American Bronze Star for his work with the 67th TRW, the citation noting:

> "At the time of the arrival of Sqn Ldr de la Perelle and the RAF Photo Intelligence Detachment, the 67th TRW was in the process of moving to another base [Kimpo]. Photo intelligence personnel were urgently needed for the move and to keep the squadron operational at both bases. Under adverse conditions, Sqn Ldr de la Perelle immediately integrated his personnel in the squadron and trained them in the procedures of the squadron. In addition, [he] organised his unit to study aerial photographs for camouflaged enemy supply installations and to detect enemy material in transit. This unit was instrumental in providing much of the intelligence information needed for air attacks in the USAF interdiction programme against the enemy in Korea . . ."

While the 67th TRW was engaged on sorties over North Korea, RB-29s of the 91st SRS conducted special missions over more sensitive areas such as the Chinese and Soviet border regions and Soviet Pacific islands. Two such special missions were flown on 8 and 11 August over Soviet-controlled Kurile Island, while another penetrated as far as Shanghai on 25 August.

CHAPTER VIII

THE MIGS RUN AMOK

September – October 1951

". . . [Wg Cdr Steege] is emphatic and loud in his statements that the Meteor is hopelessly outclassed by the MiG-15 in air-to-air fighting. This attitude, which of course does not help morale, is however largely governed by his natural desire to prevent his squadron from being badly beaten up and decimated . . ."

Air Vice-Marshal C.A. Bouchier, AOC Air Component BCOF,
to the RAF Chief-of-Staff, September 1951

When 77RAAF moved from Japan to Kimpo in July, the base was not complete. Seoul and its environs had been fought over twice during the preceding campaigns and the terminal building showed the evidence of the ravages of war. Facilities required re-building as they had been destroyed by Allied air interdiction or during the ground assault. Ironically, 77RAAF had actually targeted Kimpo during its earlier Mustang operations. Cpl Pat Melican recalled:

"77 Squadron Meteors were dispersed about two hundred yards west of the runway which ran north-south and standing on the steel matting so dear to the US Air Force. It was very good stuff, its only fault being that in severe winter conditions, and these prevailed in Korea, the steel surface would attract a coating of ice which could be a hazard to the movement of both men and machine. By September, Kimpo – the most forward USAF base in Korea – was reasonably well set up but did not boast a PX [the American equivalent of the NAAFI, only much better provisioned]. Having an acute awareness of the needs of the average GI, a variety of items normally purchased in a PX were issued free to all who came to the evening meal. Happily, this included the Australians and we were delighted to be given cigarettes or tobacco, the choice being for rolling cigarettes, smoking in a pipe or just plain chewing, plus candy, toothpaste, etc. Added to this was the weekly issue of 50 first-class English cigarettes in a sealed tin generously provided for every man in the Commonwealth forces by the famous philanthropist, Lord Nuffield. When the dreaded day arrived and the PX was a functioning fact of Kimpo life, we could still buy our cigarettes for one US dollar per carton of two hundred.

It would not be an exaggeration to say that Americans are, for the most part, compulsive givers and their generosity to us, as the only non-US unit on the base, was extensive. When the Americans discovered our winter gear, adequate for Australia but not for the extremes of the Korean winters, consisted of woollen vests and Long Johns (two sets of each), they handed out their winter clothing to every man in the Squadron and this made all the difference. Furthermore, there were not strings like signatures for items issued: this stuff was gift stuff. Then there was the matter of hospitality and this was readily forthcoming also. The Yanks didn't have Messes as we did but prefer to have counterparts called Clubs, and because the USAF didn't have NCO pilots as we did, they made our non-commissioned pilots welcome in their Officers Club, and all manner of valuable contacts both working and social were made, with fliers mixing with fliers. Our unit had an Officers Mess which, in

Kimpo, catered for all ranks of sergeant and above. The airmen had what was grandly called a Mess which was really an enlarged wooden-framed double tent which had been constructed by our pilots in their off-duty hours. We had a bar with scrounged, stolen and donated chairs and tables and a stock of the usual canteen goods for sale. We, the corporals and below, were not overlooked by the Yanks who invited every airman to enjoy the amenities of their Top Three Club, which catered for the three senior ranks of sergeant, Staff, Technical and Master. In the early days, their Club had modest beginnings but as time went by and the profits from the bar sales increased, so their premises grew in keeping with their prosperity. By the time my nine months at Kimpo had come to an end, the Top Three – sometimes called the *Honcho* Club – had prospered to the stage where there were lots of tables and chairs, bought and paid for, and a juke-box was just being unveiled! I heard later that it was a freebee and was rigged to play without the requirement of being fed with coins. The USAF other ranks were in the club business too and they were called The Little Joes. The rules only allowed them to have beer, which was very mild. On the other hand, the Top Three could sell just about anything.

I had always imagined that all the people in 77 Squadron would have been living on hard rations – bully beef, army biscuits left over from WWII and mugs of luke-warm tea – but it was not like that with Uncle Sam's tucker. You were served a cereal, fried or scrambled eggs (the latter were delicious and infinitely superior to what our RAAF cooks gave us which were generally referred to as yellow peril), great slices of apple-cured Virginia ham, toast and coffee. As to the quantity served per person, there was always a prominent sign saying 'You are welcome to seconds'. The menus varied from day to day and the Yank food was always popular with the troops. The pancakes were superb. Somewhere along the way, a few of our blokes asked if tea was ever available and sure enough, a day or so later, a great urn of tea appeared beside the coffee. The urn was great but not the tea. For those who enjoyed a strong cup of tea, it was still far too strong. Wherever the cooks obtained the tea making formula, it was not the right place. But before the matter could be rectified, quite a few Yanks had become converts to the tea-drinking fraternity and the strength of the tea remained as it was, très formidable."

There was always a good number of American spectators when the Australian Meteors took off. They were now performing like clockwork, taking off singly at three-second intervals. It was not unusual to see the 18 aircraft airborne in 65 seconds. Back in August, before the 8th FIW had moved out, this had compared very favourably with the time necessary for the single-engined F-80s, and also F-84s, to get off the ground. Taking off from Kimpo in very hot weather had proved quite hazardous for these aircraft. If a pilot doubted his ability to get off successfully, a panic button was pressed and a pair of 1,000-lb bombs and two great wing fuel tanks went bouncing down the runway. It had not been uncommon either for a stream of bullets to travel the length of the runway when these aircraft touched down. In the very hot weather, it was a thrilling sight to see a bombed-up F-80 assisted in its take-off by the operation of JATO canisters fitted on the underside of the fuselage. In wet weather it was also noticeable that the F-80s, and the F-84s, had difficulty in pulling up within the length of the runway. There was no proper overshoot and many accidents took place. It came as no surprise when it became known that the 4th FIW with Sabres was to operate from Kimpo while the 8th FIW moved down to Suwon. The runway was not much longer there, but overshooting facilities were available at both extremities.

The arrival of the 4th FIW was marked by a party given by the Australians in the tent set aside for an Aircrew Club. Food was prepared and flown over from Japan. A very happy evening followed. This afforded the Australians the opportunity to become re-acquainted with Colonel Herman A. Schmid, who still commanded the Wing, and his men. Personal contacts were renewed and new ones were made. It resulted in a very satisfactory close and co-operative liaison between the two units. The 4th FIW had the well-deserved reputation of being the foremost fighter wing in the US Air Force, although only two of its three squadrons, the 334th and 335th, were in Korea. Its other unit, the 336th, was in reserve in Japan and due to swap with the 335th during the month. The airmen and pilots of these squadrons were conscious of their reputation. The pilots seemed especially capable and their skill in taking off in pairs in their Sabres did not go unnoticed by the Australian pilots. Very soon afterwards, 77RAAF's Meteors were duplicating the performance and taking off in pairs at four-second intervals.

Colonel Schmid was a man facing some major concerns. As far back as June 1951, it had been estimated that the Communists – the Chinese, it was supposed – possessed some 445 MiG-15s against 89 F-86s in the 5th Air Force's inventory. Of these, only 44 belonged to the 4th FIW's two squadrons that were committed to Korea. While these figures were bad enough, which indicated that the American fighters were outnumbered 10:1, the front line situation was actually much worse. The Wing's maintenance and supply support system was fragmented, dispersed at several locations in Japan, and Colonel Schmid had found that in practice it required a substantial maintenance effort by his hard-working groundcrew in Korea to keep as many as half the Sabres, some 22 aircraft, flying at any one time. This meant that his pilots were potentially confronted with an enormous 20:1 disadvantage each time they flew to the Yalu. Not only that, while the F-86 numbers had remained constant, the enemy strength according to US intelligence had grown to 525 MiGs by the beginning of September. The UN pilots were facing a steadily deteriorating air-to-air situation. With their increased numbers and the safety of their sanctuaries on the forbidden side of the Yalu, the MiGs could afford to become more aggressive, and they were. In mid-August the Sabres had been able to counter the more active MiGs, often at odds, but the immediate future looked ominous. The only other unit deployed for air-to-air combat was 77RAAF. Although the Meteors had come out of the battle on 29 August with poor results – one pilot missing, one aircraft lost and another badly damaged, for no MiGs claimed – the Australian pilots were game enough, but the question was, were their aircraft good enough?

The storm broke on 1 September as the MiG pilots began to introduce new fighter tactics. As many as 90 MiGs now entered North Korean airspace at one time. Not only that, their formations were better organised and the pilots appeared more disciplined. Taking advantage of their vast numbers and capability to fly higher, the MiG pilots could evade the Sabre patrols at the Yalu and continue southwards at altitudes above 35,000 feet. If the Sabres could be avoided so easily, or were to be overwhelmed, the UN fighter-bombers would be no longer safe from fighter attack. In aerial combat that day, the 335th FIS's Maj Winton W. Marshall claimed a MiG, but the warning signs were there. A Russian pilot of the 18th GuFAR claimed an F-86 in return. The first strike for 77RAAF in September was also flown on the first day of the month, a close-escort mission by a dozen Meteors led by Sqn Ldr Wilson. They met a similar number of B-29s over Hajang-dong and escorted them to the target, the railway bridge at Sunch'on. Bombs were seen to be dropped in the centre of the railway bridge amid meagre, but accurate, heavy flak. During the second strike that day, again led by Sqn Ldr Wilson, to close-escort one RF-80 on a reconnaissance over the Sunch'on area, eight MiGs were sighted over Anju. The MiGs were heading south-west but turned to follow the Meteors, keeping a distance of about six miles to the rear. By this time the Meteors were low on fuel and they made sure they kept out of range, and the MiGs made no attempt to attack. A further ten unidentified aircraft were spotted by Flt Lt Scannell at 40,000 feet heading north-west over Anju; however, these aircraft maintained their heading and disappeared from sight.

Flak was enough for the fighter-bombers to contend with. Operation 'Strangle' railway interdiction missions now being flown by 2SAAF were directed mainly against the section of double track between P'yongyang and Sinanju. Before the threat of MiGs increased early in the month, sections of the main line between Sinanju and Sonch'on were also attacked. Other lines that received the attention of the SAAF Mustangs were the single tracks from P'yongyang to Kunu-ri, Sinanju to Kunu-ri, and Wonson to Songch'on. On 1 September, two South African flights formed part of an 18th FBG fighter-bomber formation from K-16. They were led by Capt Eager and Lt van den Bos, respectively. After cutting a section of the main railway line in three places south-east of Sonch'on, the two flights split up, looking for targets of opportunity along the main supply route. Van den Bos found 300 railway wagons north of Sonch'on and, in a devastating attack, his flight destroyed 15 of these and damaged 100 others. That afternoon the Mustangs returned to this very profitable target and Capt Eager's flight destroyed six more wagons and damaged 20 others.

2/Lt M.O. Grunder led another SAAF flight of four Mustangs as part of another 18th FBG rail interdiction mission. After making three cuts on the main line mid-way between Sunch'on and Sinanju, the flight proceeded on the usual armed reconnaissance along the enemy's main supply route. Throughout the mission they came under moderate but accurate AA fire. Towards the end of the reconnaissance, Grunder who, from all accounts, was conducting a personal vendetta against AA gunners since his close friend Ian de Jongh had been shot down two days' earlier, sighted a small wooded area south of Youn-dong that he wanted to investigate further. As he flew low over the area a burst of anti-aircraft fire was seen behind his Mustang (342) and he called on the radio reporting that he thought he had been hit. Undaunted, and followed by the rest of the flight, he proceeded to rocket and strafe the AA positions, six of which were silenced. While pulling up into the sun after a strafing run, Grunder's No2, the newly arrived Maj Barry Wiggett, lost sight of his leader. Wiggett, who was soon to take command of 2SAAF, then saw the canopy from a Mustang and some papers floating down at 1,500 feet, but there was no sign of machine or parachute. A radio check-in was carried out immediately but brought no response from Grunder. On the ground the pilots noticed two fires. One was a grass fire but the other revealed a crashed aircraft. They searched the area for 20 minutes but could not find evidence of a parachute or any sign of life near the wrecked aircraft. 2/Lt Mick Grunder was posted missing. The Americans also lost a Mustang and its pilot although 2/Lt Robert Woods of the 12th FBS survived to be taken prisoner, but the crew of a B-26 of the 13th BS flown by 1/Lt Ernest C. Oliphant were not so fortunate.

Things were happening in the ground war, too. Late in August, after the truce talks had been suspended, General Ridgway ordered his forces to begin a new series of attacks east of the Iron Triangle. This was to intensify pressure on the Communists to resume the talks and to gain the strongest possible defensive positions before any agreement was finally reached for an armistice. This offensive began on 2 September. As was always the case, the most intense fighting would be for the hills dominating the deep valley called the punchbowl, about 20 miles from the east coast. US Marines concentrated on gaining control of the Punchbowl itself while the 2nd US Infantry Division, reinforced with ROK troops, attempted to secure two ranges of hills a short distance to the west. The names of these features would tell the story – Heartbreak Ridge, for which the 2nd Division would suffer 3,700 casualties, and Bloody Ridge which would cost 2,700 more. Similar limited assaults were due to begin at various points along the front to establish a UN front line of contact that the South Koreans would be able to hold securely in the future.

Shortly after noon, 22 of the 4th FIW's Sabres became embroiled with an estimated 40 MiGs in a savage dogfight that raged for 30 minutes between Sinuiju and P'yongyang. The F-86 pilots finished the fight with claims for four MiGs destroyed for the loss of 1/Lt Lawrence C. Layton of the 335th FIS, with Colonel Gabreski getting his second MiG kill, as also did the 335th FIS's Maj Winton Marshall, who had now scored on consecutive days. For Capt Richard S. Johns it was his first victory while Capt Ralph Gibson notched his fourth. Gibson had now drawn level with 334th FIS's newly promoted Capt Richard Becker. A race was on to become the USAF's second jet ace in Korea but Gibson's chances were limited. The time was looming for the 335th FIS to trade places with the 336th FIS currently in Japan. Unbelievably, in this action the Russian pilots of the 18th GuFAR claimed no fewer than seven F-86s shot down in the area of Teiju, while the 176th GuFAR claimed two more near Syukusen.

The existence of the air rescue system was good for the morale of the UN pilots. They believed that pilots landing in enemy territory would be shot on capture, especially if they fell into the hands of North Korean militia in an area where a strike had just been carried out. Detailed air rescue data, including radio frequencies and locations of air and sea rescue facilities, were given to all pilots in pre-flight briefings. When a pilot was shot down it was the flight leader's responsibility to alert air-rescue. If the leader himself went down, then the responsibility to make contact fell to his deputy. A CAP to cover the rescue would be provided to protect the downed airman from enemy troops while he was awaiting rescue. It was also the duty of the leader, or second-in-command, to guide in the rescue helicopter, or amphibian if the man had come down in the sea, and if necessary hand over the CAP to a relieving flight.

On 5 September, the pilots of 2SAAF flew a dozen rescue sorties, losing Lt van den Bos while engaged in the rescue of an American pilot. While searching for the downed American behind enemy lines north-east of Sunch'on, small-arms fire hit van den Bos' Mustang (344) in the cooling system and his engine failed at 800 feet. The South African had to force-land, and he hastily chose the bed of a shallow stream to land in. His aircraft had caught fire while still in the air but van den Bos managed to make a successful crash-landing. He did not waste any time as he leapt from the cockpit and was seen to run for cover in a nearby ditch. Two more flights led by Lt Don Parker and Lt N. Biden arrived on the scene to provide cover. This time the air rescue system worked smoothly and about 45 minutes after being shot down van den Bos was rescued by a US Navy helicopter and flown to Wonsan harbour, where he was deposited on an American landing ship. Misfortune again struck the South Africans a few hours later while making a napalm attack on a Communist artillery position in the punchbowl area. Lt Biden was killed when his aircraft (302) failed to pull out of the shallow dive on his run-in.

Another clash between Meteors and MiGs took place that afternoon, when eight aircraft from 77RAAF led by Flt Lt Joe Blyth and Flt Lt Vic Cannon set out to escort two RF-80s on a photo-recce mission of the Sinuiju area. The unarmed RF-80s had to be covered on such missions. If trouble occurred the job of the reconnaissance pilots was to dive for the deck and get the valuable photographs home while the escort held off the attackers. Two of the original eight Meteors had aborted, one with inoperative guns and the other had escorted it back to Kimpo. After two passes over the target area, one RF-80 returned to base but the other continued photographing for almost a further 20 minutes and was able to cover the railway line from Sunch'on to Ch'onju, at which time Flt Lt Cannon sighted bogies at 12 o'clock high. There appeared to be a dozen, their red noses clearly visible as they flashed over the Meteors in the later afternoon sun.

There were actually 24 MiGs altogether, the whole of the 523rd FAR led by the deputy commander, Kapt Grigorii Okhai. The MiGs had scrambled to meet the incoming USAF raid, which they had sighted flying along the coastline, out to sea. The two groups flew a parallel course, each waiting for the other to make the first move, but nothing happened. Neither side appeared willing to make the first move. As time went by, Kapt Okhai began to worry about diminishing fuel reserves and was on the verge of returning to base, when suddenly the six Meteors were spotted flying over land at a lower altitude. Okhai ordered eight of his group to remain as high cover and another eight to follow him down to provide close cover, while his own formation of eight MiGs attacked. With his formation flying in four pairs, Okhai descended quickly from about 39,000 feet to close on the Meteors. Misjudging the differences in speed, the MiG pilots found little time to take proper aim before overshooting. Their first attack was unsuccessful, as Okhai later recalled:

> "They [the Australians] had been warned, and made a circle . . . they protected each other well. Our first attack had failed. We could not succeed that way and gave the command: 'Break up right, a half-roll attack!' The manoeuvre succeeded. Commencing fire at a distance of 400 yards, I overtook one of the Meteors with a burst from my cannons. It caught fire. Tyulyaev's, Sheverev's and Razorvin's pairs each shot down one aircraft. I set fire to one more aircraft. One of the six Meteors survived. Being well-camouflaged [sic], it dived to the ground, and we lost sight of it." [1]

Of the five victories mentioned by Kapt Okhai, only three – the two claimed by Okhai and one by Kapt I. Tyulyaev – were credited to the 523rd FAR, although it was believed by the Russian pilots that the other two Meteors were probably so severely damaged that they would have possibly crashed beyond the 38th Parallel, the line which the MiG pilots were not allowed to trespass. Claims made by fighter pilots employing dive-and-climb attacks in combat, albeit sincere, were often notoriously unreliable, as was the case on this occasion. The Meteor pilots reported that after the MiGs had swooped over them from the front, they abruptly turned 180

---

[1] See *MiG-15* by Gordon and Rigmant.

degrees and dived to attack, coming down on the rear pair of Meteors flown by Flt Lt Ralph Dawson (A77-163) and Wt Off Bill Michelson (A77-726). Flt Lt Joe Blyth (A77-385) saw them coming and yelled a warning for the Australians to break starboard as hard as they could. The MiGs came in at first in well-disciplined passes, following the Meteors in pairs. Two would fire, then pull up. The second pair would fire, then pull up, the procedure repeated by the third pair. The first six then drew off and re-grouped. The first two MiGs had come in very fast and passed swiftly ahead of the two Meteors under attack. Michelson saw a fleeting chance and fired. At the same time Dawson saw two more MiGs behind them, firing at Michelson, whose aircraft was hit and he lost control. The Meteor flipped onto its back and went into a long dive – obviously the Russian pilots thought it was doomed. Michelson himself was unhurt but he could see that his tail assembly was damaged. He made no attempt to pull out too quickly or use his speed brakes. Gently, he gradually flattened out and managed to regain control of the aircraft at 10,000 feet. Besides the damage to the tail, the starboard aileron had been hit which caused the aircraft to fly right wing low. Michelson called on the radio to let the others know that he was alive and well, and was going home. He coaxed the Meteor back up to 25,000 feet and headed for Kimpo, following the coast road.

All the other Meteors came away from the fight unscathed, the encounter having lasted about five minutes, but the pilots had been given a stinging demonstration of the superiority of the MiG in speed and manoeuvrability. Particularly impressive was their rate of climb. Flt Lts Cannon, Blyth and Dawson, in addition to Wt Off Michelson, had managed to fire bursts of 20mm cannon at the fast-moving enemy jets but could claim no positive hits, although when he saw the first six MiGs draw off to re-group, Joe Blyth had observed smoke coming from one of them. He later recalled:

"We were intercepted by twelve MiGs. Bill Michelson was ahead of me and was hit after he fired a burst. Don Armit was flying No4 to me. I wasn't sure our tails were clear and, in those fleeting seconds, I let enormous targets go by, but at speed."

Back at Kimpo, Michelson landed A77-726 successfully. Cannon-fire had punched a big hole in the port tailplane, and had caused considerable splinter damage to the centre section between the port engine nacelle and the front of the rear fuselage. The starboard aileron was damaged and its tab was left hanging by just one hinge. Following a thorough inspection, the airframe was patched up and the aircraft ferried to Iwakuni next day. A77-726 would be unserviceable for combat until 6 October.

In this latest clash with MiGs, one Meteor had been severely damaged, but little harm, if any, had been inflicted on the attackers. The MiGs had enjoyed the tactical advantages of superior numbers, greater height and surprise in both encounters, and now overall superiority of their performance had been made blatantly obvious. The Meteors were simply outclassed, especially for high altitude duties. That there had not been greater carnage was a tribute to the skill of the Meteor pilots. This raised once again the question of the wisdom of the decision to replace the Mustangs with Meteors. Although it had been realised that the Meteor was inferior in performance to the MiG-15, the full extent of this inferiority had not been known in advance and, in any case, the Meteor had been the only jet fighter available to the RAAF. Wg Cdr Steege concluded, in view of these experiences, that the rôle of 77RAAF had to be modified. After discussions with Colonel Meyer, the former CO of the 4th FIW and now the new Director of Operations of the 5th Air Force, it was agreed that the Squadron would cease to fly in MiG Alley. It would continue escorting bombers and flying combat air patrols to protect fighter-bombers over North Korea, but this would be done south of the Ch'ongch'on. This was a blow to the pride of all members of 77RAAF, and in political terms to the prestige of Australia in the air war over Korea, but at the risk of undermining the confidence of the Meteor pilots, the hard decision had been made.

On the ground, after launching his offensive into the Punchbowl area, General Van Fleet planned the seizure of the Imjin salient, up to and including the first line of major hills running north-east to south-west across it. These hills were firmly held by the Chinese. Operation 'Minden', scheduled to be launched on 8 September, would be the first step of the push with the particular aim of extending the Wyoming Line across the salient, parallel to the main enemy line which lay some 28 miles further to the north-west. The central sector of the Commonwealth Division's new front line would then be five miles north-west of the Imjin-Hantan junction. On the night of 5/6 September, it seemed that the enemy might pre-empt the attack when a large group of Chinese troops surrounded a company of the 5th US Cavalry on the north side of the Imjin and inflicted heavy losses on the Americans, and a company base of the 7th US Cavalry that was not far away was also attacked by the Chinese that night and forced to withdraw with heavy losses. Prospects of a major clash increased when several Chinese patrols of platoon strength were detected within the objective area on 6 September. In the morning, while flying the 1903 AOP Flight's first sortie over the Commonwealth Division's front, Capt Leslie Addington spotted three enemy tanks. He called for an air strike with napalm and rockets. Shortly thereafter he was relieved by Capt Derek Jarvis in another Auster, who brought in a second strike. This missed the target, however. Enemy movements continued throughout the day and later Capt Stewart-Cox, flying a further AOP sortie, sighted about 300 enemy soldiers moving across the area in a north-westerly direction. He called two batteries of artillery to engage them, and radioed adjustments as the enemy shifted to the west. He, in turn, was relieved by Capt Fitzgibbon who continued to correct fire until the enemy troops at last dispersed into scrub and broken country. The AOP pilots had proved their worth.

Meanwhile, two Meteors of the alert section at Kimpo were scrambled to intercept an unidentified aircraft. It was standard practice to have a pair of Meteors ready for such an action because of their fast-climbing capability, their initial climb rate being higher than that of the F-86s, but on this occasion there was a delay when Flt Lt Des Murphy's aircraft (A77-734) proved difficult to start. Once airborne, Murphy and his No2, Sgt Keith Meggs (A77-446) were vectored to intercept various aircraft which turned out to be three AT-6s, a C-46, a C-54, and an F7F Tigercat – all of them friendly. On another alert scramble, Flt Lt Scannell (A77-982) and his No2 intercepted two F-51s near Sibydong-ni.

When Operation 'Minden' finally got under way, the Chinese responded quickly with both infantry counter-attacks and artillery bombardments. Their artillery fire proved highly accurate and the Australians of the 28th Brigade of the Commonwealth Division had to dig in thoroughly to escape injury. On the afternoon of 8 September, one company was driven off a small hill in the objective area of their intended advance of the previous night. Heavy mortar, artillery and small-arms fire killed two Australians and wounded four others. For the next three days patrols were busily engaged in contesting with the Chinese in the area until relieved by 25th Brigade units, and eventually were able to reach their objectives on the new Wyoming Line by the evening of 12 September, fortunately for relatively few casualties. The Commonwealth Division's HQ was moved forward to a position just south of the Imjin and a new Divisional airstrip was needed. It was constructed in the paddy fields by Canadian sappers but, before it could be occupied, the area had to be dried out. This was done by burning the surface with napalm. The resulting airstrip, named Fort George, became acclaimed by all of the UN's light aircraft pilots as the best in Korea. 1903 AOP Flight relocated there on the 12th. In all, during the month, the Flight would perform 41 air shoots and flew a creditable 215 sorties.

Twelve Meteors of 77RAAF led by Sqn Ldr Wilson provided escort for B-29s bombing Sunan airfield on 8 September. The Australians did not meet any enemy fighters on this occasion, and therefore had an opportunity to observe the bombing attack, and were impressed by the accuracy of the American bombing. Three good bomb patterns were seen, one on each end of the airstrip and the third in the middle. Moderate flak was encountered but it was inaccurate and directed only at the bombers.

In air-to-air combat on 8 and 9 September, the MiG pilots used their superior numbers and employed tactics that had not previously been seen over Korea. They flew in groups of seven, eight or perhaps more – two pairs in each group – sometimes stepped up, sometimes stepped down. The Americans dubbed them "bandit trains", and often two such formations would cross the Yalu at altitudes above 35,000 feet and perhaps 40 miles apart. If they spotted Sabre patrols the MiG leader would send sections down to engage, while the others would fly south to a point high up above P'yongyang. Here they would re-form before heading back north. For them to venture as far south as P'yongyang was a sign of the enemy's increasing confidence in their superiority. On the homeward track they would engage any Sabres they found, again on their own terms and, as they neared the Yalu, a third group of MiGs would fly across to cover the withdrawal of those returning. New methods of attack were used too. Some MiGs attacked in trail formation. Others would circle, maintaining their height advantage, while waiting to make diving passes at UN aircraft which came within range. After diving at an opportune moment and making firing passes, the MiGs would zoom back upstairs. In one encounter four flights of MiGs flew line-abreast in head-on passes, all 16 aircraft blazing at a single Sabre. Colonel Gabreski, who was an expert on tactics used by the Luftwaffe in WWII, recognised that the Communists were employing a technique that the Germans had used against American bomber formations in the air war over Europe. In the heavy clash that took place on the afternoon of 9 September, 28 Sabres became embroiled in a fight with an estimated 70 MiGs. It was in this air battle that the race to be the USAF's second jet ace was settled. Captain Richard Becker of the 334th FIS and Captain Ralph Gibson of the 335th FIS each claimed, thus becoming the second and third American jet air aces of the Korean conflict. Considering the odds being stacked against them, the Sabres were still managing to give a good account of themselves. Nonetheless, the Russian pilots claimed seven F-86s shot down, two by the 196th FAR in the Anju-Teisen region, one by the 523rd FAR near Hakusen, two by the 176th GuFAR near Teisen, and two by the 17th FAR near Anju, one of these possibly falling to the commander of the 303rd FAD, Lt-General Georgii Lobov.

American rescue helicopters had to be alerted when Capt Dormie Barlow of 2SAAF suffered engine failure and was forced to bale out of his aircraft about 20 minutes after take-off. The abandoned Mustang (352) crashed just below the South African pilot as he floated down, and the resulting explosion of its bomb load caused his parachute to partially collapse. Barlow crashed heavily to earth and was knocked unconscious. When he recovered his senses, he was alarmed to find he was surrounded by a crowd of curious Koreans. Fortunately, they were friendly as he had come down on the Allied side of the lines. A rescue helicopter arrived promptly and flew him to hospital, where he was treated for a back injury. Meanwhile at Kimpo, the two readiness Meteors manned by Flt Lt Des Murphy and Sgt Bob Strawbridge were scrambled and vectored onto four unidentified aircraft near Hweangju. They made a non-firing pass and identified the bogies as American F-51s. They were then directed to the East Central Front to investigate more unidentified aircraft, only to find several L-5s operating near Kumsong. The identity of these was reported to the controller, who warned that Yak-type aircraft were reported to be in the vicinity. Unfortunately for the now-eager Meteor pilots no Yaks were sighted and, low on fuel, they returned disappointed to Kimpo. Shortly afterwards, another pair of Meteors were scrambled and once airborne the pilots contacted a forward GCI post. Flt Lt Cannon and Sgt Vance Drummond, a New Zealander serving with the RAAF, were vectored to just south of P'yongyang, and then south from there to Uijongbu and Seoul, but in these areas only friendly aircraft were intercepted: several L-5s, one C-54, two F4U Corsairs, one Mustang, and one F-80.

The evening fighter sweep for 77RAAF was cancelled, so two sections of four Meteors were detailed to find targets of opportunity on the main supply routes into P'yongyang. The second flight, led by Flt Lt Scannell, strafed and destroyed a building which exploded and probably wrecked a jeep located nearby. Shortly afterwards, they strafed and destroyed two pairs of trucks in two different locations. Throughout the area they encountered heavy concentrations of intense, accurate automatic-gunfire although no Meteors were hit. While the first flight led by Sqn Ldr Wilson (A77-15) was patrolling a road, a truck convoy was spotted. After one pass at the target, Wilson decided on another despite encountering severe AA and small-arms fire. During the second pass, an armour-piercing incendiary shell went through the front fuselage of Wilson's aircraft, immediately below the base of the windscreen, and disintegrated, wounding him in the arm. He radioed that he had been hit. The formation broke and returned to Kimpo where Wilson landed safely. He had suffered about 50 small shrapnel wounds on the right forearm and the fleshy part of the shoulder, and recalled:

"I was leading in A77-15 when I saw something suspicious under trees beside the road and turned to dive on it. At a height of about 1,000 feet I was hit by anti-aircraft fire. A projectile, not larger than 20mm, punched a neat hole in the port side (of the cockpit) just forward of the throttle quadrant and burst against the starboard side just below shoulder height. The shell broke into small fragments but one sizeable piece went though my right bicep, missing the bone and artery. Many small fragments lodged in my upper right arm, the back of both hands and a piece hit my left leg. I was wearing a Mae West over an escape waistcoat and these two items soaked up all the fragments that might have hit my body. I did not lose the use of my right hand. I turned for home and transmitted a 'May Day' which is when I discovered that a shell fragment had removed the transmit button from the throttle lever. When I put my thumb on the throttle it encountered bare wires and I got a mild shock. However, the radio still worked. I returned to base, landed and taxied to dispersal where an airman jumped up on the wing to help me from the cockpit. He grabbed my right arm, got a handful of blood and almost fainted.

After first aid by the MO, Mike Kater[2], I was taken by American ambulance, driven by a negro, to the US Army hospital in Seoul. That trip was the most terrifying part of the day. In Seoul the fragment was removed from my left leg. The next day I was taken by RAAF Medivac Dakota to Iwakuni, and thence to the British hospital at Kure. The following day my right arm was cleaned up – I think the term is debrided – but no attempt was made to fish for the tiny pieces. After a couple of days I was discharged to Iwakuni." [3]

Alarming gaps were beginning to appear in the meagre F-86 screen and through sheer weight of numbers, the MiGs were starting to break through with relative ease. On 10 September near Sukch'on, F-84s of the 8th FBS on a rail cutting bombing mission were bounced by six MiGs. The American flight leader, 1/Lt William Skliar, ordered his aircraft to turn into the attack and, as one of the Russian jets crossed his path, Skliar was able to fire several bursts at close to maximum range, claiming a probable kill. Soviet pilots participated in several air combats during the day and claimed a total of ten UN aircraft – three F-86s and five F-84s being credited to the 523rd FAR, while one F-80 and one Meteor were claimed by the 176th GuFAR, the latter awarded to Kapt Grigorii Ges. Australian records show that while one Meteor was damaged on this date, it had nothing to do with air combat. At Kimpo, a 77RAAF NCO had requested a trip in a two-seater Meteor T7 prior to his departure for Australia, and Sgt Don Armit was granted permission to arrange a flight in A77-305. They had been airborne for thirty minutes and were flying east of Seoul when the hood suddenly blew off. The Meteor returned to Kimpo, where the passenger admitted that he might have grabbed the hood opening handle during a turn, although inspection of the aircraft revealed that the hood-jettison release had not been operated.

Next day, a dozen Meteors provided close escort for B-29s detailed to bomb marshalling yards at Sinanju. The bombers, which were running a few minutes late, were met at the rendezvous and escorted over the target without incident. Bombing results appeared to be good. Two minutes after the bombers left the target, someone warned "Swept-wing bogies at 3 o'clock high". The unidentified fighters made a diving pass between the escorting Meteors and the bombers, while the Australian pilots ranged and tracked them, ready to open fire. When they were about 300 yards away they were recognised, with some relief, as American Sabres. The remainder of the trip was uneventful. The MiGs were active, however, pilots of the 523rd FAR meeting F-80s near Jyungsen, two of which were claimed shot down, one reportedly crashing near Ryuto-kuri, and the other about ten miles south-east of Jyungsen. The Americans admitted the loss of 1/Lt Sterling J. Bushroe of the 35th FBS, who was killed. The 176th

---

[2] Sqn Ldr Mike Kater MC, 77RAAF's Senior Medical Officer, was a unique and courageous character. During WWII, in New Guinea, he went absent without leave from the RAAF and disappeared into the jungle with the army. The RAAF intended to court-martial him, but when it was discovered that the audacious doctor had been awarded a Military Cross for his work while among the troops, the charge was dropped. En route to Korea he landed at Iwakuni AFB aboard a DC-4 wearing jungle greens and carrying a rifle. His unorthodox ways endeared him to those who had the privilege of knowing him, and his reputation as a surgeon in Korea was second-to-none.

[3] See *Odd Jobs*.

GuFAR also reported a clash with US fighter-bombers near Teiju, Kapt Mikhail Ponomorev alone claiming four F-84s shot down of which two apparently blew up in mid-air.

Despite the growing MiG threat, Operation 'Strangle' continued unabated with day and night pressure being exerted on the enemy, but it was starting to become costly. At first light on 12 September, Capt Frank Montanari of 2SAAF led an armed reconnaissance mission to P'yongyang. Nearing the target, the South Africans found the area enveloped in heavy cloud. Capt Montanari spotted several gaps and ordered his pilots to patrol the area while he went down low to reconnoitre a road. He ran into heavy flak and his aircraft was hit. Lt Ron Beamish, flying No2, saw Montanari's crippled Mustang (351) streaming glycol as it pulled up from the road, following which it crash-landed in a river-bed where it disintegrated on impact. There was little chance of the pilot surviving and the heavy flak prevented the remaining Mustang pilots from making a close inspection of the wreckage.

The MiG threat was growing alarmingly. On the approach of a force of F-80s and F-84s in the Anju area, the two FADs scrambled no fewer than 80 MiGs according to Lt-General Lobov:

"... we flew in such strength very seldom. Between Anju and P'yongyang, the MiG-15s intercepted several groups of fighter-bombers (up to 150 F-80s) that were attacking various targets while in visual contact with each other. Since the enemy had no fighter cover, the MiGs came down directly on the F-80s. The fighter-bombers ceased the strafing mission and engaged in air combat, but since they lost 15 aircraft within a few minutes, they turned back to their bases. The MiG-15s returned to their airfields uneventfully. Only three MiG-15s sustained minor damage. The strafing operation was frustrated." [4]

The Russian pilots in fact submitted claims for three F-80s by the 196th FAR and five by the 17th FAR, while two F-84s were also claimed shot down, one by a pilot of the 196th FAR, and another by a pilot of the 523rd FAR. This raised the tally of MiG claims for the month to a staggering 47.

That night, as usual, B-26s continued with their intruder missions. One aircraft flown by Capt John S. Walmsley of the 8th BS carried an experimental 80-million-candlepower searchlight with which to illuminate targets. The searchlight was the size of an external fuel tank. Despite being specifically adapted for the purpose, not all B-26 pilots were convinced that a searchlight offered any improvement over flares to attack enemy convoys and troop movements at night and although it offered excellent illumination over target, it was cumbersome and caused considerable drag reducing the aircraft's speed and range. There were other faults. Some lights caught fire and had to be jettisoned, while others snapped off their fixing brackets. On this occasion, when near the North Korean town of Hwangju, Walmsley and his crew found a convoy and halted it by bombing. The searchlight was then turned on and used to illuminate the enemy troops in stark relief while the B-26 repeatedly overflew the stalled convoy. Using fragmentation bombs and gunfire, the crew claimed the destruction of at least 16 trucks. Two nights later Walmsley and his crew were shot down whilst carrying out another similar operation, only his gunner surviving to be taken prisoner. For his courage and determination, Capt Walmsley was posthumously awarded the Congressional Medal of Honor. Not long after this, such operations were deemed to be impractical and the use of aircraft-mounted searchlights was abandoned.

On 13 September, USMC fliers of the newly arrived HMR-161 carried out Operation 'Windmill 1', the first-ever mass helicopter re-supply mission. US Marines were attacking northwards along the ridge system and had become involved in heavy fighting. Although making use of some 400 Korean porters, they simply could not keep up with the demands for ammunition and the need to evacuate so many casualties. HMR-161 was called in to fill the supply and evacuation gap. The unit's new Sikorsky HRS-1 helicopter could lift four to six troops with combat equipment, or up to 1,500-lb of cargo, or three to five casualties in litters. A follow-up operation named 'Windmill 2' a few days later saw ten helicopters carry out 18 flights during which a total of in excess of 12,000-lb of supplies were successfully transported.

---

[4] See *MiG-15* by Gordon and Rigmant.

These two operations proved highly successful and the HRS-1 was subsequently seen as an exceedingly practical, much-prized tool by USMC ground commanders.

That same day Flt Lt Des Murphy led a dozen Meteors to provide close-escort for B-29s bombing a railway bridge. The target was straddled with explosions but the results of the attack could not be positively determined due to smoke, dust and haze. No enemy fighters interfered with the raid, during which Flt Lt Scannell clocked up his 50th operational sortie in Korea. The MiGs were busy elsewhere, however. They broke through to the fighter-bombers again and found a flight of F-51s of the 39th FIS on a rail-cutting mission near Sambong-dong. Three of the Mustangs had already started their wing-overs to bomb the railroad tracks when, as he dived, the leader spotted three incoming MiGs from the 17th FAR and transmitted a warning to break, but 2/Lt William E. Jackson may have been either too occupied in locating his target or perhaps his radio had failed. He did not acknowledge the call to break and was jumped from behind and shot into the mud flats below. The Russian pilots reported that one Mustang blew up in mid-air and that the pilot's effects, but not the pilot, were later recovered, and that a second crashed near Nammen. It was a bad day for the Americans since, apart from the loss of 2/Lt Jackson, a second Mustang was lost when 1/Lt Leland H. Wolf's 67th FBS aircraft was seen to crash. An LT-6 spotter aircraft of the 6148th TAC Squadron flown by 1/Lt Alvin E. Crane Jr which dropped down to investigate was also shot down, as was a rescue helicopter. All four airmen were reported missing.

With all available B-26s engaged on night interdiction, the 3rd and 452nd BGs were credited with the destruction of 2,362 enemy vehicles, plus damage to 4,959 others between 25 August and 15 September. The increased results were attributed to the fact that light bomber/intruder units were putting all of their efforts into night interdiction. Although many vehicles were claimed destroyed, many others were undoubtedly getting through with their valuable cargoes. To achieve even greater success, and to have a chance of really choking the enemy's supplies, General Weyland needed more intruder-bombers. He argued that if the USAF could not increase aircraft allocations to the 3rd and 452nd BGs, then he recommended that the 126th Light Bombardment Wing, which was currently training in the United States for deployment to Europe, be given to him on loan. He promised that, when the Korean War was over, he would deploy to Europe a light bomber wing that was fully trained and combat ready.

By mid-September, when the latest 'Strangle' operations were nearly a month old and seemed eminently successful, General Weyland began to develop a relationship between the day fighter-bomber rail-cutting missions and the night-intruder operations. By now, the railway interdiction attacks had effectively reduced the main line system to single track. But what really alarmed the General were the latest developments in the air war that were posing a serious threat to the continuing successes of 'Strangle', and he candidly warned General Vandenberg that the MiGs were now hampering UN air-to-ground attacks as far southward as P'yongyang. He stated that the FEAF had a "vital and immediate" requirement for another wing of F-86s. If the USAF could not provide the wing, he recommended that one of the FEAF's F-80 wings should be converted to F-86s, and further warned:

"If the present trend continues, there is a definite possibility that the enemy will be able to establish bases in Korea and threaten our supremacy over the front lines . . ."

Lt Jan de Wet led a four-aircraft flight from 2SAAF as part of an 18th FBG railroad bombing mission on 15 September, but Lt Ron Beamish's aircraft developed an oil leak, so he aborted and headed back with Lt Lamb escorting. Along the way they dropped their butterfly bombs on Sinch'on in an attempt to silence anti-aircraft fire from a position in the village. Lt de Wet and Lt McLeod meanwhile achieved one rail cut in their allocated target area but could not follow this up with the usual armed reconnaissance along the enemy's supply lines because of cloud cover over the interior of North Korea.

Flt Lt Des Murphy led a dozen Meteors on another close-escort mission for the B-29s on 18 September, on this occasion accompanied by a two-seat Meteor T7 (A77-229) flown by Flt Lt Joe Blyth, which was carrying a US Army photographer, Sgt Gramstead, in the back seat. The whole mission went smoothly, the Meteors meeting the bombers at the rendezvous and escorting them to the target which was bombed through cloud using radar. There was no interference from enemy fighters. The B-29s were escorted to the west coast before the Meteors left them to return to Kimpo. Of these B-29 escort missions, Flt Lt Scannell later reported:

> "At the bombers' request, we had to fly a close-escort at 1,000 to 3,000 feet above the formation, and the fighters would weave in pairs or fours. The first sections would weave 3,000 to 5,000 yards in front of the formation, the second immediately above, and the last 2,000 yards to the rear. We did not like this cover at all and we frequently requested that we should fly an area cover 10,000 feet above and to the rear of the formation. The bombers would not agree to this and said that although they agreed that we would not be able to do much about stopping an attack, the morale value of having some fighters above and in sight of the bomber crews was more important."

Next day, the pilots of 77RAAF saw about 40 MiGs above them while on a fighter sweep near Anju, a town on the Ch'ongch'on. The MiGs did not usually come further south in strength than the line of the Ch'ongch'on, up to where the Australian jets had been cleared to operate, but the enemy was becoming increasingly bold. There were again twelve Meteors, in three sections of four, led respectively by Flt Lt Murphy, Flt Lt Thomas and Flg Off Thornton, plus two more Meteors further back, at 30,000 feet, acting as an airborne relay between these flights and GCI. It looked as though they might be jumped at any minute and the Australians remained alert, ready to break as soon as the call came – but this time the MiGs found other targets. A straight-wing jet, which they thought was probably an F-84, was seen smoking and burning, and soon after a parachute was observed opening. Then to the north they saw another aircraft falling in flames. Over the radio, the Australians heard American voices yelling warnings followed by bellowed instructions as they came under attack. It transpired that they were USMC F9F pilots, but the Meteors were not in a position to help. The Russian pilots were apparently from the 523rd FAR, and claimed their victims as F-86s, both of which were reported to have crashed into the sea.

Other MiGs did in fact encounter bomb-carrying F-84s of the 49th FBG up from K-2 on their way to attack a rail complex between Sinanju and P'yongyang. The American pilots had been listening to the FAC warning of "MiG trains heading south". When they saw the MiGs at one o'clock high however, they assumed that the escorting F-86s would be in a position to intercept – but they were not. Amid the increasing radio chatter came the order to jettison the bombs, pick up speed and break. Capt Kenneth L. Skeen of the 9th FBS saw a section of MiGs overshoot an attack on his leader, allowing him to open fire. He saw pieces fly off the enemy jet, accompanied by smoke and flames, before it disappeared into the thin undercast. For an instant his attention was drawn to another MiG on his left, and when he looked back to his right he saw a parachute descending and the rest of the sky deserted. All the F-84s returned safely to base, with only one aircraft showing signs of damage, and on the strength of the sighting of the parachute, Skeen was credited with a kill. Their opponents were also from the 523rd FAR, no fewer than six F-84s being claimed shot down, three of which were credited to the Regiment's commander, Podpolkovnik A.N. Karasyov. One of his victims was reported to have crashed a few miles west of Jyunan, a second west of Sensen, and the third north-east of Syanjinjio. The other three were reported down west of Syuksen, south-east of Jyungsen, with another falling into the sea. The MiGs had scored a tactical success, having forced the fighter-bombers to jettison their bomb loads and abandon the rail-cutting mission. Meanwhile, Capt Bob Rogers of 2SAAF led two flights of Mustangs as part of a 18th FBG raid on a railway bridge south of Sinanju. The attack went off as planned and afterwards Rogers led his flights southwards to reconnoitre the main supply route. Farther south, he happened upon 150 railway wagons, and the South African pilots attacked these until they had used up all of their ammunition but only made a modest claim of two wagons destroyed and 50 damaged.

The work of 77RAAF was currently being scrutinised by the AOC of the Air Component of the BCOF, Air Vice-Marshal Bouchier, who sent a report of his findings to the RAF Chief-of-Staff:

> "Following is the gist of my purely personal investigations carried out privately with Wg Cdr Steege, who commands 77 Squadron, and two flight commanders: Flt Lt Murphy, who

is Australian, and Flt Lt Scannell, who is an RAF officer and the head of the original team of three officers and one NCO pilot who came here from England in February last to convert this Australian squadron from Mustangs to Meteors.

Flt Lt Scannell of Eastern Sector of Fighter Command and Flt Lt Blyth of Training Command are the two remaining members of the team. I saw only Flt Lt Scannell. In the absence of Sqn Ldr Wilson (wounded), I judged Scannell to be the best pilot in the Squadron and his morale is high. He says he can shoot down a MiG-15 and very much wants to remain with the Squadron to complete a full tour. I strongly recommend that Scannell should immediately be authorised to stay with this Squadron, and Blyth also, if the latter volunteers.[5]

Wg Cdr Steege appears to be an excellent officer but understand he does not fly regularly, if at all, with the Squadron. He is emphatic and loud in his statements that the Meteor is hopelessly outclassed by the MiG-15 in air-to-air fighting. This attitude, which of course does not help morale, is however largely governed by his natural desire to prevent his Squadron from being badly beaten and decimated, with relatively so few Meteor aircraft behind him and with his present difficulty in getting replacement pilots from Australia. I asked Wg Cdr Steege what his reactions would be if we could send him some hand-picked experienced jet fighter pilots from England. He said he would welcome them."

The question raised in the final paragraph of Bouchier's signal brought the following weak response from the Deputy Chief-of-Staff:

"I think it would be most impolite to do so unless asked. We might perhaps ask for a few vacancies in the Squadron for RAF pilots as a favour, on the grounds that we would like our chaps to get practical operational experience on Meteors, but even that would have to be handled very carefully to avoid giving offence."

At the same time as Wg Cdr Steege was airing his views on the Meteor's performance, the Australian Minister for Air, Mr William McMahon, was announcing:

"It is perfectly true to say that the Russian MiG has a slight superiority over the Meteor in speed when flying on the level and is somewhat faster still in a dive. In other respects such as manoeuvrability the Meteor is better than the MiG . . . in dogfights they are superior to the Russian machine."

Years later, Wg Cdr Steege expanded his opinions:

"The Meteor was purchased for the RAAF for the air-to-air rôle, but you didn't have to be a Rhodes scholar to know that it just wasn't going to cope with the MiG-15. I was quite convinced of the aircraft's inadequacies before it went into operations, but of course my opinion wasn't well received by either Air Force Headquarters in Melbourne or the Royal Air Force representatives who naturally had their own ideas about the value of the British aeroplane. But the critical difference was that the RAF intended using it as a bomber interceptor, not for air combat, and it was suitable for the defence of the UK in those days. But to put it into air-to-air operations against the MiG in Korea was just asking for an entire squadron to get knocked off." [6]

On the subject of MiG supremacy, General Vandenberg brought bad news from Washington to General Weyland next day. The USAF could neither provide nor support additional F-86 squadrons in Korea. Vandenberg had been told that no more Sabres could be sent without seriously hampering the effectiveness of the US Air Defence Command and that even the present capability of supporting one Sabre wing in FEAF was questionable. An ability to support two did not exist. Aside from its inability to provide and support more Sabres in combat, the USAF Director of Operations felt that no number of additional fighter units could

---

[5] The RAF Mission's other pilot, Flt Lt Frank Easley, was about to return to the UK on domestic business; he did not go back to Korea.

[6] See *Odd Jobs*.

assure air superiority in Korea unless the source of the enemy's air supplies could be attacked. These could not because they were located safely across the Yalu in Manchuria. Likewise, Vandenberg also reported that the USAF would not, nor could not, provide or support the deployment of additional B-26s in Korea either. General Weyland had no choice but to make do with what he had. Hamstrung in this way, Weyland's gloomy predictions now loomed as imminent reality. If the additional tools to finish the job were not forthcoming, he feared whether the impetus of 'Strangle' could be maintained, particularly if the fighter-bombers could not be properly safeguarded. Because of the shortage of covering Sabres, the 5th Air Force had little choice but to call a halt to fighter-bomber interdiction in the MiG Alley area. Operation 'Strangle' was itself being strangled.

As well as the threats posed by enemy fighters and the increasing volume of flak, there were other hazards the fighter-bombers faced. 2SAAF was building a fine reputation for precision in its low-level attacks but there was a price to be paid for increased accuracy. On 20 September, 2/Lt Tom Sivertsen led a glide-bombing attack against a railway yard between Ch'onju and Sinanju. The Mustangs were carrying GP bombs with eight-second delay fuses. To make sure of hitting his target, Sivertsen delayed releasing his bombs as he came in low and flew into a mass of black earth and debris thrown up by an exploding bomb dropped from another aircraft. The undercarriage, tailplane and canopy of his Mustang (357) were badly damaged and its engine began to run roughly. He was escorted back to K-16 by a flight of American F-51s. On arrival, the airfield was cleared for him to make an emergency landing but, while turning onto his final approach, the Mustang became increasingly difficult to control and then suddenly lost power. It struck the ground at high speed before reaching the runway. Fortunately for the pilot, his most serious injuries were lacerations to the forehead. Later that day, three flights of Meteors led by Flt Lt Vic Cannon carried out a fighter sweep in the Anju area. Two other Meteors acted as relays. Eight MiGs were sighted heading south about 20 miles south-east of Anju, and another group of eight was seen just to the north of Anju also travelling south. Both groups of enemy jets were well above the Meteors but they did not attempt to make any attacks, apparently having sighted a formation of F-80s near Pengwon, three of which were claimed shot down by pilots of the 18th GuFAR. Elsewhere, an F-86 was claimed near Syukusen by the 176th GuFAR.

MiGs were as active two days later, as recalled by Sqn Ldr Dick Cresswell, 77RAAF's former CO, who was now flying a short tour with the 336th FIS as a guest of the US Government before returning to Australia:

> "I did not have enough time on the Sabre to be really happy with it. You need about 30 hours on type to really feel comfortable with an aircraft – to be really competent. We took off at 1425 and I was up one hour 20 minutes in F-86A [FU-210]. It was my 115th mission in Korea. We were 22 F-86s going up to Sinanju. Twelve MiGs jumped us. I spun and lost contact with my No1."

Two of the F-86s were claimed by MiG pilots, one being credited to the 523rd FAR, which reportedly crashed about ten miles south-west of Deeguan-dong, the other near Hakusen by a pilot of the 17th FAR. Sqn Ldr Cresswell also recalled an attempt to deal with the high-flying MiGs:

> "On one occasion the CO of the Wing and myself decided to try our own bouncing technique. We decided to climb to 47,000 feet, which you could do in the Sabre but only just. We took off behind the 16 Sabres going up towards MiG Alley in their shadow so no radar could pick us up. We climbed and climbed. The idea was that if the MiGs came across we'd go right through them from above and break them up, but my cockpit exploded and I lost the canopy. I got explosive decompression. Boy, that hurts. Although I had a G-suit on, it's a shocking thing. I was bleeding from my nose and ears, fortunately just a slight rupture of various bits and pieces. We got down pretty quickly and flew back home then and landed. I was flying again two days later. It might have been a good idea but my cockpit exploding may have stopped the Yanks trying that sort of thing again. They might have tried it again later. I don't know."

Meanwhile, a dozen Meteors were tasked to provide a close-escort for B-29s. One of the two-seat Meteors, A77-229, on this occasion flown by Sgt Keith Meggs, accompanied the escort again carrying US Army photographer Sgt Gramstead. The bombers were met at the rendezvous point and escorted to the target, which was bombed through cloud. Some moderate and inaccurate heavy flak was seen over the target from 22,000 to 26,000 feet. Shortly afterwards, GCI reported that MiGs had been despatched to intercept the bombers and they were waiting south of Anju. The Meteor pilots searched the sky but enemy aircraft were nowhere to be seen. They escorted the bombers all the way to Korea's west coast where the bomber leader finally dismissed the fighters. The mission had been a long and nervous one, and by now the Meteors were running low on fuel. Two aircraft, A77-189 flown by Flt Lt Joe Blyth and A77-385 (Sgt Allan Avery) diverted and landed at K-13. Blyth was able to return to Kimpo after refuelling but Avery had to remain overnight due to a minor electrical fault with his aircraft.

At Kimpo there was more drama. As Sgt Vic Oborn touched down in A77-616, the Meteor's starboard undercarriage leg collapsed, resulting in the aircraft swinging off the runway and it came to rest within a few feet of the GCA tent. This incident was humorously depicted in a drawing by the Squadron artist, Flt Sgt Bill Middlemiss. The cartoon showed two Americans hurriedly evacuating the GCA tent with one yelling to the other, "Hey, that blip is fair dinkum." When a crane lifted the aircraft the undercarriage was tested. It functioned properly, so it was assumed that the pilot, almost out of fuel and naturally in haste to land, had not allowed sufficient time for the undercarriage to lock down. The decision was taken not to repair the aircraft at Kimpo and it was partly dismantled and eventually transported by road to the port of Inch'on. When finally it reached Iwakuni it was found that the centre section port lower longeron had been badly damaged. A77-616 was fully operational again by the third week of November.

22 September also proved to be another bad day for the 18th FBG, with three Mustangs being shot down by ground fire. Both 1/Lt George Coyle of the 67th FBS and 1/Lt Orval Tandy of the 39th FIS baled out and were captured, while Capt James Moore of the 67th FBS crash-landed his damaged machine. Although suffering burns, he reached friendly territory. This brought the Group's losses to 12 aircraft for the month, four of which were attributable to accidents. Although the 45th TRS did not suffer any losses during the month, six of its RF-51s returned with battle damage. Next day it was the F-80s that suffered losses to ground fire, 2/Lt Lewis F. Pleiss of the 25th FIS and 1/Lt William A. Pugh of the 36th FBS both failing to return.

Nuisance raids by the slow North Korean Po-2 biplanes were to be expected during the full moon period and, on the night of 22/23 September, Kimpo received a visit shortly after midnight. Meteor A77-510 was parked with some Sabres when a fragmentation bomb exploded nearby but the resulting damage was only minor when a piece of shrapnel cut through the starboard side of the rear fuselage and travelled on through the fillet of the starboard wingroot. A prowling USMC Tigercat of VMF(N)-513 flown by Maj Eugene A. van Grundy and M/Sgt T.H. Ullom was up that night too. The radar operator was successful in making a contact, allowing his pilot to shoot down the Po-2 responsible for the attack, or possibly another, the biplane crashing in flames.

On 25 September, a routine USAF reconnaissance flight just north of the lower reaches of the Ch'ongch'on made a discovery that caused alarm. Three major airfields that were obviously capable of taking jet fighters were being prepared near Taech'on, Saamcham and Namsi, within 20 miles of each other. Up to this point, the only airfields in North Korea which the Communists were able to use regularly were those in the Sinuiju-Uiju complex on the Yalu. It appeared that this new airfield complex could be part of a strategy to extend the border of MiG Alley southwards to P'yongyang. The new airfields were situated sufficiently close to each other to be able to be defended by a single force of MiGs. Work appeared to be well advanced, almost ready for the one-and-a-third-mile long runways to be surfaced. Once they were in use, they could prove just as difficult to attack as the Sinuiju-Uiju complex. Clearly there was a high priority to render them unusable and to keep them that way but, while plans were being made for the launching of B-29 attacks, the F-86s had to prevent the MiGs from establishing air superiority over the new bases. The new airfields were intended as advance bases for the Chinese MiG units now being pushed into battle, Mao having ordered the CCAF to participate more fully in the war. As a result, MiGs of the Chinese 4th FAR had deployed to Langtou on 20 September, and two days later the advance echelon reached Antung.

In heavy aerial fighting next day (25 September), the Sabres met some of the Chinese MiGs during a combat when five were claimed destroyed. Maj Richard Creighton of the 336th FIS claimed his second kill, but honours that day went to the pilots of the 334th FIS with 1/Lt Booth T. Holker claiming two, 1/Lt Charles F. Loyd one, and the fifth shared by 1/Lts Paul E. Roach and Marshall F. Babb. In return, three F-86s were claimed by the Russian pilots who accompanied the Chinese MiGs, one of which was reported to have crashed near Son-Hang after a fight with the 17th FAR; a second Sabre allegedly blew up in mid-air during combat with the 523rd FAR, the third being credited to the 196th FAR. A Chinese pilot also claimed an F-86 shot down but one of the Chinese MiGs was lost. In 'Strangle' operations during the day, Lt Jan de Wet led four aircraft from 2SAAF on a railroad interdiction mission. The South Africans obtained two complete rail cuts in their allotted target area and during the subsequent recce from Ch'unghwa to Singye, some ox-carts were attacked. Four were destroyed by strafing but as de Wet pressed his attack home, one ox-cart exploded violently. The debris thrown up smashed his canopy and fragments cut his face, although he was able to return to K-16 and land safely.

According to Communist sources, the MiGs beat back two major air attacks by UN aircraft on the 26th. These raids were intercepted by the 303rd and 324th FADs and this time Meteors took part in the fighting without suffering any losses. The Russian pilots claimed ten UN aircraft destroyed, the kills being registered as four F-86s, three F-84s, one F-80 and two Meteors, the latter claimed by St/Lt Nikolai Sutyagin (his ninth victory, making him the leading ace in Korea on either side) and St/Lt Ivan Yakovlev (his third or fourth victory) from the 523rd FAR. No Meteors were actually lost although one was damaged in this combat. 77RAAF's records show that a dozen Meteors led by Flt Lt Vic Cannon had been given the task of escorting B-29s raiding P'yongyang. After take-off, the controller ordered them to abandon this mission and instead fly a fighter sweep over Anju. They were over Anju by 0940 and were immediately attacked by fifteen MiGs. Before the first break was called, Sgt Don Armit's aircraft (A77-949) was hit from behind. Armit tested his controls. There was no change in the flying characteristics of the aircraft so he continued to support his section leader Plt Off Ray Trebilco while the flight weathered several clashes with MiGs fighting in pairs. As the dogfight continued, a pair of MiGs dived down past the flight led by Flt Lt Cedric Thomas (A77-959) but at the same time another pair came in making a head-on firing pass. The Meteors returned fire without any obvious results before the MiGs sped by. Thomas and his No2, Sgt Vic Oborn (A77-373), saw another pair of MiGs and started a firing pass on the leader. The MiGs reacted quickly and broke, but in different directions. While the leader broke towards the Yalu, his wingman made the mistake of breaking in the opposite direction. This aircraft was singled out by Thomas and Oborn. Just to the west of P'yongyang the MiG pilot tried to turn back towards the north but found the two Meteors blocking his way, forcing him in the opposite direction. Each time he tried to turn back they headed him off. In this game of cat-and-mouse Thomas and Oborn forced the enemy pilot to fly south of P'yongyang, and into a possible trap as this was where the two reserve Meteors and a flight of Sabres were orbiting. Thomas tried to contact them on the radio to have them intercept the straying MiG, but there was no reply. Then it was too late. The MiG pilot hauled up into a climbing turn, using his aircraft's superior rate of climb, and managed to escape by flying into the sun. Having forced him so far south, the Australians considered it doubtful that he would have enough fuel for his return flight across the Yalu because it would have been necessary for him to return via the coast road to avoid other UN aircraft returning south. The reserve Meteors were flown by Sgt Keith Meggs and Sgt Bruce Gillan, who had been orbiting at 30,000 feet over P'yongyang when, amid the excited radio chatter, Meggs heard that a lone MiG was heading south:

> "I saw this swept-wing aircraft underneath. He was turning to go north. I thought it was a Sabre spare, maybe lost. I turned towards him, but of course couldn't catch him. If I hadn't hesitated and turned towards him first then I may have given a MiG a bit of a shout. He was obviously a tyro and been forced away and the Meteors had chased him south."

When Flg Off Les Reading (A77-29) and Sgt Dick Bessell (A77-446) lost contact with Thomas and his No2, they sighted six to eight MiGs just west of them at 23,000 feet although they then lost sight of these while in the turn. They then saw six Meteors orbiting and decided to try and join up but then saw ten MiGs passing from left to right below and started to initiate a roll-over attack. At that moment, six to ten more MiGs were observed just above at 26,000 feet so they broke off their intended attack. Reading and Bessell then started climbing towards four swept-wing aircraft they saw at 28,000 feet, and as they climbed a single MiG fired at them but it did not score any hits. They continued climbing to find that the four aircraft were two F-86s under attack by two MiGs. The enemy broke off as the Meteors closed in to help. Meanwhile, Flt Lt Ralph Dawson (A77-811) and Sgt Max Colebrook (A77-368) sighted two more MiGs at two o'clock and made a firing pass at the wingman without seeing any results. They had to break off their attack when they saw more MiGs on their tails. They turned after them, Dawson picking out the nearest two. He hit the leading fighter, causing liquid to steam out of its port wing. This was verified by Colebrook. The second MiG suddenly flew between his leader and the Meteors and came under attack itself, but now only one of Dawson's guns seemed to be firing. There was little choice but to break off the action. The remaining Meteors had meantime broken into fighting pairs and, amid the melee, several pilots fired bursts at the enemy jets without achieving any obvious results. At last, because the Meteors were low on fuel, Flt Lt Cannon ordered all pilots to break off the fight and return to Kimpo. Sgt Armit landed his aircraft safely and discovered that damage resulting from the shell that struck A77-949 was not severe. The port flap was holed and there were numerous small dents and cuts on the rear nacelle and rear fuselage. The Meteor was patched up and flown back to Iwakuni AFB in Japan for a more permanent repair.

The Australian pilots were elated by the results of this dogfight in which, for the first time, they had not come off second best. One Meteor had been damaged but, although no claim for a confirmed kill could be made, the MiG attacked by Flt Lt Dawson had obviously been hit and possibly badly damaged although, unfortunately, the cine-film from Dawson's Meteor could not be used for verification because the camera had not been switched on. In addition, the MiG chased south of P'yongyang was a moral victory if nothing else. In the afternoon, a dozen Meteors were up again taking part in another fighter sweep over the same area around Anju but this time, although a total of 49 high-flying MiGs were sighted, there was no fight.

Another RAAF pilot was in action against the MiGs that day, and scored a similar victory. Sqn Ldr Dick Cresswell was still flying with the 4th FIW, and recalled:

> ". . . it was an 09.29 take-off in F-86A [FU-210], my 120th mission in Korea. Fifty-plus MiGs came in at height. We were 32 Sabres and they were way up there. One Sabre was shot down [flown by 2/Lt Carl G. Barnett Jr, who was killed]. I probably damaged one MiG but got attacked again. I wasn't hit (I never got hit – except about 30 times by ground fire when I was flying Mustangs). That was a bad one. Also I was very tired. I was at the end of my time in Korea. I claimed a probably damaged MiG-15. It would've been on the gun-camera film. I assume the claim went through. I never found out. When I finished my tenth mission on Sabres I came home."

26 September was an important day for the South Africans, too. It was the anniversary of 2SAAF's departure from South Africa for the Far East. Throughout the day, the four squadrons of the 18th FBG flew 122 combat sorties and out of these the South Africans improved on their own record by flying 40 sorties. These were flown during ten close-support missions dropping napalm, attacking with rockets, and strafing entrenched Communist troop positions along the IX and X Corps fronts. Total claims for the day amounted to 13 buildings and two field guns destroyed, four buildings damaged, and an unknown number of enemy troops killed. Most of the pilots on duty flew three missions but one SAAF flight was credited with four, each sortie exceeding one hour in duration. Such an arduous programme was extremely demanding on both pilots and groundcrews. A mission flown by 2/Lt John Howe earned him an American DFC. With 2/Lt Frank Grobler as wingman, he was briefed to lead a four-aircraft close-support mission to the area of Mahyon-ni. The air strike had been called to dislodge enemy forces

strongly entrenched on a hilltop only a few hundred yards from the closest UN troops. With calm, relentless accuracy, Howe made repeated low-level attacks on the enemy troops in the face of tremendous concentration of anti-aircraft guns of all calibres, as noted in his citation:

". . . Using napalm, rockets, and .50 ammunition in a succession of highly destructive attacks, 2/Lt Howe only left the area after the armament of his flight was completely expended and he was assured that the optimum damage had been inflicted. Notwithstanding the continuous ground fire directed at the aircraft, two of which including that of the leader, were hit, 2/Lt Howe continued to display a standard of leadership above and beyond that normally expected. The success of these attacks which caused the Aerial Controller to express the highest satisfaction, attests to the leader's high personal courage, devotion to duty, and superior airmanship. The 100 per cent coverage of the target credited to the flight indicates that extensive moral and physical hurt were caused to the enemy, all of which was accomplished without injury to friendly ground elements . . ."

Naturally, there was a party to celebrate the first anniversary of the departure of 2SAAF from South Africa. It was held at the Special Service Club at K-10, and also served as a farewell to Cmdt Johann Blaauw who had completed his 100th combat sortie and handed over the Squadron to newly promoted Cmdt Barry Wiggett. As the South Africans celebrated, they could look back on a year during which the Squadron had overcome difficulties in administration, operating conditions, inter-air force co-operation and morale, to become a well-integrated, highly respected fighting unit. But at a cost. Thirty-six Mustangs had been lost and 19 pilots killed or posted missing, of whom two were POWs. There was a sequel to the party that night, when every SAAF officer attending received a confidential letter from recently promoted Brig-General Turner C. Rogers, OC 18th FBW, declaring that he took a serious view of certain forms of celebration, including the stamping of holes in the floor and the throwing of furniture and glasses!

2SAAF's celebrations were short-lived, as Lt Denis Earp's luck ran out next day. It was his 65th mission, just ten short of the 75 missions that pilots of the 2SAAF were required to fly as a tour of duty before returning home. Earp noticed an anti-aircraft gun which was firing at his flight as they were busy strafing a target north of Kaesong. He attacked this and succeeded in knocking it out, but his own aircraft (355) was hit and its cooling system severely damaged. He was forced to bale out behind the enemy's forward positions north-east of Kaesong and, as he floated down on his parachute, he attracted small-arms fire from the ground although he escaped injury except for twisting a knee as he landed. The rest of the flight began to circle the area to provide air cover and was joined by a flight of USAF Mustangs from the 39th FIS.

From the air the pilots could not see the Communist soldiers who were closing in on the downed pilot. They had camouflaged themselves with branches and moved only when the aircraft were out of sight. Earp, however, was very much aware of his predicament. The Mustangs could not stay forever and he was in the path of a Chinese search party that was spread out in three lines, exploring the undergrowth. He hid in a ditch and managed to avoid discovery but decided that his best course of action would be to move in the same direction as the search party once it had passed. Unfortunately, as he was about to leave the shelter of the ditch, a lone Chinese soldier stumbled upon him. The two startled men stood facing each other. The South African tried to draw his revolver from its holster as the soldier fumbled with the safety catch of his rifle, but it was too late. Before either man could do anything, the alarm was given. Earp was captured and for the next 23 months he was a prisoner of the Communists.[7]

Led by Flt Lt Cannon, twelve Meteors provided close escort for B-29s again on the 27th. They met the American bombers at the rendezvous point but, as they escorted them to the target, GCI reported that there were between 80 and 90 MiGs in the area. The Australians felt very conspicuous particularly as one flight of bombers, flying a little below the other, was causing very heavy contrails. It was not long before MiGs were sighted well above and they

---

[7] Lt Earp was released at the end of August 1953 and arrived back in South Africa on 19 September 1953. He remained in the service after his release and rose to become Chief of the South African Air Force with the rank of Lt-General.

watched, ready for action, as two enemy flights executed a 180 degree turn and trailed them while they were approaching the target. During the bomb run, intense and accurate heavy flak was encountered and Flt Lt Scannell's aircraft (A77-744) received a hit in the ventral tank but this was not discovered until later, after the aircraft had landed back at base. The bombs straddled the target but results could not be clearly seen due to smoke and dust. The escorting Meteors broke off just south-west of P'yongyang and returned to Kimpo. Although the MiGs followed, they had made no attempt to launch an attack on the bombers, probably due to the efforts of the Sabre screen, two of which were claimed shot down by pilots of the 196th FAR. The MiG pilots also claimed six F-84s near Anju, five being credited to the 18th GuFAR and the other to a pilot of the 176th GuFAR. There was plenty of air activity throughout the day and Plt Off Ray Trebilco and Sgt Don Armit, on airstrip alert duty, were scrambled to investigate a bogey approaching from the north, eventually intercepting a B-29 at 20,000 feet. Before returning to base they were ordered to investigate four more unidentified aircraft, which turned out to be F-80s.

That night the USMC mounted Operation 'Blackbird', the only large-scale helicopter operation carried out at night during the Korean War. HMR-161 was assigned the task of flying supplies in for Marines at the front which meant negotiating a dangerous course up a narrow winding valley near the punchbowl. It was a hairy operation flying along the valley with the mountains on either side higher than the flying altitude of the HRS-1 helicopters. The operation was also hampered by insufficient lighting on the landing zone, inadequate night instrumentation in the helicopters and a need for a night-guidance system that could direct the helicopter to the exact landing point, but nevertheless it was a success. The Marine squadron was less fortunate next day when it suffered its first loss of an HRS-1 helicopter although its crew survived.

During the afternoon of the last day of September, a dozen Meteors led by Flt Lt Cannon again provided close-escort for B-29s briefed to target a North Korean airfield. Heavy, accurate, and intense flak was encountered from the rendezvous point up to and over the target but no hits were sustained by either the bombers or the escorts. GCI reported that enemy fighters were orbiting, waiting to intercept the bomber force over Anju, but no sightings were made. Good hits were scored on the target and the Australians left the bombers over Cho-do. However, honours for the last day of the month went to a pair of F-80s of the 80th FBS on their final sortie. They found a large convoy of vehicles moving southwards and destroyed an estimated 40 trucks, although a pilot of the 16th FIS, 2/Lt William Grammer, was lost near P'yongyang.

Figures released by FEAF at the end of the month revealed that pilots of the 4th FIW had reported a total of 1,177 MiG sightings over North Korea during September, of which 911 had been engaged in combat and 14 claimed shot down. Despite the odds against them, the Sabre pilots lost only three aircraft in combat during the month. Nevertheless, the MiGs had become more aggressive and more numerous in the air, succeeding in breaking through the Sabre screen to challenge RF-80 reconnaissance aircraft and vulnerable F-51, F-80 and F-84 fighter-bombers – 5th Air Force figures showing one of each type being lost in air combat. Should the situation in the air continue to deteriorate further a serious question mark had to arise over the apparent continuing effectiveness of the Operation 'Strangle' anti-railroad campaign. Besides flying these missions, the 5th Air Force had provided a total of 2,451 close-support sorties during the month. Meanwhile, in logistical support, the C-47s of the Royal Hellenic Air Force Flight based at Ashiya AFB, flew 82 operational missions in September. The Greek's advance echelon that had been flying from Kimpo had moved to Ashiya at the end of July and the remainder of the unit had been relocated to Ashiya from Tachikawa during August in order to avoid a strong typhoon. They remained under the command of the 21st USAF Troop Carrier Squadron, as was the Royal Thai Air Force (C-47) Detachment, now at Tachikawa.

Following the committal of the Thai Detachment to operations (in July), there had been a heartening decline in the number of sick and wounded requiring evacuation from Korea each month. With the beginning of the Truce talks, the situation on the ground became more static, and the movement of airdropped and airlanded supplies to Korea became more routine. There was a concurrent decrease of cargo-load airlift into Korea, and much of the space on the outbound planes could now be used to transport troops going on leave to Japan. C-47s of the 21st Squadron, including the Greek and Thai Detachments, regularly hauled cargo to the small field airstrips in Korea. Since most of the C-46s still lacked litter straps and sanitary facilities, maximum use was made of the C-47s, which could handle 26 patients, or C-54s, which could accommodate 36. At this time, the patients were usually picked up at forward airstrips and airlifted to the field station hospital at Taegu or Pusan. Under 8th US Army regulations, patients requiring specialised treatment or hospitalisation in excess of 30 days were airlifted to allotted areas in Japan: head and chest cases went to the Tokyo area, frostbite and hepatitis victims to the Osaka area, and miscellaneous cases to the Fukuoka area.

October 1951

In a recent communication to the Communist leaders, General Ridgway had suggested the possibility of using a new site for the stalled peace negotiation meetings, rather than returning to Kaesong. In this he had the full support of General Bradley. The disadvantages of Kaesong to the UN negotiators had become blatantly obvious. This ancient Korean capital was 20 miles within the Communist lines, but three miles below the 38th Parallel. Its position gave the Communists a decided propaganda advantage. It created the impression that the Communists had gained this ground during the war and added emphasis to their demands that the 38th Parallel should be the military demarcation line. The existence of the meeting site within Communist lines also made it appear that the UN Command always had to go to them to negotiate. There were tactical reasons, too. Kaesong stood in the strategic western sector of the Korean peninsula that had the best terrain for military endeavours, eastern Korea being very mountainous. It was situated right where it impeded UN military progress further northwards. Had the meeting been held on board the *Jutlandia*, as Ridgway had initially proposed, the Communists would not have had any of these advantages and may have been more receptive to agreeing to an armistice.

It was obvious that the Communists had not anticipated a demand for moving the site, and the response of their liaison officers to the suggestion revealed a great deal of anxiety. As of the beginning of October, no official response had been forthcoming. By now many UN negotiators believed it was obvious that the real reason the Communists were reluctant to accept proposals for discussing a new site for the peace talks, was that they risked exposure over the incidents and their manufactured evidence at Kaesong back in August. General Ridgway would only resume the conference negotiations at a site that was truly neutral so that the Communists could not play any more tricks. In order to break the deadlock, but still not concede on his demands to change the location, Ridgway offered them a new proposal, one which permitted them a face-saving avenue of escape, by suggesting a meeting be held at a site selected by them but acceptable to him midway between the respective front lines. The ball was squarely back in the Communist court.

On 7 October the Communist negotiators proposed a shift of the location of talks to the village of Panmunjom, five miles to the east of Kaesong, with both sides taking responsibility for its protection, and an expansion of the neutral area to cover a rectangular zone including Kaesong and Munsan. UN military pressure no doubt helped to induce them to seize the opportunity without delay. Ridgway immediately accepted, insisting only on a smaller neutral zone. Three days later, as liaison officers from both sides were meeting to discuss the matter of resuming full-scale peace negotiations, a pair of USAF F-51s flew perilously close to the neutral zone[8], sparking a furious protest from the Communists. The senior UN Command delegate, Admiral Turner Joy, having investigated the violation, apologised to General Nam Il, his North Korean counterpart, and explained that it had resulted from an error in navigation.

---

[8] The two F-51s were intercepted by Meteors flown by Flg Off Dick Wittman and Sgt Bruce Gillan who had been scrambled from Kimpo to investigate. The F-51s were shepherded away and instructed to return immediately to Kimpo after their identification numbers (Buzz numbers) had been noted and recorded. They landed at Kimpo shortly before the Meteors returned.

He offered assurances that appropriate disciplinary action would be taken. Out of this incident the Communists then sought to lay the blame for all delays on the shoulders of the UN Command and cover up their own attempts to impede progress. The situation was delicate. Now that the Communists had agreed at last to change the site, another such incident could not be afforded. Preliminary meetings continued until finally it was agreed that peace talks should resume on 25 October.

*　*　*

Oblivious to the toing-and-froing on the political front, skirmishing in the air and on the ground continued unabated throughout the month. During the morning of the first day of October, four pilots of 77RAAF led by Flt Lt Thomas were scrambled and instructed to contact GCI for a special mission. Accompanied by two 4th FIW Sabres, GCI instructed them to fly to Po'hang and escort an incoming C-121 Constellation carrying VIPs to Kimpo. The aircraft was duly met over Po'hang and the fighters took up their positions but, shortly thereafter, the Sabres were ordered to intercept an unidentified aircraft in the vicinity. This turned out to be a C-47. Meanwhile, the Constellation landed safely at Kimpo where the VIPs disembarked, including General Omar Bradley, Chairman of the US Joint Chiefs-of-Staff, and General Ridgway, there to be greeted by General Van Fleet and Admiral Turner Joy. After a brief ceremony they were conducted on a tour of the base and before their departure were met in 77RAAF's maintenance area by Wg Cdr Steege.

Another VIP visitor to Kimpo at this time was Air Marshal George Jones, the Australian Chief-of-Air Staff, who wished to investigate adverse reports appearing in Australian newspapers about the performance of 77RAAF's Meteors. He had many questions to ask about aircraft serviceability and the availability of spares, and seemed to be impressed by the fact that the Squadron had always sufficient serviceable aircraft to meet every commitment. He also showed an interest in the Meteors' performance while carrying external ordnance. On this, the Rolls-Royce representative Mr Jock Gibb recorded:

> "Priority was once again given to the investigation of the possibility of Meteors carrying external ordnance. Some work had previously been carried out, but this was dropped when it was seen that the Meteor was not designed to carry out the ground-support rôle. An American electrical release was fitted to bomb pylons based on the type of pylon carried by the Shooting Star [F-80]. This pylon was attached to the wing tank release slip. Figures were obtained for the carrying of two 500-lb bombs and two 1,000-lb bombs. The results, which in no way compared with the performance obtained by the GAC [Gloster Aircraft Company] developed pylon, impressed the Americans . . . napalm tanks were also carried and figures quoted. Some considerable work was put into checking the flying characteristics carrying rockets. A rocket with a $6^1/_2$-gallon napalm head was developed and although no snag from the flying aspect was discovered, it was found that there was insufficient napalm to create a good blaze."

The departure of Air Marshal Jones coincided with the arrival of Wg Cdr Brian Eaton DSO DFC RAAF, OC 78 Fighter Wing in Australia, who was detailed to investigate the operational performance of the Meteor. He was checked out on the aircraft and took part in five operations during his fourteen-day stay with the Squadron, the first of which he flew on 13 October.

Meanwhile, enemy opposition in the air continued to intensify. When, in September, the 5th Air Force had received the news that it could expect no additional F-86s for air cover, General Everest was obliged to withdraw his fighter-bomber interdiction attacks from the area of MiG Alley. The fighter-bombers now concentrated on the railway lines in the zone between P'yongyang and the Ch'ongch'on. While this change narrowed the choice of rail targets, it intensified air attacks against the middle reaches of the enemy's rail network, although it also enabled the Communists to set about making repairs to airfields everywhere in North Korea and to commence the construction of an entirely new major airfield just north of the Ch'ongch'on, near Saamcham. The significance of this was ominous.

Realising this as a looming threat, the Sabre pilots of the 4th FIW intensified their shielding patrols at the Yalu, and were to fight some of the greatest air battles of the war during the first three weeks of October. Indeed, on the first day of the new month, two MiGs were claimed destroyed, one by 1/Lt Raymond O. Barton Jr of the 334th FIS and the other credited to Lt Colonel George L. Jones. Both were first kills, while WWII fighter ace Maj William T. Whisner Jr of the 334th FIS opened his Korean account with a MiG damaged. In return, MiG pilots claimed an F-86 which reportedly crashed near Jyansyan-ri after being attacked by the 523rd FAR, and an F-84 by the 176th GuFAR; this latter machine failed to return and 1/Lt Herbert E. Ritter of the 111th FBS was reported missing. Next day (2 October), a dozen Meteors led by Flt Lt Cannon again provided close-escort for B-29s bombing a railroad bridge by-pass. The eight bombers were met at the rendezvous and escorted to the bomb run. Over the target moderate but accurate flak was encountered and consequently bombing results were poor, with only one stick of bombs seen to straddle the target. Although warned that MiGs had scrambled from Antung, none were encountered and all aircraft returned safely. The MiGs were busy elsewhere, Sabres of the 4th FIW reporting several engagements during which claims for six MiGs destroyed were submitted. One was credited to Colonel Gabreski, his third kill in Korea, two others being claimed by Capt George W. Dunn of the 334th FIS, one of which was shared with 2/Lt Charles R. Spath; two more were credited to Lt Colonel George J. Ola and Capt Paul W. Bryce, while the final one was claimed by 1/Lt Loyd J. Thompson of the 336th FIS. In addition, the F-80 pilots of the 8th FBG reckoned they had also turned the tables on the MiGs, Maj John Tulloch, CO of the 36th FBS, and 1/Lt Edwin Faulconer each claiming a probable, while Colonel James Tipton, the Group Commander, claimed one damaged. Their opponents were from both the 303rd and 324th FADs and claims for five F86s, one F-84 and one F-80 were submitted, the 523rd claiming two, the 196th one, the 176th GuFAR two, and the 18th GuFAR two. An RF-80 of the 15th TRS failed to return and 1/Lt Bruce A. Sweney was posted missing.

In darkness and mist at 0300 on the morning of 3 October, Operation 'Commando' began, aimed at further straightening the UN line and showing the enemy that the UN forces were still ready and willing to go on the offensive. The 28th British Commonwealth Brigade was allotted the major task on the east central sector, the assault of Hill 355 and Hill 317, key features in the enemy's defences. After a promising start against a well dug-in enemy, determined resistance was encountered. Austers of 1903 AOP Flight were soon involved and one of these located an elusive North Korean gun site which was well out of range of the artillery. The pilot observed an AT-6 nearby but had no direct radio contact, so he circled and dived towards the position, indicating its location to the American pilot, who then called in a flight of USAF F-51s. Unfortunately, the AT-6 pilot marked the wrong position. Despite aerobatic manoeuvres by the Auster pilot attempting to reveal the real target, the gun site was not touched. Nevertheless, British stubbornness paid off next day when the Auster pilot returned and relocated the enemy battery. This time an Air Liaison Officer equipped with an R/T set was aboard. Air strikes were called in and, under a barrage of rockets and napalm, the North Koreans were obliged to evacuate the position. Within five days of the start of Operation 'Commando', Communist forces had been cleared from the area but not without a fierce fight, the British Commonwealth Brigade alone having lost 58 killed and 262 wounded during the course of the three-and-a-half mile advance against the enemy's main defence line in central Korea. The Brigade would spend the next few weeks consolidating their new position with wire and mines. It would remain the western sector front line until the eventual ceasefire in July 1953.

There was no let-up in the air, and 3 October proved to be a good day for a dozen F-80s of the 8th FBW when its pilots claimed two MiGs probably destroyed north of Kunu-ri for no losses, although a MiG pilot from the 196th FAR reported shooting down an F-84 near Takusen. It was not a good day for Lt Mike Muller of 2SAAF who was flying his 72nd mission, however. He had already survived a crash-landing in August and now suffered another unpleasant experience when his Mustang (310) was presumably hit by ground fire, which caused a major glycol leak. Escorted by three others from his flight, Muller headed eastwards but, within minutes, the engine temperature was off the clock:

"I was determined to escape before my aircraft began burning. Scrambling over the side, my right foot trapped in the cockpit and my body hung in space, flapping back and forth against the fuselage like a puppet on a string. After some frantic wriggling of the foot it came free and I shot away from the Mustang, missing the tailplane by a fraction. Waiting until clear, I pulled the ripcord. What a wonderful feeling to look up and see the parachute mushroom above me. I landed in a tree . . ." [9]

Once on the ground, Muller heard automatic rifle fire, but the enemy troops were not firing at him. It was being directed at the low-flying Mustangs who were protecting him. They remained above for an hour and a half, until relieved by a flight of USAF Mustangs. Meanwhile, Muller was warily increasing the distance between himself and the enemy troops closing in and decided to climb down into a nearby valley where the orbiting pilots would have an easier task keeping him in sight. A rescue helicopter had been despatched to the scene but had been damaged by ground fire en route and had returned to base, while one of its escorting aircraft was shot down. A second helicopter, a USN machine from the helicopter craft LST799 based in Wonson harbour, which had been sent to rescue a Corsair pilot, was near enough to be diverted to where Muller was hiding; he continued:

"I heard the welcome sound of a Sikorsky helicopter flying up the valley and to my surprise a Naval chopper appeared. It was a pleasing sight to see a bearded sailor [R/O Sherrill] lowering the rope for me and a blessed relief when he pulled me inside. The pilot [Chief Aviation Pilot C.W. Buss] glanced at me, gave a smile and thumbs-up and we were away with four Panther jets escorting us. The helicopter had been hit by small-arms fire during the rescue and the damage caused some problems when landing back on the ship. A physical examination revealed no other injuries apart from an abrasion on my chin. Less fortunate was the Corsair pilot, Leslie Downes, who I'd met on board the helicopter. He'd been rescued after baling out of his burning aircraft and was treated for second degree burns on his face, neck, wrist, knees and ankles. That afternoon I was taken to Yodo Island off Wonson harbour as the guest of a commando unit of the Royal Marines and stayed until the following evening. The unit was carrying out an operation that night so the men were dressed in combat gear and their faces blackened . . ." [10]

On returning to K-10, Lt Muller was informed that his time in Korea was over although he still had three sorties remaining of his allotted tour. While he was away, 2SAAF had chalked up a new record on 4 October, achieving 48 combat sorties which included the Squadron's 5,000th for the campaign, the latter flown by Lt Basil Wilson. On the other side of the coin, the 8th FBG reported the loss of its Adjutant, Capt Donald W. Akers, who failed to return from a sortie.

Flt Lt Max Scannell led eight Meteors to provide close-escort for an RF-80 on a recce mission from P'yongyang to Ch'ongju on the morning of 5 October. The recce aircraft was safely escorted over the target area and back to base, despite the presence in the vicinity of Anju of 20 MiGs but these were at very high altitude and apparently failed to sight the Allied formation. A few minutes later another 20-plus MiGs were sighted heading south-east from north of Ch'ongju, these similarly failing to spot the Meteors below. In the afternoon, three flights of Meteors provided close-escort for B-29s tasked to bomb the railroad bridge at P'yongyang. Results could not be seen clearly but it was believed that the bridge was hit. No enemy aircraft were sighted although the GCI reported that several MiG flights were in the area. Besides flying escort missions, 77RAAF's tedious strip alert duties at Kimpo continued. During one of these two Meteors were scrambled but, as he took of in A77-385, Sgt Frank Blackwell, a new pilot, raised his undercarriage before the aircraft was properly airborne. The Meteor bumped the runway, scraping a hole in the rear of the ventral tank and the starboard tail portion as it was leaving the ground. Blackwell landed immediately, leaving Wt Off Michelson to continue on his own during which he was vectored to intercept four unidentified aircraft that turned out to be USAF Mustangs. Although the Meteors made no contact with MiGs that day, the Sabres did. In air fighting over North Korea, Maj Creighton of the 336th FIS claimed one for his third kill, while MiG pilots claimed three F-86s, two credited to the 176th GuFAR and one to the 523rd FAR. In addition, the 18th GuFAR reported shooting down two F-84s near Eidzyu.

[9/10] See *Flying Cheetahs in Korea*.

There was another Sabre/MiG clash next day (6 October), the 4th FIW losing two F-86s with two others damaged. As a result of the battle four Meteors led by Flt Lt Cannon were ordered off to fly a CAP for an F-86 (FU-319) that had force-landed on a mud bank off the west coast, south of Anju. When they reached the area GCI directed them to cover an air-sea rescue SA-16 that was going down to recover the pilot, 1/Lt Bill N. Garrett. The amphibian successfully landed on the mudbank and was able to get off again by reversing the engines. The Meteors escorted the rescue aircraft safely away from the area without incident. In the day's actions MiG pilots claimed six F-86s shot down, two by the 196th FAR including one by Polkovnik Pepelyaev, the commander of the 196th FAR; another was claimed by Maj Sherberstov of the 176th GuFAR, who reported seeing his victim eject before his aircraft crashed into the sea. Two others were credited to the 523rd FAR, one of which allegedly crashed about 15 miles south-west of Jyungsen, the other about five miles south-west of Syajinjio, while the sixth was reported to have crashed on the coast a couple of miles north-west of Yotori, the victim of the 17th FAR. There was obviously an element of double-claiming, as this F-86 was credited to Pepelyaev because of his accurate description of his victim, which was confirmed by his gun-camera film. Polkovnik Pepelyaev recalled:

> "I hit one Sabre. As a result of a forward-cone attack, I too was hit, but sustained only one rupture hole . . . The F-86 pilot landed the aircraft skilfully. He turned out to be an ace pilot; his Sabre carried three rows of white stars, a total of 12 shot down aircraft[11]. The pilot was immediately picked up by their Air Rescue Service, which was good, unlike ours. Two or three hours later, American strike aircraft came and started bombing and shooting up the area where the F-86 had landed. At that time the tide began rising, and water covered the landing area together with the Sabre. That night our technicians pulled it to the shore, moved it away for a considerable distance, and camouflaged it as a haystack. The next night the wings of the aircraft were cut off, and it was brought to Antung. All of us had a chance to sit in the cockpit . . ." [12]

The valuable trophy was packaged in several containers and sent to Moscow, where it was studied in great detail. The results of these studies were used to develop and improve Soviet aircraft systems, particularly the MiG-15.

While on his way with others to attack North Korea's main railway line of Sonch'on on 7 October, Lt Chris Lombard of 2SAAF ran into trouble over enemy territory. He reported the failure of his electrical system and was forced to abandon the aircraft (303). The rest of his flight watched as Lombard descended safely and touched down. He was seen to lay out his parachute and walk around before the Mustangs had to leave the area due to fuel shortage. The pilots of a relief flight of F-80s reported seeing Lombard running along the river bed in company with two other figures, but when the rescue helicopter arrived the South African pilot was nowhere to be found. He had in fact been taken prisoner by the Communists.

From Kimpo on the same day Flt Lt Cannon was briefed to lead a dozen Meteors to escort B-29s attacking the P'yongyang airfield. Moderate but accurate AA was encountered as the target was being bombed and results were poor, with most of the bombs landing on the river bank at the south-west corner of the airfield. On landing back at Kimpo, Sgt Bruce Robertson's Meteor (A77-730) swung and hit a 50-gallon drum full of sand before coming to a rest. The pilot believed a tyre had burst as he touched down although investigation revealed that it appeared that he had slightly misjudged his position and undershot to such an extent that he had hit the end of the runway. The aircraft was quite badly damaged and, once dismantled, was sent to Japan for repair. FEAF Bomber Command maintained a consistent schedule of flying some eight to nine combat sorties per day against airfields and bridge targets. These missions usually comprised three flights of three, or two flights of four B-29s. Next day the Meteors again provided close-escort for two flights attacking the airfield at Songch'on. On this occasion many

---

[11] 1/Lt Bill Garrett was not an ace; the 12 victory markings on FU-319 were evidently the total number of kills awarded to this particular aircraft.

[12] See *MiG-15* by Gordon and Rigmant.

hits were observed and the whole operation flowed with routine smoothness and was considered a success. No enemy aircraft were sighted. The airfields at P'yongyang were again the targets for the Meteor-escorted B-29s on 10 October, the airfield at Sunan being attacked next day. The MiGs were conspicuous by their absence during these raids, although elsewhere during the day pilots of the 18th GuFAR claimed three F-86s shot down, two more being claimed by Capt Hwa Lung-yi of the Chinese 4th FAR. Six more Sabres were claimed on the 12th, two of these credited to the 18th GuFAR, while three were credited to the 523rd FAR and one to the 176th GuFAR; one MiG was claimed by 1/Lt Joseph R. Ellis of the 334th FIS during the clash on the 12th.

While small formations of B-29s continued to raid the North Korean airfields by day and night, 5th Air Force fighter-bombers were busy destroying the railway system faster than the enemy could repair them, but the mainly unopposed MiGs were beginning to take their toll, although a B-26 fell to a La-11 night fighter of the 177th FAR on the night of 12/13 October. Such was the menace that efforts to destroy the rail lines between Sonch'on and Sinanju had to be abandoned, while south of the Ch'ongch'on the fighter-bomber pilots faced a heavy concentration of automatic weapons sited along the railway lines. It was now necessary for flights of attacking aircraft to attempt to neutralise the flak positions to allow the main force to carry out its task without having to run the gauntlet. Although the Communists were striking back with growing vigour, 5th Air Force interdiction efforts were making substantial progress in certain areas. After 2 October, the enemy was unable to make any rail movements on the line between Sariwon and P'yongyang.

On 14 October, in a mission that was typical of those flown by the fighter-bomber pilots, Lt N. Pretorius of 2SAAF led four Mustangs on an interdiction strike. Each aircraft carried two 500-lb bombs and four rockets and, as a result of their attack, two complete rail cuts were achieved. So the routine continued, day after day, with only the weather causing any major problems. The MiGs were after the American fighter-bombers again, the 196th FAR reporting the shooting down of an F-80 which apparently crashed about 20 miles south-east of Anju. Three Sabres were also claimed, two by the 18th GuFAR and the other by a pilot of the 176th GuFAR. Apparently the USAF did not lose an F-80 on the 14th, although 1/Lt Sidney Mullikin (35th FBS) was shot down on the 9th, Capt James Treester (36th FBS) on the 11th, and 1/Lt Richard Borschel (16th FIS) on the 12th, but all three were reported to have been victims of ground fire.

During the two-day period 14-15 October, typhoon 'Ruth' swept Japan and the seas around. At Iwakuni AFB winds of up to 80mph caused considerable damage to the tentage and stores, including those of the newly arrived 1913 Light Liaison Flight also equipped with Auster VIs. To meet the increased demand for reconnaissance and liaison duties, it had become necessary to form another Auster Flight specifically for this purpose and, therefore, 1913 Flight had been formed in England under the command of Capt P.A. Downward of the South Lancs Regt, who had served with the Parachute Regiment in WWII. The Flight, although an RAF unit, combined Army officer and NCO pilots and groundcrew with RAF mechanics. Apart from Capt Downward, the pilots comprised Capt A.T.C. Brown and Capt Gordons, plus two members of the recently reactivated Glider Pilot Regiment, S/Sgt R.E. Hall and Sgt Howard Jermy. The former had taken part in glider operations on D-Day, Arnhem and on the Rhine during WWII. A normal flying tour with an AOP unit was three years but time in Korea would be restricted to 18 months. The Flight had departed the UK by sea aboard the troopship SS *Empire Orwell* at the end of August and had arrived at Kure, Japan, after a five-week journey. From Kuri it moved to Iwakuni with its eight crated aircraft. The plan was to unpack six of the Austers from their crates, take four to Korea[13], leaving four in reserve of which two would be kept assembled and ready for use. While preparations were being made, Capt Downward visited 1903 AOP Flight at Fort George in order to familiarise himself with the Division's airstrip from where his Flight was to operate. By 19 October the first Auster (VF553) had been assembled and air tested.

---

[13] The first four Auster VIs taken to Korea by 1913 Flight were VF516, VF553, VF564, and VF622; the two assembled reserve aircraft were VF547 and VF569, and the two crated machines were apparently VF613 and WE358.

Meanwhile, from Fort George airstrip, Capt Jarvis of 1903 Flight flew a Mr McBain of *Reuters* over the Commonwealth Division's front. While over the area McBain made a tape-recording to be used in a Canadian radio programme, describing the scene. Things were quieter now. Continuous flying cover by the Austers had been called off a few days earlier on completion of Operation 'Commando', when the Flight was reduced to stand-by status. The gains that had been made at numerous points all along the front gave the UN Command a line of contact that it considered could be held securely in any future enemy counter-attack. To the east US Marines had gained control of the Punchbowl, and such objectives as Heartbreak Ridge and Bloody Ridge were in American hands, but it had been costly. Since the beginning of August, UN/ROK forces had suffered some 60,000 casualties of whom 22,000 were Americans. It was estimated that the Communists had suffered 234,000 casualties but the figures were grossly inflated to make the US losses seem more acceptable and bearable but, even so, the Communists had lost large numbers of men.

Although Meteors led by Sqn Ldr Wilson, now recovered from his wounds, on a fighter sweep around Anju on the morning of 15 October failed to sight any MiGs, there was a clash next day between 4th FIW Sabres and the Russian and Chinese jets. During the heavy engagement in MiG Alley, the Americans claimed no fewer than nine MiGs shot down to record the USAF's biggest claim in a day to date for the air war in Korea. Maj Franklin Fisher claimed two to take his score to three, and Colonel Ben Preston his second. For the 334th FIS it was one each for Capt George Dunn, 1/Lt John J. Burke, and 1/Lt Orren H. Ohlinger, while another was shared by 1/Lt Clifford F. Brossart and 2/Lt Merlyn E. Hroch. The remaining two claims were submitted by 1/Lt David B. Freeland and 1/Lt Anthony Kulengosky Jr of the 336th FIS. MiGs were also sighted by Meteors escorting B-29s attacking the road bridge at Sunch'on, although these were far to the north and did not attempt to approach the bombers. Although their losses are not known, the Russian MiG pilots claimed three F-86s in this battle, two by the 196th FAR and the third being credited to a pilot of the 523rd FAR, while the 176th GuFAR reported a victory over an F-84 near Kaisen. In addition, Capt Hwa Lung-yi of the Chinese 4th FAR claimed an F-86 for his third victory.

With the MiGs being kept busy, UN fighter-bombers were able to carry out their tasks in relative safety from air attack, and 2SAAF achieved some excellent results in their close-support missions for the day. In the morning Lt Pretorius led four Mustangs against troops and mortar positions well dug in on a ridge. They attacked with napalm and rockets and then strafed. Four bunkers were destroyed and at least 25 enemy troops killed. In the afternoon a further highly successful close-support mission was flown, the quartet led by Lt W. Botha. Troops and supplies were napalmed, rocketed and strafed before more troops were discovered and attacked in a nearby valley. While landing back at K-46, Lt Piet Retief's Mustang (347) swung to starboard and snapped off its undercarriage. The aircraft was badly damaged but the pilot was unhurt. 2SAAF at this time received a number of new pilots to replace those tour-expired.

Although daylight missions against airfields in the Saamcham-Taech'on-Namsi triangle were laden with potential hazards for FEAF Bomber Command, nine B-29s of the 19th BG were sent to bomb Saamcham on 18 October, and another nine from the 98th BG were scheduled to attack Taech'on. The 19th Group formation ploughed ahead to Saamcham closely escorted by a dozen Meteors led by Sqn Ldr Wilson. Over the target area a total of 306 100-lb bombs were dropped with results appearing to be good. The raid caught the defences by surprise for no MiGs appeared to challenge the bombers. Meanwhile, the 98th Group's formation had missed the rendezvous with their intended F-84 escort and diverted to a safer secondary target. There were three scrambles of strip alert Meteors from Kimpo during the day and, on one of these, Flt Lt Cadan and Sgt Bob Strawbridge were vectored onto another pair of F-51s that had violated the restricted neutral zone. The identification numbers of these aircraft were passed on to the controller and the Mustangs were shepherded back to Kimpo. The two Australians then returned to the neutral zone and carried out a patrol during which they intercepted yet another flight of US Mustangs about to enter the area, and guided them away before they returned to Kimpo once more. Next day Sqn Ldr Wilson led eight Meteors as close-escort for B-29s briefed to attack a railway bridge at Songch'on. The mission went without incident and no enemy aircraft were sighted, but the success of the attack was not known because the B-29s had to bomb through cloud at 16,000 feet.

The task allocated to 77RAAF towards the end of October was quite considerable. It was generally necessary to provide 18 aircraft in the morning, and a similar number again in the afternoon. In each case, two of these would be flying spares, but if they were not required they would fly at altitude and relay messages back to base. They were also required to conserve fuel and be in a position to provide cover for anyone who ran into trouble and in need of escort. They also had strip alert and airfield alert duties. The airfield alert was only necessary if an attack on the airfield was deemed imminent, but it meant air and groundcrews had to be available an hour before dawn and an hour after dusk. Four aircraft had to be ready for strip alert between these times, which meant that aircraft had to be inspected and checked very early in the morning. This could be quite a job when snow and sleet froze to the mainplanes. Then, after an evening mission, the airmen had to refuel, rearm if necessary, and carry out minor rectifications before the aircraft could be dispersed. It could be around 2030 by the time the airmen ceased work for the day.

With clear fine weather on 21 October, B-29s of the 98th BG tried to attack Taech'on again but had to divert once more because of failure to rendezvous with their escort. It was left to the 19th BG to carry out that specific mission next day and, during the afternoon of the 22nd, B-29s successfully bombed Taech'on. Shortly afterwards, the F-84 escorts were drawn away from their charges by an estimated 40 MiGs and, within the next few minutes, three more MiGs dropped out of the overcast and attacked the bombers so suddenly that the startled gunners were unable to return fire. One B-29, already badly damaged by flak, was again hit, its pilot managing to keep the crippled aircraft aloft just long enough to reach the Korean coast, where all members of the crew baled out successfully. They were all subsequently rescued. The MiGs, probably from the 18th GuFAR, had scored a kill but it would seem that on this occasion they had come upon the bombers purely by chance. In fact, the three Russian pilots each claimed a bomber shot down, while others from the 523rd FAR amazingly reported the destruction of five more, of which two were credited to Maj Dmitrii Os'kin. In addition, according to available records, in this action a total of ten F-84s were credited to the MiG pilots of the 18th GuFAR (five), the 523rd FAR (two), and the 176th GuFAR (three). American losses are unknown, but did not match the Russian claims. In another action two F-86s were claimed by pilots of the 196th FAR, with a third credited to the 523rd FAR, the latter reportedly crashing about 20 miles north-east of Jyungsen, to give the MiG pilots an incredible total of 21 victories for the day. Chinese pilots were not involved in these actions, the 4th FAR having been replaced at Antung on the 20th by the 3rd FAR, while the 14th FAR was similarly being prepared to move forward.

The Russians were now getting into the full swing of things, and were able to anticipate American actions in the Saamcham-Taech'on-Namsi triangle with some degree of accuracy, and marshalled their forces accordingly. At 0900 on 23 October, eight B-29s of the 307th BG rendezvoused as arranged with 55 F-84s of the 49th and 126th FBGs and set course for the airfield at Namsi. Ahead and far above, 34 Sabres were providing a fighter screen south of the Yalu. Suddenly, at 0915, more than 100 MiGs swarmed across from Manchuria to attack the Sabres and, within minutes, the American pilots were literally fighting for their lives, effectively isolated from the action that was about to erupt further to the south. Three MiGs were claimed destroyed, Maj Richard Creighton recording his fourth kill, while Capt Ralph Banks and Lt Walter Schirra, a US Navy pilot on exchange duty with the 5th Air Force, each got their first. The Russians admitted the loss of one MiG.

The MiG pilots made good use of their superior numbers. As the leading B-29 flight turned on course to the target, another 50 enemy jets were spotted closing in. They circled some distance off, apparently meaning to draw off the F-84s, as they had done the previous day, but after a short stand off it became obvious the escort was not going to be decoyed away this time and the MiGs came hurtling down in to attack from all directions. Most of the attackers flew normal pursuit curves, but some of them dived straight through the bomber formation to deny the Americans much opportunity to open fire. All three bombers of the leading flight came under attack and the lead aircraft (No151) flown by Capt Thomas L. Shields was badly hit.

Shields held his burning aircraft on course long enough to release its bombs over the target area before making for the coast. Meanwhile the MiGs caught up with the other bombers and promptly shot down two more, in addition to severely damaging two others, and also shot down one of the F-84s. Of the two bombers shot down, Capt Robert M. Krumm's aircraft (No045) had been attacked at point-blank range, and with its port inner engine on fire it fell out of formation and crashed on a mudflat near the coast. South Korean guerrillas later found three crewmen dead inside the wreckage, and three more outside, one of whom had apparently been executed. Two others were unaccounted for. From the second missing bomber (No940) piloted by Capt James A. Foulkes Jr, only the co-pilot 1/Lt Fred Beissner survived. The crew had been ordered to bale out of the burning aircraft, Beissner coming down in the sea, from where he was fortuitously rescued after eight hours when a Mustang pilot made a sighting. He was eventually picked by by the Australian destroyer *Murchison*. The Russians believed they had achieved even greater success, recording that 56 MiGs had encountered the B-29s, and while a dozen were held in reserve, the remaining 44 from the 18th GuFAR, 176th GuFAR, and 523rd FAR swept in to attack and claimed four bombers shot down, plus three of the escort. One of the F-84s was reported to have blown up in mid-air, and a second to have crashed 15 miles north-east of Sensen; indeed, Capt John W. Shewmaker of the 111th FBS failed to return. A MiG was claimed by 1/Lt Farrie D. Fortner of the 154th FBS, and two more by B-29 gunners (Sgt Fred R. Spivey and S/Sgt Jerry M. Webb, both of the 371st BS).

While the battle raged, a dozen Meteors were flying a fighter sweep in the Anju area. They did not sight any aircraft, enemy or friendly, until several B-29s returning from the mission were spotted just south of P'yongyang. The Meteors rendezvoused and provided escort to the mouth of the Han. Meanwhile, from Kimpo, two more Meteors flown by Wt Off Bill Michelson and Sgt Frank Blackwell were scrambled to intercept incoming unidentified aircraft, being vectored initially onto four B-29s and a single F-84, before encountering two more B-29s on their way home. It was obvious that all had been in a fight, and two made emergency landings at Kimpo with dead and wounded men on board. Meanwhile, Capt Shields' crippled bomber was eventually coaxed out over the sea where Shields ordered the crew to bale out, which they did. Sadly, Shields was unable to do so and went down with his aircraft. Four Meteors had been scrambled to provide CAP for the airmen in the sea, but Flt Lt Cannon and his flight were unable to achieve any sightings apart from RAN Sea Furies from HMAS *Sydney* which were also engaged in the search. However, most of the American airmen were picked up by USAF SA-16s. Aboard one of the rescue amphibians was Sqn Ldr Kater, 77RAAF's Senior Medical Officer, who helped in the rescue of four of the airmen. He dived into the sea in an attempt to recover the body of another, who had apparently drowned, but was hampered by rough seas and the constant movement of the amphibian and was only just able to be recovered himself. On board a second SA-16, Medical Orderly Cpl D.H. Sinclair, also of 77RAAF, assisted in the rescue of another survivor. At the end of this disastrous day for the American bomber force, the 4th FIW's intelligence officer prepared a report on the proceedings, which concluded with a warning:

"In summary, three major comments can be made from the engagements on 23 October. First, there was confusion on the part of the fighter escort and the B-29s in the rally point and route of return which greatly impaired the mission of the fighter escort aircraft. Secondly, the MiGs were aggressive and in numbers which made possible the temporary supremacy of the enemy in aerial warfare over North Korea. Their tactics seemed to be well-planned, their formation appeared excellent, and their discipline appeared superior to that seen thus far in the Korean War. Thirdly, the enemy aircraft were in sufficient numbers to engage the F-86s in areas away from the bombers. These factors could well presage a new phase of aerial warfare over North Korea." [14]

Despite the battering FEAF Bomber Command had taken in the past two days, eight more B-29s set off to attack a railway bridge at Sunch'on next day, on this occasion the 98th BG aircraft

---

[14] See *Crimson Sky* by John R. Bruning.

being escorted by ten F-84s and 16 Meteors, while F-86s again provided fighter screen just south of the Yalu. The bombers successfully rendezvoused with their escorts but, as they neared the target, about 20 MiGs and Sabres in a running battle could be seen approaching from the north-west. The Russians were again reacting in strength. Pilots of the 523rd FAR had divided into two groups, one to engage the F-86s and the other to seek out the Meteors, while the 18th GuFAR was detailed to break through to the B-29s and close-escorts of F-84s and any remaining Meteors. A furious battle developed as the Sabre pilots tried to prevent the MiGs from reaching the bombers, and the Meteor pilots observed one swept-wing aircraft spinning down, apparently out of control, and one MiG trailing white smoke.

As the MiGs came closer Sqn Ldr Wilson, leading the Meteors, ordered two flights to engage and prevent them from closing on the B-29s, but the Australians had to hold their fire since there was a chance of hitting the Sabres in the confusion. In the first pass, Flg Off Phil Hamilton-Foster (A77-316) took punishing hits in the wings and fuselage. The Meteor rocked and shuddered as he fought for control. His starboard engine flamed out and the aircraft spiralled down. Nevertheless, Hamilton-Foster was able to regain control and headed back for base, flying left wing low. Meanwhile, his section leader, Flg Off Les Reading, had come under attack but avoided a similar fate:

> "Many of us felt sure, without confirmation at that stage, that Russians were flying with the Communists and that it was they who directed the engagements from high and who pounced on the stragglers. In the running fight that was taking place, my wingman Phil Hamilton-Foster and I had become somewhat separated from the main gaggle and were definitely stragglers. When Phil was shot up I would normally have escorted him out of the area, but four MiGs set upon me and worked me over in fine style. We started at something over 25,000 feet and I soon realised that I was in a spot of bother. They immediately set up individual, co-ordinated attacks – very advanced stuff, and I thought 'Bloody Russkis'. They kept it up as I turned into each attack, not always knowing where the next was coming from. They stayed with me until around 6,000 feet, when I saw an opportunity to break into a spiral dive, heading for the deck and pulling high G to thwart their gunsights. Down low, both they and I had the problem of high fuel usage and the need to gain height in order to make it back to base. I stayed among the trees for a while to be sure I had lost them, then rubbernecked my way back to Kimpo with precious little fuel aboard."

While returning to take up escort after the first break, Flt Lt Thomas (A77-741) led his flight after a pair of MiGs but they were too fast and easily escaped. As the bombers turned left over the target area, at least ten MiGs attacked from six o'clock, evaded the Meteor flights led by Flg Off Dick Wittman and Flt Lt Max Scannell and opened fire on a B-29. Cannon shells could be seen exploding with bright flashes on the fuselage of the bomber, which suffered heavy damage and began to lose height, finally crashing into the sea near Wonsan. Its crew managed to parachute out safely and were rescued from the water by US naval ships. Meanwhile, Wittman (A77-744) and Scannell (A77-383) broke their flights into the MiGs but were too late and could only fire from long range without any visible results. They returned to continue the escort and spotted a lone MiG attacking the bombers, three Meteors successfully forcing the Russian pilot to break away before Flt Lt Joe Blyth (A77-31) observed another lone MiG. He fired two long bursts and believed he had inflicted damage; he commented later:

> "I chased a MiG off Max's tail. Later, he thanked me and rightly asked why I didn't knock him down. I think it was Les Reading who described the MiG's 37mm shells as footballs. They were really impressive, I thought like tennis balls the first time I saw them."

Despite losing fuel from his damaged tanks, Flg Off Hamilton-Foster successfully carried out a one-engine landing at Kimpo, the other engine flaming out at the end of his landing run. On inspection of the damaged aircraft, it was found that a piece of the port tailplane spar was missing while another shell had inflicted a six-inch hole in the rear fuselage. Yet another shell had pierced the port mainplane, and the underside of the front fuselage was peppered with small holes. The fuel tanks had also been holed. That Hamilton-Foster had been able to fly back to

Kimpo on one engine in such a damaged condition was a testament to the Meteor's ability to absorb punishment. Shortly before his arrival at Kimpo, the two Meteors on strip alert had been scrambled to proceed to the Anju area to give assistance to F-86s low on fuel that were being engaged by MiGs. When the Meteors reached the Ch'ongch'on they contacted the American pilots, who reported that they were over the estuary searching for a downed colleague. Dropping down to render assistance, the Meteor pilots were informed by the leader of a flight of F-51s that a dinghy had been located but there was no sign of the pilot. At this point the Meteors were recalled to base. Two Sabres failed to return but both 1/Lt Fred T. Wicks and 1/Lt Bradley B. Irish were subsequently reported to be prisoners, while a third Sabre returned badly damaged although its 336th FIS pilot, 1/Lt Dayton Ragland, was not injured.

The battle over, the Russian pilots claimed a total of nine victories for the loss of one MiG. The 18th GuFAR reported shooting down one B-29 and forcing others to drop their bombs before reaching the target, while Kapt Lev Shchukin claimed a Meteor destroyed. Pilots of the 523rd FAR claimed four F-86s and three Meteors, two of the latter being credited to Maj Os'kin and one to St/Lt V. Filimonov. One of Os'kin's victims was supposed to have crashed a couple of miles north-east of Jyungsen, and the other two Meteors claimed by the unit were reported to have fallen into the sea. For the Americans, Colonel Harry Thyng shot down a MiG, a second being claimed by a B-29 gunner, T/Sgt Harold M. Setters of the 344th BS. Despite the Russian count for Meteors destroyed, Hamilton-Foster's was the only RAAF aircraft damaged in this action, while Flt Lt Blyth was confident that his claim for one MiG damaged would be confirmed by his gun-camera film. Unfortunately for him, the processed film was again useless. In his official report of this action, Flt Lt Scannell commented:

> "Flights of MiGs were engaged by the escort during the run-up to the target and by the time the formation was withdrawn, a MiG flight was able to position and carry out a high-speed line astern attack started from 10,000 feet above. The MiGs levelled out at about 2,000 yards to the rear of the formation and made their attack in a rough line-abreast formation, breaking away above and to the left. The close escort had no chance of stopping this type of attack once it had been initiated but they had been successful in stopping at least one flight of MiGs from positioning earlier during the flight."

Flt Lt Blyth was involved in a scramble next day (25 October) with Sgt Vance Drummond, the pair being directed to intercept four bogies near P'yongyang, but when 40 miles south of the plot the controller lost radar contact. The Meteors were then vectored to intercept other aircraft nearby which proved to be three USAF Mustangs. Later, 16 Meteors led by Sqn Ldr Wilson provided a fighter screen in the Anju area for F-80s attacking enemy supply routes. There was no interference from enemy fighters. Although RAAF records do not report contact with MiGs on this date, Russian sources claim that some Meteors participated in escorting B-29s on a raid, one Meteor being claimed probably shot down by St/Lt F. Malashin, the leader of a pair of MiGs from the 18th GuFAR. During the combat he noticed a Meteor, that was presumed to have been damaged, leaving the battle area escorted by a pair of F-86s. Using height advantage, he surprised the trio and attacked the Meteor. Elsewhere, another 18th GuFAR pilot reported shooting down an F-80.

77RAAF carried out another fighter sweep of the Anju area on 26 October, the 16 aircraft again led by Sqn Ldr Wilson. Approximately 60-70 MiGs were seen in various formations and though these were often in a good position to attack, they made no attempt to do so. Further north the Sabre screen was involved in heavy fighting and two MiGs were claimed shot down, both by pilots of the 336th FIS, 1/Lt Douglas K. Evans and 1/Lt Claude C. Mitson. Pilots of the 18th GuFAR were again involved, claiming one F-86 shot down, while those from the 196th FAR reported meeting F-80s near Anju. Three of the fighter-bombers were claimed to have fallen to their guns with all three American pilots being captured by Chinese forces, but six-victory ace St/Lt Fedor Shebanov was shot down and killed, probably the victim of one of the Sabre pilots although his No2 reported being attacked by F-80s. He saw Shebanov's aircraft disappear into clouds and, later, the burnt out wreck was discovered. The investigation team was told by local witnesses that the MiG came out of clouds and dived into the ground. In the cockpit was found the remains of the aircraft's first-aid kit which suggested that Shebanov may have been wounded, and had perhaps lost consciousness, before crashing.

Late that afternoon a Royal Australian Navy Firefly from HMAS *Sydney* was shot down by flak south of Sariwon, and force-landed in a paddy field about 70 miles inside enemy territory (see Chapter XIII). Four Meteors led by Sqn Ldr Wilson were sent to provide CAP over the downed airmen who were seen sheltering in a gully. As the flight flew over the crashed aircraft, the Meteors were subjected to inaccurate automatic weapons fire from the surrounding area. Wilson's flight was relieved by another led by Flt Lt Thomas, but time was running short and daylight starting to fade. All the enemy troops had to do was wait for darkness. Meanwhile they continued to fire at the Meteors whenever they swept low and Sgt Max Colebrook's aircraft (A77-385) received a hit in the port engine nacelle. He was escorted back to base by Plt Off Philp. A message from the controller informed Flt Lt Thomas that the rescue bid was being abandoned since it was getting too late, but Thomas requested permission to remain in the area while fuel lasted. Ten minutes passed. Suddenly a Firefly appeared and its pilot announced that a helicopter with an escort of two Sea Furies was coming from the carrier. It was a race against darkness. The two Meteor pilots waited until they saw the helicopter arriving before they finally turned for Kimpo, extremely short of fuel. A third flight of Meteors led by Flt Lt Scannell was also on its way, but by the time they reached the area the helicopter had already rescued the navy aviators and was on its way south. With last light it landed at Kimpo where the rescuees were checked by 77RAAF's SMO, Sqn Ldr Kater. They and the USN helicopter crew remained overnight as guests of the RAAF.

On the morning of 27 October, Sqn Ldr Wilson (A77-15) led another B-29 escort, the 16 Meteors accompanied by 32 F-84s of the 49th and 136th FBWs. The target was a railway bridge near Sinanju. Because of reports that MiG pilots were reluctant to fight over water, the bombers were routed to the target so that they stayed over the Yellow Sea as long as possible. The escort flew about 1,000 feet above the bombers and a little ahead. As they approached the target moderate but accurate flak was encountered but none of the aircraft was hit and the bombers completed their task with some accuracy. It was seven minutes after bombing that the trouble started. Two MiGs appeared and made a non-firing pass through the bomber formation from three o'clock to the rear. The main MiG force was up at about 35,000 feet. Between ten and 15 more MiGs rolled over, dived and made an attack on the formation of bombers. They came in fast, cannons firing, damaging the aircraft flown by Colonel Wolfe, commander of one of the squadrons, while gunners aboard the bombers blazed away[15]. Six more MiGs initiated a similar attack but passed beneath the bombers. Both attacks broke up in front of the bombers and climbed away. Then a single MiG made a front quarter attack and broke up into a climbing turn before rolling away. At this moment several more made feinting attacks from the flank, before two more made passes down onto the rear of the bombers which were by now ten miles out over the Yellow Sea.

As the MiGs broke from the second attack Sqn Ldr Wilson's flight turned into them, Wilson firing at two from 1,000 yards range without any obvious result. His No2, Flt Sgt Bill Middlemiss (A77-728), fired a four-second burst from 300 yards at one that was pulling up in a stall turn, but had to break off his attack when he found another on his tail. As he pulled out of the turn he went into a vertical dive, reaching Mach .84 before he was able to recover at 7,000 feet. At that level he sighted an F-84 on which he formated but soon lost sight of it again as he scouted for a lone MiG reported to be in his vicinity. Unable to sight the MiG, he located another F-84 heading southwards and joined forces, the two aircraft landing safely at Kimpo. Meanwhile, Flg Offs Reading (A77-29) and Rivers (A77-587) had also reacted to the MiG attack and made a high rear quarter interception of two of the enemy jets. They closed to 300 yards and fired before pulling up, the aircraft attacked by Reading streaming fuel from its port wing as it climbed away. Despite the damage, Reading could not close the gap:

---

[15] Six MiGs were claimed destroyed by the gunners, with Sgt Merle A. Goff of the 28th BS being credited with two, while his colleagues S/Sgt Michael Martocchia and Pfc Harry E. Ruch were each awarded one kill; Cpl Leonard B. Eversole of the 3rd BS and Sgt Leeman M. Tankersley of the 93rd BS claimed the other two.

". . . there is no doubt in my mind that it could not have made it back to base, it was losing fuel at too great a rate."

Rivers' target also made a hasty escape by diving and easily outdistanced the pursuing Meteor. As they re-grouped, the Australian pilots saw an aircraft on fire some two miles to the south-east. Flt Lt Scannell's flight had also attempted to engage the enemy, Scannell (A77-982) and his No2, Sgt Bruce Thomson (A77-464), firing fleeting bursts as the MiGs sped by, as did Flg Off Hamilton-Foster (A77-726), while Flt Lt Thomas (A77-31) and his wingman Sgt Allan Avery (A77-385) both fired at the same MiG from long range without observing any strikes. Only Flg Off Reading's claim for one MiG damaged was accepted by the 5th Air Force.

The B-29s were escorted as far as Cho-do. Four of the bombers had been damaged, Colonel Wolfe's aircraft seriously, and he decided to land at Kimpo where he touched down with his starboard outer engine on fire. After examining the damage he and his crew visited the Australians who had escorted them, and drank a few beers, thanking the Meteor pilots for giving them such good close protection. Russian pilots of the 523rd FAR claimed two B-29s shot down, both of which they believed had crashed into the sea, plus two F-84s. Another F-84 was claimed by the 176th GuFAR, and two F-86s by the 18th GuFAR.

The day was not yet over for 77RAAF. Sqn Ldr Wilson now led a dozen Meteors on a fighter sweep of the Anju area. On reaching the area one Meteor had to abort and returned to Kimpo under escort. Except for some light flak the mission was uneventful until near the end of the patrol when eight to ten MiGs were sighted flying parallel to the Meteors, between 10,000-15,000 feet above. They were just south of Sinanju. For several tense minutes the MiGs remained on the same course keeping pace, shadowing them as they departed the area. They then turned right over the top of the three flights and headed north-west, while at the same time two other formations of MiGs of similar strength passed overhead flying northwards, but there was no clash on this occasion.

For what would be the swan-song for B-29 daylight operations over Korea, the 98th BG sent eight aircraft to bomb a by-pass bridge at Songch'on on 28 October. The operation was escorted by 16 Meteors with Flg Off Geoff Thornton leading in A77-741. The Meteors escorted the B-29s to the target without mishap and a good coverage resulted from the uninterrupted bombing. GCI advised of enemy aircraft in the vicinity but there were no sightings and the mission was otherwise uneventful. In the afternoon Flg Off Thornton again led the show, taking a dozen Meteors on a fighter sweep of the Anju area. Although several groups of MiGs were reported in the area, and several were sighted high above, there was no direct contact, but elsewhere during the day MiGs and Sabres clashed, 1/Lt Robert H. Moore of the 336th FIS being credited with his first kill, MiG pilots claiming five F-86s shot down in return; the 176th GuFAR claimed three, while the 196th and 523rd FARs claimed one apiece.

The hard fact remained that despite 4th FIW's efforts to maintain a fighter screen along the Yalu, there were just too many MiGs to hold at bay. The FEAF's aging B-29s were obviously far too vulnerable when confronted by the Russian jets. At a conference held at Itazuke AFB, senior officers of the 5th Air Force and FEAF Bomber Command agreed that virtually no amount of fighter escort could keep the MiGs off the bombers. The F-84s and Meteors, when attempting to escort B-29s at bombing altitudes above 20,000 feet, had to operate so close to the Mach limits that they could not manoeuvre quickly enough to fend off attacking MiGs without losing control. The only real defence for the B-29s was the Sabre screen, but 5th Air Force simply did not have sufficient numbers of F-86s to do the job. Up until October, FEAF Bomber Command losses had been bearable but now, in one week, it had lost five bombers to flak and fighters and suffered major damage to eight other aircraft, with 55 crewmen killed or missing and a dozen others wounded. Pessimists suggested that the B-29s were finished in Korea. Facing up to the reality of the problem, Brig-General Joe W. Kelly proposed that from now on Bomber Command would operate only at night. The Sabre pilots of the 4th FIW had been harshly criticised for their apparent lack of aggressiveness, which greatly upset all concerned and obligated the unit's historian to defend its performance:

"Throughout this war, there has been a lot of speculation as to why the F-86s don't shoot down a lot more MiG-15s. From infrequent reports received here from the United States, it seems that our inability to kill a lot more MiG-15s had been laid to everything from airplane instability to gunsight trouble and lack of pilot ability or aggressiveness. Almost all the experts, except those who actually fought here, looked at everything but the thrust coming out of the tailpipe.

Give us the ability to match the MiG-15 in climb, ceiling and top speed, and we can double and triple our kill rate. Give us an advantage in these flight characteristics, and a MiG won't come south of the Yalu River after first contact. When a man goes hunting with a gun, he's got to get close enough to whatever he's after with that gun to kill it." [16]

MiGs were sighted again by the Meteor pilots during a sweep on 29 October. Just north of Anju two flights of ten and twelve were observed up to 35,000 feet, and later two more flights of even greater numbers but none of these attacked. Tense minutes followed as the Meteors edged southwards with the MiGs following, always maintaining a striking distance but then, abruptly, they wheeled to the north-west, possibly low on fuel or seeking easier targets. There were plenty of UN aircraft around, Flt Lt Blyth and Flg Off Rivers being scrambled from Kimpo to investigate. First they encountered four USN Skyraiders at 8,000 feet and then a single C-54 at 4,000 feet. These were followed by a lone Tigercat at 10,000 feet, a Corsair at 11,000 feet, four SAAF Mustangs 500 feet higher, and finally a C-47 at 5,000 feet. These missions remained tedious but necessary work, given the increased activity of the MiGs.

It was a day of mixed fortunes for 2SAAF. Cmdt Wiggett led his flight with "the greatest skill and determination" in a series of devastating runs over enemy positions resulting in complete coverage of the assigned target. An estimated 45 enemy troops were killed. For his leadership and the relentless fashion in which he both executed and directed the attacks he was awarded the US DFC. In another operation, Lt Lamb and his flight attacked mortar positions on a high ridge near the front lines. In their runs over the target they destroyed five positions and killed an unknown number of troops. Despite intense and accurate anti-aircraft fire none of the Mustangs was hit, but 2/Lt Theo Joyce failed to return from another mission near Inch'on during a railway interdiction. Colleagues saw a brilliant explosion on the side of a hill south of the town which suggested that his Mustang (340) had crashed during its bombing run. The South Africans were more fortunate next day (30 October), during a mission against an enemy command post in the village of Tosan, when Lt Joe Meiring was shot down. On arrival over the target area the FAC aircraft was shot down by ground fire, and another took its place and directed the attack. The operation was successful and the command post set on fire but, as the Mustangs completed their attack, Meiring's aircraft (354) was hit in the engine and started to stream glycol. Despite his ailing engine, he was able to reach an emergency airstrip and carry out a belly-landing, suffering head injuries in the process when his harness broke although his crash helmet saved him from serious injury. Elsewhere, MiGs of the 18th GuFAR intercepted F-84s in the P'yongyang area and claimed two shot down including one by Kapt Sergei Kramarenko. These latest claims brought the MiG total for the month to 96, which included 45 F-86s, 24 F-84s, 13 B-29s and four Meteors.

As October drew to a close, UN air superiority in Korea was more at risk than it had ever been. During the month there had been 2,573 MiG sightings in the air involving 2,166 engagements. According to credited UN claims, 32 MiGs had been destroyed – 24 by F-86s, seven by B-29 gunners, and one by an F-84 pilot – but the Americans acknowledged the loss of seven F-86s, five B-29s (plus two others too badly damaged for further use), two F-84s and one RF-80 in aerial combat. Although it was believed the Sabres were scoring more kills, the MiGs were dangerously close to taking command of the air. Moreover, FEAF bombers had so far failed to neutralise the new airfields in the Saamcham-Taech'on-Namsi triangle. Thousands of labourers rapidly refilled those bomb craters that had been made and they remained busy building other necessary airfield facilities. Encouraged by the lack of UN success, the Communists were moving aircraft across the Yalu to Sinuiju and Uiju airfields. Aerial

---

[16] See *Crimson Sky*.

reconnaissance[17] showed that for the first time about 26 MiGs were dispersed at Uiju and 64 conventional aircraft counted at Sinuiju. There had been a further increase in the size of the MiG force as well, and it was being more aggressive. Not only that, it was being equipped with the newer, higher performance MiG-15bis. Russian pilots, aided by a growing band of Chinese and North Korean pilots, had been flying the MiG in combat now for nearly a year. The Chinese pilots were gaining valuable experience by the day. The UN air forces were hurting – but so too was the MiG force. Russian ace Kapt Boris Abakumov of the 196th FAR wrote:

> "In October 1951 our medical board offered many pilots of our Division the chance to return to the USSR. Because of permanent strain on the nerves and physical strain from combat operations, many of our pilots felt a heartache that did not cease even after quite some time. Some pilots accepted the offer. Some remained, on [General] Kozhedub's request. Many pilots who left had to be given medical aid. We were exhausted from constant combat." [18]

Despite the Communists striking back in the air with vigour, the 5th Air Force's Operation 'Strangle' interdiction campaign was still making substantial progress: the railway line between Sukch'on and Sinanju was completely out of service, although the Communists made herculean efforts to keep one rail line open from Sinuiju to P'yongyang and another from Huich'on through Kunu-ri and Sunch'on to the Yangdok area of central Korea. For a week later in October the fighter-bombers managed to block both of these lines by wrecking three locomotives along the stretch of track between Kunu-ri and Sunch'on. At the end of October, however, a few days of poor weather allowed the enemy to remove the derelict locomotives and reopen this key link in their rail network. Hostile ground fire was also taking an ever-increasing toll of 5th Air Force fighter-bombers:

August 1951:	26 aircraft lost and 24 damaged
September 1951:	32 aircraft lost and 233 damaged
October 1951:	33 aircraft lost and 238 damaged

Among the aircraft lost during the month were five Mustangs of the 18th FBG, resulting in three pilots being reported missing. These were 1/Lts Newman C. Golden and George Jones of the 39th FIS, and 1/Lt Oliver E. Jones of the 12th FBS; Golden had spent some months as a POW in Germany during WWII. Another, Capt James McCabe of the 67th FBS, was rescued by helicopter after baling out. Two tactical-reconnaissance Mustangs also failed to return, from one of which Capt Leornard was rescued after baling out, but 1/Lt Grant W. Madsen was posted missing. Another TacR pilot was fortunate to return after having hit a cable strung across a valley. The 8th and 49th FBGs suffered a spate of losses during the last week of the month, 1/Lt Louis T. Esposito (35th FBS) going down on the 22nd, 1/Lt Vernon Wright (25th FIS) three days later, although he was rescued by helicopter, but 1/Lt David Warfield (35th FBS) and Capt Howard A. Wilson Jr (25th FIS) were both killed. In addition, 1/Lt Bradford Martin suffered injuries when he belly-landed his damaged 25th FIS aircraft. The especially high damage rate was placing greater burdens upon the maintenance crews, creating for them an increasing number of problems in keeping a high percentage of aircraft available for operations. Nevertheless, if the UN lost its air superiority in the next few weeks, and the intensity of hostile ground fire continued to increase at its present rate, the fighter-bombers would be under great pressure to keep to their current programme and commitment.

Although not grabbing any of the limelight or glory, the RAF Sunderland Detachment based at Iwakuni continued to carry out mainly uneventful but arduous anti-submarine patrols over the Sea of Japan in support of Task Force 77, and in the Yellow Sea as far as the Shantung Peninsula and north towards Port Arthur. Since August, when the Sunderlands resumed their patrols after a month's respite, an average of 15 patrols had been flown each month. The three

---

[17] The Americans also continued their series of clandestine reconnaissance flights over the Sea of Japan and near Vladivostok probing Soviet defences, including a sortie by an RB-45C from Yakota AFB which overflew and photographed the southern end of Sakhalin Island on 9 October 1951.

[18] See *MiG-15* by Gordon and Rigmant.

squadrons of the Far East Flying Boat Wing – 88, 205 and 209 – continued to rotate their detachments as earlier. One of 205 Squadron's pilots, Flt Lt George Chesworth, later wrote:

> "In the early months of the war, particularly when operating well north in the Yellow Sea, the Sunderland was judged to be at risk from hostile aircraft. As a result air gunners were reintroduced into the crew. However, I am not aware that any of our aircraft were attacked. Indeed, the only occasion I was ever fired on was by the US Navy ship I had been flying round all night and who had just given me permission to return to base. The only real enemy was the weather, and in the winter the associated cold. Frontal type weather with rain and often very low ceilings posed a problem in the context of the grim and forbidden terrain in and around Korea and, in particular, Southern Japan." [19]

All this meant that winter flying for the Sunderland crews could be quite exciting at times, although it was generally monotonous, boring and exhausting.

---

[19] See *Royal Air Force Historical Society Journal 21*.

CHAPTER IX

THE GOING GETS TOUGHER

November – December 1951

"Personal to Vandenberg from Thyng: I can no longer be responsible for air superiority in North-West Korea . . ."

Colonel Harrison Thyng, OC 4th FIW, to General Hoyt S. Vandenberg,
USAF Chief-of-Staff, November 1951

In Washington, General Vandenberg was already well aware of what was happening. He had flown to the Far East in late October to make a brief on-the-spot survey of the situation. After talking with FEAF commanders and reviewing all available intelligence, he came away convinced that General Weyland's reports back in September had been right. The Communist air threat was more serious than ever before. On returning to the United States he told the press, obviously still unaware of the full extent of Russia's involvement:

"Almost overnight Communist China has become one of the major air powers of the world. The air supremacy, upon which we have relied in the past, is now faced with a serious challenge . . ."

Acting on 22 October, he defied long-standing US air defence policy – which dictated that the Soviet threat to North America was more important than Americans dying in action in Korea – and ordered the Air Defence Command (ADC) to immediately send 75 F-86A/E Sabres with pilots and crew chiefs to Alameda, California. There the aircraft were to be given the best waterproofing possible in the time available and loaded aboard escort carriers bound for Japan.

On receiving confirmation that these reinforcements were on the way, General Weyland planned to use the aircraft to equip the 51st FIW at Suwon, currently still flying F-80s. An equal number of F-80 crews were to be returned to the United States in exchange. The way was thus being paved to initially equip two squadrons of the 51st FIW (the 16th and 25th FIS) with Sabres – but this would all take time. The transfer of the Sabres was to be carried out by sea, the first batch leaving California on 1 November on the USS *Cape Esperance* and the second batch on 9 November aboard the USS *Sitkoh Bay*. Meanwhile, in a second measure to meet the growing threat, the entire 4th FIW was to be stationed at Kimpo with 77RAAF and the 67th TRW. The 4th FIW's third squadron, the 335th, was to move back from Japan to rejoin the 334th and 336th FIS already at Kimpo. The month started tragically for the 51st FIW, however, when Colonel William Linton, who had just replaced Colonel Oliver G. Cellini as CO, disappeared on a flight between Itumi AFB and Tsuiki AFB.

Other moves were afoot. In Japan, two Austers of the RAF's 1913 Flight flew from Iwakuni to Ashiya where they refuelled and took off again to join up with an RAF Sunderland detailed to accompany them on the 120 mile crossing to Korea. The flying boat escort would serve to boost the confidence of the Army pilots who were undertaking such a long over-sea leg in their tiny aircraft because they knew should the worse scenario happen and they were forced to ditch, a life-guard was on hand. Not only that, it also ensured that they would be heading in the right direction. At the onset of this flight, however, there had been four Austers in the party. At 0830, Capt Downward, Capt Brown, S/Sgt Hall and Sgt Jermy had taken off from Iwakuni as planned, bound for Ashiya, but shortly thereafter the leader in VF516 had to return to base due to faulty ignition. Thirty minutes later Hall also returned to Iwakuni due to airsickness and losing consciousness. Brown and Jermy in the two remaining aircraft flew on and arrived at Ashiya at 1000 with no further incident. The Austers were immediately refuelled for the flight to Pusan. At midday, Brown and Jermy took off, met the Sunderland over Ashiya, and arrived at Pusan an hour and 40 minutes later without mishap. Downward and Hall made the crossing in the other two Austers two days later. At Pusan transit camp they linked up with the Flight's ground party which had arrived by sea a few days earlier. While the Austers set out for the US 8th Army's airstrip at Seoul racecourse via Taegu and Taejon, the ground party embarked on a landing craft and sailed to Inch'on, from where they were taken to Kimpo. On the following day Sgt R.A. Carr, the senior NCO, flew in with the rear party, together with a newly arrived reserve pilot, Sgt J.W. Hutchings, who replaced Capt Gordons. Sgt Hutchings of the Glider Pilot Regiment had recent operational experience (for which he was soon to receive the DFM), coming from 656 AOP Squadron in Malaya. Finally, on 13 November, the Flight arrived at Fort George airstrip, where it met up with the resident 1903 AOP Flight. Unhappily for the new arrivals the weather was deteriorating and heavy rain made for a poor welcome with muddy roads and a heavily muddied airstrip and dispersal area.

The second day of November was a busy one in the air. While the 335th FIS was moving from Japan back to Kimpo, Sabres of the 334th FIS clashed with MiGs over MiG Alley during which Lt Colonel George L. Jones shared the destruction of a MiG with 1/Lt Richard A. Pincoski. On the other side, Russian pilots of the 18th GuFAR and 17th FAR who were active in the vicinity also reported clashes with F-84s and Meteors, claiming two of the former and one of the latter. Sixteen Meteors led by Sqn Ldr Wilson in A77-15 were carrying out a fighter sweep in the Anju area at 17,000 feet when, over Sukch'on, a few bursts of heavy flak were noticed. Ten or twelve MiGs were then observed at 20,000 feet heading for the P'yongyang area, but no attack was initiated. Suddenly, over Sukch'on itself, an estimated 20 MiGs of the 18th GuFAR attacked the Australian formation. In the resulting battle, Kapt Nikolai Babonin, the leader of a MiG section surprised one Meteor and claimed to have shot it down. F-86s also became embroiled in the fighting and with two types of swept-wing fighters unexpectedly in the same battle, some confusion as to who was actually the enemy resulted. Flt Lt Scotty Cadan (A77-911) delivered a good burst at a pair of jets that were firing at Flg Off Les Reading's A77-29, but did not allow enough deflection. They made off in a rush. Flt Lt Joe Blyth (A77-189) fired a long burst at three MiGs being attacked by Sgt Ken Murray (A77-373), and had the satisfaction of seeing white smoke pour from the tailpipe from one and then from inboard of the enemy's wings. This MiG pulled up and disappeared to the north. Shortly afterwards, two F-86s initiated a front quarter attack on Blyth but he called them over the radio and was identified just in time. He then joined up with the Sabres and returned to base with them. Meanwhile, Plt Off Ray Trebilco (A77-744) fired a long burst at two enemy aircraft and saw black smoke streaming from one of them before it escaped.

Flg Off Geoff Thornton (A77-741) also thought he had a good chance for a kill as he sat behind his intended victim for nearly a minute, jockeying for range at about 200-300 yards, but just before firing he realised he had been following an unsuspecting Sabre. Eight more MiGs attacked Flt Lt Scannell's flight, which broke into the attack. Immediately four more MiGs attacked from the rear. Scannell in A77-982 saw tracer spraying all around this canopy but there were no hits. One or two more MiGs made head-on passes and then they all withdrew to the north, one of which was observed trailing smoke, while another swept-wing fighter was seen going down in a spin.

Examination of the gun-camera films showed a vast improvement – much to the discomfort of one of the Australian pilots. Although he thought he had been firing at MiGs, Flt Lt Cadan's film showed two Sabres in his gunsight, and examination of battle damage inflicted on one of the Sabres revealed 20mm cannon-shell damage to its fuselage. Luckily, no serious harm was done, and the incident was immortalised in a cartoon by Bill Middlemiss, 77RAAF's resident artist. Under the heading of 'Aircraft Identification', Scotty Cadan was depicted firing at two swept-wing aircraft while saying: "Oh, I just give a short burst and watch whether they fly north or south!" On a more positive note, Flt Lt Joe Blyth was credited with damaging a MiG and declared he would have hit still more, only his windscreen had been changed. He had been using one of the cracks in his old windscreen for sighting targets at 800 yards! Unfortunately, the MiG attacked by Plt Off Trebilco could not be confirmed so no claim was made. No Meteors had been lost or hit, although it seems likely that Flt Lt Scannell's aircraft may have been the Meteor that Kapt Babonin had fired on.

In October the 5th Air Force's fighter-bombers had destroyed North Korea's railway lines faster than the enemy could repair them and, in early November, a UN victory in the air war against North Korea's railroads seemed imminent, despite the growing MiG threat. The Communists could still move trains over a circuitous route south from Sinuiju to Sinanju, then east to Kunu-ri, south to Sunch'on – a slow movement because of limited serviceability of the Sunch'on bridge – and from there to Samdung and Yangdok. They could also move from Kanggye to Kunu-ri, then to Sunch'on, and thence into P'yongyang. But, on the east coast, they had no through traffic from Kilchu to Wonsan, although they were still able to shuttle trains between breaks in the tracks. In order to sever the rail routes in north-west Korea, the 5th Air Force needed only to destroy the short link between Kunu-ri and Sunch'on, a task which appeared possible with a week of intensive attack.

'Strangle' missions flown by 2SAAF from November onwards were directed almost exclusively against two short stretches of the double main railway line between P'yongyang and Sariwon, and the secondary line between Sunch'on and Hwandong-ni. The main threat facing the fighter bombers in these raids came from the anti-aircraft guns that the Communists had placed in increasing numbers along vulnerable sections of the main supply routes, but now that the MiGs were venturing south of the Ch'ongch'on more often, these were another hazard to look out for.

The South Africans had their second encounter with MiGs, east of Taech'on, on the morning of 2 November. Eight Mustangs led by Capt Amo Janse van Rensburg took off from K-46 on an 18th FBG railway interdiction mission to Yongwon, but low cloud over the airfield caused confusion after take-off, with the result that two aircraft aborted and two others returned early. The remaining four SAAF fighter-bombers carried on with the mission but near the target they found about 15 MiGs waiting for them. A pair of the enemy jets peeled away from the main group to make a pass at the Mustangs. Capt Janse van Rensburg followed the accepted practise of turning his flight in to face the attack and this caused the MiGs to break away without opening fire. Another MiG then positioned itself within striking distance above the Mustangs, although the enemy pilot did not press home an attack because the Mustangs once again turned towards him. He broke away and flew north. The clash this time was over as quickly as it had begun. On interdiction missions during the day the South Africans flew 17 sorties and achieved three rail cuts, two road cuts, destroyed an automatic weapons gun position and killed one pack animal. Meanwhile, another flight of SAAF Mustangs, along with a flight of F-51s from the 67th FBS, carried out the rôle of close-support for an ROK training exercise. This was a landing staged by a battalion of the South Korean Marine Corps in Chinhae Beach, south of K-10 airfield. The exercise was judged an all-round success.

MiGs appeared over North Korea almost every day in November. For the most part they employed a pincer-and-envelopment technique, a method they had experimented with for some time. Co-ordinated 'trains' of 60 to 80 MiGs crossed the Yalu over Antung and over the Sui-ho reservoir at altitudes above 35,000 feet. Both the 'west coast train' and the 'central train' dropped off flights or small sections to engage the Sabre patrols, but the main bodies travelled on southwards to converge over P'yongyang and begin a return trip to the Yalu. While on the way home, part of the MiG force dropped down to 15,000 feet to attack UN fighter-bombers, homeward-bound Sabres, or any stragglers they could find. To cover their mass withdrawal northwards, a new formation of MiGs usually penetrated at least as far south as Sinanju. To UN airmen it seemed that the enemy did not exploit their tactical advantages to the fullest. Many of the enemy pilots who flew in these 'bandit trains' were apparently under training and unwilling to engage in combat.

Nevertheless, the pincer-and-envelopment tactics were difficult enough to counter. One method that was employed to safeguard returning aircraft was to scramble the strip alert Meteors from Kimpo, as on 2 November, when Flg Off Dick Wittman and Sgt D.M. Robertson were sent off. The two Meteors patrolled the Anak area for some time, but with negative sightings, before they were recalled. In the next scramble, Sgt Max Colebrook (A77-728) and Flg Off Ken Blight (A77-29) intercepted a B-29 and two USMC Corsairs. After returning to Kimpo, their Meteors were immediately refuelled and just over an hour later they were up again, with Ken Blight taking his turn leading. This time they intercepted twelve F-86s, eight F-80s and two F-84s. The two Thunderjet pilots were in a very agitated mood and took strong evasive action that was viewed with some suspicion. There were often rumours of enemy pilots flying captured UN aircraft, such as red-nosed F-80s which were not USAF aircraft[1]. After the interception was made, and as the Meteors turned south, the F-84s also turned to the south and closed on the Meteors before breaking away and heading north. The Meteors turned about and followed them to make a more positive identification, but they started to draw away. Blight and Colebrook accelerated and soon caught up, observing that they carried USAF markings and yellow tails. The Thunderjets went into a port orbit and then broke to the north. One Meteor closed to intercept and the F-84s took evasive action before proceeding further north again. After this entertaining chase Colebrook and Blight returned to base.

The next day the strip alert scrambles continued. In the morning, Flg Off Wal Rivers (A77-139) and Sgt Ken Murray (A77-728) scrambled and identified one P2V Neptune[2] and a Thunderjet before they were vectored to intercept an unidentified aircraft 40 to 50 miles to the north. This aircraft was apparently well aware of the movements of the Meteor flight and the Australians were unable to make contact with it. Later, Sqn Ldr Wilson led 77RAAF's usual fighter sweep in the Anju area. The Meteors few in four flights at 16,000 feet, one piloted by Flg Off Les Reading on his 150th mission of the Korean War. Approximately ten miles south of Anju ten MiGs were sighted at 25,000 feet and almost immediately another flight of 30 MiGs suddenly appeared overhead. Two enemy aircraft dived down, attacked the flight and then headed north as more MiGs came down. Sgt Max Colebrook (A77-368) called the initial break when the first pair of MiGs was about 1,500 yards away. He pulled around and fired at about 300 yards range, with about 30 degrees deflection. No results were observed from this burst so he barrel-rolled around them and fired at 400 yards range. One MiG pulled vapour half way along its starboard wing. Colebrook continued firing until the MiGs were out of range, his target climbing away still streaming vapour. Flg Off Wittman's section was attacked by three pairs of MiGs which made non-firing passes. The flight broke and tried to turn into the attack but the MiGs were too fast. However when one pair did break, Wittman (A77-911) found he could hold them in his sights. He fired several bursts but without obvious results.

After the break, the Meteor sections began to turn tightly, and it was soon found that any aircraft lagging was immediately attacked by the MiGs waiting above[3]. Several Meteors fired on MiGs but they were not able to close in most instances. Sgt Don Armit (A77-373) lost his element leader in the first break and received hits while turning gently to find him. His aircraft received a 37mm shell through the port engine's cowling. Armit was unhurt and he carefully nursed his plane back to base. When the order came to withdraw, Flg Off Wittman turned on to a southwards heading and began to lose altitude. His wingman, Sgt Doug Robertson (A77-811), one of the new pilots, was about 1,000 yards behind so Wittman throttled back and flew straight

---

[1] It seems highly improbable that Communist forces flew captured UN aircraft into battle.

[2] Another P2V, an aircraft of VP-6, was not so fortunate a few days later when, on 6 November, near Russia's Cape Ostrovnoi in the Japanese Sea, it was intercepted by two La-11s of the 88th GuFAR flown by St/Lts I.Ya. Lukashev and M.K. Shchukin and shot down into the sea with the loss of the crew of ten. The Neptune's stated mission had been to reconnoitre weather conditions near the Siberian coast.

[3] Stragglers were always liable to be picked off by the MiGs. Milt Cottee recalled a humorous incident concerning Sgt Keith Meggs: "He was in a section of Meteors one day when he dropped too far behind. The section leader called up and said, 'Pull up Meggs.' Sections all over the sky pulled up in all directions, until he added something like, 'Reform! I said Meggs not MiGs'."

for a few seconds. Five miles north-east of Anju, Robertson reported that he was being attacked and called a break. The Meteors broke and headed south. As he returned to base Robertson found that his hydraulic system had failed and there was a fire in the port wheel well.Luckily, the fire extinguished itself before he reached Kimpo and he carried out a belly-landing at the side of the strip. An inspection of the machine revealed that a shell had cut a furrow, front to rear, between the rear of the centre section and the front fuselage. There were obvious signs of burning in the wheel bay, and the belly-landing resulted in both engine nacelles being crushed. The aircraft was only fit for breaking up into spare parts. Sgt Don Armit's damaged aircraft was not so bad. It had received a shell through the port engine's top cowling, cutting through the nacelle inner side segment. The shell went through the front main spar and nose nacelle, practically severing the port aileron control rod in the process. After temporary repairs, A77-373 was flown across to Iwakuni.

Russian pilots in action that day reported UN air raids by Meteors and F-84s convoyed by F-86 Sabres. The Meteors and most of the F-84s were intercepted by MiGs of the 523rd FAR. In the course of several combats, they claimed five F-84s and two Meteors shot down, the latter the victims of Kapt Grigorii Okhai, deputy commander, and St/Lt B. Sinelnikov. Meanwhile, the Sabres had been engaged by MiGs of the 17th FAR and one was claimed shot down. No Soviet aircraft were lost. Of these recent clashes with the MiGs, Flt Lt Scannell observed:

> "If a Meteor had the misfortune to be on its own and was the subject of the undivided attention of MiGs, it was thought that its best evasive action was a cross between the old downward aileron roll and the F-86's maximum speed diving turn. That is, a steep diving turn, preferably in a southerly direction, at high speed and with the maximum amount of G. Naturally this meant that the pilot was blacked out for most of the manoeuvre and the recovery stage could be awkward. Owing to the extremely poor rearward visibility, the best method to clear one's tail was to do a tight skidding barrel-roll as soon as sight was regained, when the pilot could view the surrounding area through the top of his canopy. It was useless trying to fight without seeing backwards. Fortunately, the MiG would not follow an aircraft below 10,000 feet for long if it was headed south, presumably because it had a long haul home against head winds."

In further clashes next day three F-86s were claimed shot down by MiG pilots in addition to two F-80s and two F-84s, the fighter-bombers being credited to the 17th FAR. Two of the Sabres were reported to have crashed into the sea. The American pilots claimed two MiGs shot down, one by Capt William F. Guss USMC flying with the 336th FIS, and the other by 1/Lt Alfred W. Dymock Jr of the 334th FIS, while newly arrived Maj William Whisner claimed one damaged. The Americans did lose two F-80s during the day, but apparently not due to MiG action. 2/Lt Michael Kovalish of the 36th FBS was reported to have been shot down by ground fire, while 1/Lt Henry Batease of the 16th FIS crashed on landing on returning from an operational sortie and was killed.

There was almost another Meteor/MiG engagement on 5 November, when a dozen Meteors were required to close-escort four RF-80s on a photographic mission over the enemy's main supply routes from Sukch'on to Anju and Junuri. They were led by Flt Lt Scannell in A77-982. The Meteors met up with two of the RF-80s while the other two were photographing the main road at Huich'on. The whole flight then joined up and commenced to photograph from Junuri to Sunch'on. At this point, as they were leaving Junuri, a formation of twelve MiGs appeared at about 35,000 feet, but when they had approached to within about 20 miles, the RF-80s descended to 8,000 feet escorted by Plt Off Ray Trebilco's flight while the remainder stayed at 20,000 feet to cover and follow them south. The MiGs did not attack. It was missions such as this that inspired the 67th TRW's historian to write:

> "On many occasions pilots of the 15th TRS showed the fighter-boys daring fortitude by sweeping in at low altitudes for photos and evading enemy aircraft in an unarmed RF-80 . . ."

From K-46 the 18th FBG flew a railroad interdiction mission which included two flights of

Mustangs from 2SAAF. After the attack on the railway the eight SAAF Mustangs flew the usual armed reconnaissance sweeps on the way home. Lt Pretorius' flight made a rocket attack on supplies in a village north-east of Sibyon-ni and followed this up by strafing during which two houses were destroyed, but one aircraft was seen to be in difficulties and apparently failed to pull out of its dive. A check over the R/T revealed that 2/Lt Critton Pappas, on his first operational flight, was missing. Pretorius led the others back to the scene of the attack and they carried out a thorough search of the area but there was no sign of the missing aircraft (363). This was not the only UN casualty during the day. Colonel Albert Prendergast, CO of the 136th FBW, was lost when he failed to return from a mission.

On 6 November the Chinese Communist Air Force made use of a lack of UN air presence to employ its Tu-2 light bombers for the first time, attacking the island of Taehwa-do in the Yellow Sea, where ROK forces were fighting North Korean marines. On this occasion they and their escorting La-11s escaped unscathed; the Chinese crews would not be so fortunate at the end of the month when a formation of Tu-2s was intercepted by Sabres. Next day (7 November) twelve Meteors led by Flt Lt Vic Cannon carried out a fighter sweep in the Anju area to cover the withdrawal of F-80 fighter-bombers, one of which had been shot down with the loss of the 35th FBS's 1/Lt Jerome Volk. The Meteors were in three flights at 25,000 feet. Over Sinanju some 16 to 20 MiGs were sighted heading southwards at 30,000 feet. No attacks were initiated. Ten more MiGs were seen in the area during the patrol but again no attacks were made. Finally, just after the recall was given and the Meteors were in the act of turning south, eight or ten MiGs initiated a sudden high-quarter attack from the north. These were aircraft of the 176th GuFAR on a 'loose hunting' mission and Kapt Petr Milaushkin of the 1st Eskadrilya claimed one of the Meteors shot down. When the MiGs attacked, the Meteor sections broke into them and fired a few apparently ineffective bursts. A pair of Sabres which had been acting as an airborne relay joined the fight unexpectedly and were attacked in error by Flt Lt Cannon (A77-31), fortunately without hitting them. Meanwhile, Flt Lt Thomas' flight held the break until the MiG attack was committed, then broke into four MiGs and opened fire but no results were observed and more MiGs came down from a circle orbiting above. The MiGs were following their usual tactics of attacking with one or two sections and leaving the main body above the fight to descend in pairs on any likely target. Several such attacks were started with the MiGs diving on a lone Meteor, but each time they were broken off before the Russian pilots could obtain a suitable firing position. Flt Lt Thomas (A77-959) and Wt Off Bill Michelson (A77-726) climbed up into the upper circle and launched their own attack on the MiGs but were forced to leave when they themselves came under attack. After about ten minutes of combat in which no hits were received, and apparently no hits scored, the Meteors withdrew and returned to base, low on fuel but in the clear. Flt Lt Scannell later wrote:

> "During the [recent series of] combats, enemy attacks were well co-ordinated and pilots found it virtually impossible to get [their] sights on a MiG before one or more MiGs descended onto the Meteor's tail. It was observed that after the initial break by the Meteors, one section of MiGs remained positioned above the area of the break and additional pairs of MiGs were sent down when Meteors relaxed in the turn."

Dawn on 8 November introduced fine warm weather for the first time in five days, and 2SAAF flew a busy 40 sorties from K-46. Probably the most successful mission was flown by Maj Ray Lyon's flight when it came upon enemy troops in the open in a valley and found more in a small village nearby. The South Africans attacked with napalm and rockets, and followed this up with strafing. Three buildings were destroyed outright and another three were left burning, with at least 15 enemy soldiers killed. None of the Mustangs were hit but an additional hazard the pilots saw just in time was a cable stretched across the valley. 77RAAF flew two fighter sweeps during the day, both in the Anju area, and the first was led by Sqn Ldr Wilson in A77-15. Arriving in the sweep area, 30-40 MiGs were sighted flying south at 30,000 feet. They obviously saw the Meteor formation at the same time and changed direction to circle overhead. The Australians continued with the sweep, watching and waiting for the first sign of action, but none was initiated. As the Meteor flight left the area eight MiGs separated from the main group and followed it south for a short distance, then turned back. The second sweep was led by Flg Off Thornton in A77-741. This time four flights of twelve MiGs were observed up at 30,000 feet. As the Meteor pilots watched, two elements separated from one enemy flight, descended to 20,000 feet and then immediately climbed back up to their original height. No reason could be seen for this behaviour. There were no further incidents but while Thornton's flight was in the target area smoke could be seen coming from the island of Uri-do and Tan-do. The Sabres were busy elsewhere, Maj Whisner of the 334th FIS claiming his first MiG, and damaging a second. Both Russian FADs were involved in the action, pilots of the 196th FAR claiming three F-86s and one F-84, reporting that one Sabre crashed north-west of P'yongyang, a second at Don-Ha-li, while the third fell into the sea, with the Thunderjet coming down a few miles south of Anju. Meanwhile, the 17th FAR claimed four more F-84s and two F-80s. It seems that Chinese MiGs may have also been involved, Capt Zhao Bao-dung and Lt Liu Yuti of the 4th FAR claiming three 'unidentified' aircraft between them. Certainly one F-86 was lost, Capt Charles W. Pratt of the 334th FIS being reported missing, but losses of F-80s and F-84s are unknown. Capt Charles Brower of the 35th FBS reported that his F-80 section had been jumped by MiGs, one of which he claimed damaged. The F-84 claimed by the 196th FAR may have been credited to Kapt Abakumov, who related:

> "I opened fire at a distance of 800 metres. My tracers hit the F-84 at the cockpit. The enemy aircraft rolled left, dropped its nose, and crashed into the sea. The sea was not deep at this location, and the aircraft tail projected up through the water . . ." [4]

During the day Flt Lt Joe Blyth, flying A77-17, and Flg Off Wal Rivers each chalked up their 100th operational sortie in Korea. Both had flown missions on Mustangs as well as Meteors. Unfortunately, celebrations were dampened when it was learned that Sqn Ldr David Wilson's wife had been involved in a car accident in Australia, and that he was returning home forthwith. Next day he was advised that he had been awarded an immediate DFC, the first such award made by the British Government in the Korean War.

Among the FACs operating at this time was Capt Louis R. Drapeau, a Canadian with the 6148th TAC Squadron. He had already been awarded the US Air Medal for taking part in 30 spotting missions. On 8 November, his AT-6 was flying near the Sanjon when he observed about 1,000 enemy troops moving south. He called in a flight of four fighter-bombers and then sat tight while his pilot made two passes to mark the enemy force. Both times the marker rockets refused to fire, and the Communist troops, apparently realising what was happening, exploded two rounds of white phosphorus at a false location to draw attention. The AT-6 pilot then dived through intense small-arms fire and marked the real target with a coloured smoke grenade, following which Capt Drapeau directed the fighter-bombers as they bombarded and broke the enemy force. For this action he was awarded an Oak Leaf Cluster to his Air Medal. Another Canadian Army observer, Capt John H. Howard from the Royal Canadian Horse Artillery, who was attached to the 6147th TAC Squadron, like Drapeau, was also awarded a US Air Medal for taking part in 30 spotting missions and, for his continuing exemplary work, he was recommended for another decoration, an American DFC. However, the Canadian Government did not grant Capt Howard permission to accept the American award since it had decreed that Canadian servicemen in Korea could only receive one foreign decoration, in line with the British position and, as he had already been awarded the US Air Medal he could not officially accept the DFC.

There was a fierce air battle between eight F-80s of the 80th FBS and more than 20 MiGs near Kuni-ri on 9 November, after which the Americans claimed two MiGs probably shot down for no loss to themselves. However, an F-80 of the 36th FBS flown by 2/Lt Thomas Hadley was shot down and the pilot killed, reportedly to ground fire but possibly the victim of a MiG pilot from the 18th GuFAR. On this same date Maj Whisner of the 334th FIS reported a second successful engagement with a MiG, while a Chinese MiG pilot claimed slight damage to an RB-45 he intercepted. Elsewhere, SAAF pilot 2/Lt Ken Whitehead had a narrow escape when he flew too low while making a bombing run. His Mustang was damaged when debris from

---

[4] See *MiG-15* by Gordon and Rigmant.

exploding bombs tore his canopy and damaged a wingtip, although the aircraft remained flyable. He was escorted back to K-16 and landed without further mishap.

For some time now there had been speculation as to when the first snow would fall. At Kimpo the RAAF Aircrew Club opened a sweepstake. The weather on 10 November was again fine and warm and it felt as though snow could be several weeks off yet. MiGs were out in force, a flight from the 17th FAR catching a formation of F-84s on a 'Strangle' mission and claiming three shot down; it was alleged by Russian sources that two of the fighter-bombers fell just south of Kosei, with the third coming down near Tsinnampo, but only 2/Lt Michael G. Rebo was reported to have been killed in this action. The Meteors flew their usual daily sweep in the Anju area, this time led by Flt Lt Vic Cannon in A77-31. Fifty high-flying MiGs were observed but they made no attempt to attack. As the Meteors were leaving the sweep area the MiGs tailed them south until just north of P'yongyang when they turned back. Next day, Armistice Day, there was a tragedy for 77RAAF when two Meteors – A77-959 flown by Sgt Doug Robertson and A77-587 flown by Flg Off Ken Blight – collided while returning from a fighter sweep around Anju. Flt Lt Cannon was leading the formation during a mission when no MiGs had been sighted. The accident occurred suddenly, 24,000 feet up in a cloudless sky near the North Korean capital, about 80 miles beyond the bomb line. Sgt Robertson was on Flt Lt Scannell's wing but he appeared to be too far away and edging further out. Suddenly he banked to starboard, apparently trying to regain formation but then hit Blight's aircraft. Following the impact, Robertson's aircraft flipped over onto its back and spiralled down. At 18,000 feet two large pieces broke off the aircraft. Then the canopy either broke away or was jettisoned as it continued spinning down. Other pilots in the section followed the Meteor down, calling on Robertson to use the ejector seat – but in vain. The aircraft crashed so far inside enemy territory that only an aerial inspection could be made. Flg Off Les Reading recalled:

> ". . . I was the closest [and] I called to whoever was leading that I would follow [Robertson] down. I tried to talk to him but could never get through to him. I lost him in cloud. I then started to head home, low on fuel. Ken Blight was checking in. He had been damaged and was trying to get back to base. Nobody had sight of him, and it was only fortuitous that having left Robbie and trying to catch up that I saw Ken bale out and was able to pinpoint him and they were able to get a chopper and pick him up . . ."

Later that afternoon a recovery party made a search for the crashed aircraft. The services of an interpreter were enlisted and, after calling at various Korean police stations and asking policemen and civilians for directions, the wreckage of A77-587 was finally discovered shortly before midnight at a village a few miles south of the Imjin. A dead Korean farm labourer was still lying within a few feet of the wreck, killed by a piece of flying debris. After extending condolences to the young man's family, the party made a hurried departure back to Kimpo. Next morning the recovery party returned to the crash scene to inspect the wreckage in daylight but, by the time the Australians arrived, the last of a group of Korean labourers were leaving the scene of the crash, loaded up with scrap dural on their A frames. It turned out to be too late for an inspection since the aircraft had already been salvaged by locals. The Koreans did however allow a search of their booty as a security measure, however. The engines and cannons, which appeared to be all that was left of A77-587, were immersed in a mud crater which was rapidly filling with water, and were thus considered beyond salvage. An effort was made to intimidate the Korean salvage gang by announcing that a bomb which was likely to explode if disturbed was buried in the remaining debris, although it was doubtful if this would be much of a deterrent in a country where wages were sixpence a day and metal was very valuable.

A few days later, after the shock of the accident had diminished, Flg Off Blight was requested to write an outline of the incident to send to the Martin-Baker Company since, as far as it was then known, this had been the first use of a Martin-Baker ejector seat in operational conditions – details of Wt Off Ron Guthrie's high-altitude bale-out on 29 August (see Chapter VII) were not known at this stage:

> "At a position approximately 20 miles off P'yongyang and at a height of 24,000 feet I felt a terrific thud which jarred the aircraft in a manner suggesting I had been hit by a 37mm

MiG burst. My first thought was to call a 'break', but the aircraft whipped instantly into a violent gyration, developing into a spin. This rather stunned me and so I could not speak over the R/T at that stage. With the fear of landing in Red territory which we were well into, I fought the controls and also thought quickly of abandoning procedure. The aircraft ceased gyrating momentarily, then commenced again, then suddenly it wallowed into a semi-stable attitude, and I found it necessary to wind on full left rudder trim. The use of the inside engine was undoubtedly my salvation during the recovery.

At this stage, having recovered my breath but still with my strength exerted to hold the aircraft, I took stock of my predicament. I saw that approximately four feet was missing from my starboard mainplane [and] my starboard jet pipe temperature gauge was right at the end of the dial. I found that with full power on starboard engine and nil power on port, full left rudder trim plus all extra rudder I could physically apply, and with the control column hard left and back, I could steer a reasonably straight course, losing height at approximately 1,400 feet per minute at 220 knots.

I was now able to contact the other pilots in the formation and notify them what I was doing and I also learnt that another aircraft had slipped into me out of the sun, causing the damage. He spun straight down to the ground. I then changed over to the emergency rescue frequency and notified my base D/F of my predicament, and they gave me a course to steer. I managed to edge round on to the approximate heading [but] after two or three minutes felt that I could hold on no longer and then retracted my gunsight, depressurised the cockpit and opened the canopy electrically. I called D/F for a position again and asked if I was yet over friendly territory, but it was two or three minutes before they could pinpoint me, so I hung on. Finally, they informed me that I had crossed the front line and I unlocked my seat, leant forward and pulled the canopy jettison lever. There was a slight suction of dirt from the cockpit floor and I looked up in time to see the canopy flying about 20 feet above and to the port side of the tailplane.

I could now see the base on the horizon approximately 20 miles away and although my left leg was numb by this time, I felt I could get a little closer; now ideas of crash-landing were running through my mind, this being possibly brought on by the fear of abandoning, plus the possibility of saving the aircraft. I experimented with the aircraft and found that even a slight alteration of the circumstances caused the aircraft to roll, and that the lowest speed that it was controllable was 190 knots. I could not control my descent as it was fatal to vary the power, so I decided against crash-landing and then looked for a suitable place to abandon. I considered the best place was over the coastal mud flats about seven miles north-west of the base, if I could reach them, as now I was down to 5,000 feet.

I was a little afraid as to whether I would be able to leave the aircraft cleanly, as I knew that as soon as I relaxed the controls, the control column would bang over to my right knee and the aircraft would whip into a spin. I felt for the seat release hoop to make sure I could reach it, then made a quick check and tightened the seat harness. When I was satisfied that all was correct, I placed my right hand above my head and lightly on the blind hoop, palm inwards, my right foot on the seat stirrup, and jammed the stick over to the left with my right knee. I then quickly wound on some heavy nose trim and simultaneously brought my left foot back to the seat stirrup and left hand up to the hoop. With both hands I smartly pulled the blind out and down.

The ejection was instantaneous and I am rather hazy as to the sensations I felt. I do remember a terrific acceleration, then a peculiar feeling of deceleration and of my legs flying out and flailing the air uncontrollably.

Soon I found myself sitting very comfortably beneath the drogue with a feeling of complacency. I was neither oscillating nor did I have any feeling of rapid descent. I was able to think clearly what I was to do next and looked down at my parachute canopy release and felt for its release, then I took a breath and turned the release of my seat harness. The seat left me immediately and I commenced tumbling uncomfortably with wind hitting my eyes; I placed my hand firmly through the parachute release D and drew it smoothly across my body and to the full extent of my right arm. In the following second or so I saw the seat falling away below me and I felt the canopy jerk me – due to straps twisted in front of my face my head was jammed back uncomfortably. I tugged at them and they sprang apart, leaving me dangling nicely under the canopy. I had little time to take in the situation before a paddy field was rushing up at me and I relaxed my body in preparation for the impact. I landed with a moderate jarring of the posterior in the sitting position, with my feet in the rice paddy and seated on my dinghy on a narrow path.

A few minutes later an American rescue helicopter picked me up and returned me to base, where I found later I was unhurt except for a few slightly strained muscles. My neck was a little sore and my nose bruised, which I think was caused by the twisted parachute straps. I left the aircraft at 4,000 feet, which I consider is just a comfortable height. Speed was about 200 knots." [5]

Reasoning that the re-opened truce negotiations at Panmunjom offered such a good prospect for peace that they ruled out large-scale ground offensives by either side, and noting that the cost of mounting new major attacks against the Chinese and North Korean defences could not be justified in terms of the limited results that would follow, General Ridgway now directed the 8th US Army to cease offensive operations as from 12 November and to begin an active defence of its front. Desultory throughout October, the 8th Army's ground forward probes were now virtually halted by its commander's latest order. With the ground forces undertaking no offensive action and with the Communist forces equally quiet, 5th Air Force had reason to expect that ground commanders would request a minimum of close air support operations, and thereby the major effort could be directed into 'Strangle' attacks. This was not to be the case, however, and on occasion air strikes were ordered against small dugouts which probably contained no more than two or three enemy soldiers. More often than not, the FACs led supporting fighter-bomber pilots against designated ground targets where no sign of hostile activity could be seen at all from the air. Nevertheless, close-support strikes in the middle and towards the end of November did pay worthwhile dividends that were apparent on occasions.

13 November proved to be of those occasions for the pilots of 2SAAF. Shortly after midday 2/Lt Frank Grobler set off from K-46 at the head of a flight of four Mustangs, being directed by an FAC to attack bunkers and trenches full of troops on the top of a ridge. On completion of a successful mission during which it was estimated that 25-30 enemy troops had been killed, the Mustangs returned to base. Soon after their return, a further flight of four SAAF aircraft led by Capt Pretorius carried out a similar attack against bunkers when a further 75 troops were believed to have been killed. Grobler's flight followed shortly thereafter, carrying out another attack against well dug-in troops. The FAC fired a white smoke rocket to mark the target but it fell too far to the west. Grobler decided that he would indicate the target to his colleagues by means of a strafing run, but encountered intense and accurate 20mm and small-arms fire. After his attack he called up saying his aircraft (365) had been hit although he was able to orbit south of the target until his flight had completed its attack, but while attempting to turn for base he lost control and was forced to bale out. Fortunately he was by then over friendly territory and was soon rescued by helicopter from a forward US Army airstrip, eventually returning to K-46 three days later aboard a light liaison aircraft. For his performance during the day's missions he was awarded a US DFC. Altogether, 2SAAF launched 32 sorties that day which resulted in the destruction of at least five enemy field positions and inflicted an estimated 128 casualties. While making a strafing attack during one of these missions Capt Cliff Collins' aircraft (327) was hit in the engine. With his aircraft streaming glycol, Collins headed south towards friendly territory but the engine caught fire before he could reach the lines and he had to bale out.

---

[5] In his letter to the Martin-Baker Company, Flg Off Blight added: "This experience, although I do not wish to repeat, has given me the utmost confidence in both the aircraft and the safety equipment, particularly the ejection seat. Under the circumstances, I would not have been confident of abandoning in the old manner, and consider if I had not been ejected I would have been badly injured or perhaps unable to release my parachute. In any case, being the first [sic] British or Aussie pilot to have used it in operations, I thank you again – and on behalf of us all extend our appreciation of the fine work the people your side of the game are doing."

Luckily, prevailing winds drifted his parachute across the lines and down into the hands of the British Commonwealth Division, where he received quite a reception from the troops who plied him with drinks until a USAF helicopter 'rescued' him and flew him back to K-46.

Around Kimpo the sky become overcast in the afternoon and light rain fell over the area. Next day (14 November) saw little activity because of continuing rain which persisted until late afternoon, but there was no snow. Rain returned next day, transforming the camp area into a sea of mud and curtailing all operational flying from Kimpo. In early November the difference between the temperature at midday and after sunset was quite extreme. It was not unusual to see pilots sitting around sun-bathing at midday, while after dark there could be ten degrees of frost. Supplies of British winter clothing were issued to the men of 77RAAF to replace the American-type which had been issued earlier. The British wind-cheater jacket, the rear of which was made like a tail-coat, looked unusual but when this tail was pulled between the legs and buttoned to the front of the thighs it proved extremely effective, especially when sitting on the wet seats of open jeeps. The British string-vest, green woollen jumper, olive green under-trousers and pile cap were very warm and much envied by the Americans. The rate of exchange was one pile cap for a B-26-type, fur-lined jacket.

Just when victory for the comprehensive 'Strangle' rail campaign seemed to be in sight, Communist counter-measures began to work. Daylight photographs had been showing a by-pass bridge at Sunch'on with two spans missing from its middle, so it was naturally assumed to be out of service, but 5th Air Force was suspicious. An RB-26 was sent there to take pictures. These photographs showed that removable spans had been placed across the bridge and the enemy was in fact using it throughout the night. It raised the question of where else the enemy was doing the same sort of thing. Enemy fighters and flak had already substantially lessened the FEAF's interdiction capabilities and, after the blood-letting over the MiG Alley airfields in late October, FEAF Bomber Command did not have the resources to do both jobs -- neutralise the airfields the Communists were building as well as destroy the bridges they were repairing. Night bombing by Shoran-equipped[6] B-29s was considered to be an option, but results from the new night bombing offensive were not very accurate at first. A bomber crew normally required as many as 35 practice drops before it became really proficient but, because of the urgency of the situation, Bomber Command only had time to give its crews eight practice drops before sending them on combat missions. Some of the problems experienced were caused by inaccurate maps. The airfields at Namsi, Taech'on, and Saamcham were not located exactly where existing maps showed them to be. This large error factor necessitated dropping a greater volume of bombs, but the bombers succeeded in damaging the three airfields faster than the enemy's labour force could effect repairs.

The Communists tried to counter nocturnal bomber attacks by using deception and cunning, as well as force. Hoping to confuse the reconnaissance aircraft when they came over following attacks, the North Korean labour teams piled circular rings of dirt on the runways to look like bomb craters from the air. This ruse was detected by an alert FEAF photographic interpreter who realised that the dummy craters were not the right size. Low-level reconnaissance verified that the craters were simply piles of loose earth, banked up on unharmed sections of runways. There was also an increasingly large volume of flak, especially along the Yalu[7]. One of the senior Allied officers of the 67th Tactical Reconnaissance Wing, Sqn Ldr Allan Simpson of the RCAF – who was employed as a Photo Intelligence Officer – wished to see for himself just what the RB-26 crews were having to experience during their nocturnal sorties over North Korea, and he requested permission from Grp Capt R.W. McNair DSO DFC RCAF (see

---

[6] Shoran was short-range navigation radar, which paired two AN/APN-2 radar ground beacon stations with an AN/APN-3 transceiver installed in the aircraft. It had initially been tried in late 1950 and had proved ineffective, but by early 1951 was being used successfully by night-flying B-26s and RB-26s, and later briefly by B-29s sent to attack North Korean marshalling yards.

[7] On the evening of 8 November, flak batteries scored against a B-29 which was flying a leaflet dropping mission along the Yalu. The pilot managed to nurse his crippled bomber to the coast where he and his crew parachuted to safety. Eight nights later a pilot of the 351st FAR(N), St/Lt V. Kurganov flying an La-11 night fighter, reported shooting down a B-26 south-east of Antung which apparently crashed into the sea.

Appendix III), Air Advisor to the Canadian Liaison Mission with the USAF at FEAFHQ in Tokyo, to accompany an American crew on such a mission. Permission was granted and, accordingly on the night of 12/13 November, he flew with 1/Lt Erwin A. Thomassen and his crew aboard an RB-26C of the 12th TRS:

> "We followed the railway line near the east coast. Our route was Kimpo-Ch'unch'on-Kojo-Wonsan-Kowon-Yonghung-Hamhung-Hungnam-Songjin-Chuuron Jang, and back to Kimpo. At the most northerly point we were about 175 miles from Vladivostok in Siberia. We made visual observation and took photographs. At points, the railway was damaged by American naval bombardment. Supply trains coming from the north would have to off-load on one side of the break in the line. Then it would be manhandled and re-loaded onto another train south of the break and sent on its way. We carried no bombs but the North Korean railway crews didn't know that. One engineer pulled into a tunnel with the caboose partly exposed at one end and the locomotive just peeking out at the other. We encountered light flak near Kowon. There were both light and heavy flak batteries operating at or near Hamhung. We sustained no damage."

A few days later Sqn Ldr Simpson received another message from Grp Capt McNair which advised him that RCAFHQ in Ottawa had cancelled authorisation for him to fly on operations and, as a result, for the remainder of his short tour with the 67th TRW he was grounded, much to his chagrin.

With US bombers unable to attack the rail and road bridges in North Korea, Chinese and North Korean repair gangs redoubled their efforts to restore those that had been cut. By 15 November the Communists had finished reconstruction of their main highway bridge at Sinanju and, under cover of darkness, they were endeavouring to complete a rail by-pass bridge at P'yongyang. With monotonous regularity UN fighter-bombers had to return again and again to attack the same targets. Rail cuts were seldom left unrepaired for more than 24 hours.

On 16 November, the pilots of a flight of three F-84s of the 154th FBS returning to Taegu after a rail interdiction operation experienced one of the most dramatic and publicised happenings of the war. They were at 33,000 feet heading south when the lead aircraft flown by Capt John L. Paladino suddenly started to turn and then went into a steep dive to the left. After dropping a few thousand feet, its nose pitched up before it went into another dive, then climbed again. At first thinking that their leader was practising evasive action, his wingmen became concerned when they realised that his oxygen equipment had probably failed. Paladino had passed out from oxygen starvation and could only survive at a lower altitude – if it could be reached without his aircraft diving out of control. Acting with courage and forethought, Capt Jack Miller and 1/Lt Wood McArthur cautiously approached Paladino's aircraft and positioned their wingtips under his wingtips on either side, and by using the flow of air thus caused were able to keep his aircraft level. Locked together in this way they tensely and gradually descended. Their quick thinking worked and at 13,000 feet Paladino regained awareness and was able to fly back to base and land safely. He emerged from his cockpit suffering a severe headache but had no memory of the 15 minutes his aircraft had been miraculously held aloft by his companions.

Next day, Strike 39 for the month of November for 77RAAF was a sweep around Songch'on led by Flt Lt Thomas. The twelve Meteors carried out their patrol without seeing any MiGs, but the enemy jets were in the vicinity, ten being sighted by the two airborne relay Meteors piloted by Flt Lt Scannell and Sgt Avery orbiting south of P'yongyang. The MiGs were at 43,000 feet. Scannell and Avery climbed to their level and turned into them, ready to engage, but the MiGs continued flying northwards. No contact was made. Thick cloud shrouded Kimpo until 1030 the following morning. As conditions improved, Flt Lt Thomas led a fighter sweep to the Sunch'on area, one of the flights being led by Flt Lt Scannell flying his 99th operational sortie in Korea (he would complete his 100th next day in A77-189 during another sweep over Sunch'on). On this date also, Flt Lt Joe Blyth completed his 105th and final operational sortie with 77RAAF[8]. Just after the flight had entered the sweep area and commenced its patrol, ten

---

[8] Flt Lt Joe Blyth returned to the UK at the beginning of December. By late 1956 he was commanding

contrails were observed high above but no enemy aircraft could be seen. These contrails were joined by eight more and then ceased, presumably as the aircraft descended below contrail level. Some minutes later pilots of a flight of F-84s were heard calling over the radio that they were being attacked by MiGs over Hich'on. By now the Meteors were low on fuel and could not go to assist. Meanwhile, the F-84s, aircraft of the 111th FBS, struggled to hold their own, losing 1/Lt John Morse Jr while 1/Lt William Cowert baled out safely over the Yellow Sea; in return a MiG was claimed shot down by the combined fire of 1/Lts Kenneth C. Cooley and John Hewett Jr. A third F-84 returned with battle damage, while the Russian pilots from the 17th FAR and 18th GuFAR claimed four F-84s shot down, and their Chinese comrades from the newly arrived 9th FAR claimed six more.

At Taegu, Colonel Gabreski had taken command of the 51st FIW, having transferred from the 4th FIW. His first job was to prepare the 51st FIW for conversion from its aging F-80s to the much anticipated F-86E Sabres that were on their way by sea from the United States. When they arrived, not only would Sabre numbers be increased, but the F-86E was expected to be a much better match for the higher performing MiG-15bis now being encountered. Meanwhile, the 335th FIS was now settled in with the 334th and 336th at Kimpo bringing the whole of the 4th FIW together at last. At first the commitment of the three squadrons to combat did not markedly increase the Wing's capabilities, because the 335th merely shared the planes already held by the other two squadrons in Korea. Patrolling F-86s of the 336th FIS sighted about a dozen parked MiGs on the ground at Uiju airfield during a sweep on the 18th. It was an opportunity too good to miss. Leaving one pair of Sabres as top cover, Capt Kenneth D. Chandler and his wingman, 1/Lt Dayton Ragland, made a devastating attack that destroyed four MiGs and left several others damaged.

The serviceability rate for operations of the older F-80s was now declining considerably. At the same time as a high operational rate was giving maintenance crews trouble and placing burdens upon them, the amount of flak damage was especially high. With flak concentration and accuracy increasing, the fighter-bomber pilots were forced to revise their tactics in order to reduce the time spent over the target to a minimum. The fighter-bomber units faced many other problems. Shortages of spare engines and inadequately programmed supply support was also severely reducing the number of combat-ready F-84s at Taegu, and aircraft of the 49th and 136th FBWs were experiencing high numbers of engine failures. The 49th FBW had converted from F-80s to F-84s in late August and all the F-80s used by the 49th FBW eventually ended up in the hands of the 8th and 51st Wings, both of which were operating out of Suwon. The 51st, having been chosen to convert to the new F-86E being rushed from Japan, now began turning over its fatigued F-80s to the 8th Wing – the old fighter-bomber's combat career was coming to an end, while the 51st FIW commenced working up its new Sabres.

Meanwhile, at Fort George airstrip, the Auster pilots of 1903 and 1913 Flights were now settled in. Cold, windy weather and the heavily muddied airstrip and dispersal area made for difficult flying and landing conditions, particularly for light aircraft. There occurred two accidents during the month, the first on 14 November when Capt O'Brennan, ADC to Maj-General Cassels and a qualified Auster pilot, who had been authorised to fly Auster VF553 for the purpose of transporting the GOC to US I Corps HQ, crashed while landing. Fortunately, neither pilot nor passenger was hurt but the aircraft sustained serious damage. A few days later, on 20 November, newly arrived Lt Joe Luscombe of the Royal Australian Artillery crashed while taking off in VF988. The reasons for the crash were determined as heavy frost on the wings, the roughness of the runway, and the fact that the aircraft was pulled off the ground too quickly. It stalled and cartwheeled to a halt at the end of the strip but, again, neither pilot nor passenger were injured. Apart from Lt Luscombe, Capts G.W.C. Joyce RA and J.A. Crawshaw RA had arrived on posting from 656 AOP Squadron in Malaya to replace Capts Corfield,

---

Footnote 8 continued 8 Squadron of the RAF in the Middle East and flew operations in Venom FB4 fighter-bombers against Egyptian forces during the Suez conflict (when he destroyed five EAF MiG-15s on the ground – see *Wings over Suez* by Brian Cull with David Nicolle and Shlomo Aloni), and later still operated in the Oman. He received the DFC and Bar to add to his AFC and Bar (and US Air Medal), making him possibly the most highly decorated post-WWII RAF pilot.

Addington and Fitzgibbon, all of whom were tour-expired. To replace the two damaged Austers, VF547 and VF569 were ferried to Fort George from Iwakuni by S/Sgt Hall and Sgt Jermy. Meanwhile, Capt Bob Begbie's time with the US 3rd Light Aviation Section was also drawing to an end, as he recalled:

"Well over two thirds of my activities were in support of American – and at times South Korean, Turkish and other UN – forces. I flew a variety of aircraft, the L-5 Stinson, L-16 Aeronca, L-17 Ryan Navion, L-19 Cessna, and the [AT-6] Harvard. My conversions ranged from the minimal to the micro-minimal and were all done in situ. The Americans . . . conceded no mystique or super ability to fly light aircraft – and that included our Harvards which, in those days, was quite a hot pursuit ship equipped with under-wing rockets. A pilot would kick the tyres, climb in, light his cigar, press the starter button, check magnetos and open up for take-off. I must say it built up confidence and promoted a rather blasé attitude towards light aircraft.

My tasks with the Americans ranged from Air OP, medical casevac, reconnaissance (often behind enemy lines in the Harvard), to VIP and liaison sorties. The Harvard recces were interesting. FGA [Fighter Ground-Attack] 'cab ranks' operated almost continuously over the battle area, piston- engines at 8-9,000 feet plus, which could, if necessary, find their own targets, but the jet FGA Panthers had to cab rank at much higher altitudes to conserve fuel. The Harvards, flown by Army pilots, would penetrate beyond that area under observation by the light AOP aircraft. This was usually a more lucrative area where movement was concerned, and the US military policy was to declare a band of territory up to a depth of a certain number of miles, a 'no-go' area for Korean civilians. This meant that anything that exposed itself, or we observed, could be attacked. As we were out of range of our artillery, our attack weapon was the FGA cab rank. If we could indicate the target and still stay at height, we did, but if not, we would ourselves dive on the target and fire our under-wing rockets. They were not terribly accurate but they provided the marker the FGA needed. The amazing thing was how long it took the Chinese to change their doctrine of passive reaction, but once they did and brought in their AA and small-arms retaliation measures, our tactics had to change. Anyway, it was exciting while it lasted and the Americans even awarded me a medal [the US Air Medal] . . ."

The pilots of 77RAAF were advised they were to fly escort for the American Vice-President, Mr Alben Barclay, who was to visit the front lines on 22 November. He and his party were to be transported from point to point in light aircraft. However, poor weather prevented the tour from going ahead as planned and the Meteors remained grounded for the day. The first fall of snow occurred in the early hours of the next day, and it was not until the 24th that the Vice-President and his party were able to carry out their tour of the front lines. Throughout the day flights of Meteors provided top cover in relays for the L-19s with their VIP passengers in the area around Kumsong, the tour being successfully and uneventfully concluded.

At K-46, 2SAAF pilots were briefed to join an 18th FBG rail interdiction mission south of Sunch'on. From the onset things went wrong. Firstly, 2/Lt Frank Grobler's Mustang went u/s on the ground but, as flight leader, he had to go on the mission so he took over another aircraft. A second Mustang then developed engine problems, 2/Lt George Krohn being obliged to taxi his aircraft out of the way. Two more Mustangs from the second flight were also unable to take off, and consequently just four of the eight aircraft joined the 18th FBG attack. However, the problem with Krohn's machine (345) was quickly rectified and he was able to get airborne ten minutes later, meeting up with flights of USAF Mustangs. Although invited to join forces with the Americans, he was determined to catch up with his own flight, advising Grobler of his intention over the radio. Over the target area, meanwhile, Grobler orbited while the US fighter-bombers attacked, and he suddenly heard Krohn advising that he was going down to bomb the target. Grobler assumed that his colleague had joined forces with an American flight after all, but Krohn did not return to base. An American pilot later reported seeing a lone SAAF Mustang heading south after the attack, but it was lagging well behind. It was therefore assumed Krohn's aircraft had been hit, and had crashed en route to base. Although MiGs were active, it would seem that he did not fall victim to one, Russian claims being for two F-84s by the 17th FAR (pilots of the Chinese 7th FAR apparently claiming seven more) and one F-86 by a pilot of the 196th FAR, which reportedly crashed into the sea near Limpo. The Americans claimed two MiGs damaged, one by Colonel Thyng of the 4th FIW and the other by Maj Marshall of the 335th FIS.

On 27 November, Maj Richard Creighton of the 336th FIS became the USAF's fourth jet fighter ace when he claimed a MiG shot down, two more being claimed by Maj George A. Davis Jr of the 334th while another was credited to 1/Lt William R. Dawson (336th FIS). On this occasion MiG pilots did not make any claims against the Sabres, although two F-84s were claimed shot down by the 196th FAR, both of which reportedly crashed near Kansokun, while the 523rd FAR reported shooting down two F-80s near Jyunan. One of the F-80s was flown by 1/Lt Rafael Dubreuil of the 36th FBS, who was killed, while his colleague 2/Lt Travis Etheridge claimed a MiG damaged in return. An F-84 also failed to return in which Maj Bernard K. Seitzinger of the 7th FBS was reported missing. Soviet records also reveal that a pair of MiGs flown by Kapt Pavel Nikulin and St/Lt N.A. Garmashov of the 176th GuFAR entered clouds to evade four attacking Sabres and when they broke through into the clear at 29,000 feet, they found eight Meteors ahead of them, one of which Nikulin claimed to have damaged before the others escaped into cloud. There were twelve Meteors on the sweep in the area of Sunch'on, with Flt Lt Cannon at their head. Upon reaching Sunch'on the Meteors patrolled for 20 minutes with no sightings until the leader of a flight of USN Panthers operating in the vicinity called up and asked if the Australians would verify the result of an attack that had been made on two trains. Cannon brought the Meteors down to 5,000 feet and found the trains, one on either approach to a bridge over a small river. Both had been damaged, and one was on fire. While carrying out this check, accurate 20mm and 40mm flak opened up but none of the Meteors was hit. At no time were MiGs encountered.

There was more heavy air-to-air fighting next day when Sabres clashed with MiGs. Maj Marshall of the 335th FIS claimed one MiG shot down near Kang-jong and shared a second with 2/Lt Samuel A. Groening near Sang-dong, while 1/Lt Dayton Ragland (336th FIS) was credited with a third but was himself shot down by another. It would seem that just about all the pilots of the 196th FAR had attacked him, claims being submitted by this unit for seven F-86s shot down, while pilots of the 523rd claimed two more. Polkovnik Pepelyaev, commander of the 196th FAR, was credited with one F-86 in this action. In the event, Ragland safely ejected but was captured and imprisoned for the remainder of the war. In addition, a MiG pilot of the 17th FAR reported shooting down an F-84 which allegedly crashed between Don-song and Sun-sen in which the American pilot was killed. The Russians also admitted the loss of one of their ace pilots, Kapt German Shatalov of the 523rd FAR, who had been credited with two F-86s, two F-51s and an F-80. It is unclear whether the following 4th FIW report related to the shooting down of 1/Lt Ragland's aircraft, although it does refer to one of the Wing's losses at around this time:

"F-86A (49-1109) was reportedly seen out of control and trailing smoke while engaged in combat with enemy aircraft . . . 1109 failed to return from this mission."

Another 4th FIW report revealed the safe return of one of its pilots who had originally opted to eject during a combat with MiGs, but had been unable to do so:

"Pilot of F-86A (48-288) during a combat mission, on the initial break while engaging a MiG-15, experienced complete boost failure while in a 5G turn at .95 Mach. A tight diving spiral was then started with G force increasing to 8Gs. At 11,000 feet the pilot, still in a tight spiral at 500 knots indicated, made the decision to abandon the aircraft. When the canopy release was actuated at 10,000 feet, the canopy charge exploded, but the aft rollers of the canopy dug in to the canopy deck forward of the seal, causing the canopy to ram in on the aircraft. This apparently acted as a speed brake and the pilot stated his speed decreased 100 knots immediately, rendering the Sabre controllable and he was able to pull out at 2,500 feet. It is believed that the excessive G forces in the spiral were the reason the canopy dug in and did not break clear of the ship. Pilot was unable to utilize the speed brakes for recovery due to loss of hydraulic pressure. The F-86 was brought in for a safe landing with no further damage noted."

The encounter generated some activity for 77RAAF. Two Meteors flown by Flt Lt J.T. Hannan, a new pilot, and Sgt Allan Avery were scrambled to intercept unidentified aircraft. When they reported to the GCI controller, he directed them to search for a downed F-86 pilot (1/Lt Ragland) who was thought to be somewhere on the west coast. After a vain search in one area for a few minutes they were vectored onto another possible location, and continued searching for half an hour without luck. Meanwhile, four more Meteors led by Flg Off Wittman took off to provide CAP for the American pilot if found. They located a burning Sabre at a position about ten miles south-west of Sinanju but their search of the surrounding area covering a ten-mile radius revealed no sign of the pilot or a parachute. It was likely that Ragland had already been captured by this time. While the search was underway, it was business as usual for the other members of 77RAAF. Flt Lt Thomas led a fighter sweep in the area of Songch'on, which proved to be uneventful, while later Flt Lt Hannan and Sgt Avery were again scrambled to chase a bogey that was eventually lost by the controller. Finally, Hannan flew a third scramble for the day on the wing of Flt Lt Cadan to investigate more unidentified aircraft which turned out to be four USMC Corsairs, two RF-80s and six F-86s.

2SAAF lost a Mustang during the day as a result of a close-support mission against two tanks. Working with an FAC, 2/Lt Peter Norman-Smith led his flight down on the target, which they attacked with bombs and rockets. During one strafing run 2/Lt Ken Whitehead's aircraft (356) was hit in the engine by ground fire and it started to leave a trail of black smoke as he pulled away. Whitehead headed for an emergency landing strip but when he arrived he found people and trucks on the runway. The only choice he had was to carry out a belly-landing in a paddy field adjacent to the airstrip, during which his aircraft was severely damaged although he emerged unscathed. Next day (29 November), while attacking a secondary target, the South Africans lost another aircraft, this time along with its pilot, Capt Amo Janse van Rensburg, who was acting as formation leader on a routine railroad interdiction mission. No flak was observed over the primary target and with some ordnance remaining the flight proceeded to a secondary target, a village south-east of Suan which the enemy used as a supply dump. This was bombed, rocketed and strafed. After pulling off the final strafing run, the Mustangs climbed away and started forming up. Suddenly they ran into intense light ground fire and Capt Janse van Rensburg's aircraft (346) was hit and began streaming a thickening white trail of glycol. He started a radio transmission but had apparently been severely wounded. Within a few seconds the Mustang caught fire and abruptly spiralled down out of control towards the ground. Lt Jimmy Parsonson, flying No3, was forced to take evasive action to avoid a collision. Lt Ken Hanson, at No4, saw that Janse van Rensburg was slumped forward in his seat as the Mustang began its final dive, hit the ground and exploded. During the month 2SAAF claimed the destruction of 200 buildings, nine vehicles and four railway rolling stock, also inflicting an estimated 300 casualties on the enemy's troops, but the cost was high.

In the Anju area a dozen Meteors led by Flt Lt Thornton sighted an estimated 40 MiGs high above, which were patrolling north and along the same line but several thousand feet above the Meteors at their 18,000 feet designated patrol height. A short time later eight big, black puffs of flak were observed to burst over Sunan, about a mile ahead. These were not aimed at the Meteors but seemed to be intended to mark their position for the benefit of the MiGs, although no attack ensued. Over Sunch'on another flight of about a dozen MiGs was seen to be patrolling an east-west line and, on two occasions, a number came down from the north-south patrol group and started to initiate attacks on the Meteors but, in each instance, they were able to evade by losing altitude slightly. The attacks were then broken off early, and the MiGs returned to their former positions. After a while the Russian pilots seemed to lose interest in the stalemate and left the Meteors alone. But that was not the end of the cat-and-mouse action as when they were on the way back to Kimpo, four Sabres flew alongside the Meteors and proceeded to annoy the Australian pilots by moving in and out, closing to 2,000 yards and, on two occasions, appeared to carry out mock attacks before breaking away. Whatever the reason for these tactics, the Australian pilots were not amused. The Americans were possibly elated since there had been a Sabre/MiG clash in which 1/Lt Vernon L. Wright of the 336th FIS had claimed a MiG shot down, although the Russians had claimed five F-86s in return, in addition to a single F-84. MiGs from both FADs were involved.

The last day of November saw the biggest USAF air combat success so far. In the afternoon 31 Sabres of the 4th FIW led by Colonel Preston sighted a formation of 12 Chinese 24th FAR Tu-2s escorted by 16 piston-engined La-11s and 16 MiGs heading for the island of Taehwa-do. It was an all-Chinese force, as Russian ace Kapt Boris Abakumov recalled:

> "Often the Chinese pilots were self-confident and flew off without our protection. Frequently, it ended in tragedy for them . . . One day when returning to base after a mission, we saw nine Chinese Tu-2s below. We landed on the airfield, and some time later three riddled Tu-2s landed. Six of them had been shot down by Sabres that attacked them over the sea when the Chinese made an attempt to bomb islands occupied by the Americans. Well, the Chinese Command should have contacted our control tower and asked us to cover the area where the Tu-2s were to operate." [9]

The American pilots submitted claims for eight Tu-2s shot down, plus three La-9s (sic) and a MiG, all without loss, although the Chinese pilots claimed seven Sabres shot down in return. Maj George Davis was credited with three of the bombers and the MiG, thus becoming an ace, as did Maj Winton Marshall who claimed a bomber and an La-9. The other claims for bombers were made by Capt Barton, 1/Lts John Burke, Robert W. Akin and Douglas Evans, while Colonel Preston claimed an La-9, as did 1/Lt John W. Honaker. There was quite a party in the 4th FIW's mess at Kimpo that night. During the day a pilot of the 523rd FAR reported shooting down an F-86 which allegedly fell into the sea, although the Americans admitted no losses. This final MiG claim raised the total Russian claims for the month to 66, one of which was credited to an La-11 night-fighter pilot, while MiG pilots claimed 29 F-84s, 24 F-86s, seven F-80s, four Meteors, plus an F6F by a pilot from the 176th GuFAR.

Early in the morning two Meteors were scrambled from Kimpo and directed by GCI to reconnoitre the airfield at Sariwon, where Plt Off Ray Trebilco and Sgt Bruce Gillan observed revetments covered with camouflage even though the airfield appeared heavily bomb-cratered. The B-29 attacks were beginning to take effect. By the end of the month the bombing effort had progressed so well that, out of all the North Korean airfields, only those at Sinuiju and Uiju were still considered to be operational. On their return flight Trebilco and Gillan were vectored after bogies but these proved to be four USMC Corsairs.

At the end of the month Air Vice-Marshal Bouchier, the RAF AOC BCOF, sent a second report to the Deputy Chief-of-Air Staff in London, extolling the strength of the Meteor:

> "One Meteor came back with no elevator controls and with only one strand of elevator trim tab remaining. Ailerons have come back with holes that you could put your head and shoulders through; pilots landing back [in this condition] have reported only that the Meteor appeared to fly slightly one wing low. Very heavy damage to tailplanes has been experienced as a result of MiG-15 attacks from the rear. Enemy shells penetrate and burst inside aircraft somewhere near the centre section of the fuselage causing considerable fragmentation damage but the Meteors always [sic] return safely to base. Only one Meteor with pilot to date is known to have been lost by enemy action."

The AOC again made the point about 77RAAF receiving an influx of experienced RAF pilots:

> "The Squadron could do with a half dozen, hand-picked, experienced Meteor flight commanders and leaders. If this could be arranged it would boost, sky high, morale in this Squadron and greatly enhance the growing reputation of the Meteor which, as you know, got off to a rather shaky start."

With the threat of an enlarged MiG Alley stretching down to P'yongyang diminished despite the growing number of MiGs in the air, B-26s and B-29s were more readily available to return to attacks against transportation objectives. A redirection of effort was sorely needed because Operation 'Strangle' was faltering. Hostile ground fire continued to take a substantial toll and

---

[9] See *MiG-15* by Gordon and Rigmant.

the 5th Air Force lost 24 fighter-bombers and 255 damaged in November. The 18th FBG lost five Mustangs, its lowest monthly number to date, in which three pilots were killed: 1/Lt Ned C. Frankart (39th FIS) on the 3rd, 1/Lt Robert J. Lucas (12th FBS) on the 12th, and 2/Lt Donald Lynd (39th FIS) in a landing accident at K-10 on the 20th.

With the arrival of winter weather, accompanied by blasts of cold air coming down from Manchuria, the Communists were beginning to break the fighter-bomber blockade of North Korea's railways. By 30 November they had completed a rail by-pass bridge at P'yongyang which permitted through rail traffic eastwards to Samdung for the first time since August 1950. This and other repair efforts led to more supplies being shifted by rail again and the USAF night intruders found correspondingly fewer enemy vehicles moving on North Korea's roads after dark. As the convoys became smaller and better dispersed, 5th Air Force claims for vehicles destroyed began to decline, although a creditable 4,571 were claimed destroyed during the month. Replying to the need, FEAF Bomber Command's B-29s commenced Shoran-guided attacks against the bridges at Sunch'on and Sinanju. However, despite this renewed effort, the Sunch'on bridges would remain functional and the rail crossings at Sinanju would never be unserviceable for more than a few days running. The month's operations were summarised in 77RAAF's records:

> "During the month of November 1951, United Nations ground forces confined themselves to holding the line won in October. This has been successful in the face of numerous counter-attacks along the entire front, the heaviest of these being in the west where several such attacks have been repulsed. In the air the interdiction effort is still being successfully maintained in the face of increasing MiG aircraft, the highest number of these yet sighted in a day being 236 aircraft on the 30 November. However, F-86 Sabres continue to inflict heavy losses on these enemy aircraft . . ."

To improve their creature comforts at Kimpo, the Australians converted the fuselage of an abandoned C-46 transport into an Australian-style snack bar, open for one and all. The windows were glazed, a buffet constructed and tables fitted to provide that quick cup of tea or coffee and sustenance for the hard-working troops. After the first snows arrived it was just plain cold, and the Australians and South Africans who were accustomed to warmer climes noticed it more than most. The snow presented some very difficult problems for the early rising groundcrews and pilots. At Kimpo some Meteors had to be readied to fly an hour before dawn. Following futile attempts to sweep the snow off, jet exhaust from the engines of one aircraft was turned onto the airframe of another but, while this melted the snow, the water that was formed ran down the bodies and wings and sometimes froze again almost straight away when it was out of contact with the warm air. This practice was considered dangerous owing to the risk of aerofoils becoming jammed with ice, so various antifreeze greases and oils were spread over the upper airframe surfaces to assist in the removal of the ice and snow but these attempts also proved futile. The only practical solution was the provision of light nylon or rayon covers with deep scallops to which strings were attached for underneath fastening. These had to be manufactured in Japan where such materials could be purchased cheaply.

Likewise at K-10 and K-46, all the Mustang crew chiefs had great difficulty with the task of winterising their aircraft. Among other things, they had to double-clamp all of the coolant lines and inspect the insulation of all the electrical wiring to ensure that they were properly protected against moisture. However, winter brought an unforeseen and more unusual problem for some of the South African pilots because of their physical size. The average SAAF pilot was larger in stature than the typical USAF pilot. Some of the bigger men found that they could not fit comfortably into the winter clothing that was supplied. If they did, wearing it would not allow them easy access into the cramped cockpit of the Mustang; or they could not properly reach the cockpit controls; or their bulk restricted the movement of the control column and so made the aircraft difficult, and therefore unsafe, to fly. These unfortunates had to be temporarily grounded.

December 1951

According to an account written many years later by Lt-General Georgii Lobov, commander of the 303rd FAD, he was responsible for a plan to 'ambush' and hopefully wipe out the Meteors of 77RAAF which, if successful, he believed might have serious political repercussions that would be felt not only in Australia but also in Britain and possibly the United States. Lobov's reasons for electing to concentrate on the Meteor squadron were political. In comparison to the massive US forces involved in the war it was only one squadron among so many, but it was the only non-American, UN unit operating jet fighters over Korea. There were, up until now, only four UN squadrons employed exclusively as fighters – the 4th FIW's 334th, 335th and 336th FIS, all flying Sabres, and 77RAAF with its Meteors. All were operating from K-14, so the Australian squadron's presence was very obvious, and the Russians were well aware of the Meteor's inferior performance.

On the morning of 1 December, two dozen MiGs of the 176th GuFAR were prepared for action. Sixteen of the pilots, mostly from the 1st Eskadrilya, had orders to attack the Meteors. The other eight MiGs were to fly top cover in order to defend the others against possible attacks by Sabres. When it was time, the MiGs were led to the north by Podpolkovnik Vishnyakov, where they cruised, waiting for the Meteors to arrive. Meanwhile at Kimpo, dawn had broken on a fine, mild day. The month's first scheduled strike for 77RAAF was to be a routine fighter sweep in the Sunch'on area, and was to be led by Flt Lt Thornton, who had recently been promoted and now had more than 150 missions to his credit. Fourteen Meteors were prepared for the sweep, with Flt Lts Scannell and Cadan leading the other two flights while Flt Lt Hannan and Sgt Strawbridge were to act as airborne relay south of P'yongyang. Shortly after 1000 the Meteors were at 19,000 feet over Suncho'n when about 40 MiGs were sighted overhead, obviously about to attack. Flt Lt Thornton watched the MiGs closely, waiting to call the break. A fast, confusing and violent battle followed. Many years later Lobov gave an account of the action:

> "When groups of fighter-bombers and F-86s appeared, 16 Meteors – practically all the surviving ones – came along behind the American pilots. Vishnyakov's group rushed forward to meet the Meteors, by-passing the would-be combat area. The Australians, refusing combat, began going away one by one toward the sea and to the south but were barred by several pairs of MiG-15s. In the course of the battle, 12 Australian Meteors were brought down. The MiGs did not sustain any losses. As a result, No 77 Squadron practically ceased to exist." [10]

Russian accounts of this combat tell of two attacks, the first of which was the unexpected assault by Vishnyakov's group diving from over 30,000 feet, and the second was made as the Meteors were trying to withdraw, apparently by the covering MiGs led by Kapt Sergei Kramarenko, who recalled:

> ". . . My six aircraft were above the strike group, aft and on the left. Having the covering group in a common combat formation, we hoped to rendezvous with Sabres and, all of a sudden, we met with Meteors. This opponent, of course, was not as dangerous. There were 16 of us and 24 of them, the whole squadron. In the first attack, my pair shot down two aircraft. The other pair struck with no success. In this hit-and-run and very dynamic air battle, we shot down 16 Meteors and did not lose a single aircraft . . . What was the reason for such an unprecedented success, besides the advantages of the MiG-15 over the Meteor? A surprise! What fighter pilots always try for: we found ourselves in the ideal situation. Before a strike attack during a turn on target, the enemy offered the tails of the aircraft to us without knowing it. And we took advantage." [11]

These recollections were made many years after the battle and this may account for the discrepancies in the stated numbers of aircraft, but at the time nine Meteors were claimed shot down by the 176th GuFAR, six of them by the 1st Eskadrilya – one each by Podpolkovnik Vishnyakov, Maj Serafim Subbotin, Kapt Petr Milaushkin, Kapt Aleksandr Vasko, and St/Lts A.F. Golovachev and F.A. Zubakin. The 2nd Eskadrilya claimed three Meteors – two by Kapt

10/11 See *MiG-15* by Gordon and Rigmant.

Kramarenko and one by the leader of the second pair, St/Lt I.N. Guliy. It was believed to have been an outstanding accomplishment achieved at just the right time and of such proportion that it would counter any adverse impact on morale caused by the American success of a dozen Chinese aircraft shot down without loss just the day before. According to Russian records the pilot of a Meteor which crashed near Gangen-ri was rescued from the sea, while the pilot of another that crashed near Ryonge was taken prisoner by Chinese forces. The remaining seven Meteors were recorded as having crashed near Gogen, Sagamen, Sung-genmen, Heng-gen, Don-senmen, Kodonmen, and Kodon.

But it was not the overwhelming success the Russians supposed. Australian records supply more specific information. Over Sunch'on the Meteor pilots reported being attacked initially by two MiGs which latched on to the aircraft flown by Sgt Don Armit (A77-949) and Sgt Vance Drummond (A77-251), the No3 and No4 in Flt Lt Cadan's flight. At the same time, two more came in from the rear after Flt Lt Scannell's flight. Sgt Armit reported MiGs attacking, his leader calling for a break to starboard, but both Armit and Drummond broke late and were not seen again by Cadan. Meanwhile, Cadan (A77-911) and his No2 Flt Sgt Bill Middlemiss were engaged by two MiGs in a high port quarter attack. In this second break, Middlemiss' aircraft (A77-559) was hit and flicked down. On reporting that his aircraft had been damaged, he was told to return to base. Cadan meantime worked his way behind two MiGs and, at 3,000 yards range, fired at the starboard MiG with no obvious result. Then two more MiGs attacked from the starboard high quarter. Cadan evaded these, and then observed two Meteors being attacked by two MiGs close behind in a tight turn. He went after these but was himself engaged by more. After successfully evading them, he found himself about five miles north of the fight with seven MiGs for company. To evade, he dived to 7,500 feet and pulled out at 6,000 feet. The MiGs pressed their attack as far down as 7,000 feet, still firing, but the Meteor was not hit.

At about the same time, Flt Lt Thornton (A77-741) chased after a pair of MiGs and fired at them without any obvious results. After the first skirmish, more MiGs came down in pairs from 26,000 feet in diving attacks. Thornton's No3, Flg Off Bruce Gogerly (A77-15), held his initial break and while doing so observed one Meteor from Flt Lt Cadan's flight in a hard starboard turn, streaming fuel. Gogerly slackened the break, still maintaining a starboard turn, and two MiGs loomed up ahead. He followed them into a port turn and, at 800 yards range, fired a two-second burst with no obvious results. The MiGs steepened their turn, but Gogerly pulled inside, closed to 500 yards and fired for five seconds, this time observing strikes on the rear fuselage and starboard wingroot of the nearest jet. Streaming fuel, the MiG pulled up to the left. Gogerly broke off the attack when two other MiGs got on his tail. A couple of head-on passes were made with this pair and then Gogerly turned starboard into two more MiGs coming in from nine o'clock. He turned to port and fired a quick burst with no obvious result and the MiGs broke away.

Gogerly and his wingman Sgt John Myers (A77-139) then found themselves alone. Gogerly saw an aircraft go down in flames and hit the top of a hill. He noted the time, 1012. Then a lone MiG was sighted just over a mile ahead and 4-5,000 feet below; Gogerly closed on him to 1,200 yards in a dive to an altitude of 14,000 feet. The MiG turned to port and then straightened out on a northerly heading and began to climb. Gogerly held him for five seconds and fired a quick burst. The MiG rolled slightly to port, recovered, and then drew away. Gogerly observed another aircraft go down in flames and strike the ground. It was 1015. Myers confirmed what Gogerly had seen and he also noticed two MiGs closing on the two Meteors flown by Flt Lt Scannell (A77-189) and his No2 Sgt Bruce Thomson in A77-29. Scannell broke south and climbed into the sun to 27,000 feet, shaking off his pursuers by doing so, but Thomson called to say that he had lost sight of his leader. It was 1011. Looking around, Scannell sighted an aircraft going down in flames from 24,000 feet and also noticed two Meteors being chased by two MiGs in a tight turn. He moved in to attack this pair but was attacked himself by more MiGs and went down to 10,000 feet. One MiG followed him down firing, then pulled away. After the break, Scannell saw a MiG pulling up with fuel streaming from it. At 1015 Scannell heard Thornton calling for a check. Everyone answered except Sgt Thomson. Scannell called him twice and received an answer to the second call at 1017. During the radio check Sgt Drummond reported he was streaming fuel and had no electrics. Scannell climbed to 30,000 feet and withdrew. He came home alone having observed two fires on the ground, well before the radio check was called.

Shortly before the radio check Flt Sgt Bill Middlemiss saw an aircraft falling in two burning pieces which crashed on a hill north of P'yongyang. He also saw a fire several miles north of this crash, when due east of P'yongyang. Then, a few minutes later at 1018, a single MiG attacked him at 10,000 feet but it did not follow as he broke to starboard. He returned to Kimpo where it was discovered that the pitot head and the forward portion of his port wingtip were crushed. Another of the returning pilots, Flg Off Wal Rivers, reported having sighted what he thought to be a Meteor, zig-zagging down and streaming black smoke shortly before the radio check. The aircraft exploded at about 12,000 feet and crashed. His wingman, Sgt Bruce Gillan, saw two aircraft flame down before the check, and observed another streaming fuel. The Australians landed back at Kimpo in ones and twos. Their faces showed the strain of combat but they were happy. It had been a desperate encounter against overwhelming odds but after the MiGs had lost their initial height advantage they did not seem to take long in turning their noses towards the Manchurian border and sanctuary. It would seem that at least one of them did not make it. Two planes had been seen burning on the ground and through the squadron check all of the Meteor pilots had been accounted for immediately after the battle. Flg Off Bruce Gogerly was credited with the Squadron's first confirmed kill and he probably made hits on another. A number of other pilots had fired on MiGs including Flt Lts Scannell, Thornton, and Cadan but, since no one could tell for certain who had shot down the second aircraft, it was credited as a Squadron kill.

But celebrations were cut short when it was realised that three Meteors had not returned. The elation began to subside. Sgt Thomson in A77-29 was tracked to within 80 miles of Kimpo by the controller well after most of the others had landed. Thomson had then asked for directions. These had been given but the message was not acknowledged. He had gone off the air. Time passed. The fuel deadline came and went. Missing besides Thomson were Sgt Armit (A77-949) and the New Zealander Sgt Drummond (A77-251). It seems probable that these two fell victim to the MiGs, while Thomson had possibly run out of fuel but was more likely to have also fallen to a MiG. Despite their first victories over the Russian jets, the jubilant mood of the pilots changed to one of growing concern for their missing colleagues.

As far as the battle can be reconstructed, it seems that during the initial attack by the MiGs of Vishnyakov's group, at least two Meteors were damaged – those of Flt Sgt Middlemiss, who managed to reach Kimpo safely, and Sgt Drummond, who reported that he was streaming fuel and had no electrics – and two others may also have been damaged; those of Sgt Thomson, who had difficulty with establishing radio contact both during and after the check, and possibly Sgt Armit, who responded to the check but was not seen again after the first break. Gogerly and Myers had witnessed two aircraft crash in flames; Scannell had seen an aircraft falling in flames and two fires on the ground; Middlemiss had seen an aircraft falling in two burning pieces and another fire several miles north of where it fell; Gillan had observed two aircraft flame down; and Rivers had sighted an aircraft he thought was a Meteor streaming black smoke before it exploded at about 12,000 feet – all before the radio check. Since all of the Meteor pilots responded to Flt Lt Thornton's call at 1015, it seems reasonable to assume that the two aircraft that had fallen in flames were MiGs (although an F-80 of the 35th FBS was also shot down), yet the Russians asserted they suffered no losses. Kapt Kramarenko's group must have attacked very soon after the check, and in the chases that followed he and Guliy claimed three Meteors shot down. Their victims were almost certainly Thomson, Armit and Drummond, the latter's aircraft at least having been already damaged in the first assault.

Two F-80s of the 35th FBS flown by 1/Lt William Womack and 2/Lt Thomas Mounts had been jumped by MiGs from the 196th FAR that morning, in about the same locality that Thomson had been flying. The Russian pilots claimed two[12] – including one by Polkovnik Pepelyaev – but only Mounts[13] was lost, Womack having managed to evade the attackers and reach Kimpo, where

---

[12] Apart from claims for nine Meteors and two F-80s, MiG pilots also claimed three F-84s and an F-86 during the day. The only USAF claim was by 2/Lt Robert E. Smith, an F-80 pilot with the 36th FBS, who claimed a MiG shot down.

[13] 2/Lt Thomas Mounts managed to eject, only to be taken prisoner.

he landed safely. The American was asked if he had seen anything of the missing Meteors. He replied in the negative. Officers of the 4th FIW tried to persuade him to bed down for the night at Kimpo, and then go on to his home base next morning, but the young pilot seemed anxious to push on that night and report the loss of his colleague. He took off in the gathering darkness, only to crash to his death into the side of a mountain, south of the airfield.

That afternoon eight Meteors were despatched, including one flown by Wg Cdr Steege, to conduct a search in the hope of finding some trace of the three missing airmen. They reported to control and then broke into four elements to conduct a wide-ranging, thorough search of the area south of P'yongyang and north of Kimpo from Chinnampo to Singye. Results were negative. It was some time later that the Squadron learned that Sgts Vance Drummond[14] and Bruce Thomson[15] were POWs but Sgt Don Armit had been killed in action. On his return to New Zealand after his release in 1953, Drummond spoke of his capture after being shot down:

> "My plane was damaged, and I parachuted to safety, landing in mountainous country. In landing, I sprained my ankle. The footprints I left in the snow were responsible for my capture 45 minutes after I had landed [he was presumably the pilot reported by the Russians as having been taken prisoner by Chinese forces after a Meteor had crashed near Ryonge]. For six days I was held in a village 30 miles outside P'yongyang, and then I was taken to a camp for officer prisoners near the Manchurian border. British, American and Turkish officers were in the camp."

Meanwhile, 77RAAF's normal duties could not be ignored and during a strip alert Wt Off Bill Michelson and Sgt Ken Murray were scrambled to intercept unidentified aircraft. They met two of the searching Meteors on their way home, and three F-80s, before being recalled to base. Flt Lt Scannell later wrote in his general report:

> "When a break was called, each aircraft turned in its own air and if a pilot was slow in initiating his turn, or did not turn hard enough, he was in trouble. The only two aircraft shot down or damaged during a fight was in the initial break. If a No2 was too close to his No1 and was forced to wait for him to cross in front and then to slip in behind, the short pause before he started to turn was long enough to enable a MiG attacking at high speed to get within firing range. With each aircraft turning in its own space it meant that some of the No2s were leading the section during the turn but this had to be accepted. I had an arrangement with my No2 that if he saw a target during a turn, he could attack and I would cover him, but I retained the right to veto."

The Australians had important decisions to make, and make quickly. The latest action had made it blatantly clear, if it had not been so before, that the Meteor was simply outclassed by the MiG. The MiG was faster, climbed better and was more manoeuvrable at high altitude. The fact that two had possibly been brought down could only be attributed to the fighting qualities of the Meteor pilots. Obviously, the Russians were not about to change their tactics. The MiGs would continue to enter MiG Alley with a height advantage and they would always be there in greater numbers. Without an aircraft to match the MiG's performance, the Australians could only look forward to more losses. There was really no choice in the matter. The anticipated loss rate of between two to three aircraft per month had been reached on the very first day of the month. Furthermore, between 3 November and 1 December, a period of just over four weeks, five Meteors had been lost and one was so badly damaged it had to be broken up for parts. This was twice the acceptable loss rate and did not include other aircraft that had suffered damage. There were also distant ramifications:

---

[14] Since Drummond was incarcerated in a camp for officer prisoners, he was presumably wearing officers' rank tabs (see Chapter I). On his return to Australia 21 months later, he remained in the RAAF and later served in Vietnam as an FAC, but sadly was lost in a flying accident in May 1967. His older brother Fred had been killed during WWII in a flying accident while piloting a Spitfire.

[15] Sgt Bruce Thomson also remained in the RAAF on his return from captivity but he, too, was to lose his life in a flying accident when his RAAF Sabre crashed in 1955.

"... the tacit admission of the Meteor's inadequacy had serious consequences; the Meteor was not only the main fighter available to the RAF, but also had been purchased in considerable numbers by many continental air forces. A serious weakness in Europe's air defence system had thus been revealed by the operations of a single Meteor squadron in far-off Korea. This was precisely the situation which RAF commanders feared when arguing against the deployment of Meteors in that theatre." [16]

In any case, there was now no strategic necessity for 77RAAF to be committed to the air combat rôle. Sabres were proving highly successful in their encounters with MiGs but, up until now, there had not been enough of them. However, with the timely entry into the arena of the F-86E-equipped 51st FIW under Colonel Gabreski, the Americans felt that they now had a chance to alter the balance of power.

At the beginning of December a visit was made to 77RAAF by the RAAF's Air Member for Personnel, Air Vice-Marshal F.M. Bladin CBE, as noted by Mr Jock Gibb:

"He [AVM Bladin] was generally known as 'Dad' by the officers and airmen and seemed to be extremely popular. He appeared to be pleased with the high morale of the Squadron in general and also the high standard of maintenance carried out. The Australian opinion of the aircraft serviceability was completely summed up by the Squadron Commander when he remarked to AVM Bladin that although they had fourteen aircraft serviceable at Kimpo they could only guarantee thirteen serviceable because every second day a daily star inspection had to be carried out. It was apparent that soon after the arrival of the second Sabre Wing at Suwon, the rôle of the Meteor was going to be changed. The loss of the three aircraft on the 1 December tended to hasten this change because there were only fourteen Meteors left in Korea and this was considered insufficient to maintain a Squadron effort."

There was an insufficient number of Meteors available to maintain a realistic effort for fighter sweeps. No one was really very surprised, therefore, when the Squadron was taken off this duty. The pilots themselves were far from happy. They wanted to pull their weight in the air war and feared they might now be out of business. There was not much space available at the crowded forward aerodromes, and it was known that only those squadrons which could justify their existence would be allowed to remain forward. Fortunately, the Meteor had good climbing capabilities, being even better than the Sabre in initial climb rate. Consequently, 5th Air Force Operations detailed 77RAAF to carry out area and airfield defence at both Kimpo and Suwon. MiGs had been reported near the bomb line and the shooting up of UN fighter bases was looming as a possibility. The Meteors could achieve height at a shorter distance from base and so would be quicker in making any altitude interceptions. It also meant freeing extra Sabres for fighter sweeps. The Squadron's task then was to be ready to scramble and intercept enemy aircraft which might be attempting a bombing raid on UN airfields. In reality, this duty would prove to be quite frustrating as well as difficult and demanding. Increased transport was necessary and the groundcrews had to be divided by trades. Also, it meant that more pilots and groundcrews had to be available before dawn and after dusk.

The new F-86Es of the 51st FIW were adorned with a rearward-slanting, black-edged yellow band on the fuselage, and black-edged yellow bands on wing and tail. The distinctive yellow bands were designed to prevent the F-86 pilots from mistaking each other for MiGs in speedy dogfights and to distinguish themselves from the 4th FIW, which had had forward-slanting black-and-white stripes on the centre fuselage of their F-86As since they began operations back in 1950. The FEAF now had 165 Sabres in the theatre, of which 127 were committed to combat in Korea. The tempo of air fighting did not let up during the first week of December and the MiGs were out in force again on the 2nd. This time they ran into the enlarged USAF Sabre screen and it was a good day for the American pilots who claimed five confirmed

---

[16] See *Odd Jobs*. Unbeknown to 77RAAF, a decision had already been taken by the Australian government to obtain a manufacturing licence for the Sabre, which was to be in a modified form using the Rolls-Royce Avon engine rather than the General Electric J47; the first Avon-powered Sabre made its maiden flight on 3 August 1953.

kills, four of them going to the 4th FIW, the scorers being Maj James F. Martin and Capt Nelton R. Wilson, both of the 334th FIS, and Major Zane S. Amell and Capt Michael J. Novak of the 335th. The 51st drew its first blood when 1/Lt Paul E. Roach of the 25th FIS, who had transferred from the 334th FIS, also claimed a MiG; in return, MiG pilots of the 17th FAR claimed three F-84s shot down, two of which failed to return including one flown by 1/Lt G. Madison. The Communist air threat was becoming more menacing. On 3 December the diarist of 1903 AOP Flight recorded ominously:

> "Three unidentified jet aircraft dropped approximately six bombs and strafed B Battery, 195 FA Battalion. In addition, three MiG-15s were seen over Seoul."

This was the first time that enemy aircraft had been so far south for quite some time and it seemed to confirm intelligence reports that the enemy intended to keep stepping up his air activity. However, the bombing and strafing attack was probably carried out by USAF aircraft in error. With regard to the MiG threat, the AOP pilots considered themselves to be fairly safe from attack; one commented:

> "We did not believe the jet fighter pilot could come down close to the ground and mix it with us."

During the day pairs of Meteors were scrambled three times from Kimpo. On the first, Flg Off Bruce Gogerly and Plt Off Alan Philp were ordered to intercept four aircraft but could not close in for identification. On the second, Flg Off Wal Rivers and Sgt Vic Oborn found a B-26 and were then instructed to search from the west coast to Haeju where a flare had been seen. Results were negative. They intercepted two F-51s before returning to base. Rivers and Oborn were up again later but again results were negative. They did, however, have time to conduct a search of the area where Sgt Thomson went missing from the fighter sweep on the 1st, but without any luck.

2SAAF and the 18th FBG continued their rail-cutting missions during December, concentrating mainly on the railway lines radiating out from Sunch'on. The Americans would lose eight F-51s to ground fire during the month with the South Africans running into their share of flak. Lt Ron Beamish must have thought that enemy gunners were singling him out for special attention. On 2 December, while flying Mustang 350, flak struck his aircraft inflicting damage to the port mainplane leading edge, wingtip and scoop. He returned to base safely, but next day history repeated itself. This time he was at the controls of Mustang 334 when ground fire hit his aircraft again, which inflicted damage to mainplane leading edge and, after he landed, bullet holes were found through the battery and inter-cooler. On another mission during the day 2SAAF suffered a serious and unfortunate mishap when 2/Lt Peter Norman-Smith led four aircraft on a typical mission. After carrying out the strike, the flight set course for the secondary target. Due to adverse weather conditions with cloud preventing any form of attack, the Mustangs headed home, flying above the overcast. Unable to locate K-46 in the poor weather, Norman-Smith called control for a course and was told to stand-by as they had an emergency situation to deal with first. As they were low on fuel, Norman-Smith decided to divert to K-16. The flight turned west. Approaching Seoul they had to tighten their formation in order to penetrate the clouds without losing sight of each other. Suddenly the aircraft flown by 2/Lt Ken Whitehead closed in too fast on his leader and his propeller sliced into the tail section of Norman-Smith's Mustang (341), severing all of the control cables. The damaged aircraft rolled over onto its back and dived inverted into the Han, where it embedded itself in the bottom of the river. Whitehead's machine (324), minus its engine and propeller, tumbled down into the river also. Everything had happened so quickly. After receiving a fix from control, the two remaining pilots, Capt John Montgomery and Lt Jack Tindall proceeded to K-16, where they landed to refuel. Just six days earlier Whitehead had walked away unscathed after crash-landing on an emergency airstrip, but not this time and his body was recovered and buried at Tangok.

Reports had reached 2SAAF concerning Lt Chris Lombard, who had disappeared after baling out two months earlier. They suggested that he had not been captured by the Communists as feared, but was in the hands of friendly guerrillas. Back on 7 October, following his bale-out, Lombard had been seen running along a river bed in the company of two other figures but, by the time a rescue helicopter had arrived on the scene, all of the men had disappeared. It now seemed possible that the two other men could have been friendly guerrilla fighters, and perhaps a belated rescue was feasible. What the South Africans did not know was that Lombard had in reality been taken prisoner, and the North Koreans were using him as bait in a plan to capture a US helicopter. The Communists had tried to gain his co-operation in their scheme by offering him the position of colonel in the North Korean Air Force, plus a safe conduct for his family to North Korea. The offer was made in person by General Nam II, the Chief of the NKAF. Following his refusal to co-operate in such a scheme, he was quartered with a Korean named Kim Dong Shik, and both were set to work on a pig farm near P'yongyang. Lombard did not know that his companion was in fact a double agent. Acting on instructions from the North Koreans, the agent used radio equipment captured or brought from South Korea to transmit his message that Lombard was in the hands of guerrillas and a rescue could be arranged. When, on 5 December, a shrill radio signal, as if someone was trying to make contact with them, was picked up by the pilots of a Mustang flight searching the mountainous area midway between Kunu-ri and Yonghung in the middle of the peninsula, not far from where Lombard had last been seen, this seemed to confirm the reports.

2/Lt Frank Grobler was entrusted with the task of making a rescue attempt since he had repeatedly led a flight of Mustangs on search missions in the area. Grobler returned to the area, this time flying a USAF Mustang specially converted to carry a passenger. He was accompanied by Lt Hong, a South Korean Army officer, who soon made radio contact with the Korean agent on the ground, and Grobler arranged a rendezvous from where Lombard could be picked up at 0800 next day. The trap was set. Next morning Grobler led the rescue mission to the rendezvous. The rescuers consisted of a helicopter covered by four SAAF Mustangs. Contact was re-established with the Korean agent and he was asked to bring Lombard into the open so he could be identified. The Korean would not comply. Suspicious of a trap, and with weather conditions too poor for the helicopter to be escorted in properly, Grobler ordered the abandonment of the rescue. Two further rescue attempts were made but each time with negative results because of poor weather. After this, the idea was given up completely, but the hope remained that Lombard would be safe in the hands of the guerrillas. The Communists were to soon announce Lombard was a POW, however, but the full story of what had actually happened to him was only discovered much later when he was released by his captors after the war.

77RAAF were now carrying out their area defence duties in flights of four aircraft. During the first scramble of the day (4 December), Flt Lt Thornton and his flight were directed to intercept ten aircraft heading north. These turned out to be USN Skyraiders, and the same aircraft were intercepted again later as they orbited over the front lines waiting to be directed onto targets. Flg Off Wal Rivers' flight was later scrambled to intercept aircraft, possibly MiGs, flying at extreme height. The GCI controller asked them to climb to 45,000 feet after a radar plot but the Meteors were unable to gain this height. Before returning to Kimpo they joined in a search for a downed F-86 pilot but without success. The American had been shot down by a MiG pilot from the 17th FAR. Over Uiju airfield that night, as searchlights coned a B-29, two MiGs attacked the American bomber and inflicted damage. Only along the Yalu were the Communists able to organise effective anti-aircraft defence against the USAF night attacks, and Uiju was defended by more than 50 searchlights, radar-controlled flak batteries and fighters.

Next day (5 December), MiGs again ran foul of the F-86s of the 4th FIW, with four being claimed destroyed, one jointly by 1/Lt Garold R. Beck and 1/Lt Ernest F. Neubert of the 336th FIS. Another was claimed by Maj Marshall (335th FIS), while Major Davis, CO of the 334th FIS, continued his spectacular run by reporting the destruction of two more. Capt Conrad E. Matson (335th FIS) damaged another. The Russian pilots claimed only one F-86 in return, this being credited to a pilot of the 18th GuFAR, although three F-80s were claimed by the 196th FAR, and three F-84s by the 17th FAR and 18th GuFAR, while Chinese MiG pilots of the 3rd FAR claimed no fewer than seven Sabres between 2-5 December; one of the F-84s lost was flown by Capt Hugh F. Larkin of the 136th FBG who was reported missing in this action. It is also believed that an F-80 was shot down. There occurred another Sabre/MiG clash next day, when 1/Lt Charles B. Christison of the 336th FIS claimed a MiG shot down, with the Russians claiming an F-86 and an F-84, the former reportedly falling near Peitunkun.

From Kimpo, 77RAAF's Senior MO, Sqn Ldr Kater, went on another search and rescue mission, his third for the month so far. From the point of view of meeting enemy opposition, the trips were usually uneventful but this time the SA-16 was subjected to anti-aircraft fire from an island just off the coast and the amphibian was hit three times, although neither crew nor passengers were injured. Meanwhile, the Australians continued their four-aircraft flights for strip alert duties. Flt Lt Thornton and his flight were scrambled to intercept unidentified aircraft but, after reporting to the GCI controller, they were directed to search for a downed aircraft. The tail of an aircraft was sighted in the water and its position reported. Sometime later, newly promoted Sqn Ldr Cedric Thomas and his flight were scrambled to investigate another plot, this time meeting an F-80. On completion of their duty, they were ordered to land at Suwon from where they were to carry out air strip alert duty. The flight was soon scrambled and directed around the Kaesong restricted area to cover a downed F-84, presumably Capt Larkin's aircraft.

Weather conditions contributed to 1903 AOP Flight having an accident at Fort George. While taking off in Auster VF639 Capt John Crawshaw crashed due to ice and frost on the aircraft's wings. The Auster developed a slight yaw to port and hit a pile of sand on the side of the runway. It was seriously damaged but both of the men on board were unhurt. Two days later, Capt Joe Luscombe operated for two hours 40 minutes over the Commonwealth Division front in VF664. He directed an artillery shoot in co-operation with an American unit and an enemy bunker was destroyed.

Overcast skies and intermittent rain prevented flying from Kimpo throughout the daylight hours of 7 December. That night a celebration was held in 77RAAF's Aircrew Club when presentations of model Meteors were made by Mr Jock Gibb on behalf of the Gloster and Martin-Baker companies to Flg Off Ken Blight for being the first (sic) pilot to eject operationally using the Martin-Baker ejection seat. Farewells were said at the same time to Flt Lt Vic Cannon and Flt Lt Max Scannell, the last member of the RAF Mission still with the Squadron. Scannell had completed 107 missions, 21 on Mustangs and the remainder on Meteors, for which he had received the US Air Medal. A DFC would follow. Cannon had completed 102 missions, 32 on Mustangs and 70 on Meteors, and was also awarded the US Air Medal. He, too, would be awarded the DFC. In honour of the whole occasion Wg Cdr Steege played his accordion and led the members of the mess in his version of the *Horst Wessel* song, much to the amazement of the American guests. Max Scannell, in his farewell speech, said that he hoped to return to Korea with an RAF squadron to assist the air effort. He emplaned for New Zealand via Australia on 10 December. It was rumoured that he was to be married in New Zealand during his leave. Thus the RAF's association with 77RAAF ended – for the moment.

8 December was an extremely cold day and 77RAAF carried out a number of scrambles. During one of these, Flg Off Bruce Gogerly in A77-741 led four aircraft to perform a special reconnaissance of Haeju airfield. The pilots were warned to check the revetments for aircraft, but found the airfield totally unserviceable; the revetments were camouflaged but appeared to be empty. While circling for the next 30 minutes, closely examining the vicinity up to the foothills to the north-east, two of the Meteors, A77-734 flown by Sgt K.G. Towner, and A77-31 (Sgt Frank Blackwell), suffered minor damage from small-arms fire. Shortly after they landed, Flt Lt Thornton led four more Meteors to cover the withdrawal of F-86s and F-80s returning from strikes through the same area. Meanwhile, operating from Suwon, Flg Off Wal Rivers and his flight scrambled to fly CAP over a downed pilot. When they arrived in the search area they found and escorted an SA-16 south along the coast before returning to Suwon. There had been a clash between the Sabre screen and MiGs, with the Americans apparently coming off second best. With no claims being submitted by the F-86 pilots, honours for the day went to the Russian pilots of the 17th FAR who claimed three of their opponents shot down, registering the crash locations as west of Jyungsen, west of Syukusen and near Podok. Next day an F-84 of the 9th FBS failed to return, 1/Lt Thomas F. Wells being posted missing, but it was not until 11 December that the Sabres and MiGs drew blood again. It was a fine warm day, the first for four days. Over the Yalu 1/Lt Donald O. Griffith (335th FIS) claimed a MiG shot down

and Capt Alfred C. Simmons (336th FIS) accounted for a second, while Maj Marshall damaged another. Their opponents from the 176th GuFAR and the 196th FAR claimed four F-86s, two credited to each regiment. One of these may have been awarded to Kapt I. Goncharov. The 35th FBS lost an F-80 during the day but 2/Lt Richard Cronan was believed to have fallen victim to ground fire.

Meanwhile at Kimpo, Air Vice-Marshal J.P.J. McCauley CBE RAAF, arrived to carry out an inspection visit of 77RAAF. After the Squadron area had been inspected, Wg Cdr Steege took him on an aerial inspection of the front lines and surrounding areas in one of the Meteor T7s escorted by two Meteor fighters. In the evening, a farewell party was held for Flg Off Les Reading and Mr Jock Gibb. Many American officers from the base joined the party. Reading had completed 165 missions during his tour of operations, 94 on Mustangs and the remainder on Meteors, and had been credited with damaging a MiG on 27 October. The announcement of his DFC was made in the new year.

12 Decmber saw 77RAAF's first ground accident since returning to operations in July. At around 0800, the jet stream of a taxying aircraft caught LAC K.A. Todd off balance and blew him into the path of another plane. He was taken to hospital where, on examination, it was found that he sustained a broken rib, abrasions to the chin and lacerations to the shoulder. Strangely, a similar incident occurred just over two weeks' later when LAC D.J. McKeever was caught in the jet stream of a taxying Meteor and injured his right ankle. The South Africans suffered a far more serious ground accident during the month, one which proved fatal. Air Corporal W.D. Patterson was standing in the refuelling area at K-46 when a refuelling truck, its windshield frosted over by the cold, knocked him down. He died in the base hospital. This was the first mishap of this nature for 2SAAF since it had arrived in Korea over a year ago.

The success or otherwise of the interdiction campaign was again under review. According to information gained from questioning captured enemy troops, Communist plans to launch a Sixth Phase ground offensive in August had been cancelled because of the air attacks against North Korea's railways. At a 5th Air Force planning conference in Seoul on 12 December, Brig-General James Ferguson, Deputy Commander of the 5th Air Force, remarked candidly in his assessment that although the enemy had made no large-scale attack, they did not know whether it was the result of the interdiction or whether he had never intended to attack. Ferguson did note, however, that intelligence believed the Communists had not been able to amass the supplies they needed for a two-week ground offensive. On the other hand, even before the onset of winter with its shorter days and longer nights, the enemy had seldom left rail cuts unrepaired for more than 24 hours. UN photo interpreters indicated that by using coolie labourers and beginning work at dusk, they could repair a rail cut within eight hours, thus opening a railway track for traffic between midnight and sunrise. When it appeared that the battered Kunu-ri to Sunch'on track defied further repair, the Communists redoubled their efforts elsewhere. South of Sukch'on on the P'yongyang-Sinanju line, Communist labourers began to restore the badly damaged rail line between P'yongyang and Sariwon. Repairs were progressing so rapidly that there was a chance they might break the fighter-bomber railroad blockade of the North Korean capital.

The 5th Air Force also lost part of its night-intruder capability when USMC Squadron VMF(N)-513 was forced to suspend its intruder operations as it ran short of aircraft and crews. When this occurred, 3rd BG B-26 intruder crews began to work with flare-dropping aircraft for attacks along the road route between P'yongyang and Sariwon. Trains were difficult targets. Locomotives never showed headlamps and could be sighted and destroyed only by crews who hunted them at low altitudes and looked for plumes of smoke or steam. Added to this, the fewer number of night intruders were finding fewer enemy vehicles moving with lights on North Korea's roads. 5th Air Force claims of vehicles destroyed would decline marginally from 4,571 in November to 4,290 in December. Since both General Ridgway and General Weyland were in favour of continuing the railway interdiction campaign, 5th Air Force had to determine how rail attacks could be most effectively carried out with declining air capabilities. Brig-General Ferguson expressed confidence that FEAF Bomber Command would be willing to help provided intelligence could find some bottlenecks in the enemy's rail system which would make worthwhile targets for the B-29s but, as it turned out, the first of these would not be found until late January 1952.

At the operational level, Lt Colonel Levi R. Chase, CO of the 8th FBW, came straight to the point when he stated that the goal of his squadrons was to achieve a maximum percentage of rail cuts in inverse proportion to personnel losses and battle damage to his aircraft. The fighter-bomber pilots were almost unanimously agreed that the way in which the 5th Air Force was scheduling its railway attacks had made them vulnerable to enemy flak. Every day, morning and afternoon, 12 to 24 fighter-bombers kept hitting targets selected on 15 or 30 mile stretches of railroad. The pilots argued that enemy gunners knew exactly when and where to expect them. Against this view, 5th Air Force Operations analysts disagreed with the contention that the Communists concentrated their flak against fighter-bomber strikes. Flak plots actually indicated that they uniformly distributed their automatic weapons along their railroad lines south of the Ch'ongch'on. Along the six main stretches of track which the 5th Air Force had been attacking, flak positions were placed at four-mile intervals. Meanwhile, the increasing volume of ground fire was lowering the accuracy of fighter-bomber attacks. According to a 5th Air Force operations analysis of F-84 attacks, only 7% of bombs dropped by them were cutting the enemy's railway tracks. Recognising that the aerial interdiction problem in Korea had become much more difficult, Brig-General Ferguson emerged from the planning conference to announce that 'Strangle' operations ought to be continued for at least 30 more days, pending on the development of more lucrative air targets.

With dawn on 13 December came the renewal of extremely cold weather and the activity of 77RAAF was limited to airstrip alerts. Sqn Ldr Thomas' flight was scrambled to fly CAP over a Sea Fury pilot from HMAS *Sydney* (see Chapter XIII) who had been downed near P'yongyang. Once airborne, Thomas was instructed to contact the leader of a flight of USAF F-51s escorting an incoming helicopter. He did this and was informed that the pick up had already been completed and that no further assistance was required. There was good news during the day for 77RAAF when it was learned that it had been awarded a Presidential Unit Citation from the Republic of South Korea. The citation was dated 1 November 1951:

> "This Squadron entered the Korean War during the first week of North Korean aggression. Flying Mustang aircraft it earned the highest reputation for itself in giving close support to military operations for over eight months of the campaign, and it won the admiration and friendship of all units it supported. It then re-equipped with Meteor aircraft and has since continued its fine record in the new rôle allotted to it with the more modern aircraft. Its performance throughout merits the highest praise."

The real action for the day took place between Sabres and MiGs high in MiG Alley. In widespread clashes, two 'bandit trains' with an estimated combined total of 150 MiGs managed to shoot down only two Sabres including that flown by 1/Lt Charles D. Hogue of the 334th FIS (the other Sabre pilot baled out near Cho-do and was rescued from the sea by a helicopter) – although the Russian pilots claimed seven, plus an F-80, with their Chinese comrades of the 6th FAR and 42nd FAR claiming one F-86 and two F-80s. In return, the USAF pilots claimed no less than 14 of the Russian jets destroyed. While many of these may have been flown by the less skilled pilots of the Chinese Air Force – one source suggests that six Chinese MiGs were lost – it was nonetheless a resounding success for the Americans. Lt Colonel George Jones, the 51st FIW's Group Commander, claimed a MiG damaged, and 1/Lt Tony Kulengosky of the 25th FIS claimed one destroyed (his second victory, having claimed one earlier with the 336th FIS), but the other victories went to the more experienced 4th FIW pilots from Kimpo. Colonel Preston scored his fourth kill, but supreme among the claimants was the 334th FIS, its aggressive CO, Maj George Davis, setting the pace with four victories and thereby raising his score to an incredible 12 in just over two weeks, while Capt Theo S. Coberly claimed two; other claims were submitted by 1/Lt Dymock (his second) and 1/Lt Pincoski (also his second although his earlier victory was shared). 1/Lt Honaker of the 335th destroyed one, his second, while for the 336th FIS, 1/Lt John P. Green Jr (his first) and 1/Lt Mitson (his second) shot down one each, and Capt Kenneth Chandler destroyed one to give himself five victories, technically making him an ace, but his score actually consisted of one air and four ground kills. If these

USAF claims over the past 14 days had any bearing on actual losses, it would seem that it was a very costly period for the MiG units. Claims had been submitted by Sabre pilots for 39 aircraft destroyed, in addition to the two by the Meteor pilots. It appeared to the Americans that, after this latest victory, the MiGs seemed to lose the urge to fight as hard as they had before. Though they still flew over North Korea in large numbers, they came at 50,000 feet, a height where they were relatively safe from the F-86s. The commander of the 196th FAR, Polkovnik Pepelyaev, may have been referring to the massacre on 13 December when he wrote:

"The condition of the Chinese pilots could be seen easily – emaciated, no adipose tissue at all, so thin and feeble. How could they withstand MiG-15 G-loads? The Chinese pilots sometimes lost consciousness, not without reason. Later I met Chinese pilots after they landed one or two regiments at Antung, after they had received a severe mauling. I think the Chinese pilots did not feel comfortable in the MiG-15 cockpit when they met Sabres or other American aircraft. It is very difficult to make a rated pilot within six months, as they [the Chinese Command] wanted for combat actions with the Americans, especially if this pilot was poorly fed and had poor physical training. If it was hard for us to fight against the Americans, what about the Chinese? Our Chinese allies were inadequately drilled for combat and suffered heavy losses. They were actually aerial targets for the Americans." [17]

One Russian air historian has written – again, not specifically about the action on 13 December – but just as revealing:

"The Joint Chinese/North Korean Air Army participated in combats since the middle of 1951. The main task of Chinese pilots was to attack bombers and fighter-bombers. Their meetings with F-86 Sabres usually ended in defeat. Once, eight MiG-15s of the Chinese 4th Fighter Air Division [Regiment] were surprised by 12 F-86s. The Chinese pilots lost brain [panicked] and all were shot down; one pilot was killed." [18]

Over MiG Alley next day (14 December), Colonel Harrison Thyng claimed another MiG, his second since taking over as CO of the 4th FIW, Lt Colonel George Jones of the 51st FIW claiming one damaged on a later mission. At Kimpo, Sqn Ldr Thomas' flight was at readiness on strip alert when the Meteors were scrambled to intercept an unidentified aircraft, which turned out to be a friendly jet but then the controller advised that a friendly aircraft (an F-84) had been shot down and ordered the flight to the area. The Australians saw an aircraft burning on the ground at the position given but there was no sign of the pilot, 1/Lt Clayton Conley of the 9th FBS. This was reported to the controller who ordered them to intercept another aircraft that turned out to be a C-47. Meanwhile, Flt Lt Thornton's flight was on strip alert at Suwon when the Meteors were scrambled to carry out a CAP for a pilot down just off the coast. On becoming airborne the controller instructed the flight to contact an ASR SA-16, but its pilot reported that he was withdrawing from the area. The Meteor flight then searched the vicinity for the next 12 minutes without any sightings before it, too, had to return to base. American losses are not known, but nine F-86s were claimed shot down by the MiGs, pilots of the 176th GuFAR being credited with four, those of the 196th FAR with two, while the 17th FAR and the 18th GuFAR claimed one each. Russian sources reported that one Sabre had crashed a mile south of Suwon, another near Redi, a third about 30 miles south of Saksu, with two falling into the sea.

The first half of a campaign known as Operation 'Rat Trap' finished on 14 December. This was the codename for an effort carried out jointly by the ROK Army and the ROKAF to eliminate the activities of Communist guerrillas behind UN lines. These guerrillas had created irritating problems for the Allied forces ever since the UN had broken out of the Pusan Perimeter at the end of the previous year. Most of the guerrillas were Communists who had infiltrated into the hills to escape capture or death during the UN drive north, from where they had been making harassing strikes, mostly at night and never causing a great amount of damage, but their very existence was intolerable and they were potentially a serious danger.

---

[17] See *MiG-15* by Gordon and Rigmant.
[18] See *Twenty Years in Combat* by Alexander V. Kotlobovkii.

The ROKAF's 1st Fighter Wing had been formed in September 1951 with a complement of 63 officers and 222 airmen. Twelve F-51s were detached from training units and used to form the nucleus of the 12th ROKAF Fighter Squadron. During the first week of October this unit had moved to K-18 at Kangnumg, and had been considered as operational for combat from 11 October. By the end of the month it had flown 236 combat sorties and followed this up with another 250 sorties in November. On 1 December, all of the Mustangs at K-18 had been flown back to K-4 to participate in Operation 'Rat Trap'. Now, with the first half of the campaign over, the 12th FS returned to K-4 to fly a week of interdiction missions along and just behind the enemy's front lines while their efforts during the operation were being assessed. Since these missions were strictly a South Korean effort, the results received little publicity, but it was concluded that they did serve to curtail guerrilla attacks on road and rail movements behind the UN lines. The 12th FS was now moved to Chinhae to set up operations ready for the second half of 'Rat Trap'. Communist guerrillas had caused problems in the British Commonwealth Division's area, too. On the night of 10/11 December, a vehicle had been ambushed by a party of the enemy some distance behind the front lines. As a result of this, the Division conducted a sweep of the whole area with the object of discovering enemy guerrillas, agents and unauthorised civilians. With 1903 Flight fully stretched with the Air OP, 1913 Flight had taken on recce tasks to ease the strain. Visual recces of enemy positions with patrol commanders, intelligence officers and specialist officers normally took place at 4,000-5,000 feet, above expected enemy AA defences, but the enemy proved hard to find because of his high standard of camouflage. The value of visual reconnaissance was soon realised and an increasing number of calls for assistance were made for such tasks as checking the state of the roads after flooding.

For months now ground fire had been taking a heavy toll of UN fighter-bombers – 115 shot down and almost 800 damaged since August – on close-support and rail interdiction missions and, by late November, both the USAF's 49th[19] and 136th FBWs were reaching the point where losses and damaged aircraft had seriously reduced their capabilities. To help them, the 116th FBW at Misawa began rotating a squadron at a time to K-2 for combat training. On 2 December, 16 F-84s from the 159th FBS flew their first sorties against a rail complex at Wonsan. In the afternoon, 12 F-84s returned to the same target and the next day they attacked Wonsan. On 6 December, after successfully completing their assigned mission, all aircraft returned to their base in Japan having flown a total of 92 sorties. Four days later, 158th FBS was given its turn to participate and left Misawa for K-2 on 12 December. Its tour would be slightly longer, lasting seven days. During this period, the squadron flew 114 effective sorties, of which 88 were by 158th FBS personnel and the balance by 136th FBW pilots flying 158th FBS aircraft. They filed claims of a dozen rail cuts, 23 buildings destroyed, one MiG destroyed and three damaged. On one of its first missions, on 15 December, a flight composed of a flight leader from the 136th FBW and three members of the 158th, was jumped by four MiGs. Capt Paul C. Mitchell, who was the Operations Officer of the 158th, succeeded in shooting down a MiG and damaging another. He reported that his first victim burst into flames and the pilot immediately ejected. The Squadron's triumph was short-lived however, for shortly afterwards it suffered the 116th FBW's first combat loss when one of its aircraft was hit by ground fire, and the pilot, Capt David J. Miller, was unable to eject before it crashed The 8th FBS also lost an F-84 and its pilot on this date, Capt Robert D. Gibb, a WWII fighter ace. It seems their opponents were Chinese MiGs of the 9th and 42nd FARs which claimed 9 F-84s and two probables.

Sqn Ldr Thomas' flight of four Meteors was scrambled from Kimpo on the 15th to intercept the usual procession of unidentified aircraft. Two separate pairs of F-51s were met and identified but then the flight was directed to contact and escort home an F-86 that had been damaged in combat. The crippled Sabre was found at 5,000 feet and escorted towards Kimpo, but on its final approach to the airfield the badly damaged aircraft crashed just two miles from the end of the runway. Thomas thought he saw the pilot eject but nobody saw a parachute open. This was apparently a victim of one of the MiG pilots, three Sabres having been claimed shot

---

[19] 49th FBG suffered its last two operational fatalities for December when 1/Lt Edgar Grey of the 36th FBS and 1/Lt Lawrence B. Kelly of the 80th FBS were killed on the 14th and 16th, respectively.

down in combat during the day, one each by the 17th FAR, 176th GuFAR and 523rd FAR. Two of the Sabres were reported to have crashed near Syukusen and Namyang.

Mustangs of 2SAAF flew a successful 'Strangle' mission on 16 December, led by Lt Ron Beamish. Each aircraft carried two 500-lb bombs and four rockets and, during their strike, the South Africans achieved two railroad cuts before being directed to attack a village where enemy troops were known to be billeted. Four houses were destroyed and six others damaged in the subsequent attack. Next day, 77RAAF pilots on strip alert at Kimpo were scrambled to investigate contrails reported over Inch'on. The Meteor flight led by newly promoted Sqn Ldr John Hannan contacted GCI on becoming airborne and was instructed to proceed to 20 miles west of Inch'on. There were no sightings. The controller ordered the flight to make a wide orbit of Suwon airfield and continue searching but again results were negative. A few minutes later a Chinese-sounding voice speaking garbled English was heard on the radio channel and was reported to Control before the flight returned to base. Meanwhile, from Fort George airstrip the Austers of 1913 Flight RAF were ordered to search for the wreckage of a crashed American C-47. It was eventually located down in a valley by Sgt Jim Hutchings. The C-47 pilot, it was later discovered, had parachuted safely behind UN lines. 1913 Flight's diariest recorded December as:

> "A month of bad weather and constantly decreasing temperatures. Open-air servicing becomes extremely difficult due to the cold and prevailing wind, this however has been somewhat relieved by the construction of a steel tube and canvas hangar. The freezing during the low night temperatures is causing vehicles to bind fast on the solid earth until they thaw out at approximately 1000. All wheels of vehicles and aircraft are now bedded overnight on boards. A Cessna L-19 aircraft has been precluded by HQ 1st Commonwealth Division from HQ 8th US Army Light Aviation Section for a conversion to this aircraft. Captain Brown is at present training as the GOC's pilot."

At the end of the month all aircraft of the Flight assisted in flying the visiting Canadian Defence Minister and his party from Kimpo up to and around the Commonwealth Division area during their stay. The Flight was now well established at Fort George, with a growing reputation for dependability and accuracy in support of the Division and, by the end of the month, had completed 280 sorties in just over six weeks. However, its aircraft, the Auster VI, had been found to be underpowered for take-off, particularly in winter conditions but it had a good short-landing capability. It was a rugged, forgiving and reliable aircraft with a high rate of serviceability, but its main drawback was the very cramped cockpit. There was only one seat in the front for the pilot and behind this, but angled to the right, was the seat for the observer or passenger. Between the two seats was installed a radio set. To say the least, it was cramped and uncomfortable for almost any passenger. With the onset of winter any increase of clothing meant that, for a large man, there was little leg-room and his head would virtually touch the roof. Soon after arrival, the Flight made a proposal for a larger bucket-type passenger seat with arm rests and it was hoped that this would increase head and leg room.

Although Kimpo was closed by fog on 20 December, the 18th FBG was able to fly missions from K-46 where the weather was bitterly cold but the sun was shining and there was remarkably little cloud. With the early morning operations over, the men of 2SAAF enjoyed a break between sorties. So far nothing else had been scheduled for them. Their aircraft were parked well to the side of the runway, more than halfway along its length. Most of the aircrew had gone to their quarters and the ground staff, with rearming and refuelling over, were either working on the Mustangs or just standing around idle. One of the American squadrons was about to take off. The SAAF airmen began to take an interest in the proceedings. Fully-loaded Mustangs were lining up for a stream take-off. Even though the runway was slippery with ice and slush, the first few aircraft got off normally, one after the other, but then the next in line started fish-tailing as it sped along the runway. As the pilot tried to straighten out by gentle application of brakes, the tail swung first to one side and then the other with increasing ferocity. Halfway down the runway one wheel brake locked and the speeding aircraft swung off to one side. The pilot cut the engine but the Mustang hurtled straight into the refuelling area. It crashed into a fully-laden petrol bowser before coming to rest. The bowser was ruptured and petrol poured out everywhere, over another bowser and over the aircraft until it stood in a pool while, in the cockpit, the pilot sat dazed.

Everyone ran for cover, expecting an explosion, all except Sgt Laurie Burgess, one of the South African armourers, who ran through the pool of petrol and leapt up onto the wing of the Mustang. Working swiftly, he opened the canopy, freed the pilot's harness and helped the still stunned American – believed to have been 1/Lt Carl McCamish of the 67th FBS – out of the cockpit to safety. After checking the pilot was unhurt, Burgess returned to the aircraft. Standing in inch-deep petrol – the ground being frozen would not absorb it – he calmly proceeded to make the rockets safe by removing the fuses from those that had been undamaged in the crash and unplugging the remainder. The whole drama was over in a matter of minutes and the take-off of the remaining Mustangs was hardly affected. Burgess' courage had not gone unnoticed, and some time later he was advised that, by direct order of President Truman, he was to be awarded the US Soldier's Medal. About two months later General Everest, GOC 5th Air Force, flew in from Japan to make the award personally, and Burgess became only the third Commonwealth holder, and the only South African, of this prestigious award.

Fine, mild weather returned on 22 December, allowing normal operations from Kimpo. The remainder of the month would bring most erratic flying conditions. A limited number of sorties were launched on any given day by both sides and often these were recalled because of icing or low clouds. What few targets that could be located were attacked by the fighter-bombers, but these were becoming fewer and fewer because the Chinese and North Koreans were digging in for the winter. 'Strangle' attacks continued as the weather permitted. On 23 December, a flight of SAAF Mustangs led by Capt Bernie Trotter achieved one partial railroad cut and two near misses before going on to strafe and rocket enemy troops reportedly located in houses nearby. Three houses were destroyed and intense 20mm anti-aircraft fire was encountered but it was inaccurate and no Mustang was hit. Despite the continuation of such attacks, 5th Air Force intelligence officers had to concede that the repair work of Communist railway gangs and bridge builders had progressed so rapidly, all key rail arteries were now back in use, and the UN fighter-bomber railroad blockade of P'yongyang had been broken. During the day Flg Off Gogerly led four Meteors in a scramble to intercept enemy aircraft and cover returning Sabres. The flight was ordered to patrol just north of Haeju, where many Sabres were seen returning to base following a scrap with MiGs, the Russian pilots having claimed two shot down in addition to an F-84. The Meteor pilots then spotted four unidentified black-painted aircraft and reported to the controller, only to be advised they were friendly. Before returning to Kimpo, Gogerly led the flight to Haeju airfield where about 20 new-looking barracks-type buildings were observed, while the airfield itself, although extensively cratered on the south-west side, appeared serviceable.

That night the B-29s returned to Uiju. Before their arrival, however, a co-operating B-26 from the 3rd BG piloted by Capt William Jessup made a preliminary attack and knocked out eight of the searchlights. When the bombers arrived they came in at various heights and times to throw off the defences, although the remaining searchlights still managed to keep them illuminated to enable defending fighters – La-11s of the 351st(N) FAR – to attack, Kapt Anatolai Karelin being credited with shooting down one of the raiders. However, the damaged bomber was able to reach its base safely, as did a second that had been damaged by flak.

Christmas Eve turned out to be another fine, mild day, allowing newly-arrived Sqn Ldr Ron Susans DFC to fly his first mission with 77RAAF, a strip alert scramble to Haeju. On the way, the starboard engine of Flg Off Wal Rivers' aircraft (A77-728) caught fire due to turbine failure. Escorted by his wingman, Rivers was able to return to Kimpo on one engine and land safely. Meanwhile, Sqn Ldr Susans and Sgt Bruce Gillan continued to patrol the Haeju area, intercepting and identifying one F-86 and four F-80s before returning to base. On Christmas Day there was no sign of the snow that had been expected for a white Christmas. Instead there was continuous rain which prevented any flying from Kimpo. By Boxing Day the continuous rain eventually turned into sleet and then to snow, again curtailing any serious flying, but by 27 December a return to more settled conditions allowed several scrambles by Meteor flights, mainly to investigate bogies in the area. During one, Sqn Ldr Hannan led four Meteors to intercept three unidentified aircraft near Sariwon which turned out to be F-84s. A few minutes later a large explosion was seen on an island just off the coast, and soon after the pilots made a rare sighting when they intercepted and identified a lone RB-45 heading out to sea at 30,000 feet. In clashes over North Korea two MiGs were claimed shot down by Sabres, one being claimed by 1/Lt Cliff Brossart of the 334th FIS, and the other by 2/Lt Kenneth A. Shealy of the 25th FIS. Their opponents were from the 17th FAR and the 196th FAR, who claimed three Sabres in return, two of which were reported to have crashed near Kijo with the third falling into the sea off Haksen. One of these may have been flown by 1/Lt William D. Bush of the 335th FIS. Next day, in further skirmishes, 1/Lt Paul Roach of the 25th FIS claimed his second MiG of the month, while Lt Colonel Jones damaged another, with the Russians claiming four Sabres shot down, two each by the 17th and 196th FARs. This latter unit claimed a further four Sabres on the 29th, the final victories of 1951 going to the pilots of the 18th GuFAR who reported shooting down three F-80s on the last day of December.

Interdiction and ground-support missions continued to be flown, subject to the vagaries of the weather. Late on 30 December, the FAC found a worthwhile target for a flight of Mustangs from 2SAAF led by Maj Ray Lyon. They were directed against dug-in troops and two machine-gun positions, which were duly napalmed, rocketed and strafed. One gun position was destroyed and possibly the other. Haze and oncoming darkness affected the accuracy of the attack. During the course of another mission, Mustang 334 flown by Lt D.R. Leathers, one of the new pilots, was hit by ground fire and slightly damaged. On landing at K-46 a bullet hole was found through the tailplane stabiliser. Apart from the two pilots killed in an air collision, 2SAAF escaped any combat casualties during December, although the other squadrons of the 18th FBG did not fare so well. Eight Mustangs were lost to enemy action, with the 12th FBS losing three pilots killed: 2/Lt Donald E. Hoffman on the 3rd, 1/Lt John A. Swanson on the 13th, and 1/Lt Clarence McGowan on the 23rd; the 67th FBS lost 1/Lt Lyle E. Moore on the 1st, and 1/Lt Grant D. Harkness on the 5th, while the 39th FIS lost Capt Robert D. Ramsey on the 10th, 1/Lt Robert L. Smith on the 14th, and 2/Lt Thurston R. Baxter on the 21st. The 45th TRS also lost a pilot, Capt Charles D. Brown being reported killed on the 17th.

The year ended with further visits by VIPs, including one by the Australian Minister for the Army, Mr Josiah Francis, who was on an inspection tour of the conditions and equipment of the Australian Army in Korea. His aircraft arrived at Kimpo, where he met members of 77RAAF, and later attended a ceremony when US Air Medals were presented to Sqn Ldr Cedric Thomas DFC, Flt Lt Scotty Cadan and Flg Off Ken Blight. Also present were Grp Capt A.G. Carr AFC RAAF, OC 91 (Composite) Wing at Iwakuni and Colonel G.S. Brown from 5th Air Force HQ, who had arrived the day before to discuss the problems that 77RAAF was experiencing in its rôle of air defence of the area.

A period of change was now sweeping through 77RAAF, with Wg Cdr Steege handing over command to Sqn Ldr Ron Susans. A number of veterans were tour-expired and new pilots arrived to take their places. Before Wg Cdr Steege departed for Australia, he wrote his final report:

> "Though results have not been spectacular, the Meteor on CAP has contributed valuably to the work of attack aircraft in enabling them to go about their task relatively untroubled by MiGs. When additional Meteors arrive, the question as to suitability for the various commitments to be met by the 5th Air Force will have to be reviewed, bearing in mind the numbers and types of United States fighters available."

Nonetheless, for the loss of four Meteors shot down in combat with the MiGs, two of the Russian jets had been claimed destroyed in return and several others damaged.

MiG pilots had continued to submit excessive claims for UN aircraft destroyed during December, these totalling 78, comprising 48 F-86s, 12 F-84s, nine F-80s and nine Meteors. Of these, 176th GuFAR claimed 27, 17th FAR claimed 26, 196th FAR claimed 13, 18th GuFAR claimed 11, and 523rd FAR claimed one single victory. These latest claims raised the number of Sabres claimed destroyed to a staggering 234 out of a total of 544 UN aircraft claimed destroyed by MiG pilots since their first victory on 1 November 1950. The USAF's admitted losses for Sabres in aerial combat was just 14. The remaining MiG claims were for 124 F-84s, 85 F-80s, 41 B-29s, 27 Meteors, 19 F-51s, eight F-94s, 2 B-26s, two RB-45s, and two USMC F6Fs. Claims by the respective regiments still operating at the end of December 1951 were:

324th FAD
17th FAR	100 Top-scorer (by February 1952)	Kapt Nikolai Sutyagin – 22
176th GuFAR	107 Top-scorer (by February 1952)	Maj Serafim Subbotin – 15
196th FAR	92 Top-scorer (by February 1952)	Polkovnik Yevgenii Pepelyaev – 19

303rd FAD
18th GuFAR	81 Top-scorer (by February 1952)	Maj Lev Shchukin – 15
523rd FAR	96 Top-scorer (by February 1952)	Maj Dmitrii Os'kin – 11
		Kapt Stepan Bakhaev – 11
		Kapt Grigorii Okhai – 11

Admitted aircraft/pilot losses during this period for these units are known only for the 18th GuFAR (18 aircraft and eight pilots), and the 196th FAR (12 aircraft and six pilots killed, plus four wounded) while it is understood that the 17th FAR lost four pilots, 176th GuFAR five pilots, and 523rd FAR five pilots. It could be assumed that the 17th FAR, 176th GuFAR and 523rd FAR lost at least 30 aircraft between them, on the basis of their pilot casualties, raising total MiG losses in combat to about 60 aircraft, to which must be added the unknown Chinese Air Force losses. Among the top-scorers of the 196th FAR (by February 1952) were Polkovnik Yevgenii Pepelyaev with at least 19 (14 F-86s, two F-84s, two F-94, one F-80), Kapt V.N. Alfeev and Kapt L.M. Ivanov with eight apiece, Maj Boris Bokach with seven (six F-86s, one F-84), Kapt I.M. Zaplavnev with six, and Podpolkovnik A. Mitusov, Kapt Boris Abakumov (three F-86s, one B-29, one F-94) and Kapt M. Muraviev (four F-86s, one F-84) with five apiece; the latter had also accidentally shot down two Chinese MiG-15s. The top-scorer for the 17th FAR (by February 1952) was Kapt Nikolai Sutyagin with 22 victories (15 F-86s, three F-84s, two F-80s, two Meteors), and for the 523rd FAR the joint top-scorers were Maj Dmitrii Os'kin, the CO, with 11 (four F-86s, two B-29s, two F-84s, one F-80, and two Meteors), Kapt Stepan Bakhaev with 11 (five F-86s, three F-80s, two F-84s, one B-29), and Kapt Grigorii Okhai also with 11 which included three Meteors, plus three F-86s, two F-84s, and two F-80s. The 176th GuFAR's top-scorer was Maj Serafim Subbotin with 15, while Kapt Sergei Kramarenko numbered two Meteors in his total of 13 victories, as did the 18th GuFAR top-scorer Maj Lev Shchukin, in addition to eight F-84s, three F-80s, one F-86 and one F-51, while Kapt Grigorii Ges of the 176th GuFAR also recorded a victory over a Meteor amongst his 10 victories. Other high-scoring pilots of 176th GuFAR included Kapt Mikhail Ponomarev, who claimed four F-84s in one day (on 11 September 1951) in his total of 11, and Kapt Petr Milaushkin with 10.

During this same period, Sabre pilots were credited with 130 MiGs, eight Tu-2s and three La-9s shot down, while a dozen more were claimed by pilots of F-80s and F-84s, and two were credited to the Meteor pilots. In addition, B-29s gunners claimed 23 more. A mixed bag of 28 Yaks, Ilyushins and La-7s were claimed by the various F-51, F-82, F-80 and F-84 units, while a B-26 crew was credited with a Po-2, to give the USAF/UN a grand total approaching 200 air victories up to the end of 1951. The 4th FIW could now boast six aces by December 1951, listed in order of achieving ace status:

Capt James Jabara	334th FIS	6 victories as at 21 May 1951
Capt Richard S. Becker	334th FIS	5 victories as at 9 September 1951
Capt Ralph D. Gibson	335th FIS	5 victories as at 9 September 1951
Maj Richard D. Creighton	336th FIS	5 victories as at 27 November 1951
Maj George A. Davis Jr	334th FIS	12 victories as at 13 December 1951
Maj Winton W. Marshall	335th FIS	6¹/₂ victories as at 30 November 1951

* * *

At the beginning of December the issue of prisoners of war had come to the fore in the peace negotiations at Panmanjom. Early in the war the US/UN Command and both North and South Korea had announced that they would abide by the terms of the 1949 Geneva Prisoner of War

Convention. To prevent a situation similar to the Soviets' holding of huge numbers of German POWs long after the end of WWII, the International Red Cross had adopted the principle that all prisoners must be repatriated without delay once hostilities had ended. However, on 3 July 1951, US Assistant Secretary of State for Far Eastern Affairs, Mr Dean Rusk, had informed America's allies that the United States wished to exchange POWs on a one-to-one basis because there was a huge imbalance. At that time, the UN forces in Korea had almost 100,000 North Korean and Chinese POWs, whereas the Communists held only about 10,000 US/UN/ROK prisoners. To return all of the POWs immediately would have been to provide North Korea with practically a whole new army in exchange for just one tenth the number. The American delegates to the Peace Conference said nothing about this change of policy even during the first weeks of December, when the negotiations turned to the prisoner-of-war issue, and in fact the Communists agreed to exchange lists of POWs only because the UN Command promised to release all prisoners as soon as an armistice was signed. This was to occur on 27 December.

The POW lists, presented on 18 December, showed that the UN Command held a total of 132,472 prisoners, of whom approximately 95,500 were North Koreans, 20,700 were Chinese Communists and 16,200 were pro-Communist South Koreans who had joined the North Korean Army. The UN Command held an additional 38,000 anti-Communist South Koreans (mostly men, but including some women) who had been recruited at gunpoint by the North Koreans; they were reclassified as civilian internees. A further 6,000 POWs had either died in captivity or escaped.

The Communists provided the UN Command with a list which revealed that 11,559 POWs were held by them in eleven camps – three near P'yongyang and eight along the Yalu. These included 7,142 ROK; 3,198 US; 919 British; 234 Turks; 40 Filipinos; ten French; six Australians; four South Africans; three Japanese, one Canadian, one Greek, and one Netherlander. The numbers did not add up. When these figures were published in the American press, they caused a great wave of moral outrage against the atrocities which they implied. The US/UN Command had officially reported 11,224 Americans as missing in action, presumed prisoners of war; the Communist figures suggested something like 8,000 Americans were unaccounted for and therefore had probably died of illness or starvation when in captivity. Nearly 80,000 South Koreans were also unaccounted for. The Communists claimed that 53,000 South Koreans had either died or else were forced to serve in the North Korean Army. Once these figures had been released it was unthinkable for the United States to agree to an all-for-all exchange, to give the Communists 132,000 men in return for 11,000.

However, the personnel of 77RAAF found some welcome news in the POW lists handed over by the North Koreans. The lists showed that Flt Lt Gordon Harvey, who had been shot down while flying a Mustang on 19 January 1951 was a prisoner in a camp two miles north-east of Sinuiju, and that Wt Off Ron Guthrie, who had disappeared on 29 August whilst flying a Meteor on a fighter sweep in MiG Alley, was there too. There was no news at this stage of Sgts Vance Drummond and Bruce Thomson, although both were also in Communist hands. The good news for 2SAAF was that four of its missing pilots were safe and being held as POWs: 2/Lt Mike Halley, 2/Lt Denis Earp, Lt Hector Macdonald and Lt Chris Lombard.

The 27 December deadline set at the Panmanjom peace talks, came and went without an agreement being signed. There would be no peace in 1951. The stumbling block was still the prisoner of war issue. Once the figure had been released when POW lists had been exchanged, the Communists soon realised there would not be an all-for-all trade off despite the terms of the 1949 Geneva Prisoner of War Convention. Meanwhile, they had taken advantage of the respite to fortify their front lines. Having secured their battle positions, they moved troops back to rearward support positions, thus reducing both the logistic support required at the front lines and their exposure to air attack. The ground war was about to begin with even greater intensity, and with it the air war, which would see many clashes between Sabre and MiG during the coming eighteen months before the guns fell silent.

Meanwhile, at sea . . .

PART TWO

CARRIER-BASED AIR OPERATIONS

Korea 1950-1951

No less important than the life and death struggle being fought in the skies over Korea by land-based UN air units, were the continuous air strikes launched by the RN and RAN aircraft carriers in conjunction with the USN and USMC aircraft carriers stationed in the Yellow Sea. The first Royal Navy carrier to participate in the Korean War was HMS *Triumph* commanded by Capt A.D. Torlesse DSO RN, which arrived off the west coast of Korea on 2 July and joined US Task Force 77. *Triumph* and her attendants were part of the British Far East Fleet based at Singapore and Hong Kong, and had been engaged in a summer cruise to Japan when called to action. Flying his flag in the cruiser HMS *Belfast* was Rear-Admiral W.G. Andrewes RN, Deputy Commander Far East Station. *Triumph* was a unit of the Royal Navy's 1st Aircraft Carrier Squadron. On board was the 13th Carrier Group commanded by Lt Cdr(P) P.B. Jackson, which comprised 12 Seafire FR47s of 800 Squadron (Lt Cdr(P) I.M. MacLachlan) and 12 Firefly FR1s of 827 Squadron (Lt Cdr(P) B.C. Lyons).

At this time the American 7th Fleet had only one carrier in Korean waters, the USS *Valley Forge*, which had a dual rôle – supporting US forces in Japan as well as the Nationalist Chinese on Formosa. Because of the commitment, *Valley Forge* was unable to carry out lengthy periods of operations off the Korean coast until reinforcements could arrive. Plans were immediately laid for the combined Anglo-American force to move into the Yellow Sea for strikes against targets in North Korea. For this purpose, Rear-Admiral J.M. Hoskins USN commanding the US 3rd Carrier Division, was in tactical command, flying his flag in *Valley Forge*. Embarked on the carrier were two jet fighter squadrons, VF-51 and VF-52, with F9F-2 Panthers, plus VF-53 and VF-54 with F4U-4B Corsairs, and VA-55 with AD-2 Skyraiders.

CHAPTER X

CARRIER AIR OPERATIONS: HMS *TRIUMPH*

July – September 1950

"I consider myself lucky as I was too shit scared to bale out over shark infested seas . . ."
Lt(P) Peter Lamb, 800 Squadron HMS *Triumph*

The British naval force was soon in action when the cruiser HMS *Jamaica* engaged six North Korean MTBs at dawn on 2 July. They were considered a threat to Task Force 77 (TF77), and five were quickly destroyed by *Jamaica* and her attendant frigate HMS *Black Swan*.

Joint operations began at dawn on 3 July with an air strike against the airfield at Haeju near Kaishu, about 120 miles from the ship, heralding the start of a determined effort by the United Nations to eliminate North Korea's small air force as an effective fighting force. The object was primarily to destroy aircraft and, secondly, installations. For the strike, *Triumph* had a large number of aircraft ranged on her deck. This meant, on a small escort carrier, that the aircraft at the head of the range did not have a full take-off run, so the four Seafires at the front were fitted with RATOG (Rocket Assisted Take-Off Gear) to get airborne. The technique was to fire the rockets as the aircraft passed a mark on the deck late in the take-off run. Firing them gave quite a push, though not as much as when using the catapult. Once airborne, the pilot jettisoned the rocket packs. Using this method was not popular because carrier operations were already hazardous enough, but by making free take-offs or using RATOG, *Triumph* could launch at 15-second intervals compared with normal catapulting at the rate of about one launch per minute.

A dozen rocket-armed Fireflies led by Lt Cdr(P) Bernard Lyons and nine Seafires also armed with rockets had the task of attacking the hangars and installations at Haeju. Taking off at 0545, they approached the airfield at low level, but about 15 miles from the target fog and low cloud forced them higher. Fortunately, the cloud cleared over the target and the attack went in as planned. No aircraft or movement could be seen on the airfield, which in fact appeared deserted. Most of the rockets were discharged into hangars and the administration area, while a few exploded on the concrete dispersal. The last section of Seafires found the target completely shrouded by black smoke. Despite instructions to stay above 600 feet during the attack, the Firefly flown by the CO was hit by a rifle calibre bullet, possibly from light flak, while the Seafire piloted by 800 Squadron's Senior Pilot Lt(P) Peter Lamb suffered hits from ground fire and sustained superficial damage to its radiator when it flew through debris thrown into the air by the explosions of its own rockets:

> "After a strike on Kaishu and getting hit several times, I managed to return to the ship and land on with the complete loss of coolant and all temperatures off the clock. Says something for the Rolls-Royce Griffin engine. I consider myself lucky as I was too shit scared to bale out over shark infested seas."

As soon as he throttled back after landing, the engine ground to a halt. It had seized and was a complete write off.

The Americans had better luck. A dozen Skyraiders, 16 Corsairs and eight Panthers from *Valley Forge* attacked major airfields around P'yongyang. Two Yak-9s bravely attempted to interfere and were shot down by Panthers flown by Ens William E. Brown and Lt(Jg) Leonard H. Plog. At least nine other aircraft were claimed damaged on the ground. Following the Panthers in, Corsairs and Skyraiders bombed and rocketed hangars and fuel storage facilities. They encountered both heavy and light flak but suffered no damage. Their only loss of the day was one of the Corsairs on CAP which caught fire and ditched close by one of the destroyers, which immediately rescued the pilot. The successful action by the Panthers inspired Rear-Admiral Edward C. Ewen USN to record:

> "It is quite possible that the early appearance of the Panthers over Northern Korea on 3 July had a quieting effect on Russian and Chinese plans to provide North Korea with large numbers of obsolescent propeller-type aircraft."

Valley Forge launched another strike in the afternoon but because her Panthers were unable to provide distant fighter cover for the proposed Seafire/Firefly strike, *Triumph* was instructed not to launch. The Fireflies were unfortunately showing up as a major handicap to operations with the American carrier because of their very restricted strike radius of only 140 miles. USN strike aircraft could attack targets at twice the distance. Even the Seafires were capable for some 200 miles but they lacked bomb-racks.

Triumph was again unable to co-ordinate her strike with *Valley Forge* efforts next day (4 July), because P'yongyang was beyond the reach of her Fireflies. She would not be able to launch her aircraft to attack such targets until the ships moved further north, although at 1100 a dozen Fireflies and seven Seafires were despatched to bomb and rocket a railway bridge between Yonan and Haeju, scoring two hits. On returning to the carrier one Firefly had to make a one-wheel landing due to a hydraulic fault, while a Seafire returned with a hole in its port overload tank, the damage having been inflicted by a spent cannon shell case ejected from another Seafire. *Valley Forge*'s Skyraiders meanwhile completed a successful mission although four of her aircraft were hit by AA fire. One of the damaged machines, on returning to the carrier, bounced over the protecting barriers with catastrophic effect – two Corsairs and a Skyraider were totally destroyed, while three Skyraiders, two Panthers and a Corsair were damaged.

After just two days of operations *Valley Forge* had to withdraw to her other commitment, covering the Formosa Straits. Because *Triumph* lacked the aircraft to conduct simultaneous defensive and offensive operations, she withdrew with TF77 and accompanied it throughout the time spent away from the combat area. The break gave the two carrier group commanders an opportunity to formulate improved procedures to co-ordinate operations. It had become apparent that the choice of targets for RN aircraft was severely limited by the Firefly's strike radius. American aircraft were proving much more versatile, both the Skyraider and Corsair being capable of carrying mixed loads of bombs, rockets and drop tanks, and they could be catapulted off deck with any combination. Among other matters, it was decided that *Triumph* would in future be responsible for defensive patrols while in company with the American carrier, leaving the US Navy squadrons to concentrate on delivering heavy attacks. This was a sensible arrangement, for as a defensive fighter the Mark FR47 Seafire was superior in every way to the Corsair and its rate of climb and endurance were better than those of the jet-propelled Panther.

Unfortunately, an inherent structural weakness of the Seafire was beginning to reveal itself. Already many had suffered wrinkled fuselages due to inevitable and unavoidable heavy landings. The wrinkling was not really visible to the human eye, but if a hand was rubbed over the skin trouble spots could be detected. The worry was that the structure was less strong than it would have been, although the Engineer Officer remarked that while they were outside the safety limits for peacetime flying, he would let them continue to fly operational sorties! For the replacement and upkeep of *Triumph*'s aircraft, it was decided to use the Fleet Air Arm base at HMS *Simbang* (the Royal Navy's shore station at Sembawang, Singapore), rather than employ a shore base in the forward area, such as Iwakuni. The Air Repair Department of the supply carrier HMS *Unicorn* was established there, with the necessary workshop equipment and stores.

TF77 returned from Okinawa to cover an amphibious landing at P'ohang scheduled for 18 July and to resume strikes on enemy-occupied territory. The landing at P'ohang by the US 1st

Cavalry Division went ahead as planned, unopposed by the NKAF, and by evening 10,000 troops, 2,000 vehicles and 2,700 tons of cargo had been put ashore. Meanwhile the Task Force, having completed its duty, headed northwards to attack targets in North Korea, where *Valley Forge*'s Corsairs and Skyraiders destroyed the country's largest oil refinery (annual output of 1.7 million barrels) during the afternoon strike, but most of the ensuing missions were against targets of opportunity such as airfields, supply dumps, road and rail traffic, and harbour installations. The majority of the NKAF's aircraft were reported to be concentrated at P'yongyang and Yonpo, and these airfields were allocated as targets for the Task Force's strike aircraft. In two attacks against P'yongyang's airfields, the American carrier pilots claimed at least 14 enemy aircraft destroyed with 13 others damaged. Next day *Valley Forge*'s pilots claimed a further 15 aircraft destroyed as a result of a raid on Yonpo airfield.

On board *Triumph* Lt(P) Peter Cane, pilot of the carrier's ASR Sea Otter amphibian (JM960), was briefed to carry out a rescue of a US Navy Corsair pilot who had been forced to ditch about 120 miles north-north-west of the American carrier's position near Wonsan. By the time Cane took off, with Aircrewman Gil O'Nion[1], he learned that the Corsair had sunk and that the pilot was in his dinghy, which was being circled by two other aircraft from his own unit. The ASR crew soon established R/T contact with the circling Corsairs and were warned that conditions would be rough for sea landing. Although visibility was poor, the dingy eventually came in view. The sea certainly was rough and, with a steep chop of between four and five feet and a wind of 20-30 knots, conditions were well outside the limits for a fragile Sea Otter. Nonetheless, Cane prepared to alight. With superb skill he held the nose up and closed the throttle to settle into a trough, but one wingtip was damaged. He taxied to the dinghy as quickly as the choppy sea would permit. Standing up in the forward hatch, O'Nion hooked a slip-line onto the dinghy and allowed it to float under the wing alongside the rear hatch. After securing the line, he moved aft and hoisted the American, Lt Wendell R. Muncie USN, into the aircraft via the rear hatch, before sinking the redundant dinghy with his knife. The rescued pilot was uninjured and obviously pleased to see them, though somewhat amazed at the archaic machine that had come to rescue him. Take-off consisted of ploughing into the sea, thumping from wave to wave without porpoising. O'Nion recalled later:

> "I cannot remember how many waves we hit. It felt like being on a roller coaster at a fairground. Seas were breaking over the top mainplane and engine, which spluttered and caught again. The last wave we hit pushed us staggering into the air."

Back on *Triumph*'s deck, where Cane had landed safely, the Sea Otter was immediately struck down in the forward lift into a hangar. Muncie took off his Mae West and handed it to his rescuer as a souvenir. For this gallant recovery, Cane was awarded the US Air Medal and O'Nion received a Mention in Despatches.

Valley Forge lost a second aircraft when a Panther crashed into the sea on take-off. On this occasion the pilot was quickly rescued by the carrier's helicopter. Meanwhile, during this day of heavy activity, Seafires flew 27 CAP sorties without incident apart from intercepting USAF aircraft bound for North Korean targets. During the final land-on for the day, the Seafire flown by Cmd Plt Dennis White caught No10 wire and, very gently, engaged the barrier. The engine was not damaged, so after replacing the propeller the aircraft was soon made serviceable. This was the second Seafire accident on consecutive days, as earlier Lt(P) Don Reid had landed off-centre and had hit the fore batting position, severely damaging the leading edge of his port wing. For *Triumph* the first warnings of the beginning of the typhoon season caused the cancellation of strikes planned for 20 July. Instead, the carrier left TF77 and headed for Sasebo to enable minor repairs to be carried out, and to take on board spare Seafires and Fireflies from *Unicorn*. She was back on station within a few days.

TF77 began a new three-day series of strikes on 26 July with the launching of some 60 sorties from *Valley Forge*. As soon as they were in the combat area, the Navy pilots, for the first

---

[1] Acmn1 Gil O'Nion had served as a TAG with 808 Squadron early in WWII, flying Fulmars from the deck of HMS *Ark Royal*.

time in co-operation with their 5th Air Force counterparts, reported to Airborne Tactical air co-ordinators to have enemy ground targets located and to be vectored onto them. Prior to this the Navy pilots had been detailed to work exclusively over precisely defined areas where they would not come into conflict with 5th Air Force fighter-bomber operations. It had, however, become clear that to enable the 8th US Army to establish a perimeter for the defence of Pusan, tactical air power would have to be used and co-ordinated on a massive scale.

Although the UN capability for waging an around-the-clock tactical air offensive against the advancing enemy was growing steadily, the employment of tactical air power still suffered from a lack of co-ordination. With carrier aircraft playing an increasing part in the fighting, it was obvious that much more could be achieved if Navy pilots were permitted to range along the entire battle line. Naval liaison officers from *Valley Forge* had discussed the problem with their Army and Air Force counterparts in the Joint Operations Centre and reached an information agreement that carrier aircraft operating under the strict control of the JOC would join the 5th Air Force's fighter-bombers in attacking targets along the whole front (see Chapter I). *Triumph* rejoined *Valley Forge* for this series of operations. With the British light fleet carrier providing all the defensive flying, TF77 was able to keep up uninterrupted continuous pressure. During this time, out of *Triumph*'s total of 168 CAP and ASP sorties, the Seafires flew some 80 CAP sorties. One of these almost ended with disaster, on 28 July, when a flight of Seafires intercepted a formation of B-29s of the 22nd BG on their way to bomb Wonsan, and flew on either wing of the rearmost bomber for several minutes. Despite their distinctive markings, the Seafires were apparently mistaken for Yak-9s by the nervous B-29 gunners, who fired on VP473/180, the aircraft flown by Cmd Plt Dennis White:

> "About mid-morning C Flight was flying CAP. The first of the bomber stream appeared on the screens heading roughly towards the Fleet and we were sent off smartly to intercept. This we did and duly reported a friendly B-29 – no trouble – and shortly afterward we were vectored to another bogey from the same direction. Same result, then another and another and so on until it became obvious to all concerned that a bomber stream was passing through the area.
>
> Ever cautious however, the Fighter Controller continued to send us to intercept as each one appeared. As we sighted the fateful one we radioed back, 'Another B-29'. The controller was unimpressed since he had us still 12 miles apart but it was quite obvious to us – huge aircraft with that enormous fin like the others we'd seen. We were ordered to get closer for a positive identification. I think they were concerned lest one of the Russian look-alikes had been slipped into the stream with evil designs on the fleet.
>
> Sometime prior to this, 'Sheepy' Lamb's radio had failed. Johnny Treacher had been signalled into the lead and I was now leading the second element with Sheepy – sans radio – on my wing. We approached the culprit about 1,500 yards out on his port side – and then, well astern, Johnny swung the flight left across his stern. At this point my engine spluttered and died – dry fuel tank. After I'd got it going again, JD [Treacher] and his wingman were about 1,000 yards out. As we drew alongside – still trailing the lead element and in a shallow dive going like the clappers – there was a sudden bang behind me.
>
> Sheepy swears I was out within ten seconds of a gaping hole appearing in my fuselage about a foot behind my head – right where an extra 30-gallon fuel tank had been added as one of the FR47 improvements – I ask you, a fuel tank for a headrest! Anyway, at first nothing seemed to have happened; the engine was going well, controls all normal. But something had happened, I told myself, as I started to turn my head to see if I could see if anything was the matter with the tail. As I did so, the whole cockpit filled with flames. I knew I had to get out fast and reached up for the hood jettison toggle. It was stuck fast. I brought my other hand up to it and pulled with all my strength; the flames seemed to follow my hands. After what seemed to be an age, the hood suddenly went with a bang. I pulled the nose up level, flipped over to inverted and undid my harness with one hand while pushing forward with the other, and shot out as good and clean as any ejector seat. I'd always known this was the best way to get out if ever I had to do, so I didn't even think about it – just did it. Lucky I did because I could have survived very little longer in there.

I went out at about 10,000 feet or so, realising my clothes were probably on fire. I did freefall for some time thinking the slipstream would blow them out. The slipstream was fanning my smouldering gear, including my parachute harness, into a bright read glow! So I pulled the ring and opened, hoping I'd get down to the water before something burned through. I spent the descent trying to beat out my gleaming harness and pulling fist-fulls of smouldering kapok out of my Mae West. I got down and into my dinghy. Treacher was unaware of what had happened behind him and had flown on. Sheepy couldn't tell him and I was too busy. Sheepy circled me going down and switched his IFF to emergency. This was spotted by *Valley Forge* who sent Treacher back to find Sheepy circling me sitting in a dinghy. Fireflies were sent to look after me and keep my position – the sea was very rough – until after about an hour the USS *Eversole* drove up and plucked me out."

Although suffering from burns to his face, arms and shoulders, White was returned to *Triumph* next day. The whole incident was kept very quiet at the time "for the sake of morale". On reflection, Dennis White added:

"It was no accident. We were fired on quite deliberately and intentionally. I could still hear them banging away with their .5s as I floated down on my brolly. They may well have taken us for Yak-9s but since we'd already looked at six or seven other B-29s in the stream, going much closer to some than this particular one, it can only be concluded that their recognition was faulty and/or they were trigger happy . . . It has been said that we made a pass at them – not true – we made no offensive move whatsoever."

In response to a formal complaint lodged by Capt Torlesse of *Triumph*, a signal was received from General Stratemeyer at USAF Headquarters, which, although expressing regret for the incident, suggested that all aircraft should keep out of gun range of B-29s! In fact, the Group's commander, Colonel James V. Edmundson, had apparently instructed his gunners to fire at any unidentified fighter within range which pointed its nose at one of the bombers. White proffered his own views:

"The reason it happened, fundamentally, which was not apparent, was that the USAF and the US Navy were at war with each other almost as much as with North Korea. They were locked in deadly conflict over the matter of budget appropriation for their respective arms of service . . . The upshot was that far from co-operating and co-ordinating with each other, the two services were barely on speaking terms.

On the day in question, the US 7th Fleet [TF77] was mounting strike operations against the North Koreans from an area in the Yellow Sea well to the north of the 38th Parallel. On the same day the USAF had laid on a raid on P'yongyang [in fact, their target was Wonsan] by a force of B-29s operating out of Okinawa. Korea was buzzing with mostly Mustangs and B-26s spreading HE and napalm like corn. On this day however these tactical forces were ordered to confine operations to south of the 38th Parallel. The B-29s were briefed that if they should see anything to the north of this it would be hostile. Nobody told them that the 7th Fleet was there and nobody told the Fleet that the B-29s were coming through their area!"

The problem of correct identification by the Americans of unfamiliar British aircraft had to be resolved quickly, particularly the difficulty of distinguishing between Seafire and Yak-9. The two Royal Navy aircraft types being operated by *Triumph* were among few UN in-line engined aircraft operating in the area, the other being the F-51D. The NKAF, on the other hand, was operating Russian-built in-line engined Yak-9s and Il-10s. A solution was reached – to paint the RN aircraft with black-and-white stripe wing and fuselage markings similar to the Normandy invasion stripes of 1944.

August 1950
On the first day of August, TF77 was strengthened by the arrival of a second USN carrier, USS *Philippine Sea*, also equipped with two squadrons of USN Panthers, two squadrons of Corsairs and one squadron of Skyraiders. Two escort carriers arrived soon thereafter, the much smaller USS *Badoeng Strait* with just one squadron of USMC Corsairs, and USS *Sicily*, also with a

squadron of USMC Corsairs.

After this eventful patrol, a short break from operations was deemed necessary to enable *Triumph* to maintain her troublesome machinery, and she left the Task Force to spend ten days at Kure. En route, flying continued with Lt(P) Peter Lamb carrying out a test flight in a Seafire which began developing engine problems. Although he was able to make a successful landing, he would have been justified in abandoning it in flight. For saving that particular aircraft, combined with the safe return of the battle-damaged Seafire earlier in the month, Lamb was later awarded the DSC. Soon after arrival at Kure, 800 Squadron's Senior Pilot, Lt Cdr(P) Tom Handley, was asked to brief the Americans on bombardment spotting, which resulted in two trips for him in a US Navy Neptune of VP-6 to give practical demonstrations. On the first he controlled Royal Navy destroyers *Cossack* and *Cockade* bombarding the port at Mokpo on 2 August; on the second trip, four days later, he assisted the cruiser *Kenya* shelling Inch'on, flying with Lt John W. Stribling USN. A second Neptune flown by Lt George B. Anderson USN carried British Army Capt Thompson RA, who similarly spotted for *Belfast*; three destroyers, including a Dutch vessel, also participated in the bombardment while four USMC Corsairs of VMF-323 from *Badoeng Strait*, circled overhead as escort; the results of these attacks directed against Inch'on railway station, an electrical works and oil storage tanks on the northern side of the city, were reported to have been very satisfactory.

With the arrival of the reinforcing American carriers, *Triumph* sailed to the Yellow Sea for a solo blockade patrol of Korea's west coast as Task Force 91 (TF91). With the Communists driving rapidly southwards to the bridgehead around Pusan, clearly the encircled land forces needed the support of an effective naval blockade of the enemy's supply ports. This therefore was the primary task of the naval forces in the Yellow Sea, preventing the enemy from supplying his forward units by sea by destroying all forms of seaborne transport. The presence of an aircraft carrier lightened the load on the surface vessels, for aerial reconnaissance and strikes reduced the need for a large number of ships on simultaneous patrol. Although the Fireflies were the principal coastal surveillance aircraft, the better combat radius of the Seafires permitted them to be used for extended tactical reconnaissance. Seafires were also used for following-up initial contact reports as well as providing pairs of aircraft either on CAP or at immediate readiness on deck. *Triumph*'s aircraft were responsible for surveillance along the west coast from Taedong on the 38th Parallel to Mokpo – a patrol line similar in length to the distance between the Thames estuary and the Firth of Forth in Scotland. In support were the cruiser *Kenya* and three destroyers.

There were few targets. The North Koreans, lacking naval strength on the scale of that available to the UN, were moving by night and remaining concealed under camouflage by day. Nonetheless, several craft spotted in the Taedong estuary were attacked by six Fireflies and six Seafires equipped with rockets. An 800-ton coaster, a minesweeper and a medium-sized freighter were claimed badly damaged, while a few junks were strafed at Chinnampo during the course of the four-day patrol.

Triumph returned to Sasebo on 16 August for 48 hours. The news of the birth of HRH Princess Anne having just been received, the carrier arrived with masthead flags flying. UN ships in harbour at the time followed suit and sent congratulatory messages. At noon, there was a parade and a royal salute was fired followed by the mandatory splicing of the main brace (the Royal Navy's tradition of issuing a tot of rum to all ranks on special occasions) to give the royal infant of a naval officer and his wife a royal welcome. After two days spent replenishing at Sasebo, *Triumph* returned to her west coast patrol in the Inch'on/Kunsan area on 18 August. The American carriers of TF77 were also operating the Yellow Sea, making the RN's Seafire CAP unnecessary. Freedom from this duty, in effect, doubled the British offensive fighter potential. There were still a few targets, and *Triumph*'s bag for the four-day operation was one patrol craft sunk in the Taedong estuary, two small motor coasters sunk at Kunsan, and several railway trucks strafed at Mokpo. On one patrol, as Lt Cdr(P) Ian MacLachlan's Seafire flight carried out an armed photographic mission as far north as P'yongyang, the North Korean capital, it met with what was later estimated to have been 75mm heavy flak, although none of the Seafires was hit. The pilots reported that the factories seemed to be working at full production but very little movement was observed on the river. On the last day of the operation, a flak position on the island of Wolmi-do, off Inch'on, was attacked with good results. Finally, the RN destroyer *Consort* carried out a bombardment of a factory at Kunsan, controlled by one of 800 Squadron's Seafires, gaining an estimated 50% hits.

USN Corsairs and Skyraiders from *Valley Forge* and the *Philippine Sea* were extremely active during this period, a total of 37 aircraft carrying out a strike against a big steel railway bridge west of Seoul on 19 August. The bridge had been targeted by fighter-bombers of the 5th Air Force and medium bombers of the FEAF since the early days of the war, yet it had survived. Although the USN fighter-bomber attack inflicted further damage, it remained intact until the night, when two spans finally collapsed into the water. The third span was demolished the following day by B-29s. Amongst those lost during the attack was the commander of the *Philippine Sea*'s Carrier Air Group Eleven, Cdr R.W. Vogel.

The Seafires aboard *Triumph* were now reduced to an availability of only nine after two aircraft had reached the limit of acceptable cumulative wrinkling, and a third was over-stressed due to an off-centre landing on the last day of the patrol. *Unicorn* had only seven replacement Seafires left, so the total number available in the Far East was now down to 16. *Triumph* was relieved by the American escort carrier *Sicily* and the routing which followed – alternating RN and USN escort carriers on the line in the Yellow Sea – was to be maintained, with a few breaks, up to the end of the war. On 23 August, *Triumph* entered Sasebo where she joined *Valley Forge* and *Philippine Sea*.

In *Triumph*'s absence, as luck would have it, RN destroyer *Comus* came under attack from two NKAF Il-10s when patrolling the Inch'on approaches, heading north-east shortly after 0700 on 23 August. The destroyer's radar had not picked up the approaching aircraft, partly because of positioning and partly because it was short-range equipment which was best used in co-operation with longer-range radar in larger ships. As *Comus*' captain, Lt Cdr R.A.M. Hennessy, emerged from his cabin in response to the order for action stations, the North Korean aircraft turned in behind the destroyer and dropped to about 100 feet above her wake. The leading aircraft opened up with cannon fire before dropping four bombs which hit down the port side, abreast of the whaler, the explosions heaving the craft upwards as water splashed down heavily onto the bridge. Hennessy ordered full-speed ahead and had commenced to alter the course violently to starboard by the time the second aircraft started to attack. It faced a hail of fire from all the destroyer's Bofors guns and the starboard Oerlikon. Bombs from this aircraft dropped ahead of the ship and did no damage. The first Il-10 returned to strafe with its machine-guns blazing before escaping by following the second into the clouds, all the time under anti-aircraft fire. *Comus* had certainly come off second best in the clash. Her forward boiler room had been holed at the waterline on the portside, and the compartment was flooded. Remarkably, there was only one fatality, Leading Stoker/Mechanic James Addison, who was killed instantly at his station in the boiler room; a second rating was wounded. Escorted by HMS *Consort* and covered by an air patrol from the American carrier *Sicily*, *Comus* slowly made her way back for repairs to the huge hole on her waterline.

When *Triumph*, in company with *Kenya* and three destroyers, sailed from Sasebo at 0900 on 26 August for four days of operations off the west coast of Korea, the Seafires, as a result of the attack on *Comus*, had to concentrate on CAP, leaving armed reconnaissance to the Fireflies. During the patrol two motor cruisers of about 100 tons were sunk by rockets near Antung, as were various small craft and motor junks lying inshore between Inch'on and the south-west point of Korea. A pontoon landing stage at Kunsan was damaged, two or three sections being sunk. Fearful of air attack, the North Koreans were becoming adept at camouflaging their presence among the islands and inlets. Lt(P) Ron Forrest and CPO Jim Churlish, while checking unfamiliar green islands, found they were in fact three gunboats covered with foliage.

On 29 August there occurred a tragic fatal accident when a Firefly failed to catch an arrester wire while landing on *Triumph* and broke its propeller on the barrier. The CO of 827 Squadron, Lt Cdr (P) Bernard Lyons recalled:

> "Lt Cdr Ian MacLachlan (CO of 800 Squadron) was killed in a ghastly accident. He was watching out of the Ops Room porthole when a Firefly engaged the barrier. The hub of one

of the propeller blades crashed through the armoured glass and hit him full in the face. A
very sad loss of a fine pilot and a good friend."

He was buried at sea, with full naval honours, off the coast of Korea that evening. His successor
to command 800 Squadron was its Senior Pilot, Lt Cdr(P) Tom Handley. Next day (30 August),
Triumph sailed for Sasebo where she met *Unicorn* which had just arrived from Pusan.
Unicorn's last 14 aircraft – six Seafires and eight Fireflies – were transferred over to *Triumph*.

During August, TF77 had lost a further five Corsairs, a Panther of VF-111 (from which the
pilot ejected, the USN's first combat use of an ejector seat), a Neptune (see Chapter II) and a
USMC OY-1 spotter, the latter while operating from K-10 together with the HO3S-1
helicopters of VMO-6. The little, two-seat spotter aircraft were very active during the month;
the crew of one, upon encountering a NKPA staff car, opened fire with their revolvers and
apparently caused the vehicle to crash. Another crew carried hand grenades which they tossed
at troops who had the audacity to fire upon them. The helicopter detachment was also kept
busy. On 10 August, one carried out a rescue mission of a USMC pilot whose damaged Corsair
of VMF-323 had crashed just off the coast. Two more Corsairs were damaged by ground fire
the following day and crashed into the sea and, again, an HO3S-1 from Chinhae rescued one
pilot but the second, who had been picked up the day before, was this time not so fortunate and
lost his life.

September 1950

TF77 withdrew for replenishment at sea on 3 September, aircraft from the two American
carriers, *Valley Forge* and *Philippine Sea*, having logged a total of 2,841 sorties in August in
support of the Pusan garrison. After replenishment, the ships proceeded northwards once more
to carry out further interdiction work, so it was again left to the 5th Air Force to bear the brunt
of the ground-attack operation.

Meanwhile, continuing the campaign to cut off supplies to the NKPA, *Triumph*, having left
Sasebo on the same date, took part in an operation against rail targets along the west coast. The
new CO of 800 Squadron, Lt Cdr(P) Handley, led his Seafires on an armed recce around
Kunsan next day, resulting in two 50-ton motor junks being strafed. A Seafire was written off
in a rare type of accident when its belly-mounted fuel drop-tank came off during catapult
launch, badly ripping the bottom skin of the aircraft's fuselage. Fortunately, the pilot was able
to land-on again safely.

The Fireflies spotted for a bombardment of Inch'on by the cruiser *Jamaica* and destroyer
Charity on 5 September, then, next day, Handley and his flight of Seafires spotted for *Jamaica*
at Kunsan, where a railway station and buildings on the airfield were bombarded. Immediately
after this, *Triumph* and three destroyers sailed for the east coast to relieve TF77 carriers which
had been withdrawn for storing and maintenance. Two days earlier there had occurred an
incident which might have had serious repercussions although, in the event, apparently did not.
A patrol of Corsairs of VF-53 from *Valley Forge* was vectored towards an unidentified aircraft
approaching the fleet. The intruder was intercepted, a twin-engined aircraft tentatively
identified as a Tu-2 or Il-4 light bomber. On spotting the Corsairs, it dived towards the North
Korean coast, its gunner opening fire. Having radioed *Valley Forge* for instructions, the
Corsairs were given permission to return fire at which Lt Ed Laney promptly despatched the
bomber, blazing, into the Yellow Sea. A nearby destroyer searched the area for survivors,
finding only the unconscious and fatally wounded pilot, who died shortly thereafter. Other
bodies were recovered from the sea and a search of their personal effects established they were
Russians. Apparently the bodies were later returned to the Soviet Union, while the Russians
explained that the aircraft had been on a training sortie and had strayed off course.

Triumph launched a dawn strike against Wonsan on 8 September, when six Fireflies escorted
by six Seafires rocketed and strafed road and rail communication. A train in Shikuogi station
blew up after being hit from a rocket fired by a Firefly, and a tunnel was damaged. After lunch,
an armed reconnaissance by six Seafires and four Fireflies located a concentration of 80 box-
cars in the goods yard at Kowon and another 40 at Yonghung. The Fireflies rocketed while the
Seafires strafed. When he returned to the carrier from this strike, Lt(P) D.I. Berry was unable

to lower the arrester hook of his Seafire into position despite carrying out a series of violent manoeuvres. After tense minutes waiting for a decision to be made on his best course of action, he was instructed to bale out. At 10,000 feet he climbed out on the wing and jumped, and almost immediately after landing in the water he was picked up, none the worse for wear, by the Australian destroyer *Bataan*.

Two other aircraft were written off during the day. The first incident involved Lt(P) R.W.T. Abraham, 800 Squadron's B Flight leader, who carried out a successful landing on one wheel, the Seafire stopping short of swerving over the portside. This latest incident reduced 800 Squadron to ten aircraft. The other accident involved Firefly MB687 which bounced on the deck, missed all the arrester wires and was only prevented from going into the deck park when the hook caught in the second barrier. Both oleos collapsed when the aircraft struck the deck, although neither Lt(P) Mortimer nor his crewman was hurt. Since there was difficulty in folding the damaged aircraft's wings, the Firefly was jettisoned overboard.

Bad weather on 9 September drastically reduced flying, only eight sorties being undertaken. It was the last day of the patrol. In the afternoon, two Fireflies and two Seafires caused considerable damage to Koryo airfield with rockets and cannon fire. At this stage 800 Squadron suffered a severe blow when it was discovered that four of its ten Seafires had suffered skin-wrinkling beyond the limit of safety, which effectively terminated the unit's capability as an operational unit. The Seafires affected included aircraft supplied by *Unicorn* a week earlier. So ended another patrol.

On 15 September the war situation changed dramatically with the largest amphibious operation since World War II – the landing of US forces at Inch'on on the Korean west coast, over 150 miles north of the battlefront, and west of Seoul. The invasion fleet was made up of 261 UN ships: 194 American, plus a further 32 leased from the Japanese by the USN; 15 ROK, 12 British, three Canadian, two Australian, two New Zealand and one French vessel constituted the remainder. The US X Corps began landing at dawn over the difficult and treacherous beaches at Inch'on. A force of Marines went in first on Wolmi-do, the island just offshore which had been bombed and strafed by USMC Corsairs from *Sicily* and *Badoeng Strait*. Strategic surprise was achieved, although a two-day preliminary bombardment had forewarned the few NKPA detachments in and about Seoul. The 1st US Marine Division advanced through light opposition with the objective of securing Kimpo airfield. Following the Marines ashore, the 7th US Infantry Division turned southwards, to cut the railroad and highway supplying the NKPA deployed against the Pusan perimeter in the south. Close support for the US ground forces making the landings was provided by USMC Corsairs. Meanwhile, strike aircraft from the larger carriers of TF77 flew interdiction missions over the roads, tracks and railway leading to Inch'on.

Triumph's part in the operation was to provide cover for the assault convoys during their passage up the west coast of Korea, and to maintain close blockade to prevent any enemy concentration by sea that could reinforce the Inch'on or interfere with the invasion. Her aircraft were assisted in this rôle by the Sunderland Detachment at Iwakuni, as recalled by Wg Cdr Dudley Burnside, commander of the Far East Flying Boat Wing:

". . . [USN patrol squadron activity] was closely co-ordinated with ours and we worked together in the blockade of Korean ports. Frequent very long patrols were carried out from Iwakuni up each coast to Korea to just off Port Arthur on one side and Vladivostok on the other. Working in co-operation with the Royal Navy and US Navy, many anti-mine and anti-submarine sorties were flown covering shipping lanes, particularly in the Tsushima Strait between the South Korean coast and Japan."

Aboard *Triumph*, 13th CAG had by now been reduced to only a dozen effective aircraft. Nevertheless, 827 Squadron's Fireflies were fitted with none-jettisonable 45-gallon external fuel tanks and configured for bombardment-spotting. The extra fuel tanks would extend their time over the target to two hours thus reducing the number of change-over flights that would be necessary. The Seafires were to be used for surveillance patrols and CAP. Patrols were flown between 13-20 September, with *Triumph* sailing just 60 miles from Inch'on when the landing took place, aircraft taking off before dawn on the 15th. Target-spotting operations by Fireflies for the cruisers *Jamaica* and *Kenya* were the only direct contribution to the landings made by RN aircraft, but offensive sweeps by both Seafires and Fireflies over the next few days found many small enemy craft along the coast. Small freighters, junks and coasters were attacked at every opportunity, particularly at Haeju and Chinnampo. Meanwhile, owing to the UN's total air supremacy, the Seafires scheduled for CAP sorties were usually retained at readiness on deck. The Firefly crews carried out daily air spotting for as long it was required. Despite many of the crews never having previously carried out this type of duty, they experienced no real difficulties. Lt Cdr(P) Lyons recalled:

> "*Triumph's* aircraft supplied air support, mainly bombardment spotting for our cruisers but also interdiction missions in the Inch'on area. At one time I had a bird's-eye view of tank battles as the US forces forced their way inland. This invasion was a complete success, which was all the more remarkable when one considers that it was planned and mounted within three months of the unexpected outbreak of the war . . ."

Although the support ships shelled targets of opportunity on the 16th, *Kenya* and *Jamaica* were not called upon that day, *Kenya* used the brief respite to take on board more ammunition from the US Auxiliary *Ryder*, which was loaded with British supplies as a back-up vessel. That day, a section of Seafires led by Lt(P) John Treacher attacked gun positions on an airfield in the Haeju area. Afterwards, following a report received from the destroyer *Charity* of two junks suspected of mine-laying activities, Lt(P) Randy von Kettle led an attack on them, destroying one and damaging the other. Early on the 17th, the NKAF appeared for the first, and last, time during the assault. At daybreak two enemy aircraft slipped in to attack the American heavy cruiser *Rochester*. After scoring two near misses with light bombs, they turned their attention to *Jamaica*. Captain J.S.C. Salter DSO OBE reported:

> "First degree of AA readiness was assumed at daylight, as usual. At about 0555 a single aircraft – taken to be friendly – flew normally and slowly from north to south down the line of ships anchored in the approach channel to Inch'on, at a height of about a thousand feet. Shortly afterwards it dived gently, passing over the US Hospital Ship *Consolation*, towards USS *Rochester*: it dropped two bombs close astern of *Rochester* and was followed by a second aircraft, which also attacked the *Rochester* with bombs. The first aircraft then wheeled around and gave the impression that she might have designs on HMS *Jamaica*: she was taken under fire with 4-inch and close-range weapons, apparently thought better of her intentions and made off over the islands to the south. The second aircraft came at *Jamaica* from a relative bearing . . . and was taken under fire with close-range weapons: the enemy returned the fire, raking *Jamaica's* port side with tracer and machine-gun fire, did a vertical bank, turned sharply to port, passed over the forecastle and crashed in the water about thirty yards from the ship. There were three casualties in *Jamaica* [one mortally wounded] . . . and there were a number of lucky escapes; one disturbing feature was the fact that the one-inch armour plating which forms the back of Y [gun] turret was penetrated by a 15mm solid armour-piercing bullet: there was one man only inside the turret and he suffered no more damage that a grazed leg but he was considerably surprised. No markings were seen [on the aircraft]: one was a Yak-3 and the other a Stormovik Il-10 . . ."

The attack put the Fleet's defences on edge and throughout the day *Triumph's* Seafire CAP was scrambled on two occasions, but both were false alarms. Meanwhile, Lt Cdr(P) Lyons' section of Fireflies co-operated with *Charity* to bombard and silence two coastal guns that had fired on an ROK vessel near Haeju. On shore, after overcoming light opposition, the 1st US Marine Division secured Kimpo airport and the US 7th Infantry Division, after sweeping south, cut the railroad and highway. Seoul was surrounded and supplies to the NKPA in the south of the peninsula were blocked.

Only one section of Seafires led by Lt(P) A.J. Tallin flew on the 18th, attacking two barges in the Haeju area, while Firefly crews carried out their routine spotting duties which they reported as becoming rather dull, being largely conducted tours of the battlefields. Next day a section of Seafires led by Lt(P) Abraham carried out an armed reconnaissance in the Chinnampo area which proved eventful. A 500-ton ship was attacked and damaged, another smaller one was damaged on the slipway, a floating crane was set on fire and, finally, a flak position was attacked. Back on *Triumph* while returning from this mission, Cmd Pilot A.R. Warren's Seafire hooked the No10 wire, thus halting its impetus before it delicately engaged the barrier. Not so graceful and much more spectacular was the return of Lt(P) H.M.A. Hayes' Firefly some time later. The Fireflies, as well as flying reconnaissance sorties, carried out target spotting for HMS *Ceylon* when she joined the bombarding force inshore. Coming back from this mission, Hayes made his approach low – a little too low. His aircraft struck the carrier's round-down knocking off the arrester hook. Unable to engage the wires, the Firefly plunged full speed into the barrier. Fortunately, there were no serious injuries. Later still, a report of a number of suspicious-looking, rice-carrying junks in the Haeju area resulted in three Seafires being scrambled to deal with them. After a lengthy search, two medium-sized junks were eventually found and attacked.

On 20 September, Lt Cdr(P) Handley led the Seafires on an armed recce around Chinnampo. With only three aircraft left, this was all they could muster for what would prove to be the last combat operation by Seafires in service with the RN. An enemy patrol craft was damaged in the Chinnampo estuary. 827 Squadron still had eight aircraft, albeit in poor condition, and they carried out a successful shoot with *Ceylon* on extensive defence works and gun emplacements near Fankochi Point on the coast west of Haeju.

With the Inch'on operation successful and the Communists in full retreat, the presence of *Triumph* was no longer essential, and on 25 September the RN carrier left the war zone bound for Hong Kong. By the time she withdrew she had been reduced to just one fully-serviceable Seafire and two Fireflies, plus eight other flyable aircraft which were unfit for missions over enemy territory. In departing, she took with her the praise of the Commander, US Navy Far East, Admiral C. Turner Joy USN, who had been impressed by the determined performance of this small carrier which had used its aircraft highly efficiently. *Triumph*'s Air Group was armed with the oldest aircraft types still in front line RN service, but by solid hard work sufficient aircraft had been made available to operate effectively on 33 days between 3 July and 20 September. Lt Cdr(P) Lyons recalled:

> "827 was the last Naval Air Squadron embarked that was operating Firefly I aircraft, and most of ours were elderly, mainly being World War II veterans. A point worthy of mention, I think, is the help we received from HMS *Unicorn*, the repair carrier, which managed to repair and supply some aircraft to us during this period. This was important, as in the case of the rather elderly Firefly Is maintenance was a problem, but by dint of hard and continuous work, the daily serviceability rate was good . . ." [2]

The Seafires of 800 Squadron had flown 245 CAP and search sorties, and 115 strike sorties during the period, losing no aircraft to enemy action and suffering very little damage from the flak, which grew in intensity and accuracy as the weeks passed. The non-combat attrition was high, however, only three aircraft surviving in flyable condition until 20 September, out of the initial dozen and 14 replacements received. Only two had been lost in flying accidents away from the ship. There had been relatively few barrier crashes resulting in heavy damage, but the rear fuselage weakness of the Seafires had taken its toll.

---

[2] See *With the Carriers in Korea* by Lt Cdr John Lansdown.

CHAPTER XI

CARRIER AIR OPERATIONS: HMS *THESEUS*

October 1950 – January 1951

"On top of old P'yongyang, all covered with flak, I lost my poor wingman, he never came back . . ."

FAA Songbook

Following the departure of HMS *Triumph* from Korean waters, she was replaced on 5 October by HMS *Theseus* under Captain A.S. Bolt DSO DSC. Aboard the newly arrived carrier was the 17th CAG commanded by Lt Cdr(P) F. Stovin-Bradford DSC. This group had more modern equipment, comprising 23 Sea Fury FBIIs of 807 Squadron (Lt Cdr(P) M.P. Gordon-Smith DSC) and 12 Firefly AS5s of 810 Squadron (Lt Cdr(P) K.S. Pattisson DSC). The Air Group had been augmented by several new pilots when leaving the Home Fleet and extensive flying training had been carried out on the way to the war zone. Arrangements were made to establish a pool of reserve aircraft and maintenance staff at Iwakuni. Another American carrier, USS *Leyte*, also joined TF77 at this time.

On 8 October, while sailing from Sasebo, there occurred an unfortunate accident on board the carrier. During that afternoon, aircraft were launched for CAP and training exercises. As Firefly WB281 flown by Cmd Plt Frank Bailey was touching down it jumped both landing barriers and collided with two more Fireflies (WB369 and WB376) in the deck park. All three were wrecked, thereby reducing 810 Squadron's effective air strength by 25% even before combat operations had started. Next day, before starting operations off the Korean coast, *Theseus'* Fleet Aviation Officer, Cdr E.S. Carver, visited the local Tactical Air Control Centre at Kimpo, to ensure that the staff there were fully acquainted with the Navy's general plan and the types of British aircraft operating in the area. It was fortunate that he did so. He was informed that 5th Air Force HQ had failed to inform the Centre of any British carrier operations taking place. Carver also discovered that there was an American helicopter rescue flight based at Kimpo, the 3rd Rescue Squadron equipped with H-5s, and he brought back information on the procedure for contacting it in case of an emergency. It would be needed all too soon.

TF91, of which *Triumph* had been part, had been dissolved following the successful Inch'on landings and became TF95.1, to which *Theseus* was now attached, responsible for blockading duties on the west coast. The Fireflies were soon in action and on 10 October they destroyed two centre spans of a railway bridge near Ch'ang-yon, Lt(P) D.A. Cook and Lt(P) G.F. Birch being credited with the main successes, but subsequent attacks on road bridges were not so successful. The Firefly flown by P3 Ray Grant returned with its windscreen damaged by debris thrown up by the bombs of his leader. On the same day four Sea Furies led by Lt Cdr(P) Stovin-Bradford attacked a stores depot about 15 miles south of Chinnampo but encountered considerable light anti-aircraft fire, the aircraft flown by Lt(P) Stanley Leonard sustaining severe damage which caused it to crash-land in a paddy field five miles from the target. Following the procedures outlined by Cdr Carver, the Kimpo Rescue Flight was contacted immediately, and an H-5 with Capt David C. McDaniel USAF at the controls was scrambled for the 125-mile flight to Ch'ang-yon to pick up the downed British pilot, the helicopter escorted by a USN Tigercat.

On the ground in the crashed Sea Fury, 26-year-old Lt Leonard was severely injured, with broken spine, two broken legs and one arm broken. He was also trapped. The fuselage of his aircraft had buckled at the cockpit, pinning him inside. Enemy troops were in the vicinity but, overhead, Sea Furies from his flight, and then a relief flight, shot up any they found to prevent them from coming too close to the crashed aircraft. Leonard drifted in and out of consciousness. One one occasion he revived and, using his broken arm, fired his revolver towards the nearest antagonists but then passed out again. After about an hour, the H-5 arrived and landed. Capt McDaniel and his airborne doctor, Lt Col John C. Shumate USAF, between them keeping the enemy at bay with bursts of fire from their automatic weapons, had to hack Leonard free. Finally safe aboard the helicopter, the injured pilot was given a blood transfusion during the return flight, which turned out to be the longest rescue mission of the war to date. The USMC Hospital Ship *Consolation*, moored offshore at Inch'on, was warned of his imminent arrival, and McDaniel landed the helicopter on the nearby beach. Lt Leonard was transferred to the Consolation, where he received prompt and excellent treatment[1]. His rescuers, Capt McDaniel and Lt Cdr Schumate, were subsequently each awarded the Military Cross by the British authorities, while Lt Cdr(P) Stovin-Bradford later flew over to Kimpo with two bottles of prized whisky for the brave helicopter crew.

By now it was clear that the enemy had largely evacuated the Haeju-Ongjin area, and the attacks from *Theseus* were switched to the port of Chinnampo. There, on 13 and 14 October, three strikes with bombs and rockets caused the destruction of dockside stores and buildings. Dive-bombing by the Fireflies was highly accurate, and the Sea Furies attacked two suspected mine-laying junks at Ho-do, severely damaging both. Similar attacks were carried out on Mongumpo, Sariwon and Chinnampo on 16 and 17 October. It was while returning from one of these strikes that P3 Ray Grant almost came to grief when the troublesome engine of his Firefly (VX428) cut as he was landing; the aircraft required an engine change, while a Sea Fury needed repairs following a barrier crash when being landed by P3 Peter Lines.

Off the west coast, naval air operations by *Theseus* had been briefly suspended to clarify the position on shore while UN troops were rapidly moving forward. During a recce over P'yongyang, the Sea Fury piloted by Lt(P) Bernard Bevans (a former WWII TAG) suffered damage to its engine from light anti-aircraft fire, although he was able to make a glide landing back on the carrier. Bad weather intervened with operations on the 19th but during the next couple of days *Theseus* was able to operate aircraft over the Shinanju-Chougju area, the only unrestricted region on the west coast. She then returned to Sasebo. Operations flown by *Theseus*' aircraft so far had clearly demonstrated the advantages and drawbacks of the new British equipment. The increased combat radius of the Sea Furies and Firefly AS5s, compared with those of *Triumph*'s Seafires and Firefly Is, was a very welcome plus. So too was the ability to launch Fireflies carrying a full bomb load regardless of the force of the wind. The Sea Furies clearly proved their accuracy with rockets but, later during the patrol, under-wing tier stowage of the weapons had to be stopped because of the damage caused to rocket posts and mainplanes during firing. Another drawback with the Sea Furies was their inability to take photographs. Rapid oiling-up of the camera lens rendered vertical photography unsuccessful and no equipment was carried for oblique photography.

As for the ship itself, the authorised storage capacity for rockets, and to a lesser degree

---

[1] Lt Stanley Leonard was told by doctors that he would be invalided out of the Navy, would spend the rest of his life in a wheelchair, and would never father children (he had married a fortnight before sailing for Korea). He set out to prove them all wrong, which he did. Having persuaded the Navy to let him stay on in non-flying duties, he eventually regained limited flying status despite the cumbersome iron frame on his paralysed left leg, and became flying instructor to the Northern Air Division. In the early 1960s he was Lt Cdr (Flying) aboard the carrier HMS *Hermes*, and later still Cdr (Flying). His final appointment was to command HMAS *Culdrose*. The father of four, he retired after 25 years service, having been awarded an OBE.

bombs, proved totally inadequate. Almost three times the normal supply of 60-lb HE rocket heads was fired but foresight and improvisation prevented any question of running short. During the patrol the crew had to catapult every operational sortie owing to aircraft loading, RATOG restriction and the deck park area. Unfortunately, on return to Sasebo, the overworked catapult became unserviceable and therefore unusable. This was a serious setback and during her next patrol, from 27 October to 5 November, *Theseus* was obliged to leave six Fireflies ashore at Iwakuni to reduce the deck park. However, she did take on board an American pilot and his helicopter to replace the Sea Otter, which required an engine change. Chief Aviation Pilot Dan C. Fridley USN was the newcomer, together with his H-5 helicopter which was soon named 'The Thing'.

807 Squadron came close to losing a Sea Fury on the 30th when P3 Richard Johnson, inexperienced in the use of RATOG, banked hard to starboard on take-off and almost became inverted. The remaining aircraft had to be flown off without rockets, bombs or drop tanks, and because of this the air rôle was therefore confined to providing CAP over the ship and over the USN minesweeping force which was then in the process of carrying out a large clearing operation at Chinnampo. At the end of this patrol only about 40 miles or so of the Korean coastline remained in enemy hands. At this juncture, as it was unlikely that incoming enemy supplies would be delivered by sea, *Theseus* sailed for Hong Kong to enable work to be carried out on the unserviceable catapult launching system.

November 1950

Commencing on 9 November and extending over the next three days, US Navy Corsairs and Skyraiders from the carriers *Valley Forge*, *Philippine Sea* and *Leyte* of TF77 succeeded in destroying two other bridges further up the Yalu at Hyesanjin as well as the road bridge at Sinuiju, but the vital railway bridge still remained standing. Cover was provided by USN Panthers. MiGs – seven aircraft from the 1st Eskadrilya of the 139th GuFAR led by Maj Mikhail Grachev – were encountered on the very first day. In his excitement just before the first engagement, Cdr A.D. Pollock, CO of VF-51 from *Valley Forge*, allegedly reported: "20,000 MiGs coming in at five feet!" The Panther pilots found that the MiGs had a better rate of climb, were faster, and were more manoeuvrable than their own aircraft, but they were less impressed by the enemy's teamwork and marksmanship. The Panthers emerged unscathed and somewhat elated when it was learned that Lt Cdr William T. Amen, CO of VF-111 aboard the *Philippine Sea*, had succeeded in shooting down a MiG, his victim none other than the MiG leader, Maj Grachev[2]. The Russian pilots reported meeting a dozen Skyraiders, two of which it was believed were shot down by Grachev before his own demise; another was claimed by Kapt Bochkov, while two of the Panthers were claimed by St/Lts Stulov and Sannikov. Another was engaged by St/Lt Bolotin but, before he could open fire, a second got on his tail, this being attacked by Lt Kumonaev, who reported that it was last seen on fire, flying in a southerly direction. Before the action was broken off, six more MiGs, from the 72nd GuFAR led by Maj Stroikov, arrived on the scene and engaged eight Panthers but without success.

There occurred another MiG/Panther clash on 12 November, on this occasion eight MiGs from the 139th GuFAR led by Kapt Bochkov meeting an estimated 20 Corsairs and Panthers at various heights between 13,000 feet and 32,000 feet. Bochkov led his section against four Corsairs, one of which he claimed shot down jointly with his wingman, Lt Shchegolev. Four Panthers attempted to intercept Bochkov's section but these were engaged by St/Lt Kolesnichenko, who claimed the leading Panther shot down as it manoeuvred onto the tail of St/Lt Stulov's aircraft. By now the MiGs were low on fuel and three carried out emergency landings at Antung. Six days later, on the 18th, the USN pilots showed their skills again. Two *Valley Forge* pilots, Lt Cdr William E. Lamb, a WWII ace with five victories, and Lt R.E. Parker of VF-52, shared a second MiG kill. A third Navy MiG kill was claimed by Ens F.C. Weber of VF-31 on Leyte later that day. Both MiGs were claimed shot down at low altitude,

---

[2] Despite claims by the USAF to the contrary (see Chapter IV), this was in fact the first MiG-15 to be shot down during the Korean War, and it had fallen victim to a US Navy fighter pilot.

but only one was lost when St/Lt Tarshinov of the 139th GuFAR crashed and was killed. Two Panthers were claimed in this action, one each by Lt Bulaev and Kapt Pakhomov.

Between the 9th and 21st, USN aircraft carried out almost 600 sorties against the Yalu bridges, but were allowed only to attack the spans on the Korean side. The *Leyte* lost one of its personalities on 4 December when Ens Jesse L. Brown, the first negro to fly for the US Navy, crash-landed his flak-damaged aircraft in a mountainous area north-west of the Chosin reservoir. With both legs broken, he was unable to free himself. The crash had been observed by a member of his flight, Lt(Jg) Thomas J. Hudner, who, with complete disregard for his own safety, carried out a wheels-up landing nearby, having radiocd for a helicopter. Brown's aircraft was burning and Hudner attempted to extinguish the fire, but the injured pilot died before he could be released. For his unselfish and gallant attempt to save his colleague, Hudner was awarded the Congressional Medal of Honor.

December 1950

Meanwhile, her catapult again operational, *Theseus* sailed northwards to provide support for the evacuation of Chinnampo (see Chapter IV), since all the American carriers were fully employed on the east coast giving support to the US Marines at Hungnam, during which at least six USMC Corsairs were lost with three of their pilots, 1/Lt Robert O. Crocker, Tech/Sgt Matthew J. Biedka, and M/Sgt Boyd T. Teague, all of VMF-312. By 5 December, the evacuation was completed with 1,800 American troops and 5,800 ROK soldiers having been taken off under the air cover of Sea Furies and Fireflies and gunfire support from five British Commonwealth destroyers. With the evacuation over, *Theseus* provided air cover for the Task Group and armed reconnaissance north of the bomb line. Winter had now set in, and conditions at sea were appalling, with frequent gales, intense cold and low visibility. But despite this, 332 sorties were flown from *Theseus* between 7 and 15 December without accident or damage. There was some excitement on the 14th when MiGs made a firing pass at the carrier's helicopter while it was airlifting a number of stragglers from the Chanyan area. The incident occurred in an interval when the helicopter's Sea Fury escort was being relieved and before the arrival of the relief flight. Fortunately, no damage was sustained.

Theseus began her fourth patrol early on 16 December, but the weather over the next two days was too poor for any flying. On the 18th, the initial sorties were delayed for an hour because the aircraft were iced up and there was snow all over the flight deck. When they did get off, the pilots found that Korea was snow-bound although there was obvious evidence of enemy movement on the roads. The Sea Furies came across a number of trucks which had evidently got stuck while trying to cross the frozen Ch'ongch'on, and these were duly strafed. The 19th was a successful day for the Sea Furies. During a series of four strikes, at least 17 trucks and three tanks were destroyed or damaged in the Hwanju-Sariwon area. After midday, low cloud base and poor visibility over the target area made rocket attacks difficult. The Fireflies, by finding holes in the clouds, combed areas along the P'yongyang-Sariwon and Sariwon-Sinmak roads and damaged a bridge. During the day Sea Fury pilot Lt(P) Tom Leece chalked up the 17th CAG's 2,000th deck landing since leaving the UK the previous May. Despite poor weather over the target on the 20th, the Sea Furies strafed buildings in Chinnampo and Sariwon, damaged a road bridge, strafed a bulldozer and damaged two oil dumps and some lorries. One aircraft developed engine trouble and Lt(P) Bill Noble had to return to *Theseus* early. The Fireflies were fitted with rockets in place of bombs and attacked bridges around Sariwon, where a pontoon bridge was put out of action.

Having refuelled from the USN's *Brown Ranger* on 22 December, *Theseus'* operations recommenced the next day with a rocket strike against Chinese troops, trucks and buildings east of P'yongyang. There was increased enemy activity on Christmas Eve but the pilots did not encounter any opposition in the air. The only damage to aircraft from *Theseus* during her period of operations was caused either by anti-aircraft fire or technical troubles. 807 Squadron pilot Lt(P) Dennis Kelly – known to his friends as John – had some nasty moments shortly after he had taken off on a strike in his heavily-laden Sea Fury (VW541). His engine began to lose power, banging and coughing alarmingly. Foremost in his mind was the rumour going around that it was impossible to ditch a Sea Fury but he had no choice but to bring the ailing aircraft down onto the freezing waters of the Yellow Sea. Against all the odds, he managed it successfully and the aircraft stayed afloat long enough to allow him to scramble out of the cockpit. He had come down some four miles ahead of *Theseus* but fortunately the ditching had been seen by the crew of the Canadian destroyer *Sioux*, which rushed immediately to pick him up. Kelly was recovered unhurt despite spending 13 minutes in the bitterly cold sea, and was flying again the next day[3].

Meanwhile, the Sea Furies inflicted an estimated 200-plus casualties on a column of troops marching south near Sariwon, apparently in preparation for an offensive that was expected to start on Christmas Day. With the start of the enemy's push, two Sea Fury strikes were launched to recce the enemy airfields at Chinnampo, Ongjin and Haeju for signs of air activity but none was found. Then, during a routine inspection, water was found in the fuel filter of a Firefly and all aircraft were grounded to check their fuel filters for water. Some of the Sea Furies were also affected so flying was reduced to CAP and anti-submarine patrols. *Theseus'* patrol finished on the 26th after another series of successful strikes, and soon after she sailed for Sasebo accompanied by her destroyer escort. During the December series of strikes, the 17th Carrier Air Group had flown 630 sorties[4]. Throughout the period, in addition to armed recces, Fireflies equipped with long-range tanks had maintained anti-submarine patrols. It was known that the small North Korean Navy had two Russian-built submarines which were believed to be operating in the Yellow Sea although neither had been sighted. A CAP had also been maintained during daylight and a staggering total of 3,000 interceptions and visual identifications were made by the Fireflies and Sea Furies. All of the aircraft intercepted turned out to be UN types, mainly B-29s, US Navy Neptunes and the odd RAF Sunderland. There were a number of changes aboard *Theseus* at this time with Lt Cdr(P) Gordon-Smith taking over command of the 17th CAG, newly promoted Lt Cdr(P) Bevans becoming CO of 807 Squadron, while Lt Cdr(P) Geoffrey Coy took over the reins of 810 Squadron from Lt Cdr(P) Ken Pattisson who became Lt Cdr (Flying).

January 1951

By 7 January, *Theseus* was back off the west coast of Korea ready to carry out her next patrol. Showers and gusting winds caused the cancellation of her first sorties. Thereafter, six Sea Furies operating in pairs flew a series of three separate strikes. North of Haeju airfield large corrugated iron-roofed buildings, reported to be housing enemy troops, were rocketed and strafed. Other buildings were left on fire. At Kimpo three rocket strikes on a storage building caused a large fire which sent black smoke billowing up to 3,000 feet. Two abandoned aircraft which seemed to be intact, a Corsair and an F-80, were strafed as were other huts and oil drums. When they landed back on board, the pilots reported that Suwon airfield appeared to have been destroyed, and that thousands of refugees were streaming south along the Suwon-Osan road. The position of junks and other minor vessels in the patrol areas was reported. Fireflies carried out an armed recce of Haeju, bombing buildings believed to be housing North Korean troops. They also photographed various alternative emergency airfields now that Kimpo was in enemy hands.

It was business as usual next day and *Theseus'* squadrons carried out armed recces in the morning. This was switched in the afternoon to close-support for the US 25th Division on the left flank of the line south of Osan. The British 29th Brigade was part of this Division. These operations were the first of their kind to be provided by the Fleet Air Arm. As they came over the target area, the pilots were allocated to an FAC who directed them onto targets in Osan and to buildings containing an enemy command post and troops nearby. The American controller was so delighted with the accuracy of the attacks, confirming that the correct targets had been destroyed, that he thanked them repeatedly.

Off the west coast, on 11 January, snow storms, low cloud and restricted visibility limited

---

[3] Lt Kelly was later killed flying a Sea Hawk jet fighter.
[4] For its work during 1950 the 17th CAG was awarded the annual Boyd Trophy for the best performance by a Fleet Air Arm unit during the year.

flying from *Theseus* to just two Sea Furies flying an armed coastal recce and a detail of Fireflies sent on close support. At Ch'ang-ni the Sea Furies destroyed four huts containing Communist troops in the centre of the village. The Fireflies found reasonably good weather over the front lines and were directed to bomb and strafe Chinese troops in front of the British 29th Brigade, where they inflicted an estimated 200 casualties. After a few days of inclement flying weather, conditions improved sufficiently on 14 January for a full day's operations, but the catapult again became unusable during the afternoon with a number of aircraft already airborne. Sea Furies could still take off but without long-range tanks and rocket armament, although the Fireflies, by using RATOG, could carry their usual armament and fuel loads. RATOG take-off was a new experience for many of the RN pilots and while no trouble was experienced in becoming airborne, jettisoning the equipment caused some damage, holes and dents, along the fuselage of each aircraft. Despite the unavailability of the catapult, 58 sorties were flown next day, the highest number so far. According to 807 Squadron's diarist, a signal was received from the Joint Operations Centre stating that the Carrier Air Group had flown more sorties than the entire 5th US Air Force on that date.

The arrival of USS *Bataan* off the west coast enabled the two aircraft carriers on that side of the peninsular to initiate operations on alternate 18-day cycles and, at the end of operations on 16 January, *Theseus* set out for Sasebo for a short rest and routine maintenance. It had been a record day with 60 sorties flown. On 25 January it was also the turn of *Theseus* to relieve *Bataan*. She was soon back in action and, next day, Fireflies attacked gun emplacements, road blocks and villages suspected of harbouring Chinese troops north-west of Suwon under the direction of the FACs. The Sea Furies concentrated their efforts in the Suwon area itself, strafing and rocketing troops and houses. Some junks were strafed in the entrance of the Han. Factories west of Kangwho were also attacked and troops and a few small craft were strafed. Over Sariwon, Lt Cdr(P) Bevans' Sea Fury was hit by 40mm flak that punched a 12-inch hole through the top of his rudder. Despite poor rudder control, he managed to return to *Theseus* and make a safe landing. He was fortunate. Not so lucky was his near-namesake, Lt(P) A.C. Beavan, a new pilot, whose Sea Fury (VR940) was seen to stall during a tight turn and fall into a spin. Helpless onlookers could only watch as it failed to pull out and crashed into the sea ten miles east of the fleet. The destroyer *Comus* was on the scene within 15 minutes, but only a few small pieces of wreckage were found. There was no sign of the pilot. *Theseus* had suffered her first fatality in Korean waters.

The Firefly crews provided another day of close air support sorties on the 27th, operating north-west of Suwon. There was also some excitement during an anti-submarine patrol when Cmd Plt R.B. Young, on his first solo patrol, spotted a suspicious submarine-like object below and attacked it with depth charges but the unfortunate victim proved to be a whale. Meanwhile, Sea Furies flew armed reconnaissance sorties along the coast to Chinnampo, and from Haeju to Seoul. While flying between Inch'on and Seoul, Lt Cdr(P) Gordon-Smith, the 17th CAG's commander, received a hit from ground fire which crippled the engine of his aircraft. He was forced to ditch near the Canadian destroyer HMCS *Nootka*, and Gordon-Smith was picked up and on deck within five minutes, uninjured but suffering from the effects of the icy water. Appropriate hospitality offered by the Canadians soon rectified his condition. During a reconnaissance of roads north and north-east of Seoul next day (28 January), the Sea Fury flown by Lt(P) Peter Keighley-Peach was hit by anti-aircraft fire:

> "We were flying down a valley, looking for anything that moved, particularly transport. I was about 200 feet high, weaving back and forth behind my leader when, the next thing I knew, there was a colossal crunching noise up the front and my engine caught fire. Ground machine-guns had hit me, and the whole aircraft started to break up. I didn't think I would get away with it if I baled out, since I was so low – yet, I couldn't climb up because of the sides of the valley. So there was nothing for it but to belly-land. I jettisoned my hood and belly-landed across a couple of paddy fields. Flames were pouring into the cockpit as I put her down. But I ran into a six-foot ridge between the two paddy fields, which knocked me out on impact and broke the aircraft in two."

Overhead, Lt(P) Ian Hamilton had seen Keighley-Peach's crash-landing in the narrow valley near Tongduch'on-ni and radioed a Mayday call to summon a helicopter. The downed pilot continued:

> "I woke up 20 minutes later, sitting outside the aircraft, watching the smoke coming out of the rear. I have no recollection whatsoever of climbing out of the aircraft. Fortunately I had switched off the petrol just before I touched down, and the fire that had been burning had stopped by the time I came to. Perhaps it was the snow jamming the holes that had stopped the fire, I don't know. I particularly wanted to hide our scrambling codes, so I immediately buried them in the snow, together with all my escape kit, my maps and my helmet. When I looked up I saw three Chinese sitting on the wall of a bombed house 200 yards away. They appeared to be looking at me. But, strangely enough, they did not fire. Seeing that I was in a bad position, I decided to hide in a wood on the other side of the valley. But, although I didn't know it at the time, I learned afterwards from one of the pilots patrolling overhead, that some other Chinese were watching me 150 yards away. All the time, by the way, I was covered by up to 16 friendly aircraft. I sat behind a tree for about an hour until I saw a helicopter coming up the valley. Then I started edging down the side of the hill, moving along some trenches. As soon as the helicopter landed I popped out from a foxhole and ran to him. I was climbing aboard just about as he was touching down. Then, as we took off, the Chinese opened fire for the first time."

Following the successful rescue, the wrecked Sea Fury was strafed to prevent it falling into enemy hands but it resisted all efforts to set it on fire. Lt Keighley-Peach was flown to Taegu for a check-up and treatment to his wounds, returning to *Theseus* at the end of the month[5]. The helicopter's crewman, Cpl Carl W. Pool USAF, was awarded the DSM for his part in the rescue.

February 1951

Off the west coast on 2 February, *Theseus'* exceptional sequence of 1,463 accident-free deck landings came to an end when the pitching deck and gusty weather combined to cause a Sea Fury to bounce down too heavily and burst a tyre. The pilot was unhurt. Next day, the last of this her sixth patrol, *Theseus* established a new daily operational record when her aircraft flew a total of 66 sorties. This was due in no small part to the work of the maintenance crews. Apart from anti-submarine patrols, Fireflies continued to attack villages and foxholes north-west of Suwon, and gun positions around Anyang-ni. Other sections pounded troop positions in the hills. The Sea Furies meanwhile carried out coastal reconnaissance in addition to surveillance of the airfields, using rockets to destroy a lorry at Haeju and blow the roofs off two warehouses in Wonum. Target spotting sorties were carried out for naval bombardments of the Inch'on area and, during one of these duties, the Sea Fury (VW554) flown by Lt(P) J.M. Pinsent was damaged by small-arms fire and he was forced to ditch in the Han estuary alongside the USS *St Paul*. The American cruiser's helicopter picked him up within a few minutes but while doing so its hoist broke and Pinsent plunged back into the icy water. A speedy second rescue attempt was successful and the British pilot, cold but otherwise unharmed, was soon safely aboard the *St Paul*. At the end of the day's flying *Bataan* took over from *Theseus* and she, accompanied by her destroyer escort, set course for Kure. During this patrol the RN carrier operated under much better weather conditions and in her eight days of operations her Fireflies and Sea Furies had flown 408 sorties. These had provided close-support for the US I Corps as well as for the usual armed reconnaissance missions around the coast, over enemy airstrips and inland supply routes.

On 12 February, accompanied by four destroyers, *Theseus* set out to return to the west coast of Korea for her seventh patrol. En route to the operational zone, relief pilots who had been taken on board at Kure were given necessary practice session take-offs and deck landings. She flew off her first missions on 14 February, when Sea Furies carried out two armed reconnaissances from Seoul to P'yongyong and from Sariwon to Haeju and Ongjin airfields.

---

[5] Lt Keighley-Peach was later awarded the DSO. His father, Captain Charles Keighley-Peach OBE DSO, was a WWII fighter ace; his grandfather was an Admiral who had been awarded the DSO in WWI.

P'yongyang railway station and other buildings were attacked with rockets and cannon-fire. There was some sporadic and inaccurate heavy AA fire with shells bursting as high at 9,000 feet. Little activity was reported, although in one attack enemy troop positions on a ridge within 500 yards of UN forces were marked with smoke by the artillery and were duly strafed, many casualties being inflicted. On returning to the carrier, the Sea Fury flown by Lt(P) F.P. Curry struck the batsman's screen while landing. Meanwhile, Firefly crews flew two strikes north-west of Seoul and two close-support missions. Directed by FACs, they bombed, rocketed and strafed troop positions found on the ridges and in dug-outs with good results being reported. Ground fire hit Lt Cdr(P) Ken Pattisson's Firefly although he was able to land safely. Three returning Fireflies accidentally discharged their guns while landing and, in one of these incidents, an aircraft handler working in the forward deck park, PO(A) J.F. Wigley, was fatally wounded by a 20mm shell. He was buried at sea with full naval honours next day.

On 15 February, the Sea Furies were again in the Inch'on area in support of the British 29th Brigade. They strafed enemy troops on the ridges, then villages around Wonju were attacked and so too were huts, railway trucks and buildings at Chowon. A coastal reconnaissance went up as far north as Ongju and found that the ice around the Chinnampo estuary and in the northern area was beginning to melt. Fireflies attacked bridges ten miles north-west of Inch'on, damaged the tracks of a railway bridge a few miles north-west of Seoul, scored hits with rockets on buildings and trucks in nearby sidings, and caused explosions in a storage dump in a village north-east of Inch'on. The engine of Lt(P) David Davis' Firefly began to run roughly during the first mission so, for safety, he flew south and landed at Suwon. To carry out temporary repairs on the crippled aircraft, an aircraft mechanic was flown from *Theseus* with spares, enabling Davis and his observer to return to the carrier. Next day a section of Sea Furies attacked barrack buildings and obliterated a road block to the east of Seoul, while two others reconnoitred as far as Ongjin airfield, attacking a field gun and vehicles in Chinnampo despite ground fire. At about the same time Fireflies attacked road and rail bridges north-west of Seoul, silencing an AA gun by strafing. Landing back on the rolling deck of the carrier proved hazardous and the sea swell caused an unusually large number of wave-offs, resulting in damage to two aircraft as they touched down.

Sea Furies again carried out armed reconnaissance sorties of Ongjin airfield on 20 February, flying as far north as Chaeryong and along the road from Sariwon to P'yongyang, where heavy flak was encountered. Enemy-held ridges in the Ch'unch'on area were strafed under FAC direction. No targets were found in the Inch'on area so the Sea Furies attacked Pupyong-ni, while Fireflies struck at railway bridges west of Hwangju, badly damaging the track and silencing an AA position. Next day heavy rain and high seas prevented any flying from *Theseus* after midday. Before this, however, Sea Furies attacked buildings at Chinnampo, troops in a valley and on a ridge at Songyueni, and buildings and troops in the village of Yangong. During one of these sorties Lt(P) Keighley-Peach had to land his Sea Fury at Suwon with engine trouble. Later, a Firefly arrived with a mechanic, the same aircraft ferrying Keighly-Peach back to the carrier. The Fireflies meanwhile damaged tracks near the railway bridges close to Sariwon and strafed stores, starting small fires. Two days later, Lt(P) K.G. Shirras returned from strafing two small locomotives at Kyomipo with his aircraft showing signs of battle damage, the Sea Fury having been hit in the ailerons by small-arms fire.

23 February was the last day of *Theseus'* seventh patrol, the Sea Furies carrying out an armed reconnaissance to Chinnampo where they blew up a shed in a brilliant blue flash. For the remainder of the day they supported IX Corps by attacking woods and ridges in the Wonju area. The Fireflies flew close-support missions as well as attacking a rail tunnel. Troops in nearby foxholes were also strafed. Cmd Plt Frank Bailey's aircraft was hit in four places by small-arms fire, but he was able to return to the carrier and land safely. At the end of the day's flying *Theseus* once again handed over to *Bataan* and set course for Sasebo, where she arrived on the 24th. Four Sea Furies and two Fireflies were taken on board in preparation for her next patrol.

March 1951

Theseus began her eighth patrol off the west coast on 4 March. The weather encountered during this patrol this time proved to be variable, ranging from flat calm to rough with strong winds that hampered flying. On one day fog prevented flying completely and altogether only 339 sorties were flown. The usual duties were carried out, including bombardment spotting and CAP, close-support for the Army, mainly in the Wonju area, and reconnaissance and ground attacks. On 12 March, during a photo-reconnaissance of Ongjin and Ch'ang-yon, Sea Furies encountered intense and accurate heavy flak south of Hwangju. This did not prevent the aircraft hangars at Ongjin from rocket attack after which a number of fires were seen, presumably among supply dumps. A floating crane was strafed at Kyomipo. Next day a railway bridge near Sariwon was the primary target of another mission. There, track was ripped up in numerous places and the line was severed to the west of Sariwon at Paengo, but the bridge itself remained intact. Later in the day, during a photo reconnaissance in the Sariwon area, the Sea Furies chanced upon a moving jeep. They toyed cat and mouse with it, chasing and strafing until they caused it to crash and burst into flames.

The Fireflies were very busy in the afternoon also. On close-support sorties they attacked foxholes and trenches on enemy-held ridges south-west of Hongch'on and a railway bridge was destroyed with 1,000-lb bombs south-east of Sariwon. Another bridge was attacked near Hungsu-ri but, while flying at about 5,000 feet, Lt(P) D.L.G. James' aircraft (WB408) was hit by anti-aircraft fire which severely damaged the port wing, obliging James to divert to K-13 at Suwon. His section leader provided escort. It was late by the time they reached the airfield and, because they would be unable to return to the carrier before dusk, the four weary British airmen had to stay overnight. David James recalled later:

> "The aircraft was hit at several thousand feet whilst climbing away from the last bombing run by, it is believed, a 40mm shell which made a large jagged hole in the port wing just forward of the port aileron. As we hadn't seen any AA fire during the strike you can imagine that Ken [Lt(O) Ken Talbot, his observer] and I were surprised to say the least. However, I reckon I was somewhat at fault as I had stopped weaving and was climbing straight at what I, indeed we, reckoned was a safe altitude. That's what complacency does for you! Anyway, after doing a slow flying test at altitude, I decided that a deck landing approach could be lethal and opted for a flapless wheeler at Suwon and happily *Theseus* agreed. We were hospitably received at Suwon where we stayed overnight in a tent heated by a roaring gasoline/petrol stove which was most efficient, but took a bit of getting used to given the way we respected 'AVgas' on board."

Lts James and Talbot were flown back to *Theseus* next day, while a repair crew started work on the damaged aircraft.

On 13 March, the last day of *Theseus'* eighth patrol, 810 Squadron lost one of its crews. Both Sea Furies and Fireflies were active during the day, the former carrying out armed reconnaissance sorties over the area from Kangsan-sa to Chinnampo, attacking workshops and leaving a junk burning in the harbour, while Fireflies attacked enemy foxholes and gun pits on the ridges south-west of Hongch'on and, later, the town itself. Two strikes were flown, the first on bridges near Hungsu-ri and the second with 1,000-lb bombs on a rail bridge east of Haeju, which was destroyed. While returning from this mission, Firefly WB269 crashed a few miles from the bridge near Sariwon. The cause of the crash was probably due to a hit by AA fire or damage inflicted by exploding bombs. Sea Furies maintained a CAP over the wreckage but could see no sign of the crew, pilot Lt(P) G.H. Cooles and his RAF observer Flt Lt D.W. Gray. They had most likely perished in the crash. On completion of flying, *Theseus* set course for Sasebo, arriving there during the following evening. During the patrol, 339 sorties had been flown, 226 offensive and 113 defensive. The usual maintenance load had accrued, to be cleared during the harbour period, including some engine changes and the reception of six replacement aircraft from *Unicorn* and Iwakuni.

Theseus began her ninth patrol on 22 March. Two days into it, her Sea Furies found several concentrations of camouflaged vehicles in the Chossan-ni and Namch'ongjom areas, some of which blew up and caught fire when attacked. During a recce of the Haeju to Namch'ongjom area Lt Cdr(P) Gordon-Smith's Sea Fury was hit by a .5-inch armour-piercing bullet that snipped off the corner of his main fuel tank, but the tank's self-sealing proved ineffective.

Although he was almost overwhelmed by petrol fumes, he diverted to Suwon where he succeeded in landing safely. On inspection of his aircraft, severe damage to the main bulkhead was discovered, and his machine had to be written-off. The Group Commander was picked up later by a Firefly and flown back to the carrier.

810 Squadron itself was scheduled for three close-support operations. During one of these, the Fireflies had to wait nearly an hour before they were cleared to attack buildings in a village 15 miles east of Kaesong, just ahead of an advancing UN tank column. The next mission entailed bombing enemy troop positions on ridges 15 miles north-east of Seoul, only 200 yards ahead of advancing UN troops. Intense flak was encountered near Sariwon and Lt Cdr(P) Coy's aircraft was hit by a 40mm explosive shell while Cmd Plt Frank Bailey's aircraft was damaged either by flak or possibly shrapnel from an exploding bomb. Both returned to the ship and landed safely, but a third Firefly landed at Suwon low on fuel.

The weather overland was cloudy on the 27th and in mid-afternoon it closed in at sea off the west coast. Because of rain and poor visibility, flying had to be suspended from *Theseus*. Having replenished at sea, operational flying recommenced on 29 March, with the Sea Furies mostly devoting the day to armed reconnaissance sorties from Haeju to P'yongyang while the Fireflies launched three bombing strikes. The second strike succeeded in collapsing one span of a double railway bridge south-east of Sariwon, while rail sidings nearby were attacked with rockets. Next day, Sea Furies encountered accurate and intense AA fire from a village near Sariwon and this reaction was rewarded by a rocket attack. Close-support missions for US IX Corps north-east of Ch'unch'on resulted in the strafing of ridges and bunkers with good results reported by the controller. Eight camouflaged trucks were damaged during an armed reconnaissance east of Nanch'onjon. The Fireflies attacked bridges and a rail tunnel, damaging the entrances to both. Escorted by Sea Furies, a strike by Fireflies using 1,000-lb bombs on a barracks east of Sariwon brought about the destruction of eight buildings and damaged twelve others, while the Sea Fury escort strafed troops and lorries. After this mission one Sea Fury had to land at Suwon airfield with a misfiring engine. On the last day of March, Sea Furies attacked Haeju harbour where six large vessels were left badly damaged, and many vehicles were destroyed or left burning near Namch'ongjom. Sea Furies again escorted Fireflies carrying 1,000-lb bombs on a mission to attack a bridge near Sariwon but this time they only scored near misses, inflicting superficial damage. Lt Cdr Coy's aircraft was again struck by AA fire, causing damage in the port wing but he was able to return safely to *Theseus*.

April 1951

The first day of April was also the last day of *Theseus'* ninth patrol. Although low cloud prevented coastal reconnaissance operations, her Sea Furies attacked the hangars at Haeju airfield and destroyed two vehicles near Namch'ongjom. In general, it appeared that the enemy had moved out of the area and numerous camouflaged revetments were found apparently deserted. In close-support missions for US IX Corps, a village north of Ch'unch'on containing a road block was attacked and trucks in a second village were strafed and rocketed. Four vehicles were destroyed and four damaged. Fireflies shot up a company of enemy troops on a ridge 30 miles north of Seoul, and strikes were made on four bridges but the only real success was the destruction of two spans of a railway bridge near Sariwon. At the end of an anti-submarine patrol, Lt(P) J.D. Nunn had to land his Firefly ashore at Suwon because of engine problems. A Royal Navy maintenance party from *Unicorn* was already at Suwon in the process of changing the mainplane of another Firefly that had landed there earlier. To enable Nunn to return to *Theseus*, they robbed this aircraft to repair his machine. Meanwhile, Lt(P) Peter Cane in the carrier's Sea Otter flew in spares and another pilot, Cmd Plt Ian MacKenzie, who was to remain at Suwon until work on the grounded Firefly was completed. When eventually made airworthy, MacKenzie flew it to Iwakuni. Later in the afternoon a bank of fog rolled in from the west and forced the cancellation of *Theseus'* last flying detail for the day. This effectively finished her patrol. She and her screening destroyers set course for Sasebo.

For future air missions over Korea, *Theseus* was directed to operate in co-operation with *Bataan* in the Sea of Japan, rather than in the Yellow Sea, and her tenth and last patrol therefore began on the opposite side of the peninsula. This move was brought about by the threat that Chinese forces were believed to be preparing for an assault on Formosa, which necessitated a redeployment of UN naval forces and the US 7th Fleet was ordered to temporarily keep most of its heavy aircraft carriers in that region. Friendly rivalry between the two carriers was to produce a general speeding up of flying operations by both. *Theseus*, with one catapult, usually managed to launch faster than *Bataan* with two. Catapulting intervals for launching Sea Furies would drop to between 40 to 42 seconds. Operations began – almost disastrously – on 10 April[6] when two Sea Furies carried out an armed reconnaissance at 4,000 feet in the area south of Wonsan. Lt(P) Tom Leece was flying VX691 as No2 to Lt(P) Charles Lavender when they saw two USMC Corsairs dive into the valley and drop one bomb each. Suddenly and without warning, the two Corsairs turned and attacked the Sea Furies. Tom Leece recalled later:

> "On recovering from the dive they must have sighted us because they started to climb in our direction. We continued a gentle Rate One turn to starboard until the Corsairs were astern and closing, when my leader ordered 'Break'. I opened the throttle fully and commenced a steep starboard climbing turn, but almost immediately there was a loud bang from the engine, so I throttled back and eased the turn as I did not realise I was being fired at. By this time the leading Corsair, which still had one bomb under his starboard wing, was dead astern of me and he opened fire. I saw many tracer flashing over my port wing and I turned violently to starboard breaking down. The Corsairs did not attempt to follow and, as the aircraft was vibrating and the starboard wing tank was on fire, I left the area and returned to the ship.
>
> I believe the Corsairs thought they had shot me down as they subsequently claimed one La-9 destroyed. When they saw me break down, on fire, they concentrated on Charlie Lavender who kept going round in a very tight turn with the Corsairs firing at him. Charlie was obviously worried about me, plus his own difficult situation, but he eventually managed to out-turn his attackers and escaped to chase after me. For my part, as I started for home, my first thought was to bale out, as I could see the starboard wing was bright red and smoke was pouring out of the back end. However, the fire suddenly went out (I learned later that the bottom of the wing tank had burned through and the remaining fuel had just dropped out) and, as the engine continued to give power and the aircraft was flyable, I continued back to *Theseus*. Charlie eventually caught up as I was flying slowly and, after a visual inspection and a slow flying check, I made a normal landing.
>
> There were 21 bullet holes in the aircraft and no right wing tank (internal, not drop). The bullets had severed some of the flying controls. There was no trim but the rest worked. My admiral was bloody mad at the US Marines: they had claimed two enemy aircraft shot down thinking we were Lavochkin La-9s despite our black and white identification stripes." [7]

When he alighted, Lt Lavender found that his aircraft had been struck in the wing by one .5-inch bullet. The Corsairs were from VFM-312 operating from *Bataan*. The American pilots were seemingly taking the rivalry between the two carriers rather too seriously.

But this was not the end of the day's exciting events for the 807 Squadron pilots. Another pair of Sea Furies were carrying out a reconnaissance in the vicinity of Kowon when they heard Lavender's call for help as he and Leece came under attack by the Corsairs. On their way to assist, Richard Johnson's machine (VW698) was hit by 37mm flak and he crashed while trying to make a forced landing in a valley. Johnson was presumed killed at the time but he was later reported to be a POW. Following this, another section searching for signs of the missing pilot also came under fire and the Sea Fury flown by Lt(E) Harry Julian was hit. With a severed

---

6 On 10 April, at Hong Kong, Vice-Admiral Sir William Andrewes hauled down his flag as Second-in-Command, Far East Station and was succeeded by Rear-Admiral A.K. Scott-Moncrieff DSO. Admiral Andrewes had recently been awarded the KBE for his service in Korea.

7 See *With the Carriers in Korea*. Of this latest recognition error incident, Lt (later Lt Cdr) Tom Leece added: "I do not know for sure what happened to them [the USMC Corsair pilots]; however, much later on, when I was flying Scimitars, I met a US Marine pilot at a party in Subic Bay who knew of the incident and told me there had been a big inquiry and disciplinary action had been taken."

port aileron control rod, he decided to head for newly-captured Kangnung airstrip where he had to land so fast with the wheels locked down that he overran and plunged into deep mud at the end of the runway. The Sea Fury tripped over on to its back but fortunately there was no fire. Julian scrambled out of the cockpit just before the aircraft settled down into the slime. He remained two days at the airfield's hospital until he was picked up later by a Firefly and flown back to *Theseus*.

Elsewhere on this action-packed day, USAF Sabres clashed with MiGs and one of the latter ditched in shallow water off Sinmi-do at the northern end of the Yalu Gulf, its pilot having ejected safely (see Chapter V). The 5th Air Force requested the commander of Task Force 95, which was operating in the area, to investigate the possibility of recovering the remains of the MiG. Thus, early next morning, Captain Brock of HMS *Kenya* was ordered to form a temporary element from ships of the west coast blockading forces and ROK patrols to undertake the task. Available information was very sketchy. Simni-do was entirely surrounded by mudbanks which, at low water, joined it to the mainland; only to the east was there a narrow channel about one mile wide with a minimum depth of seven or eight fathoms. There was little time for detailed planning and the whole operation had to be conducted on an ad hoc basis. Arrangements were made for the 5th Air Force to provide air cover and search aircraft. A helicopter and an LST to act as its base were made available, as was a salvage tug.

Kenya duly arrived off Simni-do at 1015 on 12 April, but Captain Brock was now confronted by a series of irritating delays, including a signal received from an ROK frigate which advised that Simni-do was in enemy hands. A deterioration in the weather meant that the ships had to shelter north of Taewha-do, an island south-west of the operational area. The helicopter base craft did not arrive until late evening. She had been loaded with a deck cargo of 500 drums of aviation fuel but, because of the very real danger of air attack as the search progressed, Captain Brock reluctantly ordered all but the minimum amount as required to be thrown overboard. As the fuel drums floated away, an ROK frigate swung into action to salvage as many as she could for her own purposes, regardless of risk. Meanwhile, air searches throughout the day revealed no trace of the MiG. The story was repeated next day, although an ROK motor launch, part of the search element, rescued 17 ROK paratroops with four North Korean prisoners from Chari-do, an islet west of the north point of Simni-do. This was the first Captain Brock knew of their presence. He learned they were from a force of some 20 paratroops that had been dropped on Simni-do four days earlier, without proper briefing and without signalling equipment. They had retired to Chari-do after beating off an assault by 50 North Koreans who had crossed the mudflats from the mainland. Next day he was in for another surprise when a sampan was encountered, in which was a party of armed Koreans who eventually proved to be a clandestine group under an American intelligence team on Cho-do island.

The risk of keeping so many ships operating for so long in such an exposed position was greatly increased when four enemy aircraft, identified as Yaks, appeared just after the CAP had withdrawn owing to engine trouble. Fortunately, the Yaks made no attack but, because of the increased danger, the task force began moving southwards in the evening. Early next morning Rear-Admiral A.E. Smith USN, commander of TF95, instructed Captain Brock to abandon the search for the phantom MiG. All ships were ordered southwards, but there was a complication. An ROK frigate had returned to Simni-do in the darkness, hoping to gather some last-minute information. She delayed her departure and was found by four Yaks which, this time, were armed and ready to attack. The frigate claimed one shot down and hits on a second, but was herself damaged by cannon-fire and a near miss by a 100-lb bomb. Fortunately, after some temporary assistance, she was able to proceed to Pusan under her own power. The task force was dissolved, *Kenya* returning to Sasebo, the enterprise a gallant failure[8].

---

[8] Although unsuccessful on this occasion, in July another MiG wreck was discovered and successfully salvaged (see Chapter XII). Small teams of US-led South Korean clandestine units were also involved in retrieving parts of downed MiGs at this time. Another small group of Americans and South Koreans was led by Capt Ellery Anderson MC, a former Special Air Services operative. They had been air-dropped south of Wonsan tasked to blow-up the Kyongwon railway line. Having successfully achieved this, the party made its way to a pre-designated point 120 miles to the south-east where all were safely plucked from enemy territory by two USN helicopters (see *Banner over Pusan*). Capt Anderson was later awarded the US Bronze Star for his performance.

Bridges in the Hungnam area were the targets for Fireflies on 12 April. Two spans of one bridge were knocked out and damage wreaked on another. Nearby barracks buildings and store dumps were rocketed and strafed. During a strike on a bridge near Songjin, the aircraft (WB340) flown by Cmd Plt Frank Bailey and Acm1 Jim Loveys was hit in the engine by small-arms fire. Loss of oil pressure caused the engine to seize and Bailey had to ditch about ten miles north-east of Hungnam, some 40 miles from the carrier. Escorted by Sea Furies, helicopters from *Theseus* and *Bataan* picked up Bailey and Loveys after they had spent around 40 minutes in their dinghies. During their armed reconnaissance patrols, Sea Furies attacked tanks, several of which were camouflaged and, directed by a USAF Mustang, strafed and bombed troops in dugouts near the bomb-line. Other duties they carried out included target spotting for RN and USN ships as they bombarded the coastal area of Wonsan and Sang-ni.

For *Theseus*, much of the morning of Friday 13 April was spent refuelling at sea from the RFA *Wave Chief*. True to the day and date, in a slight mishap, some of the fuel lines parted and several radio aerials on the starboard side of the ship were written off. Flying re-commenced shortly before midday in a considerable swell. During an armed reconnaissance to Hamhung, Lt(P) J.S. Humphreys' Sea Fury (VX710/118) was hit by flak. He was obliged to crash-land in a small paddy field and the aircraft skidded into an adjacent dried up river bed. Fortunately for the pilot this provided some protection from enemy small-arms fire. The remaining aircraft in Humphreys' section orbited overhead and requested a helicopter pick up from USS *Manchester* at Wonsan, about 40 miles away. Two other Sea Furies in the area escorted the helicopter piloted by Aviation Pilot Henry Cardoza USN along the way. Humphreys was picked up after about 40 minutes on the ground and carried back to the American cruiser, where he was treated for severe head injuries and a badly broken ankle. The American helicopter pilot was awarded a DSM, as was his crewman AM3 James H. Hicks. During the afternoon Fireflies attacked three bridges, knocking out two spans, while Sea Furies wrecked warehouses at Sontang-ni under the direction of a controller and attacked a village north of Wonsan, damaging buildings and strafing troops.

While Fireflies attacked various bridges in the Hungnam area with no obvious results on 14 April, Sea Furies carried out armed reconnaissance of the west coast at the same time. Visibility was poor, but they attacked the marshalling yards at Chinnampo, hitting a large number of wagons and several small craft along the coast were left on fire. Later flights attacked tanks around Hamhung and small craft near Wonsan but the flak was intense. South-west of Hungnam, Lt(P) Irwin Bowman, a Canadian from Calgary, had his Sea Fury hit by flak:

> "We were rocketing a fuel dump and trenches covered with straw in the side of a hill. We believed the Communists were hiding their trucks there during the day. We had been receiving quite a bit of anti-aircraft fire and on one of my passes, just as I pulled up, I heard a loud 'whang' and my engine conked out. I immediately looked around for a flat place to land, away from all the small villages. I finally landed near the railroad tracks that ran right into Hamhung. The plane wasn't damaged very badly and I wasn't hurt at all in the crash. In fact, the wheels-up landing was one of the smoothest I ever made." [9]

Bowman was quickly in radio contact with the aircraft overhead, and all available aircraft in the area flew RESCAP over him until a rescue helicopter could arrive. In Wonsan harbour, *Manchester*'s helicopter had just flown off to deliver a load of cigarettes, soap and sweets for another helicopter crew aboard the LST *0007*. Before the supplies could be delivered, however, *Manchester* received an emergency call from the Sea Fury flight leader. The wheels of the helicopter had just touched down aboard the LST when the pilot, Lt Roger Gill USN, was contacted to effect the rescue. In a matter of seconds the helicopter was in the air and heading north up the coast, picking up an escort of two Sea Furies on the way. Approaching the outskirts of Hamhung, a line of flak bursts suddenly appeared just in front of the helicopter. At the same time, Gill heard the British flight leader issue a warning, "Quick, get down low, they're firing at you." Gill pushed the helicopter down towards the ground and as he came around he spotted

---

[9] See *With the Carriers in Korea*.

the downed Sea Fury. On the ground, Lt Bowman could see what was happening:

> "While I was waiting for the helicopter to arrive I could hear machine-guns and larger anti-aircraft batteries firing at my wing mates circling the area. They seemed very close, just over a small ridge a short distance away. It wasn't long before I could see the helicopter approaching, and I also saw the flak bursting around it. I don't know how it ever missed being hit. The way it headed for the ground I thought it had been hit . . ." [10]

At first Gill thought the plane on the ground was the Sea Fury that had crash landed the previous day, but as he went lower he could see somebody running around the tail of the aircraft. He recalled:

> "I was still going about 100 knots and I passed right over the plane the first time. The pilot ran back around the plane and, as soon as I could get down on the ground, he climbed aboard and I started to take off. I was too nose-heavy though, and with an embankment just in front of the plane I was afraid I would crack the plane up and everybody else with it. I hollered at my crewman to jettison some of the stuff in the plane to make it lighter, and he started throwing out all the candy, cigarettes and bars of soap we had brought for the LST. The plane still wasn't light enough so finally he heaved out the big aerial camera and we took off. The last thing I remember thinking about as we headed out of the area was that with all those cigarettes, candy and soap scattered around the ground the gooks will live like kings for a while. Just as we were airborne there was another large shell burst near the plane as the North Koreans began to get our range. It seemed like a long time before we were over water again and headed back down the coast to Wonsan harbour . . ." [11]

The helicopter reached the *Manchester* just on dusk. Lt(P) Bowman was returned to *Theseus* the following afternoon. Sometime later, Lt Gill was awarded a British DSC for this rescue, while his crewman, Aviation Mechanician's Mate Thomas C. Roche received the DSM.

Operations on the 15th were reduced because of fog. Sea Furies strafed the remains of Bowman's aircraft and it was left on fire. Motor transport and troops were reported in the village of Ch'ungyang-ni and it was attacked twice, causing several fires. Fireflies meanwhile attacked bridges, destroying two spans of one about 15 miles north-west of Wonsan and a second was rendered unfit for road traffic. Two days later Sea Furies attacked Sariwon airfield and left it completely unserviceable. Light but ineffective flak was encountered near Chaeryong, where warehouses and stores dumps were attacked, while boat yards at Chinnampo and railway installations at Sariwon were also rocketed and strafed. The Fireflies bombed road and rail bridges around Haeju and Chaeryong, knocking out the centre span of one and leaving the others damaged. During the course of one attack, Lt(P) D.W. Winterton's aircraft was hit by ground fire, one bullet striking the HF aerial mast above the observer's cockpit. Next day, Fireflies loaded with 500-lb and 1,000-lb bombs continued with attacks on bridges. A span was knocked from one and the support of a second collapsed. A direct hit was scored on the support of a third bridge but the bomb failed to detonate. The Sea Furies attacked junks and stores in the dock area of Chinnampo and mine-laying junks in the estuary were attacked and damaged. During the afternoon one flight wrecked stone-crushing machinery and vehicles in a quarry near Yonan. While returning from this mission, the engine of Lt(P) Ian Hamilton's aircraft (VW582) cut and he had to ditch in the sea about 60 miles from *Theseus*. Unable to retrieve his dinghy as he scrambled clear of the aircraft before it sank, he had to spend 55 minutes in water before he was rescued. He was practically unconscious when the helicopter found him, but he made a good recovery within 24 hours. This was the fifth helicopter rescue since the carrier had sailed on 8 April and the effect of these prompt rescues maintained high morale among the aircrews.

18 April proved to be the final day of operational flying for *Theseus* before she left Korean waters for the last time. That evening the destroyer *Consort* was detached to meet her replacement, HMS *Glory*, in the Formosa Channel. Next day the weather was miserable with low cloud, limited visibility and heavy rain. A pessimistic forecast prevented flying over the

---

[10/11] See *With the Carriers in Korea*.

land so *Theseus* and her escort withdrew to Sasebo. As she entered Sasebo on the 20th, all of the carrier's aircraft were ranged on deck, and all available men were paraded to form the word *THESEUS* at the forward end of the flight deck. The helicopter, with a photographer on board, made numerous runs over the scene to record the occasion. Unserviceable aircraft and surplus stores were transferred to *Unicorn* and on arrival Admiral Scott-Moncrieff, who had accompanied the last patrol, transferred to the Headquarters Ship HMS *Ladybird*.

During *Theseus'* final patrol, her companion carrier *Bataan* had been equally busy. Corsairs of VMF-312 had started April on a bad note when their CO Maj Donal P. Frame was killed in action and his successor, Maj Frank H. Presley, was wounded on the 20th. The following day, Capt Phillip C. DeLong (a WWII ace credited with 11 victories against the Japanese in the Pacific) ran into trouble while leading a section of Corsairs on an armed reconnaissance mission near Chinnampo. The two Corsairs were searching for targets of opportunity when DeLong's wingman, 1/Lt Harold D. Daigh, announced that four aircraft were closing on the section from behind. He called the break just as DeLong shot down the lead enemy fighter, which he identified as a Yak-9. In the short engagement that followed, DeLong shot down two more Yaks and Daigh scored hits on the fourth. In the space of a few minutes, the Marines had completely turned the tables on the North Koreans.

Apart from the highlighted operations, *Theseus'* aircraft had undertaken a daily reconnaissance across Korea along the Choppeki area. During this patrol *Theseus* flew a total of 276 operational sorties, taking her total to 3,446 for the tour. The RN carrier had suffered no deck landing accidents, despite extraordinarily heavy swell on four of the days, but battle casualties turned out to be the highest so far experienced with five Sea Furies lost (one pilot missing, later reported POW, and one severely injured), plus two aircraft written off in accidents, while four Fireflies were also lost, two due to accidents, with one crew killed. Her crews were credited with the destruction of 93 junks, 152 railway trucks, 33 gun positions, plus numerous buildings, warehouses, factories, bridges, railway stations, power stations, in addition to road vehicles. The list was impressive. During these actions, in excess of half a million rounds of 20mm ammunition had been fired and 6,617 rockets launched, while 1,390 500-lb and 84 1,000-lb bombs had been dropped.

While *Theseus* had escaped relatively lightly with regard to her aircrew losses, the cost to the USN and USMC squadrons had been extremely high, however, and since the beginning of January to the end of April, 51 Corsairs alone had been lost in operations from the carriers, plus six Skyraiders, and one Panther.

On 25 April, *Theseus* sailed for Hong Kong, first doing a tour around Sasebo harbour before passing through the boom. Since her arrival in the theatre of war seven months earlier, her two squadrons had flown 3,446 operational sorties in 86 operational flying days. The main credit for this fine record was ascribed by Captain Bolt to the pilots for their high and consistent standard of flying, and to the Deck Landing Control Officers for their excellent work. Great attention had been paid to the avoidance of deck-landing, taxying and handling accidents. The US Navy was generous in its recognition of her achievements, her departure being marked by a number of congratulatory signals.

From Admiral Radford, C-in-C US Pacific Fleet :

> "I well remember that British and American carrier task forces operated together with great profit to ourselves and great loss to our enemies in the closing campaigns of World War Two in the Pacific. That this fine association has been renewed in Korea has been a source of great pride and pleasure to me and to units of the United States Pacific Fleet. The work of the *Theseus* in our joint efforts has been outstanding and a fine example to all. May you have a good trip home and many happy landings." [12]

From Vice-Admiral C. Turner Joy, Commander Naval Forces Far East :

> "*Theseus* and embarked airmen have set high standards for all aircraft carriers during their most effective tour of duty with the United Nations forces. We have admired your quiet and

---

12 See *With the Carriers in Korea*.

confident way of always doing more than the schedule called for. It has been a privilege to have such a fine unit share this campaign with us. Well done. Good Luck. God speed on your homeward voyage." [13]

From Vice-Admiral H.M. Martin, Commander US 7th Fleet:

"Your fine performance in this Korean show has added new lustre to the brilliant traditions of the British Navy. It has been a privilege to have you in the Seventh Fleet. Good luck and may we be shipmates again." [14]

Theseus' replacement, HMS *Glory*, had much to live up to.

[13/14] See *With the Carriers in Korea*.

CHAPTER XII

CARRIER AIR OPERATIONS: HMS *GLORY*

April – September 1951

"... while the next in the circus swung round in the misty air, awaiting its call and the disks of the batsman, the word of the choregrapher, to bring it home." [1]

War correspondent Eric Linklater watching Fireflies
and Sea Furies land aboard *Glory*

HMS *Glory* was commanded by Captain K.S. Colquhoun DSO, who had on board the 14th Carrier Air Group under Lt Cdr(P) S.J. Hall DSC comprising 804 Squadron with 22 Sea Fury FB11s (Lt Cdr(P) J.S. Bailey OBE) and 812 Squadron with 12 Firefly AS5s (Lt Cdr(P) F.A. Swanson DSC), plus the H-5 helicopter – ex-*Theseus* – and two USN pilots, Lt Paul O'Mara and CPO Dan Fridley. Like *Theseus*, *Glory* had carried out intensive flying training on her way out, and was ready to embark on operational sorties with minimal delay.

Her first patrol began on 28 April and the usual pattern of attacks ensued. The carrier's start was not encouraging. Low cloud and foggy weather prevented any flying until the afternoon when 15 aircraft were flown off. The weather then closed in again and brought about a tragedy. While on CAP Sea Fury VW655 piloted by Lt(P) E.P.L. Stephenson disappeared into thick cloud at 900 feet and apparently crashed into the sea near the Clifford Islands. A search by other aircraft failed to find any sign of either man or machine. Meanwhile, of the four Fireflies on close air support, two had to return because of problems with their fuel tanks. The remaining pair bombed the runway of Ongjin airfield. An improvement in the weather next day allowed *Glory* a full day of flying, with a pair of Sea Furies making the early morning armed recce up the coast, where they strafed and rocketed junks and attacked rail installations. Another section was detailed to patrol north-east of Seoul where enemy troop positions that had been marked with smoke by an FAC were attacked, while another flight attacked the villages of Yanju and Chidong-ni with rockets. Meanwhile, one section of Fireflies carried out a close-support mission while another section flew north of the bomb-line and attacked storage dumps and unused airfields. One Firefly aborted with radio trouble, but joined up with another section on the anti-submarine duty. A second Firefly then ran low on fuel and had to land at Suwon where it was refuelled and later returned to the ship. Close air support sections of Sea Furies attacked troops in the Uijongbu area next day, while two elements of Fireflies on close-support missions attacked troops in a valley and on a ridge and a third section flew north and bombed Kaesong.

May 1951
Having replenished at sea on the first day of the new month, there had been no flying for *Glory*'s aircrews. Honours for the day went to USN Skyraider crews of VA-195, one of the squadrons aboard the USS *Princeton*. They attacked the Hwach'on Dam, a structure that was 240 feet thick at the base, with each of its faces strengthened by rocks. It had already defied destruction by bombing, both by the B-29s and Skyraiders, and had weathered attacks by more

---

[1] See *A Year in Space* by Eric Linklater.

Skyraiders using 11.5-inch rockets. A decision was therefore taken to try and breach the dam by using torpedoes to destroy the floodgates that stretched between its east and west abutments. Subsequently, eight Skyraiders led by Cdr Richard Merrick were launched from *Princeton* and escorted to the target by Corsairs. They broke into two-aircraft sections, evaded AA fire, and manoeuvred around the 4,000 feet-high peaks to approach the reservoir. The torpedoes had a narrow margin for error. If they were dropped too high they would plunge into the water and sink; if they were dropped too low they would ricochet off the water. Six of the eight that were dropped struck on or near the floodgates and one gate was blown away. The dam was breached and holed on both sides. The damage caused by this, the last-ever combat use of aerial torpedoes, exceeded all expectations. Sadly, Cdr Merrick, a colourful character noted for always carrying a long-barrelled Luger pistol, a pair of binoculars and a camera on his missions, was killed in action two weeks later.

Both of *Glory*'s squadrons flew the usual pattern of armed reces on 2 May, attacking junks along the coast and railway box-cars inland, and flying close air support missions for the army. The Fireflies meantime bombed a large building in Haeju but another Sea Fury (possibly VX610) was lost when it developed engine trouble on returning from a ground-attack mission and Lt(E) Peter Barlow had to ditch in a stream north of the bomb-line. While he was swimming in the water he came under fire from positions on a nearby hillside. An American helicopter was quickly on the scene to pick him up, while Lt Cdr(P) Bailey (VX609) led the CAP. When Barlow was safely in the clear, his abandoned aircraft was strafed and set on fire by his colleagues. Barlow was flown to Seoul, damp but otherwise unhurt. Poor weather hampered operational flying over the next couple of days, and it was not until the afternoon of 5 May that sections of Sea Furies and Fireflies were able to carry out strikes, the former attacking warehouses and other buildings at Haeju, while Fireflies bombed a railway bridge near Haeju and then attacked targets in the town with rockets. The aircraft flown by Cmd Plt P. MacKerral landed at Seoul owing to damage caused to one wing by an exploding cannon. Next day junks and sampans were attacked and, when flying was completed, *Glory* set course for Sasebo for a brief two-day stopover.

By 11 May, *Glory* was back on patrol off the west coast, her Sea Furies flying armed reces along the coast and attacking fishing sampans and junks when located, before flying inland seeking trucks and stores on their way to Haeju. Meanwhile, despite serviceability problems, the Fireflies succeeded carrying out a photo-reconnaissance mission while others attacked and damaged two bridges. Overnight, the enemy's bridge repair gangs were out and the first section of four Sea Furies to arrive over the area reported that most of the bridges were back in use. Later, a miscellany of junks and sampans were attacked in the Chinnampo estuary by Sea Furies, while Fireflies attacked bridges at Wontan and Yonan. Owing to reports that the Chinese and North Koreans were using ox-carts to transport ammunition, these were now regarded as legitimate targets despite objections by some of the aircrews.

14 May was planned as a replenishment day for *Glory*, with no operational flying schedule. Then, unexpectedly, the Canadian destroyer *Nootka*, in pursuit of a number of suspicious junks, requested a CAP at dawn when her captain realised she was going to be too far to the north when daylight arrived. There were serious concerns for her safety but she managed to accomplish her task and steam south again at high speed without mishap or the need for air cover. While *Glory* was refuelling, the carrier's helicopter was airborne to allow PO(A) E.J. King, the ship's photographer, to obtain some aerial footage. Fortunately, the helicopter was near the carrier when the pilot saw a man struggling in the water. A seaman (Stoker McPherson) had fallen overboard during the refuelling operation. The helicopter swooped low and hovered over him and King volunteered to jump into the water to make room in the aircraft. Wearing his Mae West, he supported the half-drowned man and slipped a sling around his body which allowed him to be hauled up out of the water and flown back to the carrier.

Drizzle and low cloud lingered well into the afternoon of 15 May, severely hampering flying but, owing to a high risk of encountering enemy aircraft in the operating area, *Glory*'s CAP was increased to four machines. A flight of Fireflies bombed a bridge near Sariwon but failed to score any hits. The Sea Furies flew three sections of armed reconnaissance, one along the coast, one to Chinnampo, and the other north of P'yongyang where they encountered intense light and heavy flak. Lt(P) J.A. Winterbotham's Sea Fury (VW669) was hit and he had to ditch off the coast. The ditching was achieved without difficulty and Winterbotham had more than enough time to climb out safely. He swam to a nearby sampan that was crewed by friendly Koreans and they took him to a safe island. An American helicopter from LST799 picked him up and took him back to the vessel for the night. Winterbotham was returned to *Glory* next day. Despite unfavourable weather, *Glory*'s two squadrons managed to fly 155 sorties between 13 and 15 May.

There occurred another aircraft loss on 18 May when Firefly WB346/211 flown by Lt(P) Robert Williams was hit by what the pilot thought was rifle fire and he was obliged to ditch in a river inlet about six miles south-west of Onjin, and some 70 miles north of *Glory*'s position. Williams was unhurt but his observer, Acm1 Ken Sims[2], had been wounded in the arm. The latter recalled:

"We were attacking some buildings west of Haeju and I had the camera ready to photograph results when I was hit in the left arm. Lt Williams did not really know what had hit us, but I smelled a lot of cordite in the cockpit and am convinced it was from something larger, like 20mm cannon, which had exploded in my seat. I got all the bits from the seat and some wadding in my arm. On the way home the engine seized on us – the coolant tank had been hit – and we ditched, just offshore in four feet of water."

Two South Korean fishermen in a sampan speedily came to their aid and they were subsequently picked up by *Glory*'s own helicopter. The Sea Furies led by Lt Cdr(P) Bailey (VX609) meantime spotted for the cruisers in addition to carrying out armed recces of the Chinnampo area and points further north. Targets of opportunity such as buildings, junks and ox-carts were rocketed and strafed, and adjacent to the village of Kumsan-ni the British pilots saw a large sign reading WELCOME UN ARMY, which was assumed to be just another decoy for a flak trap. Next day *Glory* was relieved by *Bataan* and departed for Sasebo to seek some urgent repairs.

June 1951

On 3 June, *Glory* sailed from Sasebo to return to the operational area and relieve *Bataan* off the west coast of Korea, and her aircraft began flying the following morning when Sea Furies attacked junks at Hanch'on and Kumsan-ni, but two close-support sections were unable to operate near the front due to poor weather conditions. They were diverted instead to Kaesong where they strafed enemy troops and rocketed railway wagons. When returning from the last trip of the day, the engine of Lt(P) P.A.L. Watson's aircraft (110) failed and he made a successful ditching off Cho-do near HMS *Black Swan*; the frigate picked him up unharmed. Fireflies flew armed reconnaissance sorties, bombed bridges, buildings and troop positions on a ridge. Next day, 5 June, it was the turn of Sea Furies to have an uneventful time. Only a few stray junks were found and attacked off shore and on the land some ox-carts were destroyed. At the same time, the Fireflies demolished a railway bridge at Yonan and attacked the villages of Kamsan-ni, Sungtam-ni and Sunyang-dong causing several buildings to explode. During his sortie P3 S.W.E. Ford's Firefly (WB244) was damaged, apparently by rifle fire, but he reported that since everything seemed to be functioning normally he would land back on *Glory* rather than ditch. He was flying without an observer. On his second attempt the engine failed and the Firefly splashed into the sea, sinking almost immediately. Although the cockpit canopy was open, Ford did not have time to escape and he was lost with his aircraft.

The strikes continued unabated, both squadrons operating in the Chinnampo area on the 6th, Fireflies spotting for *Ceylon* and *Cossack* next day during a bombardment of coastal villages suspected of harbouring stores. One Firefly (WB363) was hit by flak after attacking a bridge at Hwason-ni although the pilot, Lt(P) Roi Wilson, managed to reach the coast and ditch alongside the island of Paengyong-do. Both he and his observer, Sub Lt(O) L.R. Shepley, were rescued by a shore-based helicopter, as Wilson recalled:

"I was leading a flight of six Fireflies in an attack on a bridge at Hwason-ni when we were

[2] Acm1 Ken Sims DSM, a former WWII Swordfish TAG, was on his third Korean tour, having previously flown as a member of the Sea Otter crew aboard both *Triumph* and *Theseus*.

hit by anti-aircraft ground fire causing the port wing to be perforated and, I suspect, the coolant tank, for after a matter of a few minutes the coolant temperature went off the clock. We had a lot of height when hit and so managed to make the coast. Here I had the choice of landing on the beach or ditching relatively close to the shore. As I had ditched a Firefly[3] after an engine failure in the Mediterranean during the work up period without too much bother, I opted for the ditching. It was a lovely smooth sea and the ditching must have been fairly good as we had plenty of time to get out, get the aircraft dinghy out before the aircraft sank, and were rescued by a helicopter and taken to Paengyong-do. After a typical American steak and more than a few cans of beer, *Glory*'s helicopter came in to fly Lieutenant Shepley and myself back to the ship."

Enemy troops and ox-carts were the main targets found by the Fireflies on the 8th. Elsewhere, Sea Furies attacked railway trucks and a storage dump near a factory which blew up destroying more ammunition supplies. Persistent low cloud over the target area made finding targets difficult for later sections. Next day, 9 June, was set aside for replenishment at sea but during the course of this it was discovered that the aviation fuel being pumped from the supply ship, RFA *Wave Premier*, was heavily contaminated. Sabotage was rumoured and it seemed that *Glory* might have to return prematurely to port if the situation could not be rectified at sea. It was subsequently established that the problem was caused by corrosion in a supply tank. Despite the contaminated fuel, operational flying resumed on the 10th with a combined strike by Sea Furies and Fireflies on the village of Osan-ni, which was engulfed in flames following the attack. Sea Furies led by Lt Cdr(P) Bailey (VW656) also attacked buildings on the Chinnampo waterfront, destroying several of them, while Fireflies set fire to targets in Honsan-ni and Chaeryong. The CO landed with three bullet holes in his Sea Fury. By the evening, however, it was clear that the fuel problem could not be overcome and that the patrol would have to be cut short and, therefore, the next day was rescheduled to be the carrier's last of her third patrol before returning to Sasebo.

On the last day of her third patrol, *Glory*'s aircraft revisited their targets of the day before. Another successful combined strike by both squadrons was made on troop billets in the village of Osan-ni. Fireflies also inflicted some damage to the Sariwon rail bridge with near misses, but when landing-on after this strike, Lt(P) R.H.W. Blake came in too low and his aircraft struck the carrier's round-down; the pilot survived unhurt but the Firefly was so badly damaged that it had to be written-off. Sea Furies again targeted buildings on the Chinnampo waterfront, ox-carts, troops and junks but a new type of target was allocated to them for the first time – electrical transformers, three of which were attacked and damaged. Next day, while on passage to Sasebo, the contaminated aviation fuel was transferred to another vessel, RFA *Green Ranger*. Following her arrival at Sasebo, 25,000 gallons of fresh fuel was taken on board before the carrier set off to rendezvous with *Unicorn* at Kure to embark replacement aircraft.

Glory commenced her fourth patrol on 21 June and sailed again for her station where she was to relieve USS *Sicily*, which had replaced *Bataan* as the USN's west coast carrier. This patrol was beset by difficulties from the outset. The carrier's helicopter was out of service and its loss hampered the efficiency of normal operations. As a plane-guard for deck take-offs and landings, a helicopter was in its element being able to pick up a ditched airman in a few minutes, something that a destroyer could take up to an hour to achieve. Having one destroyer employed as a plane-guard for most of the day meant that both the mobility of the force and the effectiveness of the screen were handicapped. Conscious of this, Captain Colquhoun shifted his area of operations 30 miles north of the usual position to be as near as possible to a shore-based helicopter.

When flying started on the 23rd, Sea Furies were sent on close-support missions to the eastern end of the line. This meant operating over country unfamiliar to the pilots, whilst their American counterparts from TF77 in the Sea of Japan were being sent at the same time across to the western end. Despite protests concerning this inefficient strategy, it persisted throughout the whole patrol. Fireflies bombed Chaeryong, a bridge north of Sariwon and storage dumps

---

[3] Lt Wilson had ditched VT423 in the Mediterranean on 18 December 1950.

near Chinnampo in addition to a railway bridge at Wontan. Sea Furies were less successful although next day they attacked gun positions and buildings. During one mission between Haeju and Chinnampo, 804 Squadron's Senior Pilot, Lt Cdr(P) Maurice Birrell, encountered heavy ground fire while making a low sweep and his aircraft was hit by a 20mm shell that exploded in his ammunition box, which fortunately was empty. Meanwhile, the Fireflies bombed factory buildings south of P'yongyang which were left damaged and smoking. Other buildings on an island in the Chinnampo estuary were bombed and strafed, as was the railway bridge at Hwasan-ni.

Armed reconnaissance sorties were made to Hanch'on on the 25th, searching for junks and around the local airfields from where it was believed the Po-2 biplanes were operating, although none could be found. During one of these missions, despite the distinctive black and white identification stripes that adorned the Sea Furies, Lt(P) R.H. Kilburn's flight was subjected to a firing pass by four USAF F-80s. Fortunately, the marksmanship of the American pilots was not good, and no one was hit. At Ongjin airfield the Fireflies destroyed a hangar and during another mission they bombed and strafed machine-gun positions high on a ridge, later bombing a bridge at Hwasan-ni. A Sea Fury flight on an armed reconnaissance mission to Ka-do island in the far north led to a coastal vessel being sunk next day, while, inland, five tanks were detected alongside a road and these were subjected to vigorous rocket attacks. Elsewhere, Fireflies bombed the railway sidings and sheds at Toktong-ni, and a factory on the outskirts of P'yongyang.

Having replenished at sea on the 27th, both of *Glory*'s squadrons were back in action next day. During an armed reconnaissance attack on a barracks building south of P'yongyang, Firefly WB308 flown by Lt(P) J.H. Sharp was shot down by anti-aircraft fire. It crashed in flames killing both Sharp and his observer, Acm1 George Wells DSM. Another Firefly on a strafing run after dropping its bombs on the rail bridge west of Allyong reservoir was also struck by ground fire, although Lt(P) T.V.G. Binney was able to land at Suwon for repairs rather than attempt to return to the carrier. Meanwhile, the Sea Furies were occupied with carrying out attacks on junks and ox-carts, and achieved a couple of spectacular results when one of each blew up. Next day, the Sea Furies attacked junks along the coast and buildings inland. Results were good. Because of the constant reports that the enemy was building up his air strength, Ongjin-ni airfield was reconnoitred closely where it was observed that most of the bomb craters had been filled in and it appeared that concrete floors had been laid in some of the blast pens. Elsewhere, north of Kyonipo, Fireflies made two bombing strikes on a road bridge over the river, one span being demolished as a result of an accurate dive-bombing attack by Cmd Plt Maurice Purnell, who was later awarded a DSC. It was subsequently discovered that a junk sunk by the Sea Furies during the day had been friendly. The craft had been manned by personnel belonging to a secret guerrilla organisation, five of whom were killed. It was a calculated risk that all such groups took in wartime when they worked behind the lines. The British pilots were not to blame for this unfortunate incident as those on the junk had not fired recognition signals in spite of receiving a warning burst of fire across the bow. The first operation on the 30th was a combined strike by both 804 and 812 Squadrons on villages around Ongjin-ni airfield. While Sub Lt(P) J.R. Howard was taking off on the afternoon mission, the strop came off the catapult trolley and the Sea Fury (VW565) plunged over the bows. Fortunately, the pilot survived and was picked up by one of the attendant destroyers, HMS *Constance*. The remaining launches were made using RATOG.

July 1951

At the end of the day's flying on 1 July, *Glory* set course for Sasebo once more, at the end of her fourth patrol. The passage to the port was wet and windy due to typhoon 'Kate' but, fortunately, it was too far to the north to cause any real trouble. On arrival in Sasebo, *Glory*'s aircrew were given five days leave, while her aircraft were having routine maintenance checks and the catapult was being repaired.

While *Glory* was at Sasebo, the UN naval task element operating off Korea's west coast received reports from the Joint Operations Centre (JOC) of a MiG-15 down in the water just offshore, about 40 miles north of Cho-do. It was thought most likely to be one of those shot down by F-86s the previous day. The water at this location was very shallow and there seemed no prospect of any UN ships being able to reach it. The commander of the force at that time decided to take no action apart from requesting reconnaissance planes from USS *Sicily* to search for it during their daily sorties to confirm its position.

On the morning of 10 July, *Glory* sailed from Sasebo to commence her fifth patrol and to relieve *Sicily*. Early next morning, fog and cloudy conditions made targets difficult to find for *Glory*'s aircrews on their first missions, although Sea Furies found the area around Chinnampo clear and they were able to attack buildings and junks. During the course of this mission, Lt(P) W.R. Hart made a sighting of the MiG's tailplane lying in mud near Hanch'on, about 13 miles south and slightly west of the position originally reported. Meanwhile, when breaks in the cloud cover allowed, a thorough search was made of an area west of Chinnampo from where it was suspected that enemy coastal batteries had been firing but no gun positions were spotted and the examination of the photographs taken revealed only a few camouflaged pits.

On the 13th, the Sea Furies attacked railway trucks, junks and barracks buildings. Part of the fuselage of the crashed MiG was visible for the first time and the location photographed. The wreckage was just awash at low water; it lay along a narrow channel flanked by sandbars and blocked at the southern end by a minefield. Light flak came from a junk nearby. Meanwhile, air support was given to the front line, strafing enemy troops resisting the UN forces who were within 1,000 yards of them. Elsewhere, Fireflies damaged a railway bridge north of Sariwon, and destroyed another to the west of Chaeryong. Next day, a section of Sea Furies was tasked to photograph Yondang-dong airfield, where they were greeted by heavy and light anti-aircraft fire, some of it reaching up to 6,000 feet and beyond. Examination of the photographs showed that although the airfield was damaged it was obviously still being used. Firefly crews meantime bombed Ullul and Kumsan-ni and attacked a railway tunnel on the Haeju to Sariwon line, one aircraft being damaged by ground fire although it was able to return and land safely.

Having replenished on 15 July, *Glory* was back in action next day although low cloud ruled out close-support missions and generally restricted air activity. The Sea Fury pilots reconnoitred the area around the downed MiG, checking the channels and mudflats to see if it might be accessible to small craft since Admiral Turner Joy had directed that every effort should be made to recover as much of the wreckage as possible, reminiscent of the earlier failed attempt to recover the remains of the MiG downed near Simni-do in April (see Chapter XI). Whilst keeping up this observation, three aircraft were slightly damaged by flak and all were able to return and land safely. Not so fortunate was Firefly WB380 crewed by Lt(P) Williams and Sub Lt(O) Shepley, both of whom had survived earlier ditchings. Their aircraft was hit by flak while carrying out a bombing attack north of Sariwon and it crashed in flames behind enemy lines. Neither survived. Another aircraft was lost next during an armed recce near Chinnampo, where enemy troops were rocketed and strafed. Lt(P) Hart's Sea Fury (VW661) developed engine trouble, probably due to flak, and he had to ditch his aircraft near friendly islands south of Choppeki Point. He was quickly rescued by the ROK frigate *PF61* and was returned to *Glory* by helicopter the same day.

The Sea Furies were in trouble again on the 18th. The first mission, led by Lt Cdr(P) Bailey in VR951, flew up the west coast with orders to photograph Yondang-dong airfield from 15,000 feet, which they did, and then attacked buildings and railway sidings near Osan-ni. While searching for targets in this area, two aircraft were hit by anti-aircraft fire. A shell exploded in the cockpit behind Lt(P) P.G. Young's head, but he managed to return to the carrier and land on safely. Lt(P) Peter Davis – known as Toby – was not so lucky and he had to ditch VX609 off Choppeki Point. He had great difficulty with his Mae West and dinghy and was rescued by *Glory*'s helicopter after an exhausting 90 minutes in the water. During the next mission for the day, Cmd Plt T.W. Sparke's Sea Fury (VW573) was hit by flak while attacking a gun position and he reported that the aircraft was on fire. Shortly afterwards it was seen to dive into the ground and explode, giving the pilot no chance of survival.

Glory now moved 70 miles north ready to give air cover to a force attempting to recover the downed MiG, which had been inspected by a team of CIA experts aboard an YH-19 helicopter in a daring clandestine mission. Captain W.L.M. Brown of the frigate HMS *Cardigan Bay* had evolved a salvage plan using the highest tidal ranges in the area for the month. He first proposed that two shallow draught junks be towed in at the next maximum high, lashed to the MiG at low water and then towed clear at the next high water. However, learning at a meeting with agents of various US special intelligence groups of the existence at Inch'on of a special landing craft fitted with a crane, he decided to use this instead of the junks. He planned for *Glory*'s helicopter, guided in by her aircraft, to accurately mark the position of the MiG with buoys, and for an ROK motor launch with a crew assumed to have local knowledge to lead the vessel there after dark. *Cardigan Bay* would proceed to the area of operations to provide AA support and the aircraft from *Glory* would provide low-level CAP with 5th Air Force jets giving high-level cover.

Captain Brown's plan was duly approved by the Task Group commander. The weather on the morning of 20 July was not suitable for *Glory*'s helicopter to fly but it cleared in the afternoon. Meanwhile, the passage to the vicinity of the MiG was uneventful for the ships and they arrived at 1235. There they were to await until near low water. The weather had by then improved with good visibility but there was no sign of any movement by the enemy, nor any apparent interest in their presence. At 1600, when the tide was nearly out and the channels and sandbanks were exposed to view, Lt O'Mara arrived in *Glory*'s helicopter while two Sea Furies provided cover. At low water the fuselage of the MiG could be seen and O'Mara marked it with a buoy. Shortly afterwards, the tail assembly was also evident and this was marked with a life jacket and fluorescent dye. This done, O'Mara's helicopter was escorted to Cho-do, where it landed with its fuel tanks almost empty. The two Sea Furies then returned to the scene, where the recovery craft had by then assembled. It was quickly established that, in addition to four large sections which would require the crane to lift them, there was a very large number of small pieces scattered over an area of about 400 yards radius, mostly on sandbanks. All visible small parts were eventually recovered, as were the four main sections. On board *Cardigan Bay* observing the operation was war correspondent Eric Linklater:

> ". . . the experts were waiting with tense excitement to examine the secrets of its construction. Two of them, American engineers of massive build, were aboard when we came alongside. It was the boat's crew from *Cardigan Bay* that had shared the salvage with the landing craft, and now the frigate had to escort its treasure south along the coast. I climbed down to look at the wreckage, and one of the Americans drew back the tarpaulin from the unbroken nose of the fighter, and in a language too technical for me to understand, told me how fine a piece of work it was. The fighter was Russian-built . . . but it was a lovely job for all that. Caressingly he stroked a smooth dark rib of metal, that to my untaught eye had nothing remarkable about it, and said with affectionate approval, 'That's better than we can do, or better than we have done. Yes, sir! We're going to learn plenty when we get a proper look at this.' I felt ashamed because I knew nothing of metallurgy, nothing of engineering, when to him metallurgy and engineering so clearly transcended politics and war." [4]

After three-and-a-half-hours the Sea Furies were relieved by four Corsairs from the *Sicily*, which had arrived on patrol to take over from *Glory*. During the land-on, Lt(P) D.E. Johnson hit the round-down during his first approach and on the over-shoot one wheel struck a Sea Fury in the deck park, much to the shock of the pilot in the cockpit. When he did eventually touch down, he had to do it wheels-up. Completion of the day's flying marked the end of *Glory*'s patrol and she set course for Kure. Meanwhile, the recovered portions of MiG were transported to Inch'on where they were handed over to the 5th Air Force, and *Glory* duly received a signal saying, ". . . the success of the MiG operation was entirely due to the work of *Glory*'s aircraft and helicopter, for which we are very grateful."

Late on 24 July, while still at Kure, *Glory* was prematurely ordered back to Korea to

---

[4] See *A Year in Space*. The remains of the MiG were shipped to the United States and subjected to rigorous inspection by aeronautical engineers, where it was established that it had been built in 1948 and was one of the first production batch. Bearing the serial number 120147, it had one 23mm and one 37mm cannon instead of the normal two 23mm and one 37mm cannon.

reinforce *Sicily* in a show of strength to stimulate the peace talks at Kaesong (see Chapter VII), which had stalled on the first item on the agenda. The two carriers were to concentrate their air operations on this area, to the exclusion of coastal reconnaissance missions. All available frigates and ROK vessels off the west coast were also ordered to the Han estuary. Only nine hours after receiving her sailing orders, *Glory* departed from Kure, leaving several of her aircrews ashore, some of whom were test flying replacement aircraft at Iwakuni, while others were on leave. It was not possible to embark the replacement machines, so the Air Group was short of six aircraft on this patrol. The pilots from Iwakuni were ferried by helicopter on the way out, the stragglers arriving some days later by destroyer. On the way to her new station, a patrol of four Sea Furies was again attacked by a similar number of F-80s. Only violent evasive action allowed them to escape without damage.

Unfortunately for the carriers, bad weather with 10/10th cloud cover restricted flying to just CAP duties until the afternoon of the 27th, when Sea Furies attacked villages in the coastal area from Yonan to Haeju, where an estimated 2,500 enemy troops had been reported. Weather next day was similar, thwarting the launching of air strikes until mid-afternoon. Buildings and railway sidings around Chinnampo were attacked by the Sea Furies amid light flak. During these operations there was an aircraft crash on *Sicily*'s flight deck and an incoming USN Corsair with hydraulic trouble was ordered to divert to *Glory*. For this landing, so that there could be no misunderstanding with the pilot, an American batsman was flown over from *Sicily* by helicopter. The Corsair landed safely. That evening *Glory* went to action stations when one of the escort destroyers made an Asdic contact and dropped depth charges. Oil slicks were spotted coming to the surface of the water but there was no tangible evidence. Improving weather allowed Sea Furies to fly armed recces on the 29th. An estimated 4,000-plus troops had been reported in the vicinity but, if they were there, they kept well out of sight. Besides attacking villages, *Glory*'s targets included buildings, railway trucks and a tunnel. There were no casualties and only one mishap, when the arrester hook of Cmd Plt W.F. Cockburn's Firefly snapped as he was landing and the aircraft plunged into the barrier. Rough seas, high winds and low cloud then curtailed flying from *Glory* until the afternoon of the 30th, and prevented all flying on the last day of the month.

August 1951

Daylight arrived on 1 August with low cloud and miserable weather completely blanketing the Han estuary, nullifying air operations. Captain Colquhoun used the morning to replenish *Glory*'s stocks of aviation fuel and fuel oil. The carrier had returned to her station by midday but conditions remained poor for target spotting. Nevertheless, missions were flown throughout the afternoon and evening. Off the Han estuary next day, Sea Furies carried out armed recce sorties to Kumsan-ni where reports had disclosed that rafts and boats were under construction. Junks were found and two were destroyed. Numerous others were damaged as were many buildings, one of which exploded under attack. There was only light flak but one Sea Fury was damaged although it returned safely to the carrier.

Bad weather over the next two days similarly frustrated flying activities, although on the 4th an unidentified twin-engined jet aircraft emerged for a moment through the 300 feet cloud-base, dropped a bomb that fell near HMS *Mounts Bay*, and quickly disappeared back into the murk. There was no damage but this was the first of a series of such incidents. Three days later the UN frigates engaged another jet aircraft that made two passes out of low cloud, and a similar incident occurred again two days later. After checking, it transpired that the aircraft belonged to the 5th Air Force which did not know of the friendly naval operations in the Han estuary. The frigate captains were likewise unaware that they were working under one of the fixed flight paths into Kimpo airfield. Admiral Scott-Moncrieff, who briefly visited the estuary aboard HMCS *Huron* on 11 August, remarked acidly that these incidents could only reflect upon the quality of the US Inter-Service co-ordination and briefings. That evening *Glory* was relieved by *Sicily* and sailed for Sasebo, arriving there late on the 5th.

On her arrival at Sasebo she was joined by HMS *Warrior* which had arrived with spares and replacements from the UK. On 10 August *Glory* left Sasebo for Kure and made a stop at

Iwakuni to pick up eleven replacement aircraft. She departed Kure three days later to relieve
Sicily off the Han estuary and to commence her seventh patrol. War correspondent Eric
Linklater was invited to spend a few days aboard *Glory*, as he later wrote:

> ". . . early in August I went back to sea. My instructions were to spend two or three days
> aboard the aircraft carrier *Glory*, then cruising some hundred miles westward of land. I was
> driven to Seoul airport where I found waiting for me a modest young pilot and . . . a Firefly.
> He helped me into a Mae West, and then, with some difficulty, I stuffed myself into the after
> cockpit. We took off quickly. [The carrier] looked small. It looked minute, a mere chip in
> the sea. But quickly it grew larger, and in my last sight of it before hitting, it was agreeably
> ample. With a monstrous clatter and bang we hit the deck, and a wire stretched across it
> caught our trailing hook and stopped our further progress with remarkable abruptness. I
> threw back the cockpit roof, I undid my straps, and climbing out was greeted by a
> commander whose hospitality was immediate, whose understanding was profound. 'The
> first of your duties,' he said, 'is to come to the wardroom and have some gin.'"[5]

Linklater found the sight of returning aircraft and the efforts of the batsman to assist their
landing, akin to a colourful theatrical performance:

> "A voyage in an aircraft carrier was going to be unlike voyaging in other ships. More like
> going to sea in a factory, for the bustle and din of mechanical effort went on, with hardly a
> break, from day-start till dark. The carriers were ocean factories, exporting bombs and
> rockets, but on the factory roof there was a gaiety unexpectedly reminiscent of older wars
> – of the many-coloured bunting that used to fly above the dusk of burnt powder – for on a
> flight-deck a recurrent ballet was performed. A batsman stood to one side of the stern of the
> long, narrow rectangle which was the deck of the ship, and by lowering and raising his
> coloured disks, by signalling and swaying like the conductor of an orchestra soothing a
> difficult movement, brought in the plane on its proper course ... the Firefly or Sea Fury was
> wheeled and manhandled to its proper out-of-the-way position while the next in the circus
> swung round in the misty air, awaiting its call and the disks of the batsman, the word of the
> choreographer, to bring it home." [6]

On 15 August, Sea Furies carried out armed reconnaissance sorties from Hanch'on to
Chinnampo. During the course of these, three junks were destroyed and numerous others plus
a steam tug were damaged. Two 45-gallon fuel tanks dropped on a village caused a vigorous
outbreak of fire. One Sea Fury of 804 Squadron was hit by anti-aircraft fire and two others had
engine trouble, obliging Cmd Plt W.A. Newton to divert to Kimpo while Lt(P) R.F. Hubbard
landed at Paengyong-do due to falling oil pressure. The Fireflies concentrated their attacks on
the Yonan area. Sub Lt(P) J.S. Tait, who had joined *Glory* at Kure, had an unlucky first day's
operational flying when, while landing on in the morning, he came in too far to starboard and
his aircraft struck the crane. He was in the air again in the afternoon and, as he touched down,
his propeller struck the flight deck, inflicting damage to a second machine. One of these was
believed to have been WB382/206.

Next day (16 August), Cmd Plt Newton test flew the Sea Fury he had landed at Kimpo, only
to burst a tyre and end up in a ditch. Nevertheless, he was able to return to *Glory* later in the
day. Meanwhile, other Sea Furies operating from the carrier destroyed two junks near
Chinnampo. One blew up with a bright orange flash and others were reported severely
damaged. At least four ox-carts were destroyed and a gun position with four 20mm guns was
discovered manned by troops wearing jungle greens. This was attacked with rockets and
strafed. These results were not achieved with impunity and Lt(P) Doug McNaughton's Sea
Fury (VW558/118) was hit by flak near Chinnampo, although he was able to make a forced-
landing on the beach at Cho-do, where he remained stranded for some time.

Warning of the approach of typhoon 'Marge' was broadcast during the course of the day and
all naval commanders were authorised to remove their ships from confined waters in the

---

5/6 See *A Year in Space*.

war zone. This compelled the withdrawal of all ships from the Han estuary. In the evening *Glory* moved south and for the next two days she waited off the south-west tip of Korea to see which way the typhoon would go. Admiral Scott-Moncrieff left Sasebo and transferred his flag to *Glory* while she was north of the Makau Islands and before the carrier moved to the latitude of Quelpart Island to have more sea room, all the time cruising and waiting to see what the typhoon would do. It was rumoured that the winds at the centre were in excess of 100 knots. Reports of its progress were contradictory. It was clear that it had slowed up and for the next 30 hours the weather in the Yellow Sea was perfect. Nevertheless, Admiral Scott-Moncrieff felt it was essential to keep sea room especially as *Glory*'s deck park of aircraft was a major concern but he was also worried that the enemy might seize the opportunity to lay mines in the Han estuary. On the 19th the decision was taken to try to move around to the west of the forecast track and then down south along the China coast. In the event, the nearest *Glory* got to typhoon 'Marge' was about 150 miles, but even then for two days and nights the ship rolled heavily. Winds were recorded up to 60 knots although no damage was done to any aircraft. However, all the aircraft that were on the deck were found to have salt caked everywhere and in some cases the paint had begun flaking off. *Glory* eventually arrived off Okinawa on the 21st and sailed next day for Kure.

Meanwhile, off Korea's north-eastern coast, the three USN aircraft carriers currently comprising TF77, *Bon Homme Richard*, *Essex*, and *Antietam*, altered the pattern of their interdiction attacks in accordance with instructions to co-ordinate operations with the 5th Air Force in carrying out strikes against the North Korean railway system. They strove to maintain the neutralisation of ten rail bridges and 127 highway bridges within the area they covered, and to devote the remainder of their effort to attacks against railway lines in isolated areas where the enemy would have difficulty repairing the cuts. Since the passing of the typhoon, naval operations off the west coast of Korea had resumed as normal, though the veteran cruiser *Kenya* had left the war zone to refit and recommission at Singapore. Besides the frigates in the Han estuary, other units were working in the Yellow Sea.

An unusual raid was carried out by two platoons of Royal Marines and one of stoker-mechanics from HMS *Ceylon* early on 30 August. Its object was to round up a number of enemy troops reported to be in Ch'onidon near Mongumpo. No serious opposition was expected but, as the Royal Marines deployed across the landing beach, they were subjected to accurate and heavy mortar and small-arms fire from the flanks. They returned fire and a covering bombardment from the ships was renewed while the party withdrew and re-embarked, having suffered 15 casualties, one of them serious. Heavy shelling was continued after the landing craft left the shore and aircraft called in from *Sicily* attacked and destroyed a canvas-covered position and supply dumps a short distance inland. There seemed little doubt that the enemy had been forewarned of the operation. Admiral Scott-Moncrieff ordered that such activities should be discontinued, unless it was certain that there could not be a leak of information.

Glory returned to the coast of Korea for her eighth patrol on the last day of August, this time with good weather and good visibility. She was still required to direct her main effort into the Han estuary area despite a scarcity of worthwhile targets. In a day of routine missions, both 804 and 812 Squadrons attacked junks, railway trucks and villages. Two of the Sea Furies had to make emergency landings on Paengyong-do where Sub Lt(P) Howard attempted to land his flak-damaged aircraft on the beach. The Sea Fury overturned in soft sand and came down on its back. Howard managed to burrow his way out of the cockpit, watched by a crowd of curious South Koreans. He was picked up and returned to the ship that evening in the carrier's helicopter. Both damaged Sea Furies had to be left stranded on the island, waiting for recovery later when the chance arose. It was the beginning of a hectic patrol for aircrew and their maintenance crews and although catapult trouble hampered the flying programme on two or three days, they still managed to average over 50 sorties per day.

On 3 September the Sea Furies attacked targets ranging from Taedong in the north to Yonan in the south. Numerous junks were seen and buildings reported to contain troops were blasted with rockets. Intelligence information was often a few days out of date so by the time aircraft attacked these targets on occasion the troops were no longer there. Next day, eight Sea Furies were tasked to deal with the collection of junks spotted the previous day but, unfortunately, bad weather intervened and the aircraft could not reach them in time. Only one motor junk was sunk although troops and many vehicles were strafed and attacked with rockets. Three days later, warehouses and houses in Taedong were attacked, while other flights carried out photo-reconnaissance for the recently formed British Commonwealth Division.

Glory replenished at sea during the morning of 6 September. The intention had been to fly operational missions in the afternoon but, after two shaky catapult launches, flying was called off. The two aircraft already airborne were directed to land at Kimpo. *Glory's* catapult continued to give trouble for most of the next day and all launches but the last two of the day were made by RATOG. This created a lot of additional work for the ordnance ratings. Most of these missions were for close air support at the western end of the front line. According to the FAC more than 100 enemy troops were killed during these strikes.

On the 8th, the catapult gave more trouble at first, but it was soon rectified and the practice of using RATOG was discontinued. During the day, Fireflies and Sea Furies made attacks on targets nominated by ground controllers. One of these was directed against a suspected headquarters building and was carried out with such good effect that 60 casualties were later reported, but there were some doubts about the reliability of this claim. Next day, Firefly WB381/203 failed to return from a dive-bombing attack near Haeju, Lt(P) P.G.W. Morris having been obliged to carry out an emergency landing on nearby mudflats east of Haeju. The ship's helicopter was sent to pick up him and his observer Lt(O) G.E. Legge, but the call came at an inopportune time. At that stage the helicopter did not have a full load of fuel and matters were further complicated because it also had a faulty fuel gauge. Because of these circumstances it was deemed prudent to make a precautionary landing on a small island rather than run the risk of running dry in the middle of the pick up. Cans of aviation fuel for the helicopter were ferried by destroyer to the island next morning and, once refuelled, it flew back to the carrier with the Firefly crew on board, their non-recoverable aircraft having been torched beforehand.

By day's end, a record-breaking 84 sorties (66 offensive and 18 defensive) had been flown by the two squadrons, an effort that beat the previous total of 66 sorties that had been set by *Theseus'* squadrons earlier in the year. Serviceability was kept at an outstanding 100% throughout the day, an excellent maintenance effort. Apart from the lost Firefly, only minor damage was sustained to the other aircraft and there were no casualties to personnel. With her downed crew safely returned, *Glory* sailed for Kure leaving *Sicily* to continue carrying out similar operations until the 16th, when the USN carrier completed her tour and was relieved by the USS *Rendova*.

Between 16 and 20 September *Glory* was employed off the east coast of Korea before returning to the west coast. Operations started on the 18th, with Sea Furies and Fireflies flying strikes against targets at Wonsan. Next day, strong winds and a heavy swell delayed the start of flying and later, when the carrier was in calmer water in the lee of the land, there was more frustration. Her aircraft were all set to go but the catapult broke down once again. It was a bitterly disappointing anti-climax as this was the carrier's first and last visit to the east coast and the previous day had been well up to standard with a total of 68 sorties. All aircraft had to be launched with RATOG and, by the end of the day's flying, *Glory* was obliged to return to Sasebo to collect more RATOG equipment. While at Sasebo several of her Fireflies were transferred to *Unicorn* for them to be serviced in preparation for handing over to the Australian aircraft carrier HMAS *Sydney*, which was on her way to take *Glory's* place in the line.

Glory sailed for the west coast that evening to complete her ninth and last patrol. Because only seven of 812 Squadron's Fireflies were left on board, no more anti-submarine patrols were flown. When she reached the west coast next day, the 21st, there was only time for one detail to be flown late in the afternoon. A full, but reduced, day of flying was carried out by the squadrons next day with all aircraft still being launched using RATOG. The air operations were mainly concentrated around Taedong and air support was provided for a guerrilla raid on the Amgak peninsula. The Sea Fury pilots reported that Chinnampo junk traffic seemed to have increased while *Glory* had been away, showing this to be a well-used enemy supply route, and that there were more wagons on the railways. Junks were the carrier pilots' main targets, but a large group of soldiers at Hanch'on were also attacked with rockets, causing many casualties.

Buildings and villages containing troops were also attacked though results on these were difficult to assess. During one launch, Cmd Plt J.P. Hack's RATOG failed to fire and his Firefly (WB309) plunged straight into the sea just ahead of the carrier. Hack was rescued by the helicopter but his observer, Sub Lt(O) R.G.A. Davey, was not seen again. The use of RATOG was not popular at the best of times, and due to this unfortunate accident repair work on the catapult proceeded with a greater degree of urgency. Much to everyone's relief it was tested and pronounced restored late in the afternoon.

22 September happened to be the anniversary of the ferry carrier *Unicorn*'s departure from the UK and, to celebrate this and her first visit to the operational area after many months of hard and dreary ferry work, her commander, Captain J.Y. Thompson, was permitted to proceed north across the 38th Parallel and carry out a couple of brief bombardments of enemy positions on Choppekki Point. By doing so, *Unicorn* achieved the honour of being the first aircraft carrier to carry out a direct bombardment of the enemy in the Korean War.

On 23 September, *Glory*'s Sea Fury pilots achieved another record ambition, their 1,000th accident-free deck landing. Sadly for the American carrier *Essex*, the same could not be said. A few days earlier a damaged F2H Banshee of VF-172 leapt the barriers and collided with four fortunately unarmed and unfuelled aircraft before it disintegrated into a hugh fireball. The accident claimed seven lives and injured 27 others. For *Glory*'s aircrews however, the day's missions concentrated on the increased junk traffic. Numerous junks that were obviously fully loaded were strafed and attacked with rockets. Many were damaged and one erupted in a spectacular explosion. Next day, the Sea Furies conducted a search for a reported enemy gun position. Unable to find it, they attacked instead suspected villages with good results. Later, while strafing junks in the Chinnampo area, the Air Group commander, Lt Cdr(P) Sidney Hall, reported engine trouble. The Sea Fury flight escorted him to Cho-do where he turned and headed south until he was compelled to ditch VW545 several miles from the island. *Glory*'s helicopter was despatched to pick him up and a USN air-sea rescue SA-16 was alerted. The open sea proved too rough for the amphibian to alight so the American pilot landed on calmer water in-shore and tried taxiing out from there. At this stage the helicopter arrived and won the race to pick up Hall, who had by then been in the water an hour or so. He was recovered somewhat chilled but otherwise unhurt.

The 25th was *Glory*'s last day of operations for this tour. The Sea Furies destroyed seven junks and damaged many others near Chinnampo and, during another strike, also damaged a tracked vehicle that was at first thought to be a dummy. Sea Fury pilot Lt(P) Young, who had transferred from *Theseus* when she departed, flew his 100th sortie on his last mission, while Lt Cdr(P) Frank Swanson, the CO of 812 Squadron, led the last strike following which he landed at Kimpo. He was delayed there and returned to the carrier an hour or so after the strike aircraft. The ship's band and half the ship's company turned out to see his Firefly land on – the last operational landing of the tour. With all safely gathered in, *Glory* set course for Kure. En route, time was spent servicing aircraft, in particular preparing the Fireflies for transfer to *Sydney*.

On the 27th she arrived at Kure, where she found *Sydney* berthed on the other side of the pontoon. Over the next four days, all of the Fireflies and most of the air stores were transferred to the new arrival, while the 'Ditchers Union' aboard *Glory* bade farewell to their very efficient and popular American helicopter crew, Lt Paul O'Mara and CPO Dan Fridley, before they too transferred to the Australian carrier. It had been intended for *Glory* to have her own helicopter flight, two Royal Navy Dragonfly HR1s (the British version of the S-51), and indeed VZ964 and VZ965 had arrived at Singapore aboard HMS *Warrior* in July, although they were not transferred to *Unicorn* until early September. In the event, VZ964 crashed on take-off from *Unicorn* on the 10th when a mainwheel caught the carrier's guard rail and it fell into the sea. It was proposed that VZ965 would be transferred to *Sydney*.

During her tour *Glory*'s squadrons had flown 2,875 sorties, 1,055 by the Fireflies and 1,820 by the Sea Furies. Both squadrons had suffered inevitable losses, 804 losing nine aircraft and two pilots while 812 lost eight aircraft, three pilots and three observers. In return, amongst their successes, were the claimed destruction of 679 junks, 1,261 buildings, 236 rail trucks, 25 vehicles, 60 gun positions, 794 ox-carts, in addition to bridges, stores dumps, and an estimated

1,273 troop casualties. Her aircraft had fired in excess of half a million rounds of 20mm and launched 9,240 rockets, in addition to dropping 1,514 500-lb and 1,000-lb bombs. The commander of the 14th CAG, Lt Cdr(P) Hall DSC, received the DSO as did the CO of 812 Squadron, Lt Cdr(P) Swanson DSC, while 804 Squadron's CO, Lt Cdr(P) John Bailey OBE, the RN's foremost carrier landing exponent, received the DSC (see Appendix III). Pilots and observers of the two squadrons shared 13 DSCs, while Lt O'Mara USN was made an honorary MBE.

During the period July to September, the combined USN/USMC carrier aircraft operational losses were recorded as 34 Corsairs, 12 Skyraiders, and six Panthers; these figures do not include accidents. Total USN/USMC carrier aircraft operational losses for the year to date had passed the 150 mark, although many aircrew had been saved. One gallant rescue attempt of a downed USMC pilot sadly failed when the rescue helicopter flown by Lt John Koelsh USN was shot down as the seriously burned Marine Corps pilot was being hoisted aboard. Koelsh managed to extricate his crewman and the injured pilot from the wreckage, then led them away from the scene of the crash in the hope that they, too, would be rescued. However, having evaded capture for nine days, the trio were eventually taken prisoner. Koelsh died in captivity but was awarded a posthumous Congressional Medal of Honor for his efforts.

CHAPTER XIII

CARRIER AIR OPERATIONS: HMAS *SYDNEY*

October – December 1951

". . . that hill was smothered with Chinese machine-guns. He just ran into a wall of fire. We all went into it. It's interesting to hear bullets hitting your aeroplane. It's like putting your head into a kettle drum and having somebody go bing, bing, bing, bing! Not good."

Sub Lt(P) Ian MacDonald reporting on the death of
Lt(P) Keith Clarkson DFM RAN of 805 Squadron

HMAS *Sydney*, formerly HMS *Terrible* of the Royal Navy, was unique in that she was the only carrier to be built in a Royal Dockyard – Devonport, in 1944 – a Light Fleet carrier displacing some 14,000 tons. She was handed over to the Royal Australian Navy in 1948 and was currently commanded by Captain David Harries RAN. Her arrival in the Korean theatre of war was as the result of the Royal Navy's request to the Royal Australian Navy for *Sydney* to be made available for an operational tour, thereby enabling *Glory* to give her crew a rest after months of intensive operations.

Sydney's 21st Carrier Air Group was commanded by distinguished WWII fighter pilot Lt Cdr(P) M.F. Fell DSO DSC RN (see Appendix III) and comprised two squadrons of Sea Fury FB11s – 805 Squadron (Lt Cdr(P) W.G. Bowles RAN), and 808 Squadron (Lt Cdr(P) J.L. Appleby RN) – and one of Firefly AS5s, 817 Squadron commanded by Lt Cdr(P) R.B. Lunberg RN. All three squadrons[1] included a sprinkling of former RAAF aircrew who had transferred to the RAN at the end of WWII, notably Lt(P) K.E. Clarkson DFM, 805's Senior Pilot, Lts(P) J.G.B. Campbell DFC, R.A. Wild DFC, and G.F.S. Brown DFC, all of 808 Squadron, and Lt(P) A.L. Oakley DFC and Lt(O) A.H. Gordon DFC (see Appendix III). In addition, Lt Paul O'Mara USN transferred from *Glory* with an on-loan USN H-5 helicopter.[2]

In carrying out her duties, *Sydney* was to alternate in the Yellow Sea with the American light carrier, USS *Rendova* (and later the USS *Badoeng Strait*), in a cycle of nine days on patrol and nine days for replenishment and passage to and from Sasebo. On 5 October, *Sydney* became the first British Dominion carrier to send her aircraft into action. Lt Cdr(P) Michael Fell led the first mission. Initial operations were marred by fog which prevented attacks on the primary target (ferry terminals at Taedong and a road bridge at Chinnampo) but four Sea Furies and four Fireflies attacked other targets, the former damaging buildings at Ongjin with rockets and the latter attacking a road bridge at Songwha. In addition, troop shelters and one large building were destroyed while damage was inflicted on junks, houses and rolling stock, and enemy troops harassing friendly forces were strafed. Sub Lt(P) Ian MacDonald, a Sea Fury pilot with 805 Squadron, recalled:

---

[1] All three squadrons were former Royal Navy units transferred lock, stock and barrel to the Royal Australian Navy, together with their aircraft and a sprinkling of RN aircrew and non-flying officers (see Appendix VII).

[2] It is not known if the H-5 was 'The Thing', or a different machine.

"They scrambled us early and we got off early. The catapult take-off was quite something. I never really liked it but technically it was the best way of getting airborne. It was guaranteed. Even if you lost your engine halfway down the slot you still had enough speed to pull out of the way of the ship. It wasn't the bows we were worried about, it was those big chompers down at the other end.

On the first detail, after we'd taken off, we formed up in a flight of four, finger-four of two sections. Keith Clarkson had briefed us after we had got the briefing from the Intelligence Officers. We had a quiet little huddle. He said we were bound to see this trench, a standard zig-zag trench, and we'd go in a longish line astern, fire rockets – two at a time – just to see the lay of the land. He said he wanted us to put them in the point of the vee so that the blast would go both ways – and that's what we did with 32 rockets. We then started to strafe. From the moment we did that we could see we had done a lot of damage with the rockets but there were still some fellows left sneaking away down at the western end. George [Lt(P) G.McC. Jude] spotted them doing this and he said to Keith, 'If you attack from the south-east to the north-west, we'll come in from the south-west to the north-east so that which ever section of the vee they get into, we'll catch them one way or the other.' That's what we did and I don't think there was one soldier left alive. The guerrillas got out. They weren't fired on after we'd finished. The attack lasted about thirty minutes."

Next day 32 offensive and 15 defensive sorties were flown, with one aircraft – Lt Cdr(P) Walter Bowles' Sea Fury – suffering light flak damage. A flight of Fireflies knocked out a span of a major road bridge west of Chinnampo, and several buildings were destroyed and others set on fire. The standard offensive load for the Fireflies was two 500-lb bombs, while the Sea Furies normally carried eight rockets. Two Fireflies, those flown by the CO, Lt Cdr(P) Ron Lunberg, and his Senior Pilot Lt Cdr(P) M.W. Wotherspoon RN, both had trouble with their landing hooks and ended up in the barrier when they returned from anti-submarine patrols. Only 27 sorties were flown on 7 October before flying was halted because *Sydney* had to take on fuel in the afternoon, but earlier activities included the bombing of a rail bridge at Haeju, a rocket attack on a barge south of Kyomipo and a successful impromptu air spot for the frigate *Amethyst*. Small-arms fire continued to be a major problem, and three Sea Furies returned with damage. One of these was Lt(P) P.W. Seed's aircraft (140). He and his wingman, Sub Lt(P) R.R. Sinclair, were carrying out a low level recce of Chinnampo waterfront when a 20mm shell hit Seed's aircraft, severing the elevator tab wires and rudder cable. Seed had to divert to Kimpo where he landed safely without rudder control.

After a few days of experimentation, *Sydney's* personnel had just about perfected their methods of coping with high-intensity carrier operations. Captain Harries' aim was to fly 54 sorties per day, divided into five sections. The shortness of the winter days and the distances the aircraft had to fly to their targets made more than this very difficult to achieve, despite flying off the first aircraft at dawn. Managing three squadrons, totalling some 36 aircraft, pressed *Sydney's* facilities to the limit and 20 aircraft had to be kept parked on the busy deck. These machines were manned and started up during all take-off periods so that any unserviceable aircraft in the range could be replaced immediately. An emergency party of armourers stood by to remove bombs and rockets so that the unserviceable aircraft's wings could be folded before going below for attention. As aircraft returned to the carrier they were divided into two groups: serviceable and unserviceable. Those that were serviceable were taken aft to the deck park for refuelling and rearming, and the unserviceable were either moved forward for attention on deck or taken below to the hangars. After the last fly-on, the aircraft in the deck park had to be lashed down securely to prevent them damaging each other as the ship moved. For bad weather, heavier lashings of steel-wire rope were used. Aircraft handlers had to be on deck from an hour before dawn, unlashing the aircraft and preparing for take-off, and remain on duty until dusk, often in very low temperatures with a break of only 30 minutes for a meal. Despite such long hours of hard physical work in all types of weather, there were seldom complaints.

While refuelling at sea, Captain Harries received orders to set course to the south to join up with the RN cruiser *Belfast* for passage to the east coast of Korea, escorted by five destroyers.

Admiral George C. Dyer USN, commanding TF95, had ordered Admiral Scott-Moncrieff to make a co-ordinated air and surface strike against suspected enemy positions near Kojo, 30 miles south-east of Wonsan. Scott-Moncrieff was not told either the purpose or the scale of the bombardment but he later deduced that the prime object of the strike was to provide a spectacle on the east coast for Vice-Admiral Sir Guy Russell, C-in-C Far East Station, who was visiting from Hong Kong.

The Kojo strikes began on 10 October and *Sydney*'s aircraft flew 55 sorties on the first day. Damage was estimated as seven large barrack buildings destroyed, 18 troop shelters and six boats damaged or destroyed, while the main railway line was cut in several places. Nine Fireflies were launched to strike coastal guns but these could not be located because of low cloud. While alighting back on, the Firefly flown by Sub Lt(P) Neil MacMillan suffered minor damage. The Sea Furies were also busy, strafing and rocketing troop concentrations in a village south of Kojo. In so doing, Sub Lt(P) F.T. Lane's aircraft was damaged slightly by the blast of his own rockets, while Sub Lt(P) MacDonald's machine collected a couple of bullet holes. With a maximum effort, closer targets and good weather, 11 October became an exceptional day in which *Sydney* equalled *Glory*'s record of 89 sorties in one day. Seven sections were flown from first launch at 0625 to last recovery at 1650. Sea Furies from 808 Squadron started the day with a rocket attack on a reported bivouac area, where at least two houses were destroyed and a large fire was started with smoke towering up to 5,000 feet. Throughout the day the villages of Ch'onch'on and Tonghow were targeted and severely damaged. In addition, all three squadrons spotted for shoots with *Belfast* which was joined by the battleship USS *New Jersey* and two destroyers for what would be the biggest sea bombardment of 1951. The battleship's massive 16-inch guns destroyed the villages of Kirin-ni and Singhung-ni and, during the bombardment of the latter, *Sydney*'s airmen reported seeing about 1,000 enemy troops, plus stores dumps on ridges and hills covering the beaches, apparently reinforcements being built up to oppose any landing. The day climaxed with an attack by 16 Sea Furies on these troops and it was estimated at least 200 were killed. As the ships withdrew, an ammunition dump exploded, the result of one of the many fires still burning in the vicinity. Three aircraft suffered minor flak damage. Lt(P) George Brown of 808 Squadron, a former WWII RAAF fighter pilot, recalled:

"The targets were mostly heavy guns or important store dumps. Watching the fall of fire from the air, we'd direct fire on the targets by radio. The bigger the ship the better the result. I remember spotting for an American cruiser which was 15 miles off shore and getting wonderfully good results. That was pretty good shooting. Those heavy shells landing plunk into the targets from an invisible source miles out to sea was indication enough that we had complete command of the sea. The enemy's only answer to these sort of tactics was wonderfully good camouflage. Individual soldiers wrapped themselves in straw mats and lay still for hours. They were fond of hiding guns in haystacks.

In winter the air was crystal clear, with the landscape visible for miles, sparkling with ice and snow. Mostly we could fly every day, dodging around snowstorms and bad weather. Once we used a snowstorm to sneak up on some barges near the Yalu. We were warm enough in our planes. Too hot, sometimes, in our rubber immersion suits. These were designed to keep out the cold if we had to ditch in freezing waters. Normally the deck landing parties had all the discomfort of snow and ice and bad weather. We flew around in warm cockpits and took refuge in the warmed interior of *Sydney* during our non-operational hours." [3]

A few days later *Sydney* received congratulatory signals, including one from the British Chief of Naval Staff:

"I would add my congratulations to a personal message I have received from First Sea Lord conveying his congratulations on HMAS *Sydney*'s outstanding performance on her first operational patrol."

And another from the Commander-in-Chief, Far East Station:

---

[3] See *Australia and the Korean War* by Robert O'Neill.

"Your air effort in the last two days has been unprecedented in quantity and high in quality. It has been a magnificent achievement on which I warmly congratulate you. Eighty-nine sorties in one day is grand batting by any standard, especially in the opening match."

Sydney arrived at Sasebo on the 12th to refuel and re-arm before undertaking her next patrol off the west coast. She had been in port about 24 hours when informed of a tropical typhoon called 'Ruth' heading towards Sasebo. Captain Harries was told to be at immediate notice to sail by 0900 on the 14th. The carrier's Lt Cdr (Flying) was Lt Cdr(P) Roland Hain, who remembered:

". . . Sasebo is an almost completely land-locked harbour with a narrow entrance and surrounded by hills of up to 2,000 feet in height. It had been chosen by the Imperial Japanese Navy as a typhoon anchorage and the harbour was liberally provided with buoys on mooring of great strength where, theoretically, it was possible to ride out any gale. The theory proved to be correct when enquiries were made afterwards. But the decision (to put to sea) once made could not be altered and the work of preparing for sea was commenced with all speed.

The flight deck was always a scene of confusion during these replenishment periods. Ammunition boxes piled under the crane, crates of aircraft spares, bags of potatoes and nets of cabbages, drums of lubricating oil. Somewhere a harassed aircraft artificer would be looking for a spare space and ring bolt where he could lash down his aircraft and run up the engine he had been working on, and the chief of the flight deck would be shouting at the aircraft handlers to push the aircraft along. Soon the tremendous roar of the big engine would drown all other noises, the clang of the life-warning bells, the rattle of the Clarkat tractors over the arrester wires and the shouts of the petty officers in charge of working parties. All this had to be reduced to orderliness at top speed. Ammunition was hoisted outboard again and dumped in the lighters, moveable stores were quickly stowed, drums rolled away and the largest packing cases left on the large pontoons amidships. *Sydney* carried a full war complement of aircraft which meant that after every nook and cranny in the hangar had been filled there were still 18 over that must be stowed on deck. These must be treble-lashed against the roll and pitch that was expected. While all hands worked to the utmost ability, the wind began to rise and the leaden surface of the harbour was whipped up into short, angry waves that tumbled the small boats about and lashed their crews and passengers with spray. The cloud level descended until the summits of the hills around the harbour were hidden in the flying scud and the rain began. Ashore the trees bowed and swayed . . ."

Condition 2, the second highest typhoon warning, was set at 0700. Admiral Scott-Moncrieff ordered the Commonwealth ships to put to sea where they were to remain hove-to until the storm passed. At 1030, *Sydney* slipped anchor and proceeded to sea. On clearing Sasebo swept channel some six hours later, course was altered to the west at a speed of 14 knots. The wind was from the north-east at Force 8. *Sydney* began to roll heavily, with the sea turning brown and torrential rain beating down on the crew working on the flight deck. It was soon impossible to walk upright. Anything not secured began to slide to and fro. Heavy objects that were badly secured started tugging at the wire of the rope that bound them. By late afternoon the typhoon was worsening and at 1527 a maximum roll of 22 degrees was recorded. To prevent damage, speed was reduced to two knots as she hove-to by heading up to the sea using the main engines just enough to hold her in position where it was hoped she would ride more safely. As daylight came to an end and darkness fell, heavy seas began striking the bows giant blows, and one of the cutters stowed on the galley deck was smashed to matchwood. By 2100, wind speed reached 70 knots. Lt Cdr Hain continued:

"A night of terror began. The huge seas pounded the ship and sent tremors from bow to stern and back again. The roll was jerky and violent. Water slanted across the deck and poured into the leeward sponsons, taxing the capacity of the scuppers to free them. Clinging to lifelines, small parties of men in glistening oilskins went from aircraft to aircraft on the flight deck. Wire lashings were slipping, securing lugs were being torn out and chocks, once displaced, disappeared over the side. In the hangar aircraft were riding it out uneasily, snatching at their lashings as the motion of the ship transferred the weight from one oleo leg to the other. At least down there men could see. In C Hangar, a power plant secured to the bulkhead with wire began to work loose. Men rushed at it and lashed it again before the two tons of metal tore itself loose and mangled them on its career of destruction across the hangar deck. Noise was everywhere. The boom of the wind, the creak of the working ship, the crash of mountainous seas against the ship's side, the hiss of spray on the deck. To add to the fears of all hands came a pipe – 'Fire, fire, fire' – but the outbreak was dealt with. Spray and sometimes solid sea water in exposed positions was shorting the cables. There were three more fire alarms that night. Fire is never a pleasant thing at sea, even worse in the middle of a typhoon aboard a vessel which carries thousands of gallons of high octane petrol.

Soon after midnight, at the very height of the storm, when a wind speed of 100 knots was registered, the first aircraft carried away. In the light of the 10-inch signalling searchlight, it was seen to collapse on to its belly, slide towards the side, hang there for a second, then disappear into the boiling seas astern. The undercarriage of an aircraft is not designed to take a side strain. As the ship's labouring grew worse, three more aircraft collapsed, tore themselves clear of their lashings and vanished. The men who had tended them for months watched them go helplessly. They had done everything possible to keep them, but it seemed that the forces of nature were determined to show that, when the occasion demanded, they could produce an appalling strength which made all men's efforts to counteract them puny and unavailing. As the aircraft went over the side they ruptured their long-range tanks and soon the flight deck and gun sponsons aft had something more deadly than water swilling over them. By the grace of God no spark made an inferno of the ship then.

The centre of the typhoon moved gradually away. As dawn broke, parties of men who had been sheltering in the island were sent out to re-secure what was left on the flight deck and assess the damage. Apart from the aircraft lost overboard, many others had been damaged. A Clarkat tractor had broken loose and smashed through a Bofors gun before going over the side. Two boats were stove in and some of the others damaged, while the little motor dinghy had vanished from its stowage place under the crane. In gradually clearing weather and abating seas, *Sydney* steamed back to Sasebo looking as if a Kamikaze had struck her . . ."

Only one aircraft, Firefly WB396, was actually lost overboard but six others were considered complete write-offs. Another Firefly (WB516/207), ended up in a gun sponson, while Lt(P) Guy Beange's Sea Fury (WE673/135) had made several determined attempts to plunge over the side but it was thwarted every time by the deck hook engaging a bow-spring. This caused a shower of sparks as the aircraft had somehow become live. Captain Harries stated afterwards it was the worst sea he had ever experienced. Fortunately, injuries to personnel were restricted to cuts and bruises but the material damage from the typhoon was estimated at £250,000, a huge sum in the 1950s. Other ships had suffered also. Screening *Sydney* during the height of the storm was the Dutch destroyer *Van Galen*. Captain Harries sent her a signal that she need not keep station but back came the reply requesting she stay due to the damage she had suffered. A dozen other vessels were wrecked including the USN troop transport K*ongo Maru* with 500 US troops on board, which ended up aground on Ukushima, an island 35 miles west of Sasebo. At Sasebo, most ships suffered superficial damage. At Iwakuni, one of 209 Squadron's Sunderlands (RN277) was blown ashore.

Sydney headed back toward Sasebo at about 0800, reaching harbour four hours later. Aircraft that were written off in the typhoon were sent over to *Unicorn* by lighter and exchanged for replacement machines. Two days later *Sydney* sailed for the west coast of Korea for further operations in the Han estuary area. The diarist for 805 Squadron noted:

> "The peace talks seem to be progressing so we may only be lucky enough to complete a couple of tours. However we may intimidate Kaesong one way or the other."

Operations began on the 18th, and this operational tour, which lasted until the 28th, saw the Fireflies focusing mainly on railway bridges and tunnels, while the Sea Furies went after coastal shipping and troop concentrations. 54 sorties were flown on the first day and several targets were successfully attacked by 817 Squadron aircraft. The first Sea Fury section from 808 Squadron attacked a target recommended by the 5th Air Force – gun positions and an estimated 1,500 troops at the northern tip of the peninsula near Pungsan. When they arrived no movement could be seen and the defences appeared deserted. A nearby building was strafed and rocketed. Targets on the northern banks of the Han and west of the Vesong river were attacked by 805 Squadron. Villages were rocketed and strafed but no movements were seen and no fires started, although several buildings were destroyed. Later, Fireflies dive-bombed a rail bridge north of Haeju and struck storage buildings at Sinch'on where box-cars and a barracks were strafed. On returning to the carrier, Lt(P) W.E. Dunlop's Firefly bounced on its main wheels, caught the fourth wire and its propeller pecked the deck. The same thing happened to Sub Lt(P) MacMillan. Neither aircraft suffered major damage.

53 sorties were flown against a variety of targets on 19 October. The primary target, the Han River area, was completely clouded over, as was most of Korea. Six Sea Furies of 805 Squadron led by Lt(P) Keith Clarkson were airborne at 0700 and eventually found a hole in the clouds. Rocket and strafing attacks were made on six villages causing fires in two of them. The area east of Haeju was easily recognisable by the chimney which protruded above the cloud. The same six pilots were airborne again at 1100 for a recce to Hanch'on. The weather was still poor inland so targets of opportunity along the coastal areas were attacked on the return journey, including barracks-type buildings at Kuryon-ni which were rocketed, one building being blown to pieces and the other seen collapsing. Earthworks and trenches were strafed nearby after movement was seen, after which men were observed running from the area, several of whom were strafed and apparently killed. Railway trucks at Wonum-ni were strafed until ammunition was expended and two box-cars were set on fire. Lt(P) Clarkson's aircraft collected a bullet hole, the only damage inflicted on the Sea Furies.

Lt Cdrs(P) Mike Fell and Walter Bowles, the latter a New Zealander in the RAN, led six more Sea Furies, from 808 Squadron, in a strafing attack on villages near some large pentagonal structures, which turned out to be slag heaps. Bright, orange-coloured smoke came from one house whilst another showed signs of secondary explosions. A group of men were also strafed. The flight then proceeded to Wonum-ni where more box-cars were attacked. Two direct hits on rolling stock were observed after Sub Lt(P) E.I. Webster had fired his rockets. Other targets included a camouflaged gunboat in the Chinnampo area and the factory area at Kyomipo together with junks and buildings along the waterfront. Three Sea Furies were damaged by flak, one aircraft being hit in the fuel tank, another in the engine and the third in the tailfin. Meanwhile, four Fireflies that were unable to attack their designated target, a bridge, bombed a large building at Ullyul and others struck at targets at Sinch'on and Ongjin.

On 20 October, despite the peace talks being held at Panmunjom, operations continued unabated. Poor visibility over the whole of the assigned target area resulted in a cessation of flying at 1330 after 33 sorties had been flown. Prior to that, 808 Squadron Sea Furies destroyed a large building at Yonan and aircraft from both 808 and 805 were directed to attack the Han area, where villages and woods alleged to be hiding troops were rocketed and strafed. North of the area four box-cars and five ox-carts were damaged. There were few targets regarded as being worthwhile in the vicinity but the weather was unsuitable for close-support so the Han villages received an additional 32 rockets and a few hundred rounds of 20mm cannon. In return, 40mm AA guns opened up but none of the aircraft were damaged.

In response to urgent calls from guerrilla forces, which reported a junk-borne invasion of the island of Taehwa-so in the Yalu Gulf, six rocket-carrying Sea Furies from 805 Squadron led by Lt Cdr(P) Bowles were detailed to attack motor and sail junks approximately 20 miles south-east of the Yalu. On arrival, one motor junk was seen heading for the enemy coast and this was sunk by cannon-fire. There were no survivors. More junks were observed and attacked resulting in claims for the destruction of one motor junk and six large sailing junks destroyed, plus 15 small junks damaged, this action taking place to the north and north-west of the island of Sinmi-do. Since the designated target had not been found, another six Sea Furies were sent to the area and the pilots eventually spotted three large motor junks 400 yards south of Sinmi-do. These were rocketed and strafed, causing several small explosions. One junk was armed with a machine-gun mounted aft but this was blown off during the first attack. All of these craft were left burning from stem to stern. Unfortunately, despite prior assurances that no friendly craft were in the area, two of the junks destroyed belonged to one of the UN's clandestine organisations. Because of secrecy for security reasons, the chances of occurrences like these were high, but the organisations themselves apparently deemed it an acceptable risk.

The Sea Furies also carried out their first close air support missions with the return of good weather. The pilots had been briefed to report to the ground controller for the US I Corps; on arrival, initial communications with the ground were poor but, eventually, the controller for the British Commonwealth Division asked for an attack on a village about 15 miles north-east of Munsan. This was very close to the bomb-line and since there was no FAC or smoke indication of the target available, the Sea Fury leader decided it was too risky to attack. They hit, instead, two villages further behind the bomb-line. Intense light flak was experienced but no aircraft were hit. A second section of four Sea Furies eventually located the target, entrenched troops, who were accurately rocketed and strafed. Six more Sea Furies carried out another Han area strike, during which two houses were destroyed and two others damaged. After this strike, the flight separated and proceeded in pairs to do armed reconnaissance, photographing and bomb spotting. One pair destroyed some equipment located on a ridge and strafed a village. Another pair of Sea Furies carried out a shoot with *Amethyst* but the exercise was eventually called off because no fall of shot was being observed. Later, a barracks building was destroyed and some 30 troops attacked. Meanwhile, the Fireflies were busy also. They attacked and damaged a bridge at Chinnampo, strafed a camp north of Undong-ni and the railway station at Yongwon, where rolling stock was also strafed and damaged. Altogether on 21 October, a total of 53 sorties were flown.

Having replenished at sea on the 22nd, *Sydney* was to launch a further 57 sorties next day. The Sea Furies of 808 Squadron, on the first mission, went to the far north of the Yellow Sea searching for enemy shipping. Though poor visibility restricted observation, several large sampans and junks were sighted, attacked and damaged, in addition to two troop shelters in a village south of Ch'ongju. The railway line from Ch'angyong to Chaeryong was reconnoitred and seen to be intact, while two tunnels along the way appeared to contain rolling stock. Finally, five houses were destroyed in attacks on four villages in the Imjin area. Elsewhere, Fireflies bombed railway bridges near Haeju and Ch'angyong. Other attacks were made on a railway tunnel between Haeju and Ongjin, and on targets near Sokjong-ni, while a flight of 805 Squadron's Sea Furies led by Lt Cdr(P) Bowles was despatched to the front lines for a close-support mission. I Corps sent them north to be controlled by a FAC attached to the Commonwealth Division. Communications and procedures were good this time and after the strike, the FAC indicated their target had been obliterated by rockets and cannon-fire. A signal from JOC later credited the flight with five bunkers destroyed and some 75 enemy troops killed. At 1300 Lt Cdr(P) Fell's flight was airborne and attacked targets to the east and south-east of Ongjin, where an estimated 500 North Korean troops had been reported in the target area, although no activity was seen during or after the attacks during which five houses were claimed destroyed and others damaged. A destroyed camouflaged ox-cart was scant tangible reward for the strike.

Thirteen of *Sydney*'s sorties were associated with searching for a downed B-29 crew that had baled out between Chinnampo and the Sinanju River (see Chapter IX). Sea Furies and Fireflies provided RESCAPs but it was not until 1500 that there was any sign of life when a survivor was sighted by Lt(P) Peter Seed and Sub Lt(P) Dick Sinclair. The American airman was found in water thought to be too shallow for a blockading frigate to reach him, so four 808 Squadron Sea Furies escorted Sub Lt(P) N.E. Lee's Firefly to the scene, which dropped a dinghy into which the airman was seen to climb. Despite the misgivings, the Australian frigate *Murchison* navigated through the shallows to a position close by and sent in a boat which picked the man up at 1800. Next morning, two Sea Furies acted as mine spotters and navigators for the rescue vessel as she made her way to seaward through the shallows.

High winds and difficult deck landing conditions on the 24th restricted the number of sorties to 32 as the search for other members of the downed B-29 crew continued. Two Sea Furies carried out a sweep to the north-west but nothing was seen although an F-86 was also reported to have ditched. On the return flight overland, two box-cars were attacked with rockets and a village strafed, where houses were still burning from a previous attack. With the weather unsatisfactory for operating from the carrier, flying was reduced to two combat air patrols and two RESCAPs for the remainder of the day. Although nothing was sighted over the sea leg of the patrol, approximately 20 enemy troops were found digging in as the Sea Furies returned overland, and these were strafed causing an estimated dozen casualties. The Firefly crews again demonstrated the precision of their low-level skip bombing skills during the day by placing a 500-lb bomb in the entrance of a rail tunnel. While landing on returning from this mission, Sub Lt(P) Armand Roland's aircraft caught No10 wire and entered the barrier.

The weather improved on the 25th, but the sortie rate was reduced slightly to 47 due to the carrier needing to top up its aviation fuel supply. Sea Furies of 808 Squadron carried out an armed recce to Hanch'on, which revealed no shipping, but on the return flight an enemy supply centre was rocketed and strafed. Troops were seen firing at the aircraft and during a strafing run on these, Lt(P) C.M.A. Wheatley's aircraft was hit twice and he was forced to ditch off Chinnampo. This was *Sydney*'s first combat loss. Colin Wheatley successfully abandoned his aircraft and was quickly recovered unhurt by an American air-sea rescue SA-16. He was flown to Kimpo escorted by two 805 Squadron Sea Furies. Later, another successful close-support mission was carried out with the British Commonwealth Division when six Sea Furies were directed to a village near Taegwang-ni, reported to contain troops and supplies. With the target indicated by the FAC's smoke rockets, rocket and strafing attacks were carried out despite accurate and intense AA fire. The aircraft flown by Lt Cdr(P) John Appleby, 808 Squadron's CO, was badly hit in the port wing and, as a precaution, he landed at Kimpo. Shortly thereafter, Lt Cdr(P) Fell led another Sea Fury flight to strike at houses near the Han, nine of which were claimed damaged. Two Sea Furies suffered superficial hits by anti-aircraft fire. Elsewhere, 817 Squadron was equally busy. As one flight of Fireflies attacked the rail tunnel north of Ch'angyong and backed up by strafing box-cars, another flight was busy hitting the rail tunnel north of Haeju. All aircraft returned safely.

26 October proved to be an even more expensive day for *Sydney* with the loss of a Sea Fury and a Firefly during the course of 58 sorties. The day started when four Sea Furies of 805 Squadron took off armed with two 1000-lb bombs each instead of the usual rockets. Their target was a rail bridge north of Haeju. Two near misses were recorded but no damage was caused to the bridge, which remained in service. Other targets of opportunity were strafed, including a store house and an ox-cart, while two box-cars at Chaeryong were strafed during the return flight and, when passing Haeju, two large houses were set on fire. During the next mission, Sea Furies from 808 Squadron concentrated their efforts in the area of the Han, where Sub Lt(P) Noel Knapstein's aircraft was crippled by flak. He managed to carry out a successful forced landing in the estuary, on a mudflat near a friendly island. A crowd of curious Koreans gathered to watch as a rescue boat from *Amethyst* quickly arrived on the scene. Realising that it would be completely impossible to recover the stranded aircraft, the men from the destroyer salvaged what they could and then the resourceful Knapstein sold the remnants of the wreck to the Koreans! Pocketing an immensely satisfying wad of notes to the value of 1,000 Wong, he was duly returned to *Sydney* with his pockets literally bulging where it was realised that his small fortune was just that – small. It amounted to exactly one shilling and ninepence, less than 50 cents!

Meanwhile, Sea Furies from 805 Squadron and Fireflies were also busy carrying out strikes, adding more buildings, ox-carts, box-cars, sampans and a railway bridge to the tally. On the last strike of the afternoon, five Fireflies attacked and closed both ends of a railway tunnel north-east of Chaeryong. It was while attacking this tunnel that they ran into intense flak. Sub Lt(P) Neil MacMillan, the pilot of Firefly WB316/204, later reported:

> "We were to carry out a low-level run, endeavouring to place our bombs, fused for a 25-second delay, into the mouth of the tunnel. On the run-in, I was positioned about 300 yards astern, and just below, my section leader, who was strafing the tunnel entrance as an anti-flak precaution. It was prior to releasing my bombs that I saw what I thought to be ammunition links from my leader's aircraft passing over my canopy. This was later ascertained to have been tracer from a flak position near the entrance to the tunnel. At no time during this period had I felt any hits on my aircraft.

After releasing my bombs I pulled away and at the same time my observer, Phil Hancox, informed me that we had been hit. The port nacelle tank was streaming fuel, while the starboard wing had two six-inch holes in it, one through the gun-bay, the other through the roundel. I immediately informed my section leader of the damage and asked him to come and check my aircraft for any further signs of hits. As I did this I smelt burning in the cockpit and on checking the engine instruments found the pressure to be reading zero. At this time my altitude was 1,000 feet, so I immediately switched off the engine and fuel and told my leader that I was carrying out a forced landing, there being quite a few paddy-fields in the area. I had to abandon the field I had first chosen due to high tension lines across my approach path. I chose another and my observer jettisoned our canopies. I failed to jettison my nacelle tanks. The approach and landing was quite satisfactory, the aircraft coming to rest at the intersection of two large ditches in the western corner of the field. The time of landing was 1555. The nacelle tanks remained on the aircraft and the radio was still working. However, not knowing what enemy concentrations were in the area, my observer and I cleared the aircraft at once. It was later pointed out at FEAFHQ that enemy troops had been ordered to shoot at the cockpits of forced-down aircraft for the very purpose of preventing the survivors from using the radio."

MacMillan and Hancox had crash-landed in the heart of enemy territory, some ten miles south of Sariwon and 75 miles away from the carrier. Neither man was injured but their situation was far from pleasant. It seemed extremely doubtful if *Sydney*'s helicopter could reach them and fly clear of enemy territory before nightfall. The two airmen moved about 50 yards along the ditch running east to west, MacMillan carrying his parachute and Hancox the Owen submachine-gun, his navigation bag and maps. They placed out their yellow fluorescent panels as a signal to the remainder of the flight and surveyed the scene. About 200 yards to the north-west of their position was a small group of houses and two people wearing white robes, apparently civilians, could be seen peering at the aircraft through a picket fence. They were not the main concern, however, as about a mile to the west was a knoll some 200 feet high from which a concentrated stream of automatic fire was being directed at the circling RESCAP aircraft.

On receiving the news of the downed aircraft, Captain Harries decided to make a rescue attempt despite the lateness of the day. The decision was received with enthusiasm by the on-duty American helicopter crew, CPO Arlene K. Babbitt USN and Airman Callus C. Gooding USN, and they prepared the H-5 for the mission. The helicopter lacked instruments for night flying and was unarmed so Gooding took a couple of Owen machine-guns. This marked the beginning of a remarkable rescue operation. The welcome news was conveyed to MacMillan and Hancox by one of the RESCAP aircraft which fired a green Very cartridge to tell them that help was on the way. About five minutes had passed since landing.

At this time, four of 805 Squadron's Sea Furies led by Lt Cdr(P) Fell were busy in the Han area attacking the usual targets, including some camouflaged positions and supply dumps near a railway line to the west of Kaesong. They had just rocketed an enemy HQ at Haeju, causing a thick volume of smoke to issue from the buildings, when the call came to fly RESCAP over the downed Firefly. Word had also gone out and a flight of Meteors from 77RAAF at Kimpo soon joined them. Meanwhile, the helicopter had taken off from *Sydney* and was on its way. Down on the ground, MacMillan and Hancox were heartened by the presence of the aircraft overhead and ready to defend their position if they came under attack. MacMillan wrote in his report:

"We then noticed several men situated on the knoll to the west, looking in the direction of the aircraft. Through the binoculars we identified them as enemy troops. However, they disappeared over the side of the hill and we did not see them again. 45 minutes after landing, the Air Group Commander [Lt Cdr(P) Fell] flew low over our position and dropped a message in a container, which landed about 25 feet from the edge of the ditch. The message was a welcome one, stating that the ETA of the rescue helicopter was 1730 . . ."

In his flight low over the stranded airmen, Lt Cdr (P) Fell's Sea Fury was hit by flak. He had to leave the area and divert to Kimpo where he landed safely with only about an eighth of an inch of movement on his ailerons. At 1715 the Meteors had to depart and the Sea Fury pilots also, being at the limit of their endurance, were instructed to go although Lts(P) J.H.G. Cavanagh and J.R.N. Salthouse courageously decided to hold on for a few minutes longer. MacMillan continued:

"... Hancox and I kept a look-out for signs of enemy activity and awaited the arrival of the helicopter. At 1720 we heard two bursts of machine-gun fire nearby. Looking over the edge of the ditch we saw a Chinese soldier about 100 yards away, who immediately started waving his arms about and shouting – no doubt calling on us to surrender. At that moment Observer Hancox saw the helicopter coming, so I opened fire on the soldier with the Owen gun. He very smartly dived into the ditch running at right angles to ours. I then placed the red panel alongside the yellow, pointing to the enemy. This was the Air Group's signal meaning that we were being fired on from the direction indicated. At once two Sea Furies dived and strafed the area.

By this time the helicopter was on its way down, while the aircrewman in it was firing his sub-machine-gun at the enemy troops. The helicopter landed some 20 feet from our position, alongside the ditch. I fired several rounds at the enemy position as Hancox climbed aboard, and then I followed him – at the rush. As we were taking off one of the enemy stood up to fire at the helicopter, whereupon he was shot by Aircrewman Gooding."

Lts(P) Cavanagh and Salthouse remained with the helicopter and escorted it to Kimpo. The trip was uneventful except that the last 30 minutes had to be flown in darkness. MacMillan and Hancox were already known at Kimpo, as Cpl Pat Melican of 77RAAF recalled:

"There were a few occasions when Australian pilots who had been shot down or forced down over North Korean territory were rescued by American helicopters. Two of these were from 77 Squadron and the other was a Navy pilot, Neil MacMillan, with whom I was mildly acquainted. He came into Kimpo on two occasions while I was there. The first time was when he just appeared out of the blue and taxied his Firefly onto our hard standing after having sighted the Meteors on his landing run. I walked over to find out why it had come to Kimpo and recognised him as he was leaving the cockpit. He told me that the reason for his visit was to have a bomb removed from his aircraft which had hung up, its non-release having been advised to him by another Firefly on the same mission. His flight commander had told him to have it removed because he could not be permitted to land back onto the carrier with a live bomb. At the time, the USAF base at Suwon was the nearest likely place to get the bomb removed but, when he told the tower there why he wanted to land, they said he'd have to go elsewhere because they had a lot of returning aircraft on the way back. They would be put at risk if his live bomb were to be dislodged in the landing and, maybe, create a large hole in the runway, plus a great deal of demolished Firefly wreckage which would compromise the chances of uneventful landings.

Neil was very understanding and headed for Kimpo, where he told the tower that he had an armament problem to attend to. I can still remember the look of horror on his face when I asked him, 'What bomb?' I could see no bomb and neither could he. It had obviously dropped off somewhere along the way. By this time, his observer-navigator mate was out on the tarmac and both of them got to work on their map to see just where they had been since making landfall. Neil needed access to a phone so I took them down to our Ops Officer, with an invitation to come to the Airmans Bar for a drink after they'd been fed. When he arrived later in the evening, we had another minor reunion as quite a few of the ground staff he knew from his training days were then in 77. Neil had a small problem which I was able to bring to a happy ending. He had managed to become the owner of a US issue .45 automatic but didn't have a holster for it, so I volunteered to go over to the Yank lines and scrounge one for him. This was easy as I knew a Yank who had all manner of bits and pieces that could be used for trading and, in the parlance of the business of favour, he owed me one. All told, we had a good night. His next visit was per courtesy of a Yank chopper which extracted him and his observer from imminent capture when they were shot down during a ground-attack mission." [4]

---

[4] Shortly after leaving the RAN in 1960, Lt(P) Neil MacMillan was killed in a helicopter crash.

The rescued airmen were lavish in their praise of the American helicopter crew for their devotion to duty in travelling 120 miles to effect the rescue, knowing full well that they could not return to friendly base before nightfall. CPO Babbitt and Aircrewman Gooding were each subsequently awarded the Royal Navy's Distinguished Service Medal, Babbitt also receiving the US Navy Cross, for this daring rescue. Commenting further, Captain Harries reported:

> "Apart from the fine performance of the helicopter's crew, the whole rescue organisation worked with copybook exactitude, and it was felt that the ship's Guardian Angel had had a very hard-working and successful day."

Captain Harries had researched the question of rescue very carefully, and was responsible for the introduction of fluorescent panels carried by all of *Sydney*'s aircrew. These had proved their value. On two occasions when aircraft had crashed in enemy territory, the crew of the rescuing aircraft had seen the panels long before they sighted the downed airmen. Admiral Scott-Moncrieff lost no time in recommending the general adoption of this idea to the Commander of the 7th Fleet and to Admiral Dyer.

These dramatic events brought to a close *Sydney*'s second patrol, its Air Group thus far having flown 654 sorties (474 offensive and 180 defensive) for the loss of two Sea Furies and a Firefly. A further 23 aircraft had been damaged by flak, mostly small-arms fire. This patrol had itself witnessed 389 sorties and the expenditure of in excess of 95,000 rounds of 20mm ammunition, 1,472 rockets, eight 1,000-lb bombs and 174 500-lb bombs. At the end of flying on the 26th, *Sydney* set course for Kure where she arrived two days later and where MacMillan and Hancox rejoined the carrier. She remained at Kure until 2 November for re-arming and refuelling.

November 1951

Admiral Scott-Moncrieff left Sasebo aboard *Belfast* on 3 November and embarked in the USS *Rendova* to see for himself how the Americans operated. He was given a very cordial welcome and a thoroughly enjoyable day aboard the American carrier by Captain E. Fickling USN and his officers and men. The 18 aircraft available flew 60 sorties. Operations included an air spot for a bombardment by the Australian frigate *Murchsion*, destruction of supply craft in the inland waterways, close air support for I Corps and the customary strikes in the Han estuary. The Admiral addressed the pilots, and was left in no doubt that the US Marine Corps VMF-212 was a fine unit. Admiral Scott-Moncrieff was made an Honorary member and presented with a leather jacket emblazoned with VMF-212's colourful insignia.

Meanwhile, *Sydney* departed from Kure for her third patrol off the west coast of Korea on 4 November. She relieved *Rendova* next day, when Admiral Scott-Moncrieff hoisted his flag in her for a couple of days on board before leaving for Sasebo on the 7th. On board *Sydney* was the RN Dragonfly HR1 helicopter VZ965 and its pilot Lt(P) C.W. Perry RN.

Poor weather greeted the first day of operations. Sea Furies on a FAC-controlled strike for the US 1st Cavalry Division destroyed a number of buildings, while another Sea Fury flight strafed box-cars in the Sindok area and carried out a reconnaissance in the Han area, attacking troop positions and loaded box-cars in sidings. Lt(P) Keith Clarkson led one of the 805 Squadron sections. Troop concentrations were rocketed and strafed, followed by an armed reconnaissance heading north from Pakch'on. It was during this reconnaissance that Clarkson's aircraft (WE674/103) was hit as he was making a strafing run on what appeared to be a truck. His aircraft rolled over on its back and dived into the ground, breaking into pieces. 29-year-old Clarkson from Melbourne, a successful WWII former RAAF fighter pilot, was killed. Sub Lt(P) Ian MacDonald recalled:

> ". . . Lt Clarkson was shot down. I was about 200 yards behind him when he bought it. At the bottom of a strafing run he rolled to his right, then rolled straight back and hit the ground on his back, doing about 380 knots. We assume they shot him by the way he went out of control. It was a flak trap. It looked as if it could have been a truck covered with branches. We think it was really an ox-cart. It was in a bend with a little hill nearby and that hill was smothered with Chinese machine-guns. He just ran into a wall of fire. We all went into it. It's interesting to hear bullets hitting your aeroplane. It's like putting your head into a kettle

drum and having somebody go bing, bing, bing, bing! Not good."

Although there was no sign of life, two Sea Furies carried out RESCAP over the area while the third returned to the carrier to report the loss. A few enemy troops were seen and these were strafed and rocketed. Both aircraft took hits from ground fire, one picking up a couple of 20mm holes and a bullet that nearly severed the rudder control. Running short of fuel, they diverted to land at Kimpo. In other operations, a highly successful close support mission was flown by 808 Squadron for the US 1st Cavalry Division, the Sea Furies under the direction of a FAC putting their rockets on target to within 200 yards of friendly troops. Other sections strafed box-cars in the Sindok area while, on the daily recce run to Hanch'on, several sampans were destroyed and a gun position and troop shelters were hit with rockets. The Fireflies bombed three bridges at Wonto, Yongnam-ni and to the north at Haeju, and carried out a shoot in the Han estuary with *Murchison*. It was noted with interest by the aircrew that all of the bridges and tunnels destroyed during the previous patrol had now been repaired.

Even though the weather was poor with low cloud on the 6th, a full programme of 55 sorties was flown but the effectiveness of the missions was hampered by the conditions. The day included two special operations. At dawn four Sea Furies from 808 Squadron joined *Belfast* and the Canadian destroyer *Athabaskan* in a decoy operation in the hope of drawing the fire from and therefore expose the shore batteries of Amgak, the peninsula opposite the island of Sok-to, south of Taedong. Possibly the Communists were suspicious, or had been tipped off, because the guns did not open fire and disclose their positions. The aircraft proceeded to rocket and strafe the area in general but no guns were observed. Either they were not there or they were well camouflaged. 805 Squadron's first mission called for eight Sea Furies to attack junks and small craft around the Ch'orusan peninsula and along the north side of Ka-do, where one 70-foot junk, five 40-foot junks and three sampans were destroyed, and a dozen sampans damaged. There was some light flak in the area but only one aircraft was hit. It was regarded as a quiet mission with good results. Other Sea Fury sections strafed and rocketed box-cars at Sugyo-ri, while Fireflies bombed road bridges near Mungjon-ni, Chiwiya-ri and Haeju as well as a rail bridge near Haeju. The almost immediate repair of bridges by the enemy prompted the use of dropping delayed-action bombs as well as the usual ordnance. It was hoped this would somewhat discourage the overnight repair teams. Retaliation came that afternoon with an attack on Taehwa-do, to the south of Ka-do, by eleven Chinese Communist Air Force Tu-2s, the Chinese using their light bombers for the first time while UN fighters in the south were grounded by poor weather (see Chapter IX). Following this, reports were received that the island was being invaded and ROK forces were fighting North Korean marines. It was ascertained that it was in fact Tan-do, a few miles north-east of the reported Taehwa-do, that had previously been occupied by the enemy. *Athabaskan* was ordered to support the guerrillas on Taehwa-do and was followed by *Belfast*. The two vessels subsequently evacuated air raid casualties to Paengyong-do.

With snow starting to fall on the battle front on 7 November, the *Sydney*'s Air Group flew 53 sorties, including another close-support mission for the Commonwealth Division, attacking enemy bunkers and troops. An armed reconnaissance from Haeju to Chaeryong yielded nothing but a group of box-cars, which were attacked and damaged. The last Sea Fury section attacked targets in the Han area. Guerrilla leaders had forwarded information of troops sheltering in three villages, which were targeted. Fires were started in all three with an estimated ten houses destroyed. Later, two suspected enemy vehicles were seen in another village and although hits were obtained no result was observed. The Fireflies attacked bridges at Sinch'on, Yonan and the southern end of the Allyong reservoir. One rail bridge had a span removed and a delayed-action bomb was placed on another span.

Fireflies spent the next day (8 November) bombing targets at Haeju, Wonto and west of Samch'on. Two more rail bridges were put out of action. 808 Squadron's Sea Furies carried out close-support sorties for the Commonwealth Division, being directed by a FAC onto 40 enemy troops in trenches and bunkers on a ridge. The trenches were rocketed and strafed and it was estimated that 25 troops had been killed. 805 Squadron's Han reconnaissance mission struck at two villages reported to contain troops, and two houses were destroyed with three damaged. 9

November was a refuelling day without flying but, on the 10th, *Sydney* was back on station and 55 sorties were flown. The Firefly campaign against the enemy's rail bridges continued with attacks on bridges at Sariwon, Wonto and Chinnampo, while Sea Furies attacked craft along the Chinnampo waterfront, including a 50-foot steel-hulled vessel. Two sampans and two ox-carts were also destroyed. A close-support mission for the Commonwealth Division saw six Sea Furies of 805 Squadron strike at targets allocated by the 25th Canadian Brigade.

By Armistice Day 1951, with the cease-fire negotiations seemingly close to agreement, *Sydney*'s aircraft again flew 53 sorties with almost monotonous routine, although all flights were potentially fraught with danger. Directed by a FAC, Sea Furies provided close-support to the 28th Infantry Brigade on US I Corps front, where they rocketed and strafed enemy troops in bunkers. Intense small-arms and 20mm AA fire damaged two aircraft. Fireflies meanwhile bombed a rail bridge south of Chaeryong and another, plus a road bridge, near Ongjin. Extremely bad weather on 12 November restricted the day's work to just 22 sorties, but one of these was the 1,000th operational sortie for *Sydney*'s Air Group. The Sea Furies attacked three troop concentrations in the Han area, destroying several houses and large buildings with rockets and by strafing, in addition to four ox-carts. Later, one flight of Fireflies bombed a rail bridge at Yongwon, and it was on returning from this strike that Sub Lt(P) Armand Roland recorded the 1,000th operational sortie, achieved in just 19 flying days since arriving in Korean waters.

During the last day of *Sydney*'s third patrol, Sea Furies had a successful run to Hanch'on resulting in the destruction of a junk and eight sampans, while two box-cars were destroyed when rolling stock was rocketed and strafed at Wonam-ni. A close-support mission was flown for the Commonwealth Division, and another resulted in one junk being sunk and two others damaged, plus five sampans sunk and another four damaged. Despite low cloud, the Fireflies bombed bridges at Allyong reservoir and at Wonto, and another flight dive-bombed the village of Chihyon-ni. At the end of this patrol, Captain Harries reported:

> ". . . on 13 November no railway line was serviceable in the area covered by my aircraft, each one having at least one bridge down or one line cut."

While Lt Cdr(P) Ron Lunberg, CO of 817 Squadron, noted:

> "It is of interest that over 400 Air Group sorties were flown during the last patrol, which reflects credit on everyone who helped to make such an achievement possible. It was also noted that as the aircrew gained in experience the percentage of aircraft hit by flak showed a considerable drop."

From 14-17 November, *Sydney* was at Sasebo replenishing in preparation for its fourth patrol. There, she offloaded the RN Dragonfly since it had been unserviceable for most of the patrol. By contrast, the USN H-5 seemed to be in a permanent state of serviceability.

On 18 November, the Australian carrier sailed to begin her fourth Korean patrol, this time off the east coast to take part in Operation 'Athenaeum', an attack designed to destroy the installations, defences and communications of the industrial centre and port of Hungnam, which was to be conducted by naval forces under the command of Admiral Scott-Moncrieff, now flying his flag in *Belfast*. The shore batteries at Hungnam had been markedly aggressive at considerable ranges against patrolling minesweepers and destroyers so opposition to the operation was expected. Reconnaissance photographs showed that Hungnam had been nearly devastated already by USAF bombing but there were still considerable numbers of prefabricated-type buildings in or around the area. Five air strikes were planned for each day, while anti-submarine patrols were to be carried out by USN Mariners for the duration of the operations, freeing *Sydney* from this duty.

On the morning of the start of the attack, the weather was clear. Since the large buildings and warehouses of the port were *Sydney*'s primary targets, all Fireflies and most Sea Furies carried bombs. Taking off at 0710, Sea Furies of 805 Squadron were first over the port, and for the first time in this theatre they employed dive-bombing tactics to attack targeted buildings. Five tall buildings were destroyed and six were damaged. An armed reconnaissance after this strike damaged four junks and six sampans. Although flak was generally slight and inaccurate, two aircraft returned with battle-damage. One of these, Lt(P) Oakley's Firefly (243), caught the No10 wire and ended up in the barrier, while Lt(P) M.H. Simpson's Firefly 'pecked the deck' with its propeller. After the last recovery at 1600, the ships withdrew and three rocket-firing ships moved into position and rocketed the town for 35 minutes. To Admiral Scott-Moncrieff's surprise, no enemy shore batteries had so far returned fire on the ships. He suspected that the enemy was anticipating an invasion and so holding his fire until UN landing craft were deployed. This supposition was strengthened when, throughout the night, the beaches were floodlit by the enemy and occasional star shells were fired.

Next day, 65 sorties were flown, most of them similar to the strikes of the previous day, resulting in the destruction of 29 large buildings, with many others damaged, while at least three ox-carts were also targeted and destroyed. During an attack by six Fireflies on a rail tunnel just north of Hungnam there occurred a secondary explosion and the tunnel was blocked. At 1700 the ships departed after an apparently successful operation. *Sydney*'s aircraft had flown 113 sorties in two days (78 by the Sea Furies, 35 by the Fireflies) of which 78 were strike and 38 CAP over the carrier and bombarding ships. An official release reported the success of the operation in glowing terms:

> "Shortly after dawn the ships opened fire on known AA positions to silence them before the Sea Fury and Firefly aircraft swooped down to carry out the first of ten attacks against barracks, industrial plants, stores and rail communications. Alternate with air attacks were bombardments from the cruiser and destroyers carried out with aircraft spotting the fall of shot and directing it on to selected targets. Fires were started and a large number of selected targets destroyed. In the evening the rocket ships moved slowly into positions close inshore, covered by the bombarding forces. For 35 minutes these three ships rammed their rockets down on the city area, causing much damage to war industries. During the two days over 200 tons of explosive fell on Hungnam while *Sydney*'s aircraft flew more than 100 sorties."

But 805 Squadron's diarist was sceptical about the merits of the operation:

> "From the pilots' point of view – a most uninteresting operation and we can now only wait and hope that future records will show that it was worth the effort. On completion of flying the ship set course to return to the west coast to complete our patrol."

By now winter had set in and *Sydney* spent the 22nd on passage to the west coast in deteriorating weather conditions, with rough seas, strong winds and snow showers. The remainder of this patrol was to become notable for its appalling weather. Only 31 sorties were achieved on 24 November, one flight of Fireflies being unable to reach its target, while other aircraft attacked bridges and villages as detailed. Having replenished at sea next day, *Sydney*'s aircraft were able to manage only seven sorties on the 26th when Sea Furies carried out a strike against a nominated village. However, dawn on 27 November brought with it good weather, allowing a full day of flying totalling 60 sorties. Fireflies attacked the village of Orijong which was reportedly housing Chinese troops, and four bridges – one between Ch'angyong and Sinch'on, one to the east at Ch'angyong, one at Wonto, and one between Haeju and Yonan. On returning from one of these sorties, Lt Cdr(P) Wotherspoon caused a sensation when his Firefly entered the barrier via the gun sponson aft of the bridge. During the day Sea Furies flew a close-support mission for the Commonwealth Division, successfully hitting enemy bunkers on top of a hill while other flights destroyed four houses in the Han estuary and damaged several more. Four loaded box-cars were also located and duly strafed near Sariwon. One aircraft was damaged by flak and Lt(P) P. Goldrick of 808 Squadron had to land his Sea Fury at Kimpo because of trouble with its throttle.

The 28th was the last day of *Sydney*'s fourth patrol and the weather allowed another full day's flying, with 54 sorties flown. Two more rail bridges were destroyed by the Fireflies, the bridges north and south of Allyong reservoir and at Wonto being attacked, once again making all rail lines unserviceable in the carrier's area of operation. At Hanch'on, observation posts including one appearing to have radar, were strafed by Sea Furies, which then located a large number of troops digging in near P'yongyang. These were attacked with 20mm cannon and rockets, during which many were killed. Another section strafed a box-car and a junk. The enemy always retaliated and the aircraft flown by Lt Cdr(P) Bowles and Sub Lt(P) Webster were hit by AA fire while trying to locate a flak position. Another Sea Fury flight led by Lt Cdr(P) Fell repeated the attack on the troop concentration near P'yongyang, who were again apparently caught unawares. Altogether, it was estimated that at least 100 casualties were inflicted. Due to the relative brevity of this most recent patrol, and the loss of several days due to the weather, only 270 sorties were flown. By this time, cease-fire negotiations had at last made progress, and with the demarcation of the cease-fire line at last settled, operations in the Han estuary were brought to a close on the 30th. Of these operations, Admiral Scott-Moncrieff wrote:

> "Whatever the value of these operations as a contribution to the peace talks, there is not doubt that they have maintained the prestige of the Commonwealth Navies, and the determination and resolution with which they were carried through, especially by commanding officers and navigating officers, often under unpleasant, and always under trying conditions, has been in accordance with the best traditions of the Service."

November closed with the emphasis shifting to the defence of the UN-occupied islands in the Yellow Sea. Of particular importance were Paengyong-do and Cho-do where there were air-sea rescue parties and emergency landing strips on the beaches. Apart from this support for the carrier and USAF/UN airmen, it was important to retain control of Cho-do, the Tech'ong islands and Paengyong-do as a preventative measure to guard against enemy mine-laying activities.

December 1951

Between 1-4 December, *Sydney* was at Kure preparing for her next patrol. She sailed on the 5th and, on passage to the west coast of Korea, the men of the Carrier Air Group were informed of their change in priorities. They were told that the Communists had captured all the major islands in the north of the Yellow Sea and it was suspected that the islands of Cho-do and Sokto-ri would be next to be attacked. This patrol was aimed at defending them. 805 Squadron's diarist recorded:

> ". . . An invasion is feared and besides keeping a TARCAP overhead most of our air reconnaissance will be along the waterways looking for junks and barges etc. Quite a collection of craft will be available for us to attack so the patrol will be anything but dull."

Sydney was on station and ready for operations on the 7th, and suffered two losses on the very first day. The first Sea Furies up acted as CAP for the ships patrolling off Cho-do and Sokto-ri. Next, a reconnaissance of the beaches revealed many junks and sampans but their serviceability could not be assessed until photographic coverage of the area had been obtained. A search was made for a briefed target of six 20mm guns but these were not found, while an armed recce of the inland waterways for craft capable of making an amphibious assault resulted in a number of junks being rocketed and strafed. A village was also strafed but it was in this area that Sub Lt(P) A.J.B. Smith's 805 Squadron Sea Fury (possibly WE795) was hit by gunfire and he was forced to make a wheels-up landing on the beach at Paengyong-do. The RN pilot was unhurt. While carrying out strikes against other sea craft, three more Sea Furies were hit by flak, the pilot of one of them becoming the Air Group's second fatality. Sub Lt(P) Sinclair's 805 Squadron aircraft (VX728/103) was struck during a low-level run over salt flats just north-west of Chinnampo. Over the radio he called that he had been hit and could smell burning. As he gained height to about 1,500 feet, his aircraft was seen to emit flames from the underside and start a gentle dive which increased to around 60 degrees on impact. Sinclair, a 22 year-old from Western Australia, was seen to bale out at 300-400 feet but he hit the tailplane of his aircraft while doing so and was fatally injured. A helicopter from Paengyong-do later recovered his body from the mudbank on which it had fallen. Sub Lt(P) Ian MacDonald recalled:

> "Dick Sinclair, a course mate of mine, got hit and tried to bale out. We reckon he went out the wrong way. Before we went on operations we were in Kure a couple of days with HMS

Glory and they showed us a movie that they made on an alternative method of baling out. The standard method was simple – you either undid your harness, let your canopy go, climbed half out and pulled yourself out over the port side – or you could roll on your back, trim it slightly forward and just fall out. These fellows over there came up with the idea that you'd get out of your seat, sitting face forward, let your canopy go, push the side panel out, let your Sutton harness go and then stand up and turn, put your parachute and your bottom and your dinghy out the port side, and roll backwards. Now, when we saw that, everybody on board scoffed at it, except Dick. Dick said, 'I think that's a smart way of doing it.' And we think that's what happened. Nobody else wanted to do it because there are two very sharp edges of metal there that you could very easily snag your chute on and prematurely pull it open. It was the chute that opened and dragged him onto the tailplane. They sent a chopper in and got his body back. It was a horrible day. It was obvious that he'd been killed when he hit the tailplane. We buried him the next day with full honours."

During the recovery of the body Chinese troops were spotted moving across the mud to where the burning Sea Fury had come down. They were strafed and rocketed. Several bodies remained on the foreshore. Some form of revenge had been reaped. Meanwhile, the Fireflies of 817 Squadron had one of their most successful days to date, when a flight attacked a rail bridge at Wonto and another near Allyong reservoir before they strafed stores dumps along the rail lines. A second flight bombed rail bridges at Ch'ong-dan, west of Ch'ong-dan and another west of Yonan, while a third flight attacked rail lines east of Ongjin. The day's work included six bridges down, and one rail cut and one ammunition dump destroyed, with the result that four of the seven railway lines in *Sydney*'s sphere of influence were again unserviceable. Nevertheless, it became frustratingly obvious yet again that repairs were being carried out overnight, and that the successes achieved were only temporary.

After flying 54 sorties on the 7th, *Sydney* followed this up with 51 sorties next day. During 805 Squadron's second mission, led by Lt Cdr(P) Bowles, a number of junks and sampans were sighted in the vicinity of Taedong and Chaeryong. When these sightings were reported to the command ship Bowles was subsequently advised that all were enemy craft. A strike was carried out during which two junks were destroyed and six others damaged. Since invasions of both Cho-do and Sokto-ri were anticipated, Sea Furies were employed almost continuously against anything that looked as if it could be useful in amphibious landings. Junks, barges, sampans, straw-covered craft near the coast and even large piles of logs that appeared to be for raft construction were rocketed. Rolling stock in the rail yards at Sinwon-ri was attacked, as were unusually large concentrations of enemy troops in villages. Two Sea Furies were damaged when attacking a 30-foot junk sighted in a shed on Chinnampo waterfront during an afternoon coastal recce, although both returned safely. The Fireflies continued their attacks against rail bridges and two west of Chaeryong, and others west of Haeju, were hit, as was a barracks at Ongjin. Lt(P) Oakley in flak-damaged WB358 had to make a belly-landing on the beach at Paengyong-do. Neither Oakley nor his RN observer, Lt(O) J.S. Hickson, were injured and they were entertained there by the local guerrilla leader until picked up by the Australian destroyer *Tobruk*, together with 805 Squadron's Sub Lt(P) Smith, for return to *Sydney*.

On 9 December, 54 sorties were flown. The Sea Furies operated mainly against small vessels and troop concentrations. During sorties along the coast, 11 junks and 19 sampans were destroyed or damaged. 805 Squadron flew to Hanch'on and besides damaging three junks by strafing, an AA position was hit and troops rocketed and strafed, 20 bodies being counted on completion of the attack. It was thought that many more casualties must have been caused. In the afternoon, sections from both 805 and 808 Squadrons were sent to another troop concentration that had been sighted by the Fireflies. Repeated rocket and strafing attacks were made and upward of 40 soldiers were killed. Meanwhile, Fireflies bombed a rail complex north of Chinnampo, which resulted in all rail lines south of *Sydney*'s area being cut at least once on this patrol. They also attacked barracks buildings to the north of Ongjin and a large working lead and zinc mine complex nearby. Two aircraft were damaged by flak.

There was continuing good weather next day, and once again 54 sorties were flown. The Fireflies attacked bridges north of Allyong reservoir and north of Chinnampo as well as bombing targets on the Chaeryong-san peninsula. They were also responsible for destroying two spans of a bridge on the last serviceable railway line in *Sydney*'s area, and the destruction of 22 buildings believed to be housing enemy troops. Targets for the Sea Furies were mainly troops in villages and near the city of Ch'angyong, and continued attacks on junks and sampans, while three 45-foot junks and one small craft were damaged during the Hanch'on run. Guns in a village that had fired on some friendly vessels were attacked, six houses being damaged and an AA position strafed. An estimated 130 troops were killed in the Ch'angyong area. Three aircraft were hit by small-arms fire but none of the pilots was hurt and all three aircraft returned safely to the carrier. The pattern of strikes continued next day, when a further 56 sorties were flown, mainly against troops and small vessels. The Sea Furies destroyed 35 small craft, including three junks, and a flight of Fireflies bombed targets near Ch'angyong where houses suspected of concealing some 300 Chinese troops were hit and damaged; another flight bombed a bridge at Wonto. Probably the most spectacular strike of the day was against Chinese troops outside Sinch'on, Sea Furies of 808 Squadron attacking first before those of 805 Squadron were called in, together with a flight of bomb-carrying Fireflies. By the end of the attack, the only houses left standing were on fire and it was estimated that 80% of the enemy troops must have been killed. Two aircraft received hits from light flak.

Having refuelled at sea on the 12th, *Sydney* and her aircraft were back in the fray next day. The first mission was the run by 808 Squadron to Hanch'on where the Sea Furies strafed many small craft in the estuaries, damaging three junks and five sampans. During an attack on box-cars north of Chinnampo, Lt(P) P.B. Cooper's aircraft (WE679) was hit by flak and started losing oil pressure. He headed for the coast but could not maintain altitude and, not having a suitable field in sight for a forced-landing, he baled out at 800 feet, north-west of Chinnampo. Cooper was seen to walk away along a creek bed displaying his yellow panel; he later recalled:

> "I was about to get the hell out of that exposed spot when I looked up and saw a Commo standing near a tree with a gun in his hand. So I lay down again and crept away to cover."

He did not have to hide for long. Soon afterwards a USN helicopter arrived from Paengyong-do to pluck him to safety. Later, Lt Cdr(P) Bowles led six Sea Furies from 805 Squadron on an armed reconnaissance near Uiju airfield, attacking a designated target at Naedong-ni. A large fire was started and at least four houses were destroyed. Bowles then sighted a camouflaged vehicle and during the subsequent strafing run his aircraft (possibly WE796) was hit and started to lose oil. He, too, was forced to bale out and was seen to land in shallow water. Luck was on his side, also, and he was swiftly rescued by a friendly Korean junk that happened to be nearby and taken to Paengyong-do from where he was later picked up by the same USN helicopter which had rescued Lt(P) Cooper. Meanwhile, Fireflies were busy dive-bombing a village on the Ongjin peninsula, others attacking rail bridges between Wonto and the Allyong reservoir. There was more drama during the pick up when two Sea Fury pilots acting as RESCAP for the helicopter heard a Sabre pilot say over the radio that he was heading for Cho-do and would probably bale out. His position at the time was 30,000 feet over Sinanju. The American pilot baled out five minutes after the RESCAP arrived in the area. Meanwhile, a helicopter from the USS *Manchester* had been alerted and the man was out of the water within five minutes. On returning from one of the day's missions, Lt(P) D.J. Robertson's Firefly was accidentally marshalled into the USN rescue helicopter, rendering it unserviceable for the remainder of the patrol.

For the next two days there was little flying possible due to heavy swells, high winds and snow storms. At this stage, the decision was made to hand the defence of friendly islands off the west coast of Korea to the 5th Air Force, but a difficult situation arose because of lack of inter-service co-operation. The 5th Air Force had no knowledge of the spotting procedures used with ships on the west coast. Around Cho-do and Sokto-ri, anxiety was caused by considerable air activity at night that could only have been caused by friendly aircraft. On one occasion bombs were dropped and on another an aircraft gave an incorrect IFF signal. It took 24 hours to elicit a reply from the Joint Operating Centre that no friendly aircraft had been assigned to the area, but 5th Air Force night interdiction routes passed close by and it seems probable that identification mistakes were made. However, this apparent lack of co-ordination and co-operation between the US Navy and the 5th Air Force was beginning to frustrate and concern Admiral Scott-Moncrieff, who did not enjoy the best of relations with Admiral Dyer:

> "The operations of the past three weeks bring out all the weaknesses of the American command system. The lack of any joint Service planning; the lack of a combined headquarters in Korea; the inability to work direct with other organisations and commands, except right up and down through the chain of command; the rigid command and lack of confidence in the man on the spot; the need to 'go on record' resulting in long and sometimes confusing directions; the insistence on being told every detail immediately anything happens; the appalling overcrowded signal communications causing further delay, and aggravated in the present case by the unwieldy chain of command and the objection to any signal on any policy matter being made for info' up and down the chain.
>
> A further weakness is the lack of intelligence available to me under present conditions when the local organisations who normally keep me supplied with operational intelligence are bottled up in the islands. In the meantime, some 16 (including ROK) ships . . . are tied up in yet another of these static tasks, in a vulnerable position, as a result of a threatened attack which may be launched by a few junks and a large number of collapsible boats, and is only credible having regard to the characteristics of a resourceful and fanatical enemy. This loss of naval mobility, which has been such a feature of this war, is the price that has to be paid for the insufficiency of regular soldiers to carry out static garrison duties. More particularly, it is directly the result of failure to evaluate and agree the basis of military requirements on a joint service basis. A study of recent naval operations in the light of the established principle of war' is most revealing."

Sydney was back on station on 17 December, the final day of her fifth patrol. 55 sorties were flown, mainly against suspected troop concentrations and gun positions in the Cho-do-Sokto-ri area. Fireflies, loaded with 1,000-lb bombs, dive-bombed gun positions on the Amgak peninsula. They were escorted by a flight of Sea Furies from 805 Squadron, one of which acted as spotter for the strike, but no results were observed. The other Sea Furies carried out a junk and troop reconnaissance but very little movement was discerned although during one of his observation runs, Lt(P) Salthouse's Sea Fury was hit by flak and he lost the use of his rudder and elevator trim. He was directed to fly to Japan, and after refuelling at Kure, to proceed on to Iwakuni. Other Firefly flights attacked buildings in Ullyal and rail bridges near Yanwon. Five aircraft were damaged by flak during the day. After the last land-on, the carrier headed south.

So ended *Sydney*'s fifth tour of duty in the Yellow Sea. Her CAG had logged 338 sorties but, with four Sea Furies (VX728, WE679, WE795 and WE796) and a Firefly (WB358) lost, plus a pilot killed in action, it had proved to be the most expensive patrol to date. A further 20 aircraft had been damaged by flak, no fewer than 11 being hit from one position in the Amgak peninsula. It was a relatively high rate, one for every 12 offensive sorties flown, but this was not regarded as surprising when so many aircraft were continually flying over one small area carrying out attacks. A similar trend had been noted over the Han. During the period October to December 1951, TF77's operational losses totalled a further 63 USN/USMC aircraft (44 Corsairs, 16 Skyraiders, two Panthers, and one Banshee); others were lost in accidents. The carrier war was proving to be a costly war.

Sydney handed over to the USS *Badoeng Strait* on 18 December and proceeded to Kure for replenishment and re-arming, and hopefully a pleasant Christmas. She berthed at 1130 next day. To replace the damaged H-5, a new helicopter arrived on Christmas Eve on loan from the US Navy complete with its crew, Lt Barfield USN and Ens Dixon USN. Most of *Sydney*'s aircrew spent the harbour period in and around Kure. 805 Squadron's diarist noted:

> "During these nine days in harbour, work was at a minimum and pleasure was at the maximum. From the very first day, invitations have been pouring into the mess, both privately and for the wardroom, to attend parties and dances in the various service messes or quarters. Naturally the closest liaison has been with the Australian and New Zealand army officers and between us all a rather lively Christmas ensued. Christmas Day on board saw the exchanging of presents in the wardroom – or rather Santa Claus alias David Cain

distributing same. Boxing Day, as usual, brought forth the hangovers and such like so that the two days steaming to the area will afford the unfortunates time to recuperate."

The war had to go on and, on 27 December, *Sydney* sailed again for the west coast and her sixth patrol . . . [5]

* * *

Volume Two of *With the Yanks in Korea* will continue the story of the Korean airwar, and the British and Commonwealth involvement, up to the end of the conflict in July 1953.

---

[5] *Sydney*'s sixth and seventh patrols followed a similar routine, and the latter was to be her final patrol in Korean waters, which ended on 25 January 1952. During this time one more pilot was lost (on 2 January) when Sub Lt(P) R.J. Coleman of 805 Squadron became separated from his leader and disappeared. His Sea Fury (WE686) was presumed to have crashed into the sea. *Sydney*'s final number of air sorties totalled 2,366 (of which 743 were by the Fireflies) during which time eight Sea Furies (and three pilots) were lost, together with nine Fireflies (no aircrew losses), including one lost over the side during typhoon 'Ruth'.

APPENDIX I

AIR COMBAT CLAIMS MADE BY BRITISH & COMMONWEALTH FIGHTER PILOTS KOREA, 1951

30/3/51:	Flt Lt J.A.O. Lévesque RCAF	334th FIS	MiG-15	F-86A	FU-111
16/4/51:	Flt Lt S.W. Daniel DSO DFC RAF	334th FIS	MiG-15 damaged	F-86A	FU-080
26/9/51:	Sqn Ldr R.C. Cresswell RAAF	4th FIW	MiG-15 damaged	F-86A	FU-210
	Flt Lt R.L. Dawson RAAF	77RAAF	MiG-15 damaged	Meteor F8	A77-811
24/10/51:	Flt Lt C.I. Blyth AFC RAF	77RAAF	MiG-15 damaged	Meteor F8	A77-31
27/10/51:	Flg Off L. Reading RAAF	77RAAF	MiG-15 damaged	Meteor F8	A77-29
2/11/51:	Flt Lt C.I. Blyth AFC RAF	77RAAF	MiG-15 damaged	Meteor F8	A77-189
3/11/51:	Sgt M.E. Colebrook RAAF	77RAAF	MiG-15 damaged	Meteor F8	A77-368
1/12/51:	Flg Off B. Gogerly RAAF	77RAAF	MiG-15	Meteor F8	A77-15
	Squadron victory[1]	77RAAF	MiG-15	Meteor F8s	

APPENDIX II

ROLL OF HONOUR
BRITISH and COMMONWEALTH AIRCREW
KOREA 1950-51

77 Squadron RAAF

7/7/50	Sqn Ldr G. Strout RAAF	Mustang A68-757
3/9/50	P3 W.P. Harrop RAAF	Mustang A68-753
9/9/50	Wg Cdr L.T. Spence DFC RAAF	Mustang A68-809
14/11/50	Flt Lt C. Kirkpatrick RAAF	Accident on ground
20/11/50	Flt Lt W.V. Gray RAAF	Accident on ground (14/11/50, died 20/11/50)
22/12/50	P2 D.C. Ellis RAAF	Mustang A68-726
6/1/51	P3 G.I. Stephens RAAF	Mustang A68-765
14/2/51	Flt Lt K.C. Matthews RAAF	Mustang A68-812 (collision)
14/2/51	P3 S.S. Squires RAAF	Mustang A68-796 (collision)
26/2/51	P3 K.E. Royal RAAF	Mustang A68-704
19/3/51	Sgt H.T. Strange RAAF	Mustang A68-782
17/4/51	Sgt R. Robson RAAF	Mustang A68-124 (accident)
22/8/51	Sgt R.L.R. Lamb RAF	Meteor A77-354 (collision)
22/8/51	Sgt R.D. Mitchell RAAF	Meteor A77-128 (collision)
11/11/51	Sgt D.M. Robertson RAAF	Meteor A77-959
1/12/51	Sgt E.D. Armit RAAF	Meteor A77-949

2 Squadron SAAF

2/2/51	Lt W.E.St E. Wilson SAAF	Mustang 319
7/2/51	2/Lt D.R. Leah SAAF	Mustang 307
15/2/51	Lt G.D. Doveton SAAF	Mustang 304
2/3/51	Capt W.J.J. Badenhorst AFC SAAF	Mustang 317
2/3/51	Lt D.A. Ruiter DFC SAAF	Mustang 301 (accident)
10/3/51	Capt J.F.O. Davis DFC SAAF	Mustang 321
15/5/51	Lt M.H. Rorke SAAF	Mustang 330 (accident)

---

[1] The pilots who fired at MiGs in this action can be identified as Flg Off Gogerly (A77-15), during his second engagement, Flt Lt M. Scannell AFC RAF (A77-189), Flt Lt G. Thornton DFM AFM RAAF (A77-741), and Flt Lt L.L. Cadan RAAF (A77-911).

NB: On 2/11/51 Flt Lt L.L. Cadan RAAF in Meteor A77-911 claimed a swept-wing fighter damaged, but scrutiny of his camera-gun film confirmed his victim as an F-86 of the 334th FIS, which suffered at least one 20mm cannon-shell strike.

10/6/51	2/Lt T. Liebenberg SAAF	Mustang 333 (accident)
22/6/51	Lt A.G. Frisby SAAF	Mustang 337
1/7/51	2/Lt J.P. Verster SAAF	Mustang 328 (accident)
9/7/51	Maj L.B. Pearce SAAF	Mustang 316 (accident)
23/7/51	Capt F.M. Bekker SAAF	Mustang 335
23/7/51	Lt R.M. du Plooy SAAF	Mustang 338
14/8/51	Lt C.I. de Jongh SAAF	Mustang 349
1/9/51	2/Lt M.O. Grunder SAAF	Mustang 342
5/9/51	Lt. N. Biden SAAF	Mustang 302
12/9/51	Capt F.A. Montanari SAAF	Mustang 351
29/10/51	2/Lt H.T.R. Joyce SAAF	Mustang 340
4/11/51	2/Lt C.J. Pappas SAAF	Mustang 363
24/11/51	2/Lt G.H. Krohn SAAF	Mustang 345
29/11/51	Capt A. Janse van Rensburg SAAF	Mustang 346
3/12/51	2/Lt P.I. Norman-Smith SAAF	Mustang 341 (collision)
3/12/51	2/Lt K.R. Whitehead SAAF	Mustang 324 (collision)

Royal Navy/Royal Australian Navy (aircrew)

29/8/50	Lt Cdr(P) I.M. MacLachlan RN	800 Sqn RN	Accident aboard HMS *Triumph*
26/1/51	Lt(P) A.C. Beavan RN	807 Sqn RN	Sea Fury VR940 HMS *Theseus* (accident)
13/3/51	Lt(P) G.H. Cooles RN Flt Lt D.W. Gray RAF	810 Sqn RN⎱ 810 Sqn RN⎰	Firefly WB269 HMS *Theseus*
26/4/51	Lt(P) E.P.L. Stephenson RN	803 Sqn RN	Sea Fury VW655 HMS *Glory* (accident)
5/6/51	P3 S.W.E. Ford RN	810 Sqn RN	Firefly WB244 HMS *Glory*
26/6/51	Lt(P) J.H. Sharp RN Acmn1 G.B. Wells DSM RN	812 Sqn RN⎱ 812 Sqn RN⎰	Firefly WB308 HMS *Glory*
16/7/51	Lt(P) R. Williams RN Sub Lt(O) L.R. Shepley RN	812 Sqn RN⎱ 812 Sqn RN⎰	Firefly WB380 HMS *Glory*
18/7/51	Cmd Plt T.W. Sparke RN	804 Sqn RN	Sea Fury VW573 HMS *Glory*
22/9/51	Sub Lt(O) R.G.A. Davey RN	812 Sqn RN	Firefly WB309 HMS *Glory* (accident)
5/11/51	Lt(P) K.E. Clarkson DFM RAN	805 Sqn RAN	Sea Fury WE674 HMAS *Sydney*
7/12/51	Sub Lt(P) R.R. Sinclair RAN	805 Sqn RAN	Sea Fury VX728 HMAS *Sydney*

205 Squadron Sunderland (PP107) accident 25/1/51

Flt Lt D.R. Hobdey RAF	Plt Off R.E. Baker RAF
Flt Sgt P.E.T. Brooks RAF	Flt Sgt R.F. Hodge RAF
Sgt A. J. Carpenter RAF	Sgt W. Thompson RAF
SAC R.C. Curtis RAF	SAC A.J. Kent RAF
LAC E.A. Cooper RAF	LAC W.C. Dauris RAF
LAC J. Gracie RAF	LAC D.E. Humphreys RAF
LAC P.C. McAllister RAF	LAC J.S. Olley RAF

APPENDIX III

A SELECTION OF BIOGRAPHICAL NOTES RELATING TO BRITISH AND COMMONWEALTH AIRCREW WHO SERVED IN KOREA 1950-1951

Ranks shown as at time of service in Korea; British decorations shown were awarded for service in Korea or those held prior to service in Korea.

Flt Lt John I. Adams (Bay) DFC RAAF, born 1922 at Melbourne, Australia, joined the RAAF in 1941. Posted to the UK and served with 3 Squadron RAF 1944-45 flying Tempests. Credited with six VI flying bombs, one and one shared air victories, plus two damaged on the ground. Postwar joined the BCOF in Japan and served with 77RAAF. Awarded DFC, US Air Medal. Post-Korea was CO of 76RAAF 1952-54 (AFC). Task Force Air Commander Vietnam 1968-69; CBE 1970. Commander Integrated Air Defence System Malaysia 1975-77; Chief of Air Force Operations 1978; Air Defence Commanding Operational Command 1978-79. Retired as Air Vice-Marshal 1979.

Sqn Ldr The Honourable Michael C. Adderley AFC & Bar. Born 1917, the second son of the 6th Baron Lord Norton of Fillongley Hall. Served in RAF Training Command during WWII, and was awarded his first AFC in 1941. Remained in the RAF and awarded Bar to AFC in 1948. Served in Malaya in 1950. Exchange officer USAF and served in Korea 1951 with 523rd Fighter-Escort Squadron USAF flying F-84s. Attached to Directorate of Operations FEAFHQ as Fighter Aircraft Requirements Officer 1951-52. Awarded US Bronze Star. Retired as Grp Capt OBE 1960, and died in 1992. His brother John became 7th Baron Norton on their father's death in 1961 following a horse riding accident. Ancestor Humphrey had been Master of the Wardrop to Henry VIII.

Lt Cdr(P) John L. Appleby RN joined Royal Navy in 1939. Flew Sea Gladiators and Fulmars in 1940-41 with 802 and 807 Squadrons. CO 794 Squadron 1945, CO 737 Squadron 1949. On loan to RAN as Lt Cdr in 1950 and commanded 808 Squadron (Sea Furies) on HMAS *Sydney* 1951-52. Awarded US Legion of Merit. Returned to RN in 1952.

Flt Sgt Ernest D. Armit (Don) RAAF, born 1926 at Waverley, NSW, Australia, joined the RAAF in 1944 and was under training 1944-45. Served with 77RAAF in Korea during 1951, but was posted missing, presumed killed, on air operations 1 December 1951. Awarded US Air Medal.

Flt Sgt Allan J. Avery DFM RAAF. Served as an air gunner with 625 Squadron RAF during the latter part of WWII, completing 45 ops, awarded DFM. Re-trained as pilot and flew Meteors with 77RAAF in Korea 1951-52. Received MiD and US Air Medal. Killed in flying accident 1/9/52 in Meteor T7 A77-701 (formerly A77-577).

Capt Wessel J.J. Badenhorst AFC SAAF. Served with 3SAAF Squadron in WWII. Flight commander 2SAAF Korea 1950-51. Awarded US DFC. Killed in action 2 March 1951.

Lt Cdr John S. Bailey OBE DSC RN, joined FAA in 1939. Posted to 774 Squadron (Swordfish). Joined 827 Squadron HMS *Indomitable* (Albacores). By 1943 flying Barracudas. CO 768 Squadron HMS *Argus* 1943-44; as deck landing officer for training batsmen carried out 1,290 deck landings in 15 months. Awarded OBE. Postwar flew Seafire, Sea Fury, Attacker at EPTS; posted to Service Trials Unit and flew Vampire and Meteor (had flown 41 types by January 1951). CO 804 Squadron (Sea Furies) aboard HMS *Glory* 1951-52. Flew total of 191 ops on Albacores (WWII) and Sea Furies (Korea, awarded DSC), plus 20 on F-86s while on attachment to the 335th FIS in 1952. Completed 2,282 deck landings, an unbeatable record.

Flt Lt Frederick W. Barnes DFC RAAF, born at Melbourne in 1924, joined the RAAF in 1943 and flew Kittyhawks with 77RAAF in 1945. Postwar joined BCOF Japan with 77RAAF 1946-49; rejoined 77RAAF in 1950. Awarded US Air Medal. Post-Korea with the Aircraft Research and Development Unit 1951-54 (AFC 1953); attached to 479th Fighter Wing USAF 1954-56; commanded 75RAAF and 2OCU 1963-65; OC RAAF Williamtown 1976-77; AOC Support Command 1977-79; Dep Chief of Air Staff 1979-81. Retired in 1981 as Air Vice-Marshal.

Flt Sgt Henry W. Bessell (Dick) DFM RAAF, born 1928 in Victoria, was an aircraft mechanic when he enlisted in the RAAF Air Training Corps in 1944. Discharged in 1946 and re-enlisted in 1947. Re-trained as pilot and joined 77RAAF in 1950. Awarded DFM 1951, US Air Medal. After returning to Australia served with various base units 1955-79. Retired as Flt Lt.

Lt Cdr(P) Maurice A. Birrell DSC RN, joined the FAA in 1939. Flew Hurricanes briefly with 79 Squadron RAF during the Battle of Britain (credited with one damaged). 804 Squadron later 1940, 802 Squadron 1941, then rejoined 804 Squadron when it became Catapult Fighter Unit. First pilot to be catapulted in Hurricane from CAM ship; survived twice being torpedoed. Senior Pilot 804 Squadron HMS *Glory* 1951-52 (DSC). CO 891 Squadron (Sea Venoms) 1954-56. Retired as Cdr 1971.

Maj Johann P.D. Blaauw DFC SAAF. Commanded 7SAAF 1942; CO 40SAAF (TR Spitfires) 1943 during Sicily Invasion; CO 208 Squadron RAF 1944-45 (Lt Col). Dep CO 2SAAF Korea 1950; in May 1951 deliberately force-landed his Mustang close to downed SAAF pilot to assist; both rescued by helicopter. Awarded US Silver Star, the highest award by US government to members of foreign armed forces. CO 2SAAF August 1951. Awarded US DFC, US Air Medal. Flew in excess of 500 operational sorties WWII and Korea.

Plt Off Kenneth J. Blight RAAF, born 1922 in Victoria, enlisted in the RAAF in 1940. During WWII he was with 64 Rescue Squadron and various training establishments. Served with 77RAAF 1951-52. Awarded US Air Medal. Post-Korea was with HQ Support Command 1960-63; HQ Operational Command 1963. Retired 1968 as Flt Lt.

Flt Lt Colin I. Blyth (Joe) DFC AFC RAF, born 1925 in Maidstone, Kent, joined RAF 1940 aged 15´, having falsified his Birth Certificate. Trained as Air Gunner/WoP and joined 161 Squadron in 1942, flying Whitleys on clandestine operations over Unoccupied France. In September 1942, his aircraft crashed due to engine failure; baled out and evaded capture. Returned to UK via Gibraltar, recommended for DCM but not awarded. Trained as pilot in South Africa, retained as instructor. Postwar with RAF Training Command (AFC) until posted to Japan with RAF Mission to convert 77RAAF pilots on to Meteor. Flew 100+sorties on Mustangs and Meteors, damaged two MiG-15s.

Awarded DFC and US Air Medal. On return to UK joined 63 Squadron (Meteors) 1952-54, awarded Bar to AFC; posted to 32 Squadron (Venoms) in Middle East, 1954-56. CO 8 Squadron (Venoms, 1956-58) at time of 1956 Suez conflict; destroyed five EAF MiG-15s on ground. Flew further 99 ops in 1957 (awarded Bar to DFC). Returned to UK, 23 Group 1958-62. Retired 1962, Sqn Ldr. Obtained Civil Licence, still flying commercially in 2000.

Sqn Ldr Henry E. Bodien (Joe) DSO DFC RAF, born 1916, served with 43 Squadron before being posted to 48 Squadron of Coastal Command flying Ansons. He rejoined Fighter Command in 1941 and was posted to 151 Squadron, at first flying Hurricanes, then Defiants and finally Mosquitos on night fighting duties, being credited with three victories in 1941 (awarded DFC), and another two in 1942 and 1943 (awarded DSO). RAFHQ, Hong Kong 1950. Flew B-26s with 3rd Bombardment Group USAF 1950. Awarded US Air Medal. On his return from Korea he was appointed to command 29 Squadron flying Meteor NF11s, 1951-52. Promoted to Wing Commander, but in 1954 emigrated to Canada where he joined the RCAF. He died in 1999.

Lt Cdr(P) Walter G. Bowles DSC RAN, born in New Zealand in 1920, served with RNZNVR during WWII. Transferred to RAN in 1948 and commanded 805 Squadron (Sea Furies) aboard HMAS *Sydney* 1951-52. Awarded DSC, US Legion of Merit. Retired 1973.

Wg Cdr Alan H.C. Boxer DSO DFC RAF, born in New Zealand in 1916, joined RAF in 1938. Flying instructor, Training Command 1939-42. Bomber Command 1942 and commanded one of the RAF's 'secret' squadrons (138 Squadron) flying agents and supplies into occupied Europe. Awarded DSO and DFC. Air Staff, Bomber Command until 1945; RAF Staff College 1945-46; Joint Staff MoD 1946-47; Army Staff College 1948. Exchange posting with USAF Strategic Air Command, 1949-51 including tour with 92nd BW USAF, Korea 1950, as Project Officer. Awarded US Bronze Star. Flew B-29 sorties with 307th BG. Awarded US Air Medal. CFE 1951-53; RAF Staff College 1953-55; CO 7 Squadron 1956-57; OC RAF Wittering 1957-59; Bomber Command HQ 1960-62; SASO 1 Group 1963-65; SASO HQ Bomber Command 1965-67; Defence Services Secretary MoD 1968-70. Retired as an Air Vice-Marshal, having received a knighthood.

Flt Lt Stuart Bradford (Brick) DFC RAAF, born 1923 in NSW, joined RAAF in 1942 and flew Kittyhawks with 86RAAF and 75RAAF. With 82RAAF in BCOF before joining 77RAAF. Awarded US Air Medal. CO of 76RAAF 1954-55. Became Director of Establishments, Dept of Air 1968 (Wg Cdr) but died that year.

Lt(P) George F.S. Brown DFC RAN. Served with 76RAAF (Kittyhawks) in SW Pacific area during WWII and awarded the DFC. Transferred to RAN postwar and served with 805 Squadron (Sea Furies) aboard HMS *Sydney* 1951-52. Received MiD. Commanded 805 Squadron 1952-53, Lt Cdr.

Lt(P) John G.B. Campbell DFC RAN. Served with the RAAF during WWII in the Western Desert and Italy, initially flying Hurricanes with 33 Squadron in 1942 and later Spitfires. Credited with one victory plus two damaged. Awarded DFC. Later served with 457 Squadron in Australia, flying Spitfires. Transferred to RAN postwar and served with 805 Squadron (Sea Furies) aboard HMS *Sydney* 1951-52. Commanded 805 Squadron 1956-58, Lt Cdr.

Flt Lt Victor B. Cannon DFC RAAF, born 1921 NSW, joined RAAF 1943. Flew with 64 Rescue Squadron 1944-45, commissioned 1945. Participated in Berlin Airlift 1948-49 before joining 77RAAF 1950-51 (Awarded DFC 1951, US Air Medal.). Post-Korea became CO 24RAAF 1954-56, 21RAAF 1956-58 (Queen's Commendation for Meritorious Service in the Air 1958), 77RAAF 1963, 79RAAF 1963, 77RAAF 1964-65. OC RAAF Townsville 1968-71. Retired 1976 as Grp Capt.

Lt(P) Keith E. Clarkson DFM RAN, born 1922 in Melbourne, joined RAAF 1940. Fighter pilot WWII attached to RAF, credited with five victories (two on the ground) while flying Spitfires with 72 Squadron in 1943. Awarded DFM and commissioned. Later served with 611 Squadron in the UK. Transferred to RANVR in 1945 and flew with 805 Squadron (Sea Furies aboard HMAS *Sydney*) as Senior Pilot in Korea 1951, but was killed in action 5 November 1951.

Flt Sgt Maxwell E. Colebrook DFM RAAF, born 1926 in Perth, WA. Joined the RAAF in 1944, in training establishments 1944-45. Re-enlisted 1949 and joined 77RAAF. Damaged MiG-15 in air combat. Awarded DFM, US Air Medal 1951, commissioned as Plt Off, but was posted missing, presumed killed in action 13 April 1952.

Plt Off Milton J. Cottee RAAF, born 1926 in NSW, enlisted in RAAF 1944. Re-enlisted 1948 and joined 77RAAF. Awarded US Air Medal and MiD 1950. Attached to RAF 1955-58; RAAF F-111 Project Manager Washington 1969-74. Retired from the RAAF 1976 as Grp Capt AFC.

Sqn Ldr Richard C. Cresswell DFC RAAF took command of 77RAAF shortly after its formation in 1942, and had fought in its first action, over Darwin, when he shot down the first Japanese bomber destroyed over Australian soil at night. He followed this with a second tour as CO from September 1944 to August 1945 when the unit operated from Noemfoor, Morotai and Labuan. Commanded 77RAAF for third time September 1950-August 1951. Attached briefly to 4th FIW, damaged MiG-15. Awarded DFC, US DFC, US Air Medal.

Flt Lt Ronald W. Daniel RAAF, born 1921 NSW, joined RAAF 1941. During WWII served with 35 Squadron RAF, shot down over Europe and successfully evaded. During Korean War served with 30RAAF, and later with 36RAAF (awarded AFC 1953). Resigned from RAAF 1957.

Flt Lt Stephen W. Daniel DSO DFC & Bar RAF. Born 1920 in England but lived in Scotland. Joined RAF 1938 as an airman, volunteered for pilot training in 1941. Commissioned and posted to 72 Squadron, UK and North Africa. DFC for four victories. CO February 1943, Bar to DFC for 17 victories. Posted to 219 Group, then instructor 71 OTU. Briefly with 601 Squadron September 1943, then OC 145 Squadron until 1945 (awarded DSO). Various postings postwar including spell with 603 Squadron and at CFE. Joined 43 Squadron 1949, then exchange posting with USAF 1950; joined 71st FIS (F-86s) before posting to Korea, joining 334th FIS (damaged MiG-15). Awarded US DFC and Air Medal. Post-Korea, HQ 12 Group 1952-53. OC Sabre Conversion Unit, 2TAF 1953. Remained 2TAF until 1955. Converted to Canberra bomber 1956, later to Valiant, and joined 207 Squadron 1958-60. Retired as Sqn Ldr, but died in 1982.

Capt John F.O. Davis DFC SAAF. Flew Marauders with 12SAAF during 1943-44, Italy and the Balkans, commanded the Squadron in 1944 (awarded DFC). Joined 2SAAF Korea 1950-51. Awarded US DFC, US Air Medal. Killed in action 10 March 1951.

Flt Lt Ralph L. Dawson DFC RAAF, born 1922 in Victoria, joined RAAF 1941. Served overseas and commissioned in 1944. With 77RAAF during Korean War, damaged MiG-15. DFC 1952, US Air Medal. Resigned from RAAF 1960 as Sqn Ldr.

Sqn Ldr Victor B. de la Perelle RAF, born in New Zealand in 1919. Joined RNZAF 1938 but served in RAF WWII. Flew Hurricanes with 245 and 258 Squadrons UK and Far East, 1940-42. Liaison Officer with NEI Air Force until captured in March 1942 and POW until 1945. CO 165 Squadron 1946; CO 66 Squadron (Meteors) 1946-48. OC RAF Photo Intelligence Unit attached to 67th Tactical Recon Wing Japan 1951. Awarded US Bronze Star. Retired as Sqn Ldr 1958, and died in 1983.

Flt Sgt Vance Drummond RAAF, born 1925 Hamilton, New Zealand. Enlisted RAAF 1947 and joined 77RAAF in Korea. Shot down by MiG-15 and POW 1 December 1951, released 1953. During Vietnam War was FAC with USAF TAC 1965-67. CO 3RAAF 1967, killed in Mirage accident 17 May 1967. DFC 1967, US DFC 1967, US Air Medal (12 clusters), US Bronze Star, Vietnamese Cross of Gallantry.

Lt Cdr(P) Michael F. Fell DSO DSC RN. With 804 and 800 Squadrons 1940 flying Sea Gladiators and Skuas (HMS *Glorious* and HMS *Ark Royal*); shared in destruction of three enemy aircraft in 1940, credited with two probables in 1941 and shared another in 1942 while flying Hurricanes with RNAS in the Western Desert, awarded DSC. OC 7 Naval Fighter Wing 1943-44. Awarded DSO. CO 736 Squadron, 1947-49. Commanded 21st CAG HMAS *Sydney* 1951-52. Awarded Bar to DSC. Later knighted. Retired as Admiral.

Flg Off Bruce Gogerly DFC RAAF, born 1923 NSW, and joined Australian Army in 1941; transferred to RAAF 1943 and flew Kittyhawks with 76RAAF in 1944. Re-enlisted 1948 and joined 77RAAF in 1951. Became first RAAF pilot to shoot down MiG-15, on 1 December 1951, and probably shared a second (DFC 1952, US DFC 1952, US Air Medal 1953). 91RAAF Wing 1953-54; 78RAAF Wing 1962-64. Retired 1974 as Wg Cdr.

Lt(O) Alexander H. Gordon DFC RAN, joined RAAF during WWII and served with 194 Squadron RAF late in the war, flying Dakotas in India and Burma. Awarded DFC 1945. Transferred to RAN and flew Fireflies with 817 Squadron aboard HMAS *Sydney* 1951-52. Received MiD.

Wt Off Ronald D. Guthrie, born 1925 in NSW, joined RAAF in 1943. Posted to 77RAAF in 1951 but was shot down by MiG-15 on 29 August 1951, POW; released 1953. Remained in RAAF as Controller and retired in 1979 as Sqn Ldr.

Flg Off Phillip V. Hamilton-Foster DFC RAAF, born 1920 in NSW, joined RAAF in 1941. Served in various operational and training units before joining 77RAAF in 1951. Awarded DFC (1952), US Air Medal (1951). Served in Vietnam in 1966. Retired 1967 as Sqn Ldr.

Flt Lt Gordon R. Harvey DFC RAAF, born 1923 in NSW, joined RAAF in 1942 and served with 8RAAF flying Beauforts late in the war. Joined 77RAAF 1946, then 82RAAF 1947-48 before returning to 77RAAF in 1950. Shot down and POW January 1951. Released August 1953. Awarded DFC, US DFC, US Air Medal. Thereafter, served with 78RAAF Wing in Malaya 1959-61; Air Attaché, Paris 1970-74. Retired as Grp Capt 1974.

Flt Lt David Hitchins, RAAF, joined RAAF in 1942. Flew Beauforts with 100RAAF in SW Pacific during WWII. Post-war he flew with Dakota transport squadrons, 37RAAF, 33RAAF, 38RAAF, and 36RAAF (CO). Joined Dakota Flight at Iwakuni 1947, becoming personal pilot to C-in-C BCOF. Post-Korea 34RAAF 1952-53; 38RAAF; 24RAAF (CO) 1960-63; 36RAAF (CO) 1964-68; OC RAAF Pearce 1968. Retired as Air Commodore AFC.

Plt Off Lyall R. Klaffer RAAF, born 1928 in Adelaide, joined RAAF in 1947. Posted to 77RAAF in Korea 1950-51 (US DFC, US Air Medal). Post-Korea with 78RAAF Wing, Malta 1952-53. ADC to Governor-General 1953. Flew with 16th TRS USAF in Vietnam 1965-66; Air Attaché Washington 1965-67. Retired from RAAF 1981 as Air Commodore AFC.

Wg Cdr James E. Johnson DSO & 2 Bars DFC & Bar RAF. Born 1915 in Leicestershire, joined RAFVR 1939. Posted to 616 Squadron 1941 (DFC September 1941, Bar June 1942, for seven victories, one shared); CO 610 Squadron 1942-43 (two victories, one shared); OC Kenley RCAF Wing 1943 (19 victories, five shared, awarded DSO and Bar); OC 144 RCAF Wing 1944 (ten victories, awarded second Bar to DSO, plus US DFC); OC 125 Wing 1945 (Grp Capt). Official Fighter Command top-scorer with 38 victories (actually 34 plus seven shared). OC Tactics CFE 1946; RCAF Staff College 1947; Exchange posting USAF 1948. To FEAFHQ USAF 1950, flew a dozen B-26 and F-80 operational sorties. Awarded US Air Medal and Legion of Merit. Post-Korea, OC RAF Wildenrath 2TAF 1952-54; Dep Director, Tactical Operations, Air Ministry 1954; OC RAF Cottesmore 1957-60; SASO HQ 3 Group Bomber Command 1960-63, Air Commodore; AOC Air Forces Middle East 1963-65. Retired as Air Vice-Marshal CB CBE 1966.

Lt(P) Peter L. Keighley-Peach DSO RN. Son of Capt Charles Keighley-Peach OBE DSO, WWII fighter ace, and grandson of Admiral Keighley-Peach DSO. Served with 807 Squadron HMS *Theseus* 1950-51 (DSO). CO 818 Squadron (Sea Hawks) 1957; CO 727 Squadron 1958-59.

Lt(P) Peter M. Lamb DSC RN. Born 1923, joined FAA in 1942 and trained in USA. Served with 807 and 808 Squadrons 1943-44, and 800 Squadron in Pacific in 1945. Instructor, School of Naval Air Warfare 1948-49. Senior Pilot with 800 Squadron (Seafires) aboard HMS *Triumph* during 1950, awarded DSC. Senior Pilot, Naval Test Squadron, A & AEE 1952-54 (awarded AFC). Commanded 810 Squadron (Sea Hawks) during Suez conflict of 1956, awarded Bar to DSC. CO 700 (Test & Trials) Squadron 1957-58. Retired as Lt Cdr. Chief Test Pilot Westland Aircraft (Saunders Roe Division) 1958-65; Chief Test Commander, British Hovercraft Corp, 1966.

Wg Cdr Peter DeL. Le Cheminant DFC RAF. Born 1920 in Guernsey. RAF Cranwell. OC 223 Squadron 1943-44, awarded DFC; Staff College and Instructor 1945-48; OC 209 Squadron (Sunderlands) 1949-51, awarded Bar to DFC; JSSC 1958; OC RAF Geilenkirchen 1961-63; SASO FEAF 1966-67; Chief of Staff FEAF 1967-68; Commandant, Joint Warfare Establishment 1968-70. Assistant Chief of Air Staff (Policy) MoD 1971 (Air Vice-Marshal Sir Peter).

Flt Lt Joseph A.O. Lévesque (Omer) RCAF, was born in Monteal, Canada. Joined Royal 22nd Regiment of Canada but resigned commission to join the RCAF. Posted to UK. Served as NCO pilot with 401 Squadron RCAF (Spitfires) and shot down four German fighters before being shot down and taken prisoner in February 1942. Postwar 410 RCAF Squadron (Vampires) 1947-50. Exchange posting with USAF. Went in Korea with 334th FIS (F-86s) and became first Canadian to shoot down a MiG-15. Awarded US DFC, US Air Medal. Remained in RCAF until 1965 (posted to Indo-China 1959-60). Member of research staff of Air Transport Committee.

Capt Gordon B. Lipawsky DFC & Bar SAAF. Served with 2SAAF in Western Desert in 1942; credited with one victory, plus one probable; also rescued fellow pilot who had baled out by landing nearby in Hurricane and flying back with him in cockpit. Later served with 1SAAF and shared victory in 1943. Awarded DFC 1944, Bar to DFC 1945. 2SAAF Korea 1950-51. Awarded US DFC, US Air Medal.

Grp Capt Robert W. McNair DSO DFC & 2 Bars RCAF, born 1919 in Nova Scotia. Joined RCAF 1940 and posted to UK. Joined 411RCAF 1941. Posted to Malta 1942 and joined 249 Squadron RAF (DFC for five victories). Returned to UK and rejoined 411RCAF. Served with 403RCAF 1943 before commanding 416RCAF and 421RCAF (awarded two Bars to DFC, with 16 victories to his credit). OC 126RCAF Wing 1943-44 (DSO). Remained in RCAF postwar. OC RCAF Lachine 1950. Air Adviser to Canadian Liaison Mission FEAFHQ USAF 1951-53. Survived transport aircraft crash 1953, awarded Queen's Commendation for Brave Conduct. OC 4RCAF FW Baden-Soellingen 1957 (Grp Capt). Died (leukemia) 1971.

Flt Lt Cornelius D. Murphy (Des) DFC RAAF, born 1921 in Victoria, joined the RAAF in 1943. Various training establishments 1943-45. Commissioned 1945, and served with 77RAAF 1950-51 (DFC, US Air Medal). Post-Korea CO 75RAAF 1962-63 (AFC); Senior Air Officer RAAF Butterfield, Malaya, 1963-65. Retired from RAAF 1973 as Grp Capt.

Flt Lt Carlyle R. Noble DFC RAAF, born 1919 in Victoria, joined RAAF in 1940. Posted to Middle East and served with 39 Squadron RAF and 203 Squadron RAF, and 461RAAF. Post-war served with 76RAAF 1946-50, before joining 77RAAF (awarded DFC, US Air Medal). Retired from RAAF 1960 as Wg Cdr.

Lt(P) Albert L. Oakley DFC RAN. Served with RAF 1943-44, flying Beaufighters with 254 Squadron.

Lt(P) Albert L. Oakley DFC RAN. Served with the RAF in 1943-44, flying Beaufighters with 254 Squadron. Awarded DFC 1944. Postwar transferred to RAN and served with 817 Squadron (Fireflies) aboard HMAS *Sydney* 1951-52. Retired as Lt Cdr.

Capt Hendrik O.M. Odendaal DFC SAAF. Served in Italy and Balkans 1944-45, mainly on Spitfire and Mustang fighter-bomber operations with 5SAAF. Awarded DFC 1944, Bar to DFC 1945. Joined 2SAAF in Korea 1950-51. Awarded US DFC, US Air Medal.

Flt Lt Ian R. Olorenshaw DFC RAAF, born 1920 in South Australia, joined RAAF in 1941. Served with 5RAAF, 4RAAF, 77RAAF and 83RAAF Wing during WWII; flew 126 operational sorties in the Pacific. CO 75RAAF 1949-50. Flew with 77RAAF Korea 1950-51, awarded Bar to DFC, US DFC, US Air Medal. Seconded to Royal Malaysian Air Force 1963-66. Retired in 1970 as Wg Cdr OBE.

Maj L.B. Pearce SAAF. Served with 1SAAF and 5SAAF 1942 in Western Desert flying Tomahawks. Credited with one probable and two damaged. Joined 2SAAF in Korea 1951 but killed in flying accident 9 July 1951.

Sqn Ldr John E. Proctor DFC RAF, born in 1913, joined the RAF in the late 1930s. Flew Hurricanes with 501 Squadron RAF in France and Battle of Britain 1940, and later with 32 Squadron, receiving DFC for 11 victories. CO 33 Squadron RAF in Middle East 1942; CO 352 (Yugoslav) Squadron 1944. Postwar CO 205 Squadron (Sunderlands) 1950-51 (awarded Bar to DFC). Retired 1957 as Wg Cdr. Died 1991 in South Africa.

Flg Off Wallace B. Rivers DFC RAAF, born 1924 in NSW, joined RAAF in 1943. Served with various training and operational units 1943-45. Post-war 82RAAF 1948-50 before joining 77RAAF 1950-52 (awarded DFC (1950), Bar to DFC (1952), US DFC, US Air Medal). Resigned RAAF in 1957 as Flt Lt.

Flt Lt Eric A. Roberts DFM RAF. Flew with 61 Squadron during 1942-43, awarded DFM. Attached to 67 Tactical Recon Wing Japan as Photo Intelligence Officer 1951. Awarded MiD.

Lt Dennis A. Ruiter DFC SAAF. Served in Western Desert and Italy with 2SAAF 1942-44 (Capt). Credited with three victories, two in 1942, one in 1944. Awarded DFC. Joined 2SAAF in Korea but killed in action 2 March 1951.

Sqn Ldr John F. Sach (Jack) DFC AFC RAF, born 1914 in London, joined the RAF in 1936 as an airman. Having been selected for pilot training, he was commissioned and later won the DFC while flying with Bomber Command (214 Squadron) during the early days of WWII. He was later employed as a VIP pilot, with Prime Minister Churchill as his passenger on one occasion, receiving the AFC in January 1943 (AFC). Postwar, exchange posting with USAF. Attached Directorate of Operations FEAFHQ 1950. Awarded US Bronze Star. Flew B-26s with 3rd Bombardment Group USAF 1950. Awarded US Air Medal.

Flt Lt Maxwell Scannell DFC AFC RAF, joined RNZAF in 1942. Flew Kittyhawks and Corsairs in Pacific during WWII. Transferred to RAF 1947 (AFC 1949). To Japan 1951 as commander of RAF Mission to convert 77RAAF to Meteor F8. Flew 100+ ops on Mustangs and Meteors. Shared in destruction of a MiG-15. Awarded DFC and US Air Medal. CO 68 Squadron (Meteor NF11s) 1957-59. Retired as Air Vice-Marshal.

Flt Lt Peter H.L. Scott AFC RAF. Joined RAF in 1944. Completed pilot training in USA and then served with 29 and 151 Squadrons (Mosquito night fighters) 1946-48. To CFS 1948, trained to be QFI. Central Fighter Establishment 1949. Exchange posting with USAF 1950-52. Served with 82nd FIS (F-84s) before being posted to Korea with 136th FBW (F-84s) in 1951. Awarded AFC. Post-Korea C-in-C's representative at Gloster Aircraft Co, flight-testing Javelin, 1953-56. Staff College 1959. Personal Staff of Secretary of State 1960-62. CO 31 Squadron (Canberra PR7) 1962-65, Wg Cdr. NATO Defence College 1967-69. SASO Central Reconnaissance Establishment 1970-71. Defence and Air Attaché in Paris 1972-75. Director of Air Defence MoD 1975-76. Left RAF 1976 as Air Commodore to become political Air Advisor.

Sqn Ldr Allan J. Simpson DFC RCAF. Joined RCAF prewar and posted to UK. Served with 13 Squadron RAF (Lysanders) in France 1940. Later posted to 6 Squadron RAF (Hurricane tank-busters) in Western Desert 1942. Awarded DFC. Attached to USAF Japan with 67th Tactical Recon Wing as Photo Intelligence Officer. Died 1998.

Wg Cdr Louis T. Spence DFC RAAF, born 1917 in Queensland, joined RAAF in 1940. Flew with 3RAAF in North Africa 1941-42 and credited with two air victories (awarded DFC); CO 452 RAAF at Darwin 1944-45; Dept of Air 1945-46; Instructor RAAF Point Cook 1947-50; CO 77RAAF 1950 but killed in action 9 September 1950 (Awarded Bar to DFC, US Air Medal and Legion of Merit).

Wg Cdr Gordon H. Steege DSO DFC RAAF, born 1917 in NSW, joined RAAF in 1937. During WWII served with 11RAAF, then posted to Middle East and flew Gladiators and Hurricanes with 3RAAF 1940-41 (credited with 7 air victories); CO 450RAAF 1942/43, one further victory (DFC 1943); OC 73RAAF Wing (Kittyhawks) 1943-44 (DSO). OC 81RAAF Wing 1944. Staff appointments 1944-45. Resigned from RAAF 1946, re-appointed 1950. Commanded 77RAAF 1951. Post-Korea OC RAAF Auberley, Butterworth and Edinburgh; later appointments included SEATO Senior Planners Committeee 1958-61; Director Plans, Dept of Air 1963-64. Retired in 1972 as Air Commodore.

Sqn Ldr Graham Strout RAAF, born 1921 in Adelaide, joined RAAF in 1940. During WWII flew with 12RAAF and 86RAAF, and served with various training establishments. Joined 77RAAF 1948 but killed in action 7 July 1950.

Cmdt Servas van Breda Theron DSO DFC SAAF, born 1918 Cape Province, South Africa, joined SAAF in 1938. Posted to East Africa 1940 and joined 3SAAF flying Hurricanes. Credited with five Italian aircraft shot down, plus nine on the ground. Awarded DFC. Returned to South Africa, instructor 1941-43. To Middle East 1943, CO 250 Squadron RAF (Kittyhawks) 1943-44 (DSO). Returned to South Africa and CO 2SAAF 1950-51 Korea (Bar to DSO). Returned to South Africa and to instruction duties, awarded AFC. Retired as Director of Operations SAAF (Brigadier) 1970. Managing Director Hawker Siddeley's South African operations, but died in 1986.

Sqn Ldr Cedric G. Thomas DFC RAAF, flew with 148 (Special Duties) Squadron RAF during the latter stages of WWII. Awarded DFC in 1946. Served with 77RAAF 1951-52. Awarded US Air Medal.

Plt Off Raymond E. Trebilco DFC RAAF, born 1926 in NSW, joined RAAF in 1945. Served with 77RAAF 1950-51 (awarded DFC, US Air Medal). Post-Korea 2OCU 1953-54; CO 77RAAF 1961-64; OC 2 OCU 1968-70; Defence Attaché Tokyo 1970-73; Director of Personnel Services 1973-74; OC RAAF Butterworth 1976-79; AOC Support Command 1978-80; Chief, Air Force personnel 1980-82; Administrator of Norfolk Island 1982. Retired as Air Vice-Marshal.

Lt(P) Reginald A. Wild DFC RAN. Served with RAAF during WWII in Western Desert with 112 Squadron RAF on Kittyhawks. Credited with two victories plus three damaged in 1942. Commissioned and awarded DFC. Later, flight commander with 3RAAF. Transferred to RAN postwar. Flew Sea Furies with 805 Squadron (HMAS *Sydney*) during Korean War, 1951-52. CO 850 Squadron RN 1953.

Sqn Ldr Norman F. Williams CGM, DFM RAAF, born 1914 in NSW, joined RAAF in 1941 and trained as an air gunner. Posted to UK and joined 10 Squadron RAF flying Halifaxes. Credited with shooting down Ju88 night fighter in September 1942; awarded DFM for this action, and a Bar to the DFM at the end of his tour of 30 operations. Volunteered for second tour and posted to 35 Squadron RAF, also equipped with Halifaxes. In June 1943 his aircraft severely damaged by a Ju88 night fighter. Although wounded, he claimed the attacker shot down before probably destroying a second; awarded the Conspicuous Gallantry Medal (CGM). Returned to Squadron on recovery of wounds and completed tour, having been commissioned. In 1944 he returned to Australia and joined 23RAAF on operations against the Japanese. Discharged from RAAF in 1948 as Sqn Ldr. Rejoined RAAF in 1951 and flew a few B-29 ops as air gunner with USAF before joining 77RAAF as a ground officer. Returned to civilian life in 1954.

Sqn Ldr David L. Wilson DFC RAAF, born 1916 in NSW, joined RAAF in 1940. Served with 23RAAF, 83RAAF, 85RAAF, 76RAAF during WWII. CO 81RAAF 1948-49; CO 76RAAF 1950-51; Joined 77RAAF 1951 (Awarded DFC, US Air Medal). Post-Korea became Director Personnel Services 1955-57; Air Attaché Washington 1957-59; Services Adviser Pakistan 1967-69. Retired 1969 as Grp Capt.

Flg Off Richard W. Wittman DFC RAAF, born 1924 in Victoria, joined RAAF in 1942. Various duties including 161 (Special Duties) Squadron RAF. Re-enlisted 1948 and joined 77RAAF in 1950 (Awarded DFC, US Air Medal); OC Meteor Conversion Unit 1950-54 (AFC); Weapons Officer 78RAAF Wing, Malaysia, 1960-64. Served in Vietnam with 9RAAF 1970-71. Retired 1971 as Sqn Ldr.

Wg Cdr Peter G. Wykeham-Barnes DSO DFC RAF, born 1915 in Surrey, joined RAF in 1932 as aircraft apprentice. Later, Cranwell Cadet and comissioned in 1937. Flew Gladiator biplanes and Hurricanes with 80 and 274 Squadrons 1940-41, then commanded 73 Squadron at Tobruk; awarded DFC and Bar, having been credited with 15 Axis aircraft shot down including three shared (13 Italian and two German). CO 257 Squadron 1942. Later converted to night intruders and commanded 23 Squadron (Mosquitos), gaining the DSO and Bar, and two further victories. OC 140 Wing, 2TAF 1944, and led long-range Mosquito attacks against German HQs. Postwar Chief Test Pilot at Fighter Experimental Establishment before seconded to USAF in Korea. Flew B-26s with 3rd Bombardment Group USAF 1950. Awarded US Air Medal. OC RAF North Weald and Wattisham 1951-53, NATO 1953-56; Fighter Command HQ 1956-58; Director of Operations, Air Ministry 1958-59; AOC 38 Group 1960-62; Assistant Chief of Defence Staff 1962-64; Commander Far East Air Force 1964-66; Dep Chief of Air Staff 1967-69. Retired 1969 as Air Marshal Sir Peter with the KCB OBE and AFC to add to his wartime decorations, having changed his name by deed-poll to Wykeham in 1957; he died in 1995.

USAF PERSONNEL WITH RAF/RCAF CONNECTIONS

Colonel Donald J.M. Blakeslee DFC USAF, born 1917 in Ohio USA, joined RCAF in 1940; posted to UK in 1941, he flew Spitfires with 401 Squadron RCAF and the RAF's 133 Eagle Squadron during 1941-42 and claimed three victories, two probables and seven damaged for which he was awarded the DFC. He transferred to the USAAF in 1943 and served with the 334th FIS and the 356/354th FG before taking command of the 4th FG. By the end of WWII had taken his score to 14 and one shared. Postwar he commanded 31st FG and the 27th FEW. Awards included two DSCs, the Silver Star, and a number of US DFCs and Air Medals.

Capt Charles E. McDonald MM USAF from Louisiana USA, served with RCAF during WWII, having volunteered in 1940. He reached the UK in August 1941 and joined 403 Squadron RCAF as a Sgt Plt. He was shot down on one of his operational flights but managed to crash-land near his base. A few days later (21 August 1941) he was again shot down, having claimed a Bf109 damaged first, and this time was taken prisoner, badly burned about the face and hands. A year later he managed to escape from Stalag Luft VIIIB together with two RAF pilots and a Polish Jewish member of the British Army. Helped by the Polish Resistance movement for almost a year, McDonald and two of his companions (the other having been recaptured) eventually reached Gibraltar in July 1943, from where they were flown back to England. Awarded the Military Medal for his escape (the first member of the RCAF to escape and reach England), he was commissioned in the RCAF but then transferred to the USAAF. He later saw service in China flying P-51s and was credited with two victories (one shared) flying against the Japanese. Following service in Korea, he remained with the USAF until his death on 17 November 1953. On that date, flying an F-86D of the 60th FIS, he was killed when his aircraft suffered a flame-out when on its landing approach. Rather than bale out over a populated area, he remained with the crippled aircraft and guided it to crash in open land. His act of selflessness was recognised by the posthumous award of the US Soldiers' Medal.

Capt Vasseure F. Wynn (Georgia), born 1917 in Oklahoma USA, joined RCAF in 1941 and posted to UK. Attached to RAF and served with 249 Squadron at Malta in 1942 as Sgt Plt; credited with two (one shared), two probables and two damaged. Known as 'Georgia' to his RAF/RCAF friends. Commissioned but then transferred to USAAF after his return to UK. Joined 334th FIS and promoted to Capt in 1944; claimed three Bf109s (one shared) before shot down and POW on 13 April 1944. Remained in USAF postwar, seeing service in Korea with 27th FEG (claimed MiG-15 damaged). Retired 1962 as Major. Awarded US DFC and two US Air Medals.

APPENDIX IV

RED CHUTE BAYOU
THE ADVENTURES OF FLT LT PETER SCOTT RAF

On the morning of 8 January 1951, RAF exchange pilot Flt Lt Peter Scott, attached to the 82nd FIS at Hamilton AFB near San Francisco in California, took off with three others in F-84s on the first leg of what was intended to be a series of flights across the USA during that week. The pilots were to practice navigation, let-downs at unfamiliar airfields, and instrument flying in weather conditions that were not as good as those to be found in California:

"At Albuquerque the first two aircraft refuelled and flew off to Barksdale AFB near Shreveport in Louisiana. Capt Fred Gleason and I were delayed and didn't take off for Barksdale until after dark. We let down short of our destination to burn off fuel before landing and flew around the local area at 1,500 feet in open formation about 100 yards apart. The weather was good – a broken base cloud of 2,000 feet and half a moon shining on the stretches of stagnant water below, known as bayous, and providing a home for alligators and unattractive snakes – rugged and unfriendly countryside. But my mind was elsewhere – on the bluepoint oysters we had planned to eat at the Officers Club that night, and what the town of Shreveport would be like.

Then it happened – the emergency all pilots dread the most – fire in flight. There was a muffled explosion, and at the same time, the fire warning and engine overheat lights came on. They were about two feet from my right eye and made quite an impression because I'd forgotten, at Albuquerque, to close up the iris on each of them before the night flight. Of course, we had all practised what to do in case of fire many times in the simulator. But you can't simulate fear. And when this sort of thing happens suddenly, at low level, at night, directly above a lot of water containing alligators, there is liable to be a bit of fear about. But there is one thing that can be said about being in a single-engine fighter on fire – the pilot does not have a decision to make; he uses his ejection seat and bales out.

I throttled back to stop the fuel feeding the fire, pulled back a bit on the stick to gain some height, pressed the transmitter button and said 'No1, I'm on fire'. The simulator drills told me that the next thing to do was to jettison the canopy so that I could eject. I flipped up the red cover of the canopy jettison switch and operated it. Nothing happened – and that I hadn't practised. It meant no ejection. So I rolled back the canopy, electrically, undid various connections, turned the aircraft upside down, pushed the stick forward and popped out. All this was very low for a manual bale out so I pulled the ripcord at once, and can still remember the tremendous feeling of relief as I saw the canopy deploying above me. But that feeling didn't last for more than a couple of seconds, because I went splat into the cold water of what I found out later to be Red Chute Bayou. I was near the bank and it took no time to get out – spurred on by the thought that being eaten by an alligator would make a poor ending to an exciting adventure. In fact there was little danger of this because alligators, apparently, tend to sleep in the winter – but I didn't know that at the time!

To avoid further drama I climbed up a small tree on the edge of the bayou and sat in it to wait for help. My aircraft had gone vertically into the swamp about 100 yards away and was burning merrily. So I knew they'd find me. In about two hours a convoy arrived along a reasonably dry track the other side of the bayou, headed by what turned out to be a very smart Cadillac ambulance containing the other three members of my flight – all of whom thought I'd perished in the aircraft until they heard me blowing on the whistle attached to my Mae West. One of the crash vehicles had a dinghy, which they blew up and I was paddled back to my friends across the bayou.

The journey back to Barksdale in the smart ambulance was hilarious. It contained a medicinal bottle of brandy, which the four of us polished off before turning up at the base hospital. There I was emboldened to decline the flight surgeon's offer of accommodation for the night. I was unhurt apart from a modest graze down my nose. Instead, we went off in search of some clothes – all I had was underclothes and a wet flying suit. Then the four of us went off to Shreveport at about 10pm to tell the customers of various bars and night clubs our exciting story, and pick up a good few free drinks in the process.

After a few days the Board of Inquiry decided that the cause of the accident was a broken fuel line. The colonel back at our home base told the junior lieutenant [in our group] to come back in a transport. I took his aircraft and the remaining three of us went on with our trip around the States. It was not until much later that I learnt the reason for this – to lessen the chance of an onset of fear of flying, and it worked, which was a good thing because a few months later I was in Korea."

APPENDIX V

THE MIG-15 – AND BRITAIN'S INVOLVEMENT

Britain supplied Russia, its ally against Nazi Fascism during WWII, with 55 brand-new Rolls-Royce Derwent MkV (30) and Nene MkI and MkII (25) jet engines in 1946/48 to clinch a trade deal with Moscow. A Soviet delegation which included aircraft designer Artem Mikoyan and engine designer Vladimir Klimov had travelled to England to negotiate the acquisition of the engines, despite the reservations of Premier Stalin that the British would agree; but agree they did, in the mistaken belief that the engines were obsolete. The supply of these engines reduced the British lead in jet engine technology over the Soviet Union from an estimated five years to three years, particularly when one was used to power the new MiG-15 fighter.

RAF Chiefs and Defence ministers had unsurprisingly opposed the sale, but when the Soviet trade delegation in London pointed out to Sir Stafford Cripps, the President of the Board of Trade, that Labour-controlled Britain appeared to be discriminating against Russia in its export trade policy, further urgent discussions were held with Prime Minister Attlee, as documents released in the 1980s revealed:

"The matter became of some importance to a trade agreement and the President of the Board of Trade represented to the Prime Minister that if the engines could be exported he could get the agreement through. The PM sent for the Chiefs-of-Staff and asked them, bearing in mind that the Russians could obtain the engines from some other country, if we refused to sell them, they wished to press the security objection. The Chiefs replied that as it seemed as if the harm was already done and there were strong positive reasons for exporting them, they did not wish to press the security objection, provided the licence to manufacture was withheld. The export licence was signed the same day, and the trade agreement was concluded immediately."

Later, Moscow asked for more engines and also for three Meteor jet fighters and three Vampire jet fighters, but London said the request could only be met if the Russians allowed British experts to see their aircraft. The Russians did not pursue the request.

After the alarming appearance of the MiG in North Korean skies in late 1950 – and on the Americans learning of the British deal – rows broke out on both sides of the Atlantic. An embarrassed and hassled British Ambassador in Washington telegrammed London:

"It would be helpful if you could authorise us to add (to a statement) that the 55 engines which were supplied were obsolete . . ."

But, as an RAF officer pointed out:

"The Derwent is the latest mark and will definitely not be obsolescent this year. The Nene has not been introduced into the RAF for general purposes. It has, however, been used for experimental purposes . . ."

While a senior Air Ministry official wrote in December 1950:

"Our present belief that the Nene is in the MiG-15 confirms our opinion that the acquisition of this engine has been of great value to them (the Russians). The state of the Russian jet engine development has always been largely an unknown quantity to us, but in the light of our present information, it may well be that the sale of these may well have been of appreciable value to them. We must, however, remember that in 1946, when the decision was taken, there was still a chance that the Russians would adopt a reasonable course of conduct, and that the Government did not wish to give them grounds for complaint that we were withholding from them engines which had been sold to other countries."

When it erupted onto the scene, the MiG-15 could fly faster, climb faster and dive faster than any Western aircraft. And, as believed by British sources, it was powered by the Nene MkI (designated RD-45 by the Russians), which was initially considered by the Soviets as more suitable for bomber aircraft development; it was the Derwent V, designated RD-500, which was used in various fighter projects being developed by the Yakovlev and Lavochkin design teams, specifically the Yak-23, Yak-30 and La-15. However, Mikoyan opted for the RD-45 to power his design, the Mikoyan I-310, later to be designated MiG-15, which made its maiden flight on 30 December 1947 in the hands of test pilot V. Yuganov; the second prototype first flew on 27 May 1948. Mikoyan's design had a fierce competitor in Lavochkin's RD-500-powered La-15 of similar appearance, and both types were evaluated by the Soviet Air Force. Although slightly faster and more stable at speeds approaching Mach 1.0, the La-15 was rejected on the grounds of its small wheel-base when compared to the MiG, and was also more difficult to manufacture and maintain. In 1949 the first MiG-15s entered service with the Soviet Air Force, and by the mid-1950s several units were considered to be operational. Indeed, on 28 April 1950 the MiG-15 claimed its first victory when a pilot of the 29th Guards FAR shot down a CNAF P-38.

APPENDIX VI

MUSTANGS FLOWN BY 77 SQUADRON RAAF
1945-50

RAAF No	Received by RAAF	USAAF/CAC No	Remarks
A68-121	8/48	CA-18 Mk23 1346	Scrapped 11/56
A68-123	8/48	1348	Crashed 11/57
A68-125	8/48	1350	Crashed 14/4/51 (Sgt R. Robson KiFA)
A68-130	8/48	1355	Scrapped
A68-557	5/45	F-51D 44-12496	Crashed 11/45
A68-701	7/45	44-84404	Reduced to components 11/49
A68-702	7/45	44-84405	Used as target 4/52
A68-704	7/45	44-84407	Shot down 26/2/51 (P3 K.E. Royal KiA)
A68-705	7/45	44-84409	Crashed Japan 4/9/50 (Flt Lt F.R. Coburn b/o)
A68-706	7/45	44-84410	Airframe sold to US Aeronautics Corp 2/53
A68-707	7/45	44-84412	Used as target 4/52
A68-708	7/45	44-84413	Crash-landed 15/2/51, w/o (Wt Off R. Howe rescued by helicopter)
A68-709	7/45	44-84414	Airframe sold to US Aeronautics Corp 2/53
A68-711	7/45	44-84416	Crashed 11/45
A68-715	7/45	44-84400	Shot down 20/3/51 (Sgt C. Sly rescued by helicopter)
A68-716	7/45	44-84401	Airframe sold to US Aeronautics Corp 2/53
A68-720	7/45	44-84482	Scrapped 11/53
A68-722	8/45	44-84472	Collision with RN Firefly 17/4/50 (P3 W.L. Rivers and RN pilot baled out, RN observer killed)
A68-723	8/45	44-84723	To ROKAF 11/52
A68-725	8/45	44-84725	Airframe sold to US Aeronautics Corp 2/53
A68-726	8/45	44-84728	Shot down 22/12/50 (P2 D.C. Ellis KiA)
A68-727	8/45	44-84730	Crashed 11/45
A68-729	8/45	44-84732	Scrapped 11/53
A68-732	8/45	44-84735	Sold to US Aeronautics Corp 2/53
A68-733	8/45	44-84736	Used as target 4/52
A68-734	8/45	44-84737	Sold to US Aeronautics Corp 2/53
A68-735	8/45	44-84738	Crashed 11/45
A68-736	8/45	44-84739	Sold to US Aeronautics Corp 2/53
A68-737	8/45	44-84804	Belly-landed 13/3/51, w/o
A68-738	8/45	44-84809	Reduced to components 6/48

A68-739	8/45	44-84813	Sold to US Aeronautics Corp 2/53
A68-741	8/45	44-84819	Airframe sold to US Aeronautics Corp 2/53
A68-749	8/45	44-84488	Reduced to components 9/47
A68-750	8/45	44-84489	Used as target 4/52
A68-753	8/45	44-84494	Shot down 3/9/50 (P3 W.P. Harrop KiA)
A68-754	8/45	44-84496	Ditched 11/1/51 (P3 R.O.L. Brackenreg rescued by tugboat)
A68-755	8/45	44-84497	Damaged on ground by USN Corsair 23/1/51, w/o
A68-756	8/45	44-84499	Sold to US Aeronautics Corp 2/53
A68-757	8/45	44-84501	Shot down 7/7/50 (Sqn Ldr G. Strout KiA)
A68-759	8/45	44-84505	Reduced to components 5/47
A68-760	8/45	44-84506	Scrapped 11/53
A68-761	8/45	44-84507	Damaged on ground by Beaufighter 12/45, w/o
A68-763	8/45	44-84411	Sold to US Aeronautics Corp 2/53
A68-765	8/45	44-84492	Shot down 6/1/51 (P3 G.I. Stephens KiA)
A68-766	8/45	44-84495	Used as target 4/52
A68-769	8/45	44-84502	Used as target 4/52
A68-772	8/45	44-84726	Shot down 19/1/51 (Flt Lt G.R. Harvey POW)
A68-774	8/45	44-84740	Crashed 7/50, w/o
A68-775	8/45	44-84805	Crash landed 8/50, w/o
A68-776	8/45	44-84806	Reduced to components 8/47
A68-779	8/45	44-84812	Used as target 4/52
A68-780	8/45	44-84814	Sold to US Aeronautics Corp 2/53
A68-782	8/45	44-84821	Shot down 19/3/51 (Sgt H.T. Strange KiA)
A68-783	8/45	44-84823	Reduced to components 7/47
A68-787	8/45	44-84830	Crashed 9/47
A68-791	9/45	44-84808	Crash-landed 4/1/51 (P3 W.H. Bessell safe)
A68-792	9/45	44-84810	Sold to US Aeronautics Corp 2/53
A68-793	9/45	44-84811	Used as target 4/52
A68-794	9/45	44-84822	Lost 5/56
A68-796	9/45	44-84828	Collision with A68-812 14/2/51 (Sgt S.S. Squires KiFA)
A68-799	9/45	44-84815	Scrapped 11/53
A68-801	9/45	45-11458	Sold to US Aeronautics Corp 2/53
A68-802	9/45	45-11461	Crashed 12/48
A68-803	9/45	45-11462	Crashed 13/4/51
A68-804	9/45	45-11464	Sold to US Aeronautics Corp 2/53
A68-806	9/45	45-11466	To ROKAF 11/52
A68-807	9/45	45-11467	Used as target 4/52
A68-808	9/45	45-11473	Scrapped 11/53
A68-809	9/45	45-11474	Shot down 9/9/50 (Wg Cdr L.T. Spence KiA)
A68-810	9/45	45-11479	Sold to US Aeronautics Corp 2/53
A68-811	9/45	45-11481	Collision 3/49
A68-812	9/45	45-11482	Collision with A68-796 14/2/51 (Flt Lt K.C. Matthews KiFA)
A68-813	9/45	45-11483	Sold to US Aeronautics Corp 2/53

METEOR F8s FLOWN BY 77 SQUADRON RAAF
1951

On 24 February 1951, the Light Fleet Carrier HMS *Warrior* arrived off Iwakuni with a deck cargo of 15 Meteor F8s plus two T7 trainers. These were the initial batch of 36 F8s ordered from the British Government for delivery to 77RAAF in early 1951. The remainder of the order (less WA935, which had crashed en route to Singapore on 31 March 1951), arrived aboard the *Warrior* from Singapore a few weeks later. Altogether, some 90 Meteors would be delivered to 77RAAF over the next three years, of which 54 were lost in Korea and Japan. RAAF Meteors were, for the most part, allocated random serial numbers which created obvious gaps in the serial sequence. This was probably a security measure. The later deliveries will be detailed in Volume Two.

RAAF No	RAF No	Delivery	Remarks
A77-15	WE911	3/51	Lost 1/53 (see Volume Two)
A77-17	WA964	7/51	Shot down MiG-15 and shared second 1/12/51 (Flg Off B. Gogerly) soc 10/61

A77-29	WA938	2/51	Damaged MiG-15 27/10/51 (Flg Off L. Reading); shot down by MiG-15 1/12/51 (Sgt B. Thomson POW)
A77-31	WE903	7/51	Damaged MiG-15 24/10/51 (Flt Lt C.I. Blyth RAF); sold 4/59 and scrapped
A77-128	WE908	3/51	Collided with A77-354 22/8/51 (Sgt R.D. Mitchell KiFA)
A77-139	WA949	3/51	Landing accident 10/54, w/o
A77-163	WA941	2/51	Lost 3/53 (see Volume Two)
A77-189	WA961	3/51	Damaged MiG-15 2/11/51 (Flt Lt C.I. Blyth RAF); shared MiG-15 1/12/51 (Flt Lt M. Scannell RAF); lost 4/52 (see Volume Two)
A77-231	WA944	3/51	Crashed during acceptance trials 6/51 (Sgt A.T. Stoney safe)
A77-251	WE906	3/51	Shot down by MiG-15 1/12/51 (Sgt V. Drummond POW)
A77-316	WA945	7/51	Lost 8/52 (see Volume Two)
A77-354	WA934	5/51	Collided with A77-128 22/8/51 (Sgt R.L.R. Lamb KiFA)
A77-368	WA952	2/51	Damaged MiG-15 3/11/51 (Sgt M.E. Colebrook); extant with Australian War Memorial, Canberra
A77-373	WA936	2/51	Lost 5/52 (see Volume Two)
A77-385	WE918	5/51	Damaged by MiG-15 8/5/52, crashed on landing (see Volume Two)
A77-446	WA783	2/51	Scrapped 1959
A77-464	WA958	5/51	Lost 2/52 (see Volume Two)
A77-510	WE905	7/51	Converted to PR9 1960, then to U21A (destroyed 11/68)
A77-559	WE559	5/51	Lost 1/52 (see Volume Two)
A77-587	WA939	5/51	Collided with A77-959 11/11/51 (Flg Off K.J. Blight safe)
A77-616	WA956	3/51	Lost 2/52 (see Volume Two)
A77-721	WA954	5/51	Shot down by MiG-15 29/8/51 (Wt Off R.D. Guthrie POW)
A77-726	WA957	5/51	Lost 1/52 (see Volume Two)
A77-728	WA951	2/51	Landing accident 10/53, w/o (see Volume Two)
A77-730	WA782	2/51	Landing accident 7/10/51, w/o
A77-734	WE907	5/51	MiG-15 probable 5/52 (see Volume Two); scrapped 1959
A77-735	WA942	2/51	Ditched 7/5/51 (Sgt W.H. Bessell safe); salvaged, w/o
A77-740	WA948	2/51	Landing accident 12/8/51, w/o
A77-741	WA947	2/51	Shared MiG-15 1/12/51 (Flt Lt G. Thornton); forced landing 1/52, w/o (see Volume Two)
A77-744	WA786	2/51	Scrapped 1959
A77-811	WA937	2/51	Damaged MiG-15 26/9/51 (Flt Lt R.L. Dawson); damaged by MiG-15, crash-landed, w/o 3/11/51
A77-911	WA946	2/51	Damaged F-86 2/11/51 (Flt Lt L.L. Cadan); shared MiG-15 1/12/51 (Flt Lt Cadan); lost 6/52 (see Volume Two)
A77-949	WA960	5/51	Shot down by MiG-15 1/12/51 (Sgt E.D. Armit KiA)
A77-959	WA909	5/51	Collided with A77-587 11/11/51 (Sgt D.M. Robertson KiFA)
A77-982	WA950	2/51	Lost 6/53 (see Volume Two)

Meteor T7 trainer

| A77-229 | WA731 | 1951 | Re-serialled A77-701 1952 |
| A77-305 | ? | 1951 | Re-serialled A77-702 1952 |

F-51D MUSTANGS FLOWN BY 2 SQUADRON SAAF
1950-1951

SAAF No	USAF No	Received	Remarks
301	45-11370	11/50	Ditched on operational sortie 2/3/51 (Lt D.A. Ruiter KiA)
302	45-11390	11/50	Shot down 5/9/51 (Lt N. Biden KiA)
303	45-11360	11/50	Operational flying accident 7/10/51 (Lt C. Lombard POW)
304	45-11399	11/50	Shot down 15/2/51 (Lt G.D. Doveton KiA)
305	45-11429	11/50	Crashed on take-off 4/3/51 (Lt P. Swemmer safe)
306	45-11563	11/50	Crashed on landing 30/8/51 (Maj J.P.D. Blaauw safe)
307	45-11632	11/50	Shot down 7/2/51 (2/Lt D.R. Leah KiA)
308	45-11648	11/50	Crashed 2/52 (see Volume Two)
309	44-63400	11/50	Shot down 11/5/51 (Lt J.H. Kruger rescued by helicopter)
310	44-73191	11/50	Shot down 3/10/51 (Lt M. Muller rescued by helicopter)
311	44-74168	11/50	Shot down 5/12/50 (Capt J.D.O. Davis rescued by L-5)

312	44-74432	11/50	Shot down 22/7/51 (Lt R.L. Staats rescued by USN destroyer)
313	44-74489	11/50	Shot down 30/4/51 (Lt P. Celliers rescued by helicopter)
314	44-74788	11/50	Crashed on landing 2/6/51 (2/Lt R.V. Sherwood safe)
315	44-74814	11/50	Engine failure 20/3/51 (Lt S. Armstrong rescued by helicopter)
316	44-74984	11/50	Crashed 9/7/51 (Maj L.B. Pearce KiFA)
317	44-73338	12/50	Shot down 2/3/51 (Capt W.J.J. Badenhorst KiA)
318	45-11419	11/50	Lost 4/52 (see Volume Two)
319	45-11475	12/50	Shot down 2/2/51 (Lt W.E.St E. Wilson KiA)
320	45-11704	12/50	Shot down by MiG-15 20/3/52 (see Volume Two)
321	45-11541	12/50	Shot down 10/3/51 (Capt J.D.O. Davis KiA)
322	45-11477	12/50	Force-landed to aid downed pilot, Lt J.H. Kruger 11/5/51 (Maj J.P.D. Blaauw and Lt Kruger both rescued by helicopter)
323	44-15091	12/50	Crash-landed 12/8/51 (2/Lt M. Muller safe)
324	44-73084	12/50	Collided with Mustang 341 3/12/41 (2/Lt K.R. Whitehead KiFA)
325	45-11456	12/50	Crashed on delivery 4/12/50 (Lt J.A. Joubert safe)
326	44-74344	12/50	Returned to USAF 12/52
327	44-74174	1/51	Shot down 13/11/51 (Capt C. Collins rescued by helicopter)
328	44-74718	2/51	Crashed 1/7/51 (2/Lt J.P. Verster KiFA)
329	44-73068	3/51	Crashed on take-off 29/8/51 (Lt A. Green safe)
330	44-73892	3/51	Crashed on take-off 15/5/51 (Lt M.H. Rorke KiFA)
331	44-72134	3/51	Shot down 23/7/51 (2/Lt M.I.P. Halley POW)
332	44-14930	3/51	Shot down 1/6/51 (Lt H. Macdonald POW)
333	44-74503	3/51	Crashed on take-off 9/6/51 (2/Lt T. Liebenberg KiFA)
334	44-84903	3/51	Returned to USAF 12/52
335	44-74511	3/51	Shot down 23/7/51 (Capt F.M. Bekker KiA)
336	44-72983	5/51	Crashed 26/7/51 (2/Lt J.H.G. Howe rescued by helicopter)
337	44-73049	5/51	Shot down 22/6/51 (Lt A.G. Frisby KiA)
338	44-74461	5/51	Shot down 23/7/51 (Lt R.M. du Plooy KiA)
339	44-73688	6/51	Crashed 24/7/51 (Capt H. Synman rescued by SA-16)
340	44-74757	6/51	Shot down 29/10/51 (2/Lt H.T.R. Joyce KiA)
341	44-74759	6/51	Collided with Mustang 324 3/12/51 (2/Lt P.I. Norman-Smith KiFA)
342	44-74632	6/51	Shot down 1/9/51 (2/Lt M.O. Grunder KiA)
343	44-74748	7/51	Returned to USAF 12/52
344	44-74750	8/51	Shot down 5/9/51 (Lt W. Van den Bos safe)
345	44-84867	8/51	Shot down 24/11/51 (2/Lt G.H. Krohn KiA)
346	44-63515	8/51	Shot down 29/11/51 (Capt A. Janse van Rensburg KiA)
347	44-63822	8/51	Crashed on landing 16/10/51 (Lt P. Retief safe)
348	44-84862	8/51	Lost 5/52 (see Volume Two)
349	44-72271	8/51	Shot down 14/8/51 (Lt C.I. de Jongh KiA)
350	44-14449	9/51	Shot down 1/52 (see Volume Two)
351	44-64101	9/51	Shot down 12/9/51 (Capt F.A. Montanari KiA)
352	44-74565	9/51	Engine failure 9/9/51 (Capt D. Barlow rescued by helicopter)
353	44-84863	9/51	Shot down 1/52 (see Volume Two)
354	44-84553	9/51	Shot down, belly-landed 30/10/51 (Lt J. Meiring injured)
355	44-84771	9/51	Shot down 27/9/51 (Lt D.J. Earp POW)
356	44-14297	9/51	Crashed on landing 28/11/51 (2/Lt K.R. Whitehead safe)
357	44-74745	9/51	Crashed on landing 20/9/51 (2/Lt T.M. Sivertsen injured)
358	44-84750	9/51	Shot down 1/52 (see Volume Two)
359	44-74992	9/51	Crashed 29/10/51 (Lt G. Shawe safe)
360	44-72656	9/51	Crashed on landing 10/52 (see Volume Two)
361	44-74863	9/51	Shot down 10/52 (see Volume Two)
362	44-73903	10/51	Shot down 2/52 (see Volume Two)
363	44-63853	10/51	Shot down 4/11/51 (2/Lt C.J. Pappas KiA)
364	44-84887	10/51	Transferred to ROKAF
365	44-84649	10/51	Shot down 13/11/51 (2/Lt F.J. Grobler rescued by helicopter)
366	44-84882	11/51	Returned to USAF 12/52
367	44-84902	11/51	Returned to USAF 12/52
368	44-84874	11/51	Shot down 1/52 (see Volume Two)
369	44-84761	11/51	Returned to USAF 12/52
370	44-73073	11/51	Crashed on landing 2/52 (see Volume Two)
371	44-74617	11/51	Shot down 1/52 (see Volume Two)

372	45-11707	11/51	Shot down 1/52 (see Volume Two)
373	44-74021	12/51	Crashed on take-off 2/52 (see Volume Two)
374	44-13851	12/51	Crashed 1/52 (see Volume Two)

APPENDIX VII

HMAS *SYDNEY* and HER SQUADRONS

HMAS *Sydney* was commissioned in England in December 1948, having originally been launched as HMS *Terrible* for the Royal Navy in 1944, a Light Fleet carrier of some 14,000 tons. Two RAN squadrons were also formed at the time with Australian aircrew, taking over the mantles of existing FAA units, 805 Squadron and 816 Squadron, which were intended to be equipped with Sea Fury FB11s and Firefly AS5s, respectively. Until sufficient aircraft were available, however, the Australians trained on aircraft provided by the Royal Navy. When *Sydney* eventually sailed for Australia on 4 April 1949, she had on board 27 Sea Fury FB11s (VW622-640, VW642-648, plus VW660 which replaced VW641 which had crashed before acceptance by the RAN) and 27 Firefly AS5s (VG989, VH122, VT500-504, VX371-390). These two units comprised the 20th Carrier Air Group; also on board were two Sea Otter amphibians. Two further Sea Furies were delivered by merchant vessels during 1950 (VX627 and VX661).

Sydney returned to the UK during late 1950 and embarked a further 32 Sea Fury FB11s (VX707, VX724-730, VX748-764, WE673-679) for her second fighter squadron, 808 Squadron, pilots of which had also been under training in the UK. In addition, 34 more Fireflies were embarked (WB292, WB371, WB423, WB505-510, WB516-523, WD824-840), these intended for the newly formed 817 Squadron. The two units comprised the 21st Carrier Air Group. 805, 808 and 817 Squadrons all participated in the Korean War. During October and November 1951, at the height of her involvement in the Korean War, *Sydney* embarked nine Sea Furies from RN stocks to make good losses. These were WE686, WE791, WE795-799, WF591 and WF593. Four Fireflies were also received from RN stocks (WB316, WB358, WB393, and WB396). At the end of her deployment in Korean waters a further ten Sea Furies were taken onboard *Sydney* before she sailed for Australia.

A third Sea Fury squadron, 850 Squadron, was formed at Nowra in January 1953 and operated briefly aboard *Sydney* off Korea after the end of the war but was disbanded in August 1954, her aircraft including some of the final batch of 11 Sea Furies received by the RAN (WZ642-652). *Sydney* herself returned to the UK in October 1955 and was handed back to the Royal Navy. 808 Squadron had disbanded in October 1954 but 805 Squadron lived on, being based at Nowra. In August 1955, two 805 Squadron Sea Furies (VW645 and WZ650) were involved in an unusual incident when called upon to intercept a pilotless civil Auster (VH-AET) which had become airborne from nearby Bankstown airfield after its pilot had swung its propeller, having left it in full throttle and without adequate brake control. The aircraft had taken off under its own steam, gradually gained height and had become an obvious threat to the residents of Sydney which lay in its path. Although a Meteor and a Wirraway were scrambled to deal with it, it was left to the two Sea Fury pilots to shoot it down into the sea off Broken Bay.

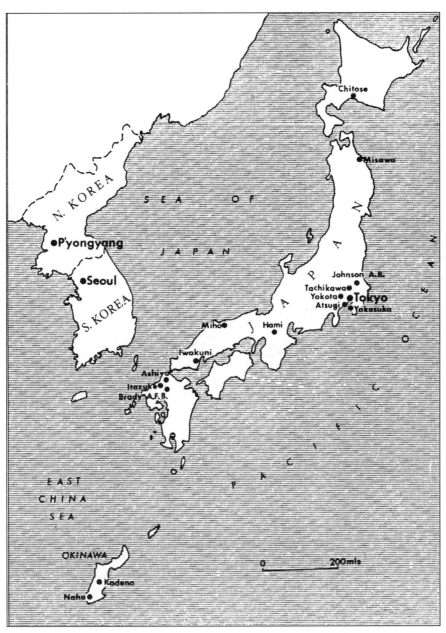

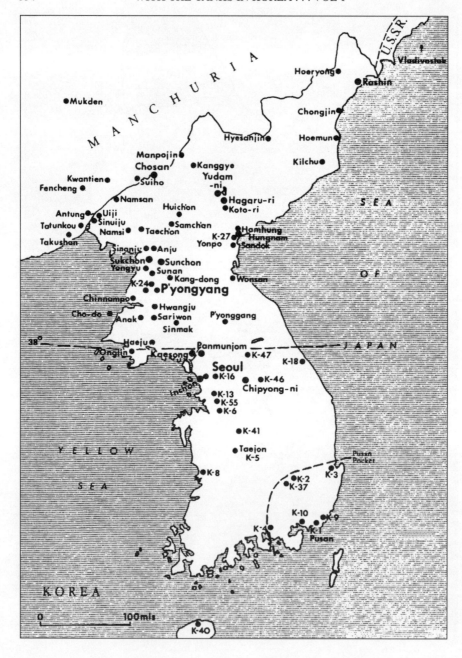

USSR

●Vladivostok

Hoeryong●

●Rashin

MANCHURIA

Chongjin●

●Mukden

Hyesanjin●   Hoemun●

Manpojin●
Chosan●   ●Kanggye   Kilchu●

Kwantien●   ●Suiho   Yudam
Fencheng ●   -ni●

●Namsan   ●Hagaru-ri
Huich'on●   ●Koto-ri

Antung●   ●Uiji
Tatunkou●   ●Sinuiju   ●Samch'an
Namsi●   ●Taech'on   K-27●   Homhung
Takushan●   Yonpo●   Hungnam
Sinanju●   ●Anju   Sandok●

Sukchon●   ●Sunchon
Yongyu●   Sunan●   ●Wonsan
K-24●   Kang-dong●
●P'yongyang

Chinnampo●   ●Hwangju
Cho-do ●   Anak●   Sariwon●   P'yonggang●
Sinmak●

38°––   Haeju●
Onglin●   Kaesong●   Panmunjom●   K-47●   JAPAN
K-18●

Seoul   K-16●   ●K-46
Inch'on   K-13●   Chipyong-ni
K-55●
K-6●

●K-41

●Taejon
K-5

●K-8   Pusan
Pocket
K-3●
K-2●
K-37●

K-10●
K-9●
K-4●   ●Pusan

YELLOW

SEA

KOREA

0   100 mls

●K-40

SELECT BIBLIOGRAPHY

Primary sources include: Unit History Sheets 77 Squadron RAAF; Commanding Officer's Reports 77 Squadron RAAF; Narrative Reports 77 Squadron RAAF; Log Books of 77 Squadron RAAF personnel; War Diary 2 Squadron SAAF (Combat Reports, Returns of Daily Missions, Affidavits of Pilots); War Diary Missions SAAF Korea (Debriefing Sheets); Unit History Sheets 1903 Independent AOP Flight; Unit History Sheets 1913 Light Liaison Flight; PRO Air 20/7798: *Combat Evaluation of the Meteor VIII*; *Report of operations with Meteor VIII in Korea*; *77 Squadron Tactical Report* (all compiled by Flt Lt Max Scannell DFC AFC RAF); MOD Historical Branch (Naval), British Commonwealth Naval Operations, Korea 1950-53, Naval Staff History BR1736(54); History of the 67th TRW USAF; Ministry of National Defence, Republic of Korea (History of the United Nations in Korea).

Published works:
Across the Parallel: George Odgers
Aerial Interdiction in Three Wars: Eduard Mark
Air War over Korea: Robert Jackson
American Caesar: William Manchester
Australia and the Korean War, Volumes One & Two: Robert O'Neill
A Year of Space: Eric Linklater
Banner over Pusan: William Ellery Anderson
Battle Hymn: Dean E. Hess
Beyond Courage: Clay Blair
Britain and the Korean War: Callum MacDonald
British Forces in the Korean War: Ashley Cunningham-Boothe & Peter Farrar (Ed)
British Part in the Korean War, The: General Sir Anthony Farrar-Hockley DSO
Canadair Sabre, The: Larry Milberry
Captives of Korea, The: William L. White
Case Studies in the Achievement of Air Superiority: Benjamin F. Cooling (Ed)
China Crosses the Yalu: Allen Whiting
China's Road to the Korean War: Chen Jian
Chinese High Command, The: William H. Whitson
Clash of Eagles: Dennis Newton
Commonwealth at War, The: Tim Carew
Crimson Sky: John R. Bruning
Cry Korea: Reginald Thompson
Drawing the Line: Richard Whelan
Duty First: David Horner (Ed)
Eastward: Sir David Lee
Edge of the Sword, The: (General Sir) Anthony Farrar-Hockley DSO
Enter the Dragon: Russell Spurr
Fly for their Lives: John Chartres
Flying Cheetahs in Korea: Dermot Moore & Peter Bagshawe
For Heroic or Meritorious Achievement: Frederic L. Borch III & William R. Westlake
For Heroism or Extraordinary Achievement While Participating in Aerial Flight:
  William R. Westlake
For Those in Peril: John Winton

Full Circle: Air Vice-Marshal J.E. Johnson CB CBE DSO DFC
F-86 Sabre: Maurice Allward
F-86 Sabre: Robert F. Dorr
F-86 Sabre – The Operational Record: Robert Jackson
Gloster Meteor: M.J. Hardy
Korea Remembered: Maurie Pears & Fred Kirkland (Ed)
Korea – The Air War 1950-53: Jack C. Nicholls & Warren Thompson
Korea – The Limited War: David Rees
Korea – The Untold Story of the War: Joseph C. Goulden
Korean Air War, The: Robert F. Dorr & Warren Thompson
Korean Diary: Frank Clune
Korean War, The: Max Hastings
Korean War, The: David Rees (Ed)
Korean War Aces: Robert F. Dorr, Jon Lake & Warren Thompson
Khrushchev Remembers: Nikita Khrushchev
Lion over Korea: David Wilson
Meteor: Bryan Philpott
Meteor, Sabre & Mirage in Australian Service: Stewart Wilson
MiG-15: Yefim Gordon & Vladimir Rigmant
MiG Alley: Larry Davis
Mustangs over Korea: David R. McLaren
Odd Jobs: Steve Eather
Our Men in Korea: Eric Linklater
Panmunjom: William H. Vatcher Jr
P-80/F-80 Shooting Star: David R. McLaren
Reminiscences: Douglas MacArthur
Sea Fury, Firefly & Sea Venom in Australian Service: Stewart Wilson
Sea War in Korea, The: Malcolm W. Cagle & Frank A. Manson
Spitfire, Mustang & Kittyhawk in Australian Service: Stewart Wilson
Spy Flights of the Cold War: Paul Lashmar
Stars and Bars: Frank Olynyk
Stalin's Eagles: Hans-Dieter Seidl
Stalin's Falcons: Tomas Polak with Christopher Shores
Story of Air Fighting, The: Air Vice-Marshal J.E. Johnson CB CBE DSO DFC
Strained Alliance, The: Robert R. Simmons
Truce, Tent and Fighting Front: Walter G. Hermes
US Air Force in Korea 1950-53, The: Robert F. Futrell
USAF Credits for the Destruction of Enemy Aircraft Korean War: Albert F. Simpson (Ed)
Wings Across the Sea: Ross Gillett
With the Australians in Korea: Norman Bartlett (Ed)
With the Carriers in Korea 1950-53: John Lansdown
Within Limits: Wayne Thompson & Bernard C. Nalty

Journals, Magazines & Newspapers include: *RAF Historical Society Journal 21*; *Journal of the RUSI No586*; *Army Air Corps Journal*; plus various issues of *FlyPast, Aeroplane Monthly, Flight, RAF Flying Review, Aviation News, Air Pictorial; Flightpath* (Australia); *Aviation Heritage* (Australia), *Australian Aviation; Despatch – Journal of the Military Historical Society of NSW* (Australia); *Paratus* (Australia); *Wartime – Australian War Memorial*; *American Aviation Historical Society Journal* (US); *Airpower* (US); *Militaria* (South Africa); *Toronto Daily Star* (Canada); Amongst Russian-language documents and articles consulted by Tomas Polak and Hans-Dieter Seidl were: *Sovetskie Letchiky Na Zashcite Neba Kitaya I Korei 1950-53 – Soviet Pilots in the Defence of Sky of China and Korea* by V.P. Naboka; *Meteopii* (Meteors) by Igor Seidov (Mir aviatsii); *Twenty Years in Combat* by Alexander V. Kotlobovskii; *Chronicle of Losses among the Fighter Elite* by Leonid Krylov & Yurii Tepsurkaev.
Via the Internet: Various websites which included 'Russian Claims from the Korea War 1950-53' (Stranka); 'Korean Air War and Surrounding Events' (compiled by Stephen L. Sewell); and 'USAF/USN/USMC Personnel Missing Korea' (PMKOR).

PERSONNEL INDEX

RAN Personnel

RCAF Personnel

SAAF Personnel

Chinese Communist Personnel